Christianity and the Contest for Manhood in Late Antiquity

In this book, Nathan D. Howard explores gender and identity formation in fourth-century Cappadocia, where pro-Nicene bishops used a rhetoric of contest that aligned with conventions of classical Greek masculinity. Howard demonstrates that epistolary exhibitions served as "a locus for" asserting manhood in the fourth century. These performances illustrate how a culture of orality that had defined manhood among civic elites was reframed as a contest whereby one accrued status through merits of composition. Howard shows how the Cappadocians' rhetoric also reordered the body and materiality as components of a maleness over which they moderated. He interrogates fourth-century theological conflict as part of a rhetorical battle over claims to manhood that supported the Cappadocians' theology and cast doubt on non-Trinitarian rivals, whom they cast as effeminate and disingenuous. Investigating accounts of pro-Nicene protagonists overcoming struggles, Howard establishes that tropes based on classical standards of gender contributed to the formation of Trinitarian orthodoxy.

Nathan D. Howard is Professor of History at the University of Tennessee at Martin. His scholarship has been supported by Dumbarton Oaks, the American Philosophical Society, and the National Endowment for the Humanities. His work has appeared in a number of edited journals and volumes, including the *Journal of Late Antiquity*, *Approaches to the Byzantine Family*, and *Studia Patristica*.

Christianity and the Contest for Manhood in Late Antiquity

The Cappadocian Fathers and the Rhetoric of Masculinity

NATHAN D. HOWARD

University of Tennessee–Martin

Shaftesbury Road, Cambridge CB2 8EA, United Kingdom

One Liberty Plaza, 20th Floor, New York, NY 10006, USA

477 Williamstown Road, Port Melbourne, VIC 3207, Australia

314–321, 3rd Floor, Plot 3, Splendor Forum, Jasola District Centre, New Delhi – 110025, India

103 Penang Road, #05–06/07, Visioncrest Commercial, Singapore 238467

Cambridge University Press is part of Cambridge University Press & Assessment, a department of the University of Cambridge.

We share the University's mission to contribute to society through the pursuit of education, learning and research at the highest international levels of excellence.

www.cambridge.org
Information on this title: www.cambridge.org/9781009088305

DOI: 10.1017/9781009090827

© Cambridge University Press & Assessment 2023

This publication is in copyright. Subject to statutory exception and to the provisions of relevant collective licensing agreements, no reproduction of any part may take place without the written permission of Cambridge University Press & Assessment.

First published 2023
First paperback edition 2024

A catalogue record for this publication is available from the British Library

Library of Congress Cataloging-in-Publication data
NAMES: Howard, Nathan D., 1971– author.
TITLE: Classical Greek masculinity and the Cappadocian Fathers : Christianity and the rhetoric of contest in late antiquity / Nathan D. Howard.
DESCRIPTION: Cambridge ; New York : Cambridge University Press, [2022] | Includes bibliographical references and index.
IDENTIFIERS: LCCN 2021063082 (print) | LCCN 2021063083 (ebook) | ISBN 9781316514764 (hardback) | ISBN 9781009088305 (paperback) | ISBN 9781009090827 (epub)
SUBJECTS: LCSH: Christian literature, Early–Greek authors–History and criticism. | Christian hagiography–History–To 1500. | Masculinity–Religious aspects–Christianity. | Masculinity in literature. | Masculinity–Greece–History. | Cappadocian Fathers–Correspondence. | Fathers of the church, Greek. | BISAC: RELIGION / Christian Church / History
CLASSIFICATION: LCC BR67 .H69 2022 (print) | LCC BR67 (ebook) | DDC 270.1–dc23/eng/20220317
LC record available at https://lccn.loc.gov/2021063082
LC ebook record available at https://lccn.loc.gov/2021063083

ISBN   978-1-316-51476-4   Hardback
ISBN   978-1-009-08830-5   Paperback

Cambridge University Press & Assessment has no responsibility for the persistence or accuracy of URLs for external or third-party internet websites referred to in this publication and does not guarantee that any content on such websites is, or will remain, accurate or appropriate.

FOR MY FATHER,
JAMES E. HOWARD

Contents

Acknowledgments	*page* ix
Note on Translations	xiii
List of Abbreviations	xv

Introduction: *Paideia*, Masculinity, and Identity	1
Bishops, *Agōn*, and Classical Masculinity	5
The Cappadocians: A Background	21
Transcendent Manhood and Asceticism in Identity Formation	35
Identity and Genre	48
Outline of Chapters	61
1 "The Sweat of Eloquence": Epistolary *Agōn* and Second Sophistic Origins	63
Second Sophistic Origins of *Agōn*	67
Epistolary Performance and *Aretē*	77
Agōn and Group Identity among Pro-Nicenes	86
2 The *Agōn* of Friendship: Sensory Rhetoric, Gift Exchange, and the Aesthetics of *Aretē*	103
Corporeality and the Soul in Sensory Rhetoric	108
"Greeting in your Honored Hand": Penmanship and *Aretē*	141
Epistolary *Agōn* as Gift Exchange	145

3 Hagiography and Masculinity: Personifications of Sacred
   Aretē   155
   Theological Background of Fourth-
   Century Hagiography   160
   Virtual Contests in Gregory Thaumaturgus
   and Caesarius   166
   Nyssen's Basil: Defender of Theological Truth   172
   Nazianzen's Basil: Campaigns against
   a Barbaric Emperor   177
   Telescoping *Aretē* from the Scriptural Past   184
   Corporeal *Aretē* in Gorgonia and Macrina   186
   Physical Beauty and *Aretē* in Family and Saints   200
   Noble Beauty and Modesty in Female Saints   203

4 *Agōn* and Theological Authority: Hagiography
   and Polemics of Identity   212
   The Eunomians as False *Pepaideumenoi*   218
   Exile as *Agōn* in the *Life of Athanasius*   231
   Basil's Voice as Theological Conditioning   244
   Macrina and Aetius as Contrasting Moderators
   of Theology   256

Epilogue: Classical Masculinity in Early Medieval
and Byzantine Christianity   272

References   278
Index   316

Acknowledgments

My study of the Cappadocian Fathers, three fourth-century bishops from eastern Rome (in Turkey), began during my doctoral studies at the University of Arkansas. Here my mentor Lynda Coon emphasized the importance of using a multi-disciplinary approach to explore the early church fathers. The best elements of this book have Lynda's imprint on them. All errors of course are my own. Lynda has been a steadfast guide, critic, and proponent during the last decade as my scholarship on the Cappadocians has evolved into the current work. Since my time at Arkansas, Lynda has continued to serve as my mentor, colleague, and friend. She has managed to navigate her support for former students such as myself, all while publishing leading scholarship in Carolingian and Early Medieval studies, chairing the Department of History at Arkansas, and now serving as Dean of the Honors College. I hope that this work will be a testament to her continuing commitment to her students, to scholarship, and to me personally, a decade and a half after I completed my dissertation.

Many others have contributed to this book by reading portions of chapters, providing suggestions, offering encouragement, sharing their own research, and by provoking me to re-think my interpretations. Among these are Paul Blowers, Leslie Brubaker, Jeff Childers, Maria Dasios, Everett Ferguson, Eric Fournier, Ed Gallagher, Kim Haines-Eitzen, Sandy Haney, Tera Harmon, Stefan Hodges-Kluck, Dan Vladimir Ivanovici, Robin Jensen, Gregor Kalas, Young Kim, Jacob Latham, Daniel Levine, Morwenna Ludlow, Brian Matz, John McGuckin, Maria Parani, Suzanne Abrams Rebillard, Adam Schor, Tina Shepardson, Anna Silvas, Arthur Urbano, Richard Vaggione, Raymond Van Dam, and Robin Darling Young. This book has benefited especially from the work of Brad Storin, both from his scholarship on Gregory of Nazianzus and his critiques of my work. Brad graciously shared with me an early draft of his translations of Gregory's correspondence, an enormous asset for the chapters on letter writing.

My book also reflects the influence of colleagues from graduate school at Arkansas, especially Aneilya Barnes, Annette Kleinkauf-Morrow, and Susan Laningham. At the University of Tennessee at Martin, my home institution, my intellectual life has been enriched through discussions during meals with Matthew Braddock, Chris Brown, John Glass, Chris Hill, Arthur Hunt, Norm Lillegard, and Sam Richardson. I have also enjoyed the support of friends that have stimulated my thinking through their own careers and interests, opened their homes during my extended periods of research, and offered camaraderie as I managed the mental transition back and forth from the fourth- to the twenty-first century. These include Jennifer Abney, Mike Cravens, Stephanie Gerdes, Becky Henderson, Sarah Kingsley Herr, Barry Jordan, Sam and Autumn Marshall, Brian and Joy Stephens, Bill and Joyce Troxler, and Robert West. The staff at the Paul Meek Library at Tennessee at Martin, meanwhile, has been exceptionally accommodating. I want to thank Dana Breland, Janie Crews Jones, Adam Kemper, Sam Richardson, and Karen White for their help, especially in acquiring copies relevant to my research, either for the library's collection or through Inter-Library Loan. The Friends of the Paul Meek Library also contributed to my work. In 2014 they awarded me the Paul Meek Library Book Award, which was used to add several new titles to the library's holdings in late antiquity and early Christianity. And in the Department of History and Philosophy, Melanie Warmath has provided steady assistance, most specifically in developing a model for the Cappadocians' family trees.

Several conferences and workshops have afforded me forums to present early stages of my project. I have delivered these papers at the International Patristics Conference in Oxford, annual meetings of the North American Patristics Society in Chicago, and the Christian Scholars Conference in Nashville. The critiques and suggestions at these gatherings have shaped this work. Equally valuable have been the informal discussions at these meetings, which always stimulate my thinking. In addition to the conferences above, I have been privileged to participate in several meetings of the Regional Late Antiquity Consortium Southeast and the Faculty Research Seminar on Late Antiquity at the University of Tennessee-Knoxville. These occasions have issued renewal and camaraderie. Thank you, Gregor, Jacob, and Tina for inviting this colleague from the northwestern reaches of the state to be a part of these workshops.

Acknowledgments

Portions of the first three chapters of this book were published earlier in the following articles: "Gifts Bearing Greekness: Epistles as Cultural Capital in Fourth-Century Cappadocia" (*Journal of Late Antiquity* 6:1 [2013]: 37–59); "Epistolary *Agōn* in the Cappadocian Fathers" (*Studia Patristica* 115:12 [2021], 11–17); and "Sacred Spectacle in the Biographies of Gorgonia and Macrina" (*Studia Patristica* 91:17 [2017]: 267–74). I am grateful to the publishers for permission to reprint excerpts from these works.

Research for this book has required study in multiple libraries besides my home institution. I am grateful to the staff of each of these for welcoming me. These libraries include the Manuscripts and Archives Research Library of Trinity College Dublin, the Chester Beatty Library, the Harding School of Theology Library, the University of Wisconsin Memorial Library, the Hodges Library at the University of Tennessee-Knoxville, and the Dumbarton Oaks Research Library and Collection. I specifically want to thank the following individuals: Jane Maxwell (Trinity); Jill Unkel and Celine Ward (Chester Beatty); Don Meredith, Sheila Owen, and Bob Turner (Harding); John Dillon and Libby Theune (Wisconsin); Doug Engle (Tennessee); and Joshua Robinson, Eden Slone, Anna Stavrakopoulou, and Alyson Williams (Dumbarton Oaks). Working with these professionals has been a highlight of my research journey. And during my travel to Cappadocia in 2014, Omer Elkay (the best travel guide in Turkey) showered me with hospitality, opening his home and family to me in Kayseri while advising me on the logistics of visiting ancient Nazianzus, Arianzus, and Nyssa.

Travel and research for this project have been made possible by support from the following institutions: the American Philosophical Society, Dumbarton Oaks, Friends of the University of Wisconsin-Madison Library, and the Marco Institute for Medieval and Renaissance Studies (UT-Knoxville). My special thanks to the Marco Institute for awarding me multiple fellowships to study at Hodges Library, particularly for the assistance of Program Coordinator Katie Hodges-Kluck. This book also would not have been possible without the commitment by administrators at Tennessee at Martin. I was the beneficiary of a year-long Reagan Research Leave by the Office of Research and Sponsored Programs in 2013–2014 and 2018–2019. In addition, the university has subsidized my study through a faculty research grant, an international travel grant, and the Ray and Wilma Smith Faculty Development award. Because of their continued support for my research, I owe a debt of gratitude to Lynn Alexander, Dean of Humanities and Fine Arts, and David Coffey, Chair of History and Philosophy.

And, of course, I would not have been awarded any of these grants or fellowships without the well-penned letters of recommendation by colleagues who have advocated for my project. I want to thank Lynda Coon, Brian Daley, Harold Drake, David Konstan, Brian Matz, and Robin Darling Young. Each has served as a reference at one time or another. In addition to writing letters of recommendation, these colleagues have reviewed my applications, discussed sources of funding, and provided words of wisdom. In addition to Lynda, who read the full manuscript, I want to express my appreciation to David Konstan for reading much of my work over the past two years. As a maven in Classics and Late Antiquity, he has been a source of invaluable counsel. And during the publishing process, I have enjoyed the best of direction by Beatrice Rehl. Her expertise and eye for detail have been exceptional. I want to thank Kaye Barbaro, Dhanuja Ragunathan, and Hemalatha Subramanian for shepherding the book through the production stage, along with Rosemary Morlin, for copy editing the manuscript. The anonymous readers, meanwhile, may be the most important contributors to this book. The comprehensiveness of their reviews surpassed my expectations. One of the evaluations, in particular, resulted in a reprioritization of thematic issues. I want these individuals to know my appreciation. The cover of the book, an image from the eleventh-century Codex 61 fol. 113r. Dionysiou, was made possible because of the graciousness of the Dionysiou Monastery at Mt. Athos. I want to express my gratitude to the community there for permission to use the image and for sending me a digitized version of it. Christos Simelidis was especially helpful by serving as a liaison between the monastery and me. Thank you for your help, Christos.

Finally, I want to thank my family for their love and perseverance throughout this project. I want to thank my brother Daren Howard and his family for their affection and support. My uncle and aunt, Leon and Marilyn Sanderson have championed this project from its beginning, when I lived with them in Memphis during research leave. They have been a source of warmth and hospitality throughout the writing. And my parents Jim and Lois Howard have been bedrocks of encouragement. They have been a sounding board, they have shown consistent enthusiasm for the book, and they have volunteered every resource to help me complete the book. My father has modeled scholarship throughout his career as a Christian minister. His commitment to preparing every sermon and Bible class through thoughtful, well-read analysis and his passion for sharing biblical knowledge with others have been an inspiration. I dedicate this book to him.

A Note on Translations

In footnotes for quotations from ancient sources, the translator's name appears in parentheses following the citation: e.g., Homer, *Iliad* 2.135 (Lombardo).
Unless otherwise noted, translations of Gregory of Nazianzus' epistles come from Bradley Storin's *Gregory of Nazianzus's Letter Collection*. In each citation I have included both Paul Gallay's numbering, first, followed by that of Storin: e.g., Greg. Naz., *Ep.* 12 (Storin 176). Gallay, *Grégoire de Nazianze: Lettres* follows the chronological scheme established by the Benedictine Maurists. Storin renumbered the epistles to reflect Gregory's original collection, which was based on groups of letters arranged by themes and personal relationships.
Most translations from *Life of Macrina* in this book come from Anna Silvas, *Macrina the Younger: Philosopher of God*. In reproducing the Greek text, however, I follow Pierre Maraval's edition, *Grégoire de Nysse: Vie de Sainte Macrine*, which has different chapter divisions than that of Silvas. Therefore, in footnotes I include the Maraval numbering, first, followed by that of Silvas: e.g., Greg. Ny. *Vit. Macr.* 31.15–20 (Silvas, 33.3).
In Chapter 4, I briefly refer to passages from Eunomius' *Apology for the Apology* (*Apol. Apol.*). This text has been preserved only in fragments from Gregory of Nyssa's refutation of it in his *Against Eunomius* (*Contr. Eun.*), a text edited and reproduced in Werner Jaeger's *Gregorii Nysseni Opera* (GNO). The fragments of *Apol. Apol.* have been organized and summarized in Richard Vaggione's *Eunomius: The Extant Works*. When I cite *Apol. Apol.*, I give its place within GNO as

well as the page number in which it appears in Vaggione: e.g., Eunomius, *Apol. Apol.* 1.346.4–11 GNO (Vaggione, 108).

Finally, I cite the epistles of Libanius according to their numbering by Richard Foerster in *Libanii opera*. In translations by Scott Bradbury, from *Selected Letters of Libanius*, I list the letter by Foerster's numbering, first, followed by that of Bradbury: e.g., Libanius, *Ep.* 482 (Bradbury 52). More recently, Raffaella Cribiore translated several of Libanius' letters in *The School of Libanius in Late Antique Antioch*. In my book, letters she translated are cited with Foerster's numbering, first, followed by that of Cribiore. Likewise, in translations by Albert Norman, from *Libanius: Autobiography and Selected Letters*, I give Foerster's number, first, followed by that of Norman.

Abbreviations

ACW	Ancient Christian Writers
AET	Abraham Malherbe, author and translator. *Ancient Epistolary Theorists*. Atlanta: SBL, 1988.
Apol. Apol.	Eunomius of Cyzicus, *Apology for the Apology*
CCSG	Corpus Christianorum Series Graeca
CH	*Church History*
C.J.	*Corpus iuris civilis*. Volume 2. *Codex Justinianus*. 11th Edition. Edited by Paul Krüger. Berlin, 1954.
Contr. Eun.	*Against Eunomius*
CP	*Classical Philology*
CQ	*Classical Quarterly*
C.Th.	*Codex Theodosianus*. Translated by Clyde Pharr. *The Theodosian Code and Novels, and the Sirmondian Constitutions*. Princeton, NJ: Princeton University, 1957.
Ep./Eps.	Epistle/Epistles
FC	Fathers of the Church (Washington, DC: Catholic University of America)
GNO	*Gregorii Nysseni Opera*. 11 vols. Edited by Werner Jaeger. Berlin, 1921–2009.
Greg. Naz.	Gregory of Nazianzus
Greg. Ny.	Gregory of Nyssa
H.E.	*Ecclesiastical History*
H-M	*Prosopographie zu den Schriften Gregors von Nazianz*. Edited by Marie-Madeleine Hauser-Meury. Bonn: Peter Hanstein Verlag, 1960.

HTR	*Harvard Theological Review*
In Basilium	Gregory of Nyssa, *Encomium on Basil*
JECS	*Journal of Early Christian Studies*
JLA	*Journal of Late Antiquity*
JTS	*Journal of Theological Studies*
LCL	Loeb Classical Library (London: William Heinemann; Cambridge, MA: Harvard University)
N.E.	Aristotle, *Nicomachean Ethics*
NIV	New International Version of the Bible
NPNF I	Nicene and Post-Nicene (First Series)
NPNF II	Nicene and Post-Nicene (Second Series)
OECS	Oxford Early Christian Studies
Or./Ors.	Oration/Orations
PG	Patrologia graeca. Patrologia cursus completus. Series Graeca. 162 vols. Edited by J. P. Migne. Paris, 1857–1886.
PL	Patrologia Latina. Patrologia cursus completes. Series Latina. 221 vols. Edited by J. P. Migne. Paris, 1844–1900.
PLRE	*The Prosopography of the Later Roman Empire*. 2 vols. Edited by A. H. M. Jones, J. R. Martindale, and J. Morris. Cambridge: Cambridge University, 1971, 1980.
SBL	Society of Biblical Literature
SC	Sources chrétiennes. Paris 1941–.
SP	*Studia Patristica*
VC	*Vigiliae Christianae*
VCS	*Vigiliae Christianae Supplements*
Vit. GTh.	Gregory of Nyssa, *Life of Gregory Thaumaturgus*
Vit. Macr.	Gregory of Nyssa, *Life of Macrina*
Vit. Phil.	Eunapius, *Lives of Philosophers and Sophists*
Vit. Soph.	Philostratus, *Lives of Sophists*

The Cappadocian Fathers and their Families

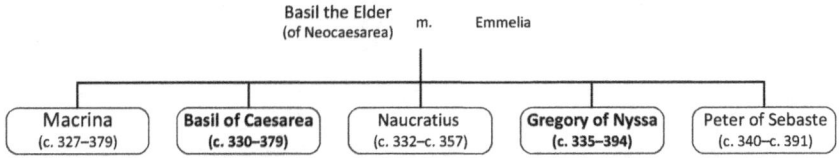

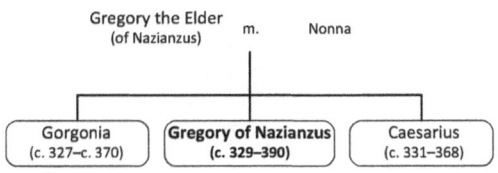

Map of Eastern Roman Empire c. 370

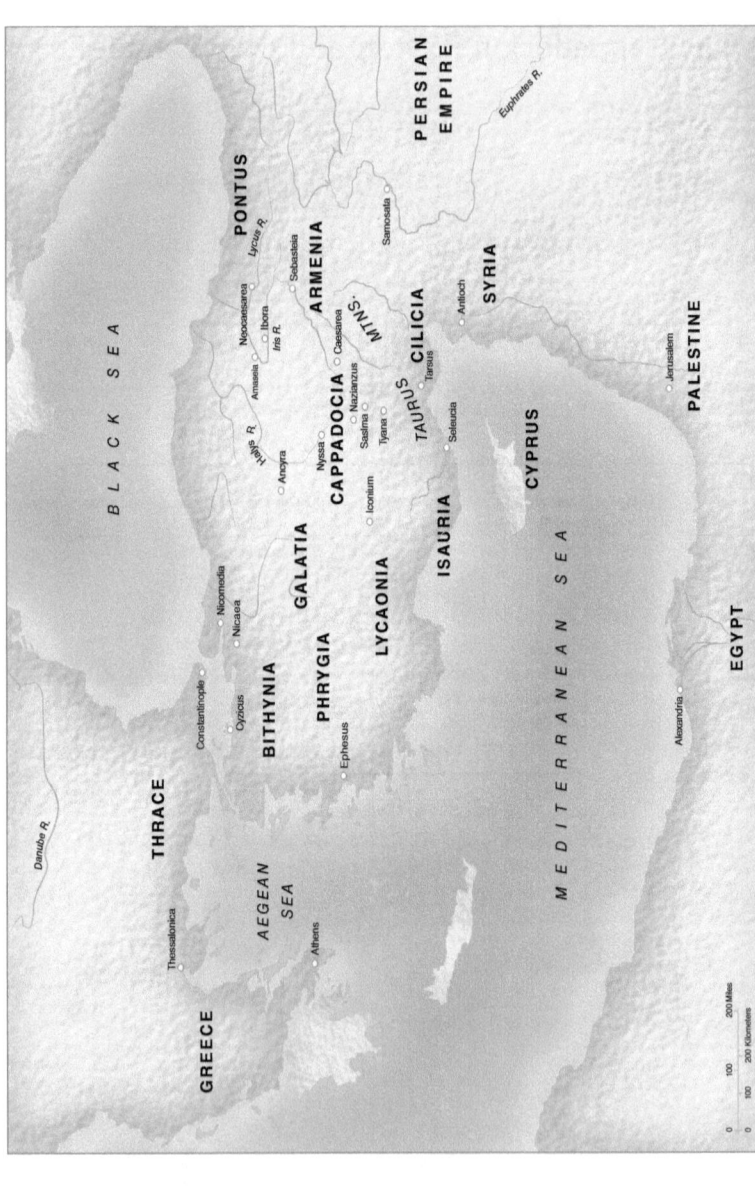

(This map design is based on an earlier version published in Raymond Van Dam, *Becoming Christian: The Conversion of Roman Cappadocia*. Philadelphia: University of Pennsylvania Press, 2003.)

Introduction

Paideia, Masculinity, and Identity

In 362 Emperor Julian (331–63) issued an edict and a letter that prohibited Christians from serving as teachers of Greek grammar, literature, and philosophy.[1] A year later, in his early thirties and recently ordained presbyter in his father's church, Gregory of Nazianzus (329–90) composed an epistle.[2] The addressee was Candidianus, governor of Cappadocia (Gregory's home province).[3] "I'm stamping the ground (κόπτω τοὔδαφος) with my feet, as it were, like the most impetuous of horses," Gregory wrote, "champing the bit, cocking my ear, chuffing hot breath (πνέω τε θυμόν) from my nostrils, gazing with ferocity (βλέπω δριμύ), shaking off the froth, yet still remaining within the corral, since the law does not permit me the race."[4] Gregory was alluding to Julian's

---

[1] *C. Th.* 13.3.5; Julian, *Ep.* 61. R. Cribiore, *Libanius the Sophist: Rhetoric, Reality, and Religion in the Fourth Century* (Ithaca: Cornell University Press, 2013), 229–37 considers the measures an attempt to draw a stark religious binary between Christian and non-Christian intellectuals; A. Kaldellis, *Hellenism in Byzantium: The Transformation of Greek Identity and the Reception of the Classical Tradition* (Cambridge: Cambridge University Press, 2007), 146–54 shows how near-contemporary authors misrepresented the legislation as an act of tyranny against Christians; and J. Stenger, *Hellenische Identität in der Spätantike: pagane Autoren und ihr Unbehagen an der eigenen Zeit* (Berlin: de Gruyter, 2009), 111–22 sees the actions not primarily as anti-Christian, but as part of Julian's larger moral reform program. Nazianzen depicts the measures as directed against Christians and as personally confining.
[2] Greg. Naz., *Ep.* 10 (Storin 230).
[3] Candidianus: R. Van Dam, "Governors of Cappadocia during the Fourth Century," *Medieval Prosopography* 17 (1996), 43–5; H–M, 51–2; and B. Storin, *Gregory of Nazianzus's Letter Collection: The Complete Translation* (Berkeley: University of California Press, 2019), 24.
[4] Greg. Naz., *Ep.* 10 (Storin 230): "law," οὐκ ἐφιέντος μοι τοῦ νόμου τὸν δρόμον.

ban on Christians teaching classical texts, exclusion from "the race."[5] Cueing the reader to imagine a caged animal, Gregory staged his restlessness. Horses were a point of pride for Cappadocians, who were famed across the Mediterranean for the quality of their stallions.[6] Equines were featured in Greek antiquity as noble animals, with a legacy in heroic combat stretching back to Homer's *Iliad*.[7] In most of the Roman empire, moreover, by the late 300s horse-racing had surpassed athletics as the most widely attended and contested sport.[8] "Shall I toss aside eloquence altogether?" Gregory then asked. "Of course not!"[9] Gregory was personifying himself as the gallant steed, unwilling to be constrained. He was also alluding to a passage from Plato's *Theaetetus* – where cavalry are preparing to race into battle – to signal that he had a natural calling to fulfill.[10] The emperor's mandates could not deter his determination to race. He was showing off his elocution, a mark of his manhood.

In expressing defiance, Gregory was protesting Emperor Julian's proscription. He was using the issue of Julian's law to fashion an identity for himself, as a challenger craving the thrill of competition. And now, having recorded his audacity, he issued a panegyric for the addressee, the governor of his homeland. Gregory admired the "power of your speech" (τοῦ λόγου τὸ κράτος), pointing out that Candidianus' just but imposing nature was manifest through his command over words.[11] He then likened Candidianus' "resolve" (στερρός) to the "pounces of lions."[12] And finally he delivered a litany of references from celebrated Greek authors

---

[5] F. Gautier, *La Retraite et le sacerdoce chez Grégoire de Nazianze* (Turnhout: Brepols, 2002), 314–17, suggests that, because of his ordination to the priesthood, he was excluded from instruction. This is not a convincing argument.

[6] R. Van Dam, *Kingdom of Snow: Roman Rule and Greek Culture in Cappadocia* (Philadelphia: University of Pennsylvania Press, 2002), 23, on the association of horses with aristocratic honor in Cappadocia; J. K. Anderson, *Ancient Greek Horsemanship* (Berkeley: University of California Press, 1961), 20–2, on Cappadocian horses as highly regarded warhorses,

[7] On Achilles' immortal horses Balios and Xanthos, *Iliad* 2.760, 16.148, 17.426, and 19.292; Xenophon, *On Horsemanship* and *Calvary Commander* on the close relationship between superior horses and combat; A. Sestili, *L'equitazione nella Grecia antica: i trattati equestri di Senofonte e i frammenti di Simone* (Scandicci: Firenze Atheneum, 2006), 50–101, gives overview of Xenophon's texts and shows that horsemanship played a crucial part of the civil and military life of the aristocratic Greek male.

[8] S. Remijsen, *The End of Greek Athletics in Late Antiquity* (Cambridge: Cambridge University Press, 2015), 87–8.

[9] Greg. Naz., *Ep.* 10 (Storin 230): "toss aside," παντάπασι καταβαλοῦμεν τοὺς λόγους.

[10] Plato, *Theaetetus* 183d.   [11] Greg. Naz., *Ep.* 10 (Storin 230).

[12] Greg. Naz., *Ep.* 10 (Storin 230).

Sophocles, Pindar, Homer, Aristophanes, and Theocritus as he praised Candidianus for his resourcefulness, justice, wisdom, gentleness, and persuasion. Gregory extolled the qualities that made a legitimate ruler, and with well-suited citations from ancient Greek authors, he flaunted his fluency. The text simulated the youthful priest as performing at an *adventus* ceremony, when orators welcomed emperors and other imperial officials to their communities.[13] Gregory thus honored Candidianus. and by recalling glorious men of honor, he brandished his intimacy with a Greek past that was – according to Julian – incongruent with his position as a clergyman.[14]

Gregory's letter illustrates the major theme in *Christianity and the Contest for Manhood*: fourth-century clergy using the rhetoric of contest as a means of identifying with classical ideals of manhood. In texts such as the preceding, Gregory and his fellow clergy Basil of Caesarea (330–79) and Gregory of Nyssa (335–94) invested themselves, family members, and fellow pro-Nicene clergy with enduring attributes of classical Greek masculinity.[15] These bishops (the "Cappadocians") represented their epistolary discourse with fellow intellectuals as emblematic of ἀρετή (*aretē*): the fortitude, the excellence, the virtue, that is, that ancient Greeks considered the product of rivalries between preeminent men. The Cappadocians penned and exchanged letters with fellow literati as part of a virtual ἀγών (*agōn*), competition that in classical Greece had included warfare, athleticism, and oratory. In hagiographic accounts (writings about saints), Nyssen and Nazianzen likewise endowed male

---

[13] For the nature of ceremony for establishing fluid relations between empire and province, and in particular the *adventus*, see S. MacCormack, *Art and Ceremony in Late Antiquity* (Berkeley: University of California Press, 1981), 15–90; on the reception of governors, A. Bérenger, "L'adventus des gouverneurs de province," in *Les Entrées royales et impériales: histoire, représentation et diffusion d'une cérémonie publique, de l'Orient ancien à Byzance*, eds. A. Bérenger and É. Perrin-Saminadayar (Paris: de Boccard, 2009), 125–38.

[14] A practice also carried out by prominent contemporary non-Christian writers. Libanius of Antioch, for instance, reached back to the classic past to celebrate the works of the fifth-century B.C. rhetorician Aristides. See R. Cribiore, "Vying with Aristides in the Fourth Century," in *Aelius Aristides between Greece, Rome, and the Gods*, eds. W. V. Harris and B. Holmes (Leiden: Brill, 2009), 263–78.

[15] To delineate between the Gregories, I use "Nazianzen," and "Nyssen." In applying the term "pro-Nicene," I am using the definition outlined by L. Ayres, *Nicaea and its Legacy: An Approach to Fourth-Century Trinitarian Theology* (Oxford: Oxford University Press, 2004), 236–40. Pro-Nicenes, that is, developed their theology using the Nicene Creed as a cipher. Ayres summarizes the principle that guided pro-Nicene arguments against rival Trinitarian theologies: "The unity of nature was understood to imply that the three persons were of equal ontological standing – all possessed the fullness of what it was to be God" (236).

and female ascetic figures with features of manhood coordinate with contest: bravery, constancy, and resolve. Such literary displays were conspicuous, an assertion of social and hierarchical authority.[16]

In the case cited above, Gregory of Nazianzus (Nazianzen) used his proficiency with ancient Greek literature to present himself as resolute and capable of matching anyone (including Emperor Julian) as an arbiter of manly deportment. His letter was an assurance to fellow intellectuals: first, that he belonged to their number; second, that he placed import on time-honored conventions of gender; and third, that with his learnedness, he was well-suited to habituate young men into leadership roles. An affiliation with a man of contest was significant in the late fourth century. Individuals and groups of intellectuals sought to claim classical Greece as part of their pedigree, a heritage that illustrated masculinity through scenes of struggle. In prohibiting Christians from teaching classical texts, Julian was symbolically emasculating church leaders such as Gregory and consequently maligning them. By declaring that clergy belonged outside this *agōn*, the emperor was declaring Christianity incompatible with classical masculinity. Gregory's performance was intended to shatter that disjunction.

But while Gregory was seeking to demonstrate his own manhood, he was not attacking the masculinity of his correspondents. Nor did Basil or Nyssen use letter writing to impugn the gender of rivals. Instead the Cappadocians participated in epistolary *agōnes* as a way of questing after the characteristics of idealized manhood. They distributed honor through literary exhibitions of correspondence, even as they were accruing status for themselves. The display of *aretē* through letters thus reflected the reciprocal nature of classical friendship (φιλία; *philia*), in which colleagues promoted a collective outlay of dignity. In managing this economy of virtue, the Cappadocians promoted confidence in the leadership of pro-Nicene Christians, believers who supported the tenets of the Creed of Nicaea, and in particular the sameness of nature in God the Father and God the Son. But in an epistolary network of intellectuals, the Cappadocians were not seeking either to isolate on an identity as pro-Nicene clergymen or to minimize the *aretē* of non-Christians. In this genre, they were attempting to gain creditability within a diverse religious community, whose affinity depended largely on a mutual sense of manhood.

---

[16] See Pierre Bourdieu's conception of *habitus*: that speech, behavior, education, and values produce social differences of hierarchy in each society. P. Bourdieu, *Language and Symbolic Power*, ed. J. B. Thompson, trans. G. Raymond and M. Adamson (Cambridge, MA: Harvard University Press, 1991), 1–12.

Within hagiographic biographies, however, the Cappadocians linked *aretē* explicitly to subjects identified as pro-Nicene Christians. Through episodes of *agōnes*, figures as diverse as third-century bishop Gregory Thaumaturgus and Basil's and Nyssen's sister Macrina were characterized as epitomes of classical masculinity and as Trinitarian (pro-Nicene) Christians. In such representations, the Cappadocians used sacred figures or family members and friends as the medium through which to tether Trinitarian episcopal leadership to classical manhood. These texts, usually delivered first as speeches to large Christian crowds, were later circulated among a wide readership of Christians and non-Christians. The Cappadocians intended these rhetorical compositions to influence a broad segment of society to correlate pro-Nicene Christianity with classical manhood. Unlike epistolary performances, where the Cappadocians shared honor with correspondents, they designed hagiographic accounts to equate manliness with pro-Nicenes, and effeminacy with doctrinal opponents. These personifications thus accentuated the Cappadocians' identity as theologians while diminishing the trustworthiness of their adversaries. As Susanna Elm argues, such literary performances were used to discredit religious rivals; in particular the non-Christian Emperor Julian, but also theological rivals *within* Christianity such as Eunomius of Cyzicus (c. 335–c. 393), the one-time bishop, critic of Nicene Christology, and frequent object of the Cappadocians' invective.[17] The Cappadocians harmonized classical masculinity and piety in their pro-Nicene subjects to authorize them against such non-Trinitarians. The hagiographic discourses placed theological persuasion front and center by staging pro-Nicene feats of *aretē* against the unorthodox, thus delineating identity *within* Christianity. In both epistolary exchange and hagiographic composition, therefore, the Cappadocians framed pro-Nicene leadership as an extension of masculinity.

BISHOPS, *AGŌN*, AND CLASSICAL MASCULINITY

By the early 370s, Nazianzen, Basil, and Nyssen all were serving as bishops in Cappadocia. Basil was elected bishop at Caesarea, capital of

---

[17] S. Elm, *Sons of Hellenism, Fathers of the Church: Emperor Julian, Gregory of Nazianzus, and the Vision of Rome* (Berkeley: University of California Press, 2012); although Elm focuses more specifically on the correct use of λόγοι (eloquence) as delineating true philosophy among rivals, my investigation into the Cappadocians' hagiography takes a similar approach. See especially Elm, 387–413.

Cappadocia, in 370. As the metropolitan bishop, in 372 he ordained Nazianzen at Sasima. The same year he appointed his younger brother Gregory (Nyssen) to an episcopal see at Nyssa. Before consecration as bishops, Basil and Nazianzen had both already served as lesser clergy: Basil, ordained as deacon in 362, and then as presbyter in 365; Nazianzen ordained presbyter at his father's church in 361. For Nyssen, his election to the episcopacy in 372 marked his first tenure as clergy. Momentarily we will turn to the familial and social background of the Cappadocians, but first an overview of the fourth-century episcopacy will show how, more generally, expectations of intellectual preparation and gender in church leaders made each Cappadocian a candidate to serve as a high-level clergyman.

During the mid-300s, bishops increasingly were conducting issues of provincial administration in association with, and sometimes in place of civic officials. In these roles, many clergy asserted status by deploying forms of cultural capital that acknowledged affinity with other provincial elites.[18] In the eastern Roman empire, most municipal offices were held by a longstanding local aristocracy (the curial class) that maintained a network of friends, patrons, and clients within the city and in other towns and provinces.[19] These individuals developed and maintained relationships, in large part, through a common social currency: a mutual acculturation (παιδεία; *paideia*) based on the study of classical Greek literature, philosophy, history, medicine, and oratory. The Cappadocians were born into families of these power brokers and each grew up studying and participating in the discourse of *paideia*. Personal honor and public status in this segment of provincial administration depended partly on playing a

---

[18] Peter Brown, *Power and Persuasion in Late Antiquity: Towards a Christian Empire* (Madison: University of Wisconsin Press, 1992), 41–7, uses the concept of cultural capital developed in Bourdieu. Brown's use of Bourdieu's cultural capital includes the language, the decorum, the rules of interaction that enabled provincial elites far removed from one another to participate in a mutual dialogue that showed respect for a shared curriculum of classical literature. Exhibiting fluency in this pedagogy was a means of participating in a collective identity that united distant parties in a common intellectual space. One of Brown's major contributions, in studying provincial administration through the framework of cultural capital, is his emphasis on well-educated bishops' ability to enter rather fluidly into influential social and political roles outside the church.

[19] S. Métivier, *La Cappadoce (IVe–VIe Siècle): une histoire provinciale de l'empire romain d'Orient* (Paris: Publications de la Sorbonne, 2005), 77–94; A. H. M. Jones, *The Later Roman Empire, 284–602: A Social, Economic, and Administrative Survey*, 3 vols (Oxford: Basil Blackwell, 1964) specifically on the *curiales*, 1:737–57.

role as a *pepaideumenos* (a performer of *paideia*).[20] Increasingly during the late-fourth century, Christian literati such as the Cappadocians – trained in *paideia* and from a heritage of provincial aristocracy – were being ordained as clergy. Such priests were thus equipped to petition various regional and imperial authorities through correspondence when the addressee understood the verbal cues that came from familiarity with tropes and references from the classical past.[21]

A cohesion based on habituation in the values of classical Greece facilitated requests for civic benefactions, exchanges of favors, personal patronage, and various forms of mediation between the Cappadocians and magnates across the eastern empire. In the early 370s, for example, Basil penned a petition regarding a fellow bishop to Aburgius, another native Cappadocian who had served as an imperial magistrate.[22] Basil spoke of honoring their common ἑταιρεία (*hetaireia*), a "brotherhood" of similarly educated men.[23] Basil reminded Aburgius of their mutual background and learning (*paideia*), which they had shared at Athens or at home in Caesarea. He praised Aburgius for his *aretē*, thus advertising his compatriot's virtuous manhood. By accentuating reciprocal nobility, Basil was reminding Aburgius of their congruity in terms of education and status. Likewise in 385 Gregory of Nazianzus mediated for his grandnephew's family in a letter to Gregory, a governor in Cappadocia.[24] Gregory suggested that men who share a love for eloquence (λόγος; *logos*) are united because of their common passion. Thus, he was seeking "from

---

[20] L. Van Hoof, "Performing *Paideia*: Greek Culture as an Instrument for Social Promotion in the Fourth Century A.D.," *CQ* 63 (2013), 387–9; S. Swain, *Hellenism and Empire: Language, Classicism, and Power in the Greek World AD 50–250* (Oxford: Clarendon Press, 1996), 6–7.

[21] C. Rapp, *Holy Bishops: The Nature of Christian Leadership in an Age of Transition* (Berkeley: University of California Press, 2005), 181–7; R. Lizzi Testa, *Il potere episcopale nell'Oriente romano: rappresentazione ideologica e realtà politica (IV–V sec. d. C.)* (Rome: Edizioni dell'Ateneo, 1987), 2–11.

[22] Aburgius: *PLRE* 1:5; Van Dam, *Kingdom*, 59.

[23] Basil, *Ep.* 33; E. Watts, *City and School in Late Antique Athens and Alexandria* (Berkeley: University of California Press, 2008), 51–3, on the nuances of the word ἑταιρεία in an intellectual context, and how the term in Eunapius' account of sophists is used to describe persons who belonged to the inner circle of a teacher.

[24] Gregory: *PLRE* 1:403; Storin, *Gregory*, 30; Van Dam, "Governors," 51–2; Gregorius had served as governor of Cappadocia Secunda or Cappadocia Prima; P. Gallay, *Grégoire de Nazianze: Lettres* (Paris: Les Belles Lettres, 1964), 86 n. 3, dates the epistle to 385 but does not specify if the recipient was, in fact, the governor of Cappadocia, or which of the two divisions he governed.

Your Friendliness (φιλία) the response that a friend would give."[25] By doing so, the governor's nobility (καλοκαγαθία) would be advertised through aiding these supplicants. Because of their common conception of *philia* ("camaraderie") – as denoted in classical texts – the bishop was reminding the governor how a Greek gentleman behaves, thus encouraging him to act befittingly.[26] The ideal of *philia*, as a shared identity based on *paideia*, formed a cornerstone of networking across the empire during the late fourth century.[27]

If an individual played the role of the *pepaideumenos* correctly with another scholar, even if the two differed in religious beliefs, he could expect a degree of respect and reasonable consideration for his requests.[28] More important than leverage gained on any single issue, by appearing proficient through displays of cultural capital, an individual acquired cumulative honor that enhanced his influence in other matters. He would be taken seriously by his peers. For centuries, the overriding premise of a curriculum in *paideia* had been to cultivate the citizen male. As fourth-century *pepaideumenoi* participated in similar disciplines as their forebears, a mutual sense of masculinity provided symmetry among a cross-section of imperial and provincial intelligentsia. Peter Brown speaks of *paideia* as the common code among the educated that allowed individuals from otherwise politically subordinate positions to interact with and persuade superiors.[29] But the less powerful person was expected to project a bold persona in order to be effective when supplicating imperial

---

[25] Greg. Naz., *Ep.* 195 (Storin 82).

[26] D. Konstan, *Friendship in the Classical World* (Cambridge: Cambridge University Press, 1997), 6–14, addresses the complexities in the Greek language for the bond that is most like conceptions of friendship in the modern western world. *Philia*, he points out, referred to affection that applied to multiple relationships, "friendship" outside of kinship groups being only one of these. The noun *philos*, he says, most closely approximates our word "friend." In other words, the more accurate and specific designation for "friendship" would be to talk about *"philia* between *philoi*." Our study will concentrate on *philia* as this latter form of friendship. That is, we will use the term *philia* about a voluntary association between individuals, involving mutual affection and commitment, and predicated on similarity of social values; and specifically rooted in mutual *aretē*.

[27] The shared identity of classical friendship, as Reeser notes, was rooted in a masculine ethos, T. Reeser, *Moderating Masculinity in Early Modern Culture* (Chapel Hill: University of North Carolina Press, 2006), 55–6; for the variant terminology of friendship between Basil and Nazianzen, K. Treu, "Φιλία und Αγάπη: zur Terminologie der Freundschaft bei Basilius und Gregor von Nazianz," *Studii Clasice* 3 (1961), 421–7.

[28] A. Schor, *Theodoret's People: Social Networking and Religious Conflict in Late Roman Syria* (Berkeley: University of California Press, 2011) 139–43; Schor uses social network theory to explain how bishops could use *paideia* as a "gateway to the Roman elite" (141).

[29] Brown, *Power*, 61–3.

figures. Knowledge of ancient texts thus was insufficient, without the attendant deportment. Elm and Arthur Urbano similarly discuss *paideia* as the matrix of spiritual and philosophic authority in the late fourth century.[30] For Christian leaders, the dividing line between orthodox and heretical came to depend on the right and wrong uses of *logoi*; here meaning philosophic reason and eloquence. For Brown, Elm, and Urbano, intimacy with the ancients enabled individuals to assert control by crafting a variety of self-representations: as powerful, civilized, erudite, philosophic, and Greek.

Christianity and the Contest for Manhood focuses on masculinity as one such configuration; a disposition that the Cappadocians understood as confirmation of *paideia* fully developed and properly used. An identity as a classical male thus overlapped with or enhanced other models of *paideia*. The issue of masculinity, for example, played a significant role enhancing one's identity as a Hellene (a true Greek). To assert oneself as a philosopher, moreover, an individual had to have excelled in a course of studies (*paideia*) that promoted manhood as a moral virtue and set forth a myriad of classical Greek persons to emulate.[31] By definition, a true Greek in late antiquity had to appear manly.[32] *Paideia* was capital through which scholars interacted, while *aretē* was the ethical character (ἦθος) of an individual whose development was bona fide and comprehensive.

The Legacy of Agōn *and the Semantics of Virtuous Manhood*

Antecedents for the cultural capital of masculinity in the fourth century appeared foremost in the earliest accounts of Greek society, where an individual gained honor by exhibiting exemplary manhood.[33] One's integrity and authority were reckoned according to his masculinity,

---

[30] Elm, *Sons*, 11–12; A. Urbano, *The Philosophical Life: Biography and the Crafting of Intellectual Identity in Late Antiquity* (Washington: Catholic University of America Press, 2013), on intellectuals competing to claim Greek *paideia* as their heritage, 6–24.

[31] Elm, *Sons*, 479–87; Urbano, *Philosophical*, 8–9.

[32] On constructing an identity as a "Hellene," a complex, multi-faceted designation in Christianity: C. Rapp, "Hellenic Identity, Romanitas, and Christianity in Byzantium," in *Hellenisms: Culture, Identity, and Ethnicity from Antiquity to Modernity*, ed. Katarina Zacharia (Aldershot: Ashgate, 2008), 127–47, and R. Dostálová, "Christentum und Hellenismus: Zur Herausbildung einer neuen kulturellen Identität im 4. Jahrhundert," *Byzantinoslavica* 44 (1983), 1–12.

[33] M. Finkelberg, "Timē and Aretē in Homer," *CQ* 48:1 (1998), 15–16; as Finkelberg shows, this notion of honor is best understood as a broader concept that included status and prestige. Finkelberg also makes an important differentiation between *timē* (honor

an identity determined not based solely on sex, but rather earned through participating in contests (*agōnes*) deemed representative of a virtuous male.[34] A man might be criticized for exuding feminine traits, for example, while a woman might receive praise for demonstrating the probity of a noble man by proving herself in a struggle. The value-laden implication of gender comes across already in the Homeric vocabulary, where idealized masculinity was imbedded in *aretē* (ἀρετή), a term used to denote stateliness and supremacy. In the Homeric epics, *aretē* involved a number of qualities ranging from valor in combat to excellence of speech.[35] Earliest examples of such idyllic masculinity appear in the Homeric warriors, who proved their bravery in matches against other combatants (e.g. Achilles vs. Hector). The action always took place in view of others, so that the warrior's virtue was made known to his chieftain and fellow combatants and he could subsequently accrue the honor befitting his deeds.[36] In these encounters, courage stood out as an index of masculinity, thus authorizing these figures as (ἀγαθοί; *agathoi*), upstanding men. The exhortation found in Homer, "Be men" (ἀνέρες ἔστε) became a commonplace in later Greek writing, as an injunction to act with courage and resolve.[37] Such acts of mettle in Homer provided an antecedent to classical *agōn*, conspicuous competition that singularized leaders. As early as the Homeric epics, moreover, legitimate masculinity appeared as a social construct achieved in solidarity with other men. Ideal manhood, that is, constituted an enterprise that was based on a consensus

allocated by others through competition) and *aretē* (virtue recognized in oneself through competition). Both were important to fourth-century bishops.

[34] J. Butler, *Gender Trouble: Feminism and the Subversion of Identity* (New York: Routledge, 1990), 170–7.

[35] W. Jaeger, *Paideia: The Ideals of Greek Culture*, trans. G. Highet, vol. 1 (New York, Oxford University Press, 1945), 3–14; on distinction of *texne* (as "art" or "craft") and comparison with *aretē* (as a moral virtue), J. Kube, TEXNH *und* APETH: *Sophistisches und platonisches Tugendwissen* (Berlin: de Gruyter, 1969), 69–78; also H. I. Marrou, *A History of Education in Antiquity*, trans. G. Lamb (New York, 1956), 95–101.

[36] J. Lendon, *Empire of Honour: The Art of Government in the Roman World* (Oxford: Clarendon Press, 2002), 32–6.

[37] For example *Iliad* 5.529; 6.112; 11.287; in classical Greek, authors used the verb *andrizomai*, also translated "play the man"; M. Jones, *Playing the Man: Performing Masculinities in the Ancient Greek Novel* (Oxford: Oxford University Press, 2012), 158–9; Jones emphasizes the moral component in the word *andrizomai*, where demonstration of ἀνδρεία (manliness) contrasts with μαλακία (softness), a sign of moral weakness; the sense of honor and resolution in this phrase comes across, for example, in its only appearance in the New Testament, where the author of I Corinthians urges readers to "stand firm in the faith, be men of courage (ἀνδρίζομαι), be strong" *(I Cor.* 16.13); e.g. Basil, *Eps.* 106, 161, Greg. Naz., *Eps.* 166, 178.

of honorable individuals,[38] thus the importance of melees between rival warriors, fighting each other in front of an audience of fellow combatants according to accepted rules of nobility. The combat was not only about "besting" the other, but also about celebrating a collective sense of virtue. *Pepaideumenoi* in late antiquity were attuned to this cornerstone of self-formation and understood that while a superior man was to embody a composite of lofty traits, status depended on those qualities that others could witness.

In classical Greek literature, the notion of valor in combat continued to give a measure of manhood; so much so, that the predominant word used to denote "manliness" (ἀνδρεία; *andreia*) also referred to the ideal of "courage."[39] The contests in the polis (city state of classical Greece) provided a variety of forums for demonstrating courage and manliness by the fifth century B.C.: melees between hoplite soldiers; rivalries between athletes; matches of wit, intelligence, and eloquence among prominent teachers and orators; and civic notables outdoing one another in publicized benevolence to their cities. The arena of struggle between preeminent persons endured for centuries as a trope in Greek literature: partly as a setting where one individual defeated or outshined the other; but more deliberately, as a staging point for exhibiting the distinctive qualities of the aristocratic male.[40] A noble individual was expected to surpass the average citizen, for example, in fortitude, endurance, and self-control. The superior conduct of an *agathos* (a brave and upright man) was made evident to others by various challenges that highlighted his dominance.

The issue of struggle as an index of honor never receded from Greek imagination. Several classical authors applied the terms *aretē* and/or *andreia* in deliberations about acquiring moral virtues. Both words resonated with overtones of masculinity. Plato and Aristotle, for instance,

---

[38] B. Graziosi and J. Haubold, "Homeric Masculinity: HNOREH and AΓHNORIH," *The Journal of Hellenic Studies* 123 (2003): 60–4, argue that in the *Iliad*, the term ἠνορέη indicated masculinity achieved in solidarity with other men, while ἀγηνορίη suggested a manhood tainted by excessive individualism.

[39] É. Smoes, *Le Courage chez les Grecs d'Homère à Aristotle* (Brussels: Ousia, 1995), 33; the word *andreia* is a post-Homeric term as Smoes points out, although the word was often used in reference to representations of courage as seen in Homer; on Homeric *agōnes* as a prototype for later Greeks, also see K. Bassi, "The Semantics of Manliness in Ancient Greece," 33, and Jones, *Playing*, 96.

[40] S. Swain, "Sophists and Emperors: The Case of Libanius," in *Approaching Late Antiquity: The Transformation from Early to Late Empire*, eds. S. Swain and M. Edwards (Oxford: Oxford University Press, 2006), 356–7.

implemented the expressions as key components of their respective taxonomies of moral philosophy, where manliness registered as an emblem of superior ethics.[41] In *Laches*, a discourse on courage (*andreia*), Plato has the interlocutors discussing the merits of fighting in armor (an act of bravery) as a way to instill an aristocratic code of behavior in young men. "For only men trained in the use of these warlike implements," the general Nicias asserts, "can claim to be trained in the contest whereof we are athletes and in the affairs wherein we are called upon to contend."[42] Here, courage (through the metaphor of combat) both forms and is informed by agonistic engagements. Plato is therefore staging a dialogue about noble manhood, where *andreia* presents the path not only to "courage," but also to its near equivalent "manliness." Aristotle similarly treats the issue of "becoming good men" as analogous to repeatedly facing danger in order to acquire bravery.[43] For Aristotle, moral goodness results from the habitual practice of virtuous behaviors. "With courage," he says, "it is by habituating ourselves to make light of alarming situations and to face them that we become brave."[44] With a coalescence of courage and manhood, Aristotle was stating that the honorable male must undergo severe training to maintain his virtue. *Aretē*, the word for moral excellence used by Aristotle, referred here to qualities expected of an upright man, achieved through trial.

The ethical implications of an individual taking part in an *agōn* likewise underpinned much of the Cynic-Stoic dialogue on acquiring virtue, a discourse that informed the use of athletic/warrior imagery in several texts from early imperial Rome. A sampling of such literature includes biographical treatises by the Hellenistic philosopher Philo (c. 25 B.C.–50 A.D.), the *Fourth Book of Maccabees*, and the New Testament epistles.[45] These

---

[41] A. Hobbs, *Plato and the Hero: Courage, Manliness and the Impersonal Good* (Cambridge: Cambridge University Press, 2000), 68–74; because manliness constituted an ethic per se, Hobbs shows, it is difficult to distinguish between the ancients' use of *andreia* as "manhood" or specifically as a moral virtue.

[42] Plato, *Laches* 182a (Lamb, 17): ἐλάττω πόνον ἔχει – καὶ ἅμα προσήκει μάλιστ' ἐλευθέρῳ τοῦτό τε τὸ γυμνάσιον καὶ ἡ ἱππική· οὗ γὰρ ἀγῶνος ἀθληταί ἐσμεν καὶ ἐν οἷς ἡμῖν ὁ ἀγὼν πρόκειται. . .

[43] Aristotle, *N.E.* 1103b26–1104a11 (Thomson); Reeser, *Moderating*, 52–5; Reeser recognizes that *aretē* in Aristotle is "coded as specifically masculine" (52); Reeser gives bravery in combat and friendship (*philia*) as examples of qualities that are public in nature, and therefore directly related to masculinity.

[44] Aristotle, *N.E.* 1104a32–1104a33 (Thomson): καὶ ἐπὶ τῆς ἀνδρείας· ἐθιζόμενοι γὰρ καταφρονεῖν τῶν φοβερῶν καὶ ὑπομένειν αὐτὰ γινόμεθα ἀνδρεῖοι.

[45] V. Pfitzner, *Paul and the Agon Motif: Traditional Athletic Imagery in Pauline Literature* (Leiden: Brill, 1967), 25–61, is an especially rich discussion of *agōn* imagery in these texts.

works redirected the spirit of competition from ventures predicated on winning glory, to struggles for overcoming the physical nature in order to live according to a higher purpose. In these cases, the writers follow the Cynic-Stoic picture of the sage who subjects his impulses to the law of reason. The *agōn* trope consequently shifts from occasions of public showmanship and honor, to battles within oneself.[46] Composing from a Judeo-Christian perspective, the writers emphasized the agency of God as essential to overcoming the passions. In addition, the ordeal to control human instincts is associated with one's piety: in Philo, through the self-control of the Patriarchs; in Fourth Maccabees, by the Jewish martyrs who overcame torture in order to commune with God; and in New Testament epistles, missionaries overcoming obstacles as they witnessed for Christ.[47]

The Cappadocians were heavily influenced by such illustrations of *agōnes*, both the mastery of the soul over bodily impulse and as visible contests in acquisition of honor and status. Our study will focus on *agōn* primarily in the latter sense, in cases where the Cappadocians cultivated *aretē* through interaction with rivals. In writings that underscored the pursuit of manly virtue, competition provided the litmus test that determined "classical masculinity," the term we are using to denote idealized manhood. Audiences for such texts valued showmanship, glory, and hierarchy along the same vein that civic gatherings had once extolled warriors, athletes, and orators. The contests, that is, certified excellence among their peers, fellow *pepaideumenoi*. Fourth-century literati were sensitive to the masculine ethos embedded in the notion of *agōn*, as training in *paideia* had made them conversant with the meaning of *aretē* and its association with public contests across a broad range of Greek epochs.[48] Within such struggles, *andreia* constituted only one element of the fuller sense of virtuous manhood. The Cappadocians thus included philosophical, physical, and spiritual excellence in coding *aretē* as masculine. And as I will argue later, even when staging *agōnes* as internal,

---

[46] Pfitzner, *Paul*, 28–35, emphasizes the variance among *agōn* motifs. On the one hand stands the context of the traditional athletic games, with its glorification of the nude body and the quest for superiority over others. On the other hand – within Cynic-Stoic philosophy – *agōn* illustrations apply to an individual's inner struggle for virtue.
[47] For example Philo, *On Joseph* 9; IV Maccabees 6:1–35, and Colossians 1:29–2:1; see analysis by Pfitzner, *Paul*, 38–48 and 57–69.
[48] T. Whitmarsh, *Greek Literature and the Roman Empire: The Politics of Imitation* (Oxford: Oxford University Press, 2004), 53.

spiritual struggles, the Cappadocians turned the experiences into exhibitions that reflected *aretē* as rooted in conventions of gender.

Second Sophistic Origins and the "Third Sophistic"

Identifying with a group that measured manhood through performance, the Cappadocians frequently gave examples of combat, athleticism, and other contests when illustrating "manly virtue" (*aretē*); thereby they reinforced their own affiliation with classical manhood, and that of their subjects.[49] The Cappadocians were informed by such techniques of asserting masculinity from their familiarity with authors of the Second Sophistic.[50] The latter is a term that scholars have applied to an intellectual movement during the first three centuries of the Roman empire when *pepaideumenoi* drew on classical Greek authors as sources for imitation, innovation, and constructions of self-identity.[51] The title was coined first by Philostratus of Athens (c. 170–c. 250), whose *Lives of the Sophists* extolled the careers of classical and contemporary sophists: individuals who taught rhetoric and who gave public displays of oratory. The sophists were celebrities of sorts who mesmerized audiences as they competed with one another to show fluency, wit, and knowledge of classical Greek philosophy, literature, and history. They were verbal warriors, intent on mastering the art of self-presentation.[52] The Cappadocians studied the

---

[49] S. Goldhill, "Rhetoric and the Second Sophistic," in *Cambridge Companion to Ancient Rhetoric*, ed. E. Gunderson (Cambridge: Cambridge University Press, 2009), 231–2, where rhetoric came to replace the leadership accorded to military heroes; and K. Bassi, *Acting Like Men: Gender, Drama and Nostalgia in Ancient Greece* (Ann Arbor: University of Michigan Press, 1998), 1–11, where Bassi, citing the influence of Michel Foucault, explains how the application of nostalgia can contribute to the preservation of gender roles.

[50] M. Gleason, *Making Men: Sophists and Self-Presentation in Ancient Rome* (Princeton: Princeton University Press, 1995), and especially the chapter on masculine deportment: 55–81.

[51] Some scholars have used the term "Third Sophistic" to designate the literary application of classical Greek themes as it continued into the fourth century. We will discuss this appellation in Chapter 1, where I maintain that it is more useful to think of the fourth century as an extension of Second Sophistic literary culture. The term "Third Sophistic," was introduced by L. Pernot, *La Rhétorique de l'éloge dans le monde gréco-romain*, vol. 1 (Paris: Institut d'Études Augustiniennes, 1993), 13–15.

[52] An excellent introduction to identity formation in the Second Sophistic is S. Goldhill, "Introduction: Setting an Agenda: 'Everything is Greek to the Wise,'" in *Being Greek Under Rome: Cultural Identity, the Second Sophistic and the Development of Empire*, ed. S. Goldhill (New York: Cambridge University Press, 2001), 1–20.

past under instructors whose intellectual lineage stretched back to these performers.[53] Studying the past through the lens of Second Sophistic oratory, the Cappadocians learned that earning an identity as a virtuous man required taking risks in front of others. They also discovered the art of tailoring the classical past to craft a self-presentation; in their case, an affiliation of ancient Greek models of masculinity within pro-Nicene Christian leadership. In letters to fellow *pepaideumenoi*, the Cappadocians mimicked elements from the performance culture of sophists; a simulation of verbal combat.

The Cappadocians differed somewhat from some of these earlier orators, however, in how they framed epistolary exhibitions. Confrontations between rival sophists often were based on zero-sum outcomes, with one opponent besting the other. In their letters, by comparison, the Cappadocians usually sought not to eviscerate addressees, but rather to uphold a code of dignity among fellow *pepaideumenoi*. In Chapter 1 we will discuss the notion of the "Third Sophistic," a term recent scholars have used to denote a revival of Greek rhetoric in the fourth century, after an abeyance in the late third and early fourth century.[54] I am not convinced there was enough discontinuity to apply the designation of a "Third Sophistic." If one does hold that a renaissance of exhibitive rhetoric took place – one similar to the Second Sophistic – it would entail two premises that distinguish it from its predecessor: first, performances among *pepaideumenoi* took place through letter exchange; and second, epistolary contests took place in view of a limited audience of correspondents and friends, and were designed to dispense honor rather than conquest. Through epistolary exchange the Cappadocians promoted their own capital, while also educating and affirming collective values.[55] The ethos of classical masculinity, that is, was made apparent in literary exhibitions that amounted to a collective intellectual enterprise. In this relationship between *pepaideumenoi*, unlike the cut-throat encounters recorded by Philostratus in *Lives of the Sophists*, literati challenged one another and confirmed a fellowship and system of values that often

---

[53] An intellectual pedigree that was itself earned by competition; Urbano, *Philosophical*, 24–6. Chapter 1 will address the Cappadocians' pedagogical connection to the Second Sophistic.
[54] For a wide variety of understandings of the term, see the different impressions of "Third Sophistic" by authors in E. Amato, ed., *Approches de la troisième sophistique, hommages à Jacques Schamp* (Brussels: Peeters, 2006).
[55] Lendon, *Empire*, 32–6.

transcended the religious controversies of their time. An epistle by Basil to Modestus, an imperial prefect, illustrates the symbiotic nature of the correspondence.[56] "The very act of writing to so great a man," Basil asserts, "is most conducive to honour (τιμή) in the eyes of the discerning; for intercourse with men who are overwhelmingly superior (ὁμιλίαι μεγίστην τοῖς ἀξιοθμένοις) to the rest of mankind affords the greatest distinction to such as are deemed worthy of it."[57] In this case Basil then proceeded to petition the prefect on behalf of clergy. But the point of "intercourse with superior men" was that an individual accrued credibility and manifested *aretē* by engaging with other men of high status.

The rhetorician Lucian of Samosata (c. 120–85) had offered similar sentiments in his dialogue on athletics. Elaborating how young men should be trained for political life, Lucian's protagonist Socrates explains "...by causing them to associate with superior men (ἀγαθῶν ἀνδρῶν συνουσίαις)...to associate with one another on equal footing, not to aim at what is base, to seek what is noble."[58] Through mingling with the elite and earning equivalent status, Lucian was indicating, a youth became socialized to assert his own authority. Writers such as Lucian viewed the pursuit of manliness as a kind of athletic endeavor. The metaphor had been common among classical authors who used analogies from sports as a parallel to becoming "best" men.[59] In both intellect and athletics, contests produced *aretē*.[60] And in both cases, the performance had to take place in public. Lucian's Solon stated that "to become a man of mark" (τὸ ἐπισημότατον γενέσθαι), it was necessary "to be pointed at with the finger as the best (ἄριστος) of one's class."[61] To excel, in other words, a runner or wrestler had to gain the recognition of the audience. A similar notion of an *agōn* had appeared in Plato's *Timaeus*, with the subject Socrates wanting to observe majestic animals "engaged in some struggle (πάθος) or conflict (ἀγών) that seems to show off their distinctive physical qualities."[62] The magnificence of these animals came into full view only

---

[56] Modestus was prefect of the East under Emperor Valens (328–78); for his role in imperial administration of Cappadocia and relationship with Basil, Van Dam, *Kingdom*, 106–35.
[57] Basil, *Ep.* 104 (Deferrari).   [58] Lucian, *Athletics* 22 (slight modification of Harmon).
[59] For example Plato, *Laws* 8.796; Aristotle, N.E. 1116a25–1116b10.
[60] J. Roisman, "Rhetoric, Manliness and Contest," in *A Companion to Greek Rhetoric*, ed. I. Worthington (Malden, MA: Blackwell, 2007), 395–7; and O. Van Nijf, "Athletics, Andreia and the Askêsis-Culture in the Roman East," in *Andreia: Studies in Manliness and Courage in Classical Antiquity*, eds. R. Rosen and I. Sluiter (Leiden: Brill, 2003), 265–73.
[61] Lucian, *Athletics* 36 (Harmon).   [62] Plato, *Timaeus* 19b (Zeyl).

when they were pushed to their limits; and only when a person of dignity could attest to their feats.

In similar manner, only with the affirmation of other *agathoi*, could an individual be counted excellent in late antiquity. This truism corresponded to the Cappadocians as letter writers, "verbal athletes" who sought intellectual validation from educated audiences.[63] "Virtue should be paraded (ἐπιδείκνυμι) before me," Nazianzen wrote to the Cappadocian rhetorician Eudoxius, "like the most valiant of athletes (τῶν ἀθλητῶν οἱ γενναῖοι) before their trainers."[64] It is not surprising that intellectuals used references to ancient Greek athletics. The ideal of courage, of unmediated manhood, was most visible in these heroes of sport.[65] Physical feats offered gritty demonstrations of fortitude. Such illustrations made for poignant rhetoric in the late fourth century, as orators became increasingly susceptible to accusations of artifice and duplicity.[66] The Cappadocians often used the language of corporeal strength, thus presenting an image of raw masculinity that contravened any hint of contrivance. The exertions that authors put into composition, moreover, mirrored the sense of achieving manhood by constantly learning and applying its ideals. The biographer Plutarch (c. 45–125) taught that "character is a habit long continued (τὸ ἦθος ἔθος ἐστὶ πολυχρόνιον), and if one were to call the virtues of character the virtues of habit, he would not seem to go far astray."[67] The appearance of having manly virtue came in large part from the advertised quest to achieve it. Participating in a dialogue on *aretē*, in other words, validated the writer according to classical standards of manhood.

The exchange of epistles constituted one such *agōn*, like oral contests of the Second Sophistic, in that the writer could be embarrassed or otherwise discounted if he failed to meet the expected erudition of his audience. But these contests, unlike oratorical duels, were witnessed primarily by a limited audience of fellow literati. Francis Gautier has convincingly argued for a major transition in the fourth century from

---

[63] Fellow fourth-century intellectuals referred to "athletes of eloquence": R. Cribiore, *Gymnastics of the Mind: Greek Education in Hellenistic and Roman Egypt* (Princeton: Princeton University Press, 2005), 220–5, for discussion of rhetoric as part of physical training.
[64] Greg. Naz., *Ep.* 174 (Storin 111); Eudoxius: Storin, *Gregory*, 25; *PLRE* 1:290.
[65] D. Hawhee, *Bodily Arts: Rhetoric and Athletics in Ancient Greece* (Austin: University of Texas Press, 2005), 10–17, shows the intersection of athletics and rhetoric. Both enabled the citizen male in classical Greece to exhibit beauty of mind and body.
[66] A. Puertas, *The Dynamics of Rhetorical Performances in Late Antiquity* (London: Routledge, 2018), 62–3.
[67] Plutarch, *Moralia* 3a (Babbitt).

a culture of oral display to one increasingly of written performance.[68] With further valorization of the text, the writings of *pepaideumenoi* came under the scrutiny of smaller, more homogenized audiences. Gregory of Nyssa compared such occasions to a banquet reserved for invited guests. He referred to his letter from Libanius of Antioch, for example, as a "ticket for a feast" (σύμβολον ἑορτῆς).[69] In other words, Gregory was part of a circle privileged to share and discuss a missive that was designed to tantalize fellow literary mavens. This made for a significant difference from the performance culture of the Second Sophistic, where declamations – set speeches meant to entertain – often took place in a much more public venue. In an epistolary *agōn* there was no need for vocal applause or mass approval and therefore no need to pander to inferiors. Libanius (314–90) was one of the most well-known and respected rhetoricians of the eastern Mediterranean. He was an individual whose opinion carried weight among intellectuals. But Gregory's interaction here was limited primarily to Libanius, along with students and associates with whom he may have shared the work. Gregory was opening himself to the assessment of others, such as Libanius, referees who like himself were specialists in the craft of epistolary composition.[70] The judgment of epistolary performances came, therefore, not through the unfiltered response of populist audiences, but among a very limited segment of society.

Classical Masculinity

A prevailing theme throughout our study is the hierarchical nature of late Roman society. The priority that late-antique *pepaideumenoi* placed on maintaining a male identity provides an example of such ordering, as well as the care taken to differentiate and maintain the boundaries between male and female. In order to illustrate this taxonomy of gender, social theorists have mapped out the general contours of Greco-Roman masculinity, a full treatment of which falls outside the scope of this study.[71] These scholars have identified pervasive elements of manhood as depicted

---

[68] F. Gautier, "Le Carême de silence de Grégoire de Nazianze: une conversion à la littérature?" *Revue des Études Augustiniennes* 47 (2001): 97–110.

[69] Greg. Ny., *Ep.* 14 (my translation).

[70] M. Ludlow, *Art, Craft, and Theology in Fourth-Century Christian Authors* (Oxford: Oxford University Press, 2020), 8–10.

[71] Much of the scholarship has used the model of "hegemonic" and "subordinate" masculinity set forward by R. W. Connell, *Masculinities* (Cambridge: Polity, 1995), 77–80.

in literature stretching from the fifth century B.C. through the fourth century A.D. I denote these attributes as "classical masculinity," a term that will include a number of recurring features outlined below.[72] The central premise of "classical masculinity," as used here, is that manhood was defined through a series of repetitive performances that guarded against other identities.[73] Classical manhood involved appearing inherently male rather than female; dominant rather than passive; public rather than private; rational rather than passionate; self-controlled rather than indulgent; free rather than enslaved; and fully Greek rather than barbarian.[74] These binaries are not exhaustive of the distinctions that made for the ideal male, but the literature of the classical world bears these out as fundamental to his gestalt. The model male thus attempted to maintain a bearing that resisted the collapsing of established gender mores. More important than any single virtue associated with gendering is the reality in antiquity that representations of maleness conveyed moral superiority. The differences underscored the hierarchical foundations of east Roman society.

Many elements of idealized manhood applied both to western and eastern Rome, as public displays of oratorical skill and political success were acclaimed in both parts of the empire. The elite male of both ancient Greece and Rome was acutely aware of his corporeal representation and aspired to certain standards of strong body. One important difference between classical Greek and Roman masculinity does call for emphasis. On one hand, in Latin society, individuals acquired fame through performances involving the voice, the most noble bodily instrument.[75] Other physical demonstrations in public, however, were acceptable only for the low-born or slaves. Serving as the source of spectacle usually implied objectification, something akin to the passivity of penetration.[76] It was

---

[72] S. Rubarth, "Competing Constructions of Masculinity in Ancient Greece," *Athens Journal of Humanities and Fine Arts* 1.1 (2014), 21–32, emphasizes that no uniform definition of manliness applied in ancient Greece. The model emphasized in this study corresponds most closely to the idea of "hegemonic masculinity" set forth by Connell; see above.

[73] A concept analogous to that in Butler, *Gender*, 170–7; I will use "masculinity" and "manhood" interchangeably. Manhood, in this study, does not represent a physical state of being, but rather a persona developed through behavior and appearance.

[74] Reeser, *Moderating*, 66, states that, in Aristotle, a lack of virtues was encoded as effeminate, a point that helps when thinking about maleness at this time.

[75] E. Gunderson, *Staging Masculinity: The Rhetoric of Performance in the Roman World* (Ann Arbor: University of Michigan Press, 2000), 59–72.

[76] See D. Fredrick, "Mapping Penetrability in Late Republican and Early Imperial Rome," 236–40 and C. Bartin, "Being in the Eyes: Shame and Sight in Ancient Rome," 216–25, in

more respectable for western Romans, then, to be a spectator at athletic games than a participant.[77] And soldiering, while it could lead to promotion and officer rank, did not necessarily denote high status. In classical Greece, on the other hand, a man merited esteem not only because of his vocal prowess, but also because he showed excellence of body (a symbol of moral beauty) in athletic competition.[78] The struggle with opponents both increased and exhibited his manly virtue. Likewise, from the Homeric warrior to the citizen hoplite, in Greek literature the soldier was emblematic of valor.[79] The Cappadocians thus used the trope of physical contest in constructions of manhood in a way that western Romans may have found counterintuitive.

Addressing gender in early Christianity, David Brakke and L. Stephanie Cobb have called attention to prevailing elements of classical masculinity in their treatments, respectively, of desert monks and early Christian martyrs.[80] The Egyptian monks that form Brakke's study engaged in combat against demons in an agonism that was implicit in the Christian faith: as Light against Darkness and Good versus Evil. The authors of these hagiographic accounts depict monks' victory against demons as an internal conquest of the passions that subsequently sanctioned the ascetics as spiritual overseers. Invested with the trappings of a Greek athlete, through the pen of the hagiographer, the monks' endogamous *agōn* is translated into a public battle. The narratives thus delineated the monks as indicative of maleness even though as ascetics they lacked the qualities of "real men."[81] Brakke's study is instructive for our inquiry because, like the desert monks of his focus, the Cappadocians were closely associated with asceticism: practicing it themselves and/or

---

The Roman Gaze: Vision, Power, and the Body, ed. D. Fredrick (Baltimore: Johns Hopkins University Press, 2002).

[77] For an excellent summary of differences regarding spectacle between the Latin West and Greek East, Remijsen, *End*, 323–30; Lendon, *Empire*, 43; Pfitzner, *Paul*, 17.

[78] D. Konstan, *Beauty: The Fortunes of an Ancient Greek Idea* (Oxford: Oxford University Press, 2014), 38–9; Hawhee, *Bodily*, 19–20.

[79] J. Roisman, *The Rhetoric of Manhood: Masculinity in the Attic Orators* (Berkeley: University of California Press, 2005), 105–13; M. Stewart, *The Soldier's Life: Martial Virtues and Manly Romanitas in the Early Byzantine Empire* (Leeds: Kismet, 2016), 43–6, makes a convincing argument that martial prowess remained the definitive mark of manhood in the early Byzantine empire.

[80] D. Brakke, *Demons and the Making of the Monk: Spiritual Combat in Early Christianity* (Cambridge, MA: Harvard University Press, 2006) and L. S. Cobb, *Dying to Be Men: Gender and Language in Early Christian Martyr Texts* (New York: Columbia University Press, 2008).

[81] Brakke, *Demons*, 10–13, 182–3.

writing about it. To inspire confidence among their congregations and their peers, they tied asceticism to manhood. Cobb, meanwhile, interprets martyrologies from the first three centuries as identity-forming texts for Christian communities. Authors appropriated Greco-Roman constructions of gender, Cobb says, to illustrate Christian martyrs as the noble male: showing agency, courage, endurance of pain, and self-control during their executions.[82] Cobb concludes that these martyr texts enabled early Christian communities to imagine their identity as believers as equivalent to that of the noble male, with Christians always appearing more manly than their non-Christian counterparts.

Brakke's and Cobb's uses of gender theory influence my approach to the rhetoric of *agōn* in the Cappadocians, particularly in their explanations of how contests against opposing forces revealed the manhood of the monk or martyr. My study of epistolary display, however, will emphasize more than theirs the correlation between the role of contest and the Cappadocians' inclusion in a group united by a mutual sense of hierarchy; one that often overrode religious differences. So, on the one hand, I interpret the Cappadocians' epistolary interchanges with *pepaideumenoi* as exercises that promoted *aretē* in both parties, rather than as a conquest that diminished the honor of a rival. My study of the Cappadocians' hagiographic literature, on the other hand, more closely follows the trajectory of Brakke and Cobb. In these occasions of self-representation, the Cappadocians align more deliberately with Christianity, and more specifically with the pro-Nicene party of believers; with displays of *aretē* in pro-Nicene saints highlighting its absence in non-Trinitarian rivals. The contests in these biographies, that is, constitute exhibitions of manliness (pro-Nicene orthodoxy) versus effeminacy (heresy); much more akin to the self-fashioning of monks versus demons and of martyrs against persecutors, pagans, Jews, and apostates.

THE CAPPADOCIANS: A BACKGROUND

The Cappadocians make compelling subjects for a study of gender in late antiquity. Their understanding of male and female was formed, like other believers, through scriptural teachings that came through family and church. Few other Christians, however, were exposed to the complex ideology of manhood that they acquired through training in *paideia*.

---

[82] Cobb, *Dying*, 20–4, 51–4.

Each therefore was conversant with the protocols of deportment and hierarchy according to the model of the classical male. They were in the minority of priests from such a position, as eastern Romans whose status was made possible by their birth into provincial nobility and their aristocratic education. Similar backgrounds, mutual networks of friends, and associations with other provincial elites resulted in comparable career paths among the three, as well as analogous perceptions of self-representation in church leadership.

Under the heading "The Cappadocian Fathers," the 2005 edition of the *Oxford Dictionary of the Christian Church* described Nazianzen, Basil, and Nyssen as "The three brilliant leaders of philosophical Christian orthodoxy in the later 4th century."[83] Much of the historical scholarship on the Cappadocians has emphasized how these theologians articulated a philosophical model for conceptualizing the Godhead. In Trinitarian discourse the Cappadocians delineated the simultaneous unity of nature and individuality of persons in the Father, Son, and Holy Spirit. It is little surprise that the three have traditionally been linked. Basil and Gregory of Nyssa were brothers, while Basil and Gregory of Nazianzus became close friends during early adulthood during their education at Athens. Both Nyssen and Nazianzen, we have seen, were appointed bishops by Basil. And along with interacting within a similar social sphere, each of the three engaged in extensive refutation of teachings that opposed their own "orthodox" theology. Each wrote extensively, for example, against Eunomius of Cyzicus (and his proponents), a native Cappadocian (mentioned earlier) who held that the Son and the Father differed according to nature. Although among themselves the Cappadocians ascribed to similar tenets of Trinitarian theology, the three varied on the nuances of a doctrine that was eventually declared "orthodox" at the Council of Constantinople in 381 (after Basil's death). In the past twenty years, scholars have increasingly investigated the distinct theology of each bishop, with careful attention to avoiding a correlation with the other two merely to deliver a singular "Cappadocian theology."[84]

---

[83] *The Oxford Dictionary of the Christian Church*, ed. F. L. Cross, third edition ed. E. A. Livingston (Oxford: Oxford University Press, 2005), 285.

[84] C. Moreschini, "Is it Possible to Speak of 'Cappadocian Theology' as a System?" *SP* 95 (2017), 139–63, discusses the trends in scholarship over the past century and finds that recent scholarship has overwhelmingly discouraged thinking of Cappadocian theology as "organic" or "uniform." The differences are particularly striking, Moreschini emphasizes, between Nazianzen's theology and Nyssen's and Basil's (140). The

Similar care is in order when addressing the Cappadocians as members of a social group whose status often elided religious discrepancies. To this end, intensive biographical studies of the bishops have opened vistas into the complex personalities of each and the influence that shaped their portrayal of the divine and their social interactions.[85] Several commonalities make it useful, however, to recognize among the three a corresponding conception of masculinity. The three clergy came from wealthy, notable provincial families. Each accordingly was raised in the study of *paideia*, with an emphasis on rhetorical performance as an index of manhood and status. The result was that they came to belong to a nexus of imperial and provincial officials who enjoyed a congruity of cultural formation; a common core of values that formed their character while crossing religious lines. We will treat the education of each Cappadocian in the next section, but first we will address their family dynamics and how that heritage shaped their expectations and literary construction of priestly office.

Nazianzen was born to a family that owned substantial land at Arianzus, a village in southwest Cappadocia near the town of Nazianzus. As a wealthy landowner, his father (Gregory the Elder) was a member of the curial order (the landed gentry) and served as a *decurion* (town councilor) of Nazianzus before he was ordained a Christian bishop there in 328. Nazianzen's mother Nonna earlier had converted his father to Christianity from a religious sect called the Hypsistarii, which may have been a synthesis of a form of Judaism and worship of Zeus; a Hellenized monotheism, that is. Nazianzen had a younger brother Caesarius, who studied at Caesarea in Cappadocia and later Alexandria, Egypt on his path to becoming a physician. Caesarius' successful career included service in the imperial government under emperors Constantius II (r. 337–61), Julian (r. 361–3), and Valens (r. 364–78).

---

following are representative of a tendency to identify differences in the theology among the three: M. DelCogliano, *Basil of Caesarea's Anti-Eunomian Theory of Names: Christian Theology and Late-Antique Philosophy in the Fourth-Century Trinitarian Controversy* (Leiden: Brill, 2010), A. Radde-Gallwitz, *Basil of Caesarea, Gregory of Nyssa, and the Transformation of Divine Simplicity* (Oxford: Oxford University Press, 2009), S. Hildebrand, *The Trinitarian Theology of Basil of Caesarea: A Synthesis of Greek Thought and Biblical Truth* (Washington: Catholic University of America Press, 2007), C. Beeley, *Gregory of Nazianzus on the Trinity and Knowledge of God: In Your Light We Shall See Light* (Oxford: Oxford University Press, 2008).

[85] For example P. Rousseau, *Basil of Caesarea* (Berkeley: University of California Press, 1994) and J. McGuckin, *St Gregory of Nazianzus: An Intellectual Biography* (Crestwood, NY: St. Vladimir's Seminary, 2001).

Nazianzen also had a sister, Gorgonia, who followed in her mother's footsteps by marrying a prominent provincial notable, whom she also converted to Christianity. Gorgonia's grandson Nicobulus (Nazianzen's grandnephew) later became a protégé under Nazianzen, receiving correspondence from Nazianzen as well as a gift comprising a collection of both Basil's and Nazianzen's epistles. In addition, Nazianzen had a first cousin Amphilochius (the Younger), a native Cappadocian who was ordained around 374 as bishop of the major city of Iconium in the province west of Cappadocia, Lycaonia. Along with having familial connections to Cappadocia, Amphilochius looked to Basil as a kind of episcopal mentor.[86] Gregory himself first entered the priesthood in 361 when he was ordained by his father at Nazianzus. In 372 Basil appointed Gregory as bishop of Sasima, an indecorous position in a small town that created a rift between the two. Although designated bishop at Sasima, Gregory served here only intermittently, and instead assisted his father at Nazianzus. He later served as bishop for the pro-Nicene community at Constantinople from 379 to 381, where he presided over the Council of Constantinople for part of 381. However, he later returned to Nazianzus under inglorious circumstances in 381, where he ministered to his deceased father's congregation for a few years before retiring near the family's land at nearby Arianzus.

Basil and his younger brother Nyssen likewise were born into a prominent provincial family from Pontus.[87] Basil was ordained into the priesthood in Caesarea of Cappadocia, as an assistant to the bishop, in 362. He was consecrated bishop there in 370, following the death of his predecessor Eusebius. Gregory first entered the clergy in 372, when Basil appointed him bishop at Nyssa. At the time, he had been a teacher of rhetoric. Their father Basil the Elder, a renowned rhetorician, and mother Emmelia owned land in three Roman provinces: Cappadocia, Pontus, and Armenia Minor (at one time, Pontus and Armenia Minor had been part of one larger Cappadocian province). Their sister Macrina, eldest of the siblings, was betrothed to a Pontic lawyer, a union likely designed to consolidate the power of two local scions. Her fiancé died, however, and

---

[86] For details of his life, K. Holl, *Amphilochius von Ikonium in seinem Verhältnis zu den großen* (Tübingen: Mohr Siebeck, 1904); R. Van Dam, *Families and Friends in Late Roman Cappadocia* (Philadelphia: University of Pennsylvania Press, 2003), 143–5, 185, on Amphilochius' close relationship with Basil and his potential place as a "Fourth Cappadocian Father."

[87] A. Silvas, *Gregory of Nyssa: The Letters*, VCS 83 (Leiden: Brill, 2006), for an excellent, succinct overview and chronology of the family, 1–57.

Macrina subsequently devoted herself to a life of virginity and managing a community of female ascetics. As we will see later, she played a role in Nyssen's formation of asceticism and theology. Macrina, Basil, and Nyssen had two other brothers, Naucratius and Peter. The former excelled as a student of rhetoric, seemingly in line to succeed his father as a gifted orator and teacher. Instead, he abandoned his apparent legacy and chose to renounce the civic life in favor of living off the land while caring for a community of elderly persons near his family estate in Pontus. He died there from a hunting accident. The youngest brother Peter grew up largely under the supervision of Macrina and later was ordained bishop of Sebaste in Armenia Minor.

The Cappadocians as Pepaideumenoi

The *curiales* (the provincial aristocracy) represented an order that expressed a sense of collective manhood by emphasizing expectations of patronage. An element of singularity that defined this group came through the education that taught eloquence of tongue and pen. As youths, the Cappadocians read the scriptures and learned theology from family members and, presumably, from leaders in the local church. But the future priests also were groomed from adolescence to be able to exhibit *aretē* among a peer group that spanned the boundaries of the eastern empire. Through a rigorous upbringing in *paideia* the three were initiated into an association that prepared them for public speaking, for the deportment of a civic leader, and the agonistic environment in which he lived.[88] Basil studied rhetoric as a youth under his father, a teacher of rhetoric himself. Nazianzen enjoyed a comparable familial introduction through the guidance of his uncle Amphilochius the Elder (father of Gregory's cousin Amphilochius the Younger), an accomplished orator who had been a fellow student with Libanius.[89]

A major literary source for the educational pursuits of Basil comes from the oration honoring Basil (after his death) that Nazianzen composed in the early 380s.[90] In it Gregory exalted his friend, but he also used the piece to highlight his own exceptional pedagogy.[91] Gregory's

---

[88] Gleason, *Making*, 21–4.   [89] Van Dam, *Families and Friends*, 53.
[90] Greg. Naz., *Or.* 43.
[91] F. Norris, "Your Honor, My Reputation," in *Greek Biography and Panegyric in Late Antiquity*, eds. T. Hägg and P. Rousseau (Berkeley: University of California Press, 2000), 149–53.

self-portrayal here, among his other works, has contributed to his legacy as one of the most accomplished Christian rhetoricians of late antiquity.[92] Indeed, George Kennedy has considered this oration one of the greatest of the ancient world.[93] As he chronicled the various places and forms of instruction in the oration, Gregory gradually crafted a picture of the masculine nature of *paideia* in Basil, himself, and in the settings where they learned. For example, in describing Basil's tutelage under his father, "whom Pontus put forward at that time as its common teacher of virtue (κοινὸν παιδευτὴν ἀρετῆς)," Gregory characterizes Basil as "running close at the side of his father, with the ardor of a colt (ἐν πωλικῷ τῷ φρυάγματι)," an image of him developing to match his father, the rhetorician, as an intellectual stallion.[94] After Basil and Nazianzen had completed studies under family, by their mid-teens they entered school at Caesarea (Cappadocia) in 345/46, where they probably first met. Praising the city in the oration (Gregory was delivering it at Caesarea), Gregory portrays Caesarea as "no less the metropolis of eloquence than of the cities which she rules and which have submitted to her power."[95] Caesarea thus is accredited as patron over client towns and as the epicenter of eloquence. Both depictions resonate with supremacy. Basil's and Gregory's renown thus benefits from schooling at such a place. Following schooling here in Caesarea, Nazianzen continued study at Alexandria in 347/48, while Basil moved to Constantinople, where for a brief period he came under the instruction of the rhetorician Libanius.[96]

---

[92] M-A Calvet-Sebasti, "Comment écrire à païen: l'exemple de Gregoire de Nazianze et de Théodoret de Cyr," in *Les apologists chrétiens et la culture grecque*, eds. B. Pouderon and J. Doré (Paris: Beauchesne, 1998), 369–81; R. R. Ruether, *Gregory of Nazianzus: Rhetor and Philosopher* (Oxford: Clarendon Press, 1969); and older works: E. Fleury, *Hellénisme et Christianisme. Saint Grégoire de Nazianze et son temps* (Paris: Beauchesne, 1930) and M. Guignet, *Saint Grégoire de Nazianze et la rhétorique* (Paris: Picard, 1911).

[93] G. Kennedy, *Greek Rhetoric Under Christian Emperors* (Princeton: Princeton University Press, 1983), 235–8, writes that many consider Gregory the "Christian Demosthenes," referring to the fourth-century B.C. Athenian orator.

[94] Greg. Naz., *Or.* 43.12 (McCauley). This phrase recalls a similar saying in Plutarch, *Moralia* 136A (Babbitt). Plutarch advises young men to take care of their bodies so that "[Their bodies] May run like weanling colt beside its dam." In other words, well-kept bodies will contribute to a well-developed soul.

[95] Greg. Naz., *Or.* 43.13 (slight modification of McCauley).

[96] Whether or not Basil studied under Libanius remains a disputed issue, but some scholars believe that he did. See discussion in R. Cribiore, *The School of Libanius in Late Antique Antioch* (Princeton: Princeton University Press, 2007), 100–4; Rousseau, *Basil*, 57–60. Based on the evidence, cited in Cribiore and Rousseau, it seems certain that Basil studied, at least for a period, under Libanius. A related, and more complex problem, is the

The two Cappadocians both finalized their rhetorical apprenticeship at Athens, "patroness of all that is excellent," where each resided for multiple years from about 349 to 358 (with Basil leaving around 356/7).[97] As we will see in Chapter 1, this was an atmosphere where aspirations of manhood were constantly made or lost through competitive display. Here they also observed advanced techniques of presentation from instructors such as Prohaeresius and Himerius, highly esteemed sophists in the early-fourth century.[98] These teachers were commemorated by Eunapius of Sardis (a late-fourth century sophist, historian, and student of Prohaeresius) in his biographical account of the great philosophers and sophists of the fourth century.[99] These were the provincials-made-good, whose influence in the local aristocracy had grown to extend across the eastern empire. Gregory associated Basil and himself with the fame of their teachers. "For our masters were known wherever Athens was known," Gregory explained, "and wherever they were the subject of report or conversation, so were we."[100] The tutelage of instructors such as Prohaeresius, in turn, placed them in the lineage of the prestigious third-century orator Julianus, mentor to Prohaeresius.[101] The ideal of intellectual descent was no word play. It was a legitimate source of meaning for a *pepaideumenos*. That Julianus hailed from Cappadocia, moreover, made the connection that much more germane. From studying under literary virtuosos, who were themselves successors of performative

---

epistolary exchange between the two. Most scholars believe most, if not all, of the correspondence is a forgery. But see Rousseau and Cribiore above for some letters that may be real. For a more detailed discussion on the forgery see L. Van Hoof, "Falsification as a Protreptic to Truth: The Force of the Forged Epistolary Exchange between Basil and Libanius," in *Education and Religion in Late Antique Christianity: Reflections, Social Contexts and Genres*, eds. P. Gemeinhardt, L. Van Hoof, and P. Van Nuffelen (London: Routledge, 2016), 116–30; especially see concluding remarks (124–5), where Van Hoof points out that the forgery indicates the popularity of rhetoric in the late fourth century into at least the early sixth century.

[97] Greg. Naz., *Or.* 43.14 (McCauley).
[98] On the competitive world of teaching in the life of Prohaeresius, Watts, *City*, 55–9, and R. Penella, *Greek Philosophers and Sophists in the Fourth Century a.d.: Studies in Eunapius of Sardis* (Leeds: Francis Cairns, 1990), 81–90; R. Penella, *Man and the Word: The Orations of Himerius* (Berkeley: University of California Press, 2007), 1–16, for excellent introduction of Himerius with translation and analysis of hisorations; T. Barnes, "Himerius and the Fourth Century," *CP* 82 (1987), 206–25, on Himerius' far-reaching influence, including on the Cappadocians, and his association with Libanius and Emperor Julian.
[99] Eunapius, *V. Phil.*, for Prohaeresius, 485–93 (the lengthiest entry of the work) and Himerius, 494–5.
[100] Greg. Naz., *Or.* 43.22 (McCauley).   [101] Eunapius, *V. Phil.*, 483–5.

celebrities, Basil and Nazianzen were initiated into the legacy of proving masculinity through exhibition. The skillsets that that they took away from Athens informed their thinking, writing, and speaking for the rest of their careers. But perhaps more affective was the sense of community and pedigree among *pepaideumenoi* they came to understand; it was a gathering in which it appears that sophists usually taught, without bias, Christians and non-Christians.[102]

Gregory of Nyssa's early exposure to the world of rhetoric took a different course than that of Basil or Nazianzen. Patristic scholars have long recognized that elements of Second Sophistic culture shaped the philosophy of Nyssen.[103] Few have acknowledged his excellence of rhetoric, however, in comparison to Nazianzen and his brother Basil. A number of factors have mitigated his standing as a master of the word in relation to the latter two: significantly fewer of his letters have survived; no extant orations celebrate his career; and his reputation as a mystical theologian has tended to overshadow his rhetoric.[104] Perhaps most importantly, the documentation on his education in eloquence is not detailed or straightforward. On this last point, Morwenna Ludlow has shown that Gregory composed epistle 13 (to Libanius) partly as a calculated effort to record his own rhetorical mastery as acquired in a non-traditional manner.[105] The letter itself represents a literary attestation of his pedagogical success, even while its ambiguity makes it difficult to say with precision how long he studied with any given teacher. Nyssen did study in a standard way, as teacher and pupil, under Basil. A point that Gregory makes in his letter, however, is that he also learned under Libanius in the sense that Basil passed his knowledge of Libanius' teachings on to Gregory. Gregory also sat at the foot of Libanius, metaphorically, by reading his texts. Nyssen came by his rhetorical skill textually, he asserted, the same way that he was introduced to the Christian faith

---

[102] For example Watts, *City*, 62–4.
[103] L. Méridier, *L'influence de la seconde sophistique sur l'oeuvre de Grégoire de Nysse* (Paris: Libraire Hachette, 1906).
[104] Van Dam also points out that in a listing of theologians noteworthy for both classical and biblical erudition, the early fifth-century Christian priest and historian Jerome included Basil, Nazianzen, and Amphilochius, but excluded Nyssen. Van Dam, *Families*, 185, referring to Jerome, *Ep.* 70.
[105] M. Ludlow, "Texts, Teachers and Pupils in the Writings of Gregory of Nyssa," in *Literature and Society in the Fourth Century AD: Performing Paideia, Constructing the Present, Presenting the Self*, eds. L. Van Hoof and P. Nuffelen (Leiden: Brill, 2014), 85–7; also Cribiore, *School*, 100.

through the writings of the New Testament authors.[106] Such claims make it difficult, therefore, to know how much formal training Gregory had, or if he studied at Caesarea or abroad. That he underwent significant instruction seems certain. His facility in eloquence translated into an early career as a teacher of rhetoric, during the early to mid-360s. It was a position that he savored and in which he appears to have thrived until he turned to service within the church upon his ordination in 372.[107]

Agathoi *and Performance*

In *paideia* an emphasis on the conventions of manhood shaped how young men came to perceive society and their responsibility in it as *agathoi*, the Homeric appellation that singled out, "the brave and upright." An immersion in philosophy, on one hand, enabled the Cappadocians to contribute to the complex Trinitarian discourse of the fourth century. The training also helped them to apprehend the significance of Christian asceticism through Greek antecedents. Attaining eloquence, on the other hand, equipped them with the dexterity of self-presentation and the ability to navigate the world of mediation and discourse.[108] Individuals that had mastered the art of persuasion represented superstars in the society of the well-educated. They were a source of pride for their teachers and their students, also bringing glory to the city where they resided as well as their hometown. These were living conduits of Second Sophistic culture who stood out as verbal combatants who left indelible impressions on ambitious adolescents.

Yet the occupation of a sophist could be a source of denunciation against an intellectual. Some confusion emerges because, by the late 300s, it had become a commonplace for philosophers to distinguish themselves from sophists and to distance themselves from a craft that

---

[106] Ludlow, "Texts," 85–91; I call the reader to Ludlow's nuanced discussion of his education, which also treats the mimetic nature of his training.

[107] Famously chastised by Nazianzen, in Greg. Naz., *Ep.* 11 (Storin 81), for his apparent ambition. B. Storin, *Self-Portrait in Three Colors: Gregory of Nazianzus's Epistolary Autobiography* (Oakland: University of California Press, 2019), 167–8, makes the point that Nazianzen was criticizing Nyssen, not for his rhetorical interests, but for identifying primarily as a rhetorician instead of serving as priest.

[108] Goldhill, "Rhetoric," 232: "Rhetoric [was] a fundamental medium for the circulation of ideas, the circulation of power, the performance of the self in the public life of the empire."

they criticized as seeking political influence rather than truth.[109] This reality, however, needs to be understood with a degree of context. The very individuals who disparaged sophistry often were themselves rhetoricians who were seeking to elevate their own arguments (or careers) against the rivals they were vilifying.[110] In fact, among the educated, accomplished sophists garnered high praise. A brilliant speaker stood out as the classical male par excellence, unflappable because he had excelled during tense oratorical displays.[111] He was a "made man." He had earned his badge of honor as a triumphant member of the provincial elite, as an advanced member who commanded respect across the eastern empire, or who had even ascended to a position of authority as part of the imperial government.[112]

Years of studying and exercising the art of verbal exercises in this context contributed to a self-perception in the Cappadocians that they belonged to an exceptional circle and held an extraordinary place in society. The cumulative effect of a young man's accomplishments in the world of *paideia* was to make rhetorical display for him a kind of moral imperative. The breadth of this training came to define a group identity among *pepaideumenoi* that held up eloquence – specifically Greek elocution – as a kind of moral outcome. Libanius praised one young man for understanding the merits of rhetoric. "Though he lives among boys who are asleep and who presume eloquence is nothing," Libanius states, "...he didn't entertain this opinion in his own soul, but holding the conviction that those without a share in culture were no better off than slaves."[113] For Libanius, an ability to communicate well through the beauty of the Greek language was a mark of sophistication and superiority. In a number of his writings, Libanius warned against the threats that the study of law and Latin posed to *paideia*; not because these subjects were inherently detrimental, but because they took the brightest young men of eastern Rome away from their true calling of immersion in the

---

[109] R. Lim, *Public Disputation, Power, and Social Order in Late Antiquity* (Berkeley: University of California Press, 1995), 61–2.

[110] Among the uninitiated, on the other hand, it is easy to see why many harbored suspicions of these clever speakers. Brown, *Power*, 44–5, characterizes the effects of their speeches as a form of magic, an apt analogy for how, for example, an imperial official might feel when coerced into a policy through a well-crafted speech.

[111] Gleason, *Making*, xxiv. [112] Van Hoof, "Performing," 387–9.

[113] Libanius, *Ep.* 666 (Bradbury 77), 114–5; the Cappadocians wrote scores of letters of recommendation, an art they learned from the same models that informed Libanius. On Libanius' abilities in this regard, Cribiore, *School*, 112–18 and P. Petit, *Les étudiants de Libanius* (Paris: Nouvelles Editions latines, 1957), 158–61.

classical Greek tongue.[114] Nyssen bemoaned the same issue in a letter to Libanius. Gregory lamented that students were "deserting the Greek language for the barbarian (τὴν βάρβαρον γλῶσσαν), becoming mercenary soldiers and choosing a soldier's rations instead of the renown for eloquence."[115] As "mercenaries" (studying Latin) the youths were devoting themselves to a foreign program, rather than their own supreme heritage. The problem did not involve merely a threat to the livelihood of persons such as Libanius, or the loss of centuries-old traditions. Rather it imperiled the identity of a governing elite who were united through *paideia*.[116] For *pepaideumenoi*, participating in literary contests – following in the footsteps of Greeks of lore – meant being true to their nature. In a world where idealized manhood was synonymous with probity, it was serious business to fulfill one's calling. And it was a destiny to be exercised and celebrated over and over with colleagues.

Agōnes *of Munificence*

As part of the local aristocracy, the Cappadocian Fathers came from a dynastic tradition that emphasized civic munificence as an aspect of competition. It was a practice indicative of a social class preoccupied with classical notions of masculinity. The idea of *leitourgia* (service to the public) was rooted hundreds of years into the Greek past, when the wealthiest members of the polis provided entertainment, education, temples, and other amenities to enrich their home city. In return, donors received public recognition through inscriptions and speeches that honored them in acts of collective gratitude.[117] The philanthropy

---

[114] B. Schouler, "Hellénismos et humanisme chez Libanios," in *Hellenismos: quelques jalons pour une histoire de l'identité grecque: actes du Colloque de Strasbourg, 25–27 octobre 1989*, ed. S. Saïd (Leiden: Brill, 1991), 270–2.

[115] Greg. Ny., *Ep.* 14 (Silvas): "mercenary soldiers," στρατιωτικὸν σιτηρέσιον ἀντὶ τῆς ἐν τῷ λέγειν δόξης αἱρούμενοι; Silvas recognizes that the "barbarian" here represents the Latin language.

[116] R. Van Dam, *The Roman Revolution of Constantine* (Cambridge: Cambridge University Press, 2007), 191, describes the attitude, that "even if the imperial administration was to be Latin, the dominant literary and rhetorical culture in the eastern provinces should remain Greek."

[117] S. Holman, *The Hungry are Dying: Beggars and Bishops in Roman Cappadocia* (Oxford: Oxford University Press, 2001), 21–5, defines *leitourgia* as part of the gift economy of ancient Greece, where patrons acquired status through giving to the poor. This understanding of patronage, she rightly argues, continued with the bishops' programs of poverty relief.

provided a visible platform for local dynasts to engage in a kind of macro-*agōn*; a municipal setting that is, where families competed to outdo one another in benefiting the city and thus to win fame.[118] This kind of public display mirrored the exhibition of *aretē* that Greek culture celebrated in individuals. The expenditures represented renown and served as a visible marker of who were the "best" families.

By late antiquity, many members of the curial order were finding expectations of municipal service increasingly burdensome and imperial legislation in the fourth century frequently dealt with the issue of decurions (council members) who were trying to withdraw from the curial order or otherwise gain exemption from curial duties.[119] Many studies of this issue suggest that decurions were attempting to evade their long-established responsibilities because increasing financial burdens – coupled with a decline in the number of decurions – made the position untenable; more or less punitive, an imposition.[120] The evidence also shows that, when in 313 Emperor Constantine exempted clergy and monks from financial obligations associated with curial status, many provincial notables joined the priesthood to escape fiscal duties.[121] While largely an accurate account of the situation, this portrayal of the transition of curial status does not adequately recognize the deep-seated system of principles on which the role of decurions was based.

One matter to consider, which goes understated, is that many individuals continued to consider the status as decurions a distinction and were willing to make financial sacrifices because of the honor associated with the position.[122] Imperial legislation to stem the flight of *curiales* should not be taken to indicate that every region and local political climate faced the same issues. Another point to consider is that patronage by provincial elites could and did continue after transitioning out of the local governing order. In other words, even though many provincial aristocrats secured exemption from curial status, many of these individuals continued to advocate for their home communities. Former decurions who came to serve the imperial administration, for example, could still provide valuable assistance to their homes, only now from a different position. Basil's boyhood friend Sophronius, for example, rose from the ranks of a

---

[118] O. Van Nijf, "Festivals and Benefactors," in *Benefactors and the Polis: The Public Gift in the Greek Cities from the Homeric World to Late Antiquity*, eds. M. D. Gygax and A. Zuiderhoek (Cambridge: Cambridge University Press, 2020), 243–50.
[119] See the many laws in *C.Th*. Book 12 and Justinian's *C.J*. Book 10.
[120] An interpretation advocated by Jones, *Later*, 1:751–61.
[121] For example *C.Th*. 16.2.2.   [122] Rapp, *Holy*, 283–4.

well-to-do family in Caesarea to serve as a high-level magistrate in the imperial court under Emperor Valens.[123] Basil's letters to Sophronius suggest both a continuation of their friendship during this time and Sophronius' desire to help his native province.[124] Many of the *curiales* who became clergy, moreover, remained in a position to carry out service for their countrymen.[125] Although many did join the clergy to evade the liabilities of their class, there is no reason to believe that most who joined the priesthood thereafter dismissed their identity as civic benefactors. In the case of the Cappadocian Fathers, after they became prelates, they continued to support their communities through a spirit of *euergetism*, even though the acts of good will came now through an office within the church. Many *curiales* who became church leaders remained connected to their hometowns and cities. They had been raised to take pride in their hometowns and they were ever conscious of familial and personal reputation regarding their commitment to the city. They did not forfeit that awareness when they became clergy, a distinction that was based on providing for the people.

Perhaps the most notable example of such tangible bounty was the huge complex, including a hospital and hospice, that Basil built at Caesarea 372.[126] The site included apartments for bishops, guests, the needy, and the poor, and the sick were treated and fed by physicians and nurses.[127] The undertaking represented a reconstruction of civic munificence along the lines of classical Greek society, but now reoriented under Christian governance. The display of philanthropy held chief place in the virtues of Greek kings as celebrated by rhetoricians such as Dio Chrysostom (c. 40–c. 115).[128] Beyond such a concrete example as Basil's charitable building project, each of the Cappadocians also mediated on behalf of individuals, groups, and sometimes the entire towns

---

[123] Van Dam, *Kingdom*, 141–2.   [124] Basil, *Eps*. 32, 76, 96, 192, 272.

[125] Nazianzen provides a helpful, albeit complex, example of how a clergyman might also maintain loyalty to his hometown and continue to support it, at various junctures of his career and in varying positions. See N. McLynn, "Curiales into Churchmen: The Case of Gregory Nazianzen," in *Le trasformazioni delle élites en età tardoantica*, ed. R. Lizzi Testa (Rome: L'Erma di Bretschneider, 2006), 277–95.

[126] Traditionally called the *Basiliad*; Greg. Naz., *Or*. 43.35,63; context and description in Rousseau, *Basil*, 139–42; and S. Giet, *Les Idées et l'action sociales de Saint Basile* (Paris: Gabalda, 1941), 417–22.

[127] Holman, *Hungry*, 72–5.

[128] B. Daley, "Building a New City: The Cappadocian Fathers and the Rhetoric of Philanthropy," *JECS* 7 (1999), 432–5, with Daley citing Dio Chrysostom, *Or*. 2.74–7.

where they served as priests.¹²⁹ By composing and sending epistles of intercession to various imperial and provincial officials, teachers, and other clergy, the Cappadocians acted as benefactors.¹³⁰ These occasions made for a synthesis of charity and public display, with advertising of philanthropy coming through the circulation of letters of mediation or receiving praise from the delivery of orations (usually at the funeral) that called attention to the noble deeds.

The responsibilities of the curial order toward their town, moreover, had been predicated in part on cooperation among a small percentage of civic leaders. Even though individual decurions vied with one another in acts of patronage, ultimately the local magnates were engaging in a collective effort to benefit their home community. They respected each other's efforts, that is, and recognized a special bond that elevated their families as select leaders. The sentiment mirrors the complementary regard of authors in epistolary exchanges. The idea that a singular class of citizens should best govern the polis was ingrained in members of the local aristocracy and that sentiment did not shift when members joined the church government.¹³¹ As church leaders, the Cappadocians often presented their liberality as the charity befitting a follower of Christ.¹³² Acts of compassion for the less powerful made for an integration of values expected equally of a believer and a local magnate.¹³³ Letters of intercession by the Cappadocians activated a societal hierarchy that required the cooperation of a superior group of individuals for the well-being of the people. The epistles were indicators of a class affiliation and its shared values. In a nexus of civic and provincial elites that crossed religious lines, the Cappadocians continually identified with peers through beneficence.

---

[129] For example Basil, *Eps.* 94, 196, 284; Greg. Ny., *Ep.* 25; Greg. Naz., *Eps.* 140, 141, 147.

[130] R. Van Dam, "Self-Representation in the Will of Gregory of Nazianzus," *JTS* 46 (1995), 142.

[131] McGuckin, *Gregory*, 98–9, makes an especially strong case, for example, that Nazianzen opposed church leaders who advocated a sense of social egalitarianism within the church (and society).

[132] Van Dam, *Kingdom*, 49.

[133] Perhaps a tension the Cappadocians faced, however, was securing benefits for those in need, publicizing these acts as philanthropy, but also avoiding flaunting their charity; a premise laid out in Jesus' command to his followers. For example Matthew 6:2–4: "So when you give to the needy, do not announce it with trumpets, as the hypocrites do in the synagogues and on the streets, to be honored by others. Truly I tell you, they have received their reward in full . But when you give to the needy, do not let your left hand know what your right hand is doing, so that your giving may be in secret. Then your Father, who sees what is done in secret, will reward you" (NIV).

Gestures of good will towards their towns and congregations reflected the virtues of provision and protection. These acts of good will indicate a spirit of kindheartedness and social consciousness. In challenging other powerful individuals and families through euergetism, the Cappadocians also propagated their standing as *agathoi*: *pepaideumenoi* who applied contests of patronage and beneficence to the greater good. These were attributes that recalled the idealized male: powerful, competitive, and devoted to others besides himself.

TRANSCENDENT MANHOOD AND ASCETICISM IN IDENTITY FORMATION

Over the last three decades, much of the scholarship on manhood in the late Roman world has addressed identifications and practices within early Christian literature that destabilized gender roles.[134] These studies have placed special attention on early scriptures that cast doubt on traditional differences between the sexes, as when the author of the epistle Galatians claimed "There is neither male nor female, for you are all one in Christ."[135] The central figure in the Christian faith was a tortured and crucified savior; seemingly a representation of emasculation according to Greco-Roman standards that frowned on portrayals of male victimization.[136] The recurring story of the Old and New Testaments, moreover, emphasized the force of omnipotent God, while downplaying the inherent power of the individual human. Currents like these in the sacred texts, when evaluated against archetypes of masculinity that upheld immutability, impenetrability, and agency, suggested a faith that effeminized men. Scholars over the past two decades have argued, however, that manhood in early Christianity is best understood as transcending the conventions of Greco-Roman society. According to such explanations, Christianity gave rise to a new version of masculinity, a spiritualized maleness that was not

---

[134] For example E. Johnson, *She Who Is: The Mystery of God in Feminist Theological Discourse* (New York: Crossroad, 1992); J. Hopkins and E. Dieckmann. *Feministische Christologie: Wie Frauen Heute VonJesus Reden Können* (Mainz: Matthais-Grünewald Verlag, 1996); and for gender fluidity in medieval conceptions of Christ, C. Walker Bynum, *Jesus as Mother: Studies in the Spirituality of the High Middle Ages* (Berkeley, CA: University of California Press, 1982).

[135] Galatians 3:28 (NIV).

[136] M. Gleason, "By Whose Gender Standards (If Anybody's) Was Jesus a Real Man?" in *New Testament Masculinities*, eds. S. Moore and J. Anderson (Atlanta: SBL, 2003), 326.

confined by worldly constructs.[137] This "new" sense of gender, however, still provoked anxiety in a society that was hyperaware of the correlation between manhood and power. Below we explore theology and practices within Christianity that posed potential problems of gender in late Roman *pepaideumenoi*. We will see throughout *Christianity and the Contest*, however, that the Cappadocians did not ascribe to alterations that subverted classical norms of manhood. Rather they invoked transcendent representations of maleness within certain identity groups, notably in discourse on asceticism and theology. But through other textual frameworks, in letters and in hagiography, they reoriented these identities to integrate them into traditional conventions of masculinity. In doing so, the Cappadocians reinforced the habitus of *pepaideumenoi*, thus expanding the breadth of masculinity in pro-Nicene Christianity and allowing for a spiritual adaptation that completed the classical male.

Transcendent Masculinity

Although some personifications of classical masculinity occur in the early Christian literature and Jewish authors from the second-Temple period, recent investigations have highlighted how Christian writers either challenged or transmuted such ideals.[138] Brittany Wilson has determined, for example, that New Testament teachings reconfigured masculinity and that many of the principal males in scripture did not conform to gender conventions of noble Greco-Romans.[139] Perhaps most markedly, in the Christian scriptures the lines blurred between established masculine and effeminate behaviors. This paradigm for thinking about gender in Christianity holds especially true in the field of late antiquity. Virginia Burrus has offered examples about how fourth-century pro-Nicene

---

[137] S. Elm, "Family Men: Masculinity and Philosophy in Late Antiquity," in *Transformations of Late Antiquity: Essays for Peter Brown*, eds. P. Rousseau and M. Papoutsakis (Farnham: Ashgate, 2009), 287–8, cautions that scholars have tended to equate masculinity that did not fit traditional standards as a subversion of classical manhood. She warns that this model does not fit well in the work of Nazianzen, who illustrated that agency could be achieved in multiple contexts.

[138] C. Conway, *Behold the Man: Jesus and Greco-Roman Masculinity* (Oxford: Oxford University Press, 2008), 53–8, discusses how Philo of Alexandria, for instance, depicted Moses as a male according to Greco-Roman conventions. Conway also illustrates how the Markan Jesus – as emasculated victim – represented an alternative to the classical ideal, 100–4.

[139] For example B. Wilson, *Unmanly Men: Refigurations of Masculinity in Luke-Acts* (Oxford: Oxford University Press, 2015), 8–9.

Christian authors reconfigured gender roles as part of a Trinitarian discourse meant to combat heresies.[140] Burrus argues that by invoking a series of contradicting, relational roles – alternating between feminine and masculine depictions – these authors set forth a masculinity associated with the Godhead that transcended worldly manhood. Among other instances, Burrus explores Gregory of Nyssa's treatises *On Virginity*, *The Life of Macrina*, and *On the Soul and the Resurrection*.[141] In *On Virginity*, Gregory exalted the practice of renouncing marriage – seemingly a rejection of the generative role of the male. This behavior represents a perfected manhood, however, when Gregory re-channels erotic desire (often read as a feminine vice) through pursuing (ascending to) the divine Father, the very essence of masculine virtue. And in *The Life of Macrina* and *On the Soul*, Gregory recounted his own spiritual quest under the guidance of his "manly" sister Macrina. Undergoing a series of gender inflections through the figure of Macrina, Gregory (and the reader) fully matures in spiritual understanding.[142] In these cases, Gregory ushers a fully realized standard of manhood that emerges out of encounters that are not bound to worldly constraints of gender. Writers such as Gregory inverted gender norms as a method of theological articulation and/or adaptation to political and social circumstances.[143] Using Burrus' phrasing, I call these new modes of virility, collectively, "transcendent masculinity." These ways of being male proved essential in thinking

---

[140] V. Burrus, *"Begotten, Not Made": Conceiving Manhood in Late Antiquity* (Stanford, CA: Stanford University Press, 2000), 3–5.

[141] Burrus, *"Begotten,"* 84–97, 112–23.

[142] This is a prime case of a male author using a female as an instructive device borrowed from Plato, a common theme in patristic authors such as Gregory of Nyssa. E. Clark, "A Lady Vanishes: Dilemmas of a Feminist Historian after the 'Linguistic Turn,'" *CH* 67 (1998), 22–30.

[143] M. Kuefler, *The Manly Eunuch: Masculinity, Gender Ambiguity, and Christian Ideology in Late Antiquity* (Chicago: University of Chicago Press, 2001), attests a similar notion of transformed manhood in his survey of bishops from the senatorial class in late western Rome. For Kuefler, clerics from the ranks of the aristocracy found the demands of Christianity increasingly acceptable as Christian intellectuals supplanted elite masculinity with a new spiritual manhood. This development mirrored the decline in the political hegemony of senatorial aristocrats, their gradual subordination to an autocratic imperial government, and their consequent "unmanning." Among many relevant examples, Kuefler cites the recurring image of bishop as "bride of Christ" as indicative of the seeming confutation of gender roles. By assuming a place of submission to Christ, clergy forfeited the traditional active place of the male. But through this intimate association with the divine, Christian writers posited, the bishop accrued moral authority over others. So, despite a semblance of effervescence, the priest's hegemony increased.

about the Godhead, understanding the individual's response to the persons of the Trinity, and amplifying spiritual authority.

In another study on Gregory of Nyssa, Raphael Cadenhead has further problematized the issue of gender in Nyssen's theology. For Cadenhead, Gregory's portrayal of gender in his later writings must be read in the context of the culmination of spiritual maturation, where male and female characterizations no longer apply. Through an investigation into Gregory's *Life of Moses* and *Commentary on the Song of Songs*, Cadenhead claims that masculine and feminine features are not concretized in Gregory's notion of spiritual ascent, but rather are labile.[144] Thus readers cannot map onto Gregory's representation of the sexes the value-laden dichotomy of masculinity and femininity found elsewhere. The "female" Soul, for example, alternately exudes fleshly passion (corrupted earthly desire) and spiritual passion (the culmination of spiritual ascent), according to its stage in the progress toward maturity.[145] Thus, "feminized" passion evokes neither an altogether positive nor negative valence, but can be read as either depending on context. For Gregory, Cadenhead states, the spiritually realized versions of the male and female soul lack the very contours that distinguish them in the earthly realm.

Cadenhead builds on the work of Verna Harrison, who argues that for each of the Cappadocians, the distinctions of gender applied only temporarily, in this life. In the divine, according to Harrison, the Cappadocians believed there was no distinction between male and female. Therefore, they did not compartmentalize virtues as male or female since they believed that humanity was designed to strive for a genderless eschatological state. Harrison subsequently points to cases of the Cappadocians undermining traditional gender norms. As part of his vision for a perfect society, Harrison writes, Basil depicts female martyrs and ascetics as soldiers and athletes (male roles), thus opening for

---

[144] R. Cadenhead, *The Body and Desire: Gregory of Nyssa's Ascetical Theology* (Oakland: University of California Press, 2018), 141; E. Muehlberger, "Simeon and Other Women in Theodoret's *Religious History*: Gender in the Representation of Late Ancient Christian Asceticism," *JECS* 23:4 (2015), 585–6, 594, posed a similar thesis. In an investigation of fifth-century Syrian bishop Theodoret's *Religious History*, Muehlberger asserts that Theodoret supplied conflating imagery of the sexes to reinforce his claim that men and women are the same in nature. In a number of examples, Theodoret marks the merit of ascetic superstars with qualities culturally understood as specifically female. Thus, Muehlberger cautions, scholars must be careful not to assume that late Christian asceticism focused on maleness as a determinant of excellence.

[145] Cadenhead, *Body*, 145–6.

Christian women new dimensions of spirituality.¹⁴⁶ According to Harrison such countercultural depictions reflected Basil's conception of men and women as equal and united in nature. Meanwhile Harrison cites Nazianzen's characterizations of his mother Nonna and sister Gorgonia to show leadership of pious women over men in his own family.¹⁴⁷ Such reversals of gender expectations support Harrison's claim that the Cappadocians emphasized new opportunities for women to participate in spiritual excellence; for in their version of a person's perfect state, neither male nor female exist.

Cadenhead and Harrison maintain that spiritual advancement ultimately transcends gender altogether in their subjects. As Burrus has shown, meanwhile, Nyssen conceived of the Trinity using a series of gender transposals and he also inscribed himself into accounts that placed his sister Macrina as his spiritual guide. But Burrus also continues to note that even in an alternate form, masculinity continued to provide an index of spiritual strength. So, while Harrison and Cadenhead emphasize a dissolution of the sexes in the Cappadocians, Burrus focuses on a reimagination of masculinity in theological discourse. Although Burrus differs from Cadenhead and Harrison on Nyssen's use of gender, each has interpreted Gregory's categorization of gender in theology as minimalizing male predominance in the sphere of the soul. The contributions of these three late antique scholars thus has advanced our understanding of how the Cappadocians reoriented the conventions of gender.

These important assessments, however, do not fully account for how the Cappadocians understood male and female. It is here that I offer a counterbalance to interpretations that deprioritize classical ideals of masculinity in the Cappadocians. These bishops, we will see, engaged with a variety of groups and settings. I do not want to minimize the extent to which these bishops reframed gender when expounding on matters of theological and spiritual importance. But in much of their writing, the Cappadocians emphasized an identity rooted in enduring features of masculinity. In these compositions, the Cappadocians marked *aretē* as signifying attributes of maleness and a sign of superior virtue present primarily in men. When Basil exhorts a fellow *pepaideumenos*, to "play the man (ἀνδρίζου)," or when Nazianzen admonishes a correspondent, "Let's become men (ἄνδρες γενώμεθα)," they leave no doubt to the ethical

---

¹⁴⁶ For example Basil, *Ep.* 207; cited by Harrison in V. Harrison, "Male and Female in Cappadocian Theology," *JTS* 41 (1990), 445.
¹⁴⁷ Harrison, "Male," 454–5, referencing Greg. Naz., *Ors.* 18 and 8.

categorization of gender.[148] In such cases, the disparity between male and female undergirds discussion of moral excellence. An understanding of epistolary exchange as an *agōn* provides an alternative model of gender than what we see in the Cappadocians' treatment of the metaphysical; one that is more traditional and limiting and more practically applied in the world of social and political networking. And even in the realm of the numinous, the Cappadocians maintained dichotomies of gender so that when they inverted male and female, it made for more dramatic effect. In attributing masculine virtues to female protagonists in hagiography, for example, the spiritual supremacy in the women works so well because of the anomaly of a female embodying virile traits. Thus, Nyssen's *Life of Macrina* illustrates Macrina's noble attributes by showing that she overcomes her nature as a woman.[149] Gender then remains operative for Gregory, with his sister embodying manhood and thus rising to a higher status as a manly woman.

Burrus and Cadenhead make provisions in their studies that masculinity remained an integral feature of Nyssen's social construction; that is, outside of spiritual discourse (and within it, for Burrus), the hierarchy of masculinity continued to feature in Nyssen's thought. Harrison shows less appreciation for this alternative in her emphasis on the dissolution of gender in the Cappadocians. Specifically, Harrison states that the social norms that formed their ethical ideals "came from the ascetical movement, not the aristocratic οἶκος."[150] Harrison suggests that Nazianzen personifies Nonna and Gorgonia as dominant, for example, because he believed the virtues of men and women were the same. I argue, against this assessment, that portrayals of Nonna and Gorgonia (we will see) attest to Nazianzen's prioritization of male over female.[151] As the audience's liaison to these "manly" women, Gregory secures the *aretē* that distinguishes his mother and sister from "femaleness." Consequently, these personifications reinforce, rather than diminish, societal emphasis on gender and hierarchy. Harrison asserts, moreover, that scholars are mistaken to specify male virtues as committed to personal excellence and civic leadership, with female authority limited to the domestic sphere.[152] Again, however, Harrison's point holds true primarily for the Cappadocians' discourse in some contexts, but not for their self-fashioning as *pepaideumenoi*, patrons, and networkers among imperial

---

[148] Basil, *Ep.* 106 (Deferrari); Greg. Naz., *Ep.* 178 (Storin 116).
[149] Greg. Ny., *Vit. Macr.*   [150] Harrison, "Male," 456.   [151] Greg. Naz., *Or.* 8.5.
[152] Harrison, "Male," 455.

and provincial authorities. Particularly in characterizations of *agōnes*, they encoded the contests and the participants as male, and by association, as socially powerful. A significant segment of audiences understood classical manhood as a sign of legitimate authority. Harrison is right to emphasize the influence of asceticism on the Cappadocians' view of gender, but they were equally influenced by the aristocratic ethos in which they were raised.

Asceticism and Preservation of Manhood

If a valorization of classical masculinity remained central to Cappadocian social theory, the problem still remains of reconciling instances in the Cappadocians' asceticism and theological discourse when they appear to have subverted manly deportment. While contemporaries may have found Nyssen's use of gender destabilizing, Nazianzen and Basil also seemingly compromised expectations of masculinity through their behaviors. Nazianzen narrated multiple occasions of his retreating from the duties of pastoral office.[153] Although he presents these departures as motivated by pursuit of spiritual and intellectual revitalization, the fact that he writes apologetically about the acts gives the impression that he was concerned about his reputation.[154] He was susceptible to charges that he had abandoned his sacred ministry; moreover, such flights mirrored an evasion of civic responsibility, a definitive mark of effeminacy.[155] Somewhat similar to Nazianzen, Basil suffered notoriety later in life due to an absence early in his career, when he had departed prematurely from a synod at Constantinople in 360. Critics of this apparent avoidance mocked Basil for fleeing a "contest concerning ultimate matters," an unmistakable jab at his manhood.[156] And although championed by later generations of Christians for his monastic rule,

---

[153] Greg. Naz., *Or.* 2, *Or.* 26, and *Concerning His Own Life*, 265–336; 1745–95; *Concerning His Own Affairs*, 261–307.
[154] On Gregory's awareness of reputation, Norris, "Your Honor," 140–59; J. Bernardi, *La Prédication des pères cappadociens: le prédicateur et son auditoire* (Marseille: Presses universitaires de France, 1968), 238–46.
[155] Kuefler, *Manly*, 129.
[156] Eunomius, *Apology for the Apology*, in Greg. Ny., *Contr. Eun.* 1. (phrase translated in Kopecek) T. Kopecek, *A History of Neo-Arianism*, vol. 2 (Cambridge, MA: Philadelphia Patristics Foundation, 1979), 301; also see circumstances of departure in Kopecek, 299–305.

Basil was susceptible to accusations of unmanliness because of his association with dubious ascetic communities.

Each of the Cappadocians, in fact, presented potential foils to the conventions of classical masculinity because of their writings on, and personal experiences with, asceticism.[157] Andrea Sterk's treatment of monasticism is revealing on this issue. Sterk's investigation of imperial legislation in the late-fourth century shows that most state authorities regarded monks as the antithesis to traditional civic leadership, as nuisances to the polis that needed to be controlled.[158] That such ascetics were marginalized from the city corresponds to general conceptions, until the fifth century, that they constituted a source of effeminacy.[159] Basil's emphasis on ascetic discipline and his idealization of the monk-turned-bishop later contributed to a legitimization of asceticism that came about in the fifth century. He investigated asceticism in a number of regions and he contributed to a series of regulations that later were collated into a rule.[160] His ideals of ascetic life, however, evolved over many years and the nuances of development were not always easily discernible. Consequently he would have been susceptible to criticisms for his early-life connections to Eustathius of Sebaste, a bishop from Armenia who promoted a radical form of asceticism censured at the ecclesiastical council of Gangra (c. 355).[161] Later in life, Basil came to view Eustathius as a bitter theological adversary and heretic. But because he had once admired the man, Basil may have been suspected of advocating similar excesses, which included criticisms of marriage. Meanwhile, Basil and Nazianzen both were liable to charges of effeminacy because of not marrying and begetting children. By committing to a life of virginity, opponents might

---

[157] M. Stewart, *Soldier's Life*, 162–5, argues against interpretations that depict asceticism as a new form of Christian masculinity as early as the fourth century.

[158] A. Sterk, *Renouncing the World Yet Leading the Church: The Monk-Bishop in Late Antiquity* (Cambridge: Harvard University Press, 2004), 163–74.

[159] D. Brakke, *Demons*, 182.

[160] See an overview of its development in A. Silvas, *The Asketikon of St. Basil the Great* (Oxford: Oxford University Press, 2005), 130–43.

[161] One of Basil's earliest extant letters (c. 357) shows his admiration for Eustathius, *Ep.* 1 (Deferrari), where Basil speaks of "following you [Eustathius] as a lamb follows the shepherd's staff held out before it." On Basil and Eustathius, Rousseau, *Basil*, 73–6, and J. Gribomont, *Saint Basile: évangile et église. Mélanges* (Bégrolles-en-Mauges: Abbaye de Bellefontaine, 1984), I:95–106. The date of the council is disputed: see Silvas, *Asketikon*, 486 n.1 and T. Barnes, "The Date of the Council of Gangra," *JTS* 40:1 (1989), 121–4. Based on the evidence cited in Barnes' analysis, it seems likely that the council took place in the mid-350s.

propose, the ascetic forfeited the sexual dominance of the male that was the foundation of the social order.

Basil and Nazianzen also spent long periods of ascetic solitude in the province of Pontus (near Basil's family land) in 358 and 359 – and Gregory, later at Seleucia, from 375–8 – further reinforcing the image of a manhood that contravened the norms for an elite male. Someone who avoided civic society seemingly contradicted a life of public performance, the very premise that defined classical manhood.[162] The gender of such a person might be called into question because his gesture, stance, voice, and language – his very self – was not engaging in visible contest. And Gregory of Nyssa compounded the problematic implications of gender in his account of his brother Peter working alongside his sister Macrina in overseeing a community of virgins in Pontus during the early 360s.[163] Such coordinated leadership could be construed as seemingly undermining the social hierarchy of male over female by empowering Macrina but diminishing Peter's standing.[164] More disruptive yet, was Gregory's depiction of his sister as spiritual guide for the younger Peter, with Macrina serving during Peter's adolescence, as his "father, teacher, guardian, mother, counsellor of every good."[165] The piety of his sister, and subsequent deference of his brother, offered a lesson in personal meekness and spiritual well-being over social hierarchy. Such narratives of asceticism thus constituted a novel sense of manhood: submission to the true male Christ, commitment to a virginal life, and forfeiting earthly authority in favor of spiritual power. This form of spiritual virility eventually gained favor within the eastern Roman church, which came to understand monastic discipline as congruent with episcopal sovereignty.[166] But in the

---

[162] G. Clark, "The Old Adam: The Fathers and the Unmaking of Masculinity," in *Thinking Men: Masculinity and Its Self-Representation in the Classical Tradition*, eds. L. Foxhall and J. Salmon (London: Routledge, 2011), 173.

[163] Greg. Ny., *Vit. Macr.* 12 (Maraval). The development of this ascetic community under Macrina took place over many years and stages. On its complex formation, S. Elm, *"Virgins of God": The Making of Asceticism in Late Antiquity* (Oxford: Clarendon Press, 1994), 78–105.

[164] E. Clark, *Reading Renunciation: Asceticism and Scripture in Early Christianity* (Princeton: Princeton University Press, 1999), 37–8 on how monastic leadership offered some aristocratic women the potential to engage in patronage, a function normally reserved for males.

[165] Greg. Ny., *Vit. Macr.* 12.10 (Silvas).

[166] D. Brakke, *Athanasius and the Politics of Asceticism* (Baltimore: Johns Hopkins University Press, 1995), 104–10, on Athanasius' attempts to bind the bishop and the monk through his *Life of Antony*. Sterk, *Renouncing*, 178–82, locates closer affiliation between monks and the church hierarchy from the late-fourth to sixth centuries, by

late 300s, this consonance was still emerging. The Cappadocians were instructing on exercises of societal and sexual renunciation at a time before ascetic rules had been codified and normalized for clergy or laity. The image of transcendent masculinity embodied by ascetics thus potentially subverted the established social order of male over female.[167] Thus the Cappadocians were met with the challenge of preserving an identity as classical males at the same time that they advocated forms of transcendent manhood that apparently contradicted such claims. In fact, as we will see later, the Cappadocians framed asceticism in hagiographic biographies as engagement in *agōnes*, thus emphasizing both piety and *aretē*. They were attempting to construe spiritual austerity as a manly enterprise.

Self-Representation and Identity Formation

As they expounded on spiritual themes, Basil, Nazianzen, and Nyssen also projected a persona of masculinity based on their training in *paideia*, more evident in some genres than in others. Studied only through the focus on their metaphysics, the Cappadocians would seem to have relinquished characteristics of the paradigmatic male. But the complexity of self-representation within *paideia* allowed for multiple roles in late-antique bishops.[168] So while much of the philosophic pedagogy elevated *aretē* within a spiritual discourse as a form of transcendent manhood, the Cappadocians were equally educated in a past that extolled the male as exhibiting *aretē* in the civic sphere: the soldier, the athlete, and the civic leader. By emulating figures of prominence from classical Greece, the Cappadocians also performed *aretē* as an exhibition of social merit, thus signaling their role as *agathoi*.

In much of their correspondence, we will see, they framed their epistles as performances that mimicked the competitive zest of an *agōn* and the verbal jousting in the Second Sophistic. This pattern of self-presentation shows up across the careers of each of the Cappadocians, from Basil's early correspondence in the 350s to Nazianzen's prolific literary output in the 380s. The Cappadocians thus contributed to a discourse of reconfigured

---

which time church historians were elevating the role of monks as a training ground for future bishops.
[167] K. Cooper, *The Virgin and the Bride: Idealized Womanhood in Late Antiquity* (Cambridge, MA: Harvard University Press, 1999), 82–3, illustrates that this was a major cause of concern, even among Christian social elites.
[168] R. R. Ruether, *Gregory*, 7–11.

manly behaviors (such as asceticism) in certain contexts. In other forums, however, they reinforced a code of masculinity that involved exhibiting rhetorical merit in contests among fellow intellectuals.

And when the Cappadocians engaged in practices that seemed at odds with male decorum, they managed these occasions to promote an image of contest, thus preserving a virile identity. In 381, for example, Nazianzen withdrew from Byzantium, where as a pro-Nicene bishop he had presided over the Council of Constantinople. The inglorious departure culminated in his return to the family estate in Cappadocia, where he embarked on a forty-day period of silence during the Lenten season of 382. Critics could maintain that such an act of silence defied the Greco-Roman expectation that a virtuous man should remain active in public affairs. The verbal stillness thereby might have compromised an image of assertion.[169] Yet, Gregory engaged in a major literary campaign during the quietude, thus rehabilitating his ecclesiastical image after his tenure at Constantinople.[170] Instead of silence representing a time of evasion, as Brad Storin points out, Gregory turned the occasion into a period of activity, thus situating himself in a struggle to redeem his reputation. In similar manner, I argue, Gregory and the other Cappadocians reoriented the ascetic endeavors of their hagiographic subjects to appear as contests consonant with virility. By situating these saints in an *agōn* setting, the Cappadocians signaled affiliation with arenas of strength. They thus associated the saints and themselves – as friends or family – with the *aretē* of bygone heroes. They were framing Christian leadership through a reference they knew well, the classical Greek past. While deploying the theme of transcendent manhood in certain contexts then, and quite possibly because of that role, the Cappadocians remained vigilant to reinforce images as superior men according to traditional norms. In doing so, the Cappadocians established depth to the Christian form of manhood, refashioning maleness to apply equally well to the civic sphere and the spiritual.

Identity Theory as a Category of Analysis

Brakke's and Cobb's uses of identity formation, discussed earlier, prove helpful for understanding how early Christians were instructed to

---

[169] Jones, *Playing*, 53; on how silence could potentially emasculate.

[170] B. Storin, "In a Silent Way: Asceticism and Literature in the Rehabilitation of Gregory of Nazianzus," *JECS* 19:2 (2011), 242–7, directing readers to Gregory's epistles 107–14 and 116–19.

perceive desert monks and martyrs as manly according to Greco-Roman norms. Such categories of analysis are especially applicable for understanding variant representations of masculinity in the Cappadocians and other early Christian writers. Other recent forays into identity theory also are useful for thinking about texts where the Cappadocians seem to have elided religious differences. Éric Rebillard, for example, has investigated north Africa in the third to fifth centuries and asserted that Christians here did not always regard religious allegiance as more significant than other social categories to which they belonged. Rebillard states that these individuals held to a variety of group category memberships and that no fixed hierarchy governed the sets. Rather a person gave salience to category membership depending on context and circumstances.[171] Kendra Eshleman, meanwhile, has applied identity theory to sophists and Christian leaders of the early Roman empire. She has determined that community formation for both groups was established in a strikingly similar manner. To *belong* to a group, Eshleman asserts, an individual had to exhibit cognitive, ritual, and ethical standards that differentiated him or her from outsiders. For early Christian leaders, this mechanism sanctioned orthodox members of the faith against heretics based on an evaluation of texts and behaviors that corresponded to the dominant theology. Sophists similarly included or excluded associates based on meeting aesthetic criteria – namely in style of speech – that were judged sufficiently superior over the ordinary person.[172] Although Rebillard was focusing largely on laity, and Eshleman's treatment precedes the fourth century, their assessments apply to the Cappadocians, who activated multiple group memberships and who used epistolary exchange as a means of situating themselves within the groupness of *pepaideumenoi*.

The sophist Libanius offers a fitting non-Christian example of how *pepaideumenoi* often asserted a category of membership outside of faith groups. In his writings, Libanius rarely defined himself according to his faith or called attention to religious allegiance as an essential category membership. While occasionally Libanius did acknowledge his own religious identity and that of others, more often he expressed congruity with others based on civic patronage and rhetorical excellence.[173] His regard

---

[171] É. Rebillard, *Christians and Their Many Identities in Late Antiquity, North Africa, 200–450 CE* (Ithaca: Cornell University Press, 2012), 7–8, 78–85.

[172] K. Eshleman, *The Social World of Intellectuals in the Roman Empire: Sophists, Philosophers, and Christians* (Cambridge: Cambridge University Press, 2012), 7–15.

[173] I. Sandwell, *Religious Identity in Late Antiquity: Greeks, Jews and Christians in Antioch* (Cambridge: Cambridge University Press, 2011), 132–43.

for these features in the life of a provincial notable served, in many ways, as his source of self-fashioning. Libanius makes for an intriguing comparison with the Cappadocians because, like his Christian counterparts, he established his identity through exhibitions of eloquence and correspondence with fellow *pepaideumenoi*. While the Cappadocians often underscored their pro-Nicene Christian affiliation, they also engaged literati specifically as part of an identity group based on mutual *paideia* (and *aretē*), with no reference to their faith. In this sense, they appear more synonymous with Libanius than with many of their fellow clergy, a point that should come as little surprise.

Apart from religious differences, the Cappadocians and Libanius shared many commonalities. Libanius was born into a curial family at Antioch. He studied at Athens, taught at Constantinople, and eventually settled as a teacher of rhetoric at his hometown, where for forty years he attracted many of the most promising young students of the eastern provincial aristocracy, including numerous Christians.[174] Although there is limited documented interaction between him and the Cappadocians (such as Basil's study under Libanius), they participated in similar intellectual circles. The fact that Libanius and the Cappadocians were so alike in relation to a specific group category, despite fundamental faith differences, shows how powerful any single identity could be. By way of comparison, Emperor Julian, a friend of Libanius, held the same appreciation for Greek literature, philosophy, and history as the Cappadocians. But whereas Libanius accepted religious divergences in colleagues and students as long as they showed mutual respect, Julian drew a firm line between those he considered the rightful heirs of *paideia* (Neo-platonic philosophers) and Christian intellectuals such as the Cappadocians. The latter, in Julian's view, had chosen to be Christians, an identity that in his eyes was mutually exclusive with the culture of *paideia*, which was permeated with the exploits of Greek divinities.

---

[174] Petit, *Étudiants*, 14–17. On the religious setting at Antioch, A. J. Festugière, *Antioche païenne et chrétienne* (Paris: de Boccard, 1959), 35–47; Cribiore, *Libanius*, 182–5, shows that Libanius interacted with and instructed numerous Christians. In many cases, a shared love of literary culture glossed over religious differences. But his tolerance seems to have been limited to Christians who offered similar quarter to pagans. C. Shepardson, *Controlling Contested Places: Late Antique Antioch and the Spatial Politics of Religious Controversy* (Berkeley: University of California Press, 2014), 190–6, argues that he issued scathing abuse, for example, on Christian ascetics who disrupted civic life by attacks on temples.

IDENTITY AND GENRE

Although the Cappadocians issued writings from numerous genres, in *Christianity and the Contest* we will concentrate primarily on epistles and hagiographic texts. These choices best demonstrate alternative means by which the Cappadocians established identity and they also show variations in group memberships to which they belonged. On one hand, by composing epistles the Cappadocians affiliated with classical manhood as actual participants. The act of writing and exchanging letters with other literati constituted an act of contest in and of itself. When Basil wrote to one recipient of the "mental labor" (πόνος διανοίας) and "share in your toils" (ἐκοινώνησας τῶν καμάτων), he was reiterating the dynamism of letter exchange.[175] In one sense, the epistle was a record of the deed that had already manifested virtue. In hagiographic accounts, on the other hand, the Cappadocians asserted identity by authoring narratives and thereby serving as overseers of a tradition of sacred *aretē*. The writer acquired a persona as manly through familial ties, friendship, or theological similarity to his subject/s. Gregory of Nyssa prefaces his *Life of Gregory Thaumaturgus* by claiming that the same power (δύναμις) fuels the person who recounts great deeds and the individual accomplishing the feats.[176] His statement is representative of how hagiographers perceived their role as conduits between listeners/readers and the lives of saints shared with them.[177] Control over the sacred life, that is, attested to the author's own virtue.

Epistolary Exchange and Participation in Agōnes

Through epistolary exchange, more so than hagiographic narratives, the Cappadocians activated the broadest spectrum of identities. Evidence of their divergent audiences is recorded in the extant correspondence of each clergyman: for Nazianzen, over 240 epistles; for Basil, some 330 missives; and for Nyssen, thirty letters (and assuredly many more, not preserved).[178] The huge majority of these surviving letters were written when

---

[175] Basil, *Ep.* 135 (Deferrari).   [176] Greg. Ny., *Vit. GTh.* 1.1.

[177] D. Krueger, *Writing and Holiness: The Practice of Authorship in the Early Christian East* (Philadelphia: University of Pennsylvania Press, 2004), 191.

[178] On relative dearth of extant letters for Nyssen, Silvas, *Gregory*, 58–61; A. Radde-Gallwitz, "The Letter Collection of Gregory of Nyssa," in *Late Antique Letter Collections*, eds. C. Sogno, B. Storin, and E. Watts (Berkeley: University of California Press, 2017), 110. Radde-Gallwitz's theory is especially intriguing, that fewer of

the authors were serving as bishops. Most of the others date from earlier clerical office. No one category neatly summarizes the roles played by the Cappadocians in these interactions. For some addressees, they wrote as ascetics; for others, it was as family members; in many cases – after ordination – it was as bishops and caretakers of congregations; and often it was as *pepaideumenoi*, who exchanged social and civic capital with one another.[179]

So although our study concentrates on the Cappadocians asserting manhood through *agōnes*, this element of identity sharing does not apply to every addressee. Basil, for instance, wrote to a congregation at Satala (in Armenia) to introduce a bishop he appointed there.[180] With typical erudition, he admonishes the Christians there to welcome the prelate. But in this case, he shows less concern with the conventions of classical manhood than we see in correspondence with audiences consisting primarily of *pepaideumenoi*. Likewise, each of the Cappadocians corresponded with women, some of whom were exceptionally educated and who wielded significant social and economic influence. Although these encounters constituted literary performances in their own right, the Cappadocians did not engage the addressees with the same reference to manhood evident in other letters.[181] Contrary to Basil's letter to the Satala church is his petition, on behalf of family friend Domitian, to Governor Andronicus (probably of Armenia Prima).[182] The letter is a show-piece as well as a mediation. Basil follows epistolary tropes by stating his desire to see Andronicus in person, justifying his absence, and staking a position of humility. He follows by vouching for Domitian, underscoring his personal connection to the man, and suggesting a natural affinity between his client and the governor, whom Basil praises as "your Virtuous self (τὴν σὴν ἀρετήν)."[183] Basil finalizes the letter

---

Nyssen's epistles were collected because there was never a contemporary biography for him, and fifth-century church historians often left him out of discussions when treating Basil and Nazianzen.

[179] A. Schor, "Becoming Bishop in the Letters of Basil and Synesius: Tracing Patterns of Social Signaling across Two Full Epistolary Collections," *JLA* 7:2 (2014), 308, where Schor cites a wide variety of social roles for Basil, as evidenced in his correspondence.

[180] Basil, *Ep.* 103.

[181] P. Allen and B. Neil, *Greek and Latin Letters in Late Antiquity: The Christianisation of a Literary Form* (Cambridge: Cambridge University Press, 2020), 132–4, on Cappadocians' female correspondents.

[182] Basil, *Ep.* 112; on Andronicus as governor of Armenia, Van Dam, *Kingdom*, 234 n. 22.

[183] Basil, *Ep.* 112 (Deferrari).

by likening the governor's potential favor for Domitian to that of Persian king Cyrus the Great favoring Croesus, king of Lydia. Instead of destroying Croesus after defeating him, Cyrus had befriended the noble ruler.[184]

The letter to Andronicus was likely to have been read by fellow *pepaideumenoi* and to have been judged according to the standards of a contest; it was a different kind of letter than the one he sent to the church at Satala. Basil begins the letter as the weaker party seeking assistance; by the end, however, through use of rhetorical flourish and a moral example from Greek historian Herodotus, Basil ascends to a role as philosopher and instructor by directing the governor on the appropriate course of action. Basil has seemingly inverted the power relations and has now become the agent of policy. In this example, Basil is adhering to the ideal of masculinity in his specified reader, an individual conversant in *paideia*. He has coordinated his identity to the situation. In the other example, the letter to congregants at Satala, he dictates from a position as their spiritual shepherd. He writes as a bishop in both letters, but his audience calls for different claims to authority. These two examples are intended to show how the Cappadocians adapted their persona according to group membership: in the first case with Basil, as a spiritual overseer accredited by his bishopric at Caesarea; in the second, as an intellectual confirmed through his posture as a classical male. This is not to say, however, that the Cappadocians were concerned about self-portrayals of gender only when it came to *pepaideumenoi* (Christian or non-Christian). Rather, it is to say that the Cappadocians emphasized certain ideals according to the group/s they were addressing. And so, when we talk of the genre of letters, only a portion of the Cappadocians' missives constituted literary exercises consciously reordered as *agōnes*.

A few characteristics of epistolary exchange suggest why letters were instrumental for projecting a variety of identities across a network of friends and associates. Perhaps most significantly, the letter (I use "epistle" and "letter" interchangeably) was a notoriously flexible form of communication. The Cappadocians addressed all manner of issues in their correspondence: doctrinal clarification; spiritual consolation; personal patronage; mediation for cities; securing supplies; and many other matters. They were writing oftentimes in response to specific petitions. But although the Cappadocians often were composing according to a specific purpose, these occasions enabled them to display breadth of

---

[184] Herodotus, *Histories* 1. 87–8.

knowledge, cleverness, and familiarity with protocols of correspondence. The premise of sending a letter, normally, was that the author was participating in a dialogue with the addressee, thus bridging a spatial gap and sustaining a relationship.[185] Certain conventions applied to letter writing, but these varied according to purpose and audience and were not applied consistently to the same extent as other kinds of rhetoric.[186] The epistolary corpora of the Cappadocians thus shows that the letters were designed to fit the station, education, faith, and even region of individual recipients.

Recent investigations in the fields of letter collection and network theory show that the Cappadocians were hyperaware of coordinating their correspondence based on particular affiliations with addressees.[187] Adam Schor, for example, has analyzed Basil's correspondence and mapped a network of his correspondents based on features of group identity. "Non-ascetics just did not hear from Basil about his monastic life or teachings;" Schor writes, "clerics heard nothing about classical culture, and other elite contacts...heard either Christian or classical literary discourse, but rarely both."[188] Schor's point is that Basil used social cues to signal the mutual identity with his addressees, and these signs were distinct and deliberate. Brad Storin, meanwhile, has illustrated that Gregory managed his letters as a form of autobiography. Storin focuses on Gregory's self-editing and collating his and Basil's voluminous letter collections after his departure from the Council of Constantinople in 381. Looking back on his episcopal career, Storin argues, Gregory coordinated these epistolary collections to create a single self-portrait; an image that highlighted his eloquence, philosophy, and friendship with Basil. By arranging letters according to addressee, purpose, and intended self-portrayal, Gregory was able to choreograph his image without

---

[185] H. Koskenniemi, *Studien zur Idee und Phraseologie des greichischen Briefes bis 400 n. Chr.* (Helsinki: Suomalainen Tiedeakatemia, 1956), 35–46; and as Margaret Mullett points out, "Every letter must be interpreted in terms of what is known of the recipient as well as the writer" (18). For this reason, among many others she cites, epistles do not fit neatly into discussions of genre. M. Mullett, *Theophylact of Ochrid: Reading the Letters of a Byzantine Archbishop* (Aldershot: Ashgate, 1997), 18–24.

[186] M. Trapp, *Greek and Latin Letters: An Anthology with Translation* (Cambridge: Cambridge University Press, 2003), 34–42.

[187] Overview of network analysis, Mullett, *Theophylact*, 163–75.

[188] Schor, "Becoming Bishop," 316; also see treatments of Basil's and Nyssen's letter collections in Radde-Gallwitz, "The Letter Collection of Basil of Caesarea," and "Letter Collection of Gregory of Nyssa," *Late Antique*, 69–80, 102–12.

violating an implicit rule among literati: that writing about oneself insinuated vanity.[189]

Storin's emphasis on Gregory's letters as an "epistolary autobiography" builds on the work of Neil McLynn, who recognized that Gregory was creating a self-serving narrative by arranging his and Basil's letter collections.[190] Gregory's epistolary self-representation thus was following other instances of self-writing, notably complementing his famous funeral oration for Basil (*Or.* 43), which succeeded so well that it has remained the definitive account of the two men's friendship. McLynn and Storin show that a skilled *pepaideumenos* could effectively negotiate epistolary exchange throughout his life to create base elements of a larger identity. Each letter, that is, formed a micro-rendition of himself that he could later, potentially, build into a fuller portrait. Other literati mirrored Gregory in that when "contesting" with other *pepaideumenoi* through letter exchange, they created similar partial-portrayals. Gregory was exceptional, however, in that circumstances and resources were such later in his life that he could take these elements and neatly order the nuances of his larger profile.

The particularity of epistles also comes out in the very process of epistolary exchange. Unlike orations, for example, letters were designed overtly for one recipient, the addressee. The text was, in theory, planned for one person. The process, of course, was much more complex. The delivery, receipt, and reading of a letter supplemented the text to create a multi-sensory, sometimes ceremonial experience.[191] Even the letter itself – the papyrus – served as a material memory of the occasion.[192] Ultimately, over time a much wider group might come to read the epistle.[193] The text, however, was implicitly composed for a much smaller group of readers and listeners than public speeches; even if in reality the author knew that the letter would be disseminated. The ability to specify rhetoric for an audience thus enabled the Cappadocians to project an identity for a

---

[189] Storin, *Self-Portrait*, 12–15.
[190] N. McLynn, "Gregory Nazianzen's Basil: The Literary Construction of a Christian Friendship," *SP* 34 (2001), 183–7.
[191] Mullet, *Theophylact*, 32–9.
[192] H.-J. Klauck and D. Bailey, *Ancient Letters and the New Testament: A Guide to Content and Exegesis* (Waco, TX: Baylor University Press, 2006,) 49–58, discuss papyrus as an aesthetic element of the letter.
[193] L. Stirewalt, *Studies in Ancient Greek Epistolography* (Atlanta: Scholars, 1993), 3, and P. Rosenmeyer, *Ancient Epistolary Fictions: The Letter in Greek Literature* (Cambridge: Cambridge University Press, 2001), 9, on the extension of letters.

certain addressee without calling into question other roles. The letter would be shared with others, but the individuals made privy to this missive would likely have been part of the group membership intended by the author.[194]

While oral forms of public presentation had long served as an index of manhood, moreover, letter writing set in motion a skill set that demanded an alternate performance. Epistolography underwent a number of innovations during the Second Sophistic and, like the themes of declamations during this period, letters increasingly alluded to classical Greek themes and conformed to Atticism, classical Greek literary style.[195] But during the second and third centuries, the most celebrated platform for recreating the ancient Greek world of eloquence came in public speeches. The cultural arbiters of the second and third centuries, as depicted by authors such as Philostratus, gained acclaim because of oratorical mastery. It was during the fourth century, by contrast, that letter writers were emerging as cultural icons, a mantle formerly enjoyed by sophists. With fewer opportunities for oratorical exhibitions based strictly on classical themes, letter writers enacted similar rhetorical contests. Epistolographers, however, had to stage an *agōn* on pen and paper and bring to life the rhetorical combat. The trope of absence, a standard feature in epistolary exchange, was only part of the author's larger task of staging human actions through the written word. Whereas the oratorical clashes of the Second Sophistic took place in public view, authors of letters used the pen to usher a virtual *agōn* so that readers could still "see" the rivalry unfolding.[196] Thus, epistolary authors initiated a sequence of kinetic events: from using the pen to write; to recreating a visual experience on paper that touched the audience's senses; to having the missive delivered and read to the recipient. The ability to orchestrate such literary encounters constituted an evolving form of eloquence, a mark of *aretē* applied to individuals and groups equipped to understand the meaning of such exchanges.

---

[194] Greg. Ny., *Ep.* 14, again where Gregory refers to an epistle from Libanius as a "ticket for a feast."

[195] O. Hodkinson, "Better than Speech: Some Advantages of the Letter in the Second Sophistic," in *Ancient Letters: Classical and Late Antique Epistolography*, eds. R. Morello and A. D. Morrison (Oxford: Oxford University Press, 2007), 283–300; Trapp, *Greek*, 31–3; Rosenmeyer, *Ancient*, 255–60.

[196] Hodkinson, "Better," 298–9, states that the flexibility of epistles allowed for a kind of rhetoric based on using competing genres, thus mimicking conventions from several performative models.

The Cappadocians also accentuated group membership among *pepaideumenoi* in letters by invoking illustrious persons from classical Greece; referents they rarely used in speeches to predominantly Christian audiences. While late antique bishops used saints to "think with" – to explore a doctrine or to elucidate scripture – some clergy also spoke through classical figures to hold up values.[197] The Cappadocians used references from the Hellenic past, for instance, to proffer models of *aretē*. In a letter to an addressee named Antiochanus, Gregory of Nyssa likened himself to Alexander the Great.[198] According to Gregory, the Macedonian king was most admired by people of understanding because he boasted not of his victories but rather "saying that his treasure was in his friends."[199] Gregory then stated that he surpassed the Hellenistic monarch in riches because of his own storehouse of intimates, exemplified by the fact that Antiochanus was a greater friend than Alexander had ever had. Moreover, Gregory said, Antiochanus had proven himself noble by always "contending within yourself to exceed in virtue (ἀρετή)."[200] Gregory added that "it is the mark of those who are nobly wealthy (τῶν καλῶς πλουτούντων) to know how to use what they have."[201] Gregory uses the figure of Alexander to cast himself as an authority on manhood and friendship. This expertise provides him leverage as he is about to detail how a friend should act. *Pepaideumenoi* had been taught that *aretē* could only be achieved through continual cultivation and demonstrations of honor. Here Gregory acclaims Antiochanus, through the medium of Alexander, and subsequently introduces a young man who was bringing a

---

[197] On speaking through female saints, see E. Clark, "Women, Gender, and the Study of Christian History," *CH* 70 (2001), 395–426. J. Connolly, "Like the Labor of Heracles: *Andreia* and *Paideia* in Greek Culture Under Rome," in *Andreia*, 292, similarly recognizes the tendency of sophists to illustrate current political issues through allusions to the history of the classical past.

[198] Greg. Ny., *Ep.* 8; this comparison was a *synkrisis*, a standard rhetorical feature that set two praiseworthy subjects side by side. See Aelius Theon, *Progymnasmata* ("Rhetorical Exercises"), 112–15.

[199] Greg. Ny., *Ep.* 8 (Silvas): τὸν θησαυρὸν ἐν τοῖς φίλοις ἔχειν; the phrase is found in Plutarch, *Moralia* 326d–45b; P. Maraval, *Grégoire de Nysse: Lettres*, SC 363 (1990), 175 n.2. notes that this was a common saying among fourth-century rhetoricians: Libanius, *Or.* 8.9, and Themistius *Or.* 16.203; on this specific anecdote, also Libanius, *Progymnasmata* 43–5 and Aelius Theon, *Progymnasmata* 100.

[200] Greg. Ny., *Ep.* 8 (my translation). Maraval, *Lettres*, 174–5 n. 1, notes that this sentiment echoes thoughts by near contemporary Neo-platonic philosophers, that the virtuous individual must fight to control his own passions. He cites Porphyry, *On Abstinence* 3.27.11.

[201] Greg. Ny., *Ep.* 8 (Silvas).

personal request on some matter. He then asked Antiochanus to receive the petitioner as a friend, "to show to him my treasure," meaning to receive him with the same grace and amity as the great Macedonian general.[202]

By framing the letter through a reference to Alexander, Gregory was calling forth Antiochanus' awareness of this archetype of Greek manhood. Gregory also was reorienting the significance of the world conqueror, in this case presenting him as a metaphor for how Gregory valued colleagues.[203] The choice of Alexander was significant for multiple reasons. First, Alexander exemplified a valorized Greek past. Thus, he represented a historical marker for Gregory, a site in which the bishop could reify his authority based on an individual who typified bravery, self-restraint, and sagacity.[204] Second, he personified Greekness. Alexander had subdued the "barbaric," unmanly Persians and ultimately spread Hellas across the eastern Mediterranean and west Asia. Speaking through Alexander, Gregory was trumpeting a non-Christian Greek past in a way that showed his reverence for it. Third, Gregory was choreographing an affiliation (*philia*) with Antiochianus based on similar background and education, an affinity outlined, among others, by Alexander's teacher Aristotle.[205] This nexus stood as an antecedent to the fourth-century community of *philoi* (of Greek *pepaideumenoi*). Finally, Gregory was demonstrating his cleverness. Gregory issued multiple layers of meaning through his personification of Alexander, thus suggesting that only well-educated readers would fully comprehend the sentiments. The missive constituted a well-crafted exemplum of Gregory's own *aretē*.

---

[202] Greg. Ny., *Ep.* 8 (Silvas).

[203] R. Webb, *Ekphrasis, Imagination and Persuasion in Ancient Rhetorical Theory and Practice* (Farnham: Ashgate, 2009), 19; Webb says that "readers were encouraged not to approach texts as distanced artefacts with a purely critical eye, but to engage with them imaginatively, to think themselves into the scenes"; also P. C. Miller, *The Corporeal Imagination: Signifying the Holy in Late Ancient Christianity* (Philadelphia: University of Pennsylvania Press, 2009), 62–9.

[204] Plutarch, *Life of Alexander*, on self-restraint, 4.8–9; on courage and wisdom, 6.1–7; R. Preston, "Roman Questions, Greek Answers; Plutarch and the Construction of Identity," in *Being Greek*, 90; see a similar strategy in Latin authors in C. Chin, *Grammar and Christianity in the Late Roman World* (Philadelphia: University of Pennsylvania Press, 2007), 142–55.

[205] For example Aristotle, *N.E.* 8; D. Konstan, "Problems in the History of Christian Friendship," *JECS* 4:1 (1996), 82–113, especially 98–106; C. White, *Christian Friendship in the Fourth Century* (Cambridge: Cambridge University Press, 1992), 13–60.

Hagiographic Biography and Agōn

The Cappadocians carved out multiple personas for themselves in epistles, depending on addressee and purpose. At first glance, it appears that in orations they reached out to audiences strictly based on religious allegiance; in their capacity as clergy so it seems. While most of their orations were intended for Christian listeners and readers, including the biographical texts to be discussed, they also embedded within these works elements of *aretē* befitting the classical male. Such depictions were meant to register across multiple group identities, including the lay Christian and the non-Christian intellectual.

Our focus thus turns to how the Cappadocians merged classical ideals of masculinity into portrayals of hagiographic figures. Here I define "hagiography" as a literary form of ancient biography that exalted individuals – in this case, already deceased – because they represented spiritual excellence. As such, hagiography forms only one example of what is broadly considered ancient biographical literature, which will include any text that focused on the life of an individual.[206] Examples include encomiums, funeral orations, and *bioi* (lives). The issue of genre is complex and each of the preceding forms of biographical literature has been categorized by others as a separate genre with specific conventions.[207] I have chosen to refer to them collectively as biographic literature because the Cappadocians did not hold fast to rhetorical categorization when treating individuals. In Nazianzen's oration for Basil, for example – which manifests many of the standard tropes of a funeral oration – Gregory does not limit himself to classical models and, with an emphasis on Basil's Christian faith, Gregory also departs markedly in content from classical precedents.[208]

---

[206] I follow Swain in treating biographical literature in this larger sense: S. Swain, "Biography and Biographic in the Literature of the Roman Empire," in *Portraits: Biographical Representation in the Greek and Latin Literature of the Roman Empire*, eds. M. Edwards and S. Swain (Oxford: Clarendon Press, 1997), 1–2.

[207] I want to call attention to the promising study by Allison Gray, *Gregory of Nyssa as Biographer* (Tübingen: Mohr Siebeck, 2021), which was published at the proof stage of this book. Also, an excellent, concise overview of biography in the Greek world up to the fourth century of the Roman empire is the series of lectures in A. Momigliano, *The Development of Greek Biography* (Cambridge, MA: Harvard University Press, 1971); more recently, see "Introduction" in T. Hägg, *Greek Biography*, 1–28, which gives attention to biography in late antiquity and discussions on the problematic nature of genre and distinctions among forms of biography; and on various rhetorical genres, Kennedy, *Greek Rhetoric*.

[208] The conventions of the funeral oration, however, form the backdrop to many hagiographies. On the rules of individual funerary eulogy, see third-century rhetorician

Meanwhile, scholarship on biographical literature in antiquity has increasingly recognized that speeches and texts were designed to uphold ideals represented by the subject, rather than merely as a historical chronicle of that person's life.[209] The authors recounting the lives of great men and women (in this case, saints), then, served not solely as proprietors of a historical past, but rather as the conduit of the noble characteristics exemplified by their subjects. Biographical literature thus makes for an especially informative source for recognizing deployment of group identity – based on certain core values – and specifically the gendered dimensions of classical antiquity. A couple of points differentiate our study of hagiography by the Cappadocians from that of their epistolography. First, the concentration will be on biographical sources only by Nazianzen and Nyssen. Unlike their much larger epistolary output, each composed only a few works of biographical nature, while no such account of a near contemporary by Basil has survived.[210] Second, the extant biographic texts serve as a point of comparison with the epistles because the former spoke to a broad Christian audience while the latter had a more singular readership. Overt references to classical *aretē*, as found in epistles to *pepaideumenoi*, appear less frequently in biographic texts. Most of the texts were first delivered orally (to a body consisting primarily of Christians) in a church, at a large funeral gathering, or to a monastic community.[211] Even Nyssen's *Life of Macrina* – somewhat of an anomaly – although composed as a letter with a specific addressee, was circulated and read in Christian liturgical settings.[212] The biographical works, therefore, offer a version of masculinity directed to a predominantly Christian gathering.

Menander Rhetor 420. See discussion of Menander and the rules and topoi of funeral orations in L. Pernot, *La Rhétorique*, 134–73.

[209] The deeds of the hero, that is, illustrated his virtue. P. C. Miller, *Biography in Late Antiquity: A Quest for the Holy Man* (Berkeley: University of California Press, 1983), 8–15, 57–65; also L. Coon, *Sacred Fictions: Holy Women and Hagiography in Late Antiquity* (Philadelphia: University of Pennsylvania Press, 1997), xv–xvi.

[210] Unlike Nazianzen and Nyssen, Basil did not compose hagiographies of contemporary saints (that survive, at least), although he did produce two homilies on earlier martyrs: *On the Martyr Gordius* and *On the Forty Martyrs of Sebaste*. See Introduction and texts in *"Let Us Die That We May Live": Greek Homilies on Christian Martyrs from Asia Minor, Palestine and Syria (c. AD 350-c. AD 450)*, eds, J. Leemans, W. Mayer, P. Allen, and B. Dehandschutter (London: Routledge, 2003).

[211] The extension of Hellenistic rhetoric, as Norris points out, thus becomes an expected work of the church. Norris, "Your Honor," 153.

[212] A. Silvas, *Macrina the Younger: Philosopher of God* (Turnhout: Brepols, 2008), 101–2 and on biography, P. Maraval, *Grégoire de Nysse: vie de sainte Macrine*, 32–4.

In hagiographic accounts, the Cappadocians extolled family and friends who epitomized piety, unwavering faith, pro-Nicene doctrine, and close relationship with Christ. Therefore, the authors cited heroes and heroines from biblical scriptures as correlations to their subjects. The association was appropriate to the religious identity of the audience. In his *Encomium on Basil*, for example, Gregory of Nyssa, places his brother in a lineage of God's chosen exponents of divine truth: Abraham, Moses, Samuel, Elias (Elijah), John the Baptist, and Paul.[213] "...this man of God in our own generation, the great vessel of truth," Nyssen wrote, "Basil, is numbered among the aforementioned saints; since his subsequence in time in no way hinders either his lofty longing for God, nor the divine grace in its perfecting of his soul."[214] By alluding to biblical figures, Nyssen designates Basil as a man favored by God. Subsequently Nyssen establishes Basil in the context of the theological controversies of the fourth century, with his brother standing up for true (pro-Nicene) Christianity against false believers (non-Trinitarians).[215] The biblical scriptures, whose holy persons were familiar to many Christian laity, provided the foundational referent to link the contemporary Basil with his divinely appointed predecessors; and likewise, for directing believers to associate Basil's sacred identity with Nyssen – the mediator of Basil's life.

Even when foregrounding their subjects' spiritual heritage, however, the Cappadocians also invested saints with actions and characteristics that insinuated affiliation with classical masculinity. The case above, Nyssen's depiction of Basil, gives one such occurrence. In rendering his brother as a proponent of pro-Nicene orthodoxy, Nyssen locates Basil within an *agōn* setting, a theological battleground. He illustrates the *aretē* indicative of an *agathos*, with Basil "struggling (συμπλεκόμενος) with rulers, associating (συμμίσγων) with generals, speaking boldly (παρρησιαζόμενος) to emperors, proclaiming (βοῶν) in the assemblies."[216] Basil confronts even the most powerful rivals, never shying away from the task with which God has entrusted him. Nyssen's Basil thus belongs to two cultural traditions: manifestly, as part of a sacred lineage from the Old and New Testaments; and indirectly, as a personification of classical *aretē*

---

[213] Greg. Ny., *In Basilium* 4–7.   [214] Greg. Ny., *In Basilium* 8 (Stein).
[215] D. Konstan, "How to Praise a Friend: St. Gregory of Nazianzus's Funeral Oration for St. Basil the Great," in *Greek Biography*, 164.
[216] Greg. Ny., *In Basilium* 10 (slight alteration of Stein). Coon, *Sacred*, xvii–xviii; Coon argues that in hagiography, males are represented as proving their sanctity through exemplary deeds, whereas female holiness more often is manifested in conquest over her corrupted self.

embedded in his contest for religious truth. The cipher of Basil, as an epitome of a classical combatant, was an act of exhibitionism coordinate with classical showmanship. In praising Basil, Gregory was excelling in a literary *agōn*.

The men and women that occupied the hagiographic narratives of Nyssen and Nazianzen thus attuned listeners and readers to biblical predecessors while setting them in contests. The accounts amplified Nyssen's and Nazianzen's status because, as authors, they served as caretakers of traditions of sanctity.[217] And addressing issues of contemporary Christianity, Nyssen and Nazianzen used the saints to think about current beliefs and behaviors, first through the pious actions of the saint, and second as an extension of the biblical paragons that they represented.[218] But in these settings, the Cappadocians still staged an *agōn*, with the competition often couched in the form of theological struggle, ascetic self-discipline, or nobility when facing death. Here the authors embedded classical virtues in the subjects of hagiographic accounts. Biblical heroes and heroines, along with the fourth-century saints that followed them, were infused with attributes of classical virility. Biblical figures such as Abraham, Moses, Elijah, and Paul – and by association saints such as Macrina, Basil, Gregory Thaumaturgus, Gorgonia, and Caesarius – were recast and empowered with classical *aretē*. They were subsequently set forward as models of Christian leadership as envisioned by pro-Nicene bishops. In such illustrations, classical masculinity merged with the piety of saints to create a vision of the new *agathoi*, pro-Nicene bishops.

As stated previously, Susanna Elm highlights the damning orations that Nazianzen delivered against individuals he deemed most counter to his vision of a pro-Nicene governed empire. At stake in such orations, according to Elm, was an outline of who was divinely equipped to guide the state in matters of true philosophy. Gregory directs much of his vitriol, therefore, against the anti-Christian Emperor Julian, the consummate "other" of Gregory's legitimate Christian ruler. Gregory likewise condemns the influence of Eunomius, a threat from *within* Christianity because of his distorted training in *paideia* and anti-Trinitarian polemic.[219] Gregory thus lays out the antithesis of divine direction.

---

[217] S. Swain, "Biography and Biographic in the Literature of the Roman Empire," in *Portraits*, 33, on the importance of bishops controlling its representative saints through literary construction of their lives.
[218] Clark, "Lady," 26–30.   [219] Elm, *Sons*, 259–65, 348–53.

Nazianzen's and Nyssen's hagiographic biographies, I argue, complemented such anti-Trinitarian polemic by accentuating the pro-Nicene identity of their subjects. Not only do the Cappadocians emphasize the Christianity of their protagonist families and friends, but they carefully denote them as pro-Trinitarian. And whenever the saintly figures of the narratives encounter non-Nicenes, the authors juxtapose the two groups of Christians, with pro-Nicenes embodying all that is male and pious, and non-Nicenes as effeminate and ungodly. In such conflicts, the *agōnes* do not involve any sense of reciprocal virtue, as was typical in letters. In Nyssen's *Encomium on Basil*, for example, Basil battles and defeats his heretical opponents much like a victory of Good over Evil. There is no mutual questing for virtue, as in epistolary exchange, but rather total opposition to a malicious group within Christianity. Because the Cappadocians viewed theological rivals as a threat to the true faith and their vision of leadership, they treated them as antagonists; the antithesis of *aretē*.

In the contest between manhood (orthodoxy) and effeminacy (heresy), hagiography also allowed for a reversal of audience expectations. Basil's and Nyssen's sister Macrina, for instance, features as the embodiment of Christian *aretē*, thereby attesting to the primacy of pro-Nicene leadership and doctrine. Nyssen's account of Macrina highlights her piety, self-denial, and spiritual leadership. Congregants hearing the *Life of Macrina* were left to consider the sanctity of the virgin whose life was intertwined with pro-Nicene Christianity. Gregory further encapsulates the Trinitarian ideal within Macrina by investing her with a character that surpassed her (subordinate) nature as a woman.[220] Macrina's masculine persona is unmistakable, even though Gregory also holds her up as a model of Christian femininity. Her femaleness, in other words, is preserved but also imbued with elements of manhood.[221] Christian *pepaideumenoi*, as well as non-Christians familiar with the narrative, would understand the implications of Gregory's "manly" virgin sister. She represents both a model of holiness for women and laity and the embodiment

---

[220] From the outset of the *Life*, Gregory establishes that Macrina exceeds her nature as a woman: "The subject of the tale was a woman – if indeed she was a 'woman,' for I know not whether it is fitting to designate her of that nature who so surpassed nature." Greg. Ny., *Vit. Macr.* 1.3 (Silvas): οὐκ οἶδα γὰρ εἰ πρέπον ἐστὶν ἐκ τῆς φύσεως αὐτὴν ὀνομάζειν τὴν ἄνω γενομένην τῆς φύσεως.

[221] Cobb, *Dying*, 92–3, demonstrates how authors used duality of gender in stories of female martyrs to accentuate features such as fortitude in the women, while situating them in appropriate roles.

of Trinitarian belief. In Caesarea and Constantinople, where the Cappadocians were vilifying non-Nicene clergy, Macrina posed an especially appealing figure of true faith. As Nyssen and Nazianzen condemned the teachings of Eunomius, in particular, personifications of sacred *aretē* in persons such as Macrina were designed to win support for the Trinitarian cause.

OUTLINE OF CHAPTERS

Based on the preceding categorization of sources, *Christianity and the Contest* is divided into four chapters, with two chapters based on evidence from epistolary exchanges and two chapters focused on biographical literature. Chapter 1, "The Sweat of Eloquence," considers the epistolary discourse of the Cappadocians as a simulation of an *agōn* and subsequently as a locus for conspicuous display of *aretē*. An investigation into the androcentric culture of the Second Sophistic shows that the Cappadocians' epistolography mimicked exhibitions of eloquence by orators; performances that are framed through pen and paper as similar acts of exertion. Chapter 2, "The *Agōn* of Friendship," explores an aesthetic of manhood coordinated through a synthesis of classical friendship and Christian fellowship. The Cappadocians participated in an *agōn* of sensory rhetoric, using highly descriptive imagery of the body in letters to acknowledge mutual virtue in correspondents and to activate shared identities. In framing *philia* (friendship) through the trope of absence, and portraying union of souls through sensory language, the authors moderated materiality and reordered it as masculine. Friendship is reinforced when the Cappadocians represent letter exchange as a form of gift-giving and cultural capital.

Chapter 3, "Personifications of Sacred *Aretē*," investigates the convergence of courage and sanctity in third-century bishop Gregory Thaumaturgus, Basil, Macrina, and Gorgonia. The Cappadocians staged scenes of struggle from classical literature and Christian scriptures to personify these pro-Nicenes as friends of God and heirs of the classical Greek *agathoi*. By authoring these hagiographies, the Cappadocians moderated an aesthetic that synthesized holiness and manhood. Finally, Chapter 4, "*Agōn* and Theological Authority" situates hagiographies of fourth-century Nicene bishop Athanasius of Alexandria, Basil, and Macrina into the Cappadocians' polemic against theological rivals. Nyssen and Nazianzen emphasize their protagonists' speech as authoritative and true, reflecting *aretē* acquired through ascetic feats that are refashioned as classical contests. The feats were meant to authorize the theology of pro-Nicene bishops, while invalidating that of their non-Trinitarian adversaries.

In his study on identity formation, Arthur Urbano emphasized that many Christian *pepaideumenoi* did not view themselves as outsiders despoiling the Greeks of their intellectual heritage. Rather, they were part of an insider's game, asserting themselves as legitimate heirs of certain philosophical schools.[222] *Christianity and the Contest* argues that a similar awareness guided the Cappadocians' self-representation as males, as they used a rhetoric of *agōn* to exhibit *aretē* and to integrate it into the episcopacy. As stated at the outset, from the perspective of the Cappadocians, Emperor Julian was seeking to "un-man" Christian intellectuals. Although his program against Christian teachers was short-lived, it jeopardized the shared learning space that Christians and non-Christians had enjoyed for decades. It also brought immediacy to the issue of manly image that Christian *pepaideumenoi* already perceived as imperiled. From Julian's death in 363 until the end of their lives (Basil – 379; Nazianzen – 390; Nyssen –394), the Cappadocians continued to rehabilitate *paideia* and its privileging of classical masculinity. Through exhibitions of *aretē* and a continual dialogue on manhood with other *pepaideumenoi*, the Cappadocians propagated the ideal of a societal leadership of *agathoi*, persons whose piety had merged with their standing as noble males. They envisioned these individuals as serving within the pro-Nicene episcopacy. By harnessing the rhetoric of manhood, the Cappadocians preserved this aspect of their cultural heritage as part of their church leadership and lent credence to Trinitarian Christianity.

---

[222] Urbano, *Philosophical*.

I

"The Sweat of Eloquence"

Epistolary Agōn *and Second Sophistic Origins*

In 382 Gregory of Nyssa composed an epistle for the Cappadocian sophist Stagirius, who had previously sent a letter asking Gregory, in his capacity as bishop, to order rafters for a house.[1] Stagirius had jested that bishops "are difficult to catch in a net (δυσγρίπισον);" shifty, that is, and difficult to obtain favors from.[2] Gregory replied with ridicule. He feigned applause for Stagirius, praising him for extracting the phrase of "catching in a net" (γριπίζω) from some "secret sanctuary of Plato."[3] Gregory was mocking him for applying such a fanciful and obscure term.[4] Gregory then quipped that the art of sophists "consists of levying a toll upon

---

[1] Stagirius' letter is found in the corpus of Gregory's epistles as Greg. Ny., *Ep.* 26; Stagirius: B. Storin, *Gregory of Nazianzus's Letter Collection: The Complete Translation* (Berkeley: University of California Press, 2019), 39; A. Silvas, *Gregory of Nyssa: The Letters*, VCS 83 (Leiden: Brill, 2006), 202; *PLRE* 1:851; H-M, 57–8.

[2] Greg. Ny., *Ep.* 26 (Silvas); for the meaning of this phrase, from the word δυσγρίπισον, see Silvas, *Gregory*, 202 n. 416 and P. Gallay, *Grégoire de Nysse: Lettres*, SC 363 (1990), 301 n. 3. This letter appears either to have influenced, or been influenced by, a strikingly similar epistle (most likely falsely) represented as sent from Basil to Libanius (Basil, *Ep.* 348).

[3] Greg. Ny., *Ep.* 27 (Silvas): ἐκ τῶν Πλάτωνος ἀδύτων.

[4] Similar improprieties had been specified by famous rhetoricians such as Lucian of Samosata (c. 120–80), who criticized the use of ambiguous words. See Lucian, *Lexiphanes* 24 and *Professor of Public Speaking* 17. E. Gunderson, *Staging Masculinity: The Rhetoric of Performance in the Roman World* (Ann Arbor: University of Michigan Press, 2000), 153–5, shows that Lucian considered such overwrought use of phrases an indication of effeminacy; S. Swain, "Sophists and Emperors: The Case of Libanius," in *Approaching Late Antiquity: The Transformation from Early to Late Empire*, eds. S. Swain and M. Edwards (Oxford: Oxford University Press, 2006), 378, points out that Eunapius criticized the use of obscure phrases even in the sophist Libanius (Eunapius, *Vit. Phil.*, 496); and see the emphasis on clarity in letters by Philostratus *On Letters* 2.257.29 and Pseudo-Libanius, *Epistolary Styles* 47–8.

words," and he indicted such teachers for "putting up their own wisdom as merchandise just as the harvesters of honey do with their honeycombs."[5] Gregory was insinuating that Stagirius pandered his craft. Such antics did not authorize him (according to Gregory) to stereotype bishops as shifty.

Gregory continued by accusing Stagirius of "making a parade (ἐμπομπεύων) of your Persian declamations."[6] The implication was that Stagirius was writing in an overly theatrical style that many literati associated with eastern decadence.[7] Gregory completed his response by stating that he had ordered rafters of equal number to the Spartans who fought at Thermopylae – an allusion to the number "300" as chronicled by Herodotus.[8] The rafters, he stated, were of good length and they "cast a long shadow" (δολιχόσκιος), a Homeric epithet drawn from the *Iliad* that referred to the powerful spears hurled in combat between Paris and Menelaus.[9] Thus he countered the sarcasm in Stagirius' petition by answering that he would fulfill the request with his patronage, which he likened to a weapon. Whereas Stagirius had approached him with flamboyance, Gregory was satisfying the entreaty with a supply of durable materials. And he was equating the provisions to the courage of hoplites at Thermopylae against a larger Persian force.[10] The metaphor issued a contrast to Stagirius' display of affectation and underscored Gregory's use of Atticism – a manner of writing that represented the antithesis to Asianism.[11] In this exchange, Gregory was one-upping his competitor.

---

[5] Greg. Ny., *Ep.* 27 (Silvas). The phrases are reminiscent of an account in which a Cynic philosopher at Athens commented on a chair of rhetoric: "Lollianus does not sell bread but words." Philostratus, *Vit. Soph.*, 1.23 (Wright).

[6] Greg. Ny., *Ep.* 27 (Silvas).

[7] T. Whitmarsh, *The Second Sophistic* (Oxford: Oxford University Press, 2005), 50–4. B. MacDougall, "Arianism, Asianism, and the Encomium of Athanasius by Gregory of Nazianzus," in *Rhetorical Strategies in Late Antique Literature: Images, Metatexts and Interpretation*, ed. A. Puertas (Leiden: Brill, 2017), 105, shows that, in other contexts, Nazianzen suggested a "connection between the allegedly effeminate rhetorical style of the Asianists and the theology, language, and mores" of heretics.

[8] Greg. Ny., *Ep.* 27 (Silvas).

[9] Greg. Ny., *Ep.* 27 (Silvas); Herodotus, *Histories*, 7.60 and 8.24–5; *Iliad* 3.346, 355; Silvas, *Gregory*, 204, on meaning of δολιχόσκιος.

[10] Gregory uses exempla from classical literature and biblical scriptures throughout his writings. A useful record of these cases, organized by genre, is K. Demoen, *Pagan and Biblical Exempla in Gregory Nazianzen: A Study in Rhetoric and Hermeneutics* (Brepols: Turnhout, 1996).

[11] Whitmarsh, *Second*, 50–4.

Gregory's epistle is representative of the performances that he, Basil, and Gregory of Nazianzus scripted in select correspondence. They often deployed allusions and witticisms that resonated within the community of eastern Romans who had been trained in *paideia* – a curriculum of Greek history, philosophy, and literature that young men were expected to master in order to develop into a cultivated civic leader.[12] Through passages from these readings, authors spoke to fellow *pepaideumenoi* in a dialogue that exalted their mutual *aretē* – the manly demeanor embodied by Greek protagonists as far back as the world of Homer.[13] In the letter above, initially it appears that Gregory is abusing Stagirius. In fact, he was engaging his colleague in a clever exhibition that only certain educated readers could fully comprehend. The transaction was an acknowledgment of their mutual eloquence, education, and status. Speaking through exempla from the heroic past, Gregory was signaling Stagirius' sophistication and that of other readers who were familiar with the conventions of letter exchange.[14] The premise of this camaraderie was facility in the culture of classical Greece, an arena that cultivated upright men (*agathoi*). "A noble deed, or a saying worthy of remembrance, or the polities of men who have surpassed (ὑπερπεφυκότων) all their fellows in natural endowments," as Basil said, "are a treasure house of the soul."[15] For Basil, the Greek past issued a repository of *agathoi* through whom he and other educated individuals could define their own deportment. Literary stratagems and references to the great deeds of ancient Greeks, that is, provided a means to uphold an affiliation with fellow *pepaideumenoi* and to show affinity with valiant Hellenes of other eras.[16]

---

[12] R. Cribiore, *Gymnastics of the Mind: Greek Education in Hellenistic and Roman Egypt* (Princeton: Princeton University Press, 2005), 225–44.

[13] Analogous to the literary culture described in C. Chin, *Grammar and Christianity in the Late Roman World* (Philadelphia: University of Pennsylvania Press, 2007), 15–25; Chin shows that late antique Latin Christian authors such as Ausonius and Jerome marked "cultural competence" by creating an identity in the present rooted in venerated authors from the past. A. Spira, "Volkstümlichkeit und Kunst in der griechischen Väterpredigt des 4. Jahrhunderts," *Jahrbuch der österreichischen Byzantinistik* 35 (1985), 55–73, points out similar uses of the classical past in sermons of patristic writers.

[14] A. Schor, "Becoming Bishop in the Letters of Basil and Synesius: Tracing Patterns of Social Signaling across Two Full Epistolary Collections," *JLA* 7:2 (2014), 298–305.

[15] Basil, *Ep.* 74 (Deferrari).

[16] A literary strategy recommended in epistolary handbooks by fourth-century rhetorician Julius Victor, *Art of Rhetoric* 27 and Pseudo-Libanius, *Epistolary Styles* 50. Also M.-A. Calvet-Sebasti, "Comment écrire à païen: l'exemple de Gregoire de Nazianze et de Théodoret de Cyr," in *Les Apologists chrétiens et la culture grecque*, eds. B. Pouderon and J. Doré (Paris, Beauchesne 1998), 369–81, explains the benefit of Christian bishops aligning with classical traditions when possible.

The interchange between Gregory and Stagirius recalled the verbal sparring prevalent in the Second Sophistic (c. 100–250) – an intellectual movement in which public displays of erudition entertained audiences and garnered fame or dishonor depending on the merits of the performance.[17] The encounter thus reenacted the contests of the ancient Greek polis, where years of strenuous mental and physical training singularized civic leaders.[18] Here, athletes and soldiers from the past presented models of *aretē* for current *pepaideumenoi* such as Gregory and Stagirius – individuals who required an arena to emulate the courage of their forebears.[19] Epistolary exchange represented one such setting, where the Cappadocians recreated a discourse – with roots in Homeric society – that validated elite males.[20] This chapter thus examines epistolary exchange as a recontextualized form of agonism. The Cappadocians framed epistolary discourse, I argue, as an exercise in competition, thus identifying themselves and a select group of correspondents that circulated honor through reenactments of classical performance. In this endeavor, they vied with fellow *pepaideumenoi* to moderate masculinity. Consequently, these clergy reinforced the *habitus* – the values, dispositions, and

---

[17] S. Goldhill, "Rhetoric and the Second Sophistic" in *Cambridge Companion to Ancient Rhetoric*, ed. E. Gunderson (Cambridge: Cambridge University Press, 2009), 228–41; T. Schmitz, *Bildung und Macht: Zur sozialen und politischen Funktion der zweiten Sophistik in der griechischen Welt der Kaiserzeit* (Munich: Beck, 1997), 50–63, following Bourdieu's emphasis on cultural currency, credits superior performance in *paideia* as a means of sociopolitical advancement.

[18] W. M. Bloomer, "Schooling in Persona: Imagination and Subordination in Roman Education," *Classical Antiquity* 16 (1997), 57–78, states that such exercises "with their projection of idealized social and family order are a kind of social comfort, a reassurance to and from the elite as well as linguistic training of that elite," 58; N. Nicholson, *Aristocracy and Athletics in Archaic and Classical Greece* (Cambridge: Cambridge University Press, 2005), 2, states that in addition to educating young men, athletics also delineated the best citizens and provided a context to exhibit superiority.

[19] R. Cribiore, "Vying with Aristides in the Fourth Century," in *Aelius Aristides between Greece, Rome, and the Gods*, eds. W. V. Harris and B. Holmes (Leiden: Brill, 2009), 263–78, maintains that elite audiences "found some comfort in commiserating with 'the best of the Greeks'," referring to the fifth-century B.C. rhetorician Aristides; K. Bassi, *Acting Like Men: Gender, Drama and Nostalgia in Ancient Greece* (Ann Arbor: University of Michigan Press, 1998), 4, describes a similar dynamic in her study of ancient Greek drama, which she characterizes as nostalgia for "a reunion with the normative masculine subject of antiquity."

[20] Bassi, *Acting*, 43–5; K. Eshleman, *The Social World of Intellectuals in the Roman Empire: Sophists, Philosophers, and Christians* (Cambridge: Cambridge University Press, 2012), 1–20, on social formation through ancient referents.

expectations – of a provincial aristocracy that identified itself with cultural and political preeminence in eastern Roman communities.[21]

In encounters such as the one above, the Cappadocians accentuated their own pedagogical heritage – a program that associated eloquence with manhood and moral excellence. As this chapter will show, eloquence was a fortitude born out of late antique pedagogy. On several occasions, the Cappadocians crafted a masculine persona using similar strategies of self-fashioning as found in Second Sophistic orators. Unlike their predecessors, however, the Cappadocians tried to outdo their correspondents in rhetorical imagination, but they did not seek to emasculate them. In the culture of epistolary exhibition, showmanship was about group identity. Emphasis, in fact, was placed on acknowledging a sense of manhood in others; a kind of consensus of dignity that was notably lacking in Second Sophistic oratory, in which "winners" and "losers" were determined on how one individual bested the other in a performance. The Cappadocians, by way of comparison, championed exemplary manhood in their literary rivals. They issued repeated demonstrations of epistolary skill, for example, and they prompted other *pepaideumenoi* to join them. By excelling in these virtual bouts, which stimulated *aretē* through simulations of exertion, clergy proved their mettle and registered themselves as heirs of cultural authority in eastern Rome. In spurring authors to showcase their abilities, moreover, the Cappadocians established themselves as arbiters of *aretē* by praising, rebuking, and evaluating performances. Through each of these endeavors, the Cappadocians were aligning the identity of pro-Nicene clergy with that of the classical Greek male.

SECOND SOPHISTIC ORIGINS OF *AGŌN*

Through the lens of Second Sophistic writers, the Cappadocians observed the contested nature of manhood in ancient Greek literature. Indeed, such

---

[21] On the concept of *habitus*, P. Bourdieu, *Language and Symbolic Power*, ed. and intro. J. Thompson, trans. G. Raymond and M. Adamson (Cambridge, MA: Harvard University Press, 1991), 14–20, how *habitus* shaped interaction between imperial and provincial administrators; P. Brown, *Power and Persuasion in Late Antiquity: Towards a Christian Empire* (Madison: University of Wisconsin Press, 1992), 3–70; C. Vogler, "L'Administration impériale dans la correspondance de Saint Basile et Saint Grégoire de Nazianze," in *Institutions, société et vie politique dans l'empire romain au IV siècle ap. J.-C., actes de la table ronde autour de l'oeuvre d'André Chastagnol* (Paris, 20–21 janvier 1989), eds. M. Christol, S. Demougin, Y. Duval, C. Lepelley, and L. Vogler (Rome: École Française de Rome, 1992), 447–64.

authors formed the conduit through which fourth-century literati learned and applied ancient texts to their own time. We cannot know for sure how much access the Cappadocians had to *complete* manuscripts of Homer, Herodotus, Euripides, Plato, or any other ancient authors.[22] Much of the reading of such authors came through teachers whose own intellectual pedigree had acquainted them with Second Sophistic literature and perhaps who had recommended acquiring portions of specific ancient texts. Knowing the reading lists of these writers remains a dubious task, although some resourceful studies have shed light on the collections of authors such as Plutarch, Lucian, Dio Chrysostom, and Aelius Aristides.[23] In a number of cases these writers probably possessed nearly complete texts from some authors, with fragments of others.[24] Even though these writers did not usually have complete works at their hands, they often held significant excerpts at their disposal in the form of abridged texts, compendia, and books of rhetorical exercises. As late as the fourth century, *pepaideumenoi* were still drawing allusions and references from the resources they acquired through traditional oral learning (instructor to pupil). Even Emperor Julian, who enjoyed a substantial library, relied on handbooks and anthologies for many of his

---

[22] We do, however, have an excellent idea of the wide range of classical and biblical sources they used. For example Demoen, *Pagan*, shows the expanse of Gregory's sources. Critical editors of the Cappadocians' works have identified similar scope in Nyssen and Basil. We also have a few snapshots of the Cappadocians' bibliographic collection. In Greg. Naz., *Ep*. 31 (Storin 126), Nazianzen sends a volume of Demosthenes' texts to a friend and he mentions that he does not have Homer's *Iliad*. Likewise, Gregory loans his collection of Aristotle's epistles to a friend, and ultimately lets him have it as a gift. (Greg. Naz., *Ep*. 234; Storin 191).

[23] For example, J. F. Kindstrand, *Homer in der Zweiten Sophistik. Studien zu der Homerlektüre und dem Homerbild bei Dion von Prusa, Maximos von Tyros und Ailios Aristeides* (Stockholm: University of Uppsala Press, 1973), shows that many of the writers of the Second Sophistic believed that Homer was divinely inspired and that the *Iliad* (more so than the *Odyssey*) was almost universally known and cited by scholars. Although most writers did not have full texts of Homer, because of the primacy of his epics they knew most of the narrative. G. Anderson, "Lucian's Classics: Some Short Cuts to Culture," *Bulletin of the Institute of Classical Studies* 23 (1976), 59–68, on the other hand, has argued that Lucian's reading knowledge of the ancients was much more minimal than often thought; that he primarily used clichés and popular tropes. If he had full texts available, that is, he did not use them.

[24] W. Helmbold and E. O'Neil, *Plutarch's Quotations* (Oxford: American Philological Association, 1959), viii, makes this case for Plutarch. He owned a prominent collection of Hesiod and Pindar, for instance, but likely used compendia for many of his other sources.

quotations.²⁵ In crafting rhetoric, habituation into the culture of *paideia* had required young men to memorize and use set phrases. Many likely owned abridged books and anthologies that contained these references, but few likely owned complete versions of the works that informed their rhetoric. When in need of help, a trusted friend or mentor would have provided a more probable source of recall.

That is not to say, however, that all collections were limited only to small selections, nor to rhetorical exempla. Erudition was learned through a variety of genres and esteemed authors. An accomplished student would learn eloquence from the orator Demosthenes, but also through Plato, one of the most widely acclaimed prose writers of late antiquity. Some fourth-century literati did have the means to amass significant personal libraries, although their writings might not include quotations or references from them. Libanius, for example, probably had an extensive library, even though his writings reflect only a selection of the texts.²⁶ Nevertheless, discovering a direct line from fourth-century *pepaideumenoi*, to Second Sophistic authors, to classical writers, is usually impossible. Even tracing the use of Second Sophistic authors in the Cappadocians can be difficult. It was a literary convention for *pepaideumenoi* often to cite authors without naming them.

Yet these authors played a much more pivotal role than merely passing on the actual written works of the classics. They transmitted passages, and sometimes entire texts, to their fourth-century heirs. But more importantly, fourth-century authors such as the Cappadocians learned from earlier generations of *pepaideumenoi* how to engage with the canonical ancient writers. In the Second Sophistic, imitation (μίμησις) of classical authors involved maintaining the vitality of a venerated past while also showing discrimination and creativity when applying ideals from its great minds.²⁷ An element of selectivity and innovation was expected rather than mindless repetition.²⁸ More important than knowing the exact texts transmitted from Second Sophistic authors is understanding that their

---

²⁵ J. Bouffartigue, *L'Empereur Julien et la culture de son temps* (Paris: Institut d'Études Augustiniennes, 1992), 111–25. Julian's library was especially noteworthy for its holdings on Homer and Plato.

²⁶ R. Cribiore, *The School of Libanius in Late Antique Antioch* (Princeton: Princeton University Press, 2007), 159.

²⁷ T. Whitmarsh, *Greek Literature and the Roman Empire: The Politics of Imitation* (Oxford: Oxford University Press, 2004), 55–60.

²⁸ Whitmarsh, *Greek*, 88, says that literary *mimēsis* provided "a fundamental means of constructing the cultural status of the present."

successors similarly applied the writings in order to create value and identity. Morwenna Ludlow's recent work on the craft of rhetoric is helpful for understanding how fourth-century literati adapted literary techniques from both Second Sophistic and contemporary authors. Ludlow observes that the Cappadocians viewed themselves as members of a community of literary craftsmen in much the same way that other skilled workers considered themselves as part of a group belonging to a workshop.[29] These writers learned pedagogical traditions to some extent by interacting with their counterparts, many of whom had studied under teachers from an alternate lineage of teachers, others having labored under the same instructors. Consequently, epistolary writers were introduced to models not only through direct study of the ancients but through collaboration and competition with fellow *pepaideumenoi*. A synergy based on emulation and adaptation from likeminded authors thus provided the Cappadocians a framework for building their own version of masculinity through the medium of the classics. Because Second Sophistic authors themselves had been ever vigilant about crafting identity in an *agōn* setting, the Cappadocians found their hermeneutics of the classics especially compelling.

Rhetoric as Weapon

Education in classical rhetoric, however, was not for the faint of heart. Various fourth-century authors recorded the violence associated with schools of grammar, where teachers disciplined young men with beatings and other forms of corporal punishment.[30] The militant nature of pedagogy continued into the advanced schools of rhetoric and philosophy, where aggression was manifested in brawls among students and between pupils of rival teachers.[31] Even when the discord did not erupt into physical blows, schools were pervaded by an underlying spirit of combat. Recounting Basil's and his own time at Athens, Gregory of Nazianzus described the students as "difficult to restrain" (δυσκάθεκτοι) because of the intense performances of rhetoricians and rivalries between instructors

---

[29] M. Ludlow, *Art, Craft, and Theology in Fourth-Century Christian Authors* (Oxford: Oxford University Press, 2020), 222–32.

[30] Cribiore, *Gymnastics*, 65–73. Cribiore cites the example of Augustine, in *Confessions* 1.9, bemoaning the "racks, claws, and other torments...we schoolboys suffered from our masters," 68.

[31] Eunapius, *Vit. Phil.* 483–4; Himerius, *Or.* 4.9; Libanius, *Autobiography* 19–21.

and pupils of different schools.³² Even within one's own learning community, young men were subjected to force and intimidation by the very classmates that recruited them to their teacher. Gregory relates the initiation of students at Athens – really a form of hazing – where newcomers were verbally assaulted and cowed into submission by more advanced disciples.³³ The student under duress was drawn into an argument and forced to defend himself against the ridicule of his besiegers. In a similar situation, fourth-century sophist and historian Eunapius writes that new arrivals faced "jokes and laughter at their expense" during their initiation into a school.³⁴ A young man's cleverness and ability to respond to scorn were immediately put to the test. His reaction served as a measure of how he could handle pressure. In such contexts, it is understandable that students would come to view oratory as a form of warfare.

In the andro-charged atmosphere of late-antique instruction, occurrences like this one socialized the youths into a world where erudition was linked to toughness and eloquence derived from conflict. Intellectual content was only one element of an experience that drew the young student out of adolescence. This combative setting was rooted in the conventions of the Second Sophistic, in which the overriding path to respect came through giving mesmerizing oratorical displays. Through public speeches, individual rhetoricians had vied with one another to outdo others in winning arguments, displaying creative wordplay, and otherwise showcasing their talents.³⁵ Extemporaneous speaking and delivering declamations (set speeches) served as two vehicles for advertising one's masculinity within civic space.³⁶ Consequently, many individuals within this movement conceived of their craft in terms redolent of athleticism and warfare, standard forums of ancient virility. Philostratus, for example, described the eloquence of sophist Polemon of Laodicea (c. 90–144) as "passionate and combative (θερμὴ καὶ ἐναγώνιος)...like the trumpet at the Olympic games."³⁷ Speaking with gusto was as much physical as it was mental. Polemon is depicted as thinking the same about his talents. He once encountered a gladiator, "dripping with sweat out of sheer terror," upon which he remarked "You are in as great an agony as

³² Greg. Naz., *Or.* 43.15 (McCauley).   ³³ Greg. Naz., *Or.* 43.16.
³⁴ Eunapius, *Vit. Phil.* 486 (Wright).
³⁵ Schmitz, *Bildung*, 97–135, considers such cases as representative of Greece's ubiquitous culture of competitive display.
³⁶ M. Gleason, *Making Men: Sophists and Self-Presentation in Ancient Rome* (Princeton: Princeton University Press, 1995), 103–21.
³⁷ Philostratus, *Vit. Soph.* 542 (Wright).

though you were going to declaim."[38] Polemon considered the pressure of public discourse as tantamount to a life-and-death battle. Likewise, Philostratus relates how Herodes Atticus, a rhetorician contemporary with Polemon, scoffed at the struggles of boxers, runners, and wrestlers. "Let the athlete who is a runner receive a crown for running faster than a deer or horse," Herodes says, "and let him who trains for a weightier contest (μέγαν ἆθλον) be crowned for wrestling with a bull or bear, a thing which I do every day."[39] The gladiator and the runner face formidable challenges, Philostratus is showing, but the level of their difficulty pales in comparison to rhetorical combat. In these anecdotes, Philostratus elevates mastery of oratory to the severest form of duress. He issued such statements of hyperbole in order to liken his own skill to the daring of the greatest athletes and soldiers, males from the past who accrued highest honor because of great feats accomplished within both soul and body.

In this constellation of verbal warriors, sophists often likened eloquence to weapons. Polemon, for example, praised his teacher Scopelian's "power of persuasion as though it were the arms of Achilles."[40] On another occasion, when asked his opinion of Polemon's eloquence, Herodes responded, "The sound of swift-footed horses strikes upon my ears."[41] Such was his impression of the effect of Polemon's words that he envisioned the roar of running stallions. In an invective that Herodes launched against freedmen in Athens, moreover, Philostratus says that the sophist "shot forth at them every weapon (κέντρον) that his tongue could command."[42] And Aelius Aristides (117–81), one of the most celebrated orators of his day, analogized effective verbal skill to "strong, sound, and firm weapons."[43] These assertions indicated that an effective performer had to master the ability to persuade with words in order to excel and to win fame. Students thus were continually conditioned to think about elocution as a tool infused with masculinity, a means of besting others, meriting honor, and assuming an identity akin to the athletes and warriors of the past. The biographer Plutarch similarly ascribed human qualities to the orations of Demosthenes, calling them "bold" (παρρησία) and "noble" (εὐγένια).[44] By imbuing Demosthenes' speech with characterizations befitting a warrior, Plutarch was raising his oral skills to a level on par with the deeds of celebrated soldiers, runners, and wrestlers. In memorizing narratives such

---

[38] Philostratus, *Vit. Soph.* 541 (Wright).
[39] Philostratus, *Vit. Soph.* 554 (Wright).
[40] Philostratus, *Vit. Soph.* 536 (Wright).
[41] Philostratus, *Vit. Soph.* 539 (Wright).
[42] Philostratus, *Vit. Soph.* 549 (Wright).
[43] Aristides, *Or.* 34. 19 (Behr).
[44] Plutarch, *Life of Demosthenes* 12.7 and 13.6 (Perrin).

as Homer's epics, moreover, aspiring sophists learned that the most striking speeches came out of the mouths of the most prominent heroes such as Achilles, whose potent words matched his exploits in war.[45] Under the cumulative militarization of rhetoric, literati came to consider powerful speech as synonymous with manhood.

The Cappadocians and the Second Sophistic

Writers of the Second Sophistic thus remained keenly aware of self-presentation and committed themselves to acquiring a manly persona through verbal performances. In Philostratus and concurrent authors, *agōnes* of combat and sport were recast as contests of words. About a century after Philostratus completed his *Lives of the Sophists*, *pepaideumenoi* continued to use eloquence as an index of status and social authority. In certain circles, that is, verbal performance revealed not only an individual's command of language, but also his character.[46] Speaking of his and Basil's days at Athens, Gregory of Nazianzus commented that young men were obsessed with rhetorical skill. He compared their fascination to the electric atmosphere of a horse race, where the students "leap up, they shout, raise clouds of dust, they drive in their seats, they beat the air."[47] The orators-in-training witnessed declamations with the zeal of spectators at the hippodrome. By the late fourth century, horse-racing had become the leading spectator event in athletics. The activity was full of danger and horses, as we saw in the Introduction, were synonymous with contest and warfare. Horse-racing thus served as a suitable metonym for rhetorical performances, where individuals strained for victory. Gregory sets himself and Basil, moreover, in the hysteria of the intellectual competition. "It was important to each of us," he says "to be the first to master our studies (πρὶν ἐπιστῆναι)."[48] The friends attempted to outdo each other and subsequently both excelled in study and performance of *paideia*. They contested not to express dominance over each other, but rather to push each other's scholarly limits.[49]

---

[45] J. Fredal, *Rhetorical Actions in Ancient Athens: Persuasive Artistry from Solon to Demosthenes* (Carbondale: Southern Illinois University Press, 2006), 20.

[46] A. Puertas, *The Dynamics of Rhetorical Performances in Late Antiquity* (London: Routledge, 2018), 58–60.

[47] Greg. Naz., *Or.* 43.15 (McCauley).   [48] Greg. Naz., *Or.* 43.15 (my translation).

[49] A concept similar to Hebrews 10:24, "Let us consider how we may spur one another on toward love and good deeds" (NIV).

Describing such rivalries as physical in nature was useful since identity was tied to both corporeal and noetic superiority, a legacy from ancient Greece. The theme of contention thus formed a backdrop for the way the two future Cappadocian bishops pursued a curriculum that included bodily comportment. In this manner, they followed in the footsteps of Prohaeresius (276–c. 368), one of their teachers at Athens and a leading sophist of the early/mid fourth century.[50] Under instructors such as Prohaeresius, a Christian and probably a native Cappadocian, Gregory and Basil came to consider eloquence and manhood as outcomes of an *agōn*.

According to the biographer Eunapius – himself a student of Prohaeresius – his mentor had enjoyed the companionship of a devoted friend Hephaestion, who accompanied him to Athens during their studies in the early 300s. Here they were "rivals for the highest honors of rhetoric."[51] In an antecedent to Gregory's depiction of the friendship between Basil and himself, Prohaeresius and Hephaestion pushed each other to succeed in scholarship and performance. The rivalry played only one part in what became a series of agonistic and antagonistic encounters that earned Prohaeresius repute across eastern Rome. Eunapius recounts a contest in which Prohaeresius competed against other candidates to succeed his former teacher as chair of rhetoric in Athens.[52] The vitriol of the affair was magnified by the fact that the aspiring teachers were already engaged in a tendentious campaign to draw the best and highest number of students to their school.[53] Prohaeresius eventually won the position despite facing widespread opposition. Eunapius made reference to the *Iliad*, insinuating that Prohaeresius' victory in speaking correlated to the martial prowess of Greek heroes such as Achilles.[54] Eunapius thus narrated the affair as a military engagement, with Prohaeresius winning because of the superior weapon of his words. Prohaeresius prevails in other contests in the biography, and Eunapius repeatedly uses warlike

---

[50] Prohaeresius: E. Watts, *City and School in Late Antique Athens and Alexandria* (Berkeley: University of California Press, 2008), 48–78 and R. Penella, *Greek Philosophers and Sophists in the Fourth Century A.D.: Studies in Eunapius of Sardis* (Leeds: Francis Cairns, 1990), 79–94.

[51] Eunapius, *Vit. Phil.* 487: φιλονεικοῦντες δὲ ἀλλήλοις εἰς πενίαν καὶ περὶ τῶν ἐν λόγοις πρωτείαν.

[52] The procedure was dependent on the selection by the town council and the proconsul. Similar accounts appear in Lucian's *The Eunuch* and Augustine's *Confessions*. See Watts, *City*, 54–6. For a different description of the contest see Penella, *Greek*, 85–6.

[53] This recruitment was especially important because transfers of students to other teachers was considered unacceptable at this time. Watts, *City*, 57.

[54] Eunapius, *Vit. Phil.* 488; *Iliad* 24.410–610.

terminology to denote his victorious declamations: the opposition "stricken by a thunderbolt (σκηπτοῦ πληγέντες);" his adversaries "defeated in a regular pitched battle (μάχη);" and Prohaeresius rising to speak, "like a war-horse summoned to the plain" (ὥσπερ ἵππος εἰς πεδίον κληθείς).[55] Eunapius elevates Prohaeresius – over his rivals – by characterizing his performance as forceful, as violent. Prohaeresius thus epitomizes the orator-as-warrior persona that informed Basil, Gregory, and through their influence, Gregory of Nyssa, during their rhetorical training. The young men were conditioned to think that verbal acumen was a definitive sign of strength and disposition. Gregory of Nazianzus could later look back at the end of his life and recognize the extremes of this culture, but as he matured into adulthood, he had come to revere the transformative power of words on which his teachers and fellow students had thrived. With Gregory and Basil immersed in an educational culture predominated by sophists such as Prohaeresius, they came to think of eloquence as an issue of war, and a key component of masculinity.

A Third Sophistic?

This absorption with performative masculinity from the first three centuries relates to current discussions about the concept of a "Third Sophistic."[56] A number of scholars have applied this term to a revival of classical rhetoric sometime during the fourth century, after many factors had mitigated the role of display oratory in the latter third century.[57] One school of thought holds that political and social factors – such as the Christianization of the Roman empire – diminished the significance of oral presentations that were based on classical Greek philosophy and erudition.[58] Enduring standards of elegance continued, this interpretation

---

[55] Eunapius, *Vit. Phil.* 490, 490, 492.
[56] L. Pernot, *La Rhétorique de l'éloge dans le monde gréco-romain* (Paris: Institut d'Études Augustiniennes, 1993), 13–15, describes the fourth century as the period when the church developed into the primary social institution around which rhetoric was oriented. See the balanced introduction to the term "Third Sophistic" by Fowler and A. Puertas in R. Fowler, ed. *Plato and the Third Sophistic* (Boston: de Gruyter, 2014), 1–26.
[57] For a wide variety of understandings of the term, see the different impressions of "Third Sophistic" by authors in E. Amato ed., *Approches de la troisième sophistique, hommages à Jacques Schamp* (Brussels: Peeters, 2006) .
[58] P.-L. Malosse and B. Schouler, "Qu'est-ce la troisieme sophistique?" *Lalies* 29 (2009), 161–224; S. Swain, *Hellenism and Empire: Language, Classicism, and Power in the Greek World AD 50–250* (Oxford: Clarendon Press, 1996), 6–13; 104–9.

suggests, in the schools and in the churches, with bishops supplanting the once-venerated sophists as the centerpiece of the civic spaces.[59] Ancient texts, then, were used as a literary model for the new civic (and sacred) elite, but they no longer dictated social norms. Such explanations, I believe, overstate change in the prevalence and context of rhetorical display in the fourth century.[60] I am sympathetic to the explanation that shifts occurred, thus changing the impetus for and sources of rhetoric. And the nuances of literary and oral exhibitions demand scrutiny according to chronological, cultural, and religious context. Nevertheless, *as a movement distinct from the Second Sophistic*, the designation of a Third Sophistic is not an ideal category of analysis for studying the Cappadocians. The main problem involves interpretations that fourth-century Christian *pepaideumenoi* applied ancient Greek conventions of rhetoric but eschewed the values of pre-Christian Hellenic sources. Such contentions represent too sharp a dichotomy between the textual traditions that informed the Cappadocians. Such renditions also isolate on the Cappadocians' identity as Christians, without adequately exploring the overlap and congruity between their faith and training in *paideia*. The correspondence of the Cappadocians demonstrates continuity with Second Sophistic authors both in the focus on self-representation and the thematic content applied to craft that image. These bishops engaged in forming a self-identity among fellow *pepaideumenoi* that was based on early Greek ideals of manhood. They appear preoccupied with promoting a very similar ideal of struggle that had been in place to validate civic and imperial elites for the better part of the preceding three centuries.

The proposition of a Third Sophistic makes the most sense, I believe, in that exhibitions of *aretē*, for example, were increasingly re-directed from the zero-sum contests of the first three centuries to a more deliberate preservation of manhood and a collective set of values that certain

---

[59] A. Puertas, "From Sophistopolis to Episcopolis: The Case for a Third Sophistic," *Journal for Late Antique Religion and Culture* 1 (2007), 31–42, is representative of this position.

[60] Other criticisms of this view: L. Van Hoof and P. Nuffelen, "The Social Role and Place of Literature in the Fourth Century AD," in *Literature and Society in the Fourth Century AD: Performing Paideia, Constructing the Present, Presenting the Self*, eds. L. Van Hoof and P. Nuffelen (Leiden: Brill, 2014), 8–12, argues for an uninterrupted continuation of a literary performative culture outside of school and church; R. Cribiore, *Libanius the Sophist: Rhetoric, Reality, and Religion in the Fourth Century* (Ithaca: Cornell University Press, 2013), 35–8, finds the concept of the "Third Sophistic" problematic because it sets forth a break between two periods without explaining connections between the two; and Watts, *City*, 13–15.

Christians and non-Christians alike favored. The most significant difference between fourth-century *pepaideumenoi* and Second Sophistic orators may be in the arena in which classical manhood was primarily established. For the former, contests did not primarily take the form of oral delivery, but rather through participation in an epistolary *agōn*.[61] Displays of bombast in public gatherings may not have aligned with the overall image the Cappadocians wanted, one of humility and selflessness as expressed in the scriptures.[62] They relished the give-and-take bravado of manly rivalry, but they generally limited the most conspicuous cases of contention to written transactions with fellow cognoscenti. An epistolary *agōn* was suitable for a persona of self-assertion because it allowed for showmanship, but only among the select. The verbal duels of the Second Sophistic were less applicable to the image they projected to larger audiences. For these groups, the Cappadocians more often presented themselves as philosophers, chosen by God to guide others through spiritual and theological insight.[63] A widespread perception in late antiquity held that philosophers mastered discourse in pursuit of truth, while sophists concerned themselves foremost with reputation.[64] Composing and exchanging epistles provided a means to engage in an affair of honor among a limited coterie that included sophists, but without parading in a sense of self-involvement that might appear unbecoming for clergy. As they drew on *paideia* as a mechanism for promoting a certain image, moreover, the Cappadocians were also embracing an ethos of competitive merit upon which they themselves had been raised. Classical authors were not mere wordplay but rather a substantive part of the bishops' vision for Christian leaders.

EPISTOLARY PERFORMANCE AND *ARETĒ*

In a perspective inherited from their intellectual predecessors, fourth-century *pepaideumenoi* believed that *aretē* had to be earned and it had

---

[61] F. Gautier, "Le Carême de silence de Grégoire de Nazianze: une conversion à la littérature?" *Revue des Études Augustiniennes* 47 (2001), 97–110, argues for a significant shift in performance milieu among fourth-century *pepaideumenoi* from oral delivery to one judged on the written word.

[62] For example II Chronicles 7:14; Proverbs 11:2; Philippians 2:3–4; I Peter 5:5; Romans 12:3.

[63] S. Elm, *Sons of Hellenism, Fathers of the Church: Emperor Julian, Gregory of Nazianzus, and the Vision of Rome* (Berkeley: University of California Press, 2012), 418–22.

[64] R. Lim, *Public Disputation, Power, and Social Order in Late Antiquity* (Berkeley: University of California Press, 1995), 61–4.

to be proven an indefinite number of times. And like declamatory speaking, writing epistles as an exercise in showmanship was a male-centered enterprise that resonated with power.[65] In letters to educated addressees, the Cappadocians appealed to two timeless truths: first, that great persons are made out of conflict. And second, that ancient Greece provided episodes of *agōnes* that illustrated authentic manhood. The courage evident in figures from the past, therefore, was to be celebrated and relived in the words and deeds of correspondents. Among company that recalled the Greek past as a crucible of masculinity, the Cappadocians depicted epistolary exchange as bodily duress, similar to how earlier savants had personified public speaking as corporeal labor. The ideal male of ancient Greece had accrued status not only through mental distinction, but also through physical feats. Epistolary composition was imagined, therefore, as a contest along the lines of warfare and athletics. Intellectual and somatic discipline, that is, went hand in hand.

Gregory of Nazianzus, for example, called to mind the "sweat of eloquence" (οἱ τῶν λόγων ἱδρῶτες) when he reminisced to childhood friend Philagrius about their studies in rhetoric at Athens.[66] Gregory responded to Basil in similar fashion after receiving a letter from him: "Eloquence! Athens! Virtues! The sweat produced by eloquence!"[67] Gregory was acknowledging their shared education and praising Basil for the epistle, a clear demonstration of Basil's power with words. The famous rhetorician Libanius similarly praised one of his students, who "on hearing Aeschylus' remark that in mortals virtues are born from toils...considered sweating over his books (τοὺς περὶ λόγους ἱδρῶτας) more pleasant than carousing."[68] For *pepaideumenoi*, the exacting nature of literary sophistication deemed the intelligentsia worthy of glory, thus reinforcing the social hierarchy. Sweat carried overtones of manhood as it represented the effects of struggle. For athletes, it was a badge of courage, like a warrior shedding blood. It was proof that an individual had been through a taxing experience. The trope of struggle had deep-seated roots in the Greek intellectual sphere, where in mythology certain gods and humans had originated from climactic conflicts.[69] In Greek consciousness, themes of discord and austerity were associated with monumental

---

[65] P. Rosenmeyer, *Ancient Epistolary Fictions: The Letter in Greek Literature* (Cambridge: Cambridge University Press, 2001), 26–7, describes the "naturalization" of letter writing by Greek authors. She writes that "it is Greek, male, and put to practical or artistic uses."
[66] Greg. Naz., *Ep.* 30 (Storin 127).   [67] Greg. Naz., *Ep.* 46 (Storin 11).
[68] Libanius *Ep.* 175 (Bradbury 92); reference to Aeschylus, fragment 340.
[69] For example Hesiod, *Theogony* 170–210, and Aeschylus, *Prometheus Bound* 610–740.

events and qualities. In *Gorgias* Plato indicated that the virtue of a thing – tool, body, soul, or animal – came about through structure and correctness.⁷⁰ The proper use of rhetoric, he insinuated, was attainable only through rigorous testing. Eloquence could be acquired only at much cost. The telos of an individual likewise was dependent on having risen to the challenges that confronted him. As Gregory repeated refrains about sweating and toiling, he was prompting readers to remember the sacrificial nature of their positions.

Illustrations of bodily strain, in particular, conveyed the severity that distinguished *agathoi* from others. In an epistle from the late 360s or early 370s, about the time of his ordination as bishop, Basil penned his thoughts about rulers and the benefits of education: "If a man has sweated much for eloquence (λόγων ἱδρώσαντος), if he has directed the government of nations and cities...I consider it right and proper that his life be placed before us as an example of virtue (ὑπόδειγμα ἀρετῆς)."⁷¹ Eloquence acquired through toil was authentic, trustworthy. It was fitting to associate such speech with worthy leaders. We will see later, in castigations of theological rivals, that the Cappadocians portrayed another form of eloquence, which was earned at minimal cost, and therefore defective and fake.⁷² For Basil, true fluency of speech involved hardships that qualified a man for the confrontations of public office. His notion of strict pedagogy, "sweating for eloquence" (λόγων ἱδρῶν), corresponded to the theme of severity in his *Address to Young Men*, a text in which Basil instructed young Christian men on the merits and challenges of studying ancient non-Christian literature.⁷³ Basil stated that the path to excellence was "rough at first and hard to travel, and full of abundant sweat and toil..."⁷⁴ Basil applied a concept from Hesiod, an eighth-century Greek poet, who had famously personified *Badness* as near to humanity, common, and within easy access. *Excellence*, he juxtaposed, had been established by the gods as attainable only through intensive labor.⁷⁵

---

⁷⁰ Plato, *Gorgias* 506d.   ⁷¹ Basil, *Ep.* 24 (slight alteration of Deferrari).
⁷² Chapter 4.
⁷³ This text is notoriously difficult to date. See P. J. Fedwick, "A Chronology of the Life and Works of Basil of Caesarea," in *Basil of Caesarea: Christian, Humanist, Ascetic: A Sixteen-Hundredth Anniversary Symposium*, ed. P. J. Fedwick. vol. 1. (Toronto: Pontifical Institute of Mediaeval Studies, 1981), 18–19.
⁷⁴ Basil, *Address to Young Men* 5.3–4 (Deferrari): ὅτι τραχεῖα μὲν πρῶτον καὶ δύσβατος, καὶ ἱδρῶτος συχνοῦ καὶ πόνου πλήρης.
⁷⁵ Hesiod, *Works and Days*, 287–92.

Hesiod's portrayal of the Good and Bad suggested that moral rectitude comes through exertion. Basil replayed this sentiment as he reminded students of the story of Heracles. This Greek hero, at the same age as these young men now were, had to choose between two roads, one easy (leading to Vice) and one hard (Virtue). Heracles chose the latter, which was full of "countless sweating toils and labors," but by following it, he became a god.[76] Basil was recalling Lucian's elaboration on this notion, when he depicts the honest, masculine orator following a "path, narrow, briery, and rough, promising great thirstiness and sweat," with the effete sophist taking the road that is "level, flowery, and well-watered."[77] The former, that is, pays the price of an exacting regimen that created a person of substance, of authenticity. He earns respect. The latter, lacking resolve, emerges through a succession of luxury and pretension as a "delicate and charming platform-hero."[78] Lucian categorizes the unproven orator more or less as an actor. In the ancient world, theatrical performers garnered suspicion because recurrent stereotypes cast them as gender fluid or feminine, as well as deceitful.[79] They were not to be respected or trusted. Keying off Lucian, Basil deployed this metaphor to distinguish the virile, well-tried man from the womanish, untested figure. He was calling attention to the long-held dichotomy that linked manliness to harshness and femininity to softness. His world of *agathoi* belonged to individuals who had proven themselves by overcoming tribulations.

Scholarship in the past twenty-five years has emphasized similar correlations between gender and rhetorical training in the ancient world. For Maud Gleason, the regimen that went into succeeding as a speaker was a "calisthenics of manhood," while Rafaella Cribiore has described *paideia* as a mental versus physical *askēsis*. Cribiore cites several references to Libanius talking about pedagogues as "gymnasts of the mind" and "athletes of the *logoi*."[80] Such epithets reflect the literary and compositional exercises of epistolary writers. Years of preparation had earned literati the

---

[76] Basil, *Address to Young Men* 5.14 (Deferrari): ἱδρῶτας μυρίους καὶ πόνους καὶ κινδύνους διὰ πάσης ἠπείρου τε καὶ θαλάσσης; Xenophon, *Memorabilia* 2.1.21.

[77] Lucian, *Professor of Public Speaking* 7 (Harmon): "narrow road," στενὴ καὶ ἀκανθώδης καὶ τραχεῖα, πολὺ τὸ δίψος ἐμφαίνουσα καὶ ἱδρῶτα. See analysis on the trope of the hard road by Gunderson, *Staging*, 153–4.

[78] Lucian, *Professor of Public Speaking* 7 (Harmon): ἁβροῦ καὶ ἐρασμίου ῥήτορος.

[79] Gunderson, *Staging*, 112: "The orator is associated with truth and spirit; the actor with fiction and the body."

[80] Maud Gleason, *Making*, xxii and 159–68; Cribiore, *Gymnastics*, 128, 222. Cribiore cites references to this terminology in Libanius' *Eps.* 140 (Cribiore 8), 309, 548, and 1020; *Or.* 23.24, 11.187, 12.54.

honor of showing off their superior craft and establishing their inclusion in a community of similar intelligentsia.[81] If training for oral performances enabled Second Sophistic speakers to manifest virility, composing epistles offered occasions for clergy to assert their own literary expertise and to validate their credibility by celebrating epistles from well-versed writers. Sporting imagery underscored the contested setting in which the Cappadocians participated. "For who is such a coward and so unmanly, or so inexperienced in an athlete's labours, that he is not strengthened for the struggle," Basil wrote to a colleague. "For you were the first to strip for the noble course of piety."[82] In classical Greece, the gymnasium provided the setting for the strict regimen that cultivated athletes and soldiers.[83] The prominent place of the gymnasium in the polis testified to its importance to society. It was a place that was unequivocally male, the proving ground for future leaders and combatants. Fourth-century literati could not fight in the ancient battles like a Homeric warrior or pursue victory in an Olympian race.[84] But through writing and receiving epistles, *pepaideumenoi* proved their worthiness as successors to former heroes, thus linking themselves with paragons of manhood from a venerated past.[85] An epistolary *agōn*, that is, served as their gymnasium and stadium; a crucible of masculinity unsullied by gender fluidity attendant to sites such as the theatre. Textual fluency became a measure of individual excellence, simulating the corporeal splendor attributed to Greek athletes. The aesthetics of eloquence were mimetic and, according to Nazianzen, requiring constant fashioning by "good artists who train their students with lots of demonstrations."[86] *Pepaideumenoi* had to be challenged in order to exercise their manhood to full potential. Authors believed that physical resilience and mental facilities derived from similar

---

[81] Ludlow, *Art*, 8–10.
[82] Basil, *Ep.* 222 (Deferrari): "first to strip," προλαβόντες γὰρ ἐναπεδύσασθε τῷ τῆς εὐσεβείας σταδίῳ.
[83] D. Hawhee, *Bodily Arts: Rhetoric and Athletics in Ancient Greece* (Austin: University of Texas Press, 2005), 30–9, 110–3.
[84] On the warrior ideology and military measure, see J. Roisman, *The Rhetoric of Manhood: Masculinity in the Attic Orators* (Berkeley: University of California Press, 2005), 105–29.
[85] For examples of performative literature rooted in classical Greece, see R. Thomas, "Performance and Written Literature in Classical Greece: Envisaging Performance from Written Literature and Comparative Contexts," in *The Anthropology of Performance: A Reader*, ed. F. Korom (Malden, MA: Wiley Blackwell, 2013), 26–35.
[86] Greg. Naz., *Ep.* 71 (Storin 150): τοὺς ἀγαθοὺς τῶν γραφέων μιμούμενος οἳ τῷ παραδεινύναι τὰ πολλὰ τοὺς μαθητὰς ἐκπαιδεύουσι.

regimens. The parallelism came in part from the fixation on athletics and *agōn* by authors such as Lucian. "The more one draws it [strength] out by exertions (πόνοι)," Lucian wrote, "the more it flows in."[87] Metaphors of exertion worked well because writing at the sophisticated level of these individuals presented a struggle both with others and within oneself. The conventions of the epistle made it a most personal form of writing, mimicking the face-to-face interaction of wrestlers and warriors. Like the *agōn* of warfare and sport, epistolary exchange depended on training, determination, and risk. Fellow literati shared, discussed, and evaluated the texts, thus holding letters up to scrutiny. Above all, composition called for an active role on the part of the writer and demanded that he respond to complex circumstances through a vast repertoire of models while using the encoded language of the elite.

Recurrent Epistolary Composition and Character Formation

An ongoing image of masculinity required diligence and it also depended on constant self-fashioning. The element of perpetual contest was a trope rooted in Second Sophistic emphasis on early Greek exhibitions of *aretē*. The nature of epistolary *agōn* among fourth-century *pepaideumenoi* likewise involved repeated demonstrations of ability. Orators of the preceding centuries had periodically declaimed, mediated, and otherwise delivered public speeches to nurture and prove their superior deportment. Sophists of the first three centuries called to mind the intellectual setting of the ancient polis, where the ritualized exchange of words formed a cornerstone of reciprocity between companions. Classical Athens, for example, was pervaded by images of men facing each other while engaging in combat, music, and sports.[88] The ubiquity of the theme of struggle prompted the citizen male to remember that he would reach his telos as an *agathos* – the brave and upright leader – only by challenging others. Authors such as Plutarch, moreover, correlated the "virtues of character" to the "virtues of habit."[89] Excellence of character, that is, was achieved through recurrent performance. And although silence could signify self-control in certain settings, within the traditional realm of civic life, vocal performance formed the core of leadership ability in a

---

[87] Lucian, *Athletics* 35 (Harmon).   [88] Fredal, *Rhetorical*, 8–12.
[89] Plutarch, *Moralia* 2a–2b (Babbitt).

pepaideumenos.⁹⁰ With few exceptions, refusal to engage in verbal confrontations (or later, in written exchanges) was damning to anyone striving for *aretē*.⁹¹ Such acts of evasion showed temerity, and perhaps most importantly, unwillingness to hone one's skill and advertise his own manhood. The Cappadocians framed epistolary exchange among literati in a similar way, as an ongoing exercise in fashioning self-identity. "Wells become better for being used," Basil told one correspondent. "At no time cease writing us and urging us to write."⁹² The entreaty couched a medical theory, by famed physician Galen (130–210), that muscles ("wells") of the human body grow stronger when exerted regularly.⁹³ Basil's premise was consistent with Galen's view that exercising the human body contributed to an overall high level of health and rational conduct. Basil considered the symbiosis of body and intellect as relevant to his point here: that mental acumen improves when literati correspond often. Productions of eloquence, of manhood, would reinforce *aretē*, and consistently remind an *agathos* of his purpose.

The mutual performances of letter writing reminded correspondents that their lineage of masculinity stretched deep into the past. With the pressing business that many administrators faced, the Cappadocians sustained their own sense of *aretē* by inviting others to join the *agōn*. Basil once received a letter from a colleague who was "discontented with the care of public business."⁹⁴ Libanius similarly told a governor, "I assumed that you'd no longer be so reliable writing as a result of your office and the inundation of business."⁹⁵ In both cases, Basil and Libanius used opportunities to interact with the correspondents, thereby sustaining self-assurance among them and also attesting to their own *aretē*. Like Libanius, the Cappadocians networked with a wide array of literati, both Christian and non-Christian, to establish conventions for their idealized *agathos*. Such analogies alerted well-educated readers to the lessons to be drawn from studies that may have been neglected. Literati were

---

⁹⁰ M. Jones, *Playing the Man: Performing Masculinities in the Ancient Greek Novel* (Oxford: Oxford University Press, 2012), 52–3. On verbal stillness as a rhetorical strategy, B. Storin, "In a Silent Way: Asceticism and Literature in the Rehabilitation of Gregory of Nazianzus," *JECS* 19:2 (2011), 225–57.

⁹¹ R. Van Dam, *Families and Friends in Late Roman Cappadocia* (Philadelphia: University of Pennsylvania Press, 2003), 136, on the breach of protocol and reputation when not responding to letters.

⁹² Basil, *Ep*. 151 (Deferrari): "wells," τὰ φρέατά φασιν ἀντλούμενα βελτίω γίνεσθαι.

⁹³ Galen, *Hygiene* 1.3.2 (Johnston, 243).   ⁹⁴ Basil, *Ep*. 299 (Deferrari).

⁹⁵ Libanius, *Ep*. 800 (Bradbury 134).

challenged to return to a nostalgic past from where they might draw on their cumulative wisdom and take up the pen.

Correspondence was verbal gamesmanship, moreover, a contest that stirred authors to engage their talents rooted in a lifetime of study and practice. It became a commonplace, in fact, to demand further letters from a fellow *pepaideumenos*. After receiving a letter from Libanius, Nyssen responded by insinuating that Libanius planned to stop corresponding: "Since even with farmers...approval of the labours they have already performed is a great incentive to further labours (τὴν προθυμίαν τὸ τῶν πονηθέντων)...on this account write so that we may stir you to write back."[96] Gregory was pleading with Libanius to pick up the pen. The exchange of letters here is like a ritual dance, with Gregory imploring Libanius to keep up the competition. It was through opportunities like this, after all, that Gregory could hone his own *aretē* and signify his manhood. In this way letter writing provided an arena that was instrumental to socializing aristocratic men even while it allowed for self-presentation. Nazianzen once told his cousin Amphilochius that his letter "implanted in my soul a harmonious lyre...with your countless writings (μυριάκις γράφων)."[97] Amphilochius' recurring correspondence, Gregory says, exerted a cumulative effect on him. The lyre was an instrument mastered as part of *paideia*, and it was associated with Homeric Greek warriors, as for instance, in the god Apollo. Gregory was asserting that Amphilochius had tested him and reminded him of his own *aretē*. Gregory honored his cousin through encomiastic verse, thereby reciprocating Amphilochius' mental efforts and brandishing his own prowess. Interchanges such as this one allowed authors the opportunity of self-presentation. They provided a recipient an opportunity to project a self-directed identity by showing off his dexterity in a way that might otherwise appear as self-praise.

Oratorical performances of the Second Sophistic often have been characterized as a zero-sum game, with only winners and losers.[98] As such, they were antagonistic encounters. The Cappadocians and other fourth-century writers, by contrast, imagined correspondence as a continual working out of mutual *aretē*. For instance, Gregory of Nazianzus prodded Eudoxius,[99] a Christian teacher of rhetoric from Cappadocia, by boasting "Let me conquer (νικῶ) you with friendly

---

[96] Greg. Ny., *Ep.* 14 (Silvas). [97] Greg. Naz., *Ep.* 171 (Storin 190).
[98] Whitmarsh, *Second*, 38. [99] Introduction, n. 64.

letters."¹⁰⁰ Gregory seemingly evokes an encounter of contention and triumph over Eudoxius, and he imbues the exchange with overtones of opposition. He clarifies the spirit of his sparring, however, by saying "I wouldn't make a show of myself...if I didn't regard your friendship as a great thing."¹⁰¹ His bravado, that is, constitutes an affirmation of his and Eudoxius' friendship (*philia*). Such expressions of friendship pervaded epistolary *agōnes*, thus providing a mechanism for cultivating *aretē* in participants. For Aristotle, demonstrations of *aretē* provided the cornerstone of *philia* – specifically as an association of *agathoi*. Repeated acts of *aretē*, applying this model, ushered a constant benefit to a friend and reminded him of the foundations of their camaraderie.¹⁰² And like mutual bestowals of honor among friends in the Homeric epics, letter exchange confirmed the bond while also crediting the status of each party.¹⁰³ Gregory approached Eudoxius with a similar understanding of friendship. "It is necessary to prod you to write," Gregory says, "as one does a colt with a strap."¹⁰⁴ He likened Eudoxius to a stallion that had been prepared for battle, a subject of ancient manuals by historian Xenophon here used as an analogy of the power *pepaideumenoi* achieved through mutual rhetorical exercises.¹⁰⁵ Gregory was provoking Eudoxius as part of a joint quest for virtuosity, not as a castigator but as an ally.

The zeal for struggle was based on a distinction between two forms of strife, a notion established in Hesiod's *Works and Days*.¹⁰⁶ One kind of struggle caused enmity and warfare, a concept obtained in our modern sense of antagonism. The other made individuals efficient, hard-working, and led to prosperity, a notion embedded in agonistic practices. In the latter, the clash between participants made each stronger. This mutually beneficial gamesmanship had once formed the core of the athletic festivals that honored the gods. Approaches to rhetoric in ancient Greece, as Debra Hawhee argues, often were undergirded by such Greek athletic concepts of competition.¹⁰⁷ Individuals raised in *paideia* had been trained

---

¹⁰⁰ Greg. Naz., *Ep.* 174 (Storin 111): Νικῶ σε τοῖς φιλικοῖς.
¹⁰¹ Greg. Naz., *Ep.* 174 (Storin 111).
¹⁰² Aristotle, *N.E.* 1156b–1157a28: on ideal friendship rooted in *aretē*.
¹⁰³ W. Donlan, "Political Reciprocity in Dark Age Greece: Odysseus and his *hetairoi*," in *Reciprocity in Ancient Greece*, eds. C. Gill, N. Postlethwaite, and R. Seaford (Oxford: Oxford University Press, 1998), 51–2.
¹⁰⁴ Greg. Naz., *Ep.* 174 (Storin 111): "prod to write," διεγεῖραί σε πρὸς τὸ γράφειν.
¹⁰⁵ Xenophon, *Horsemanship* and *Calvary Commander*.
¹⁰⁶ Hesiod, *Works and Days*, 11–16. Later referenced as foundational to virtue by Plutarch. *Moralia* 77d.
¹⁰⁷ Hawhee, *Bodily*, 21–7.

in the art of eloquence: to recognize it; to compose it; and to prize it. Having participated in rigorous exercises, *pepaideumenoi* were equipped to write ornate epistles and to share with others the virtues of the ancients. But these skills were meant to be put on display and had to be practiced regularly. Thus, agonistic rhetoric often was adumbrated by metaphors of questing. Libanius, for example, explained to an imperial official, "I'm hunting (θηρεύω) for friendship through a letter...in order that a man who is a gentleman (καλὸς καγαθός) should not elude me."[108] Libanius' pursuit of *philia* called forth the reader's own chasing after *aretē*, the cornerstone of epistolary *agōn*. An image of hunting posed an activity consistent with the development of young men in *paideia*.[109] And here, the trophy achieved from the hunt included both virtue and noble companionship. Towards the end of his life, in the mid 380s, Nazianzen similarly signified camaraderie with Timothy, perhaps a young man he planned to ordain into the priesthood: "I've always been a noble hunter (τῶν καλῶν θηρευτής) of noble qualities," Gregory told him. "I discovered your eloquence," Gregory continued, "with my own eloquence."[110] Nazianzen affiliated himself with the young man through the language of combat, with the chase after eloquence representing the mutual disposition that he perceived in Timothy. On another occasion, Nazianzen staged martial-like behavior, inciting the aforementioned Eudoxius to "tame your great wrath, Achilles, and once again set your stylus, that ashen spear of yours, in motion for me."[111] Gregory deployed imagery and epithets from the *Iliad* that recalled heroic behavior: the discipline of a warrior to control his anger; and the incentive to take up arms at the appropriate occasion. Gregory exhorted Eudoxius to take up his own weapon, his pen, and to weather the contest of written exhibition.

AGŌN AND GROUP IDENTITY AMONG PRO-NICENES

As the Cappadocians generated epistolary contests, they were reinforcing an identity that cut across religious lines. These letter exchanges activated

---

[108] Libanius, *Ep.* 510 (Bradbury 36).
[109] Xenophon, *On Hunting* 1.2.6 ff.; Jones, *Playing*, 22–3, observes that Xenophon placed value on hunting as a means of producing a man who is temperate.
[110] Greg. Naz., *Ep.* 164 (Storin 223); Timothy: Storin, *Gregory*, 41.
[111] Greg. Naz., *Ep.* 176 (Storin 113): "stylus in motion," κίνησον αὖθις ἡμῖν τὴν γραφίδα, τὴν σὴν μελίαν; same Eudoxius as above; as Storin points out, allusions to "wrath" and "spear" come from *Iliad* 9.496 and 20.272.

a code of behavior that correlated the spirit of competition with the integrity and wisdom to guide; assets often emphasized in non-Christian sources. Thus, the Cappadocians are notable for activating their group identity as *pepaideumenoi* with many non-Christian correspondents. But the Cappadocians also expected fellow pro-Nicene Christians to excel in the *agōn*; as an indication that Trinitarian believers embodied the true, masculine version of Christianity. In a letter to native Cappadocian and Christian Philagrius (same as above), Basil called on him to send many letters, writing at every pretext, because he composed "from a pure tongue" (ἀπὸ γλώττης κεκθαρμένης) and he was "one of those refined by his speech" (οἱ τὸν λόγον χαρίεντες).[112] Basil urged him to write because his letters exemplified his manhood. His style of composition, "pure" and "refined," showed that he was above the theatricality of those sophists who craved popular appeal.[113] In other words, he needed no validation. He was sure of himself and a speaker of truth. In one of his later letters, Basil likewise urged the Christian catechumen Nectarius "to maintain a continuous correspondence with us by letter."[114] Nectarius had emerged from the eastern Roman provincial aristocracy, and may already have been serving as Praetor of Constantinople.[115] Basil rejoiced that "from childhood [Nectarius] was known to us for his noble qualities" and had now gained fame for "practicing every manner of virtue (παντοίας ἀρετῆς)."[116] Acknowledgments of such literary skill and requests for more epistles advanced a dialogue among Christian *pepaideumenoi* to reinforce this element of manhood in thought and practice. These were oft-repeated literary tropes of praise, but the adulation served a purpose for clergy. The exercises forced Christian literati to think about continual engagement with fellow *agathoi* as a moral code to inform their manner as imperial, provincial, and civic church leaders. This dialogue imprinted on the minds of Christian *pepaideumenoi* patterns of self-assertion, boldness, and forceful speech.

While treating epistolary *agōn* as an expression of group membership, the Cappadocians included friends and family in these configurations of

---

[112] Basil, *Ep.* 323 (Deferrari).
[113] Puertas, *Dynamics*, 64–6, emphasizes that speech was most often the decisive element others used to determine an individual's identity as a philosopher as opposed to a rhetorician.
[114] Basil, *Ep.* 290 (Deferrari).
[115] Nectarius: Storin, *Gregory*, 33, the same Nectarius who later succeeded Gregory of Nazianzus as Bishop of Constantinople in 381 (See Chap. 4); H-M, 126–8; *PLRE* 621.
[116] Basil, *Ep.* 290 (Deferrari).

identity. Philagrius was one such person.[117] Philagrius had been a close friend of Nazianzen's younger brother Caesarius (c. 331–68) before the latter died unexpectedly. After Caesarius' death, Gregory of Nazianzus took a significant interest in Philagrius' development, perhaps as a way of honoring his deceased sibling. Gregory and Philagrius, who had studied together as youths, exchanged a series of epistles in the many years following Caesarius' passing. In one of these, Gregory recalled the delights of their student days in Athens: "the cities, the lectures, the table, the poverty, 'the things proper to the lovely time of life,' as Homer says, whether games or studies, the sweat of eloquence, the teachers we had in common..."[118] Gregory was recalling an experience when, as unproven pedagogues, the two had labored to acquire virtue. Although the training had been demanding, both could reflect on an experience that enabled them to discern truth and gave them the ability to defend their beliefs and actions. Gregory pressed Philagrius to keep alive the days of his studies in Greek literature and philosophy, directing him to "Do me the honor of composing a letter."[119] Gregory was calling him to action. Philagrius was enjoined to take up his instrument of writing and to apply it as an operation of his virtue. Gregory was activating the memory of their shared intellectual past because he wanted Philagrius to maintain the aptitudes that had made him prominent. In reviving this program from adolescence, Gregory was normalizing a rhetoric of competition for his fellow believer.

Arbiters of Eloquence

In spurring other authors to showcase their literary workmanship, the Cappadocians contributed to their own status by issuing judgments of style from a position of proven ability. They were attempting to confirm their place in a hierarchy of savants by challenging others to put forward their best work. They were showing judiciousness as they summoned others to compose, again and again excelling in the literary *agōn* even as they were enjoining others to participate. And they were resourceful, drawing on a litany of rhetorical devices and incorporating classical

---

[117] Philagrius: J. McGuckin, *St Gregory of Nazianzus: An Intellectual Biography* (Crestwood, NY: St. Vladimir's Seminary, 2001), 164–5; Storin, *Gregory*, 35 n.120; and Van Dam, *Families*, 145–6.
[118] Greg. Naz., *Ep.* 30 (Storin 127); reference to *Iliad* 3.175.
[119] Greg. Naz., *Ep.* 30 (my translation): κίνει τὴν γραφίδα καὶ χαρίζου τὸ ἐπιστέλλειν.

themes and references. They exhibited their own talents and then they praised others, directing them to compose while later commenting on the elements of their craft. This rhetoric of arbitrating among correspondents placed them in roles as cultural moderators.

A case in point appears in Nazianzen's correspondence with his grandnephew Nicobulus (the younger), grandson of Gregory's sister Gorgonia.[120] In the early 380s, retired after having now served two decades as a priest, Gregory sent Nicobulus a letter that offered guidelines for writing epistles.[121] Gregory advised him to use highly stylized language sparingly so that the words would not come across as unnatural. Gregory was discouraging him from adopting Asianic wordplay, a form associated with affectation and emotion.[122] Gregory prescribed use of more reserved verse and he advised Nicobulus to craft with "beauty, adornment, and polish"[123] through the use of "adages and proverbs and sayings, as well as of jokes and riddles."[124] These were elements that ancient theorists had advocated in order to make the author come across as erudite, yet conversational and at ease.[125] The ideal epistle would reflect a sense of apparent effortlessness of action, an indication that the author was a naturally gifted writer and speaker whose words came easily.[126] His eloquence, that is, should appear innate. It would also reflect an ability to draw on ancient authors and their wisdom in a demonstration of imaginative application.

---

[120] Nicobulus: McGuckin, *Gregory*, 6–7; B. Storin, *Self-Portrait in Three Colors: Gregory of Nazianzus's Epistolary Autobiography* (Oakland: University of California Press, 2019), 1–4; Van Dam, *Friends*, 58–60; we have several extant letters by Gregory intervening on behalf of his grandnephew and another five addressed specifically to him: Greg. Naz., *Eps.* 127, 167, 174–7, 187, 188, 190, 191, 192, 195, 196; primarily related to Nicobulus' education and career: Greg. Naz., *Eps.* 51–5.

[121] Greg. Naz., *Ep.* 51 (Storin 3).

[122] Swain, *Hellenism*, 22–4, points out that the charge of "Asianism" was first used by Roman orators as a source of stylistic criticism, but among Greeks, mainly as a geographic designation. Whitmarsh, *Second*, 49–51, says that Second Sophistic authors often used it as the antithesis of "manly" Attic oratory. In correspondence among *pepaideumenoi*, the term was used in this latter way, pejoratively. MacDougall, "Arianism," 105, shows that Gregory equated this style with effeminacy. It makes sense, then, that he was advising his grandnephew against this form of eloquence.

[123] Greg. Naz., *Ep.* 51 (Storin 3).

[124] Greg. Naz., *Ep.* 51 (Storin 3), trans. by B. Daley, *Gregory of Nazianzus* (London: Routledge, 2006), 177–8.

[125] See Demetrius, *On Style* 223; Seneca, *Moral Epistles* 75.

[126] Greg. Naz., *Ep.* 51 (Storin 3); Gregory uses the metaphor of an eagle, whose grace comes so naturally that it does not know it is beautiful.

Gregory sent other letters to Nicobulus, including one in which he answered the young man's request for a collection of his epistles. Gregory complied by sending copies of his letters to his grandnephew. He stated that the missives were bound together by a sash, "designed not for love but for eloquence."[127] He shows his cleverness by differentiating the band holding together his assemblage of letters against a sash used by Aphrodite in the *Iliad* to seduce men through magical charms and sweet talk.[128] Here Gregory puts Nicobulus to the test, challenging him to interpret this allusion from the Homeric epic. Gregory was staking claim to a manly persona and passing it on to his protégé. He was teaching that speech was multivalent and indicative of a person's essence. He advised Nicobulus on the purpose of performance, defining it not as a matter of indulgence, but as an assertion of forcefulness.[129] The manly writer, in the same way as the manly orator, was expected to present himself in a manner that set him apart from those who were garrulous. Gregory characterized his own style as "instructive in maxims and precepts whenever possible," a feature apparent throughout his correspondence that showed his affinity for the ancients.[130] He augmented his collection of epistles by including in the gift his compilation of Basil's letters.[131] The two sets of letter collections – his own and Basil's – provided a model for the young Christian *pepaideumenos*.

Recent scholarship has shown that authors also sometimes gathered and organized their epistles in order to shape a personal identity.[132] As Brad Storin has shown, this is exactly what Nazianzen did when sending

---

[127] Greg. Naz., *Ep.* 52 (Storin 1).
[128] *Iliad* 14.210–20. On sash reference, Storin, *Self-Portrait*, 115.
[129] See similar discussion by Dio Chrysostom, *Or.* 33.2–7 and Plutarch, *Moralia* 2a–2b.
[130] Greg. Naz., *Ep.* 52 (Storin 1). A trope among Second Sophistic authors. For example Lucian, *Athletics* 21–2.
[131] See Greg. Naz., *Ep.* 53 (Storin 2). P. J. Fedwick, *Bibliotheca Basiliana Universalis: A Study of the Manuscript Tradition, Translations and Editions of the Works of Basil of Caesarea*, vol. 1, *The Letters* (Brepols: Turnhout, 1993), xix–xxxi, on how Basil may have arranged his own collection. Further discussion on Basil's organizational strategy: A. Silvas, "The Letters of Basil of Caesarea and the Role of Letter-Collection in their Transmission," in *Collecting Early Christian Letters: From the Apostle Paul to Late Antiquity*, eds. B. Neil and P. Allen (Cambridge: Cambridge University Press, 2015), 119–23. A. Radde-Gallwitz, "The Letter Collection of Basil of Caesarea," in *Late Antique Letter Collections*, eds. C. Sogno, B. Storin, and E. Watts (Berkeley: University of California Press, 2017), 69–80. Radde-Gallwitz expounds on Fedwick's proposal that Basil had a filing system that made a circulation of batches possible (e.g. for use by Nazianzen), 71–5.
[132] Storin, *Self-Portrait*, 1–4; for examples of Basil's social signaling, Schor, "Becoming," 307–16.

his and Basil's epistles to Nicobulus. In this case, Gregory intended to fashion himself as dynamic, eloquent, and closely allied to the now deceased Basil. The collection also created an epistolary biography for Basil and redounded to his literary merits.[133] As a recent recipient, Nicobulus could lay claim to distinction as a *literatus*; as could his associates, who would be helping him decode style and allusions within the texts.[134] All were participating in a contest to show off their scholarship. The cumulative outcome was that in addition to providing archetypes for letter writing, Gregory was also delivering to his grandnephew a mechanism of socialization. From this literary treasure, Nicobulus could follow his grand-uncle's career and discover the temperament that enabled him to thrive in a host of identities.

Neil McLynn contends, moreover, that Gregory sometimes paired letters from Basil with one or two of his own.[135] McLynn's point is that Gregory "answered" Basil's responses on a variety of issues with his own remedies, thus casting Gregory as favorable by comparison. Another purpose to this strategy, I would argue, is that by placing letters in apposition to each other, Gregory framed the dialogues specifically as *agōnes*, as competitions between two preeminent colleagues. It was a point not to be lost on the young student. Basil's demeanor as priest, patron, and litterateur, through his letters, worked alongside that of Gregory to model the *aretē* that Gregory was trying to make known to Nicobulus. Gregory used the two sets of missives to create a profile of a Christian *pepaideumenos*. He was showing how well-studied Christian authors write and act. Finally Gregory asked Nicobulus to compensate him by giving back "the very act of writing as well as the profit that you glean from what I write here."[136] Nicobulus was commanded to show reciprocity by contributing to the epistolary dialogue, where he could prove his own merits and carve out his own persona. Gregory was affording his nephew the opportunity to improve as a writer, and in so doing to advance as an author. He was acculturating him into a select social milieu by urging him to join the *agōn*.

---

[133] Basil, *Ep.* 231 (Deferrari), had once told Amphilochius, "there was nothing to prevent my letters from being as it were a daily record of my life, from recounting to your Charity the happenings of each day."

[134] Storin, *Self-Portrait*, 1–4.

[135] N. McLynn, "Gregory Nazianzen's Basil: The Literary Construction of a Christian Friendship," *SP* 34 (2001), 186.

[136] Greg. Naz., *Ep.* 52 (Storin 1).

Gregory showed equal command as he corresponded with more seasoned *pepaideumenoi*, such as Nicobulus' teachers. In about 383 Gregory intervened in a dispute between the rhetorician Stagirius (see beginning of chapter) and Stagirius' rival, the Cappadocian teacher Eustochius. The two were competing to mentor Nicobulus.[137] Eustochius believed that Gregory had encouraged Nicobulus, who was studying with Eustochius at the time, to approach Stagirius about working under his tutelage. Acquiring promising students meant prestige and income for teachers, and so Eustochius may have been denouncing Gregory's alleged interference. Responding to Eustochius, Gregory first acknowledged the artistry and frankness of his letter: "O Odysseus, how fiercely you strike me down (με καθίκεο)...discharging your sophisms (κατασοφιστεύω) against me."[138] Eustochius is designated a Greek warrior, who has engaged Gregory in verbal display. The banter, as Gregory portrayed it, assumes the manner of a military affair. And Gregory ultimately one-ups his friend by assuming the role of Agamemnon, who in the *Iliad* served as a voice of reason and calm against the impetuous and bellicose Odysseus (here played by Eustochius).[139] After acknowledging Eustochius' skill, Gregory employed his own spirited address by trying to play peacemaker between Eustochius and himself and between Eustochius and Stagirius. He chastises Eustochius for abusing his talents as when calling Stagirius a "Telchine" – in Greek mythology, one of the original inhabitants of Rhodes who used magic for harmful purposes. "Engaging in the giving and taking of head butts (κυρίσσω)," Gregory scolded, "is totally contentious and inappropriate."[140] Here again, Gregory depicts the discourse as violent in order to highlight his colleague's disposition. In this chastisement, Gregory monitors and rectifies Eustochius for not carrying himself as an *agathos* should. He is demonstrating his acute discernment of elite demeanor. Gregory then cited an admonition from the *Iliad* to give great discretion to whatever word you speak.[141] Gregory took advantage of the dispute to play the role as instructor of an instructor. In the same letter, Gregory praised, rebuked, and educated Eustochius. The interplay was a

---

[137] On this rivalry see N. McLynn, "Among the Hellenists: Gregory and the Sophists," in *Gregory of Nazianzus: Images and Reflections*, eds. J. Børtnes and T. Hägg (Copenhagen: Museum Tusculanum Press, 2006), 215–9.

[138] Greg. Naz., *Ep.* 190 (modification of trans. in Storin 105); Eustochius: Storin, *Gregory*, 27; H-M, 78–9.

[139] Storin, *Self-Portrait*, 114; *Iliad* 14.104.   [140] Greg. Naz., *Ep.* 190 (Storin 105).

[141] Greg. Naz. *Ep.* 190 (Storin 105); *Iliad* 20.250.

form of gamesmanship, with Gregory speaking a code that Eustochius understood. The epistle was meant to ease the tensions between the three parties, and through it Gregory enhanced his own image as pedagogue.

Gregory took the same approach on a separate occasion in a letter to Stagirius. The rhetorician had incurred an unspecified misfortune that Gregory had addressed in another letter.[142] Stagirius had replied, presumably explaining his reaction to Gregory's letter. After examining the missive, Gregory composed yet another response, commending Stagirius for overcoming adverse circumstances.[143] "You valiantly (γενναίως) rose up to the altercation like quite the sophist."[144] Gregory then deployed a *synkrisis* (a rhetorical device), comparing Stagirius to Achilles' horses Balios and Xanthos in the *Iliad* following the death of Patroclus, Achilles' beloved companion.[145] After having been brought to tears by the demise of their master's comrade, the steeds were emboldened by Zeus, who breathed might into them so that they returned to battle. "You lifted up your head and shook off the dust," Gregory proclaimed.[146] He was crediting Stagirius for overcoming the hardship, a behavior befitting a nobleman. Gregory was also suggesting that his own counsel had contributed to Stagirius' gallantry. Subsequently Gregory urged Stagirius to "desire the plains, the weapons, and exhibitions;" that is to return to his career of teaching, writing, and speaking.[147] Gregory now comes across as counselor and exhorter. He has elevated himself to the place of mentor for the accomplished rhetorician. Gregory charges Stagirius to "act like a man (ἀνδρίζου), and practice philosophy against the suffering" and he emphasizes that "judging sailors from the shoreline is no great feat."[148] It was time for Stagirius to return to action, to play his

---

[142] Greg. Naz., *Ep.* 164 (Storin 223).
[143] R. Gregg, *Consolation Philosophy: Greek and Christian Paideia in Basil and the Two Gregories* (Washington: Catholic University of America Press, 1975). Gregg explores philosophical schools of thought about how a noble man should respond to grief. The genre of classical consolation stretched deep into the classical past and the conventions in the literary trope of consolation provided another means of exhibiting *paideia*.
[144] Greg. Naz., *Ep.* 166 (Storin 226).
[145] *Iliad* 17.426–80: Balios and Xanthos; on *synkrisis*, G. Kennedy, *Greek Rhetoric Under Christian Emperors* (Princeton: Princeton University Press, 1983), 25, 31, 234–36 and Libanius, *Progymnasmata*.
[146] Greg. Naz., *Ep.* 166 (Storin 226).
[147] Greg. Naz., *Ep.* 166 (Storin 226): αὖθις πεδίων ἐπιθυμεῖν καὶ ὅπλων καὶ ἐπιδείξεων.
[148] Greg. Naz., *Ep* .166 (Storin 226).

role as instructor of young men; not from the sidelines, but as a contender. Gregory cast himself as an experienced combatant who had endured hardship and could thus speak as a reliable source. Moreover, Gregory inserted himself into the narrative by playing the same role as Zeus in the *Iliad*. Whereas the latter had breathed resilience into Achilles' horses, now Gregory was doing the same to Stagirius. This parallelism was sure to have registered with Stagirius and to give a sense of Gregory's self-assurance.

On some occasions, the Cappadocians also solicited addressees to write by inscribing them into the Homeric or classical past. Late in the 380s, for instance, Nyssen crafted an epistle for Eupatrius, a *scholasticus* (a legal official in the imperial service) and a native of Pontus or Cappadocia. Gregory assumed the identity of Laertes (King of Ithaca in the *Odyssey*), as he compared Eupatrius and his father to Odysseus and Telemachus (the son and grandson of Laertes).[149] "You and your wholly admirable father honored me, as they did Laertes," Gregory wrote, "contending in friendly rivalry for the first prize (φιλοφροσύνη περὶ τῶν πρωτείων διαγωνίζεσθε) in showing us respect and kindness, pelting me with letters..."[150] Gregory respected Eupatrius and his father in this characterization of them as brave warriors. The pair had competed for a "prize" based on who had sent the most excellent and numerous epistles to Gregory. Gregory likened their missives to projectiles used in battle, here equating their correspondence to the victory that Odysseus (as Eupatrius' father) and Telemachus (as Eupatrius) won, using spears, over Penelope's suitors. The father-son duo had proven their mettle, and thus Gregory recasts them as earlier Greek heroes. Nyssen continued to heap praise: "I shall be a judge favourable to both of you, awarding to you the first prize (πρωτεῖα) against your father, and the same to your father against me."[151] Here Gregory assumes the position of critic, adjudicating the skills and labors of his correspondents, and acknowledging them both as victors. He finalizes his gratitude by admiring Eupatrius' writing style: "But you, by entertaining us in youthful fashion with your brisk and sprightly language shall restore youth to our old age."[152] Gregory declares his appreciation for the multiple epistles he received. Even as he extols Eupatrius and his father, he portrays them as attempting to outdo

---

[149] *Odyssey* 24.514–15; see Silvas, *Gregory*, 149 n. 189.
[150] Greg. Ny., *Ep.* 11 (slight modification of Silvas).   [151] Greg. Ny., *Ep.* 11 (Silvas).
[152] Greg. Ny., *Ep.* 11 (Silvas).

each other, thus further acknowledging them as virtuous. And as Gregory recognizes the merits of his colleagues, his position as Laertes – great warrior and sire to Telemachus and Odysseus – reminds readers that he has right to make judgment. By creating an imaginative narrative, Gregory recognizes their mutual commitment to an economy of honor grounded in Homer's *Odyssey*. He signals that he shares in their knowledge of noble Greeks from antiquity. And by equating father and son with these paragons of manhood, he recognizes his addressees as descended from their pedigree. It is a lineage that he, too, can claim through his success in the *agōn*.

In the world of late antique *paideia*, the Cappadocians deemed eloquence an extension of manhood. So, by sustaining an image as judges of literary style, they cast themselves as arbiters of *aretē*. Similar tropes of authority informed the discourse on both epistolary *agōn* and elite male bearing. Nazianzen, for example, adopted the place of referee over provincial administrators and eminent intellectuals. In 382 he expressed his support of Olympius, a Christian governor of Cappadocia: "I have confidence in you..." Gregory stated. "For intelligence (σύνεσις) and manliness (ἀνδρεία) guide your office..."[153] Gregory appraised Olympius' rule and subsequently certified the comportment in his fellow Cappadocian. In correspondence among elites, social hierarchies were based partly on the execution of language. Gregory was sanctioned to assess a man of high rank because his elocution identified him as a man whose opinion counted. Gregory also praised the attributes of Eudoxius (same as above), who secured his standing, according to Nazianzen, by avoiding the unsavory features of vile wordsmiths who lack sophistication. Gregory approved that his colleague did not have the "repulsive voice" (φωνὴ μιαρά) or "vulgarity" (ἀγοραῖος) of social climbers who ultimately betray their baseness.[154] Gregory contrasted Eudoxius with Greek poet Aristophanes' parody of a sausage-seller who was made into a demagogue; a man lacking all the requisite qualities of a just political leader.[155] Here Gregory affirmed Eudoxius' high birth, a mark often associated with noblemen against the inadequacies of social climbers. Because of Eudoxius' background of financial and social security, he was not slave

---

[153] Greg. Naz., *Ep.* 140 (Storin 210); Olympius: Storin, *Gregory*, 35; R. Van Dam, "Governors of Cappadocia during the Fourth Century," *Medieval Prosopography* 17 (1996), 64–6.

[154] Greg. Naz., *Ep.* 178 (Storin 116).   [155] Aristophanes, *Knights* 5.140–229.

to fame, riches, and political power, obsessions that indicated an absence of discipline and pedigree.[156] In commendations such as this, Gregory garnered respect as an accomplished critic of noble demeanor. He recognized and articulated the qualities of Eudoxius that distinguished him from less admirable sophists. Thus, Gregory acquitted himself as a connoisseur of virtue.

Managing Masculinity: Exhortations to "Play the Man"

In the preceding letter, Gregory issued an injunction that moored *aretē* specifically to its masculine affiliation. He admonished Eudoxius "Let's become men (ἄνδρες γενώμεθα)."[157] All of the characteristics that dignified Eudoxius appear to be subsumed in this dictum. The maxim, which was probably taught in early pedagogy, also recurred in Basil's letters. For instance, Basil exhorted a Christian soldier, probably an officer "to play the man, and be strong."[158] The counsel held multiple meanings here: to fight valiantly; to serve as a model of discipline for those under him; and to remain faithful to God during the ugliness of combat. Basil used the same phrasing when writing to Amphilochius of Iconium after his consecration as bishop in 374, enjoining him to "play the man" (ἀνδρίζου) and to act as "a wise helmsman (κυβερνήτης) who has assumed the command of a ship."[159] Basil had supported his friend's election to the episcopacy and here he proffered the words of a mentor. The admonishment to "be men" came from the battle-charged atmosphere of the *Iliad*, where, for example, the Greek hero Ajax and King Nestor exhorted soldiers to stand their ground in battle.[160] "Be men, my friends," Ajax urged the Greeks, "and show some shame."[161] Ajax, in this account, shows intrepidity as he rouses the men to action. The Athenian commander Themistocles, likewise, exhorted the Spartan commander Eurybiades to "be a brave man" (ἀνὴρ ἀγαθός) by engaging the Persian fleet at Salamis during the Second

---

[156] Roisman, *Rhetoric*, 163–85.   [157] Greg. Naz., *Ep.* 178 (Storin 116).
[158] Basil, *Ep.* 106 (Deferrari): ἀνδρίζου τοίνυν, καὶ ἴσχυε; the phrase "play the man" appears in other classical epistles, notably in the context of exhortations to endure misfortune, e.g. Cicero, *Letters to Friends* 5.18.
[159] Basil, *Ep.* 161 (Deferrari).
[160] *Iliad* 15.561 and 15.661. See K. Bassi, "The Semantics of Manliness in Ancient Greece," in *Andreia: Studies in Manliness and Courage in Classical Antiquity*, eds. R. Rosen and I. Sluiter (Leiden: Brill, 2003), 33, on the significance of men putting their bodies to the test in view of their leaders.
[161] *Iliad* 15.560–1. (Lombardo): ἀνέρες ἔστε, καὶ αἰδῶ θέσθ' ἐνὶ θυμῷ.

Persian War.[162] To have avoided the conflict here would have proven the Spartans cowards. Basil also is using martial imagery when he correlates Amphilochius' responsibility to "assuming command of a ship." As overseer of the church at Iconium, Basil was stating, Amphilochius would be responsible for steering the congregation clear of the "winds of heresy" and "briny and bitter waves of error."[163] The spiritual and civic duties in the office of bishop demanded the same poise as the master of a seagoing vessel. Basil stressed the point to Amphilochius, while speaking with the latitude of a veteran warrior.

In late antique epistolography, authors reserved the phrases "play the man" or "be a man" specifically for exhorting fellow *men* to act according to the conventions of the elite male. In other literary and theological works, the Cappadocians accentuated *aretē* in female family members. But they did not urge women – even saintly figures – to "be a man." As we will see in later chapters, for example, Macrina was not expected to behave according to the conventions of noble manhood. It would have been unseemly to prompt her to act outside her physical nature. So, although Macrina does, in fact, demonstrate *aretē* through her actions, her behavior exceeds societal standards, thus making her even more noteworthy. The epistolary forum of *aretē*, however, was a predominantly male space, with less allowance for gender fluidity. In this context, Gregory and Basil issued the charge "be men" as a reminder of expectations for *agathoi*, both individual and collective.

Basil and Nazianzen also called to mind the ideal of Greek heroes as they reprised such analogies of fearless warriors. Their use of this trope issued especial weight because it resonated with two features most *pepaideumenoi* treasured: a sense of hypermasculinity; and harkening back to an age that, seemingly, witnessed manhood in its purest form. In her investigation of ancient Greek theatre, Karen Bassi makes a convincing case that such longings for an imagined ideal age colored the tastes of audiences in classical Athens. Bassi observed that depictions of collective masculinity were modeled after the individual actions of a hero or "best man" (ἄριστος ἀνήρ). Such evidence anticipated and informed later conceptions of manhood as an abstract ethical quality.[164] Fourth-century *pepaideumenoi* were following their predecessors in self-identifying with the past. Both looked back to classical Athens, where citizens valorized the warrior age of the Homeric epics. The elite masculine

---

[162] Herodotus, *Histories* 8.62 (my translation).   [163] Basil, *Ep.* 161 (Deferrari).
[164] Bassi, "Semantics," 34.

ethos, "being men," was best captured in ancient scenes of heroism, episodes that stimulated self-awareness of the elevated place of a singular community.[165]

The Cappadocians impressed this expectation onto fourth-century pro-Nicene literati, thus underscoring a self-assurance resonant with nobility and courage. In a letter to Adamantius, a Christian priest, Gregory accentuated such martial-like valor by likening his correspondent to Cynegirus and Callimachus – Athenian generals at the Battle of Marathon.[166] Adamantius, we learn, had requested tablets that contained the text of Herodotus' *Histories*. Gregory told him that studying these courageous Greeks suited him because of his "longstanding intimacy" (παλαιά συνήθεια) with them.[167] Adamantius was perpetuating the excellence of the Greek commanders' fortitude by inspiring confidence in followers and providing stability for his church. Gregory cast him as an Athenian commander, emboldening congregants by standing up to Persia, the invading force at Marathon. Persia, the historical enemy of Greece, symbolized softness, laxity, and indulgence in the church and community. In other words, Gregory personified Adamantius as a source of surety and spiritual exactitude for his congregants. Employing the Herodotean binary between the hardened rigor of "western" Greece and the soft luxuriousness of feminized "eastern" Persia, Gregory applied this moral categorization to accentuate *aretē* in a fellow clergyman.

Nazianzen likewise emphasized mutual *aretē* in his correspondence with Ablabius, a teacher of rhetoric who converted to Christianity later in life. "You speak impressively (σοβαρός), hold a strong gaze (μέγα βλέπειν)," Gregory said, "and walk proudly and loftily (βαδίζειν ὑψηλὸν καὶ μετέωρον)."[168] These attributes, Gregory reminded him, befit the resolve of Miltiades, Cynegirus, Callimachus, and Lamachus, four Athenian generals, three of whom led troops at the Battle of Marathon.[169] Gregory was cueing readers to recall the ideal persona of manly orators based on Second Sophistic tropes. The picture of Ablabius was one of a virile speaker: projecting a strong voice; playing an active

---

[165] Bassi, *Acting*, 315.   [166] Greg. Naz., *Ep.* 235 (Storin 235).

[167] Greg. Naz., *Ep.* 235 (Storin 235; my translation). On longstanding intimacy, see Aristotle, *Rhetoric* 1.15,13–15.

[168] Greg. Naz., *Ep.* 233 (Storin 141); Ablabius: Storin, *Gregory*, 18, and Silvas, *Gregory*, 187–8.

[169] Storin, *Gregory*, 215 n. 160: Herodotus, *Histories* 6.94–140; Lamachus served in the Peloponnesian War: Thucydides, *History* 4.75.1–2, 6.49–50, 6.101–3.

role through his gaze, rather than taking on a passive presence; and showing confidence through his gait and posture. Gregory also was associating Ablabius' verbal *aretē* (his rhetoric) with military heroics of a definitive period in Attic history, when Greece – as the civilized world – was battling the forces of tyranny and barbarism. The oblique juxtaposition between the commanders of Greece and their unnamed Persian counterparts reinforced the manly persona that Gregory was putting on display. It was an enduring practice in Greek rhetoric to delineate something by setting it against its antithesis. Gregory deploys this strategy as another part of the cumulative image he was constructing. In both references to Persia, moreover, Gregory was also alluding to heresy as a danger to the church. As we will see later in other genres, Gregory portrayed non-Nicene theologians as effeminate. It was incumbent on a Christian *agathos* to gain the confidence of fellow *pepaideumenoi* by taking on an unmistakably masculine posture. Gregory makes Ablabius out to be one such individual.

The Cappadocians also evaluated the elegance of their educated colleagues as a way of enhancing their own image as literati. Because sophistication was aligned with masculinity, arbitrating literary dexterity translated into measuring virility. They situated themselves as analysts of other *pepaideumenoi*, as experts at defining standards of *aretē*. An *agōn* was a contest to establish and affirm the credentials of elite males. At stake was justification to specify exactly how to act like a man. The Cappadocians attempted to certify themselves as paragons of *aretē* as they delineated elements of virtuous conduct among correspondents. By calibrating *paideia* as an aspect of episcopal office, the Cappadocians positioned pro-Nicene clergy to attain credibility among fellow provincial officials. Success also aligned one with a course of ideal maleness that stretched back indefinitely into the Greek past. They inherited this veneration for the historical male from preceding generations of eastern Romans and adopted it as part of their own identity.

The Cappadocians thus re-inscribed the heritage of *agōn*, subsequently integrating the ideals of classical manhood into the collective consciousness of the church and identifying them within the pro-Nicene episcopacy. Through epistolary exhibitions, the Cappadocians promoted a masculine persona that harked back to the heroes of an idealized Greek past. By compelling *pepaideumenoi* to compose letters, and by holding up certain values embedded in Greek lore, they were forging a convergence of clerical authority and masculinity. The association of eloquence with manhood derived from their years of training in *paideia*: from the volatile atmosphere of studies in Athens; from the example of teachers such as Prohaeresius; from the curriculum and oratorical contests of the Second Sophistic that informed their conceptions of agonistic rivalry; to the exertions through which they composed letters. Unlike the antagonistic backdrop of oratory, however, the Cappadocians used correspondence with fellow *pepaideumenoi* to exalt mutual *aretē*. They prompted others to write, judged on style, and celebrated letters with the same spirit that characterized alliances between colleagues in ancient Greece. Having been prompted to exhibit ideals of manliness, correspondents were expected to uphold standards expected of noble men: sacrifice, courage, charity, patronage, justice, and clemency.

While refashioning *aretē* that was visible in figures from ancient Greek literature, the Cappadocians upheld attributes that complemented the character of bishops outlined in scriptures, such as the emphasis on temperance (νηφάλιος) and self-control (σώφρων) in I Timothy and Titus.[170] In doing so, they made it clear that the classical male ideal aligned with pro-Nicene visions of church guidance. When Nazianzen wrote to his cousin Amphilochius, bishop of Iconium, in 373, he commended him for his direction of the church there. "The command of Your Inimitable Virtue is not barbarian," Gregory says, "but Greek and even Christian."[171] Acknowledging the two cultural traditions that formed Amphilochius' intellectual and social makeup, Gregory converged the two as preconditions of an effective leader. Neither Gregory nor the other Cappadocians consistently publicized to laity so specific a vision of a church hierarchy that reoriented *aretē* as a condition of the pro-Nicene episcopacy. In communications to the larger church body, in fact, the Cappadocians ushered caution about values external to scriptural teachings. But here, for a restricted readership, Gregory prompts his cousin (and other readers) to understand the subtle message: that the qualities of the classical male applied to a Christian hierarch. Greek and Christian together contravene that which is barbaric, meaning that a civilized state is both Greek and orthodox (pro-Nicene). As bishops moderating epistolary contests, the Cappadocians established themselves as part of an "insider's game" among the intellectual elite.

---

[170] I Timothy 3:2; Titus 2:5.
[171] Greg. Naz., *Ep.* 62 (Storin 185): Οὐ βάρβαρον τὸ ἐπίταγμα τῆς ἀμιμήτου σου καλοκἀγαθίας, ἀλλ' ἑλληνικόν, μᾶλλον δὲ χριστιανικόν.

And in inciting other Christian *pepaideumenoi* to show off their literary skills as an *agōn*, the Cappadocians normalized *aretē* as a virtue of their episcopal office.

The Cappadocians used correspondence as the primary medium to cultivate a masculine identity because letter writing signified strength. While Second Sophistic *pepaideumenoi* had depended on oral performances to assert identity, many speakers had been accused of compromising their manhood by going too far with theatricality, pandering to crowds in order to curry favor. By the late fourth century, ambivalence about such sophists remained a commonplace; so much so that *pepaideumenoi* went to great lengths to justify their rhetoric as a medium for expressing philosophy.[172] They were not merely entertaining that is. Letter writing helped to maintain an image as a self-directed individual, not a crowd pleaser, because the primary audiences were also conversant in the standards of *aretē*. It was not a setting of the indiscriminate masses. It was a forum where no one could successfully masquerade as a man. The epistolary arena was a sacred space for virtuous men. No pretenders were allowed.

Composing epistles for fellow literati, the Cappadocians called to mind their own adolescence and young adult lives, where they had struggled to gain command of eloquence. They prompted addressees to do the same. These compositions kept alive a past that resonated with stability and power. Expertise in crafting these texts indicated superior discipline and knowledge of what made for effective leadership. For generations of eastern Roman leaders, Greek language, literature, history, and philosophy had informed and validated legitimate authorities. Imperial and civic leaders, teachers, aspiring young *pepaideumenoi*, and novice priests – the individuals who read these letters – would find in the Cappadocians an acute awareness of the masculine ethos that underpinned eastern Rome. The Cappadocians were attempting to conserve the culture of *paideia*, which had preserved symmetry between Roman and local rule for centuries. A limited class – defined by birth, education, and most importantly, competitive trials – provided the foundation for brokering relations across the empire. With their widespread correspondence among literati, the Cappadocians set themselves at the forefront of

---

[172] A. Puertas, *The Dynamics*, 65, gives an especially strong illustration about how the Christian philosopher-rhetorician Themistius negotiated these two categories of his intellectual make-up.

this social and political reality. Their correspondents could see in pro-Nicene episcopal leadership a comparable version of the archetypical *agathos*. The Cappadocians shared with fellow provincial aristocrats a sense of duty to develop and place *agathoi* into positions of civic authority. In doing so, they may have played a missional role by drawing non-Christians to the pro-Nicene fellowship. By playing the part of the classical male, the Cappadocians offered a version of Christian leadership that appealed to individuals who longed for continuity with the Greek heritage of eastern Rome. Because fellow *pepaideumenoi* had been trained in the same general curriculum, there was a confidence that they would uphold the values embedded in higher Greek culture. Participating in epistolary *agōnes* allowed the Cappadocians to interact seamlessly with *pepaideumenoi*, both non-Christian and Christian, and to correlate such conceptions of manhood with clerical office. They were cultivating provincial leaders and claiming the conventions of gender in *paideia* for the church.

2

The *Agōn* of Friendship

Sensory Rhetoric, Gift Exchange, and the Aesthetics of Aretē

Beginning with earliest literature in ancient Greece, exhibitions of manhood were associated with the ideal of friendship. As we saw in Chapter 1, late-fourth century *pepaideumenoi* manifested *aretē* through epistolary performances that were portrayed as contests. Authors often denoted manly excellence using imagery of battle as a means of upholding the attributes of *agathoi*, the brave and upright. As early as the Homeric world, however, the most prominent combatants had distinguished themselves not only through martial prowess, but also by executing alliances with fellow noble warriors through reciprocal acts of honor and material benefits. In the *Iliad*, for example, the Trojan champion Hector and the Hellene Ajax fought each other with spears and lances before reaching a truce. They then exchanged gifts to mark their mutual respect and declaration of friendship, an act that would enshrine the memory of their courage and sense of honor.[1] Familiar with such demonstrations of status, the Cappadocians simulated similar models of camaraderie, as well as manifestations of friendship denoted in later epochs.

Greek philosophers of the classical and Hellenistic ages had outlined the principles of *philia*, a concept that included love between friends and that shared elements with earlier ideals of *xenia* (ξενία); the latter understood primarily as guest friendship or friendship related to extended family.[2] In one version of *philia* that became particularly influential, Aristotle held that in transactions of ideal friendship, parties had to be

---

[1] *Iliad* 7.295–315.
[2] M. Finley, *The World of Odysseus* (New York: Viking Press, 1954), 103–9.

approximate social equals.³ Colleagues showed generosity and affection to each other in a bond predicated on each having a quality that indicated similar goodness.⁴ And, in a comparable portrayal by Plato, there were qualities in a friend that made him stand out from ordinary persons, whether his desire for the ideal of the Good (the Beautiful) or his pursuit of virtue.⁵ Fourth-century *philoi* (friends) most often made reference to *philia* as an affective attachment between such *agathoi*. As late as the fourth century A.D., if one wanted to identify as a member of the educated elite in eastern Rome, he needed to demonstrate familiarity with the rules of such *philia*

The Cappadocians followed the conventions of friendship in letters to fellow *pepaideumenoi* as they expressed reciprocity, honor, and attraction based on an aesthetic of body and soul. Epistolary interchanges of friendship translated into a relationship dynamic that echoed elements of an *agōn*. Vying with other *pepaideumenoi*, the Cappadocians staged contests of penning letters to convey affection. Nazianzen likened the meeting of virtuous men to the case of one singer coming across another.⁶ Instead of confronting a rival based on jealousy, the man will value him as "a fellow practitioner of one's own craft."⁷ The individual is overcome by excitement, Gregory says, because he has found a person of similar nature to help strengthen himself. Gregory's prescribed reaction for friendship is instructive for understanding how friendship often mirrored *agōn* rhetoric. The logistics of *philia* in the fourth century offered writers a platform on which to exhibit the protocol of friendship bonds and their pursuit of *aretē*. Because many friends rarely encountered each other in person, they faced the obstacle of separation from their kindred souls. *Pepaideumenoi* thus fastened on the trope of absence as they used rhetorical models and creative invention in epistles to maintain intimacy across distance and time.⁸ Correspondence among *philoi* served as a platform of

---

³ Aristotle, N.E. 1158a31–b17.
⁴ D. Konstan, *Friendship in the Classical World* (Cambridge: Cambridge University Press, 1997), 49–52, 93–9.
⁵ Plato, *Lysis* 216c–19b on *philia* as desire for the Good and Aristotle, N.E. 1156b, on *philia* based on *aretē*. On implications of these differences, C. White, *Christian Friendship in the Fourth Century* (Cambridge: Cambridge University Press, 1992), 22–8.
⁶ Greg. Naz., Ep. 195 (Storin 82).   ⁷ Greg Naz., Ep. 195 (Storin 82).
⁸ H. Koskenniemi, *Studien zur Idee und Phraseologie des greichischen Briefes bis 400 n. Chr* (Helsinki: Suomalainen Tiedeakatemia, 1956), 38–42, based his epistolary theory on the premise that the fundamental purpose of letters was to create *parousia* (presence) between sender and addressee. Every premise of letter writing in the ancient world, he says, must extend from this point.

performance, an *agōn* of friendship that promoted *aretē* in writer and addressee. When Nazianzen boasted to a correspondent that he was "conquering (νικάω) him with friendly letters," he was alluding to a contest that was meant to celebrate his own achievement, while bringing honor to both parties by announcing shared status.[9] The *philia* relationship served as an additional realization of masculinity as individuals attempted to outdo each other in formulating friendship through the medium of an epistle.

Declarations of friendship provided especially promising opportunities for self-representation. When Nazianzen composed his funeral oration on Basil, he was writing about himself even as he applauded Basil.[10] The lives of the two friends were so closely bound that chronicling Basil's deeds inevitably meant that Gregory's own accomplishments would be shown. Although Gregory was memorializing Basil through an oration, this strategy of self-writing applied to correspondence as well. When one praised noble characteristics in a friend or stated affection for him, the implication held that he too, because of similarities among *philoi*, shared those features. Perhaps as importantly, while the Cappadocians took part in an *agōn* of affection, they were contributing to a dialogue that offered opportunity to push the boundaries of friendship rhetoric. In Nazianzen's oration on Basil, Gregory wrote concerning their friendship that "I am at a loss for words and know not which way to turn..."[11] Gregory was quite right, that knowing how to praise a friend – or for that matter how to convey affection among friends – presented a challenging task.[12] Rhetorical models of epistolary theory laid out protocols for letters to friends, but the genre allowed for flexibility. Although they had access to handbooks that addressed letters of friendship, the Cappadocians had ample room to expand and create methods of articulating affection for *philoi*. Consequently, the Cappadocians drew on classical rhetoric and philosophy and specimens from fellow *pepaideumenoi*, but also language derived from biblical texts. Even in letters of friendship to non-Christian

---

[9] Greg. Naz., *Ep.* 174 (Storin 111).
[10] D. Konstan, "How to Praise a Friend: St. Gregory of Nazianzus's Funeral Oration for St. Basil the Great," in *Greek Biography and Panegyric in Late Antiquity*, eds. T. Hägg and P. Rousseau (Berkeley: University of California Press, 2000), 160–1.
[11] Greg. Naz., *Or.* 43.14 (McCauley, 39).
[12] Christian authors faced the additional problem of knowing which vocabulary to use when discussing friends: to accentuate friendship (*philia*) a classical concept based on mutual *aretē*; or charity (*agapē*) (a bond, in the New Testament, sealed as a gift of grace). Konstan, *Friendship*, 156–66.

pepaideumenoi, the Cappadocians sometimes used phrases derived from sacred scripture.

In letters of friendship based on mutual *paideia*, the Cappadocians often emphasized bodily beauty and materiality. Attention to the somatic by authors of the Second Sophistic had returned audiences to an age when bodily appearance provided an index of aristocracy. Speaking in a discourse on masculinity, they harked back to relationships among males that often equated manly virtue with both friendship and aesthetic superiority.[13] Such figures manifested appeal in their bodies as a consequence of the exercising and competitions through which they acquired excellence. The body, that is, testified to their manhood, an ideal that had to be exhibited through performance and control. While orators created a virile gestalt through bodily movements, letter writers mimicked such comportment through the text.[14] Epistolary writers emphasized a rhetoric of appearance, materiality, and movement as a virtual encounter between author and the addressee. Using sensory rhetoric, the Cappadocians participated in the male-centered dialogue of friendship, consequently reinforcing their *aretē*. And as a reenactment of classical friendship, as a return to manly virtue in early Greek literature, the Cappadocians often used a rhetoric of gift exchange to punctuate the honorific rivalry of epistolary composition. Here again, the letters – as gifts – made for metaphors of presence. The language of "giftedness" pervades letters to friends by the Cappadocians. In such depictions, the authors associate the gift with the giver, with correspondents acclaiming satisfaction at receiving "likenesses" of the sender. Utterances of physical delight reinforced the simulation of a face-to-face encounter, while sensory language challenged recipients of letters to match the inventiveness.

The institution of friendship, like other social protocols, varied according to the group identity shared by individuals. Carolinne White, in her treatment of Christian friendship, showed that fourth-century Christian authors formulated a theory of friendship based on classical ideals of *philia*, adapting many tenets of it for a faith community whose scriptures reflected only elements of the concept. According to this theory,

---

[13] D. Hawhee, *Bodily Arts: Rhetoric and Athletics in Ancient Greece* (Austin: University of Texas Press, 2005), 20–1.

[14] P. Rosenmeyer, *Ancient Epistolary Fictions: The Letter in Greek Literature* (Cambridge: Cambridge University Press, 2001), 4–7, for example, treats the letter primarily through the lens of self-representation.

philia – as a reciprocal bond between social equals – held minimal influence on Christian authors of the first three centuries.[15] For White, a heightened Christian emphasis on constructing friendship networks emerged in the fourth century and corresponded to the expanding social status of the faith.[16] Many of White's conclusions inform my treatment of friendship in this chapter. One point of difference, however, is that I am scrutinizing the Cappadocians not as distinct from non-Christian *philoi*, but as part of that coterie of individuals across the East trained in *paideia*. This latter group included Christians and non-Christians, and both were familiar with the conventions of classical friendship. White argues that many fourth-century Christian authors were guided by an armature of friendship that modified or subordinated *philia* to fundamental teachings in the New Testament, such as the practice of *agape*, loving persons unconditionally. My work, however, concentrates on the Cappadocians interacting with other *agathoi*, guided equally by tenets of *philia* and *agape* – sometimes overlapping; sometimes discordant – depending on their affiliation with the addressee. This subject thus involves investigating their friendships with Christians and non-Christians without showing conscious primacy of a single basis for relations. With the former group, we will see, the Cappadocians forged ties based on *philia*, but deepened and magnified by another element of congruence, their shared faith; with the latter, meanwhile, often no reference to religion is made.

This chapter thus examines letters of friendship through the lens of identity theory.[17] Occasions to compose epistles for fellow *pepaideumenoi* provided authors the opportunity to advertise their own verbal dexterity, thus acknowledging their own sophistication and honoring recipients with rhetorical keepsakes.[18] In this sense, I suggest that the Cappadocians participated in a dialogue analogous to that between

---

[15] White points out exceptions, such as Clement of Alexandria, see White, *Christian*, 3.
[16] White, *Christian*, 4.
[17] Letter exchange by clergy served many purposes. Separated by distance, rugged terrain, illness, and burdens of office, clergy corresponded as a way of sharing important information with family and friends, imperial magistrates, fellow *pepaideumenoi*, bishops, monks, and Christians under their guidance. See M. Mullett, "The Classical Tradition in the Byzantine Letter," *Byzantium and the Classical Tradition*, eds. Mullett and R. Scott (Birmingham, 1981), 85–92; on difficulties of travel in Cappadocia: R. Van Dam, *Kingdom of Snow: Roman Rule and Greek Culture in Cappadocia* (Philadelphia: University of Pennsylvania Press, 2002), 14–16; on value of epistles for information, R. Pouchet, *Basile le Grand et son univers d'amis d'après sa correspodance: une stratégie de communion* (Rome: Institutum Patristicum Augustinianum, 1992), 30–4.
[18] Rosenmeyer, *Ancient*, 102.

ancient Greek athletes and the epinician poets who celebrated their victories in verse. The poets who praised the athletes for their feats penned victory odes as gestures of respect, compensating champions for the glory that their achievement had brought to the city and to its leading citizens.[19] This "traffic in praise" served as a form of social currency that re-integrated the victor into the local aristocracy and externalized the collective status of the *agathoi*. As the Cappadocians sent letters of friendship to a network of associates, they too engaged in an economy of honor. In so doing, they identified themselves as individuals who valued *philia* and the mutual questing for *aretē* that united friends.

CORPOREALITY AND THE SOUL IN SENSORY RHETORIC

An ongoing theme throughout letters of friendship, largely determined by the execution of epistolary exchange, involved the rhetorical representation of corporeal presence. Because of the physical separation from correspondents, authors used literary strategies to orchestrate accessibility.[20] In sacred texts, Derek Krueger has shown, the words often stood in place of a person, with the text signifying either author or subject.[21] The Cappadocians applied corporeal identity to their writing, not only in personifications of the holy, but also as they choreographed virtual presence for fellow *pepaideumenoi*. In the Christological debates of the fourth century, the Cappadocians accrued social authority through their ability to use this rhetorical form in multiple genres. By eliding the spiritual and the corporeal through classical and biblical tropes, they also contributed to an adaptation of friendship suited to late-antique *pepaideumenoi*.

Expressions of *philia* in the Cappadocians' letters are best understood in the context of the "material turn."[22] According to this idea, Christians

---

[19] L. Kurke, *The Traffic in Praise: Pindar and the Poetics of Social Economy* (Ithaca: Cornell University Press, 1991), 92–105.

[20] D. Krueger, *Writing and Holiness: The Practice of Authorship in the Early Christian East* (Philadelphia: University of Pennsylvania Press, 2004), 156, where Krueger understands a number of early Christian texts as a "consummation of textuality and embodiment."

[21] Krueger, *Writing*, 151–6, gives examples of each, including the famous example in the Gospel of John where Jesus (the *Logos*) becomes flesh. As Krueger states, "The Father's missive is the body, the Word made flesh," 152.

[22] P. C. Miller, *The Corporeal Imagination: Signifying the Holy in Late Ancient Christianity* (Philadelphia: University of Pennsylvania Press, 2009), 3–4, defines the material turn as "a shift [occurred] that reconfigured the relation between materiality and meaning in a positive direction."

increasingly welcomed the potential efficacy of human faculties because of social and political changes in the fourth century. After the legalization of Christianity in 313, believers increasingly viewed the world as a favorable place for encountering God, and Christians re-valued senses as a way of experiencing the numinous.[23] Although scholars have discussed the material turn primarily as it related to humanity's connection to the divine, this reorientation of the material world also affected how *pepaideumenoi* crafted a rhetoric of friendship. For the Cappadocians, we see in letters of friendship noticeable attention to the human body. They drew on a deep reservoir of sources to mediate presence through imagery of the body: epistolary handbooks, literary exercises from the Second Sophistic, ancient writers, multiple philosophical schools, and finally, biblical texts. In crafting these texts, the Cappadocians thus vied with correspondents to depict corporeality as a medium for friendship.

Recurring references to the body in letters of friendship relate to the material turn; namely, the place of the soul as a basis for *philia*. In ancient Greek literature, friendship was often expressed as magnetism between two persons based on affinity of souls.[24] Late eastern Roman authors continued to specify friendship in such terms. In his funeral oration for Basil, to cite one fourth-century example, Nazianzen proclaimed their *philia*: "We seemed to have a single soul animating two bodies."[25] Here Gregory described his affection for Basil as mutual pursuit of *aretē* visibly manifested by the union of their souls. In ancient Greece, the soul was recognized as the part of the self that commanded the thoughts of a person, the functions of the body, and potential union with the divine. But unlike modern interpretations of the soul that stress a binary between soul and body, the soul was generally conceptualized as part of the material realm. It was best understood as a hierarchical entity situated high upon, but belonging to, the same spectrum on which the body

---

[23] S. A. Harvey, *Sensing Salvation: Ancient Christianity and the Olfactory Imagination* (Berkeley: University of California Press, 2006), 57–9, who first introduced the "material turn."

[24] For example Plato, *Lysis* 214a–15c; Aristotle, *N.E.* 1166a; this denotation of friendship harmonizes with the bond depicted between David and Jonathan in I Samuel 18:1: "The soul of Jonathan was knit to the soul of David and Jonathan loved him as his own soul." See White, *Christian*, 47.

[25] Greg. Naz. *Or.* 43.20 (McCauley, 44). A phrase derived from Plato's characterization of the soul in *Symposium* 189c–93e. Here, according to the subject Aristophanes, the primeval form of humans consisted of a body with two souls. The worldly state of bodies (each with one soul) resulted from Zeus dividing each primeval human into two persons.

resided.²⁶ In a status-based society, where even the components of a person were ranked along a continuum, the soul served as the foundation for friendship among the best citizens. Encountering the soul in a *philos* thus did not constitute strictly a metaphysical action, but rather an engagement that occurred through a pathway of senses that had been properly conditioned. The body proved instrumental in constructions of manhood, particularly during the fourth century as Christian *pepaideumenoi* were appraising physicality more favorably. Masculinity was exhibited, in part, through language that magnified the body and its many nuances of excellence.

The Cappadocians infused abundant corporeal imagery into letters in which they were underscoring friendship with *pepaideumenoi*. Basil, for example, assessed the nobility of a man by noting that his strength of body (ῥώμη τοῦ σώματος) matched the virtue of his soul (ἀρετή τῆς ψυχῆς).²⁷ Basil issued a consonance of body and soul, a recurring theme in many of the Cappadocians' letters. The long periods of absence from friends offered opportunity for dramatic effect in letters. It was often during these times that the Cappadocians used bodily metaphors both to connect with other *agathoi* and to attest to individuals' *aretē*. Nazianzen observed that the qualities of good and bad men should be as obvious as sight detecting the difference between gold and stones.²⁸ The innermost nature was evident to the eyes. Or in the case of distance between persons, words on paper served as the sensory stimuli that made known the person. When friends were separated, it was necessary to orchestrate the workings of the senses in order to recreate an avenue to the soul. Letters provided the medium of bringing the person virtually into the presence of the friend. "For an author constructs a letter primarily as an image of his soul," read a second-century epistolary handbook. "In every other composition it is possible to discern the writer's character, but none so clearly as in the epistolary."²⁹ The Cappadocians composed epistles consistent with this theory, staging connections to friends through a carefully crafted rhetoric of the senses. Letter writers of the New Testament had accentuated similar confidence in the text to bridge distance and time. The writer to the church at Colossae stated: "Though I am

---

[26] D. Martin, *The Corinthian Body* (New Haven: Yale University Press, 1995): on modern categorizations of body and soul, as influenced by René Descartes, 3–6; on the hierarchy of the self, 29–34.

[27] Basil, *Ep.* 269. (Deferrari).   [28] Greg. Naz., *Ep.* 22 (Storin 103).

[29] Pseudo-Demetrius, *Epistolary Types* 227 (Malherbe, *AET*, 19); modification of Malherbe's translation.

absent from you in body, I am present with you in spirit,"[30] and the first letter to the church at Corinth read: "Even though I am not physically present, I am with you in spirit."[31] A desire for presence was based on mutual beliefs and backgrounds that drew individuals to one another. In New Testament letters, this community was reckoned as *koinonia* (fellowship) between followers of Christ; in letters among *pepaideumenoi*, it was framed as classical *philia* (friendship); and in missives to Christian *pepaideumenoi*, elements of both appeared.[32] By addressing the issue of absence in epistles, the Cappadocians developed an aesthetic that merged elements of both identity groups according to the recipient.[33] Subsequently, many features of New Testament letters and fourth-century epistles among *philoi* overlapped.

Authors of the fourth century, however, placed more valence on the body as an indicator of a person's disposition than had earlier Christian writers. The Cappadocians often used the metaphor of text as body, and specific parts of the body as conduits to the soul. Basil, for example, told Maximus the Philosopher that "words are images of the mind."[34] Consequently, Basil stated, he was able to know Maximus: "We have learned to know you from your letters, as truly as, according to the proverb, from the claw of the lion."[35] For Basil, the correspondence

---

[30] Colossians 2:5 (NIV). On absence, also Philippians 1:27, 2:12; II Corinthians 10:1, 11; 13:2, 10. On Paul's use of emotion in this regard, L. M. White, "Rhetoric and Reality in Galatians: Framing the Social Demands of Friendship," in *Early Christianity and Classical Culture: Comparative Studies in Honor of Abraham Malherbe*, eds. J. Fitzgerald, T. Olbricht, and L. M. White (Leiden: Brill, 2003), 307–50.

[31] I Corinthians 5:3 (NIV). See commentary in S. Stowers, *Letter Writing in Greco-Roman Antiquity* (Philadelphia: Westminster Press, 1986), 58–60. On the trope of absence as related to factionalism and unity in Corinth, see M. Mitchell, *Paul and the Rhetoric of Reconciliation: An Exegetical Investigation of the Language and Composition of I Corinthians* (Louisville, KY: John Knox, 1991), 151–71.

[32] B. Storin, *Self-Portrait in Three Colors: Gregory of Nazianzus's Epistolary Autobiography* (Oakland: University of California Press, 2019), 82–99, outlines several of these "clusters," based on identity, that determined his arrangement. For a correlation on the theme of separation and *amicitia* (friendship) in a fourth-century Roman poet, see D. Trout, *Paulinus of Nola: Life, Letters and Poems* (Berkeley: University of California Press, 1999), 198–218. Also White, *Christian*, 146–63.

[33] White, *Christian*, 19, points out that conceptions of both *koinonia* and classical *philia* were influenced by Pythagorean notions of community.

[34] Basil, *Ep.* 9 (Deferrari): Εἰκόνες ὄντως τῶν ψυχῶν εἰσὶν οἱ λόγοι. On images and memory, M. Carruthers, *The Craft of Thought: Meditation, Rhetoric, and the Making of Images, 400–1200* (Cambridge: Cambridge University Press, 1998), 60–77, 118–22.

[35] Basil, *Ep.* 9 (Deferrari). Here Basil refers to Lucian, *Hermotimus* 54, where Hermotimus recalls that the renowned sculptor Pheidias calculated the size of a lion merely by looking at the claw. See Deferrari, *Basil: Letters*, 1:93 n. 4.

constituted an intimate encounter.[36] Although he could not enjoy the physical person of Maximus, Basil did experience a connection to him through a material imprint of his thoughts. The text forms an extension of Maximus' body, like an appendage. The words are treated, therefore, as Maximus himself, and are treated with according honor. And responding to an epistle from Ambrose of Milan, Basil rejoiced that he could be united with the western bishop through letter, which allowed him to know the "beauty of the inner man."[37] It was easy to become acquainted through letter, Basil suggested, because words reflected a variety of discourse and an abundance of the heart.[38] An epistle paralleled actual presence, these specimens suggest, because it offered an avenue into the inner person through words that allowed the reader to penetrate the author's mind.[39] In addition to the influence of *paideia*, which exalted the body as an index of virtue, Basil also drew on scriptural considerations of conduct: "What we are in our letters when we are absent," the writer to the Corinthians wrote, "we will be in our actions when we are present."[40] This passage plays on the trope that an honorable person's words match his deeds; the implication being that the behavior of a person can be gauged in a letter.[41] Basil's sentiments to addressees such as Maximus and Ambrose, through written text, revealed his own inner self in an exchange of personal emblems. The text, therefore, animated the correspondent. As if summoning the person, reading the letter enabled a recipient to commune with the sender.

These letters contributed to the convergence of *aretē* in Basil and his addressees, as they publicized similarity of soul and mutual recognition. The soul was believed to be the prime site of manliness in an individual. It

---

[36] On simulating presence between friends see A. Wilcox, *The Gift of Correspondence in Classical Rome: Friendship in Cicero's Ad Familiares and Seneca's Moral Epistles* (Madison: University of Wisconsin Press, 2012), 133–51.

[37] Basil, *Ep.* 197 (Deferrari): τοῦ ἔσω ἀνθρώπου τὸ κάλλος.

[38] Matthew 12:34. See Wilcox, *Gift*, 155. Discussing Seneca's correspondence, Wilcox writes: "And when the text becomes a virtual person, then the self that resides in the body…gains by transference into the text a kind of invulnerability, stability, and immortality."

[39] On this point in the letters of Ambrose of Milan, see J. H. W. G. Liebeschuetz, "Letters of Ambrose of Milan (374–97), Books I–IX," in *Collecting Early Christian Letters: From the Apostle Paul to Late Antiquity*, eds. B. Neil and P. Allen (Cambridge: Cambridge University Press, 2015), 98.

[40] I Corinthians 10:11 (NIV).

[41] For example *Iliad* 9.442–3; Aristotle, *N.E.* 4. 6 (1126b 11); Plutarch, *Moralia* 328b.

housed the place from which courage, temperance, and justice issued.[42] A body directed by a noble soul, moreover, revealed the superiority of the individual and displayed the earmarks of the physical discipline that had nurtured its excellence. In the respected discipline of physiognomy, a component of *paideia*, individuals learned to ascertain a person's nature based on his/her bodily characteristics, especially the face.[43] Treatises on physiognomics dating as far back as the fourth century B.C. held that the body and soul followed the same form, and that subsequently corporeal features projected a person's disposition.[44] Many *pepaideumenoi* were raised to consider the body as a gauge of ἦθος (moral character), with corporeal members providing a channel to the soul. Polemon of Laodicea's compendium on physiognomy shows the continuity of a science that informed Second Sophistic literati, and later, late-antique intellectuals.[45] In the hypercompetitive culture of the Second Sophistic, a series of behavioral rules created a need for mutual inspection.[46] Polemon's *Physiognomy*, in part, met that demand by outlining the contours of moral strength as evidenced by appearance. It also constituted yet another avenue of besting an opponent by discrediting him. Manuals on physiognomics gave standards, moreover, for denigrating a target based on manifestations of deficient masculinity.[47] In the late-fourth century, however, the Cappadocians altered the use of rhetoric that impugned a man based on appearance. Instead they often employed similar categorizations but reoriented them into a source of praise by extolling bodily merits that gave evidence of *aretē*. Beauty of body corresponded to grandeur of soul and thus merited careful inspection. So whereas sophists of Polemon's day had focused on appearances of femininity in opponents

---

[42] For example Plato, *Laches* 192c; Hippocrates, *Airs, Water, Places* 24; Thucydides, *History* 2.40.3.

[43] G. Frank, *The Memory of the Eyes: Pilgrims to Living Saints in Late Antiquity* (Berkeley: University of California Press, 2000), 146–7, argues more specifically, that the eyes were considered the most decisive site in a cluster of signs because of its place atop the corporeal hierarchy; Martin, *Corinthian*, 18–19, 33–5.

[44] Pseudo-Aristotle, *Physiognomics* 805a, a fourth-century B.C. treatise falsely attributed to Aristotle.

[45] Polemon, *Physiognomy*.

[46] S. Swain, "Polemon's Physiognomy," in *Seeing the Face, Seeing the Soul: Polemon's Physiognomy from Classical Antiquity to Medieval Islam*, ed. S. Swain (Oxford: Oxford University Press, 2007), 131.

[47] M. Gleason, *Making Men: Sophists and Self-Presentation in Ancient Rome* (Princeton: Princeton University Press, 1995), 46–7.

114 Christianity and the Contest for Manhood

to show how they differed from such individuals, the Cappadocians lauded appearance in correspondents to accentuate similarities of manhood.

The Erotics of Epistolary Agōn

Based on the axis of soul and body, harmony between friends often resonated with sensuality. In some missives, the Cappadocians framed longing for the soul of a friend as an erotic pursuit. In these cases, bonding through the soul – the highest level on the corporeal spectrum – attested to the collective *aretē* of *agathoi*. Nazianzen, for example, wrote to Governor Olympius of Cappadocia, that "my yearning for your company burns hot," a panegyric of sorts indicating the governor's virtue and Gregory's need for his beneficence.[48] After receiving a letter from one correspondent, Basil offered up a similar encomium: "I had conceived with respect to your holy and guileless soul what I may call an amatory disposition (ἐρωτική)."[49] And Gregory of Nyssa recounted his correspondence with the rhetorician Stagirius as "making me burn with greater longing for your friendship."[50] These were statements of pleasure derived from the essence of the addressee and the letter representing that individual's spirit. Attraction to the virtuosity of such persons showed that the Cappadocians shared in their *aretē*.

In many epistles, the Cappadocians also used references to bodily movements to magnify *philia*. Nyssen, for instance, compared "letters of reconciliation" (γράμματα καταλλακτήρια) to "affectionate embraces" (ἀγαπητικαὶ περιπλοκαί);[51] for Nazianzen, a friend's epistle caused him to "run to, greet, and embrace" him.[52] And another time Nazianzen received a letter from Philagrius. The latter —as we saw in the last chapter—had been a companion of Gregory's brother Caesarius, who had died only two years earlier.[53] For Gregory, the missive activated memories of Caesarius and summoned his brother into his presence. "I embrace it [the letter] and kiss it (ἀσπάζομαι)," Gregory writes, "as if

[48] Greg. Naz., *Ep.* 142 (Storin 202): ὁ πόθος τῆς σῆς συντυχίας θερμός; on the relationship between Gregory and Olympius, see Van Dam, *Kingdom*, 84–6.
[49] Basil, *Ep.* 124 (Deferrari). The addressee, Theodorus, has not been identified.
[50] Greg. Ny., *Ep.* 28 (Silvas): πρὸς μείζονα πόθον τῆς φιλίας ἐκκαίουσα; on Stagirius see Chap. 1 n. 1.
[51] Greg. Ny., *Ep.* 16 (Silvas).
[52] Greg. Naz., *Ep.* 195 (Storin 82): προσδραμὼν καὶ περιπτυξάμενος καὶ τὰ ἐπιβατήρια προσφθεγξάμενος.
[53] Philagrius: see Chapter 1 n. 117.

I expect to see him [Caesarius], to be with him, to talk with him."⁵⁴ The letter had the effect of creating an image of his deceased brother. Gregory found the emotional impact so powerful, he suggests, that it warranted a response to match his ecstasy. In this case, he created a reply that augmented his emotion through a picture of corporeal action. The valuing of the body, as both an emblem and extension of the soul, enhanced the language that authors used to affirm friendship. In this paradigm the body no longer epitomized baseness or shame, but rather now pointed to that part of the person that both imbibed in and transcended the corporeal. The Cappadocians spoke of loving colleagues by using semantics of passion. These somatic allusions constituted a noble response because the affection was based on similitude of virtue.

The outcries of joy above punctuated fondness between correspondents through scenes replicating corporeal union. In scripting bodily pleasure as a metaphor for *philia*, the Cappadocians were inspired by texts that extolled sexual love, for example Song of Songs. "How beautiful you are and how pleasing, O love, with your delights!" the author of the song wrote.⁵⁵ Throughout this Old Testament text, the writer acted out a sequence of passionate exchanges between lovers.⁵⁶ The Cappadocians drew parallels from Origen's interpretation of this literature, which treated erotic love as allegorical, as "marriage" with the Divine.⁵⁷ In somewhat approximate manner, the Cappadocians treated epistles as embodied (textual) extensions of the forms (the person), with the letter thus allowing for spiritual/intellectual union between correspondents.⁵⁸ "Though so far separated in body," Basil likewise wrote to a fellow bishop, "[you] have united yourself to us by letter (συνῆψας ἡμῖν

---

⁵⁴ Greg. Naz., *Ep.* 30 (Storin 127).   ⁵⁵ Song of Songs 7:6.
⁵⁶ A. Louth, "Eros and Mysticism: Early Christian Interpretation of the Song of Songs," in *Jung and the Monotheists: Judaism, Christianity, and Islam*, ed. J. Ryce-Menuhim (London: Routledge, 1994), 241–54, gives an insightful discussion of Origen's and Nyssen's interpretations of Song of Songs.
⁵⁷ Origen, *On the Song of Songs*; Nyssen is largely indebted to Origen's work for his own homilies on Song of Songs. Nyssen did, however, differ in significant ways. For instance, as Richard Norris points out: "He [Gregory] does not share the Platonist distaste for that which is unlimited and therefore indefinable. As Plato himself at least hinted, Gregory sees the ultimate Good as that which is 'beyond being' and therefore as infinite, beyond intelligibility. Hence he does not perceive mutability or finitude simply as the source of evil." See R. Norris, *Gregory of Nyssa: Homilies on the Song of Songs* (Atlanta: SBL, 2012), xxxvii.
⁵⁸ Krueger, *Writing*, 133, states that texts could serve as substitutes for the body, without opposing the body. Krueger's chapter on textual bodies, 133–58, fleshes out "the materiality of texts rendering writing akin to bodies."

σεαυτὸν³ διὰ γράμματος), and embracing us...have engendered in our souls an ineffable affection."⁵⁹ The epistle substituted for Basil's colleague, thus approximating a semblance of mutual love.

Such expressions of love appeared in epistolary theory and across a variety of letters; it was a fondness based on a mutual interest between correspondents. "I love your beautiful and loving form, and am not ashamed of loving," read a sample letter from an undated epistolary treatise. "For the love of beauty is not shameful."⁶⁰ Models such as this influenced letter writers throughout the first four centuries. The apostle Paul, to cite one example, wrote to the church at Philippi, "God can testify how I long for (ἐπιποθῶ) all of you with the affection of Christ Jesus."⁶¹ Similar sentiments appeared frequently among contemporaries to the Cappadocians. Emperor Julian told the philosopher Iamblichus "I was yearning for thee and thou didst set ablaze my heart, already aflame with longing for thee."⁶² Julian likewise urged the sophist Priscus, "When can I see you again and embrace you?"⁶³ And Libanius praised a colleague's letters as "many and beautiful...and revealing that affection for me (ἐμὲ φίλτρον) flourishes in you."⁶⁴ In each case, these admissions of love indicated a common identity that endeared the addressee to the writer: for the New Testament writer, the community of believers at Philippi reflected the living body of Christ; for Julian, the wisdom of an extraordinary philosopher; and for Libanius, the eloquence of a fellow sophist. In each case, overtones of eroticism served a higher role of drawing the author to a worthy source of love.

For the Cappadocians, such passionate reactions applied to variant situations. On some occasions, the Cappadocians communicated the emotional intensity of a friendship through hyperbolized bodily response. These sentiments mimicked elements of eroticism, thus amplifying deeply rooted relationships based on *aretē* on some occasions, and in others, faith. Basil, for example, "shuddered at the sight of" a letter from one correspondent, and he considered another epistle "as water has been to us, poured upon for their mouths, oft times is to race-horses, when at high midday with greedy breath they suck in the dust of the middle course."⁶⁵ Nyssen told an addressee that "even the thorns (ἄκανθας) of your words

---

⁵⁹ Basil, *Ep.* 91 (Deferrari).
⁶⁰ Pseudo-Libanius, *Epistolary Styles* 91 (Malherbe, *AET*, 81).
⁶¹ Philippians 1:8 (NIV).
⁶² Julian, *Ep.* 77 (Stowers, 65): ἐγὼ δέ σε μαόμαν, ἂν δ' ἔφλεξας ἐμὰν φρένα καιομέναν πόθῳ.
⁶³ Julian, *Ep.* 5 (Wright).   ⁶⁴ Libanius, *Ep.* 1124 (Bradbury 137).
⁶⁵ Basil, *Ep.* 3. (Deferrari); Basil, *Ep.* 222 (Deferrari).

are a pleasure."⁶⁶ And Nyssen responded to another letter with exaggerated excitement: "You have roused (παρεκίνησας) even me, an old man, to skip about and yes, you stir those who do not know how to dance, to dance!"⁶⁷ This latter case shows Gregory praising the writer, the rhetorician Stagirius, for the wittiness of his composition, placing Gregory in the role of arbiter of eloquence and allowing him to project emotion through words. In these missives, the Cappadocians recounted their fulfillment as extreme bodily responses. Exaggerations of physical satisfaction enabled writers to share the joy of a relationship rooted in greatness of soul. Such literary displays corresponded to an elevation in the status of the body, in the fourth century, as an instrument for extending into the sphere of the incorporeal.

The use of erotic imagery seems to exemplify the Platonic theme of graduating from a lower realm of being to a higher plane. The inference according to this impression, would be that sentiments of sensual desire actually hold little value for the actual corporeality of the person; rather, physical appeal merely draws one to the most transcendent part of the physical person, the soul. As Jostein Børtnes points out in Nazianzen's oration on Basil, for example, the love shared by Gregory and Basil smacks of pure Platonism, insofar as *erōs* (ἔρως) appears in the *Symposium*, *Phaedrus*, and other works.⁶⁸ Yet Børtnes also observes that *erōs*, as portrayed in the *Symposium*, unites two individuals in a kind of mentor-protégé relationship. He states that Gregory and Basil's bond, by way of comparison, is construed in terms of equality and therefore cannot be fully attributed to Platonism.⁶⁹ Kathy Gaca offers another relevant point that shows the limitations of Platonic influence on the examples of *erōs* in friendship that we have cited. Gaca delineates between Platonic *erōs* and early Stoic *erōs*. A key difference, she asserts, comes from the Stoics' rejection of Plato's metaphysical dualism. Whereas Platonic *erōs* devalued physicality, in other words, the Stoics supported a "holistic conception of the human soul, body, and the cosmos at large."⁷⁰ Under the Stoic paradigm, the body holds a significantly higher value. Taking Gaca's taxonomy into account, it seems that the Cappadocians were heavily influenced by early Stoic theories of *erōs*, as much or more than Platonism.

---

⁶⁶ Greg. Ny., *Ep.* 28 (Silvas); Song of Songs 2:1–2.   ⁶⁷ Greg. Ny., *Ep.* 27 (Silvas).
⁶⁸ J. Børtnes, "Eros Transformed: Same-Sex Love and Divine Desire: Reflections on the Erotic Vocabulary in St. Gregory of Nazianzus's Speech on St. Basil the Great," in *Greek Biography*, 184.
⁶⁹ Børtnes, "Eros," 186–7.
⁷⁰ K. Gaca, *The Making of Fornication: Eros, Ethics, and Political Reform in Greek Philosophy and Early Christianity* (Berkeley: University of California Press, 2003), 63–4.

The basis for *erōs* in these letters, moreover, must also be understood as part of an *agōn* that correlated supremacy of character to corporeal sublimity. The Cappadocians' emphasis on cultivating *aretē* in relation to the body comes across repeatedly in letters based on *philia*. They proposed an aesthetic of manhood derived from the tradition of *paideia* in the Second Sophistic, in which writers recalled ancient authors who celebrated beauty (κάλλος) in men as a mark of aristocracy, bravery, and overall excellence. Dio Chrysostom, for example, often coupled beauty of body and the attributes that made up ideal manhood.[71] "For it is not only virtue (ἀρετή) that is increased by commendation," he writes, "but so is beauty (κάλλος) likewise by those who honour and revere it."[72] Dio furthermore has one of his subjects calling a man fortunate for "possessing beauty," which he applauds chiefly, listing only secondarily, and by association, acquisition of courage (ἀνδρεία), physical strength (ἰσχύς), and temperance (σωφροσύνη).[73] For Dio, a man's beauty confirms his excellence. Listing his virtues merely adds further illustration. Such physical comeliness was most evident, for Dio, in athletes.[74] In classical Greece, athletes and soldiers exemplified contestants in *agōnes* among the best men. It comes as no surprise, then, that fourth-century authors identifying with representations from that era alluded to attributes of the body that directed focus to the soul. These individuals considered *philia* as a testimonial of an aesthetic that advertised their place in the social and political hierarchy. The Cappadocians thus applied rhetoric of the body as a portal to reach their absent *philoi*. Or more accurately, they used corporeal features as a nucleus for the *aretē* that they were admiring in friends, and by extension, themselves. In the following illustrations, the Cappadocians repeatedly turned to sight, hearing, and touch as avenues for acclaiming this congruity.

The Eyes

"Beauty addresses itself chiefly to sight," stated third-century philosopher Plotinus.[75] This characterization of vision was consistent with other hierarchical orderings of the senses. Plato, for example, specified the eyes

---

[71] For example Dio Chrysostom, *Ors.* 21, 28, 29.
[72] Dio Chrysostom, *Or.* 21.2 (Cohoon).   [73] Dio Chrysostom, *Or.* 28.12 (Cohoon).
[74] See especially, Dio Chrysostom, *Ors.* 28 and 29; S. Remijsen, *The End of Greek Athletics in Late Antiquity* (Cambridge: Cambridge University Press, 2015), makes this point clearly, 255–8.
[75] Plotinus, *Enneads* 1.6.1 (MacKenna): τὸ καλόν ἐστι μὲν ἐν ὄψει πλεῖστον.

as the keenest faculty, as the sense most capable of perceiving beauty.[76] In addition, Plato named the eyes as the first organ fashioned by the gods, and set upon the face, at the top of the body, in an honorary position as a vessel to the soul.[77] Aristotle meanwhile attributed the stirrings of *erōs* – often coupled with pursuit of beauty (κάλλος) – to the pleasure derived from sight.[78] And Aristotle also treated vision as first among the other senses suitable for perceiving the soul.[79] The eyes, moreover, triggered the imagination so that the written word could be translated into another corporeal experience like taste or touch. In this way, vision commanded the other sources of sense perception.[80] To speak of seeing the soul of an individual implied an intimate act that spoke highly of the object viewed; and that closely approximated actual presence.

In a classification that privileged eyesight, the Cappadocians spoke of epistles as canvasses on which to observe the souls of correspondents. Basil, for example, often talked of letters as reflections of his addressees.[81] He told Ascholius, Bishop of Thessalonica, that he could "observe even your very soul reflected by your words as by a mirror."[82] Basil likewise discerned Count Jovinus, noting that "no painter can grasp so accurately the characteristics of the body as words can portray the secrets of the soul (τῆς ψυχῆς τὰ ἀπόρρητα)."[83] The epistle from Jovinus revealed to Basil the count's "soundness of character (τὸ τοῦ ἤθους εὐσταθές), genuineness of worth, and integrity of mind."[84] Jovinus' letter, that is, represented an aura of this Roman official. "In truth words are images of the mind," Basil wrote in another missive.[85] In these cases, Basil considered the text in the epistle as a visual metonym for the author. Through reading their writing, that is, he enjoyed access to their souls in a manner synonymous with viewing them with his own eyes.

---

[76] Plato, *Phaedrus* 250d; D. Konstan, *Beauty: The Fortunes of an Ancient Greek Idea* (Oxford: Oxford University Press, 2014), 70, discussing this passage, reflects that for Plato, it was "sight that triggers our recollection of the beautiful."

[77] Plato, *Timaeus* 45b.

[78] Aristotle, *N.E.* 1167a3–4. On discussion of *erōs* as connected with *kallos*, Konstan, *Beauty*, 67.

[79] Aristotle, *On the Soul* 2.7; on the privileged place of sight, Frank, *Memory*, 122–3.

[80] Miller, *Corporeal*, 102–4.

[81] R. Van Dam, *Families and Friends in Late Roman Cappadocia* (Philadelphia: University of Pennsylvania Press, 2003), 133–8.

[82] Basil, *Ep.* 165 (Deferrari): σου καθορᾶν τὴν ψυχήν, οἷον δι' ἐσόπτρου τινὸς τῶν λόγων διαφαινομένην.

[83] Basil, *Ep.* 163 (Deferrari).   [84] Basil, *Ep.* 163 (Deferrari).

[85] Basil, *Ep.* 9 (Deferrari): εἰκόνες ὄντως τῶν ψυχῶν εἰσὶν οἱ λόγοι.

The Cappadocians were well-versed in replicating the presence of a person through the trope of viewing them, a rhetorical commonplace they shared with earlier and contemporary literati. "If pictures of our absent friends are pleasing to us..." the first-century Stoic Seneca wrote, "how much more pleasant is a letter, which brings us real traces, real evidences, of an absent friend!"[86] Libanius, meanwhile, believed that effective epistolary composition should allow an addressee to imagine the author so well that he could see him gesturing, joking, and laughing as if he were next to him.[87] And Emperor Julian presented a lengthy excursus to one official about the art of crafting semblance of a subject. He compared the image he received from a letter to the imprint placed on small seals placed on official documents.[88] Julian was referring to the practice of using the impression of a person on a seal to authenticate identity. His point was that the epistolary text was so well conceived that it denoted the author's nature. Each of these writers elevated the text to equivalence with the body, with sight providing a window into the inner person. Such awareness correlates to what Patricia Cox Miller calls "visceral seeing," where corporeality contributed to visual imagination that was based on evoking emotional response.[89] The authors above credited their colleagues, who revealed themselves to a select audience through texts that suggested visual encounter. The recipients of these letters also recommended themselves as having the requisite ability to see, in the text, the surplus meaning intended by their comrades.

In order to accentuate a visual aesthetic, the Cappadocians also correlated textual embodiment to pleasing stimuli from nature.[90] Nyssen, for

---

[86] Seneca, *Moral Epistles* 40.1 (Malherbe, *AET*, 29): "Si imagines nobis amicorum absentium iucundae sunt, quae memoriam renovant et desiderium falso atque inani solacio levant, quanto iucundiores sunt litterae, quae vera amici absentis vestigia, veras notas."

[87] Libanius, *Ep.* 354 (Bradbury, 117). Libanius also produced his own handbook on rhetorical exercises, which included discussion and models of *ekphrasis*: Libanius, *Progymnasmata*.

[88] Julian, *Ep.* 67. On camaraderie with a distant figure through portraiture see R. Cribiore, "Vying with Aristides in the Fourth Century," in *Aelius Aristides between Greece, Rome, and the Gods*, eds. W. V. Harris and B. Holmes (Leiden: Brill, 2009), 266. Cribiore discusses Libanius' *Epistle* 1534 (Norman 143), where the author appeared to commune with fifth-century B.C. rhetorician Aristides. Libanius "depicted himself as sitting beside a portrait of the orator [Aristides] while reading his works, as if he were trying to capture the true essence of the writer and the man by taking in both his features and his words."

[89] Miller, *Corporeal*, 14.

[90] R. R. Ruether, *Gregory of Nazianzus: Rhetor and Philosopher* (Oxford: Clarendon Press, 1969), 98–103, on Nazianzen's use of nature imagery. Ruether argued that Gregory

example, accentuated the appeal of a friend's words by saying that, like a rose, it elicited pleasure for "lovers of the beautiful (φιλοκάλοι)."[91] Gregory used pleasing imagery, the hue of a rose, to praise his colleague for his epistle, which "contained the flower of your discourse."[92] Gregory compared his friend's letter – an embodiment of the man – to the delight of viewing flora. The rose was a privileged flower in the ancient Greco-Roman world. It was an oft-used motif in literature and artistry to indicate dazzle, color, and brilliance, while also serving as the subject of festivals associated with death and rebirth.[93] The appeal stands out in Old Testament literature as well, where the "Rose of Sharon" evoked erotic allure between lovers in Song of Songs.[94] Gregory's point that his colleague's letter appealed to "lovers of the beautiful" insinuated that the text demanded a standard of high taste in readers to fully appreciate its merits.

Such imagery of the natural world worked particularly well to convey emotions because, like the body, it provided an allusion to the inner person through a material medium, one that was both relatable and unifying. Analogizing elements of nature to an individual's words further accentuated the impact of epistolary performance. Basil told a fellow bishop on one occasion that his letter prompted the same feelings as sailors caught in a storm at sea would feel if they glimpsed a beacon fire on the shore.[95] In the ancient Mediterranean, travel by sea was perilous and storms were notoriously frequent. Basil was as gratified to see his colleague as if he were an imperiled mariner who found a pathway to safety through firelight. This picture of rough waters would have resonated with the correspondent, along with the excitement of the shore light to which Basil likened his letter. The depiction also brought to mind the recurring use of brightness as a New Testament metaphor, where light (φῶς) revealed the glory of God, contrasted goodness with the darkness of evil, and unveiled the mystery of Christ.[96] The fact that meaning came only through light ushering from the divine indicated extraordinary quality. Through its luminosity, individuals were made privy to something

---

placed a premium on natural beauty, but only "apart from man and his works." He held a high regard for nature, in other words, "no matter how negative he may be about the material part of man's nature," 98.

[91] Greg. Ny., *Ep.* 28 (Silvas).
[92] Greg. Ny., *Ep.* 28 (Silvas): τὸ μὲν ἄνθος εἶχε τοῦ λόγου τοῦ σοῦ.
[93] Miller, *Corporeal*, 73–4.   [94] Song of Songs 2:1.   [95] Basil, *Ep.* 100.
[96] For example Matthew 5:14, John 12:46, I Cor. 4:5, Ephesians 5:8, 13.

otherwise hidden. Basil insinuates that his correspondent's words, too, were uncommon and pregnant with purpose.

Metaphors of light and of mirrors may also have related to implications of the visionary exchange between friends. Nyssen told fellow bishop Otreius, that "in the sweetness of your letter I beheld the most distinct image of your truly beautiful soul."[97] Gregory then added, however, that this experience did not satisfy him. "Our constant participation in the sun does not blunt our longing to behold it," he explained.[98] Gregory's point was that seeing Otreius constituted an ongoing activity, that "participation" could not be satisfied by a single occasion. The mechanics of eyesight, as many ancient philosophers theorized, involved direct contact between the eye and the object under view. A visual stream enabled a ray to extend from the eye to the object, whereby the object then reflected the light, returning an image of itself back to the sender.[99] An individual, that is, *reached out* through the eyes to connect with another person, thus bringing the likeness of that person back to his brain.

Such conceptions inferred vision between individuals as active and reciprocal, elements that also signified the nobility of the friendship. "The eyes have the courage to reach out to visible objects and do not wait to be acted on by them, but anticipate the meeting," stated Philo of Alexandria, a first-century Hellenistic Jewish philosopher.[100] In the way that theorists described this operation, the eyes issued kinetic motion. To look closely at a person of equal standing was tantamount to engaging him in a confrontation, with the potential of conferring status on him. Vision engineered an active gesture, that subsequently provoked a friend to participate in the face-to-face meeting where he *met* the gaze of his counterpart. As Georgia Frank has observed about theories of vision in late antiquity, "the most enduring theories were those that incorporated notions of contact, penetration, and even collision."[101] In the context of one friend laying eyes on another, the operation of eyesight enabled one to observe the soul of his friend, who in turn would match the deed with his own gaze. Unlike viewing between persons of unequal rank – where gaze could denote objectification – eyesight between friends accentuated

---

[97] Greg. Ny., *Ep.* 18 (Silvas): "sweetness," ἐν τῇ τῶν γραμμάτων γλυκύτητι.
[98] Greg. Ny., *Ep.* 18 (Silvas).
[99] Plato, *Timaeus* 45c (Zeyl): "Like makes contact with like and coalesces with it to make up a single homogenous body...This happens wherever the internal fire strikes and presses against an external object it has connected with."
[100] Philo, *On Abraham* 150 (Colson).   [101] Frank, *Memory*, 125.

the dignity of each. When the Cappadocians stated that they were discerning a friend through their eyes, they were choreographing sensory rhetoric that matched the temperament of one friend to the other. In an *agōn* of the eyes, the viewer acknowledged forcefulness in his coeval and prompted him to reply with his own assertion of visual meeting.

Visual imagery, moreover, was not limited to expressions of presence among separated friends. In addition to simulating encounters through a rhetoric of vision, the Cappadocians also commended and challenged friends through use of *ekphrasis* (ἔκφρασις), a literary method of using physical description to make the reader or listener able to see a place, an action, a work of art, or a person.[102] This technique had been taught to aspiring orators during the Second Sophistic as a means of engrossing audiences through dramatic effect. Renowned teachers such as Aelius Theon (first century), Hermogenes of Tarsus (late second century), Aphthonius (fourth century), and Menander Rhetor (fourth century) prescribed the use of visualization in writing and speaking so that authors could regulate the feelings of readers or listeners.[103] In *ekphrasis*, speakers and writers learned to make the subject matter vivid (ἐνάργεια) for the audience.[104] The goal was not merely to make the picture seem real, however, but to produce an emotional impact by involving the listener.[105]

In letters exchanged with *pepaideumenoi*, the Cappadocians created *ekphraseis* to regale, to provoke, and to give testament of the correspondent's own erudition. Nyssen, for example, composed illustrations of subjects as diverse as landscapes and architecture.[106] "I have also apprehended many things," Gregory writes, "through the word-pictures (λόγοι ὑπογραφαῖ) in the accounts of the ancient writers."[107] In this letter to his friend Adelphius, Gregory established the power of "word-pictures," as

---

[102] R. Webb, *Ekphrasis, Imagination and Persuasion in Ancient Rhetorical Theory and Practice* (Farnham: Ashgate, 2009), 61–86, on the variety of possible subjects depicted through *ekphrasis*.
[103] Aelius Theon, *Progymnasmata* 118–80, Hermogenes, *Progymnasmata* 22–3, Aphthonius, *Progymnasmata* 117–9, and Menander Rhetor, 1.365, 2.188–23.
[104] Aelius Theon, *Progymnasmata* 118.1.7.
[105] Webb, *Ekphrasis*, 87–106, for an excellent discussion of *enargeia* as an exercise for managing emotions.
[106] V. Limberis, *Architects of Piety: The Cappadocian Fathers and the Cult of the Martyrs* (Oxford: Oxford University Press, 2011), 53–96, discusses in great depth several examples of the Cappadocians using *ekphrasis* in variant contexts.
[107] Greg. Ny., *Ep.* 20 (Silvas).

an aid for assessing the beauty (καλός or κάλλος) of his friend's home.[108] As he continued in this long letter, through vibrant detail of numerous features of Adelphius' domicile, Gregory complimented his colleague's home town and villa at Venota in Cappadocia.[109] It was a gesture of Gregory's fondness for his addressee. In praising the details of the estate, Gregory was also applauding the sophistication of Adelphius. The physical structures and surroundings illustrated the man's greatness.[110] Such intricate representations held that both author and addressee were cultured viewers who could decode the subtle meaning embedded in narrative description. The dynamics of gazing on a subject of splendor held that educated viewing required an individual not only to see beauty, but to recognize and appropriately respond to it. Only persons of refinement, who had undergone the exertions that nurtured a shared aesthetic, could adequately write about and appreciate true beauty. Inviting an addressee to "see" through one's own eyes, then, conferred status on both author and recipient; the author by showing an ability to draw his friend into the scene, and the recipient by intimating that he knew how to respond to the prompt.[111]

Along with exhibiting sensory creativity, an *ekphrasis* publicized friendship and its sense of reciprocity. In one case, for example, Basil petitioned his countryman Martinianus to come to the aid of Cappadocia. In the intercession, Basil staged scenes of physical duress as part of a literary display based on corporeal detail. Martinianus was a retired nobleman from Cappadocia who had served at the court of Emperor Valens, the current ruler.[112] The ostensible purpose of the letter, from the early 370s, was to convince Martinianus to use his influence to

---

[108] On a similar practice in Nazianzen's orations, J. Børtnes, "Rhetoric and Mental Images in Gregory," in *Gregory of Nazianzus: Images and Reflections*, eds. J. Børtnes and T. Hägg (Copenhagen: Museum Tusculanum, 2006), 37–57.

[109] A. Silvas, *Gregory of Nyssa: The Letters*, VCS 83 (Leiden: Brill, 2006), 182–4 for discussion of this site and its geographic and historical significance.

[110] Limberis, *Architects*, 66–8, specifies Nazianzen's *ekphrasis* on his father's church (Greg. Naz., *Or.* 18.39), in the funeral oration for his father, as a prime example of his ability to associate the beauty of description with the virtue of a person (his father).

[111] M. Ludlow, *Art, Craft, and Theology in Fourth-Century Christian Authors* (Oxford: Oxford University Press, 2020), 61; S. Goldhill, "The Erotic Eye: Visual Stimulation and Cultural Conflict," in *Being Greek Under Rome: Cultural Identity, the Second Sophistic and the Development of Empire*, ed. S. Goldhill (New York: Cambridge University Press, 2001), 157–67, alerts readers to the social hierarchies involved in aesthetics.

[112] Martinianus: Van Dam, *Kingdom*, 120–1 and *PLRE* 1:564. And see Nazianzen's epitaphs on him, 104–17, in *Greek Anthology*, vol. 2, ed. W. R. Paton (Cambridge: Harvard University Press, 1970), 104–17.

counteract Valens' decision to divide Cappadocia into two smaller provinces: Cappadocia Prima (east) and Cappadocia Secunda (west).[113] Martinianus' homeland, Basil wrote, was urging him (Basil) to protect her from this harmful agenda, which he likened to incompetent physicians who made wounds worse because of their ineptitude. As a maltreated patient, Cappadocia had "become ill under such dissection" and was "weakened by sickness."[114] The body as a metaphor for society was a rhetorical device with deep roots in classical rhetoric.[115] The author of I Corinthians used this commonplace when he put forward the body as an analogy for the church, with its diversity of members (and spiritual gifts).[116] Basil likewise integrated a mythological illustration into his corporeal picture, stating "that like Pentheus, she has been torn asunder by veritable Maenads, demons in fact."[117] In classic lore, King Pentheus of Thebes had opposed and dishonored the god Dionysus. The god of wine's powerful and ecstatic female followers (the Maenads) subsequently tore apart Pentheus limb by limb.[118] The picture of the monarch, dismembered in a heinous frenzy, presented Martinianus with a vibrant picture of upheaval in Cappadocia.[119]

Basil embellished the agony to heighten the reader/s' awareness of the emperor's harmful policy. The current capital of Caesarea, under the arrangement, would be left as the only city in its new province (Prima). As metropolitan bishop of Caesarea, Basil was losing significant political and ecclesiastical authority because another metropolitan bishop would now serve over Secunda. Moreover, the partition meant that several of the *decurions* (civic councilors) of Caesarea would be transferred to the new province.[120] These local notables were the financial patrons of Caesarea and their relocation would have been an economic blow to Basil, who helped to oversee resources provided by them.[121] A calculated depiction

---

[113] Van Dam, *Kingdom*, 28–38, for a detailed overview of this policy, its consequences, and the ultimate compromise that Valens decided; also, T. Kopecek, "The Cappadocian Fathers and Civic Patriotism," *CH* 43 (1974), 293–303.
[114] Basil, *Ep.* 74 (Deferrari).   [115] Martin, *Corinthian Body*, 92–6.
[116] I Corinthians 12:12–31.   [117] Basil, *Ep.* 74 (Deferrari).
[118] Euripides, *Bacchae* 1290–1404.
[119] Nazianzen uses the *topos* of the Maenads in much fuller description, in *Or.* 35, as a depiction of unruly heretics. In that instance, he emphasizes the effeminacy of their behavior and he includes the presence of an effete man dancing in their midst. See Ruether, *Gregory*, 101–2.
[120] Van Dam, *Kingdom*, 28–30.
[121] On administration at the local level, S. Métivier, *La Cappadoce (IVe–Vie Siècle): une histoire provinciale de l'empire romain d'Orient* (Paris: Publications de la Sorbonne,

of bodily suffering was meant to stir Martinianus to take action against the measure.[122] A graphic account of misery for the whole of the community dramatized the issue and called Martinianus to action. The overall illustration indicated apocalyptic-like devastation.

Basil scripted a disease-riddled form, moreover, to humanize the deleterious effects of the administrative change. Wishing that he (Martinianus) could have seen "with your own eyes the melancholy sight (σκυθρωπά)," Basil played the proxy for his friend, re-creating the scene in a manner that would make Martinianus experience the outrage.[123] If Martinianus could witness the disaster, Basil stated, he would protest the tragedy, "stirred by the very vividness of what you had seen."[124] Martinianus was compelled to share the lively imagery with sympathetic friends and, if advocating for Basil, with imperial officials who had access to Valens. Basil punctuated these bodily images by pleading with Martinianus "not to ignore our country when she has fallen to her knees (προσκυνέω)."[125] The collective suffering of Cappadocia was manifested as a supplicant prostrating himself or herself before a superior, an act connoting submission and respect. This ceremony was meant to provoke Martinianus to act in loyalty, both as friend and countryman, appealing to his duty to protect his motherland. By personifying Cappadocia as a humble petitioner, Basil also presented his friend with the golden opportunity to come to its defense. The letters he sent would have been copied and circulated or posted. By appealing to Martinianus through a creative display, Basil offered a tribute to his colleague's status both as a cultured viewer and a patron – a man endowed with the ability to bring relief to Caesarea. Martinianus was expected to savor the artistic touch that Basil put into this illustration; to comprehend that he was being credited as a connoisseur of visual rhetoric. Basil enhanced his own status through imagination and eloquence while also creating a platform for his friend to showcase his merits.

In orchestrating visual encounters with friends and bringing to life places and events through ocular imagination, the Cappadocians established their

---

2005), 94–108; and on duties of decurions, A. H. M. Jones, *The Later Roman Empire, 284–602: A Social, Economic, and Administrative Survey* (Oxford: Basil Blackwell, 1964), 724–31.

[122] Basil, *Ep.* 74 (my translation): "For the danger is not marginal," Basil writes, "since with the removal of the most powerful members, the whole body will fall."

[123] Basil, *Ep.* 74 (Deferrari).

[124] Basil, *Ep.* 74: ἀπ' αὐτῆς τῆς ἐναργείας[7] τῶν ὁρωμένων συγκινηθείς.

[125] Basil, *Ep.* 74 (Deferrari).

facility at governing the most highly esteemed of the senses. At the top of the hierarchy of instruments of perception, the eyes provided individuals reliable images ranging from nobility within the souls of friends, to beauty in nature, to catastrophic circumstances besetting an urban community. By deploying the dynamism of sight, the Cappadocians asserted control over readers' emotions, an effect for which *ekphrasis* was particularly compelling. Regarded as highly rhetorical pieces, the letters were designed to evoke a real visceral response, whether affirming friendship or calling attention to a plight that only the reader could remedy. The brilliance of such creative writing should not detract from the reality that in the ancient world such powerful conveyances, based on age-old commonplaces, held significant affect for intended audiences.[126] These literary exhibitions befitted *pepaideumenoi*, the addressees of these letters who were regarded highly enough to be counted worthy both of appreciating the literary craftsmanship and replying with a comparable oeuvre.

The Voice

In the preceding letter, Basil played not only on visual effect, but also on aural sensations as he equipped readers to imagine the people's need for redemption.[127] He wrote: "For the gatherings of old, the orations, the conversations of learned men in the market-place, and all that formerly made our city famous, have left us."[128] This lamentation closely followed a topos used by second-century orator Aelius Aristides.[129] Aristides had written to emperors Marcus Aurelius and Lucius Commodus seeking assistance for the city of Smyrna after destruction by earthquake in 178. Basil was echoing for Caesarea the regrets fashioned by Aristides, that his

---

[126] Ruether, *Gregory*, 96, regarding the pitfall of discounting the author's feelings in a rhetorical work: "The mind-sets of a culture do not merely affect the window-dressings of its ideas; they affect the way the people in the culture think, and...experience things."
[127] S. A. Rebillard, "Let Me Cry Out in Tragic Voice: Gregory of Nazianzus' Use of Tragic Pathos," Paper Presentation at the International Conference on Patristic Studies, Oxford, 2015, on poetic use of the voice to convey emotion.
[128] Basil, *Ep.* 74 (Deferrari).
[129] Aelius Aristides, *Or.* 19.3. (Behr): "The harbor, which you saw, has closed its eyes, the beauty of the market place is gone, the adornments of the streets have disappeared, the gymnasiums together with the men and boys who used them are destroyed, some of the temples have fallen, some sunk beneath the ground. That which was the most beautiful city to behold and bore the title of 'fair' among all mankind has been made the most unpleasant of spectacles, a hill of ruin and corpses."

city retained little semblance of its former greatness. The mark of a respectable polis was a thriving *agora*, a public sphere where declamations educated, entertained, and celebrated the community's collective values. These recitals, along with discussions among wise men, presented the din of a healthy citizen body and the cornerstone of collective masculinity. But now, Basil said, "we hear but one sound – the voices of men demanding payment and those being confronted for debt, of men lacerated with whips."[130] This juxtaposition was striking: oratorical performances and philosophic dialogues before the division; with chaos and cries of pain afterwards. The divergence in sounds emanating from the polis parodied the binary between the Greek words for sound: φωνή (an articulate utterance; voice) in the former case, and ψόφος (an indiscernible sound; noise) in the latter. Basil thus rendered the declining conditions and disorderliness of the city to the reader through auditory metaphors. Yet hope remained for Caesarea (and Cappadocia). Basil called on Martinianus to assert his influence with the imperial court, "with that voice of yours and with that righteous boldness of speech (παρρησία)."[131] The bishop caricatured his addressee as the embodiment of force, of civility, and of manhood. He was a living antidote to a provincial body whose lowly state had been brought into focus by the deterioration of its orality. And the strength of his own voice held the key. Basil summoned his colleague as a mouthpiece to deliver his homeland from barbarity.

Basil's portrayal of Martinianus' speech as salvation for Caesarea provides an example of the Cappadocians participating in a community of *aretē* through rhetorical approximations of the voice. The Cappadocians made repeated affirmations of *philia* based on references to speech. In so doing, they drew attention to the corporeal feature that *pepaideumenoi* correlated most closely to manhood and to the soul. In philosophy and rhetoric, the voice served as an indication of the essence of the speaker. "For as a rill of water reveals its own true source," Basil stated, "so the nature of one's speech shows the character (χαρακτηρίζει) of the heart that brought it forth."[132] Basil here reflects the designation of a person's words as a gateway to the soul, a tenet expressed in texts such

---

[130] Basil, *Ep.* 74 (modified translation of Deferrari). [131] Basil, *Ep.* 74. (Deferrari).
[132] Basil, *Ep.* 134 (Deferrari). Treatises on physiognomics were also used to determine gender traits in an individual by evaluating the voice. See Pseudo-Aristotle, *Physiognomics* 807a.

as Plato's *Phaedrus*.[133] In *Lives of the Philosophers*, likewise, third-century biographer Diogenes Laertius depicted Pythagoras' unorthodox teaching method, whereby the sixth-century B.C. philosopher taught his disciples for five years behind a veil, making them listen to his speeches without ever seeing their teacher.[134] Through this practice, the students were familiarized with their master's disembodied voice, which took on its own corporeal form for the pupils, and came to represent the person of Pythagoras.[135] Meanwhile the Old and New Testaments abound with passages where the presence of Yahweh is made known by his voice: for example, when speaking to Moses from out of a burning bush and on Mount Sinai; talking from a cloud, when acknowledging Jesus as his Son in the Transfiguration account; and reaching down to the apostle Peter, from the heavens, to instruct on his mission.[136] In these cases, the essence and presence of God were authenticated through his spoken word. The voice of God, moreover, is set forth in the scriptures as an indication of inherent power: thundering over mighty waters, breaking the cedars of Lebanon, shaking deserts, and striking with lightning.[137] Through such renderings of the voice that controlled naturalistic phenomena, humanity was able to experience the awe of divine Yahweh.

Nazianzen likewise recognizes the potency of the spoken word in a letter to Themistius, one of the most prominent orators of the late fourth century. "The spear distinguishes the Spartans," Gregory writes, "the shoulder blade the Peloponnese, eloquence the great Themistius."[138] The Spartans were noted for their military prowess; the mythical king Pelops was famed for his ivory shoulder, fashioned by the gods; and here, Themistius is discernible because of his fluency. In a nod to Themistius' manhood – comparing his identifying trait to martial and athletic superiority – Gregory recognizes him through his command of words. *Pepaideumenoi* were trained to believe that the delivery of a speech reflected their inner person.[139] In the case of Themistius, his diction

---

[133] Plato, *Phaedrus* 270–3. [134] Diogenes Laertius, *Lives of the Philosophers* 8.15.
[135] J. Porter, "Rhetoric, Aesthetics, and the Voice," in *Cambridge Companion to Ancient Rhetoric*, ed. E. Gunderson (Cambridge: Cambridge University Press, 2009), 93.
[136] Bush and Mount Sinai, Exodus 3:4 and 19:19; Transfiguration, Matthew 17:5; Peter, Acts 10:13–15, 11:7–9.
[137] Psalm 29:3–8; on thunder, also I Samuel 2:10, Job 37:5, and Psalms 77:18, 104:7.
[138] Greg. Naz., *Ep.* 38 (Storin 152). Themistius: Storin, *Gregory*, 39; H–M, 160; *PLRE* 1:889–94; R. Penella, *The Private Orations of Themistius* (Berkeley: University of California Press, 2000), 1–45.
[139] E. Gunderson, *Staging Masculinity: The Rhetoric of Performance in the Roman World* (Ann Arbor: University of Michigan Press, 2000), 63–4, discusses first-century

confirmed his *aretē*. The congruence of speech and identity was further reinforced from teachings in the gospels. Jesus warned that speech (*logos*) ushers out of the heart of a person.[140] Jesus further illustrated speech as an overflow of the heart.[141] This concept applied to epistolary composition as well, where text simulated the voice. Spoken words, now imprinted on paper, made epistles an ideal conduit both for self-representation and for substituting for dialogue in person.[142]

According to Basil, individuals deprived of meeting face-to-face could still enjoy "conversation by letter (γράμματος ὁμιλίαν), whereby it is possible to perceive, not only the physical appearance, but the disposition of the soul itself."[143] The text of an epistle served as a record of the voice, an image of speech.[144] A nexus between author's voice and the message came to mind as the recipient of the letter read the text aloud, the standard practice of reading in the ancient world. In an almost mystical way, the words of the epistle conjured up the author (an effect not fully appreciable in our modern world that enjoys live conversations by phone and face-to-face interactions through the Internet). On another occasion, Nazianzen bemoaned separation from the company of his friend Sophronius, compelling him to write so that Gregory could find satiety through "the shadow of a conversation in a letter."[145] Here "shadow" (σκία) implied presence, immediacy, deriving from Sophronius' (potential) written words.[146] Elsewhere, in his autobiographical poetry, Gregory

---

rhetorician Quintilian's teachings that the soul both disciplined the body and was made manifest in the body.

[140] Matthew 16:18.   [141] Luke 6:45.

[142] This was a common epistolary theory among *pepaideumenoi*. "What could give me greater pleasure, failing a tête-à-tête talk with you," Cicero wrote to a friend, "than either to write to you, or to read a letter of yours?" (*Letters to Friends* 12.30.1; trans. in Malherbe, *AET*, 27). Likewise, fourth-century rhetorician Julius Victor counseled to write "as though you were conversing with the person present." (*Art of Rhetoric* 27; trans. Malherbe, *AET*, 65).

[143] Basil, *Ep*. 220 (modification of Deferrari). Liebeschuetz, "Letters," 98, on this trope in the letters of Ambrose of Milan.

[144] J. Porter, *The Origins of Aesthetic Thought in Ancient Greece* (Cambridge: Cambridge University Press, 2010), 335–54, calls the practice of "vocal writing" a prominent issue for ancient Greek writers, who went to great lengths to approximate the flow of speech when composing text.

[145] Greg. Naz., *Ep*. 93 (Storin 98): σκιὰν ὁμιλίας τὴν ἐν τοῖς γράμμασιν. Sophronius: Storin, *Gregory*, 38; Van Dam, *Families*, 141–7.

[146] Gregory of Nyssa used similar terminology, the "shadow" of the Incarnate Word, in a homily on Song of Songs. He referred to the passage Song of Songs 2:3 where the Beloved rests in the shade – the presence – of her Lover (Greg. Ny., *Homilies on Song of Songs* 2:3b). On the use of "shadow," see Norris, "Gregory," li.

consistently used the metaphor of the tongue to represent the totality of the physical self. Gregory portrayed the voice as combining within itself the physical and spiritual elements of a person.[147] For Gregory, access to the voice – through oral or written medium – provided reality and intimacy with absent friends. The tongue served as an entrée into the inner realm of an individual, as well as the nodal point of the body and the soul. Among *pepaideumenoi*, who were trained to consider the voice as the fulcrum of their manhood, letters replicating speech solidified oneness between author and addressee.

Whereas representations of the voice heightened awareness of friendship, the silencing of this instrument suggested a possible barrier between individuals. This fact may account for apparent misunderstandings in a series of epistolary exchanges between Nazianzen and correspondents in spring 382. Gregory had imposed on himself a period of silence during Lent that spring, a project that he categorized as an ascetic endeavor.[148] Gregory responded to friends who apparently were questioning his announced program of silence. For these associates, the decision to suppress speech may have suggested that Gregory was insinuating a fissure in their friendship; such was the symbolism of the voice between *philoi*.[149] Against concerns from both friends and criticisms from adversaries, Gregory defended his ascetic regime, thus assuaging anxiety that he was compromising *philia*.

To one friend, for example, Gregory contrasted his silence to the frivolous speech of the masses. He analogized this disparity to the beautiful singing of a swan, who reserves its melodies for its own kind, against the indiscriminate chirping of swallows, who sing for anyone. Gregory acknowledges his correspondent's own "sweet-sounding tongue" (εὐγλωττίας) while also advocating restraint in order to avoid excessive or flippant verbosity.[150] The control mentioned here directed Christian readers to discussion of symmetry between speech and conduct as laid out in the third chapter of the epistle James.[151] Readers of James are warned to tame the tongue, to bridle it as if a beast. It is a bodily member

---

[147] S. A. Rebillard, "Speaking for Salvation: Gregory of Nazianzus as Poet and Priest in his Autobiographical Poems," Ph.D. Dissertation, Brown University, 2003, 144–56.

[148] A complex series of circumstances set the background for Nazianzen's rhetoric of silence, in the aftermath of his time at Constantinople. These issues are explored fully in Rebillard, "Speaking," 130–228 and B. Storin, "In a Silent Way: Asceticism and Literature in the Rehabilitation of Gregory of Nazianzus," *JECS* 19:2 (2011), 225–57.

[149] On cultivating *aretē* through continuous conversation, Plutarch, *Moralia* 31f.

[150] Greg. Naz., *Ep.* 114 (Storin 156). [151] Rebillard, "Speaking," 149.

described as a "fire."[152] The admonition is that it is better to be slow to speak because such restraint bespeaks overall composure.[153] Such quietness is recalled in Plutarch's admonition that timely silence is superior to speech.[154] In Gregory's letter, he was promoting his own withdrawal from negative company while also praising the beauty of voice in his colleague. Likewise, Gregory explained to another correspondent, "I have placed a guard (φυλακή) on my mouth."[155] While Gregory was explaining his silence as an exercise in asceticism – an act of purification as a priest – the severity of the act also punctuated the function of the voice as an apparatus of cohesion between friends. Only a person with familiar sound could fully recognize the virtue in an equal. Speech acted as a bonding agent between individuals and had to be managed with caution.

References to the voice of friends, moreover, played a role in verbal sparring between correspondents. Nazianzen alluded to the voice as a testament of *aretē* through the metaphor of weaponry. For Gregory, the tongue was an instrument befitting a warrior. "Fear lest my tongue be set in motion against you," he taunted one friend.[156] In a missive to bishop Amphilochius, his cousin, Gregory acknowledged the armament wielded by his kinsman, "using a voice as the knife (ξίφος)."[157] Meanwhile Gregory indicted his friend, the rhetorician Eustochius, for "discharging your sophisms (κατασοφιστεύω) against me," comparing his verbal combat to the feats of Odysseus.[158] And, in a letter to Stagirius, Gregory equated "the tongues with which you attack and wound each other" (the verbal attacks) to the weapons of the Homeric warrior.[159] These statements are consistent with a common theme in Gregory's writing, that the voice is a dangerous force.[160] Here, in the context of correspondence with fellow *pepaideumenoi*, such assertions underscored the manhood shared by author and addressee. By attributing potency to the voice, a likeness of the soul, Gregory was acclaiming the authority of these individuals.

The Cappadocians' preoccupation with the voice shows not only insight to conceptions of virility, but also an acute awareness of

---

[152] James 3:1–6.   [153] James 1:19.   [154] Plutarch, *Moralia* 10e–10f.
[155] Greg. Naz., *Ep.* 118 (Storin 89).
[156] Greg. Naz., *Ep.* 113 (Storin 155): φοβοῦ τὴν γλῶσσαν.
[157] Greg. Naz., *Ep.* 171 (Storin 190).
[158] Greg. Naz., *Ep.* 190 (Storin 105; my translation).
[159] Greg. Naz., *Ep.* 192 (Storin 227): τὰς γλώσσας, αἷς ἀλλήλους βάλλετέ τε καὶ τιτρώσκετε.
[160] Rebillard, "Speaking," 158–67, examines the danger of the tongue in Gregory's poetry.

hierarchy.¹⁶¹ As signposts of eloquence, the letters contributed to the Cappadocians' spiritual authority and also authorized them to take their place among the cultural powerbrokers of society. The missives involved the same care with which Second Sophistic orators managed their voices in order to thrill audiences with mesmerizing performances while safeguarding reputations of manliness.¹⁶² While texts on rhetoric from the first three centuries laid out guidelines for regulating speech, authors from that period also established a lineage between themselves and practitioners of verbal arts from the past. Plutarch, for instance, gives the account of famed Athenian orator Demosthenes (fourth century B.C.), who on occasion isolated himself in a cave for two or three months to cultivate his voice.¹⁶³ This pedigree of orality linked the culture of verbal performance to the age of the Greek polis and restored its association of speech to physical strength. The voice was to be trained and exercised, but also nurtured as a wrestler or runner would his arms and legs. For authors such as Plutarch, self-representation of voice and gender was achieved in contest with rival speakers.

In a similar way, as the Cappadocians brought attention to the voices of friends, they were drawing focus to their own strength of speech. Ancient treatises on sense perception contributed to the practice of considering one's own voice in relation to others, as did the inherent sense of reciprocity that guided friendships. Aristotle taught that sound could only occur when two objects struck each other; without the contact, hearing could not take place. These objects, moreover, had to be solid to cause reverberation.¹⁶⁴ The voices cited in the Cappadocians' correspondence shared a quality that made them discernible to other *agathoi*. The implication held that these individuals shared a firm substance that amplified the force of each other's voices. This transference of sound also depended on the πνεῦμα (*pneuma*) within each person, the agent of perception – correlating to the breath – that enabled the voice to navigate the channels of the body into the soul.¹⁶⁵ The physics of speaking and hearing,

---

¹⁶¹ L. Coon, *Dark Age Bodies: Gender and Monastic Practice in the Early Medieval West* (Philadelphia: University of Pennsylvania Press, 2011), 66–72. In a study on masculinity in monastic communities of Carolingian Europe (700 and 800s), Coon has shown how the tongue came to denote hierarchy within the Benedictine Rule. As heirs of the Roman orators, lectors (readers) were judged by bodily deportment, fluency of speech, and mastery of classical Latin.
¹⁶² Gleason, *Making*, 45–7.   ¹⁶³ Plutarch, *Demosthenes* 849.
¹⁶⁴ Aristotle, *On the Soul* 2.8.
¹⁶⁵ Martin, *Corinthian*, 21–2; S. Hodges-Kluck, "Religious Education and the Health of the Soul according to Basil of Caesarea and the Emperor Julian," *SP* 81 (2017), 94–6, refers to Plato's *Timaeus* 47c–3 and Plutarch, *Moralia* 38a–b for beliefs about the effects of

therefore, mirrored the rhetoric of *agōn*. *Aretē* could only be achieved in contest with another honorable individual, just as voices had effect only when projected against a commensurate force. The breath that produced voice constituted the core of a person, a portal to his soul.

Correspondence among friends, moreover, was spurred on by the willingness to reciprocate a show of affection received from a colleague; and with it, the opportunity for self-representation. In other words, a letter from a friend simulated a coveted conversation, thus creating intimacy based on access to the soul and allowing the recipient to exhibit his own voice. Nazianzen, as a case in point, told Amphilochius that "you've become my good plectrum (πλῆκτρον ἀγαθόν)... with your countless writings."[166] Gregory meant that Amphilochius' correspondence had incited him to write, to perform. Gregory thus was depending on a "plectrum" (Amphilochius' letters) to "pluck his lyre" (move his pen) so that he could "make music" (compose letters). In a kind of symbiotic relationship between metaphorical voices, each brandished a written display of oratory, a symbol of his highly regarded speech. A Pythagorean adage held that friends share all possessions.[167] In this case, the comrades were bestowing rhetorical merit on each other in a kind of literary confrontation. The collaboration came off as a contest of rhetorical one-upmanship, but in actuality it allowed each to show off his excellence. Symbolizing the voice through letters thus provided means for *philoi* to activate their collective physical eminence (the voice), as well as their figurative high place in the social hierarchy.

The Hands

While orchestrations of visual and aural connection suggested union of souls among *philoi*, the Cappadocians applied another rhetoric of materiality, the sense of touch. Referents to a variety of corporeal imagery helped to make the text appear as an extension of the author. Of sensory depiction, characterizations of the hands best simulated physical connection between author and addressee.[168] Touch suggested movement, and

---

hearing. Because hearing molded the innermost soul, Hodges-Kluck states, Basil was vigilant to monitor the speech to which Christian ascetics were exposed.
[166] Greg. Naz., *Ep.* 171 (Storin 190).   [167] Porphyry, *Life of Pythagoras* 33.
[168] On the function of hands, Van Dam, *Kingdom*, 92–4; Krueger, *Writing*, 87–90; and Gunderson, *Staging*, 74–5.

by correlation, activeness.[169] Scripting a manual connection, it seems, placed the author in front of the addressee. "I propose the law that bids fathers to be honored..." Nazianzen told the Christian *pepaideumenos* Epiphanius, "...receive my letter with the right hand of friendship (δεξιὰν φιλίας)."[170] The "right hand of friendship" plays on a trope found also in the epistle Galatians, with Gregory substituting the word φιλία (friendship) for κοινωνία (fellowship among Christians).[171] Here Gregory identifies himself and the addressee according to their *philia*, with Gregory also making allusion to a biblical passage about honoring parents.[172] The clasping of hands signaled friendship as early as the *Iliad*. When the Greek Diomedes and the Trojan Glaukos learned that their grandfathers had established *xenia* (guest friendship) with each other, the two warriors reaffirmed their ancestors' friendship through handclasp.[173]

Gregory and Epiphanius, therefore, had the opportunity of playing out the scripture about children honoring parents by upholding their grandfather's bond. And they could do so through shaking hands, a mark of friendship rooted in Homeric text. But the onus for friendship was left to Epiphanius. Gregory entreats Epiphanius to join an *agōn* of friendship, inviting Epiphanius to respond, and to write often, "turning me into a spearman, even as an old man."[174] Nazianzen was characterizing himself as the wise king Nestor of the *Iliad* and *Odyssey*[175] Nestor was a warrior and masterful speaker, revered among Greeks for his eloquence and sagacity and also famous for wielding spears. Epiphanius' repeated correspondence would provide Gregory the opportunity to display *aretē*, much as Nestor had been privileged to do. Whereas Nestor had hurled spears and provided sage advice, Gregory would be casting letters. So Epiphanius would be reaching out his hand to accept that of Gregory, if he reciprocated the letter with one of his own; an epistle that he would craft with his hand. The epistle would constitute his handshake. The

---

[169] A. Corbeill, *Nature Embodied: Gesture in Ancient Rome* (Princeton: Princeton University Press, 2003), 20: "Even more than the lips, head, and face, the hands provide the readiest opportunity for participation in the world."

[170] Greg. Naz., *Ep.* 239 (Storin 92). Epiphanius: Storin, *Gregory*, 25; H-M, 64. Gregory alludes to a passage from Ephesians 6:1–4 about children honoring their parents and fathers raising their children in the instruction of the Lord.

[171] Galatians 2:9.   [172] Ephesians 6:1–2.   [173] *Iliad* 6.220–45.

[174] Greg. Naz., *Ep.* 239 (Storin 92): ποιήσεις καὶ γέροντα αἰχμητήν, οὐδὲν τοῦ Νέστορος ἀγεννέστερον.

[175] See *Iliad* 1.248; 2.370; and 4.293 and *Odyssey* 3.157, 343. Storin, *Self-Portrait*, 114–5, characterizes references to Nestor as a model for Gregory's own participation in *paideia*.

reference to scripture in this letter, along with the citation of the *Iliad*, shows Gregory enlisting and merging two identity groups as he exemplifies his own understanding of *aretē*. Overlapping honor and friendship from the New Testament and Homer, Gregory frames a fourth-century version of friendship.

Symbolism of hands worked especially well in letters of mediation, as for example, when Gregory of Nazianzus asked for assistance from Asterius, a magistrate under the governor of Cappadocia (381–2) and a *philos* to Gregory based on mutual *paideia*.[176] Gregory's grandnephew Nicobulus, the client for whom Gregory was petitioning, delivered the epistle and read his uncle's words aloud before Asterius: "I set this man under your hands (ὑπὸ τὰς σὰς τίθεμεν χεῖρας), and through your hands under those of the governor."[177] Through the physical extension of the letter in his hands, Nicobulus showed that he (and his uncle) was "reaching out" for help.[178] In this sense the outstretched hand offered submission and a potential alliance.[179] The text of the epistle constructed a movement that Nicobulus fulfilled. The letter and the performance both honored the magistrate as they acknowledged him as a patron, a role normally held by powerful individuals. In deliveries of letters such as this one, the messenger used hands to complete an actual physical encounter. The courier coordinated body language – gestures, posture, and facial expressions – to match the text. And messengers carried out other actions described in the text, as when Basil's courier placed an epistle before the prefect Modestus, thus "casting it [the letter] before you in lieu of the olive branch."[180] From earliest Greek myth, when Athena claimed Athens for herself by planting an olive tree, the olive had symbolized superiority.

---

[176] On Asterius' erudition, see another letter to him: Greg. Naz., *Ep.* 156 (Storin 137); Storin, *Gregory*, thinks Asterius was an assessor or possibly a governor, while R. Van Dam, "Governors of Cappadocia During the Fourth Century," *Medieval Prosopography* 17 (1996)," 41–2, says that we cannot know his office; A. Schor, *Theodoret's People: Social Networking and Religious Conflict in Late Roman Syria* (Berkeley: University of California Press, 2011), 156–79, talks about similar use of body language and patronage in epistolary performances by Theodoret, bishop of Cyrrhus from 423 to 457.

[177] Greg. Naz., *Ep.* 147 (Storin 134; my translation); on letters read aloud, Libanius, *Eps.* 779 (Bradbury 107) and 1173 (Bradbury 50).

[178] See a fuller discussion on "Hands" in this regard in Van Dam, *Kingdom*, 92–4.

[179] Corbeill, *Nature*, 20–4; A. Boegehold, *When a Gesture Was Expected: A Selection of Examples from Archaic and Classical Greek Literature* (Princeton: Princeton University Press, 1999), 23–4; Plato, *Republic* 468 b7.

[180] Basil, *Ep.* 111 (modification of Deferrari's translation): ἵνα ἀνθ' ἱκετηρίας αὐτὴν προβαλλόμενος.

Olympic athletes wore olive crowns as testament of their victory. And because of its status as the best gift, it also served as a peace offering. Basil's envoy parodied a verbal supplication by holding out the letter as one such token of peace, equating his own epistle to a present of great value. Using his hands as an augmentation of Basil, the messenger played the manual link, a corporeal nexus of *philia*.

The messenger thus contributed to a materializing of the communication, which began with the author composing the text and ended with the addressee receiving the epistle from the envoy. Authors often put much thought, then, into the choice of who would carry a letter.[181] About one messenger, for example, Basil wrote: "[He] can act as a living epistle (ἐπιστολὴ ἔμψυχος) both to him who writes and to him who receives."[182] Nazianzen likewise sent a letter to a recipient by commencing "It's pleasant to address friends, and even more pleasant to do so through friends."[183] "Fortunatus, the one placing this epistle into your hands," Nazianzen stated in another letter, "is a friend and member of my household."[184] The *philia* relationship between author and addressee was consummated through a third associate, who closed the circle of friendship.[185] The messenger served as the final link, the human element, thus providing congruence between author and addressee based on a shared ideal.[186] The boundaries ran fluid in this interplay between person, text, and physical object, with each element of the epistle seemingly complementing the others. The intermediary enhanced the connection because he presumably was familiar with both parties.

Using such imagery of the hands to sustain *philia* and convey presence was a technique derived from an upbringing in *paideia*. "So far as possible," Aristotle had taught, "the poet should even include gestures

---

[181] Van Dam, *Kingdom*, 14–16, shows that authors faced significant challenges in communicating by letter, ranging from difficulties of travel to availability of trustworthy messengers. The latter issue could be especially problematic when the author needed somebody suitable to expound on the contents of the missive. On complaints about difficulties of weather or messengers: Basil, *Eps.* 48, 95, 112, 121, 198, 199, 200 and Greg. Naz., *Eps.* 42, 129, 133.
[182] Basil, *Ep.* 205 (Deferrari). [183] Greg. Naz., *Ep.* 227 (Storin 130).
[184] Greg. Naz., *Ep.* 84 (modification of trans. in Storin 171).
[185] Similar personifications of epistles appear in the New Testament, where for example the author of II Corinthians states: "You yourselves are our letter, written on our hearts, known and read by everyone," II Corinthians 3.2 (NIV).
[186] Schor, *Theodoret's*, 35–8, 157–63, especially 36, where Schor calls couriers "extensions of the bishops themselves;" M. Mullett, *Theophylact of Ochrid: Reading the Letters of a Byzantine Archbishop* (Aldershot: Ashgate, 1997), 32–9; J. Muir, *Life and Letters in the Ancient Greek World* (London: Routledge, 2009), 10–13.

in the process of composition: for assuming the same natural talent, the most convincing effect comes from those who actually put themselves in the emotions."[187] Along with creating immediacy, as directed by Aristotle, depictions of the hands carried a moral component. In the classical tradition, the right hand served as a manual embodiment of integrity.[188] Nyssen used this understanding, for instance, when he distinguished between principled and duplicitous behavior through the metaphor of opposing hands. "So instead of their hope of the right hand (τῆς δεξιᾶς ἐλπίδος) that we dangle before them, we brush aside the souls of those who hope in us through left-handedness (σκαιότης) of what we actually do."[189] By acting in a "right-ward" way, Gregory advocated acting in a consistent manner and securing honorable interactions; a contrast to the "left-handedness" of slander and accusation. And in the Homeric epics, aside from securing friendship, the right hand symbolized reassurance and dependability.[190] *Pepaideumenoi* thus recognized the nuances involved in rendering variations of the movement of hands. Even the choice of using the right or left hand, or direction of movement with the hands, carried ethical implication.

In Christianity and Judaism, moreover, hands had a long heritage of showing sanctity. For many of the Cappadocians' correspondents, symbolism of the hands mirrored the interplay of intellectual and religious identity. Amphilochius of Iconium proves instructive on this point. Amphilochius shared a number of similarities with his cousin Gregory, as well as with Basil and Nyssen.[191] Like his fellow Cappadocians, he excelled in *paideia*, even beginning his career as an orator and lawyer.[192] He too was appointed a bishop later in life, in his mid thirties, when he

---

[187] Aristotle, *Poetics* 1455a 22–31 (Halliwell, 50).
[188] Euripides, *Medea* 496–9, where Medea reminds Jason of the promises he made with his right hand; voting also was carried out through a raising of the right hand, as in Aeschylus, *Suppliants* 605ff.
[189] Greg. Ny., *Ep.* 16 (Silvas). See Silvas, *Gregory*, 160 n. 226.
[190] D. Lateiner, *Sardonic Smile: Nonverbal Behavior in Homeric Epic* (Ann Arbor: University of Michigan Press, 1998), 20–1; Homer, *Odyssey* 508–9.
[191] He also received letters from each of the Cappadocian Fathers; e.g. Greg. Ny., *Ep.* 25; Greg. Naz., *Eps.* 9, 13, 25, 26; Basil, *Eps.* 150, 161, 176, 188.
[192] Amphilochius (the younger): P. Rousseau, *Basil of Caesarea* (Berkeley: University of California Press, 1994), 258–63; Van Dam, *Families*, 142–52, who studies Amphilochius' letters with Basil and Nazianzen through the lens of the complex relationship between the latter two. Van Dam contends that Nazianzen, early in their relationship, often alluded to classical themes when writing to Amphilochius, but that Basil concentrated only on issues related to his role as churchman. It appears, then, that Gregory and Basil were activating different shared identities with Amphilochius.

was ordained in 374 at Iconium of Lycaonia. In 375 Basil sent a letter to the recently consecrated Amphilochius. "...when I took into my hands the letter of your Piety, I straightaway became forgetful of everything," Basil wrote, "since I had received symbols of both the sweetest voice of all to me and also the dearest hand."[193] Basil celebrated his fulfillment from holding the missive from his friend, which had a multi-sensory impact. This dual portrayal of his friend's presence, through voice and hands, intensified his expression of joy in meeting Amphilochius through letter. Amphilochius was prompted to understand the surplus meaning of the hands here as a testament to his identity and sanctity.

First, hands had played an identifying role in the gospels, as in the New Testament account of the post-resurrection Jesus appearing to the apostle Thomas. In that account Jesus verified himself to the skeptical disciple: "Put your finger here; see my hands. Reach out your hand and put it into my side."[194] Jesus' own hands bore the signs of his crucifixion, the most significant sacrifice in the Christian faith. Thomas' touching Jesus' hands and pierced side registered as an intimate moment and a confirmation of Jesus' words. In a comparable manner Gregory of Nyssa simulated recognizing a fellow bishop Otreius through touch: "I fancied I was looking at you in person..." as "Again and again I took your letter into my hands for the pleasure of it..."[195] Like Basil's letter to Amphilochius, Gregory intimated that the hands of a righteous person served as an agent of discernment. Second, the analogy of letter as hand in Basil's letter also underscored their office as priests, in which the laying on of hands symbolized sacred authority.[196] In the Old Testament, the patriarch Jacob (Israel) blessed Ephraim by placing his right hand on his head, and Moses invested Joshua with the leadership of Israel (the nation) by placing hands on him.[197] In the New Testament, Jesus' followers recognized his ability to heal with touch, and the apostles designated ministers by laying on hands.[198] Manual imagery in letters to fellow clergy thus

---

[193] Basil, *Ep.* 217 (Deferrari): καὶ τῆς φωνῆς τῆς πασῶν ἐμοὶ ἡδίστης καὶ χειρὸς τῆς φιλτάτης ὑποδεξάμενος σύμβολα.
[194] John 20:27 (NIV). See discussion in Krueger, *Writing*, 178–9.
[195] Greg. Ny., *Ep.* 18 (Silvas): καὶ πολλάκις ὑφ' ἡδονῆς ἐπαναλαμβάνων τὰ γράμματα.
[196] S. A. Rebillard, "The Speech Act of Swearing: Gregory of Nazianzus's Oath in *Poema* in 2.1.2 in Context," *JECS* 21 (2013), 182.
[197] Jacob, in Genesis 48:18; Moses, in Numbers 27:18.
[198] Jesus, Matthew 9:18; Apostles, Acts 8:17.

conveyed purity and sacred presence, qualities the Cappadocians often called to mind in pro-Nicene *pepaideumenoi*.[199]

Allusion to the consecrated role of hands also comes across in epistles to other Christian *philoi*. Gregory of Nazianzus provides one such occurrence in a letter from 381 or 382 to Procopius, a Cappadocian magistrate and a Christian.[200] Gregory explained that he wanted to meet with Procopius in person, but that sickness prevented it. The next best thing, he said, would be to "approach you by letter, give you my right hand (δεξιόομαι), embrace you, and confidently ask about my fellow deacon Eugenius..."[201] In the Old Testament, the right hand denoted the power and omnipotence of Yahweh.[202] Thus to sit at the right hand of the Lord, as the Psalmist David set forth, insinuated divine authority.[203] The hand served as a manifestation of authenticity, an extension of Gregory himself. When Procopius read Gregory's letter, he visualized Gregory reaching out to him with his own right hand – a symbol of potency – grasping that of Procopius in a gesture of mutual regard; an affinity based on manliness through closeness to God. The mutual clasp of the right hand thus underscored the amicable, intimate substance of the exchange, as well as signifying an act of one powerful man acknowledging another.

These examples show how the Cappadocians deployed illustrations of hands and touch to publicize friendship with others. These portrayals advertised their understanding of corporeal imagery, whose meaning had been developed in Homeric literature and later classical and Hellenistic Greece. Simulations of gesture and touch referred readers to social cues known through study in *paideia*. For Christians, moreover, rhetoric of the hands activated an additional identity, as an avenue of expressing holiness that was prevalent in the scriptures. Subtleties in these depictions underscored the Cappadocians' command of sensory rhetoric: "reaching out" with the hands as a form of petition; receiving a letter with the "right hand of friendship" to emphasize trust. Such measured use of corporeal

---

[199] Corbeill, *Nature*, 20–4; on purity of hands, see A. Angenendt, "Mit reinen Händen: Das Motiv der kultischen Reinheit in abendländische Askese," in *Herrschaft, Kirche, Kultur: Beoträge zur Geschichte des Mittelalters – Festschrift für Friedrich Prinz zu seinem 65 Geburtstag*, G. Jenal, ed. (Stuttgart: Hiersemann, 1993), 296–316.

[200] Procopius: Storin, *Gregory*, 37; Van Dam, "Governors," 66–7; Gallay, *Lettres*, 2.18 n.1.

[201] Greg. Naz., *Ep.* 129 (Storin 179). Suzanne Abrams Rebillard brought to my attention that Gregory also uses imagery of the hands in his poems. For example, he wrote "Receive these offerings, spoken by my hand," in *Poem* 2.1.34. (translation Rebillard).

[202] Exodus 15:6, Psalm 17:7, 44.3, Isaiah 41:10.

[203] Psalm 110.1; and see reference by the apostle Peter in Acts 2:34.

features testified to the Cappadocians' literary merits. Imagining various physical attributes as emblems of the full person also sent a message to fellow *pepaideumenoi*. With touch generally viewed as the most terrene of all the senses, the Cappadocians showed willingness and ability to elevate the importance of even the most mundane parts of the body. In the preceding examples, the hands exceeded their material limits by creating access between friends and signifying mutual noble character and/or sanctity. Audiences reading these letters – texts that placed the hands in a positive role – would understand that the Cappadocians held to concepts within *paideia* that placed value on the *total* body as a bridge between persons and as a potential index of *aretē*.

"GREETING IN YOUR HONORED HAND": PENMANSHIP AND *ARETĒ*

Among the simulation of sensory encounters, handwriting posed particularly discernible evidence of identity, thus issuing proximity between friends.[204] Through knowledge that the author of the letter had dictated the text, scripted it, or signed and handled the letter, recipients spoke of epistles as actual encounters. The act of putting pen to paper – whether real or metaphorical – held meaning as a direct bond between correspondents. Basil, for example, called a letter from Amphilochius: "a symbol of the dearest hand" (χειρός τῆς φιλτάτης).[205] Likewise when Nazianzen urged his colleague Philagrius to "put that stylus into motion" (κίνει τὴν γραφίδα) Gregory was asking him to share in a connection created by movement of the hands.[206] His stylus, his pen, provided a conduit between the man himself and Gregory. With the voice understood as the essence of an individual, the written text served as a physical manifestation of the message spoken and recorded on paper. The recipient of the letter thus engaged with the author through the imprint of his voice, as transmitted on the paper. The hand often attained sacred status in hagiography as "the mechanism of composition."[207] A trope in some biblical

---

[204] Fourth-century poet Palladas of Alexandria: "Nature, pleased with the customs of friendship, invented tools so that those absent could be united: the reed-pen, paper, ink, a person's handwriting;" Palladas, *Anthology* 9.401, trans. Rosenmeyer, *Ancient*, 19; R. Cribiore, *Gymnastics of the Mind: Greek Education in Hellenistic and Roman Egypt* (Princeton: Princeton University Press, 2005), 245–7, on evoking presence through writing.
[205] Basil, *Ep.* 217 (Deferrari). [206] Greg. Naz., *Ep.* 30 (Storin 127).
[207] Krueger, *Writing*, 86.

texts correlated the pen and the tongue, as when the Psalmist stated "My tongue is the pen of a skillful writer."[208] The pen and the writing surface were also associated with memory.[209] Receiving personally written or autographed letters then represented a particularly intimate venture. "For the greeting in your honoured hand (τῆς τιμίας χειρός)," Basil told an addressee, "I hold in greater esteem than many letters."[210] Basil was expressing his affection by insinuating the excellence of his colleague's hand as a metaphor for his identity.

Expressions of pleasure at receiving a handwritten letter often were idealizations. Such statements were meant to recognize the merits of the author who sent the letter, his exceptional penmanship (acquired through *paideia*), and the hope that he did, in fact, write the entire text. In reality, many *pepaideumenoi* employed stenographers or calligraphers to whom they dictated the message.[211] Dependency on this group – whose ranks included women and specialists – made epistolary composition a multi-faceted process that cut across socio-economic and gender divides.[212] Generally, putting pen to paper, however, did not lend itself to individuals who were asserting status. The Cappadocians only rarely etched the words themselves.[213] More often they signed the letters or made short notes to the recipient in the marginalia.[214] Even though knowledge of *how* to write well denoted prestige, many authors had servants or paid experts trained to carry out the specialty.[215] It was a valuable and time-consuming skill that was usually delegated to expert scribes.[216] The very

---

[208] Psalm 45:1 (NIV). See Krueger, *Writing*, 179.   [209] Carruthers, *Craft*, 96–103.
[210] Basil, *Ep.* 146 (Deferrari).
[211] H.-J. Klauck and D. Bailey, *Ancient Letters and the New Testament: A Guide to Content and Exegesis* (Waco, TX: Baylor University Press, 2006), 55–60.
[212] See K. Haines-Eitzen, "Girls Trained in Beautiful Writing: Female Scribes in Roman Antiquity and Early Christianity," *JECS* 6 (1998), 629–46.
[213] On this point, see the examples of Libanius and Julian, who made special comment on the exceptions when they did write in their own hands: Libanius, *Ep.* 1223 (Bradbury 104) and Julian, *Ep.* 5.
[214] G. Constable, *Letters and Letter-Collections* (Turnhout: Brepols, 1976), 16–20; E. Dekkers, *Les Autographes des pères latins*, in *Colligere fragmenta: Festschrift Alban Dodd* (Beuron: Beuroner Kunstverlag, 1952), 127–8.
[215] W. Harris, *Ancient Literacy* (Cambridge, MA: Harvard University Press, 1989), 248–51; and H. Hagendahl, "Die Bedeutung der Stenographie für die spätlateinischen christliche Literatur," in *Jahrbuch für Antike und Christentum* 14 (1971), 24–38.
[216] K. Haines-Eitzen, *Guardians of Letters: Literacy, Power, and Transmitters of Early Christian Literature* (Oxford: Oxford University Press, 2000), 61–4; K. Vössing, "Schreiben lernen, ohne lesen zu können? Zur Methode des antiken Elementarunterrichts," in *Zeitschrift für Papyrologie und Epigraphik* 123 (1998), 121–5.

fact that they could enlist stenographers to write while they dictated was an indication of rank.

When an individual with stenographers penned the entire text of a letter, therefore, the gesture added meaning because the author invested more of himself than was standard. The Cappadocians most likely *did* write in their own hand to many *pepaideumenoi*, to those with whom they were most deliberately exhibiting mutual erudition. "The ancients were in the habit of writing to their closest friends," stated one epistolary handbook, "or at least in most cases of adding a subscription, in their own hand."[217] For elites, then, to write in their own hand communicated to the addressee a special intimacy.[218] In this manner, the Cappadocians approached *philia* in much the same way that New Testament authors had spoken of fellowship with believers. The apostle Paul, for example, had written to congregations, "I Paul write with my own hand," and "See with what large letters I write."[219] By pointing out his own handwriting, Paul was accentuating *koinonia* with his audiences. Like earlier Christian writers, the Cappadocians were asserting an identity with a specific group, in this case with *philoi*. And likewise, they recognized that individual handwriting contributed to a sense of intimacy and recognition. Periodic correspondents would have known each other's writing from former letters, enabling them to discern the authenticity of a missive based on the signature of the author.

Penmanship, moreover, testified to status among *philoi* who participated in a common aesthetic. "Do you, then, my son, make your strokes perfect," Basil instructed a correspondent, "and punctuate your passages to match them."[220] Basil was advising the addressee to write with a steady hand, to make firm and clear letters. Penmanship, like other forms of *paideia*, testified to an individual's status.[221] The stroke of a hand could indicate confidence or uncertainty, not unlike the posture or voice of an

---

[217] Julius Victor, *Art of Rhetoric* 27 (Trapp, 189).

[218] M. McDonnell, "Writing, Copying, and Autograph Manuscripts in Ancient Rome," *CQ* 46 (1996), 469–72, 490–1.

[219] "With my own hand," comes from Philippians 1:7–8, Colossians 4:18, and Philemon 19. "large letters," comes from Galatians 6:11 (NIV).

[220] Basil, *Ep.* 333 (Deferrari): ὦ παῖ, τὰ χαράγματα τέλεια ποίει, καὶ τοὺς τόπους ἀκολούθως κατάστιζε.

[221] For a corollary to this culture that associated penmanship with honor, see T. LaMarre, *Uncovering Heian Japan: An Archaeology of Sensation and Inscription* (Durham, NC: Duke University Press, 2000), especially 93–115.

orator.[222] In directing the youth to write correctly, Basil was figuratively advising him to behave as an *agathos*. In a similar epistle Basil enjoined the addressee: "Write straight ('Ορθὰ γράφε) and keep straightly to your lines; and let the hand neither mount upwards nor slide downhill...For that which is slantwise is unbecoming."[223] In other words, Basil was recommending to write level across the page to avoid laxity. On one hand, this was practical instruction, making reading easier. On the other hand, precision of handwriting represented certitude. Steadiness of hand demonstrated composure. And in a culture of *paideia*, with its rhetoric of restraint, handwriting mimicked larger displays of bodily control.[224]

In another letter, Basil explained that he had not reciprocated in correspondence because he did not have any calligraphers or shorthand writers available.[225] He was unwilling to send an epistle that lacked the expected measure of penmanship. Basil also urged his colleague, the rhetorician Leontius: "If your hand is slothful, you need not even write, for someone else will do it for you."[226] Basil was not so much warning Leontius, but rather disclosing a standard of quality that both should appreciate because of their training. By demanding a certain standard from Leontius, Basil was casting himself as an arbiter of penmanship.[227] Likewise Gregory of Nyssa bemoaned that "We Cappadocians are poor...especially in those able to write."[228] He apologized to his addressees for being late to send a treatise to them. "This [lack of writers] indeed is the reason for the long delay," Gregory explained.[229] Basil's and Nyssen's stated hesitancy to compose letters in their own hand testifies less to their unwillingness to write, but rather more to a lofty criterion they held. This concern to produce ornate texts indicated rigor, thus contributing to a self-image of facility and exactitude.

---

[222] G. Cavallo, "Greek and Latin Writing in the Papyri," in *The Oxford Handbook of Papyrology*, ed. R. Bagnall (Oxford: Oxford University Press, 2009), 101–48, for different scripts, including the ornate styles used for literary texts. It is easy to identify with Basil's point, since it is easier to read a handwritten note with clear, rather than shaky, letters.

[223] Basil, *Ep.* 334 (Deferrari).

[224] On writing as a physical activity, Carruthers, *Craft*, 102–3.   [225] Basil, *Ep.* 134.

[226] Basil, *Ep.* 20 (Deferrari).

[227] See C. Rapp, "Christians and their Manuscripts in the Greek East in the Fourth Century," in *Scritture, libri e testi nelle aree provinciali di Bisanzio: atti del seminario di Erice (18–25 settembre 1988)*, eds. G. Cavallo, G. de Gregorio, and M. Maniaci (Spoleto: Centro italiano di studi sull'alto Medioveco, 1991), 131–43.

[228] Greg. Ny., *Ep.* 15 (Silvas).   [229] Greg. Ny., *Ep.* 15 (Silvas).

EPISTOLARY *AGŌN* AS GIFT EXCHANGE

Emphasizing excellence in the corporeal features of colleagues, including references to tangible elements such as handwriting and the letter itself, pointed to the superiority of soul that formed the bonds of friendship. A similar reference to aesthetic appeal also applied when the Cappadocians spoke about correspondence with *philoi* by using the language of giftedness.

The Cappadocians often framed epistolary exchange as a form of gift-giving, thus configuring letter writing as an exercise in reciprocity.[230] In doing so, they reenacted an economy of honor that was embedded in the social interactions among Greeks that, like athletics, resonated with competition. The practice of gift exchange had been instrumental for establishing and maintaining *philia* as far back as the *Iliad* and *Odyssey*, when warriors delivered prestige and signified nobility through the bestowal of lavish items like tripods, gold, weapons, or even women.[231] These exhibitions were a means for Homeric heroes to acknowledge mutual *aretē*; most often, bravery in battle. In the example cited earlier, the Greek warrior Ajax and Trojan Hector traded sword, scabbard, and belt after a particularly heated encounter. Hector initiated the transaction, telling Ajax that their fellow soldiers would say, "They fought each other in soul-devouring strife, but agreed to part in the spirit of friendship."[232] The gesture was meant to bring glory to each and to celebrate the encounter as an epitome of valiant combat. The Cappadocians affirmed similar ideals of valor through conferring letters that celebrated eloquence. Like using sensory rhetoric to create intimacy, speaking of letters as gifts prompted the reader to understand the affective meaning behind the missive. The exercise of epistolary exchange thus was imbued with emotional and personal connection and was understood as sharing part of oneself.

---

[230] N. Howard, "Gifts Bearing Greekness: Epistles as Cultural Capital in Fourth-Century Cappadocia," *JLA* 6:1 (2013), 37–59, on letters as gifts, with epistolary exchange cultivating an identity informed by classical Greek literary culture.

[231] Finley, *World*, 61–5; 95–8; see examples of gift-giving and honor in Homeric society in the following passages from Homer: *Odyssey*, 4.590–605; 1.311–8; 24.274–85; *Iliad* 112.310–21. On the complexities of gift exchange see M. Mifsud, "On Rhetoric as Gift/Giving," *Philosophy and Rhetoric* 40:1 (2007), 92–4; my association of epistolary exchange with gift-giving has been influenced especially by M. Mauss, *The Gift: Forms and Functions of Exchange in Archaic Societies*, trans. I. Cunnison (New York, 1967) and K. Polanyi, *The Great Transformation* (Boston: Beacon, 1968).

[232] *Iliad* 7.299–310 (Lombardo).

For the learned, letters of literary merit constituted precious items, as well as a stimulus to respond in kind with works of erudition. Artful missives aroused readers, often eliciting joyful responses such as Basil's laughter at the message contained in an epistle from Candidianus, a governor of Cappadocia.[233] Perhaps the finest gift one could bestow came in the form of declaring the beauty of a letter received. Basil and Nazianzen repeatedly expressed the satisfaction they derived from skilled writers. Gregory called a letter from Bishop Theodore of Tyana "a festival" (ἑορτή) and he acknowledged that the author had granted a "pre-festival" (προεορτάζω) by allowing him to anticipate its arrival.[234] Festivals provided a site for highly charged rhetorical orations in late antiquity, similar to an *agōn* of athletic competition. These gatherings furnished occasions of excitement and drama, truly pleasurable and instructive for a *literatus*. Gregory was alluding to this point, that Theodore's letter would deliver a showpiece of verbal finesse, a testament of literary competence within the episcopacy. The "pre-festival" of anticipating this treasure brought its own exhilaration. Around 383 Gregory likewise told Bishop Helladius of Caesarea, Basil's episcopal successor, that he took pleasure (ἥδομαι) in his letter, calling it a fitting gift.[235] Gregory informed other writers that receiving epistles from them cheered (εὐφραίνω) him.[236] Basil told separate addressees that they should know how much pleasure (εὐφροσύνη) their letters had brought by their tone and tenor.[237] And he remarked to another that the epistle caused him to read it with pleasure (ἡδέως) because of the author's wisdom.[238] Recurring utterances of satisfaction reflected the tastes acquired through rhetorical training, thus accentuating a shared valorization of the aesthetics of epistolary exchange. Author and recipient understood these texts as symbols of rarefied intellect, of honor.

Epistles composed for audiences of *pepaideumenoi* were select goods whose standards were established by a limited circle and whose exchange

---

[233] Basil, *Ep.* 3; Candidianus: see Introduction, n. 3. Libanius and Julian similarly described epistles as gifts. For example Libanius, *Ep.* 604 (Bradbury 33) and Julian, *Ep.* 63.
[234] Greg. Naz., *Ep.* 115 (Storin 66); Theodore: Storin, *Gregory*, 40; Van Dam, "Governors," 69–73. B. MacDougall, *Gregory of Nazianzus and Christian Festival Rhetoric*, Ph.D. Dissertation, Brown University, 2015, 134–41, for an example of Nazianzen himself as a brilliant festal orator, and the imaginative and emotional appeal of these occasions.
[235] Greg. Naz., *Ep.* 172 (Storin 44); Helladius: Storin, *Gregory*, 30–1; Gallay, *Lettres*, 2: 158 and Van Dam, *Kingdom*, 35–7.
[236] Greg. Naz., *Eps.* 66, 74.   [237] Basil, *Eps.* 134, 159.   [238] Basil, *Ep.* 244.

was restricted.[239] Letters of distinction, according to George Dennis, were "small *objets d'art*, carefully articulated...so finely crafted that the recipient would want to show it, rather read it, to his friends."[240] These texts functioned as symbols of honor because the restrictions and complexity of their acquisition, the specialized knowledge required for their consumption, and their nexus to other literati limited them to a small circle.[241] According to Basil, even brief letters, when well written, equaled "tokens of magnanimity."[242] In other words, an epistle could serve as a means of conspicuous consumption, to signal social status of author and recipient. The words in the epistle were only part of a larger gift of prestige presented to the addressee. After hearing the letter read, the listeners passed it around, analyzed it, discussed it, and debated its rhetorical merits. In the Introduction, we saw that Gregory of Nyssa felt honored to receive a letter from Libanius. Referring to that letter, Gregory remarked that the epistle "became the private wealth of each" (ἴδιος ἑκάστου πλοῦτος ἐγίνετο) with whom he shared it.[243] Gregory referred to the letter as private wealth because its esotericism limited it primarily to an audience of educated readers.[244] As the letter "passed through the hands" of Gregory's friends, some memorized the text by repeatedly reading it, while others copied the contents.[245] Each, in some way, participated in the occasion, thus marking inclusion in the noble gathering and allowing him to show off his high tastes.

Libanius' epistle represented for Gregory a token of his fellowship with one of the most highly respected scholars/teachers of the day. The gift was a prize to be shared with friends because it represented a literary treasure.[246] The letter held personal significance because it was a testament of Libanius' abilities and labor, and thus an extension of himself. The epistle

---

[239] For Latin similarity see Chin, *Grammar*, 20–1.

[240] G. Dennis, "Gregory of Nazianzus and the Byzantine Letter," in *Diakonia: Studies in Honour of Robert T. Meyer*, eds. T. Halton and J. Williman (Washington, DC: Catholic University of America Press, 1986), 5.

[241] A. Appadurai, "Introduction: Commodities and the Politics of Value," *The Social Life of Things: Commodities in Cultural Perspective*, ed. A. Appadurai (Cambridge, 1986), 36–8.

[242] Basil, *Ep.* 12 (Deferrari): σύμβολα ὄντα τῆς μεγάλης σου διαθέσεως; individual honor was enhanced by circulating the epistle. See R. Starr, "The Circulation of Literary Texts in the Roman World," *CQ* 37:1 (1987), 213–23.

[243] Greg. Ny., *Ep.* 14 (Silvas).

[244] I. Morris, "Gift and Commodity in Archaic Greece," *Man* 21:1 (1986), 1–15.

[245] Greg. Ny., *Ep.* 14 (Silvas).

[246] Appadurai, "Introduction," *Social Life*, 11, suggests that "gift," with its spirit of reciprocity and sociability must be juxtaposed to "commodity," a good largely free from moral or cultural constraints.

preserved Libanius' exertion in producing the text. The animistic quality subsequently formed a nexus between Gregory and Libanius and a third party of readers. Epistles exchanged among *pepaideumenoi* were intimate statements that solidified a cultural hierarchy of educated Greco-Romans. These missives were gifts that resisted commoditization because they remained singular, accessible only to a select few who could adequately evaluate their stylistic significance.[247] And perhaps most significantly, these gifts issued a medium for literati to celebrate their roles as advocates of the Greek literary heritage. Gregory's exchange of letters with Libanius acted as a common ground between a Christian and non-Christian, who both were ascribing literary interplay as a source of social refinement.

When Gregory of Nyssa touted the letter he received from Libanius, he was not issuing hollow praise. To participate in the exchange of cultural capital, *pepaideumenoi* had to sustain their own image as scholars. Epistles were intrinsically dear to educated members of society because crafting masterful rhetorical works was no easy enterprise. An epistle could be a source of entertainment, information, and instruction. It was also a product, valuable for its workmanship. Someone of significant stature had put effort into its construction. It involved time necessary to consider a message appropriate for the circumstances and the audience. In some cases, it would have necessitated approaching scholars whom the writer could consult for rules of Attic grammar and to proof-read the finished product. An epistle engaged the reader, calling one to reflect on the creative use of enduring authors such as Euripides and Plutarch. One can imagine the smile that a witticism pooled from an ancient source evoked. Recipients who needed clarification would have turned to associates to discuss specialized language and couched references. Thus, the letter educated the audience, even as it incorporated the addressee into the circle of enlightened readers. Writing at this level was an effort. The result was a work of art that promoted a shared aesthetic.

Messengers delivering the epistles accentuated the nexus between correspondents partly through their own performance. The physical letter (usually papyrus) constituted only one part of the transaction.[248] Couriers who elaborated on the message enhanced the textual encounter. In doing so, the courier contributed to the similitude of virtue that the letter was

---

[247] I. Kopytoff, "The Cultural Biography of Things: Commoditization as Process," *Social Life*, 73–81.

[248] Klauck, *Ancient*, 63–4, considers the papyrus (the paper) as a constituent part of the letter.

meant to acknowledge between parties. Authors sometimes suggested that the messenger – often described as beautiful or noble in his or her own right – embodied attributes of the sender and receiver, thus completing the transaction of *aretē*. Basil, for example, once received a letter from Magninianus, an imperial magistrate.[249] The courier Icelium played a crucial role as a go-between, partially because she provided Basil an opportunity to answer in panegyric form. Basil responded: "The most decorous of women, Icelium, our common daughter, by delivering the letter, has increased our joy."[250] This woman completed the symbolic visit of Magninianus to Basil (through the letter) by manifesting in herself the merits of her sender, "not only being a living image (ἔμψυχος εἰκών) of your Excellency, but also by displaying on her own part every care for virtue (ἀρετή)."[251] As a "living epistle," as Basil called her, she fulfilled the "function of a letter," thus adding gravitas to the transaction.[252] The delivery of an epistle by the envoy was part of the gift, sometimes involving a formal presentation in which the speech, clothing, and body language of the messenger worked together to create a multi-media experience.[253] Such elaborate procedures of exchange celebrated the gift, humanized the interaction, and added gravitas to an act that resonated with high culture.[254] Icelium's own demeanor enhanced Basil's letter, presumably as she carried out in Magninianus' presence Basil's idea of comportment. In a world where *aretē* was expected foremost in men, Icelium's performance as a woman intensified the abundance of virtue shared between the two male correspondents. As Magninianus' daughter, possibly by blood but more likely symbolically, Icelium was the ideal stand-in before his episcopal friend.[255]

Although all epistles of literary merit were valued, a certain gradation implies that certain gifts likely carried more prestige than others. The number of literary references and their familiarity among scholars, for example, could affect the regard for an epistle. Inserting several uncommon allusions demonstrated the author's high level of labor in composing the epistle by singling out distinct references. More obscure passages also

---

[249] Magninianus: Deferrari, *Basil: Letters*, 4:274–5; Rousseau, *Basil*, 104; *PLRE* 1: 533.
[250] Basil, *Ep.* 325 (Deferrari).   [251] Basil, *Ep.* 325 (Deferrari).
[252] Basil, *Ep.* 314 (Deferrari).
[253] Schor, *Theodoret's*, 35–8; Mullett, "Classical," 85–92; also P. Hatlie, "Redeeming Byzantine Epistolography," *Byzantine and Modern Greek Studies* 20 (1996), 228–9.
[254] Hatlie, "Redeeming," 229.
[255] Basil, *Ep.* 325 (Deferrari) reads "...rewards await you from the Lord God the Master for having reared such children."

indicated the addressee's deeper knowledge of the ancients, as did metaphors, because they would have necessitated an ability to recognize them. An epistle with a few famous phrases from Homer, for example, might present less status than one that included cryptic sayings from more esoteric sources. The latter would indicate an advanced level of *paideia* for author and addressee. It designated a person as part of a limited group endowed with the precious ability to comprehend the text.[256] Receiving this kind of epistle advertised one's comprehensive familiarity with the Greek literary heritage.

To augment epistles, authors sometimes included other gifts along with the letter. These tokens of appreciation could include wine, books, maps, poetry, and other imaginative items.[257] Along with showing kindness, augmenting an epistle with another present could accentuate the message of the gift. Writing to Olympianus, a late-fourth century governor of Cappadocia, Gregory of Nazianzus indicated that he was including a gift with the letter.[258] He stated: "The little volume that you got from me, Aristotle's epistles...let it stay with you as a gift appropriate for an eloquent person and a nice reminder of our friendship."[259] A literary collection from Aristotle constituted a precious prize. Olympianus could have displayed the famous philosopher's work or shared it with associates to show himself as a man of learning. Coupled with the tablet, Gregory's letter defined Olympianus as an honorable individual, worthy of acknowledgment that he was conversant with early epistolary rhetoric.

Because letters from *pepaideumenoi* constituted precious gifts – as works of literature, products of ornate handwriting, and embodiments of respected authors – addressees often assembled and copied the missives.[260] Recipients placed these epistolary treasures in collections as symbols of mutual refinement and historical markers of social interaction with fellow elites.[261] Thus the material letter served as an artifact – a

---

[256] Letters among *pepaideumenoi* were designed primarily for a limited audience, rather than a broader public. Rosenmeyer calls correspondence used in this way an example of writing that is "widely referential, a reflection of the culture and the purpose which produce it," Rosenmeyer, *Ancient*, 28.

[257] Wine: Synesius, *Ep.* 134; Books: Synesius, *Ep.* 154; also Julian, *Ep.* 32; Maps: Julian, *Ep.* 7.

[258] Olympianus: *PLRE* 1: 642; see Van Dam, "Governors," 63–4.

[259] Greg. Naz., *Ep.* 234 (Storin 191).

[260] For discussion of several edited collections see M. Trapp, *Greek and Latin Letters: An Anthology with Translation* (Cambridge: Cambridge University Press, 2003), 12–27.

[261] M. Mullett, "Writing in Early Medieval Byzantium," in *The Uses of Literacy in Early Medieval Europe*, ed. R. McKitterick (Cambridge: Cambridge University Press, 1990),

precious commodity and a commemoration of the composition process and delivery that could be recalled again and again.[262] Epistles were testaments of the long journeys required by messengers to deliver them and also represented the ceremonial reception. The preserved letter thus constituted an ongoing animation of the author by recalling the encounter. Authors sometimes had copies made of the letters they were sending, a recognition of the intellectual, spiritual, and material value of the epistle as well as a record of often substantial correspondence.[263] Gregory of Nazianzus, as we saw in Chapter 1, gathered copies of his and Basil's letters and delivered them, on request, to Gregory's grandnephew Nicobulus.[264] The corpora served as a literary tool to instruct the young man in epistolary eloquence, but it also provided Nicobulus with an account of his granduncle's life – an autobiography – as well as a biography of Basil.[265]

Honor for the addressee of an epistle depended on words that identified the individual's integrity and set forth expectations that he would manifest exemplary behavior by helping colleagues. Gregory of Nazianzus included one such reference from Homer when he wrote to Eutropius, proconsul of Asia around 370 to 372.[266] He praised Eutropius as a high official and as well-educated, yet still mindful of his friends (τῶν φίλων μὴ ἀμέλει) (in the sense of shared culture) while holding public office.[267] In a citation that honored their common cultural heritage and Eutropius' status, Gregory compared the proconsul's behavior to that of two young warriors in the *Iliad*, who maintained their friendship even when tested by the hardships of war. The warrior ethos, that is, remained alive in the correspondence between the two. Gregory accrued renown by aligning himself with a man so conversant with honor. His bond with the governor, moreover, was based on the same valor that banded together ancient combatants.

183–4; Muir, *Life*, 185–97; essays by A. Silvas, "The Letters of Basil of Caesarea and the role of Letter-Collections in their Transmission," 113–28, W. Mayer, "The Ins and Outs of the Chrysostom Letter-Collection: New Ways of Looking at a Limited Corpus," 129–53, and A. Schor, "The Letters of Theodoret of Cyrrhus: Personal Collections, Multi-Author Archives and Historical Interpretation," 154–71 in *Collecting Early Christian Letters*.

[262] Rosenmeyer, *Ancient*, 116–17.   [263] Liebeschuetz, "Letters," 97–100.
[264] Greg. Naz., *Eps*. 52, 53.   [265] Storin, *Self-Portrait*, 1–4.
[266] Eutropius: Gallay, *Saint Grégoire*, 1:89 n.3; *PLRE* 1:317–18; Jones, *Later Roman Empire*, vol. 2, 367–8, 504–5.
[267] Greg. Naz., *Ep*. 71 (Storin 150).

The exchange of epistles between Eutropius and Gregory punctuated their *philia*, in this case in reference to an association of *agathoi*.[268] Alliances such as this one illustrate the dealings between provincial leaders in what has been described as an economy "embedded in a matrix of personal relations" where the economy and state are "constituted by networks of moral ties sanctioned by public opinion and tradition."[269] In eastern Rome, the give-and-take interactions in the friendship dynamic between cultured men remained rooted in reciprocity. The process of giving with the expectations of a return gift marked the very index of the masculine economy.[270] In this system, one that had predominated in the Homeric world, individuals gave liberally in anticipation of the public honor that would return to them because of their beneficence.[271] Leaders familiar with protocols from ancient Greece understood this practice because it had been the foundation of the Hellenic society that they treasured and that marked their own status. Underscoring this heritage, the Cappadocians were participating in the same honorific economy of gift-giving that they idealized in the world of Homer.[272] As with other *pepaideumenoi*, they paralleled givers of exquisite gifts, who created fame and gained loyalty by dispensing honorific wealth to others. In this sense, the Cappadocians continued to establish themselves as arbiters of *aretē* among their addressees.

The examples of friendship relations from this chapter show an aesthetic that advanced the Cappadocians' ideals of masculinity. In a discourse of friendship, the Cappadocians composed epistles that recognized mutual *aretē* in *philoi*, while exhibiting their own command of a rhetoric of the senses. They shared in an epistolary *agōn* of friendship with fellow Christian and non-Christian *pepaideumenoi* by using conventions predicated on an ethos of reciprocity. In these exhibitions, the

---

[268] D. Konstan, "Reciprocity and Friendship," in *Reciprocity in Ancient Greece*, eds. C. Gill, N. Postlethwaite, and R. Seaford (Oxford: Oxford University Press, 1998), 279–85.
[269] Konstan, "Reciprocity," 282–3.
[270] H. Cixous, "Sorties: Out and Out: Attacks/Ways Out/Forays," in *The Newly Born Woman*, eds. H. Cixous and C. Clement, trans. B. King (Minneapolis: University of Minnesota Press, 1986), 87–92.
[271] Mifsud, "On Rhetoric," 102–5.
[272] W. Donlan, "Political Reciprocity in Dark Age Greece: Odysseus and His Hetairoi," *Reciprocity in Ancient Greece*, 51.

Cappadocians participated in a dialogue that reckoned *aretē* as an outcome of encounters with fellow *agathoi*. Manhood was achieved, that is, through engagement with other virtuous men. Expressions of *philia* similarly held that camaraderie between noble individuals was based on reciprocity and intimacy between men of high character. The exchange of these letters, rooted in the practice of emulating presence, enabled the Cappadocians to apply a wide array of self-representations. In framing *philia* through the trope of absence, and portraying union of souls using sensory language, the Cappadocians valorized elements of materiality as means for expressing masculinity.

References to corporeality accentuated a level of fellowship according to the identity of the correspondent, allowing the Cappadocians to deploy scriptural or classical allusions to maintain intimacy according to shared background. Assigning *aretē* to Christians through a variety of references, the Cappadocians signaled a bond shared by faith and social affinity. With non-Christians, moreover, the Cappadocians used letters to reinforce their participation in a network based on a sense of masculinity founded in *paideia*. Like a "traffic in praise," to use Leslie Kurke's terminology, these letters circulated honor to recipients and reified a hierarchy of men trained in a similar habitus. An emphasis on the aesthetic appeal of bodily features in friends, even assertions of erotic attraction, indicates belief of a certain Beauty of both soul and body that gave testimony to their excellence. Authors likewise complimented the physical appearance of messengers and the magnificence of the penmanship in the letters, while portraying the missives themselves as precious gifts; all further examples of a nexus between resplendent materiality, masculinity, and hierarchy.

By activating sensory reaction as an index of *aretē*, the Cappadocians ascribed higher value to materiality than had pre-fourth century clergy. In doing so, they contributed to a shift in the use of materiality as a rhetorical medium. In these interactions, they deployed sensory language that imbued the body with surplus value. The Cappadocians imagined the senses, therefore, as a means of creating identity and hierarchy. Such attributions of status are representative of the adaptation of figural language by early Christian writers.[273] A rhetoric of sensory imagination, Averil Cameron has posed, enabled Christian apologists to use tangible concepts to talk about a God who was, by nature, transcendent.

---

[273] A. Cameron, *Christianity and the Rhetoric of Empire: The Development of Christian Discourse* (Berkeley: University of California Press, 1991), 53–68.

A rhetoric of friendship – based on sensory language – similarly equipped Christian intellectuals to define ideal masculinity. Exerting expertise in sensory dialogue, the Cappadocians replicated perception, ranging from sight and voice – the highest esteemed senses – to touch, the most animalistic.[274] The eyes, the voice, and the hands of the *agathos*, that is, were configured as instruments of sanctity and virtue. Through this elevation of corporeal imagery, the Cappadocians participated in *aretē* with correspondents, thus broadening a community based on pro-Nicene masculine identity.

[274] Frank, *Memory*, 123. On rankings of the senses, Aristotle, *On the Soul*, 2.7–11.

3

Hagiography and Masculinity

Personifications of Sacred Aretē

At the beginning of his *Life of Gregory Thaumaturgus* (the "Wonderworker"), Gregory of Nyssa sets forth the correlation between performing commendable acts and writing about them. "As I see it, one and the same power is required both for achieving virtue in deed (ἔργον) and for describing what is good worthily in a speech (λόγος). Consequently the same ally must be called upon for help as the one through whose aid he achieved virtue in his lifetime."[1] Accomplishments and accounts of exploits, Nyssen was saying, should derive from the same source.[2] Throughout the rest of the narrative, Nyssen illustrates how this origin, "the grace of the Holy Spirit," incites the protagonist Thaumaturgus to carry out divine endeavors.[3] In recounting the life of this third-century east Roman bishop, Nyssen depicts Thaumaturgus (c. 210–70) as a man of action, whose feats authorize his primacy. The subject is a doer as much as a speaker, an index of nobility often cited in the works of famed Greek orator Demosthenes and later reiterated in Second Sophistic authors such as Plutarch.[4] Set in an arena of

---

[1] Greg. Ny., *Vit. GTh.* 1.1 (Slusser).
[2] D. Krueger, *Writing and Holiness: The Practice of Authorship in the Early Christian East* (Philadelphia: University of Pennsylvania Press, 2004), 27–9, argues that the author of a hagiographic account, by mediating the narrative, participates in a holy enterprise. His writing thereby connects him, mimetically, to the spiritual authority of the saint.
[3] Greg. Ny., *Vit. GTh.* 1.1 (Slusser).
[4] J. Roisman, *The Rhetoric of Manhood: Masculinity in the Attic Orators* (Berkeley: University of California Press, 2005), 139–41, points out that Demosthenes placed high importance on speech, but taught that the surer index of character and manhood came from deeds. He cites, for example, Demosthenes, *Or.* 2.12: "All words, apart from action,

spiritual conflict, Thaumaturgus assumes a place once occupied by ancient Greek paragons of manliness, the athlete and the soldier.

By delineating the kinetic elements of Thaumaturgus' career, with attention to his performing beneficent miracles, Nyssen brings the bishop into focus as a champion of the people. For readers and listeners of the sacred biography, Thaumaturgus comes across as a man of deeds, who proves soundness of truth through public demonstrations of faith rather than what Nyssen dubs the "subtlety of speech" (περινοία τῶν λόγων) of false philosophers.[5] Nyssen warns audiences to be skeptical of the "artificial conceit of the wordsmiths" (τεχνικὴ τῶν λογογράφων).[6] By way of comparison, Thaumaturgus confirms truth through strength derived from God. He poses a virile persona by appealing to the legacy of gallantry embedded in the imagination of eastern Romans. Nyssen makes Thaumaturgus' piety an extension of *aretē* acquired through multiple contests. Through moderating the narrative, Nyssen stations his own episcopal office in the realm of an *agōn*. The connection is made even more suitable because Thaumaturgus served in Pontus, the province where Nyssen and Basil's grandparents had lived and suffered under Roman persecution. Both Nyssen and Basil magnified familial ties to Thaumaturgus: Basil, by tracing the family pedigree of faith back to their "spiritual father" Thaumaturgus;[7] Nyssen, by shaping the narrative so that elements of Thaumaturgus' career mirrored those of Basil and himself.[8] Thaumaturgus appears as the intrepid competitor, "like an athlete who, since he has enough experience from competition and strength from training, strips confidently for the race."[9] He comes across as a veteran competitor, hardened against the wiles of opponents, thus giving him power to suppress numerous challenges from demons. Embattled by the forces of evil, he was subjected to multiple trials and emerged victorious. Through miraculous feats against demonic forces – expelling them from a

---

seem vain and idle" (Vince). Also, Demosthenes, *Or.* 10.3, 18.57, 122. See the sentiment as expressed in Plutarch, *Moralia* 80e and 84b.

[5] Greg. Ny., *Vit. GTh.* 2.13 (Slusser).   [6] Greg. Ny., *Vit. GTh.* 5.41 (Slusser).

[7] See Basil, *Ep.* 204; R. Van Dam, *Families and Friends in Late Roman Cappadocia* (Philadelphia: University of Pennsylvania Press, 2003), 28, argues that because Basil was writing to Christians at Neo-Caesarea (the city in Pontus ministered by Thaumaturgus), he drew attention to the link between Thaumaturgus and his grandmother Macrina the Elder, who had preserved the regional history of Thaumaturgus.

[8] R. Van Dam, *Becoming Christian: The Conversion of Roman Cappadocia* (Philadelphia: University of Pennsylvania Press, 2003), 78–9.

[9] Greg. Ny., *Vit. GTh.* 4.33 (Slusser): καθάπερ τις ἀθλητὴς ἀρκοῦσαν πρὸς τοὺς ἄθλους ἐμπειρίαν τε καὶ δύναμιν ἐκ παιδοτρίβου κτησάμενος, θαρσῶν ἀποδύεται πρὸς τὸ στάδιον.

sacred temple, for example – Thaumaturgus flexed his dominance and piety.[10] As Thaumaturgus encounters various tests, Nyssen casts him as a seasoned athlete.[11] Nyssen paints the picture of a chiseled runner, oiling himself before toeing the starting line. Thaumaturgus takes the posture of an Olympian who welcomes the opportunity to race. He cuts an imposing figure for audiences who were taught to find in pro-Nicene bishops a bastion of truth in the fluid theological climate of the late-fourth century church. This same audience had been socialized to imagine the pinnacle of manliness in the Greek tradition. Nyssen was speaking to this sensibility.

Previously we examined epistolary exchange as an exercise in cultivating *aretē* through exhibitions of *paideia*. These manifestations of mutual refinement took place among a limited group, for individuals endowed with the training to decipher the beauty of eloquent composition, penmanship, and delivery. But as this chapter will bear out, the Cappadocians also issued demonstrations of *agōnes* for a larger public. Gregory of Nazianzus and Gregory of Nyssa, for example, penned narrative biographies of family members and bishops from past and present. These texts, which were delivered orally to civic audiences, associated high standards of masculinity with the office of pro-Nicene clergy.[12] The works, which are difficult to categorize into one genre, took the form of oration, encomium, and letter.[13] In most cases, the Gregories presented the biographies to large gatherings, in churches, or at funerals. As in their correspondence, the Cappadocians used these opportunities, in part, to associate leaders of the pro-Nicene faith with conventions of classical manhood. But in public speeches, which reached much broader audiences, the Gregories set their subjects in various contests that would

---

[10] Greg. Ny., *Vit. GTh.* 5.36. Here Nyssen uses the trope of struggle against demons as a backdrop for emphasizing maleness in Thaumaturgus. See D. Brakke, *Demons and the Making of the Monk: Spiritual Combat in Early Christianity* (Cambridge, MA: Harvard University Press, 2006), 7–14.

[11] Greg. Ny., *Vit. GTh.* 4.33.

[12] J. Bernardi, *La Prédication des pères cappadociens: le prédicateur et son auditoire* (Marseille: Presses universitaires de France, 1968), 238–46, for example, shows that Nazianzen was concerned to build a favorable image of his fellow bishops while preserving his own high esteem.

[13] See discussion of biographic literature in Introduction. For an overview of difficulties of genre, L. Pernot, *La Rhétorique de l'éloge dans le monde gréco-romain*, vol. 1(Paris: Institut d'Études Augustiniennes, 1993), 288–95; F. Norris, "Your Honor, My Reputation," in *Greek Biography and Panegyric in Late Antiquity*, eds. T. Hägg and P. Rousseau (Berkeley: University of California Press, 2000), 143, as an example of the problem of isolating genre, discusses the difficulties of classifying Nazianzen's oration for Basil, because of Nazianzen's skill at mixing genres.

appeal to the expectations of a diversity of listeners, many of whom were illiterate.[14] In these hagiographical accounts, I maintain, Nazianzen and Nyssen accentuated manliness and nobility primarily as features of pro-Nicene bishops and their families. They personified subjects as virile heroes and heroines situated in a setting of contention that demanded courage, endurance, and boldness. And they confirmed their own status as *agathoi* and superior theologians by mediating masculinity for listeners and readers. By endowing family, friends, and pro-Nicene bishops with virility, the Gregories created an aesthetic based on a conflation of piety, class, and deportment.

In eastern Rome, individual performance supplied the matrix that determined civic influence, with public displays of *aretē* serving as validation of nobility. The Cappadocians interacted in a sphere that required competitive zest: in promotion of asceticism and their own self-discipline; in theological disputes; in civic patronage; and in displays of *paideia*. The Gregories therefore infused the protagonists of their biographies with victory in epic struggles. The authors subsequently offered the subjects of their accounts as paragons of triumph in competition. Raised in a culture of leadership that extolled hard-earned success, the Gregories turned to texts that exemplified masculine, aristocratic church leaders.[15] They personified their heroes and heroines as athletes and warriors, icons of endurance and contention. Unlike epistolary composition, where the exchange of letters itself constituted an *agōn*, in biographic narratives the Cappadocians staged the struggle in the lives of the characters. Family and friends, that is, became virtual actors in a showcase of virility that spoke for the author's vision of the episcopacy and theological orthodoxy.

Scholars have rightfully interpreted imagery of an *agōn* in hagiographic texts as a typology for understanding the exertions of the martyr and the ascetic.[16] The Cappadocians applied the motif of struggle, in part,

---

[14] R. Van Dam, "Hagiography and History: The Life of Gregory Thaumaturgus," *Classical Antiquity* 1:2 (1982), 279, points out that meeting the expectations of a diverse, even polyglot audience, was often as important as the content of the speech.

[15] K. Bassi, *Acting Like Men: Gender, Drama and Nostalgia in Ancient Greece* (Ann Arbor: University of Michigan Press, 1998), 3–4, shows the same tendency in the ancient Greek poets, who sought congruity with masculine subjects from the past; Bernardi, *Prédication*, 311, has also recognized this rhetorical strategy in the Cappadocians.

[16] For example E. Castelli, *Martyrdom and Memory: Early Christian Culture Making* (New York: Columbia University Press, 2004), 90–1, discusses a classic case of such imagery in her analysis of the *Passion of Perpetua*, a third-century Latin martyr text; B. Shaw, "Body/Power/Identity: Passions of the Martyrs," *JECS* 4:3 (1996): 278–81, likewise

Personifications of Sacred Aretē

to bodily sacrifices of saints. The use of sports metaphors aligns with imagery of the runner and the boxer, for example, in I Corinthians: "Therefore I do not run like a man running aimlessly; I do not fight like a man beating the air. No, I beat my body and make it my slave..."[17] Christians generally understood the passage as a directive about submitting the body to the bidding of the Holy Spirit. The contest, that is, constituted a venture in sanctification.[18] In the New Testament, analogies of an *agōn* were used to indicate personal participation in the blessings of the Gospel, with the winner's prize represented as salvation in Christ.[19] In such uses, the trope of an *agōn* did not include the cult of beauty, the spirit of mutual *aretē* gained through competition, or the individual honor that one established for himself; all of which had been prominent in the ancient athletic games and recast in the culture of *paideia*.[20]

Confining the athletic metaphor to its biblical contexts, however, does not fully account for the way that Christian *pepaideumenoi* used the trope of exertion. The Cappadocians, for example, did not use allusions to rivalry strictly about spiritual contention. The Gregories also referenced the athlete and the warrior in reenactments of public disputation, a primary locus of an *agōn*, as well as in accounts of saints who were manifesting holiness through their bodies. While these depictions called forth a symbolic spiritual melee, they also reinforced a code of ancient rhetoric that treated contest as a testament of status and discernment. Through the protagonists in the Cappadocians' hagiographic biographies, the masculine ethos of *pepaideumenoi* merged with the piety of the saints. Accordingly, the Cappadocians were characterizing the biographical subjects as engaged in heated rivalries where honor,

---

explains that the author of 4 Maccabees used the martyr-as-athlete trope to show that the power of the martyr came through control of the body.

[17] I Corinthians 9:26–7 (NIV).

[18] R. R. Ruether, *Gregory of Nazianzus: Rhetor and Philosopher* (Oxford: Clarendon, 1969), 90, states: "In the athlete image we see classical culture transmuted and put at the service of a different value system from the system of *aretē* which first produced it."

[19] S. Remijsen, *The End of Greek Athletics in Late Antiquity* (Cambridge: Cambridge University Press, 2015), 286, states that in the scriptures the "noble athlete" topos was used "namely to explain how the good Christian could reach heaven, or metaphorically, the victory crown." A similar point is made by V. Pfitzner, *Paul and the Agon Motif: Traditional Athletic Imagery in Pauline Literature* (Leiden: Brill, 1967), 106–7.

[20] Pfitzner, *Paul*, 48, also shows that in *agōn* language from the Old Testament, the naked body constituted a source of shame, to be hidden from man and God; unlike its place in Greek athletics.

authority, and theological doctrine were at stake; and where audiences would authenticate legitimate sources of leadership as the foundation of the social hierarchy of the fourth-century church.

This chapter investigates the shaping of sacred manhood in six hagiographic accounts. The narratives of Thaumaturgus and Caesarius promote the ideal of the Christian *pepaideumenos* as an athlete, contending not only within himself, but against impious rivals that magnify his own virtue. The two eulogies for Basil, meanwhile, show a combatant, hardened through the rigorous training of *paideia* and descended from a genealogy of God's prophets and chosen leaders. And the chronicles of Gorgonia and Macrina situate the foundations of sacred *aretē* within the family, as linked to the ascetic bodies of female siblings whose corporeal suffering is reoriented as masculine piety. While treating these subjects, however, the background of fourth-century theological struggle must be established. The acrimony involved in these doctrinal debates relates to a key difference between the rhetoric of *agōn* used in epistolary composition and that of hagiography. In the former, I have argued, the Cappadocians staged virtual contests as a means of publicizing cultural capital for both parties, writer and addressee. The manhood of each was acknowledged. We have referred, on the one hand, to the evocation of contest in this sense as "agonistic." In hagiographic biographies, on the other hand, the writers construed *agōnes* between theological rivals as zero-sum battles of "antagonistic" duels. The encounters, in other words, resulted in a victor and a defeated; a right and a wrong; an accrual of *aretē* for one and a diminishing for the other. In this sense, honor was not circulated, as was the case among epistolary correspondents. Rather, pro-Nicene saints take their place as personifications of sacred *aretē*, while their enemies – often cast as opponents of Trinitarianism – play the counterpart as effeminate enemies of God.[21]

THEOLOGICAL BACKGROUND OF FOURTH-CENTURY HAGIOGRAPHY

The hagiographies discussed in this chapter promoted variant identities: the *pepaideumenos*; the civic leader; the ascetic; the noble Christian woman; the

---

[21] L. S. Cobb, *Dying to Be Men: Gender and Language in Early Christian Martyr Texts* (New York: Columbia University Press, 2008), 5–6, argues that early Christian martyr texts established their subjects as more masculine than pagan counterparts. In Cappadocian hagiography, the protagonists outstrip the masculinity, more specifically, of heretical faith groups.

Christian; and the Greek. These identities were formed against the backdrop of theological struggles over Christology during a twenty-year period (from 360 to 381) that was especially divisive and complex. In most cases, the authors of the biographies ushered idealizations not merely of sacred virtue, but of a distinctly *pro-Nicene* persona. The men and women, that is, represented the superiority, trustworthiness, and rightmindedness of pro-Nicenes – Christians supporting a theology predicated on the creed of the Council of Nicaea in 325. In some instances, the Christological struggle was set as a sub-theme of the narrative, as for example, in the depictions of Thaumaturgus, Gorgonia, and Macrina. In others, theological confrontations with opponents took the foreground and played a major role in constructing the image of the saint, as in Nyssen's and Nazianzen's portrayals of Basil against Nicene adversary Emperor Valens (r. 364–378). The contours of the divide between pro-Nicenes and opponents are complex and fall outside the scope of our study. An overview of the major lines of the Trinitarian debate, however, will help to clarify why Nyssen and Nazianzen went to great lengths to script sacred heroes and heroines as pro-Nicene.

In 359 Emperor Constantius II (r. 337–61) convened twin councils at Seleucia and Ariminum, where leaders discussed strategies for reaching a consensus on a Trinitarian doctrine that would replace that of Nicaea in 325. Over the course of the thirty-five years since Nicaea, in eastern Rome bishops had increasingly opposed the statement in the Nicene Creed that the Father and Son share the same "essence" (*ousia*). Dissenters to Nicaea generally favored an understanding of the Son as subordinate to the Father, a claim that was undermined by the declaration in the Nicene Creed that the Son derived from the "same essence" (ὁμοούσια; *homoousia*) as the Father. Church leaders opposing Nicene language held wide-ranging beliefs about the similarity of the Son to the Father. By the 350s they came to be labeled collectively as Homoians, because most were willing to admit in unspecified terms *only* that the Son is *like* (ὅμοιος; *homoios*) the Father. Constantius himself ascribed to Homoian Christology, favoring the doctrine in part because it offered flexibility of interpretation; something of use to an emperor seeking religious consensus.[22] He thus supported bishops who held this view and colluded with them during the councils

---

[22] P. Rousseau, *Basil of Caesarea* (Berkeley: University of California Press, 1994), 96–9 and L. Ayres, *Nicaea and its Legacy: An Approach to Fourth-Century Trinitarian Theology* (Oxford: Oxford University Press, 2004), 133–5, attribute the prevalence of the Homoians during this period to a desire on the part of many bishops, along with Constantius, to reach a consensus on Christology.

of 359. Despite major opposition by western pro-Nicene bishops, first the Council of Ariminum, and later Seleucia sent recommendations to Constantius calling for a new universal creed that accorded with Homoian tenets. By early 360, Constantius held a small council in Constantinople that approved a new creed, which notably disavowed any use of *ousia* (essence) to relate the Son to the Father. Basil, who was not yet a priest, attended the council to offer opposition to the Homoians. He did not speak out against Homoian arguments, however, and ultimately he departed early when it became apparent that bishops leading the resistance would lose. Later his legacy suffered because of the retreat.[23]

Two other notable outcomes of 360 help to explain why the Cappadocians fashioned pro-Nicene hagiographies.[24] First, in 360 the prominent Homoian Eudoxius of Antioch was made bishop of Constantinople and Eunomius (born in Cappadocia) was made bishop of Cyzicus. We met Eunomius earlier and we will return to Eunomius, and his mentor Aetius, in more detail in Chapter 4.[25] Eunomius' consecration in 360 shows the diversity within the Homoian camp. He advocated a greater dissimilarity between the Father and Son than most Homoians reckoned, by emphasizing that the *ousia* of the Son and of the Father was not only separate, but also dissimilar. Eunomius' position thus represented a blatant case of ἑτεροὐσια (*heterousia*), that is considering the Father and Son of separate essences. It was largely against figures such as Eudoxius and Eunomius, we will see, that Nyssen and Nazianzen characterized their versions of pro-Nicene saints. Also in 360, the council banished leading bishops, such as Basil of Ancyra and Eustathius of Sebaste, who had advocated for inclusion of *ousia* terminology in the

---

[23] M. DelCogliano and A. Radde-Gallwitz, *St. Basil of Caesarea: Against Eunomius* (Washington: Catholic University of America Press, 2011), 10–11. Also, S. Hildebrand, *The Trinitarian Theology of Basil of Caesarea: A Synthesis of Greek Thought and Biblical Truth* (Washington: Catholic University of America Press, 2007), 21, who points out that Basil's timidity at the council was highlighted in texts by Eunomius and then, later, by the Heterousian church historian Philostorgius. Reference to this slight toward Basil appears in Gregory of Nyssa, *Contr. Eun.* 1.9 and Philostorgius *H.E.* 4.12.

[24] Ayres, *Nicaea*, 156–66, offers a compelling account of the events leading up to the council and its outcomes. My assessment of the background to the council of 360 is based on his narrative.

[25] R. Vaggione, *Eunomius of Cyzicus and the Nicene Revolution* (Oxford: Oxford University Press, 2000), 14–26, discusses the background of Aetius and his formative influence on Eunomius. Eudoxius: Van Dam, *Families*, 121; a native Cappadocian, but not the same Eudoxius from Introduction and Chap. 1.

new creed. Eustathius, at this time, was a mentor of sorts to Basil (Caesarean), having introduced Basil to eastern Christian monasticism.[26] Basil of Ancyra and Eustathius had come to be known as Homoiousians because they pushed for inclusion of the phrase "similar in essence" (ὁμοιούσια; *homoiousia*). Thus, they offered accommodation with the Homoians while preserving the close approximation of the Son to the Father. Basil himself concurred with the Homoiousians' emphasis on accentuating the similarity of essence, though his theology was not strictly the same as theirs.[27]

Although he later had a major falling out with Eustathius, Basil (Caesarean) likely began moving closer in his theology to Homoousian (same *ousia* in Father and Son) Christology in response to the machinations of 360, his friends' failure at the council, and his observation of the extremes that Homoianism permitted for individuals such as Eunomius. Homoiousianism had allowed for somewhat of a compromise for individuals who leaned toward the unity within the Godhead. The Christology of Homoiousians made provisions for distinguishing among the persons in the Trinity and asserting similarity of *ousia*, but without avowing absolute sameness of substance. By 365, Basil completed *Against Eunomius*, a polemic that rejected the anti-Trinitarian arguments of Eunomius, the Heterousian.[28] Following this composition, Basil appears to have followed a path from 365 until the early 370s, leading him closer to the thought of Homoousian bishop Athanasius.[29] Except for several forced periods of exile, Athanasius had been Bishop of Alexandria in

---

[26] Rousseau, *Basil*, 73–6.

[27] An enduring interpretation has held that Basil was Homoiousian until later in his career. This presumption was resisted as early as A.-M. Ritter, *Das Konzil von Konstantinopel und sein Symbol* (Göttingen: Vandenhoeck and Ruprecht, 1965), 270–93. More recently Hildebrand, *Trinitarian*, 20–1, cautioned against equating Basil's theological tradition precisely with either that of Basil of Ancyra or Eustathius, particularly in his hesitancy to subordinate the Son to the Father. And Mark DelCogliano, "The Influence of Athanasius and the Homoiousians on Basil of Caesarea's Decentralization of 'Unbegotten'," *JECS* 19:2 (2011), 197–223, makes the most convincing case yet that it is incorrect to identify Basil as Homoiousian. DelCogliano argues that Basil was heavily influenced by Homoiousian theology, but did not sympathize with all its tenets. DelCogliano argues that much of the confusion has come because the theology of strict Homoousian Athanasius of Alexandria was mediated to Basil through the writings of Homoiousian bishops.

[28] I follow the dating based on chronological arguments of DelCogliano and Radde-Gallwitz, *Basil*, 28–33.

[29] Although there is little evidence for Athanasius' direct influence. And Basil's program of unifying moderate factions in the Trinitarian controversy never met with the approval of Athanasius. See Hildebrand, *Trinitarian*, 26–7.

Egypt since 326. He had been an extremist in the eyes of many Homoiousians and Homoians alike during the mid-century disputes, as he had been unwilling to compromise on his theology and he overemphasized the oneness within the Godhead to the detriment of distinguishing between the three persons. Having witnessed the distortions that came out of Homoianism, however, Basil was coming to see the benefits of using the Nicene Creed as a cipher for the phraseology of a theology that would ensure the Son's eternal participation in the Father's existence.

When the Homoian Emperor Valens took the throne in 364, Basil and Nazianzen both took part in the Trinitarian dispute at the church of Caesarea during the emperor's visit there in 365 (discussed below). At this point, Nazianzen had been a priest for only four years, as an assistant to his father Gregory the Elder, the bishop of Nazianzus. Basil, meanwhile, had been ordained as priest at Caesarea two years earlier. The memory of the debacle at Constantinople in 360 would still have been fresh on his mind when he completed his *Against Eunomius* in 365, around the same time as Valens' visit to Cappadocia. Basil's involvement in the Trinitarian controversy expanded after he was consecrated bishop of Caesarea in 370. Among the pro-Nicene bishops that he installed at various sees were included Gregory (at Nyssa) and Nazianzen (at Sasima) in 372. During the 370s, until his death in 379, Basil composed numerous theological writings and corresponded with numerous churches and clergy on Trinitarian doctrine.

While Nazianzen and Nyssen corresponded with others about theological matters and completed treatises before 380, most of their doctrinal output dates between 379 (the year of Basil's death) and 382. Four of the hagiographic biographies treated in this chapter coincide with this period. Both Gregories assumed a more visible role in Trinitarian discussions from 380 onward. For Nyssen, greater contribution seems to have corresponded to his role within the family, taking up where his brother Basil had left off after his death. Nyssen had already experienced harassment for his pro-Nicene beliefs, having been exiled for a two-year period by one of Emperor Valens' officials in 375.[30] He was no stranger to Trinitarian

---

[30] A. Silvas, *Gregory of Nyssa: The Letters* (Leiden: Brill, 2006), 31–2, contends that the banishment resulted ostensibly from financial mismanagement, but in reality the vicar Demosthenes exiled Gregory as a measure against his intransigence in religious matters. Demosthenes, and perhaps Valens as well, seem to have taken a hard line on religious policies early in their involvement with the Cappadocians. This rigidity, as we will see, changed to an administrative policy of utility much less driven by religious considerations.

theological battles. Nyssen and Nazianzen became more heavily involved in matters of imperial church orthodoxy in the early 380s partly due to Valens' exile and later reinstatement of pro-Nicene bishops, and partly because of the policies of Emperor Theodosius I (r. 379–395), who ruled eastern Rome following Valens' death. Valens had restored pro-Nicene bishops to their respective sees shortly before his death in 378. This unexpected measure presented a complication for Christian communities across the eastern empire, as many cities now had rival pro-Nicene and Homoian bishops.[31] By promoting the moral character of former pro-Nicene saints through hagiographic orations, the Gregories were advocating for their current colleagues. Theodosius, meanwhile, supported pro-Nicene Christianity and in 381 he convened a council of pro-Nicene bishops at Constantinople to create a consensus among imperial churches based on the Nicene Creed of 325.[32] Nazianzen, in fact, would serve as president of the council for part of its duration. Leading up to, during, and after the Council of Constantinople (completed in 381), Nyssen and Nazianzen delivered their most prolific output of theological writings.[33] A major outcome of the council was the creation of a new creed, based on but expanding on the Nicene version of 325, that confirmed a Homoousian Trinitarian theology while anathematizing "Eunomians," "Arians," and "Pneumatomachi."[34] This conclusion represented a major

---

[31] A. Radde-Gallwitz, *Gregory of Nyssa's Doctrinal Works: A Literary Study* (Oxford: Oxford University Press, 2018), 17.

[32] Ritter, *Das Konzil*, 50–133, shows that this purpose was only one of many reasons for the council. Ritter's seminal work on the council in its ecclesiastical, political, and social context remains an essential study. Ritter, *Konzil*, 116–20, and J. McGuckin, *St Gregory of Nazianzus: An Intellectual Biography* (Crestwood, NY: St. Vladimir's Seminary, 2001), 234–7, point out prior examples of Theodosius attempting to reach a consensus regarding Christian doctrine. Constantinople, therefore, was not unique.

[33] McGuckin, *Gregory*, 311–69, provides a helpful chronology and a manageable, nuanced account of the council, with Nyssen's and Nazianzen's involvement in the council itself and work in Constantinople in the period leading up to it.

[34] T. Kopecek, *A History of Neo-Arianism*, vol. 2 (Cambridge, MA: Philadelphia Patristics Foundation, 1979), 514, shows that these terms are used as polemic to condemn persons who believed differently than the affirmed doctrine: the "Eunomians" are indicted as followers of the teachings of Eunomius of Cyzicus; the "Arians" as followers of the teachings of Arius, an early-fourth century priest in Alexandria condemned by Homoousians as the originator of Heterousian doctrine; and "Pneumatomachi," for individuals who denied the divinity of the Spirit. The statement of faith from the Council of Constantinople itself does not survive, but the Trinitarian orthodoxy from the council is preserved in a letter included in Theodoret, *H.E.* 5.9. See the translation in Ayres, *Nicaea*, 258.

symbol of Theodosius' policy to unite the empire around pro-Nicene doctrine, while marginalizing heterodox opponents.

The hagiographic biographies of Nyssen and Nazianzen must be understood according to this context, with most of these texts dating within a year either side of 381. By this time, both bishops were veterans of the vitriol between pro-Nicenes and Homoians, with each holding animus toward the Heterousian Eunomius and his supporters. Both were invested in the heated contests that were taking place in public orations as attempts to sway the masses and *pepaideumenoi*. The issues surrounding the Christological debates, therefore, remained in mind as they composed biographical accounts. It was to the advantage of the pro-Nicene party, therefore, for Nyssen and Nazianzen to cast their protagonists as representatives of Homoousian belief. By aligning the moral impetus of manhood with the party of pro-Nicenes, Nyssen and Nazianzen added credence to their Trinitarian teachings. Preoccupation with pro-Nicene heroes and heroines, moreover, did not cease immediately following Constantinople. Nazianzen's personification of Basil in 382 also was based largely on Basil's (and Gregory's) defense of pro-Nicene orthodoxy. Although the Council of Constantinople confirmed a pro-Nicene creed for the church, the result did not end Homoian or Heterousian movements in eastern Rome.

VIRTUAL CONTESTS IN GREGORY THAUMATURGUS AND CAESARIUS

In his life of Thaumaturgus, Nyssen specified attributes that made the third-century Pontic bishop appear as a champion.[35] "He [Thaumaturgus] was filled with boldness (παρρησία) and confidence (θάρσος)," Nyssen writes.[36] Nyssen set this phrasing against the backdrop of athletic imagery that remained valorized among late antique audiences.[37] Participation in sports

---

[35] For an overview of Thaumaturgus and the affiliation of Nyssen's family with him: S. Mitchell, "The Life and *Lives* of Gregory Thaumaturgus," in *Portraits of Spiritual Authority: Religious Power in Early Christianity, Byzantium and the Christian Orient*, eds. J. Drijvers and J. Watt (Leiden: Brill, 1999), 99–139 and R. L. Fox, *Pagans and Christians* (New York: Alfred A. Knopf, 1987), 517–42.

[36] Greg. Ny., *Vit. GTh.* 4.33 (Slusser).

[37] Remijsen, *End*, 281; Van Dam, "Hagiography," 306, points out that athletics carried significant popular appeal: for honoring the aristocracy that funded the games; for bringing pride to native cities of athletes; and, of course, for enabling the athlete to put his excellence on display.

in classical Greece combined with artistic and intellectual proficiency to civilize young men.[38] A fundamental purpose of athletics was to expose the youngster to bodily and mental duress in order to toughen him. Engaging in sporting contests thus promoted a consensus of virtue among *pepaideumenoi*.[39] These confrontations were limited, for much of the Hellenic past, to Greek citizens and to individuals with sufficient means to prepare. Presaging the education of upper-class fourth-century males, earlier Panhellenic games represented a showcase of superior ethnicity and class.[40] The famous epinicians (victory odes) of Greek poet Pindar (c. 522–c. 443 B.C.) focused on aspects of individual performance that resonated with collective aristocratic values, particularly on proving status through accomplishment.[41] "Steep is the path of the arts but now, as you offer this prize, be bold – shout it straight out," Pindar proclaims, "for this man was born by the gods' will with hands full of strength, feet able, and eyes brave!"[42] In the Greek polis, the athletic hero was the best the city had to honor the gods.

Nyssen was creating a ballad like this fifth-century B.C. prototype, showing his own hero as a veteran of severest trials. "Thus [Thaumaturgus] undertook his struggles – for his whole life in the priesthood deserves to be called nothing less than struggles or contests (ἀγῶνες καὶ ἄθλοι) in which through faith he combatted every power of the Adversary."[43] Throughout Nyssen's narrative, Thaumaturgus undergoes tests of his faith and virtue, with each one further molding him into a worthy defender. These bouts recall the tests put to Jesus and his disciples, such as when the devil tempted Christ in the desert, with Jesus thwarting every approach.[44] After one similar victory over demons, Nyssen relates, Thaumaturgus entered the city "with confidence and boldness," his power proven through his successful contest of good over evil.[45] Thaumaturgus had faced a nefarious peril, the kind of threat against which only a seasoned church leader could contend. His entry into the

---

[38] O. Van Nijf, "Athletics, *Andreia* and the Askêsis-Culture in the Roman East," in *Andreia: Studies in Manliness and Courage in Classical Antiquity*, eds. R. Rosen and I. Sluiter (Leiden: Brill, 2003), 273.

[39] D. Hawhee, *Bodily Arts: Rhetoric and Athletics in Ancient Greece* (Austin: University of Texas Press, 2005), 16–17.

[40] Van Nijf, "Athletics," 273: "Masculinity put on display was seen as a civic value *par excellence*."

[41] L. Kurke, *The Traffic in Praise: Pindar and the Poetics of Social Economy* (Ithaca: Cornell University Press, 1991), 87–92, 108–11, 167–70, 252–60.

[42] Pindar, *Olympian Ode* 9 (Burnett). [43] Greg. Ny., *Vit. GTh.* 4.33 (Slusser).

[44] Matthew 4:1–11. [45] Greg. Ny., *Vit. GTh.* 6.42 (Slusser).

city after victory symbolized his proper place within the civic sphere, much like an athlete returning to a hero's welcome. With antecedents in scripture and Greek epinician poetry, Nyssen's account presented a man approved by God and seasoned through spiritual conflict, made relatable in worldly terms of noble competition. Thaumaturgus is reoriented as a contestant of high rank, bringing honor to his town and to fellow *pepaideumenoi*.

In the account, moreover, Gregory synchronizes Thaumaturgus' battles to the current fourth-century Christological debates by identifying him as a protagonist of pro-Nicene doctrines.[46] Writing in 380 or 381, immediately before the Council of Constantinople, Gregory shows that Thaumaturgus anticipated the role that Gregory (Nyssen) himself was now assuming in defense of Trinitarian orthodoxy.[47] Nyssen says that Thaumaturgus received a "mystagogy" (μυσταγωγία), a divine vision, that came to form his Trinitarian theology.[48] Like Moses, having written down the law after receiving it from Yahweh on Mount Sinai, Thaumaturgus penned the words; in his case, inscribing them on the walls of the Neo-Caesarean church in Pontus as a testament to his third-century congregants.[49] The tenets of this revelation adhered to the fundamental principles of pro-Nicene belief in the 380s, concluding with a statement reminding readers that "there is nothing created or subservient in the Trinity, nor anything introduced which did not exist before but came later."[50] Gregory thus transported Thaumaturgus into the late fourth century as a virtual ally, as an alter ego in his attempt to sanction pro-Nicene theologians. After recounting the origin of the saint's confession, Gregory continues the narrative of Thaumaturgus as an emboldened competitor now equipped to overcome heretical wickedness.

Nazianzen likewise deployed the metaphor of athletic excellence in the oration on his brother Caesarius. Unlike most male figures of Cappadocian biographies, Caesarius never served as bishop and showed

---

[46] L. Abramowski, "Das Bekenntnis des Gregor Thaumaturgos bei Gregor von Nyssa und das Problem seiner Echtheit," *ZK* 87 (1976), 145–66, demonstrates that Nyssen projected his own doctrine onto Thaumaturgus.

[47] See discussion in M. Slusser, *St. Gregory Thaumaturgus: Life and Works* (Washington: Catholic University of America Press, 1998), 15; Abramowski, "Bekenntnis," 162, suggests a date after Constantinople; Bernardi, *Prédication*, 308 and Van Dam, "Hagiography," 277, date the work to 380, just before the council. I follow Van Dam's argument and dating, believing that Nyssen used the text to reinforce the pro-Nicene position before the council.

[48] Greg. Ny., *Vit. GTh.* 4.31. [49] Greg. Ny., *Vit. GTh.* 4.32; Exodus 20: 1–26.

[50] Greg. Ny., *Vit. GTh.* 4.32 (Slusser).

no aspirations for clerical office at any time in his life. But Gregory's portrayal of his sibling, who died and was memorialized in 368, may have served as a model for later eulogies, even clergy. In this work Gregory negotiates a balance between expectations of masculinity and personal piety. As an unmarried male who died young, Caesarius was lacking in conventional masculinity as he had not been a father and had not served as a patron.[51] The young man also did not exude the fortitude that came by spiritual austerity, having never lived as an ascetic. With Caesarius lacking the background usually associated with manly figures, Gregory had to compensate to transform his younger sibling into a persona for the Christian civic order. Gregory thus focuses on Caesarius serving as a living metaphor of male-centered *paideia*. He was an embodiment of the rhetoric and philosophy that Christian *pepaideumenoi* increasingly were claiming as legitimate heirs.

Caesarius epitomizes the conflation of sanctity and classical erudition. It was a synthesis that Nazianzen would re-visit fourteen years later in a eulogy for Basil. Gregory promotes his brother by stressing that in scholarship, he bested everybody.[52] He is unmatched intellectually. Gregory emphasizes his brother's proficiency across academic disciplines ranging "from geometry and astronomy" to "arithmetic and mathematics, and in the marvelous art of medicine."[53] He mastered the content in all areas of scholarship and he appeared especially adept in the public realm, where Gregory tells the audience of "his boldness with rulers, his contests and discussions in behalf of the truth in which he engaged with many, not only in the dialectic manner, but also with unusual piety and fervor."[54] Gregory punctuates Caesarius' genuineness in the last clause as an indictment against teachers – perhaps the Eunomians – who base their doctrines on a series of syllogisms. Gregory considers such individuals as disingenuous and effete. Caesarius comes across as the consummate orator of the Second Sophistic, brilliant in the realm of public disputation. But at every turn in his illustrious career, Caesarius was driven by his faith, with his

---

[51] V. Limberis, *Architects of Piety: The Cappadocian Fathers and the Cult of the Martyrs* (Oxford: Oxford University Press, 2011), 194. S. Elm, "Family Men: Masculinity and Philosophy in Late Antiquity," in *Transformations of Late Antiquity: Essays for Peter Brown*, eds. P. Rousseau and M. Papoutsakis (Farnham: Ashgate, 2009), 287–300, contends that lack of fatherhood in his own life, as well in that of Caesarius, incited Nazianzen to create a philosophical family for himself.

[52] Greg. Naz., *Or.* 7.7 (McCauley).   [53] Greg. Naz., *Or.* 7.7 (McCauley).

[54] Greg. Naz., *Or.* 7.11 (McCauley): "boldness," πρὸς τοὺς ἄρχοντας παρρησίαν; "contests," ἀγῶνας καὶ λόγους; "piety," εὐσεβῶς τε καὶ διαπύρως.

paideia informed by his holiness. Gregory was disclosing that, although he did not hold sacred office and he never lived as an ascetic, Caesarius stood as a pillar in the Christian empire. He never had a bride, but his masculinity took an even better form as instead he made sacred pursuit of knowledge his passion.[55] As outstanding scholar, physician, and orator, the youthful Cappadocian was enlisted into the imperial administration, where at the court of the notorious non-Christian Emperor Julian, he faced an epic challenge to his faith and his intellect.[56] Julian attempted to turn his Christian courtiers from their beliefs, especially targeting Caesarius: "seducing (ὑφελκόμενος) some by bribes, some by dignities, some by promises..."[57] In this proem to an ordeal of conviction, Gregory sets up Julian as a duplicitous villain, whose temptations, his "witchery of words" (γοητεία τῶν λόγων) plan to undermine Caesarius' reliance on Christ.[58]

Gregory places the contest in a virtual arena, cueing the audience "to enjoy the narration, as the spectators at the marvelous happening."[59] Thus the proper setting has been made to enable Caesarius to assert manliness and to advertise his truthfulness. Gregory identifies his brother first as a "noble warrior" (γεννάδας) and then characterizes him as an athlete, a role that according to Second Sophistic philosopher Dio Chrysostom (c. 40–c. 115) surpassed even soldiering as a path to achieving manhood because of the multiple virtues it produced.[60] Gregory designated Caesarius as "an athlete ready to contend (ἀγωνίζεσθαι) in word and deed against a contestant who was capable of both."[61] In ascribing this role to his brother, Gregory re-directs audience attention to his brother's heritage. The gymnasium was closely linked to the other components of education – rhetoric, literature, deportment – that produced the elite males of Hellenic society.[62] Caesarius appears as the well-rounded intellectual, ready to outdo his rival, and he subsequently refutes

---

[55] Elm, "Family Men," 295.
[56] On this episode see McGuckin, *Gregory*, 115–6, 159–62.
[57] Greg. Naz., *Or.* 7.11 (McCauley). [58] Greg. Naz., *Or.* 7.11 (McCauley).
[59] Greg. Naz., *Or.* 7.12 (McCauley).
[60] Greg. Naz., *Or.* 7.12 (McCauley); Dio Chrysostom, *Or.* 29.8 (Cohoon): "There is scope for courage alone in warfare, whereas athletics at one and the same time produce manliness, physical strength, and self-control."
[61] Greg. Naz., *Or.* 7.12 (McCauley).
[62] J. König, *Athletics and Literature in the Roman Empire* (Cambridge: Cambridge University Press, 2005), 47–63: "The gymnasion [sic], then, was regularly associated with the inculcation of the rhetorical, literary and musical skills which were seen as central to civilized elite identity" (51).

Julian's arguments to dissuade his beliefs: "With logical turns and niceties...he [Caesarius] foiled all his [Julian] verbal subtleties (τὰς ἐν τοῖς λόγοις πλοκάς) and every hidden and open attempt."[63] In this explanation, Gregory disparages the "verbal subtleties" of Julian as a form of trickery meant to seduce his brother. He thus paints Julian with shades of prostitution. Furthermore, Caesarius outperformed his adversary, in the "stadium...with spectators on both sides."[64] This was a significant detail included because noble manhood, according to ancient Greek theories of gender, had to be revealed in competition with others, in a public forum. The "victory with Christ who overcame the world," as Gregory calls it, also served as an exercise in discrimination for the crowd listening to the story, who were called to recognize God's interpreter through the contest.[65] Thus Caesarius, a guide for those whom Gregory calls of "manly thought," was validated as a savant, above all else obedient to Christ.[66] Manliness and faithfulness merge in this epithet, with triumph in contest revealing the coalescence of *aretē* and piety.

Further into the biography, after explaining that Caesarius had died from disease, Gregory exhorted listeners to take comfort in knowing that his brother had been freed from the travails of life. In a final commentary on Caesarius' peace in death, Gregory alluded again to his learnedness:

> He will make no oratorical display? No, but he will be admired for his oratory. He will not study the works of Hippocrates and Galen and their adversaries? No, but neither will he be afflicted by diseases or experience personal grief at others' misfortune. He will not expound the works of Euclid and Ptolemy and Hero? No, but neither will he be pained at the pompous boasts of uncultured men. He will make no display of the doctrines of Plato or Aristotle...or an Epicurus, and I know not of what others of the venerable Stoa and Academy? No, but neither will he be concerned about solving their specious arguments.[67]

Caesarius had earlier withstood the test of his manhood and belief, remaining unmoved by Julian's enticements.[68] In this final record of disciplines that his brother would no longer be practicing, Gregory underpins the comprehensiveness of Caesarius' intellectual might. So

---

[63] Greg. Naz., *Or.* 7.13 (McCauley). [64] Greg. Naz., *Or.* 7.12 (McCauley).
[65] Greg. Naz., *Or.* 7.13 (McCauley), quoting John 16:3; P. Struck, "The Ordeal of the Divine Sign: Divination and Manliness in Archaic and Classical Greece," in *Andreia*, 168–9, shows that in classical Greece and Rome, tests to determine affiliation with the gods were based on ordeals that measured "notions of manliness – effective leadership, courage, and decisiveness" (169).
[66] Greg. Naz., *Or.* 7.20 (my translation). [67] Greg. Naz., *Or.* 7.20 (McCauley).
[68] II Thessalonians 2:2.

not only does Caesarius defeat the emperor in a contest of persuasion (as earlier depicted), but even in death his record exceeds that of the philosopher-emperor. In addition, Gregory favors his own sense of manhood by escalating that of his brother. Caesarius had no wife and no children to carry on his legacy. These issues mitigated his image as an ideal male, a relevant point since Gregory shared the same limitations. But Caesarius overcame any apparent deficiencies by proving himself through public confrontations against the most powerful of officials. He left no children as a legacy, but his record as a formidable Christian apologist made for a fitting progeny. Large audiences listening to Gregory's polished delivery of the eulogy could not help but notice the potency of his own words. Nor would many fail to recognize that Gregory epitomized most of the same attributes of the saintly *pepaideumenos* he was praising. Gregory was grafting his brother's bravery onto himself.

Like Nyssen's biography of Thaumaturgus, Nazianzen places Caesarius in a theological setting: here, striving against an enemy of Christianity; a ruler villainized as trying to unman Christian intellectuals by demoting their authority as *pepaideumenoi*. Gregory was writing five years after Julian's death in 363, with Valens now early in his tenure as emperor in eastern Rome. At the outset of our study, the reader may recall, Gregory penned a letter that defied Julian's proscription of Christian teachers of *paideia*, an emasculation. The portrait of Caesarius provided another exhibition of sacred *aretē*, with Gregory ridiculing Julian's former program by showing the superiority of a steadfast Christian *pepaideumenos*. Gregory was still only a presbyter currently – not a bishop yet – but he was still acutely aware of the importance of depicting Christian leaders as *agathoi*. In the oration, Caesarius surpasses Julian in all exercises of the mind. And in all realms of philosophy and rhetoric, Caesarius excels through his faith in God – a noted contrast with Julian. The point is unmistakable, that Caesarius' Christian manhood exceeds that of the vanquished non-Christian.

NYSSEN'S BASIL: DEFENDER OF THEOLOGICAL TRUTH

The contest of intellectual strength also takes center stage in Nyssen's encomium on his older brother Basil. Here *aretē* converges with holiness, in this case illustrating Basil's defense of theological truth against Heterousian opponents. But in this case, Nyssen favors military analogy; perhaps to accentuate the gravity of the battle. Even as Gregory extols his brother, he proves his own mastery as a rhetorician, combining elements of hagiography and invective to highlight Basil's virtues while denigrating his opponents. Gregory characterizes Basil throughout the account as "the noble soldier of Christ" (γενναῖος τοῦ Χριστοῦ στρατιώτης).[69] Enlisting his brother as an agent of the Divine, Gregory presents Basil as engaged in an ongoing struggle against the "master of mankind's deception," who perpetrates "idolatry, persuading by his own clever sophistry (σόφισμα)...to consider God something created because he is called by the name of Son."[70] Gregory sets the stage for his hero by attributing the doctrines of Basil's rivals, the Heterousians (Eunomians), to the designs of Satan.[71] The reference to "clever sophistry" was made unmistakable to readers who knew that Heterousians were criticized by pro-Nicenes for misconstruing biblical terminology in order to delineate between the essence of the Father and the Son. But Gregory goes one step further, leaving no doubt to the identity of the adversary. He names Arius, Aetius, Eunomius, and Eudoxius, specifically, as agents of the Evil One's "wickedness."[72] Each favored Christology that subordinated the Son to the Father because of their disparate substances. In the encomium, the doctrinal enemies appear to have swayed the emperor (Valens), the highest magistrates, and the masses to accept their beliefs, leaving the pro-Nicene Basil standing alone to press for God's truth. Gregory subsequently designates Basil as a new Elijah, the Old Testament prophet who had struggled, as one man, against the evil king Ahab and his army of pagan priests.[73] Ahab had led Israel away from worship of the *one* God, to the idolizing of *many* false gods; a charge of malfeasance that Gregory is pinning on his theological opponents. Like Elijah, Basil fights to protect his people, the church at Caesarea and beyond, from malicious teachings threatening the ecclesial body.

In the start of the eulogy Gregory establishes Basil as "a skilled chieftain (ἀριστεὺς περιδέξιος) arming himself against his adversaries."[74] By identifying his brother as a man of war, Gregory establishes him as the paragon of civic loyalty and manhood. In ancient Athens, the military

---

[69] Greg. Ny., *In Basilium* 2.3–4 (Stein).   [70] Greg. Ny., *In Basilium* 9.5–10 (Stein).
[71] It was a commonplace among opponents of Heterousians of the late fourth century not only to mock them by calling them "Eunomians," but also to brand them "Anomoeans" (from the Greek ἀνόμοιος, "unlike").
[72] Greg. Ny., *In Basilium* 10.1–5 (Stein).
[73] Greg. Ny., *In Basilium* 10.1–10; I Kings 18:1–40.
[74] Greg. Ny., *In Basilium* 1.15–20 (Stein).

ethos was predicated on facing danger head on, holding to one's position, and never letting down fellow soldiers. This notion also underpinned the image of a desirable citizen, who was expected to put the needs of the polis above his own.[75] A man who took up arms for his city exuded responsibility and reliability. By comparison, an individual shirking military duty warranted the collective scorn of the populace and putative action.[76] In addition, Gregory places Basil in a position as "chieftain," a commander of troops and consequently, an imposing figure. As far back as the *Iliad*, chieftains such as Agamemnon and Hector merited a special connection to the Divine that sanctioned their word based on manly actions.[77] Basil could be trusted, that is, because he had earned the loyalty of warriors. He had proven himself.

In the contest, Gregory sets Basil as sturdy in his dogma, while Heterousians are depicted as unsteady in their beliefs, even though they outnumber him and enjoy imperial support. Here the manliness of Basil as a *pepaideumenos* comes across, with Basil standing forth "never like a reed and uncertain of purpose."[78] Against weak-minded foes, the Caesarean bishop imbues a constancy that he confirms in metaphorical combat: "struggling with rulers (ὑπάρχοις συμπλεκόμενος), associating with generals, speaking boldly to emperors, crying out in assemblies."[79] Gregory punctuates his determination to stand up for truth opposite the most formidable offices and in the most demonstrative platforms. Basil is rendered as a warrior, "escaping the grasp of close combatants," a characterization that held affect for individuals who had been trained to consider their own manliness through the values of the ancient Greeks.[80] Fighting in close proximity carried symbolic weight in ancient combat. Face-to-face skirmishes, in full view of fellow citizen-soldiers, constituted the supreme site to prove courage and to verify oneself as an *agathos*.[81]

---

[75] Roisman, *Rhetoric*, 106, 129, says that the hoplite ethos promoted masculine values such as stamina, strength, self-sacrifice, cooperation, service to the state, and comradeship in arms.
[76] Demosthenes, *Or.* 21.55–7.   [77] *Iliad* 2.60–90. See Struck, "Ordeal," 175–81.
[78] Greg. Ny., *In Basilium* 14.1–4 (Stein).
[79] Greg. Ny., *In Basilium* 10.5–10 (Stein). Exuding *parresia*, frankness of speech, showed that Basil was standing up to tyranny, a trope widely admired among fourth-century elites. R. Flower, *Emperors and Bishops in Late Roman Invective* (Cambridge: Cambridge University Press, 2013), 25–7, notes that speaking boldly against authority gained admiration from fourth-century *pepaideumenoi*, whatever their religious identity; an argument also set forward in P. Brown, *Power and Persuasion in Late Antiquity: Towards a Christian Empire* (Madison: University of Wisconsin Press, 1992), 61–70.
[80] Greg. Ny., *In Basilium* 10.10–12 (Stein); Bassi, *Acting*, 248, states that in classical drama, playwrights prompted spectators "to look back through time to see themselves as men and as Greeks."
[81] A point emphasized by K. Bassi, "The Semantics of Manliness in Ancient Greece," in *Andreia*, 33–4, and Roisman, "Rhetoric," 132.

Homer is his most descriptive and laudatory of fighting in close ranks, where he says sounds of crashing shields and helmets filled the air.[82] Soldiers experienced in such melees garnered honor and respect from their comrades, thus enabling them to command other troops. Achilles' courage in hand-to-hand combat, for instance, gave him standing among his fellow warriors and enabled him to rouse his men.[83] Citizens who avoided the infantry, however, were met with scorn, as when Demosthenes belittled the defendant Meidias for refusing to use the weapons of a foot soldier.[84] Instead of accepting the charge of a hoplite, Demosthenes alleges, Meidias was guilty of "riding on a saddle with silver trappings, imported from Euboea, taking with you your shawls and goblets and wine-jars."[85] Such behavior was a clear indication of softness, of evading duty, and alienating peers. With an account of close-rank combat, Gregory confirms the daring of his brother against the Heterousians, whose Meidias-like cowardice reveals their lack of moral strength. Basil's courage, therefore, is placed on full display for the spectators of the encomium, who are prompted to see in him a legacy of fortitude stretching back to earliest Greek chronicles.

These close encounters of Basil commented, moreover, on his wisdom, a virtue correlative to his fearlessness, whereby he confronted even Emperor Valens, supporter of Homoian Christianity.[86] Although Nyssen and Nazianzen often isolated on the Heterousians as the enemy, they also vilified Homoians, such as Valens. The Homoians, in their estimation, represented the broader group that had compromised the unity of the Son and the Father, with the Heterousians the most egregious in their error. "What was the bold speech (παρρησία) with Valens on our teacher's part?" Gregory asks. "That he should leave the faith inviolate and undefiled, the violation of which became a curse to all the world."[87] Basil comes across as an indefatigable proponent of pro-Nicene theology. Again, deploying martial imagery, Gregory says that "Many times he arrayed himself against the Amalekites, using prayer as his shield."[88] Basil perpetually defied the Homoians, here branded as the Amalekites,

---

[82] *Iliad* 12.354; on courage in Homer, R. Balot, *Courage in the Democratic Polis: Ideology and Critique in Classical Athens* (Oxford: Oxford University Press, 2014), 199–203.
[83] *Iliad* 20.361–3 (Lombardo): "Greeks! Close this ground and engage the enemy man to man. I want to see some spirit."
[84] Demosthenes, *Against Meidias* 21.133 (Vince).
[85] Demosthenes, *Against Meidias* 21.133 (Vince).
[86] R. Van Dam, *Kingdom of Snow: Roman Rule and Greek Culture in Cappadocia* (Philadelphia: University of Pennsylvania Press, 2002), 109–12, N. Lenski, *Failure of Empire: Valens and the Roman State in Fourth Century A.D.* (Berkeley: University of California Press, 2003), 252–5.
[87] Greg. Ny., *In Basilium* 14.15–18 (Stein).   [88] Greg. Ny., *In Basilium* 22.3–5 (Stein).

ancient enemy of Israel. From the time of Moses and Joshua, to the reigns of King Saul and David, the Israelites had warred against this people from southern Canaan, a nation believed to have descended from Esau's descendants.[89] Gregory's depiction of Basil's campaigns against the Amalekites correlates to a fight by God's chosen people (Israel) against a bastard branch of that lineage; with Basil representing pro-Nicene (true) Christianity versus the false Heterousians. Basil thus is linked to Israelite commanders by his campaigns against enemies of God. His valor, like that of biblical protagonists, derived from his dependence on the Almighty. Like Moses, Joshua, Saul, and David, his actions played a salvific role for his people. And in the fashion of ancient Hellenic warriors and philosophers, he accrued fame for himself by protecting his people and delivering assurance: "And like a beacon to wanderers on the sea at night, he shone above the Church and turned all to the straight course."[90] Deploying sensory rhetoric, Nyssen equates Basil with light, a metaphor for revelation. Basil was trustworthy because he was valiant.[91]

Basil's defiance also corresponded to Homeric warriors and archaic hoplites accruing renown for holding their ground. In the *Iliad*, Greek general Nestor implored his soldiers to stay in place and fight by considering that their families and homes depended on their refusing to retreat.[92] This exhortation appealed to men of all ranks, whose basic manhood demanded protecting what they held dearest.[93] Aristides likewise compared noble speakers to soldiers who stood firm together, thus showing respect to their mutual cause.[94] The portrait of Basil echoed the tropes of martial courage, boldness of speech, and unyielding fervency.[95] The crowd was asked to consider "would he [the audience] approve of his

---

[89] Exodus 17:8–16; I Samuel 30:1–2; II Samuel 1:5–10.
[90] Greg. Ny., *In Basilium* 10.3–7 (Stein).
[91] Plutarch, *Demosthenes* 10.3 (Perrin): Plutarch's maxim, attributed to Demosthenes, held that "a single word or nod from a man who is trusted has more power than very many long periods."
[92] *Iliad* 15.700–5. For similar cases, see 9.230–40 and 12.435–40.
[93] Demosthenes, *Or.* 60.27 (DeWitt), where Demosthenes honors the fallen Greek soldiers at the Battle of Chaeronea: "The considerations that actuated these men one and all to choose to die nobly have now been enumerated – birth, education, habituation to high standards of conduct."
[94] Aristides, *Or.* 34.22 (Behr).
[95] Balot, *Courage*, 199–203, and É. Smoes, *Le Courage chez les Grecs d'Homère à Aristotle* (Brussels: Ousia, 1995), 18–20, show how the notion of courage in Homer, as an element of warfare, was adapted to the political sphere in classical Greece.

noble birth, which is called such through flesh and blood?"[96] Gregory does not fixate on his brother's [and his own] pedigree, but he intimates that *aretē* harmonizes with faith and lineage. "Now what is the noble birth of Basil?" he asks. "His family was intimacy with the Divinity."[97] Gregory thus underscores the affiliation between authority and class, with the knowledge that his audience would discern the correlation between birth, gender, and power. Basil's gentility thus fuses with sanctity to augment his standing. Through attributes of manhood, bloodline, and sacred affinity, he earns the trust of the people.

NAZIANZEN'S BASIL: CAMPAIGNS AGAINST A BARBARIC EMPEROR

In another oration for Basil, delivered three years after Nyssen's encomium, Gregory of Nazianzus similarly described his friend as a soldier holding firm against forces of heresy. Nazianzen proclaimed this eulogy, at least portions of it, at Basil's former see in Caesarea.[98] We will discuss the immediate context of its delivery in greater detail in Chapter 4. Gregory scripts Basil as a fusion of hoplite and *pepaideumenos*, engaged in a "contest which he undertook...on behalf of God, to overthrow the heretics."[99] Through his characterization of Basil, Gregory represents manly deportment as pivotal to the victory of the embattled pro-Nicenes. Subsequently, listeners are guided to affiliate pro-Nicene theologians with masculinity, truth, and sophistication. And with Basil appearing as the consummate Hellene, the masses receive the message that doctrines heterodox to pro-Nicene Christianity construe effeminacy, falsehood, and barbarism.

Early in the narrative, Nazianzen recounts his and Basil's time together as students at Athens, an atmosphere where "those expert in sophistry (περιττοὶ τὰ σοφιστικά) and purveyors of arguments...are held in high esteem."[100] It is a toxic atmosphere, Gregory is saying, where individuals compromise truth in order to push forward their personal agendas. On

---

[96] Greg. Ny., *In Basilium* 24.3–6 (Stein).   [97] Greg. Ny., *In Basilium* 25.11–14 (Stein).
[98] On date and audience, N. McLynn, "Gregory Nazianzen's Basil: The Literary Construction of a Christian Friendship," *SP* 34 (2001), 178–80.
[99] Greg. Naz., *Or.* 43.71 (McCauley).
[100] Greg. Naz., *Or.* 43.16 (McCauley). On the academic climate here and student hazing rituals: A. Wenzel, "Libanius, Gregory of Nazianzus, and the Ideal of Athens in Late Antiquity," *JLA* 3:2 (2010), 268–81.

his arrival at this city, Basil had to defend his beliefs and give a favorable account in a contest of intellect against a gathering that Nazianzen depicts as surreptitious. One group tried to humiliate the newcomer. The "dissembling and crafty" Armenian neophytes at Athens attempted to humiliate Basil through a series of contentious questions designed to exploit his lack of experience in debate.[101] The Armenian students, from the eastern fringes of the empire, may have represented Greek characterizations of the East as duplicitous and fearful of honorable battle tactics. Regardless of their stratagems, Basil bested the clique. "And full of ardor (προθυμία), to describe him fully in the words of Homer, he drove in confusion those proud youths by his reasoning, and did not cease smiting them with arguments (παίων συλλογισμοῖς) until he had completely routed them and gained a crowning victory."[102] Gregory casts Basil as a fusion of philosopher and Homeric warrior confronting an overwhelming enemy.[103] In this analogy, Gregory turns a contest of rhetoric into a site of combat between the Armenians, who depend on wiliness to win, and Basil, who triumphs through honorable warfare (using philosophic truth). Basil's victory over the assailants not only confirms his courage, but also testifies to his moral superiority by showing him a person of substance who cannot be overcome by cunning or pressure.[104]

A greater part of the text, moreover, furthered the theme found in Nyssen's eulogy, of Basil – in his capacity as priest, but before his episcopacy – safeguarding the church against imperial threat. This narration also involved the actions of Nazianzen himself, who came to Cappadocia with Basil in 365 to confront Emperor Valens, who had been interfering in matters of pro-Nicene churches there.[105] "An emperor too fond of gold and most hostile to Christ" instituted a series of policies to

---

[101] Greg. Naz., *Or.* 43.17 (McCauley): κρυπτός τι καὶ ὕφαλος.
[102] Greg. Naz., *Or.* 43.17 (McCauley).
[103] M. Jones, *Playing the Man: Performing Masculinities in the Ancient Greek Novel* (Oxford University Press, 2012), 118–9, gives evidence of the fusion of warrior and orator in the rhetoric of the ancient Greek novel.
[104] J. Connolly, "Like the Labor of Heracles: *Andreia* and *Paideia* in Greek Culture Under Rome," in *Andreia*, 288.
[105] My purpose here is not to re-visit the specific policies of Valens in Cappadocia and eastern Rome. For analysis of his interactions with Basil and Nazianzen at this stage, see McGuckin, *St. Gregory*, 142–5 and Rousseau, *Basil*, 135–7. The following address Nazianzen's literary construction of relationship with Basil: Norris, "Your Honor," 140–59; D. Konstan, "How to Praise a Friend: St. Gregory of Nazianzus's Funeral Oration for St. Basil the Great," in *Greek Biography*, 160–79; and McLynn, "Gregory," 178–93.

Personifications of Sacred Aretē 179

undermine pro-Nicenes in Cappadocia.[106] This reference to Valens suggested a ruler guided by decadence, with a love for wealth belying softness, baseness, and moral turpitude. The "hostility to Christ" denoted his support for a Christology that diminished the status of the Son in the Godhead. In fighting against this theology, Basil was defending the honor of Christ. "He [Basil] gained in one quarter, held his ground in another, and drove back the attack in a third."[107] The foray calls to mind the Battle of Thermopylae, with Basil assuming the role of Spartan king Leonidas.[108] Valens' forces, who favor the Homoian party, retain an identity as Persians, as barbarians assaulting Hellas and spreading chaos. Basil's Trinitarianism therefore takes the mantle of that which is Greek and civilized. In this valiant resistance, Basil became "a strong wall and a rampart," and an "axe breaking the rock to pieces."[109] Gregory infuses the clash with these phrases from the Hebrew prophet Jeremiah, thus framing Basil's protection as a holy war against the foes of God, with Basil similarly playing the mouthpiece of Yahweh. The picture contained religious and ethnic undertones that spoke to a broad audience. The details of this initial incursion are obscure, but the embattled pro-Nicene bishop Eusebius at Caesarea – under whom Basil served as priest – remained in office afterwards. So Nazianzen recounts it as a strategic victory for Eusebius, Basil, Gregory, and the pro-Nicene party. After a series of rhetorical debates between Homoian agents of Valens and supporters of pro-Nicene Christianity led by Basil and Nazianzen, the "base men that they were, they were basely put to shame."[110] Gregory proposes, then, that the officials sent to carry out the emperor's plan came from weak-minded functionaries, who were no match for a people emboldened by the "sincerity of their belief."[111] Basil was represented, alongside Nazianzen himself, as the spirit of pro-Nicene clergy in Cappadocia – and in neighboring provinces – in their determination to uphold Trinitarian theology despite imperial interference.[112]

---

[106] Greg. Naz., *Or.* 43.30 (McCauley).
[107] Greg. Naz., *Or.* 43.31 (McCauley) for "barbarian invasion" and 43.32.
[108] Herodotus, *Histories* 7, 198–239.
[109] Greg. Naz., *Or.* 43.32 (McCauley): γίνεται τοῖς μὲν τεῖχος ὀχυρὸν καὶ χαράκωμα, τοῖς δὲ πέλεκυς κόπτων πέτραν; see Jeremiah 1:18 and 23:29.
[110] Greg. Naz., *Or.* 43.33 (McCauley).   [111] Greg. Naz., *Or.* 43.33.
[112] Greg. Naz., *Or.* 43.33 (McCauley). Where Gregory places himself alongside Basil as defender of Cappadocia: "They [Valens' deputies] learned," Gregory writes, "that, of all men in the world, the Cappadocians were not to be lightly despised."

Writing in 382, about four years after the emperor's death, Nazianzen scripted Valens as a religious counterpoint to bring into focus Basil as manly, Greek, and orthodox. Gregory heightens the role of the emperor in the Trinitarian controversy, and the looming threat of his visit to Cappadocia in 365, in order to issue a suitable foil against which he can construct Basil's heroism. Basil (and Eusebius and Nazianzen) had right to be anxious about the imminent arrival, considering recent punitive actions against non-Homoians in 365.[113] In actuality, however, the series of events in Cappadocia in 365 proved far less menacing than presented in the narrative. Valens had been driven more by ambitions of concord across the empire than by his commitment to Homoian Christianity.[114] He showed pragmatism in his religious policies and preferred achieving consensus with bishops of dissenting camps rather than using force or exile to achieve unity. This tendency to avoid unnecessary conflict comes across in the emperor's visit of 365. Although the Homoiousian bishop Eusebius of Caesarea represented opposition to Homoianism, Valens took no steps to remove him from office. Noel Lenski rightly attributes this decision, not to a heated showdown where Homoiousian clergy bested the emperor (or his officials) in dialogue, but rather to the fact that neither Eusebius nor Basil had been condemned by the Homoian council at Constantinople in 360.[115] They had both been present, but they were exempted from punishment, along with Dianius, bishop of Caesarea in 360.[116] Neither had been outspoken against the Homoian position taken at Constantinople and neither appeared to pose a major danger in the estimation of Valens, who was traveling through the region on a journey with his army to the Persian frontier. In 365 Valens also was facing an insurrection by one of former Emperor Julian's generals, Procopius. To secure more favor, Valens recalled several non-Homoian bishops from exile.[117] It would not have made sense for the emperor to force out Eusebius at Caesarea at this time. Valens was acting out of expediency at Cappadocia more than religious fervor. Basil had only been a priest for three years, and Nazianzen four, upon Valens' arrival. Each would have been eager to assert his ability in theological disputation, but at this time it seems doubtful that public debate determined the outcome of events. Yet

---

[113] McGuckin, *Gregory*, 180–3.
[114] H. C. Brennecke, *Studien zur Geschichte der Homöer: Der Osten bis zum Ende der Homöischen Reichskirche* (Tübingen: Mohr Siebeck, 1988), 181–242, shows that Valens' pragmatism applied to his general religious policies, not just in relation to Christianity.
[115] Lenski, *Failure*, 242–7.   [116] Rousseau, *Basil*, 100–1.   [117] Ayres, *Nicaea*, 168–70.

by overstating the polemics in the emperor's visit, with pro-Nicenes keeping their places in the church because of their powerful rhetorical display, Gregory raises Basil and himself as unyielding in their guardianship of what was right.

Later in the biography, after Basil's election to the see at Caesarea in 370, Valens again sent officials to Cappadocia. After his initial designs in Cappadocia failed, Gregory states, the emperor could not accept that he "should be worsted (ἥττω ὀφθῆναι), in the sight of all, by a single man and a single city."[118] The allusion here is to the performative nature of rhetorical competition, where a public figure established, or compromised, his masculinity through actions that took place in view of the citizenry.[119] The metaphorical loss of battle for Valens – one that seems largely overstated – mirrored loss of face for the classical orator. A blow to the emperor's reputation, it seems, drives Valens' ambition to restore his honor in Cappadocia; perhaps akin to the experience of Persian king Darius, who vowed to return to Greece after his setback in 490 B.C. during the first Persian invasion of Greece. Valens is guided not by piety, therefore, but by hubris. Gregory then designates the emperor as a notorious villain from the collective memory of his audience. Valens is matched with "the King of Persia, when he was making his expedition into Greece, and glowing with passion and pride as he led men of every race against the Greeks."[120] Already having impugned the heretic emperor's masculinity, Gregory further undermines his reputation here by equating him here to Xerxes, the Persian ruler who commenced the second invasion of Greece in 480 after his father Darius' death. Valens now has been cast as an ethnically tainted anti-hero, an intruder, an impious outsider, and even a coward. Xerxes, some would remember, suffered infamy because in addition to being a lover of luxury, he did not actually fight in the war against the Greeks. Such display of timidity stoked opprobrium in citizens who located virtue foremost in the courage of combat.[121] An irony of this rhetorical denunciation was that Valens actually spent much of his career as emperor defending the eastern Roman frontiers against Persia; a reality suppressed in Nazianzen's vilification of the deceased emperor.

---

[118] Greg. Naz., *Or.* 43.44 (McCauley).
[119] E. Gunderson, *Staging Masculinity: The Rhetoric of Performance in the Roman World* (Ann Arbor: University of Michigan Press, 2000), 71–2.
[120] Greg. Naz., *Or.* 43.45 (McCauley).
[121] Flower, *Emperors*, 58–60; Balot, *Courage*, 206–14; J. Roisman, "The Rhetoric of Courage in the Athenian Orators," in *Andreia*, 32–6.

Like the ancient Persian monarch Xerxes, Gregory insinuates, Valens sent his deputies (the vicar Demosthenes and the prefect Modestus) to carry out his plans.[122] Included in the ranks of this delegation were "those from the women's apartments who are men among women and women among men, whose only manliness was their impiety."[123] This unflattering gender reversal echoed the words of Xerxes when decrying the conduct of the Persian navy at the Battle of Salamis, the key victory in the Greek defense against the second Persian invasion of 480: "My men have turned into women, my women into men."[124] Gregory maligns Valens under a long-held Hellenic reproach of Persians, their gender instability. Moreover, Gregory calls one of Valens' servants (Demosthenes) "Nabuzardan," the name of a Babylonian general placed in charge of Judea following the Babylonian conquest and deportation of Jews by King Nebuchadnezzar in 586 B.C.[125] This charge aligns the emperor's officials with a foreign power that had intruded into a holy land (Judah) and thus violated sacred territory; here recast as Cappadocia. Valens' agents have been branded as both oriental and enemy to God's people. Gregory's scathing caricature of Demosthenes and Modestus serves to foreground Basil's manhood and justice of cause, rather than reflecting the actual level of hostility between bishop and emperor's delegates.[126] Gregory's attempt to denigrate the emperor through such a damning analogy also benefited from the fact that Valens was alleged by other opponents to not speak fluent Greek. This mark of boorishness, in addition to his reputation as a man of ill temper and laxity, discredited him among *pepaideumenoi*.[127] In demonizing Basil's adversary, Gregory directed attention to the otherness of Valens and the Homoians, an alterity confirmed by their effeminacy. Thus, Gregory vilified him as

---

[122] Demosthenes: PLRE 1:249; Modestus: PLRE 1:605–8.
[123] Greg. Naz., Or. 43. 47 (McCauley). An unflattering trope of an emperor under womanly influence. Flower, *Emperors*, 103, observes that effective invective criticized an individual for being controlled through persons who were less than masculine.
[124] Herodotus, *Histories* 8.88 (De Sélincourt).
[125] Greg. Naz., Or. 43.47. On Nabuzardan: Jeremiah 39:9–11 and II Kings 25:8–20, Greg. Ny., *Contr. Eun.* 1.131–9, and discussion in Van Dam, *Kingdom*, 110 n. 34.
[126] Van Dam, *Kingdom*, 110–30, argues that like Valens, Demosthenes' actions should not be interpreted as driven mainly by animus to Basil or the Homoousians. Instead, he was motivated in church dealings by his concern to secure bishops in Cappadocia and Armenia who fit best into his military and diplomatic policies. Van Dam characterizes Modestus as a career administrator, driven by personal ambition. He was particularly flexible in his religion, adapting his own sympathies to his service under Constantius, Julian, and Valens.
[127] On disposition of Valens, Ammianus Marcellinus, *History* 29.1.10–27.

emasculate and barbaric, the antithesis of Greekness and a paragon of heresy. Gregory thereby exploited any perceived lack of civility in Valens to promote Basil as the epitome of Hellenism and manliness. Nazianzen ensured listeners that Basil was grounded in a substantive regimen that endowed him with credibility. His subject was "superior to threats, deaf to arguments, incapable of persuasion."[128] The Caesarean had been rendered impervious to fallacies or force. When the prefect Modestus tried to intimidate him into acquiescing to change his theology, Basil contravened him. "No one...has ever spoken in such a manner and with such boldness to me,"[129] the prefect responded. Through this personification, Gregory held up Basil as an authentic source of divine guidance. He thus feminized the uncultured, foreign Xerxes and his cronies, while validating *paideia* as a masculine, pro-Nicene enterprise.

In Basil's biography, Gregory orchestrated *paideia* as an arena of war, with the Caesarean bishop outdoing others because of his sanctity, elegance, and boldness. As in the earlier anecdote about Valens' travels to Cappadocia in 365, Gregory framed the emperor's subsequent encounters with Basil with similar vitriol. When Valens returned to Cappadocia in 370 and then again in winter 371/372, he likely put substantial pressure on Basil to accept Homoian doctrine. But, as we saw in his earlier visit, again the emperor did not press the issue to the level of conflict suggested in Nazianzen's hagiographic narrative. First, the social context of Caesarea under Basil in the early 370s indicates that the emperor was acting out of sensibility by not strong-arming him. Basil had recently established his renowned charitable complex and his overall administration of Caesarea had gained Valens' confidence; so much so, that Valens offered Basil support that included enlisting his advice on the ecclesiastical reorganization of Armenia before a Roman strike on Persia.[130] These do not seem like the actions of a ruler obsessed with doctrinal conformity.[131] Second, the portrayal of Valens as the primary driving force behind Homoian attempts to dismiss or correct Basil is exaggerated. From the time of his baptism, Valens was heavily influenced by Homoian clergy. That is not to say that he was weak-minded, but that on many occasions

---

[128] Greg. Naz., *Or.* 43.51 (McCauley).   [129] Greg. Naz., *Or.* 43.50 (McCauley).
[130] Ayres, *Nicaea*, 222–3; Van Dam, *Kingdom*, 131–2, shows that Basil's role in the Armenian church during Valens' rule ultimately proved ineffectual.
[131] Brennecke, *Studien*, 220–2.

while others were thinking on matters of faith, Valens was concentrating on other issues to stabilize eastern Rome.[132] A close reading of Basil's biography bears out that unnamed priests accompanying Valens were more concerned to enforce Homoian orthodoxy than the emperor. Valens was not the consummate foe to Basil.

Here literary license played a hand in Gregory's personification of the ideal pro-Nicene bishop. An emperor obsessed with imposing heresy on the pro-Nicenes made for a much more compelling figure on which to elevate Basil. Such a figure, arrayed with all the finery of a near eastern king, made the juxtaposition of Basil's *aretē* more striking. Nazianzen focused on a collective sense of masculinity in Basil in order to categorize *paideia* as a benchmark of Greekness in pro-Nicene church leadership.[133] He made the Caesarean bishop a hero, in the vein of ancient Greek corollaries, who offered reason and stability in the midst of circulating teachings. Audiences were provoked to affiliate the Cappadocians and other pro-Nicene clergy as successors to the paragons of manhood, individuals authorized by their bearing and the truth of their teachings. Public debate remained the proving ground, the litmus test, of the authentic philosopher. The performer, that is, had to prove his worthiness. He was always under judgment.

TELESCOPING *ARETĒ* FROM THE SCRIPTURAL PAST

Nazianzen and Nyssen thus inscribed conventional elements of male authority into characterizations of saintly bishops. But they also accentuated classical features of masculinity by injecting such features into scriptural persons. In doing so, they reoriented patriarchs, prophets, and apostles to mirror classical expectations of *aretē*. Throughout the laudation on Basil, for instance, Nyssen deploys *synkrisis* by likening Basil to saints that preceded him.[134] Through these analogies, Gregory transposed classical attributes of masculinity not only onto Basil, but also onto biblical heroes. "With each kind of knowledge [sacred and profane], with

---

[132] Lenski, *Failure*, 244–6.
[133] With *paideia* as a fundamental part of the episcopacy. See Norris, "Your Honor," 143–4 and Bernardi, *Prédication*, 238–46.
[134] On *synkrisis*, Aristotle, *Rhetoric* 1368a. See G. Kennedy, *A New History of Classical Rhetoric* (Princeton: Princeton University Press, 1994), 138, 202, 205 and Ruether, *Gregory*, 106, 113, 121. On affiliating an individual with classical or biblical heroes from the past, Flower, *Emperors*, 23–5.

both he [Basil] conquers his opponents," Gregory writes, "destroying by the transcendence of his wisdom the deceit of the Egyptians [Homoians]."¹³⁵ And later, Basil "imitates the valor of Moses which he worked against the Egyptians."¹³⁶ In Gregory's recounting, Basil succeeds Moses as defender against idolatry, taking a stand against doctrines that diminished the divinity of Christ the Son. Gregory paints Homoians as Egyptians, polytheists, and enslavers of God's people. Later, Gregory shows Basil imitating the prophet Elijah, whose rigorous life – "a manner of living austere...and unaffected dignity" – is juxtaposed against the comforts of his oppressors.¹³⁷ Like his Hebrew predecessor, who opposed the prophets of the pagan god Baal, Basil shuns all ostentation, thereby hardening himself for battle with the Homoians. And in similitude to John the Baptist, who embraced a life of severity, Gregory states "that he [Basil] considered an effeminate and luxurious mode of life inimical, in everything seeking fortitude and manliness (τὸ καρτερικὸν καὶ ἀνδρῶδες) instead of pleasure...with fasts and acts of self-control disciplining the body."¹³⁸ Basil comes across in one personification as a wilderness dweller, tempered by God to face resistance in the city. John the Baptist meanwhile, is made into a figure of the polis. Audience members are directed to imagine a skilled orator instead of an uncouth hermit. "John spoke boldly to Herod," Gregory says, "and this one [Basil] to Valens."¹³⁹ As John had criticized the king of Judea during the time of Jesus, so also Basil had confronted the Homoian emperor.

Nazianzen also enrolled Basil in a lineage of righteous predecessors. Gregory states that whereas Noah had preserved the seeds of the new world in the ark, Basil made his city an ark of safety, "sailing buoyantly over the waters of the heretics," and saving the whole world.¹⁴⁰ Gregory praised the ladder of Jacob as a path to the Divine, yet Gregory applauded Basil even more for not only seeing a ladder, but also climbing it "by his gradual ascents in virtue."¹⁴¹ Gregory likewise identifies Basil with Job, the prophetic figure from the Old Testament famous for enduring tremendous suffering. Like this pillar of faith, "Basil was tried and prevailed,"

---

[135] "With each kind of knowledge": Greg. Ny., *In Basilium* 1.15–17 (Stein); "deceit of Egyptians": 4.20–7 (Stein).
[136] Greg. Ny., *In Basilium* 20.15–20 (Stein): "valor," τοῦ Μωϋσέως τὴν ἀριστείαν.
[137] Greg. Ny., *In Basilium* 16.4–12 (Stein): "living austere," βίος κατεσκληκώς.
[138] Greg. Ny., *In Basilium* 13.5–15 (Stein).   [139] Greg. Ny., *In Basilium* 14.5–10 (Stein).
[140] Greg. Naz., *Or.* 43.70 (McCauley); Genesis 6–9.
[141] Greg. Naz., *Or.* 43.72 (McCauley); Genesis 28:10–22.

Gregory writes, "unshaken by the attacks of his many assailants and winning a decisive victory over the tempter."[142] The "assailants" referred not only to the tests of faith ushered by Satan, but also the faulty wisdom issued by Job's wife and friends.[143] The prophet made for a particularly apt counterpart to Basil, who comes across as a dissenting voice, because Job's constancy in the midst of afflictions revealed the truth of his words. In Nazianzen's commentary, Job's spiritual strength collapses into the fortitude evidenced by Basil's resilience as he protested the imperial stratagems of Valens. As a patron, moreover, Basil outdid Joseph, dispenser of grain in Egypt, because while the Hebrew restored bodily sustenance, the Cappadocian "provided all men and all times with spiritual food."[144] The statement may also have served as an allusion to the concrete provisions of food that Basil furnished through his charitable complex at Caesarea. And whereas Joshua had commanded the Israelite army and distributed land from the promised territory, Basil led a military force "saved by the faith" and he distributed "lots and abodes close to God," which were more precious than the earthly counterparts of Palestine.[145] Through extended parallels with scriptural gallantry, Nyssen and Nazianzen engineered a pedigree that merged sanctity and *aretē*. They authorize Basil not only by making him virile, but also by gendering his scriptural forerunners according to classical norms. In these biblical paragons of virtue, the Gregories vivified the correlation between distinction induced by *paideia* and firmness of faith acquired through the bodily mortification of saints. They telescoped biblical corollaries into their own age, thereby empowering audiences to sense an immediacy in the saints and to discern a common heritage between sacred heroes of the past and their heirs, the pro-Nicene episcopacy.

CORPOREAL *ARETĒ* IN GORGONIA AND MACRINA

While setting forth Basil as an exemplar of pro-Nicene manhood, Nazianzen and Nyssen also amplified ideals of classical masculinity in biographies of sacred women. These subjects, however, were not situated in the gymnasium, the assembly, or the battlefield – conventional sites of

---

[142] Greg. Naz., *Or.* 43.72 "tried," πεπείραται καὶ νενίκηκε; Job 1–2, 42. [143] Job 4–31.
[144] Greg. Naz., *Or.* 43.72 (McCauley); Exodus 41:39–57.
[145] Greg. Naz., *Or.* 43.72 (McCauley). Joshua 13–19.

an *agōn*. Instead the Gregories concentrated on the bodily suffering and imminent death of the protagonists in a domestic setting as a means of unveiling piety and *aretē* in traditionally female contexts. As Verna Harrison has argued, the Cappadocians' characterizations of female family members imbued them with fortitude and vigorous leadership within the household. Their virtue, therefore, mirrors that of their male counterparts, but its display differs from that of noble men based on societal conventions of gender.[146] Nazianzen delivered a funeral oration in 370 for his sister Gorgonia, while in 380 or 381 Nyssen penned a biography of his sibling Macrina that circulated in the form of a letter.[147] A similarity in content between the two works signals not only faithfulness to biographical conventions, but also Nyssen's dependency on his friend's earlier piece.[148] In these chronicles, through exertions that mimicked the acts of martyrs, Gorgonia and Macrina manifested dispositions that merged holiness with a habitus of composure and courage.[149]

Graphic portrayals of beleaguered female bodies often issued a voyeuristic-like enterprise in the ancient world. But the Gregories reoriented scenes of apparent passive suffering into showcases of agency, thus affording readers a privileged look into the ordeal of their sisters as a way of highlighting manliness in their family and themselves.[150] L. Stephanie

---

[146] V. Harrison, "Male and Female in Cappadocian Theology," *JTS* 41 (1990), 453–5.

[147] P. Maraval, "La Vie de Saint Macrine: continuité et nouveauté d'un genre littéraire," in *Du héros païen au saint chrétien (Strasbourg 1–2 déc. 95)*, eds. G. Freyburger and L. Pernot (Paris: Institut d'études augustiniennes, 1997), 133–8, shows that by writing the *Life of Macrina* in letter format, Gregory enjoyed more flexibility in composing the account. The expectations of funeral orations, for example, were usually more binding than epistles.

[148] S. Holman, "Healing the Social Leper in Gregory of Nyssa's and Gregory of Nazianzus's "περιφιλοπτωχίας," *HTR* 92 (1999), 284–5, gives examples of other cases when the two authors worked together and read each other's works; G. Frank, "Macrina's Scar: Homeric Allusion and Heroic Identity in Gregory of Nyssa's *Life of Macrina*," *JECS* 8.4 (2000), 515–6, sets out similarities and differences between the works. Frank points out that Gorgonia's portrait is largely dependent on biblical women as models. Because Macrina's identity is not rooted in such exempla, Frank maintains, Nyssen may have been cueing readers to imagine heroic paragons from non-scriptural sources. Frank is not convinced that Nyssen was familiar with Nazianzen's oration on Gorgonia.

[149] For example Castelli, *Martyrdom*, 138–46, in her analysis of the fifth-century text *Life and Miracles of Saint Thecla*, shows how authors used martyrdom accounts to map specific identities onto the memory of a saint. Shaw, "Body/Power/Identity," 278, likewise equates the impression caused by the martyr – " an aura of aristocratic demeanor" – with the victorious athlete who acquires status through exercising his body.

[150] D. Frankfurter, "Martyrology and the Prurient Gaze," *JECS* 17:2 (2009), 230–4, on the potential of pornographic appeal in martyrologies and the agency imputed to the

Cobb's treatment of early martyr texts is especially instructive on this point. Martyrologies of female saints, she observes, often produced graphic imagery of women's bodies, much more so than in men. This seeming fixation on the body maintains the close association of femininity and the body.[151] Giving as an example the martyr account of the female saint Perpetua, Cobb argues that the vulnerability of the female body serves as a mechanism for inversion, allowing the author to call attention to the remarkability of the female saint's masculine bearing. Cobb shows that Perpetua, while placed in a seemingly defenseless position, took control of her situation. Through her actions, she claimed the power of her oppressors for herself by redefining her martyrdom as an exhibition of *her* authority.[152] Nazianzen's and Nyssen's narratives are based on many of the same features of such martyrologies in that they reverse scenes of passivity in the bodies of female subjects so that they instead indicate force of will. Gorgonia's and Macrina's painful encounters suggested an internalized agonistic setting. But in the literary hands of Nazianzen and Nyssen, their battles were waged in the public eye, and therefore marked with performativity.

The two accounts chronicled the deeds of female agonists: women whose virility was made conspicuous and rendered accessible to laity. Their *agōnes* paralleled the strict regimen of rhetorical exercises and philosophy that cultivated Greek literati.[153] Like athletes or warriors, moreover, Gorgonia and Macrina were put to a test of strength. Only their trial was endogenous, a battle within the human body and against a female nature that was pushed to surpass its limits.[154] Confronting and overcoming excruciating ordeals, and dying with honor, the women stood for

---

anti-Christian punishers. D. Fruchtman, "Modeling a Martyrial Worldview: Prudentius' Pedagogical Ekphrasis and Christianization," *JLA* 7:1 (2014), 135–8, emphasizes the hagiographic author's duty to use *ekphrasis* to reframe the suffering body to exude an ideal of strength.

[151] Cobb, *Dying*, 110.   [152] Cobb, *Dying*, 105–10.

[153] But the female *paideia* that enables success has a different focus. Jones, *Playing*, 35–40, argues that in the ancient Greek novel, for example, female protagonists are endowed with similar control over emotion and quick wit as the men. But the women direct their *paideia* toward chastity and marriage rather than in public exhibitions.

[154] E. Giannarelli, "La biografia femminile: temi e problemi" in *La donna nel pensiero cristiana antico*, ed. U. Mattioli (Genoa: Marietti, 1992), 223–45. J. McInerney, "Plutarch's Manly Women," in *Andreia*, 321–8, explains that in Plutarch's conception of gender, women's virtues are inseparable from their bodies and therefore most visibly expressed corporeally.

an idealized valor associated with heroes from the past.[155] Narratives of ascetic, bodily endurance in female saints underscored the somatic *aretē* that provided stability in the public realm of contentious debate. Nazianzen's account of his sister Gorgonia and Nyssen's eulogy of his sibling Macrina are representative of an identity that Susanna Elm calls the "new masculinity" of the late Roman world and that Virginia Burrus designates "transcendent manhood."[156] In this interpretation of late antique gender, the self-image of Christian men came to depend less on a place in traditional roles as soldiers or statesmen, and more on an inward re-direction of self-control and courage.[157]

This conception of masculinity, I propose, constitutes an augmentation and a cornerstone – rather than an overhaul – of classical masculinity in Christian *pepaideumenoi*. The "transcendent manliness" of internalized *aretē* enabled the new civic elite of the episcopacy to participate as sanctified individuals in the sullied world of public disputation. This alternative form of manliness depended on the influence that holy women such as Gorgonia and Macrina had on male siblings.[158] Burrus, for example, states that Nyssen is concerned "to incorporate the female into the domain of a transcendentalized subjectivity that will itself subtly transform male social roles and reshape the society of men."[159] In the context of inward, bodily refinement, the sisters were ideal sites for male bishops to orchestrate *aretē*. They were uncompromised by the world of *paideia*, an intellectual battleground susceptible to misapplication, as portrayed in Emperor Julian. Gorgonia and Macrina thus were instrumental in sanctifying their brothers in the public realm. These portraits correlated the piety of female saints to classical ideals of manhood.[160]

---

[155] D. Brakke, "Lady Appears: Materializations of 'Woman' in Early Monastic Literature," in *The Cultural Turn in Late Antique Studies*, eds. D. Martin and P. Miller (Durham, NC: Duke University Press, 2005), 25–39.

[156] S. Elm "Gregory's Women: Creating a Philosopher's Family," in *Gregory of Nazianzus: Images and Reflections*, eds. J. Børtnes and T. Hägg (Copenhagen: Museum Tusculanum Press, 2006), 174. V. Burrus, *"Begotten, Not Made": Conceiving Manhood in Late Antiquity* (Stanford, CA: Stanford University Press, 2000), 5.

[157] M. Kuefler, *The Manly Eunuch: Masculinity, Gender Ambiguity, and Christian Ideology in Late Antiquity* (Chicago: University of Chicago Press, 2001), 124.

[158] K. Cooper, *The Virgin and the Bride: Idealized Womanhood in Late Antiquity* (Cambridge, MA: Harvard University Press, 1999), 11–17, makes the crucial point that a man's public image was grounded in his participation in the private sphere: the influence of women.

[159] Burrus, "Begotten," 83.

[160] Such characterizations were not limited to women from the Cappadocians' own families. In Nazianzen's *Oration* 15, Ludlow has shown, Gregory similarly invests the mother of the

In the theological battleground of the late fourth century, the Cappadocians represented themselves and pro-Nicene Christianity, more generally, as an extension of the fundamental sacralized masculinity evident in their pious sisters. The Gregories excelled in public contests, therefore, because they had been shaped first by spiritual *agōnes*. The Gregories branded pro-Nicene *pepaideumenoi* as leadership guided both by piety and self-honor, as commemorated collectively by east Roman communities.

Nazianzen's Oration on Gorgonia: "Courage Surpassing Men of Noble Heart"

In the oration on Gorgonia, Nazianzen fashioned a synthesis of holiness, resolve, and hierarchy. Gregory adduces *aretē* at its core within the person, with Gorgonia embodying the ideal of courage through internal and external struggle and dependence on God. Early in the narrative, Gregory establishes the oration as an exercise in self-reflection: "In praising my sister, I shall be relating the wonderful deeds of my own family."[161] Gregory's introduction establishes the panegyric as a public performance, a quest for personal and family honor. The praise of Gorgonia's virtues contributes to an idealization of the Christian *pepaideumenos* whose nobility is illustrated most strikingly through a woman who exceeds her limitations: "more courageous not only than women, but even than men of noble heart."[162] While instructing listeners and readers on noble bearing, the portrait also upholds the social order within the church by calling attention to Gorgonia's reverence for priestly office.[163] Gregory calls attention here to episcopal rank, thus indicating that through the spiritual heroine of his sister, he is also confirming clerical authority.[164] He presents Gorgonia's *aretē* as a result of conflict,

---

Maccabean martyrs (2 Maccabees and 4 Maccabees) with the attributes of a classical male hero. M. Ludlow, *Art, Craft, and Theology in Fourth-Century Christian Authors* (Oxford: Oxford University Press, 2020), 163–7.

[161] Greg. Naz., *Or.* 8.1 (Daley).

[162] Greg. Naz., *Or.* 8.13 (Daley): ἢ τοῦτο μὲν οὐ μόνον γυναικῶν, ἀλλὰ καὶ ἀνδρῶν ὤφθη τῶν γενναιοτάτων ἀνδρικώτερα; on the atypical nature of such virtue in a woman, Kuefler, *Manly*, 20.

[163] Greg. Naz., *Or.* 8.11 (Daley): "Who has given such honor to priests?" Gregory writes, recalling the gravity of episcopal office as set forward in I Timothy 3:1.

[164] L. Coon, *Sacred Fictions: Holy Women and Hagiography in Late Antiquity* (Philadelphia: University of Pennsylvania Press, 1997), 11–13, argues that a major

thus recalling exhibitions of manhood that came through confrontations. And yet her display of valor remained circumscribed, as he maintains that her acts of piety took place in secret.[165] Despite exuding manly attributes, Gorgonia retains her decorum as a noble woman, avoiding outward discourse and "remaining within the proper limits (πρεπωδέστατον) of reverence."[166] The publicity of her deeds comes not of her own accord, but through Gregory. She preserves her status as an aristocratic matron: a woman of power and dignity. She participates in an *agōn*, thereby confirming the foundation and expression of *aretē* within Gregory's family, but without undermining audience expectations of social order.

Having established Gorgonia as unobtrusive, Gregory gradually develops a testament of her contest that shows her surpassing *agathoi* in *aretē*. In the first half of the *bios*, Gregory impresses on listeners that Gorgonia exceeded all others in σωφροσύνη (*sōphrosunē*), a sense of temperance and modesty that distinguished the upright in both men and women.[167] This attribute, one of the four principal virtues famously outlined by Plato, signaled her piety and social preeminence and placed her in a taxonomy of moral qualities associated with manliness.[168] The idea of restraint points the audience to the overriding theme in the narrative: Gorgonia's management of body, mind, and emotions in all circumstances. Gregory shows a progression of Gorgonia's resolve, culminating in the final sections of the oration with a visible manifestation of composure when she was beset by bodily pain.[169] Gregory recounts a gruesome accident that resulted in a debilitating injury for his sister: "the mad mules who ran away with her carriage, that unexpected swerve, the irresistible speed, the awful wreck."[170] The results were disturbing: "Everything in her was crushed and broken: bones and limbs, internal and external parts."[171] Gregory's account mimicked elements of an *ekphrasis*, re-enacting the harrowing experience in order to evoke awe in the audience, to magnify the extent of the anguish, and to underscore

---

theme in early-western Christian hagiography of female saints involved including anecdotes that reinforced the male authority within the ecclesiastical structure.

[165] Greg. Naz., *Or.* 8.12 (Daley). [166] Greg. Naz., *Or.* 8.11 (Daley).
[167] Greg. Naz., *Or.* 8.8.
[168] For example Plato, *Republic* 4.426–35 and *Phaedo* 69C. Here I interpret Gregory's use of *sōphrosunē* in the classical sense of "moderation" rather than the more countercultural "self-denial" that asceticism sometimes represented. See Cooper, *Virgin*, 56–67, on translating it in the latter way.
[169] Connolly, "Like," in *Andreia*, 309–10, points out that Aristotle associated the chief of virtues, *andreia* (courage), specifically with endurance of pain: Aristotle, *N.E.* 1117b.
[170] Greg. Naz., *Or.* 8.15 (Daley). [171] Greg. Naz., *Or.* 8.15 (Daley).

Gorgonia's calm demeanor.[172] By orchestrating sensory imagination, Gregory prompts listeners to see the carnage, to hear the body shattering. The recounting is a literary feat, one that held potential to victimize Gorgonia, if not managed well.

Instead Gregory framed the atrocity in a manner that redounded to the tenacity of Gorgonia; that showed victory over tragedy. Crowds who otherwise would have been scandalized by such graphic harm to a genteel woman conversely receive encouragement and inspiration from Gorgonia.[173] Virginia Burrus captures the sentiment well, saying that Gregory "converted a potentially senseless accident into a triumphant spectacle of martyrdom."[174] The injury served as a medium to reveal her faith and courage, subsequently turning the event into an arena to showcase her command.[175] Her reaction to the calamity punctuates her nobility. She maintained her modesty by refusing to have a physician examine her, Gregory notes, thus exhibiting decorum even at the point of death.[176] The term used here for decorum, κόσμιος, conveyed moderation and good order. It was the ideal of maintaining peace in the polis and discouraging excess in citizens. Individuals who participated in public venues of an *agōn* required such composure. The same concerns had preoccupied Second Sophistic orators during presentations, but never to the degree that Gorgonia exemplified under such harrowing conditions. In showing Gorgonia rejecting standard medical treatment, moreover, Gregory alludes to the personal nature of her tribulation, with the discipline of *paideia* coming within herself – as subject to Christ – rather

---

[172] J. Mossay, *La Mort et l'au-delà dans Saint Grégoire de Nazianze* (Louvain: Publications Universitaires, 1966), 27–31, discusses Gregory's rhetorical technique in the funeral oration. Ruether, *Gregory*, 94–105, on other cases of Gregory's use of *ekphrasis*.

[173] R. Barrett, "Sensory Experience and the Women Martyrs of Najran," *JECS* 21:1 (2013), 94–5, argues in his study of sixth-century women martyrs at Najran that the use of sensory imagery held an important place in the sacramental and liturgical practices of the Syriac church.

[174] V. Burrus, "Life after Death: The Martyrdom of Gorgonia and the Birth of Female Hagiography," in *Gregory*, ed. Børtnes, 161–3, gives a comprehensive analysis of Gregory's narration of the accident.

[175] A. Crislip, *Thorns in the Flesh: Illness and Sanctity in Late Ancient Christianity* (Philadelphia: University of Pennsylvania Press, 2013), 101–3, and Brakke, *Demons*,190–2, describe a similar development in the fifth-century *Life of Syncletica*. According to Crislip, "Syncletica's illness (or weakness) is but a ruse in her battle with the devil, serving to reveal her 'manliness'" (102). Brakke states that Syncletica's endurance of horrific bodily affliction "brings her internal virility to the surface" (191).

[176] Greg. Naz., *Or.* 8.15 (Daley).

than from typical treatment. Christ becomes her cure. The discipline of medicine is subsumed in the power of the Savior, where worldly learning is transmuted into the realm of holiness. Gregory thus develops Gorgonia's anguish as a signifier of steadiness and courage during misfortune.

Gorgonia's tribulations in the oration, moreover, recall the trials ubiquitous in martyr acts. Like stories of early Christian martyrdoms, Gregory used vivid visual passages to recreate acute bodily suffering as a demonstration of faith that corroborated her courage. By directing attention to Gorgonia's body as a testament of her self-control, Gregory maintains her feminine persona (her materiality) and even stresses her masculinity.[177] Gregory re-inscribed the violence of martyrdoms onto Gorgonia in the form of the carriage accident, where corporeal damage provided a context to exhibit constancy. The severity of her discomfort amplified her strength as part of an epic struggle. The equanimity with which she faced pain and possible demise paralleled the "noble death tradition" in accounts of ascetic discipline (φιλοσοφία) in martyrs and saints.[178] Curbing one's emotion as a measure of masculinity had antecedents stretching back to Homeric warriors, as well as martyrologies.[179] Gregory then records her unexpected, amazingly fast recovery, one that brought awe to the crowds. Her suffering now reads as a display of faith, and a public testament of endurance.[180] After she was healed miraculously from the crash, Gregory states that his sister left a story of posterity, "revealing faith in the midst of pain and toughness (καρτερία) in the face of adversity."[181] Gregory declares that whatever the obstacle – whether sin, the "deceptive serpent" (Satan), or death – Gorgonia overcame them all through her self-mastery (ἐγκράτεια).[182] "Toughness" and "self-mastery" were distinguishing features of

---

[177] Cobb, *Dying*, 110–1; B. Shaw, "Body/Power/Identity," 274.

[178] C. Moss, *Ancient Christian Martyrdom: Diverse Practices, Theologies, and Traditions* (New Haven: Yale University Press, 2012), 26–9. On the use of the term φιλοσοφία as a referent to Christian asceticism: A. Silvas, *Macrina the Younger: Philosopher of God* (Turnhout: Brepols, 2008), 163–7; A. M. Malingrey, *"Philosophia": Étude d'un groupe de mots dans la littérature grecque des présocratiques au IVe siècle après J.C.* (Paris: Klincksiek, 1961); and G. Bardy, "'Philosophie' et 'philosophe' dans le vocabulaire chrétien des premiers siècles," *Revue d'ascétique et de mystique* 25 (1949), 97–108.

[179] Moss, *Ancient*, 27–8, on occurrences in Homer: *Iliad* 21.122–3 and *Odyssey* 11.489–91. Cobb, *Dying*, 65 on occurrences in *Martyrdom of Polycarp*: 3:1, 5.1, 12.1.

[180] Greg. Naz., *Or.* 8.15.   [181] Greg. Naz., *Or.* 8.15 (Daley).

[182] Greg. Naz., *Or.* 8.14 (Daley).

pepaideumenoi: celebrated in the hoplite and the athlete; and extolled repeatedly as part of the oral culture in the Second Sophistic. Pedagogy for young men was designed to develop these features in civic leaders, who would excel in the public domain. But in the case of Gorgonia, *aretē* was expressed in the private life of a matron and put on display only by an extenuating circumstance.

Gregory affirmed longstanding conventions among *pepaideumenoi* by chronicling how Gorgonia took command of her predicament. As Gorgonia prepared to die, sometime after recovering from the carriage crash, she offered words of encouragement to her family and friends on her deathbed, thus "turning her last day into a festival."[183] This statement shows Gorgonia moderating events, even in her last hours. Her final act has her assuming the role of patron, issuing an opportunity for family and friends to gather for an occasion of guidance. Instead of lamenting the end of physical life, she closed out her days by playing the part of teacher, providing wisdom and cause for celebration. In Gorgonia, audiences found a female paradigm of *aretē*. She remained situated in a domestic setting – dutiful to family and respectful of her place – but nevertheless she emerged out of her trials as a stabilizing presence in the church and the polis. She was brought into public view through the mediation of her brother, who relates both her decorum as a pious woman and the maleness of her fortitude. Gregory invoked his sister as his own source of pedagogy, with Gorgonia serving as an emblem of discretion and determination that formed a basis for episcopal resolve.

Nyssen's Life of Macrina: The "Manly Virgin" and "Unconquerable Athlete"

Gregory of Nyssa issued a similar picture of struggle in his *Life of Macrina*. He calls his sister "an unconquerable athlete," recalling the imagery he used in the encomium on Basil and also infusing her figure with the aura of a martyr.[184] This epithet invests Macrina with *aretē* that

---

[183] Greg. Naz., *Or.* 8.21 (Daley): πανηγύρεως ἡμέραν ποιησαμένη τὴν τελευταίαν.

[184] Greg. Ny., *Vit. Macr.* 14.27 (Silvas, 16.5). E. Muehlberger, "Salvage: Macrina and the Christian Project of Cultural Reclamation," *CH* 81:2 (2012), 282, states that Gregory re-defined the Christian notion of martyrdom in this text by making "brave struggle the key component." Muehlberger observes that this re-definition of martyrdom was aided by the flourishing cult of Thecla, an ascetic who had been counted as a martyr for her bravery, even though she did not die.

would normally not be ascribed to a woman.[185] Macrina thus takes on the role of a competitor, a place usually attributed to male heroes. The *agōn* motif plays a prominent part of the narrative, with Macrina's manly virtue coming to view in a contest. From the outset of the biography, Gregory shows that his sister was not constrained by her sex, "for I know not whether it is fitting to designate her of that nature [female] who so surpassed nature."[186] This statement underscores the moral implications of gender in the narrative. For late antique audiences, Macrina's assuming a masculine persona served as a straightforward testament of her superiority. But Macrina's exhibition of manliness takes on a much different look than that of her brother Basil, who confronted a heretic emperor and defended against external foes. Whereas Basil exhibited defiance against a nefarious ruler, Macrina personifies courage by exuding faith and composure within her body.[187] In his sister's ordeal, the debilitating effects of a progressing illness bring to the forefront Macrina's strength. Gregory devotes the last twenty chapters to a malady that resulted in her demise, the death itself, and the aftermath. These passages alternate between graphic portrayals of Macrina's declining health and imminent passing, and her words of comfort and wisdom to Gregory. After learning of her affliction, Gregory came to the house where Macrina was staying and discovered that his sister was "not lying on a bed or couch, but on the floor, on a board strewn with sacking."[188] Even in a debilitating state, she refused any aid. Thus, Macrina would not tolerate an easing of the discomfort. The rigors of her faith and will remained unshaken. She surpassed any signs of effeminacy, with physical malaise unable to diminish her will.[189] As a woman, Macrina was expected to adhere to concerns of the flesh, but Gregory shows her reversing such commonality as she embodies the passage from Romans, "setting her mind on the things of the Spirit."[190] After setting the stage for the performance and relating the severity of the disease, Gregory proceeds to take readers on a journey into his sister's triumph over tribulation.

---

[185] Harrison, "Male," 445, reminds us that Christian spirituality made this self-conception possible in women.
[186] Greg. Ny., *Vit. Macr.* 1.15–20 (Silvas, 1.3): οὐκ οἶδα γὰρ εἰ πρέπον ἐστὶν ἐκ τῆς φύσεως αὐτὴν ὀνομάζειν τὴν ἄνω γενομένην τῆς φύσεως; Galatians 3:28.
[187] V. Burrus, *The Sex Lives of Saints: An Erotics of Ancient Hagiography* (Philadelphia: University of Pennsylvania Press, 2008), 72–6.
[188] Greg. Ny., *Vit. Macr.* 16.13–20 (Silvas 19.1).
[189] On exceeding the female nature, Kuefler, *Manly*, 30.   [190] Romans 8:5 (NIV).

Over several lines of text, Gregory intensifies Macrina's symptoms as he conveys her declining state in rich description: the fever "consuming her vital force;"[191] the "short and laboured breathing;"[192] the dryness of her tongue; her voice giving out; and the trembling of her lips.[193] During the unfolding of these symptoms, Gregory facilitates for readers a visual experience of his sister's deterioration. But in a drama that offered otherwise explicit imagery, he turns grim fascination into a celebration of comportment. As Macrina nears death, Gregory characterizes her celebratory demeanor, "as a runner who has passed his adversary and already draws near to the end of the stadium, when he draws near to the prize and sees the victor's crown...and calls out his victory (νίκην εὐαγγελίζεται) to his supporters among the spectators."[194] The metaphor invests Macrina with agency as she takes control over the events unfolding. Rather than an athlete performing as a source of objectification, she uses her circumstances as a runner who incites spectators to celebrate with her. The connotation is that like the apostle Paul, she has "fought the good fight, finished the race, and kept the faith."[195] The achievement for Macrina is endogenous, a corporeal subjection that in this context yields to the will of Christ. Yet it is also exogenous in that, through Christ, she manages the condition of her body as a testimony of her piety. She does not act as a victim to her disease.[196] To the contrary, she manages the crisis so that she serves as an instrument of instruction.

Throughout the affliction, Macrina repeatedly emerges dominant because her soul overcomes her plight. In the mist of pain, Gregory states, she remained fixated on "lofty philosophy" (ὑψηλοτέρας φιλοσοφίας).[197] This phrase shows Macrina exceeding the materiality associated with her femininity. Although she was enfleshed in a beleaguered body, her preoccupation was toward extracorporeal matters. Thus, through the adversity she accrued understanding of the Divine and she comes to serve as a source of reason. Macrina's reaction to her own circumstances of illness and imminent death shows her mastery of bodily passion and guidance of soul. By giving evidence of such quietude, moreover, Macrina acts as an instructor on grief for the community of virgins that she was overseeing,

---

[191] Greg. Ny., *Vit. Macr.* 18.7–9 (Silvas 20.4). The *ekphrasis* of illness appears similar to the dramatic effect created in Nazianzen's account of Gorgonia.
[192] Greg. Ny., *Vit. Macr.* 22.8–15 (Silvas 24.1). [193] Greg. Ny., *Vit. Macr.* 25.1–17.
[194] Greg. Ny., *Vit. Macr.* 19.25–8 (Silvas 21.5). [195] I Timothy 4:7 (NIV).
[196] Cobb, *Dying*, 106, where Cobb writes about Perpetua: "She is not the passive object of the audience's voyeurism; rather, she controls it."
[197] Greg. Ny., *Vit. Macr.* 17.20–5 (my translation).

as well as to Gregory himself.[198] Playing the part of a patron, she mediates for these loved ones between the world of pain and the heavenly sanctuary where her soul now resides.[199] Nyssen personifies Macrina as the Hebrew sage Job, whom Gregory credits for containing the pain within his body as he remained true to his faith.[200] And like Job, Macrina's voice imparted divine wisdom. Even in her weakest state, she discoursed "on the soul and explained the cause of our life in the flesh."[201] A woman teaching on the soul's dominance over body ushers the converse of normality. By imparting this philosophical role to his sister, Gregory shows that Macrina exceeds all that is base; she stands outside (and above) hierarchy. Gregory offers Job as a paradigm for his sister because his very identity was equated with wisdom in the midst of suffering, and his subjugation of the body.[202] Like the Hebrew sage, Macrina looked beyond her torment, so that she "kept her mind unimpaired in the contemplation of the higher things, in no way hindered by her great weakness."[203] Gregory accentuated Macrina's exceptional composure as she faced death with stoic resolve in the last chapters. During suffering, she remained a force of equanimity and a masterful teacher.[204]

In Macrina, beleaguered and secluded from the polis, Gregory located the meeting-place of the Divine and the corporeal, a coming together that served as an extrapolation of *aretē* in a less civic forum. Her flesh was refashioned into a model that instructed Christian *pepaideumenoi* on spiritual probity. Despite her pain, Macrina remains unnerved as she rouses Gregory with "beautiful words" (καλοί λόγοι).[205] Gregory emphasized the aesthetics of Macrina's speech as a contrast to the unpleasantness of her symptoms, and also as symbolic of her noble nature. Under the weight of a life-draining disease, Macrina's fullness comes into view as her voice replaces her failing body as the seat of her identity.[206] Although her strength is "wasted by fever," nevertheless she delivers such a lesson to her brother that his "soul was elevated by her words above human nature

---

[198] Greg. Ny., *Vit. Macr.* 26.1–15 (Maraval); J. W. Smith, "A Just and Reasonable Grief: The Death and Function of a Holy Woman in Gregory of Nyssa's *Life of Macrina*," *JECS* 12 (2004), 71–9.
[199] Smith, "Just," 80–3. [200] Greg. Ny., *Vit. Macr.* 18.5–10 (Silvas 20.3).
[201] Greg. Ny., *Vit. Macr.* 17.20–30 (Silvas, 20.5). [202] See Job 1–3.
[203] Greg. Ny., *Vit. Macr.* 18.10–15 (Silvas 20.4). [204] Greg. Ny., *Vit. Macr.* 20.6.
[205] Greg. Ny., *Vit. Macr.* 22.10–15 (Silvas 24.1).
[206] J. Porter, "Rhetoric, Aesthetics, and the Voice," in *Cambridge Companion to Ancient Rhetoric*, ed. E. Gunderson (Cambridge: Cambridge University Press, 2009), 93, on the rhetoric of the voice becoming a body.

and set down through the guidance of her discourse within the heavenly sanctuary."²⁰⁷ As she lies on her death bed, Macrina takes on the role of instructor for Gregory by lecturing him on divine purpose and the resurrection. Gregory states that her teaching provided solace and that he remained obedient to her as if she were his tutor.²⁰⁸ Macrina was equipped for the task with ease of speech (εὐκολία), which flows "with complete ease like water streaming downhill from a fountain unimpeded."²⁰⁹ Here, Macrina's eloquence reflected refinement through trial, which enabled her to speak with the grace and force of a *pepaideumenos* even though she had not received training for public speaking. By expressing Macrina's sanctity through the power of her speech, Gregory illustrated her devotion as the source of her discourse, one richer in erudition and depth than that of celebrated orators. Her manliness derived from her faith. Indeed, as we further discuss theological conflict in Chapter 4, Gregory will frame Macrina as a metaphor for theology that derives from sacred *aretē*.

Under highest duress, Macrina assumed the mantle of philosopher as she regulated the passions of her brother, comforting Gregory by "the sweetness of her words" (καταγλυκαίνω).²¹⁰ Yet she remains laity and female, subservient to her priestly brother. At one point, in her weakened condition "she [Macrina] raised herself on her elbow" and "placing her hands on the floor and leaning out from her pallet as far as she could, she did me [Gregory] the honour of a reverence."²¹¹ Even in the throes of pain and death, Macrina showed Gregory respect according to his rank as bishop. Gregory depicts his sister as a "manly virgin," the ideal aristocratic Christian woman, but she still honored social and gender hierarchies.²¹² So while Macrina emerges as the paragon of ascetic virtue

---

²⁰⁷ Greg. Ny., *Vit. Macr.* 17.28–30 (Silvas, 20.2).
²⁰⁸ Greg. Ny., *Vit. Macr.* 19.1–10 (Silvas 21.2).
²⁰⁹ Greg. Ny., *Vit. Macr.* 18.20-2 (Silvas 20.6).
²¹⁰ Greg. Ny., *Vit. Macr.* 22.1–3 (Callahan, 178).
²¹¹ Greg. Ny., *Vit. Macr.* 17.1–6 (Silvas 19.2).
²¹² S. Elm, "*Virgins of God*": *The Making of Asceticism in Late Antiquity* (Oxford: Clarendon Press, 1994), 135, emphasizes that Macrina is represented as a "manly virgin" in regard to her soul, while retaining her feminine appearance. On aristocratic nature of Macrina, E. Clark, "Holy Women, Holy Words: Early Christian Women, Social History and the 'Linguistic Turn,'" *JECS* 6:3 (1998), 413-5, says that by maintaining the boundaries of the ecclesial hierarchy, Gregory encouraged laity, especially women, to relate to Macrina's piety while retaining episcopal authority. See Coon, *Sacred*, 148: "...holy women dutifully and submissively served charismatic men precisely because their spirituality was distinct from and subordinate to that of sacred males."

and a stabilizing spiritual force for her family and her community, Gregory also has her underscoring the status of the episcopal office. Imbuing a female protagonist with masculine virtues accentuated the features for a learned audience that had come to associate female figures with didactic functions. The virtual nature of this model, moreover, did not threaten the system of class and distinction embedded in the culture of *paideia*.

In these two biographies, Nazianzen and Nyssen inscribed onto their sisters qualities that paralleled features of *paideia*: for Gorgonia, deference and resolve; for Macrina, boldness and eloquence. Both authors reoriented somatic duress as a means of highlighting control of one's body, command of circumstances, and piety. The Gregories used the agonies and the corresponding bravery of Gorgonia and Macrina as a rhetorical display of sacred *aretē*, transforming their sisters from subjects of scopophilia into paragons of elite demeanor and sanctity. The performances in these female saints spoke to a core element of *paideia*, the internal battle in oneself to keep passions and desires at bay. The theme closely mimics the words of Nyssen, commending a fellow *pepaideumenos* for "contending within yourself (ἑαυτὸν ἁμιλλάομαι) to exceed in virtue (ἀρετή)."[213] Macrina's triumph illustrates the contest within individuals, the mastery of body that a Christian *pepaideumenos* must acquire before engaging in outward combat. The authors propose that from a transformative, disciplinary regimen, an individual matures into a source of spiritual authority that can translate into the public realm. Macrina, like Job, exceeded in sagacity during the affliction, as if the physical adversity triggered deeply buried insights.

The illustration of such self-comportment worked best in a martyrological setting, that is, in a place where their bodies were subjected to a severity that disclosed supreme courage. A setting characterized by excessive distress, with women under the siege of corporeal affliction, was the paradigmatic locus to highlight the ideals of *paideia*. It was the consummate inner agonistic arena. Gorgonia and Macrina accordingly manifested virile deportment. They opened vistas for audiences to contemplate the Divine while reaffirming a Greek heritage rooted in aristocratic virtue. The synthesis of sanctity and *aretē* in these accounts was itself a rhetorical

---

[213] Greg. Ny., *Ep.* 8 (my translation). P. Maraval, *Grégoire de Nysse: Lettres*, recognizes that this phrase echoes thoughts by a near contemporary Neo-platonic philosopher, that the virtuous individual must fight to control his own passions. Porphyry, *On Abstinence* 3.27.11.

display, one that credited the authority of the authors who are serving as gatekeepers of family traditions. In these lives, the erudition of the Gregories – their *paideia* – merged with the self-mastery and piety of their sisters. The biographies embedded the language of self-mastery in the unconventional place of holy women, who have now been reoriented to stand for literary refinement and decorum.[214] Gorgonia's and Macrina's comportment thus validated their own *aretē* and that of their brothers as they sacralized classical virtue.

PHYSICAL BEAUTY AND *ARETĒ* IN FAMILY AND SAINTS

In addition to recounting the deeds of hagiographic subjects, the Gregories also alluded to corporeal features of *aretē* in the persons. The composite they were creating in hagiography included characteristics of virtue that came through sensory experience. Gregory of Nazianzus, for example, called attention to the "beauty and stature (κάλλος καὶ μέγεθος)" of Caesarius.[215] In physiognomy, height usually connoted an imposing figure. Ancient writers often paired size and attraction in characterizations of great accomplishments, as when Plutarch described the success of Roman general Scipio Africanus as "exploits transcendent in magnitude and splendor."[216] Caesarius' appearance similarly correlated to his deeds. Excellence, many believed, could be observed just by looking at an individual. Appearance was especially effective in reflecting a hero's martial and athletic prowess, thus augmenting an individual's noble actions.[217] In the context of late antiquity, corporeal appeal was associated with the rigorous training (*paideia*) that equipped individuals for participation in an *agōn* of philosophy, oratory, and theological debate.[218] Conversely, an ungainly body and gawky facial expressions

---

[214] Cooper, *Virgin*, 60: Referring to asceticism, Cooper posits that "an exhibition of supreme self-control...was precisely the token by which Christian accession to power could be bought."

[215] Greg. Naz. *Or.* 7.5. (McCauley).

[216] Plutarch, *Fabius Maximus* 26.3 (Perrin): πράξεις ὑπερήφανοι τὸ μέγεθος καὶ τὸ κάλλος; D. Konstan, *Beauty: The Fortunes of an Ancient Greek Idea* (Oxford: Oxford University Press, 2014), 84, on describing praiseworthy actions as "beautiful."

[217] Aristotle, *Rhetoric* 1361b. G. I. C. Robertson, "The *Andreia* of Xenocles: *Kouros, Kallos* and *Kleos*," in *Andreia*, 65–74, cites numerous examples from ancient Greek literature where fame is linked both to outstanding appearance and outstanding excellence.

[218] Ludlow, *Art*, 188, recognizes a related correlation in Basil's and Nyssen's homilies, where "moral status, beautiful bodies, and effective public speech all align."

signaled a lack of preparation.²¹⁹ Beauty, that is, could serve as a marker of sophistication. No other accoutrements, not "folds of silk," "woven robes of transparent linen," or "costly perfumes," were used to enhance the resplendence of Caesarius' "beautiful (καλός) body."²²⁰ He was "adorned with manliness alone" Gregory proclaims.²²¹ Nazianzen juxtaposed his sibling against the external trappings of an effeminate man. Gregory then presented his departed brother with the only worthy accessory, "adornment (κόσμος) at my hands," a speech designed to preserve "more clearly than pictures the image of our beloved."²²² Gregory asserted that his words surpassed sight, the most privileged of the senses, as a medium for capturing the essence of Caesarius. Such is his surety that his hands play the part of the mouth and the eyes, penning both vision and orality. Gregory characterizes his narrative as a gift, thus calling attention to his own fluency and emphasizing his place as a conduit between his own eloquence and his brother's virtue.²²³

Gregory of Nyssa offered a similar rhetorical display as he underscored Basil's beauty.²²⁴ Gregory compared his encomium on Basil to the efficacy of signet rings, where "the wax which is impressed by the signet has transferred the beauty which lies within the groove upon itself, having received the impression of the whole character of the signet in its own mould."²²⁵ The trope of the signet ring comes from Polemon of Laodicea, who applied this metaphor to urge scholars to assess individual disposition based on an overall impression.²²⁶ Gregory was portraying the greatness of his brother as beyond conventional commemoration. His virtue, so it seemed, could not be adequately praised. This avowal was a commonplace in Greek panegyric, when speakers feigned inability to extol subjects. But rather than remaining diffident in the matter, Gregory then authorized himself to complete the task, as "the one who

---

²¹⁹ Connolly, "Like," in *Andreia*, 296.   ²²⁰ Greg. Naz., *Or.* 7.16 (McCauley).
²²¹ Greg. Naz., *Or.* 7.16 (slight alteration of McCauley): ἀρετῇ μόνῃ κοσμούμενος.
²²² Greg. Naz., *Or.* 7.16 (McCauley).
²²³ Greg. Naz. *Or.* 7.4 (McCauley): "My gift is a speech."
²²⁴ Ludlow, *Art*, 186–7, points out that in both Basil's and Nyssen's homilies on the Forty Martyrs of Sebaste, the authors praise the physique of their protagonists. By contrast, she says, John Chrysostom's homily on the Forty Martyrs depicts the soldiers' pre-transformation bodies as weak.
²²⁵ Greg. Ny., *In Basilium* 26.2–7 (Stein).
²²⁶ Polemon, *Physiognomy* 1.1.168. trans. in M. Gleason, *Making Men: Sophists and Self-Presentation in Ancient Rome* (Princeton: Princeton University Press, 1995), 34. See Gleason's extended treatment of Polemon and physiognomy: *Making*, 21–54.

points out the beauty moulded upon the wax."²²⁷ Gregory consequently served as moderator of his brother's *aretē* because he alone could fully denote Basil's comprehensive nature, having shared kinship with the Caesarean and having succeeded him as a prominent authority within the pro-Nicene party of Asia Minor. Gregory consequently fashioned himself as a *pepaideumenos* par excellence.

On other occasions, the Cappadocians directed audiences to notice the appearance of their subjects, but only momentarily. In these cases, the authors complemented manifestations of nobility (pedigree, education, and actions) with brief summaries of physical appeal. Nazianzen, for instance, accentuated corporeal features through phrasing that was ostensibly dismissive of the body. In his oration on Basil, he prefaced a long account of Basil's outstanding qualities seemingly by negating discussion of the Caesarean's somatic superiority. "Beauty (κάλλος) and strength (ῥώμη) and size (μέγεθος), in which I see most men delight, I shall leave to those who are interested in them."²²⁸ These were issues, Gregory suggested, best left to experts. Their fascination with somatic features, he implies, involved momentary interest for the sake of evaluation.²²⁹ Men were supposed to be above excessive preoccupation with the body, an aspect of humanity that Greek literature generally ascribed to female concern. Therefore, Gregory would not enervate himself by engaging in a protracted discussion of Basil's bodily merits. But before moving forward in his vaunting of Basil's great deeds, Gregory alluded to Basil's corporeal supremacy. "Not that he [Basil] was inferior even in these points [beauty, strength, and size] to those small-minded men who are busy with the things of the body."²³⁰ Thus, while nullifying the issue, Gregory artfully wove Basil's physical prowess into the narrative. By feigning to minimalize the corporeal, Gregory directed attention to his friend's appearance by stating that he would not speak about his bodily magnificence. Gregory manipulated the issue of physicality to affirm Basil's supremacy without showing inappropriate fixation on the topic. The audience was prompted to recall the age of the gymnasium, where bodily appearance *did* register individual *aretē*.

Including references to a vigorous bodily image was a useful part of these portraits because late antique eastern Romans still associated appearance with personality and moral assessment. Especially for

---

[227] Greg. Ny., *In Basilium* 26.9–10 (Stein).   [228] Greg. Naz., *Or*. 43.10 (McCauley).
[229] Greg. Naz., *Or*. 43.10 (McCauley). He calls them "unskilled athletes, who waste their strength in vain and minor contests."
[230] Greg. Naz., *Or*. 43.10 (McCauley).

pepaideumenoi – who delved into the science of physiognomy – personality, deeds, and bodily form concurred. In the biography of his sister Macrina, Gregory of Nyssa recounted acts of service by his older brother Naucratius.[231] In this case, the corporeal depiction of his sibling communicated more than the short record of his life, with Gregory noting that Naucratius "surpassed the others in good fortune of nature, in beauty of body, in vigour, and in the speed and facility in any task."[232] These features credited him to audiences. The somatic distinction scripted here recreated the verbal description by Aristotle of an Olympic victor, whose image radiates inherent superiority.[233] It also paralleled the Homeric epithet for the hero Achilles in the *Iliad*.[234] Details of Naucratius' actions extrapolated the manly excellence denoted by his appearance. It naturally followed, therefore, when Gregory said that Naucratius gave "such proofs of his own studies in a public assembly that the entire audience in the theatre was moved," or that he "tamed his own youth" and "subdued his youth."[235] These features of control were already evident in Gregory's portrait of Naucratius' sublime appearance. Noble beauty and achievement were counterparts.

NOBLE BEAUTY AND MODESTY IN FEMALE SAINTS

In biographies of female family members, the Gregories also attended to issues of corporeal eminence, but in a way that characterized the place of the body differently than in accounts of males.[236] In Nazianzen's oration for Gorgonia and Nyssen's life of Macrina, the authors illustrated their sisters' responsibility in controlling access to their beauty. In the case of Gorgonia, Nazianzen infused the account with examples of αἰδώς, respectful modesty. "Her very lack of ornament," Gregory writes, "was her beauty."[237] Further in the text Gregory accentuated her hesitancy to appear in public or to be made accessible to male observation.[238]

---

[231] Greg. Ny., *Vit. Macr.* 8.
[232] Greg. Ny., *Vit. Macr.*.8.1–4 (Silvas, 10.1): φύσεως εὐκληρίᾳ καὶ σώματος κάλλει καὶ ῥώμῃ καὶ τάχει καὶ τῇ πρὸς πᾶν ἐπιτηδειότητι διαφέρων τῶν ἄλλων.
[233] Aristotle, *Rhetoric* 1361b 14.   [234] For example *Iliad* 9.623.
[235] Greg. Ny., *Vit. Macr.* 8.15–30 (Silvas, 10.1–5).
[236] Differences between Nazianzen's depiction of physical appearance in Caesarius and Gorgonia: T. Hägg, "Playing with Expectations: Gregory's Funeral Orations on his Brother, Sister, and Father," in *Gregory*, ed. Børtnes, 142 and M. Guignet, *Saint Grégoire de Nazianze et la rhétorique* (Paris: Picard, 1911), 200–5.
[237] Greg. Naz., *Or.* 8.3 (Daley).   [238] Greg. Naz., *Or.* 8.9.

Gregory made this point immediately after his depiction of the woman of valor in the book of Proverbs, the idealized wife who is juxtaposed against the dishonorable woman who seeks the attentions of men through lascivious means.[239] Unlike this profligate woman, Gorgonia privatized her physical beauty. As a woman showing the comportment of a man, Gregory says, Gorgonia deserved to hold a place of public honor.[240] Her virtue authorized her. Yet, her temperance would not allow it. She represented a woman of strength, merging the attributes of *aretē* with the maternal duty of her Proverbs corollary. On the issue of bodily decorum, Gregory devotes a lengthy excursus, part of which appears in the translation below by Brian Daley:

> ...neither the extravagance of flowing, diaphanous robes was hers, nor the charm and glitter of stones that color the air around them and light up the forms that bear them. She was not concerned with the arts and trickery of painters, nor with cheaply bought beauty; she had no dealings with the earthly creator, God's rival, who conceals God's creation with treacherous colors and spreads shame by the honors he bestows, setting forth the divine form as an idol of lewdness for hungry eyes, so that spurious beauty might steal away the natural image meant for God...Highlights and eye shadow, the fleeting prettiness of living portraits, she left to women of the theatre and the public square.[241]

For Gorgonia, the human body, "the divine form," represented an analogue to that of the Creator and should not be corrupted by artifices, particularly those that provoke lust. Such trappings, the fare of ill reputable women, were especially beneath a woman of her high birth. Like a teacher guided by *aretē*, Gorgonia stood for authenticity and stability, unlike "the arts and trickery of painters," or "highlights and eye shadow," here alluding to the deceptions of crafty wordsmiths. Gregory was insinuating that his sister, a pro-Nicene matron, contrasted with unmanly Heterousian theologians, here couched as harlots. As a blood relative, Gregory was claiming the certitude of his sister for himself. Gregory used the description of Gorgonia's unobtrusiveness, moreover, to allude to a theology of creation, "the natural image meant for God;" an ontological status meriting human relation with the Divine. More directly, Gregory showed his sister as preserving her God-bestowed beauty, while discouraging visual allure caused by embellishments. The eyes,

---

[239] Greg. Naz., *Or.* 8.9 (Daley); woman of valor, Proverbs 31:10–31.
[240] Greg. Naz., *Or.* 8.9 (Daley) "doing a woman's tasks with a man's endurance."
[241] Greg. Naz., *Or.* 8.10 (Daley).

ancient scholars believed, were the breach through which *ērōs* (passionate desire) entered a person.²⁴² Women of honor, therefore, took care to avert any affectation that might draw the prurient gaze of men. Those occupied with ostentation – heretics, that is – signified penetrability and lack of manhood.²⁴³

Like Nazianzen, Gregory of Nyssa gave prominence to his sister's physical appearance as a facet of her *aretē*. Nyssen shows how, unlike classical characterizations of female vanity, beauty in Macrina testified to her integrity. As far back as the Homeric world, Greeks had equated bodily beauty in women with desire and danger. In the mythical judgment of Paris, the goddesses Hera, Athena, and Aphrodite engaged in a competition to win the designation as the "fairest one." These three exhibited their beauty to the judge Paris in a contention that set forth in motion events leading to the Trojan War. In this story, the women participated in an *agōn*, conventionally designated as a male venture, but here devolving into a contest of concupiscence. The goddesses were cast as instigators, an act that in the consciousness of Greek audiences represented an upsetting of the social order. The anecdote fueled the notion that the feminine nature lacked sexual control, with the goddesses participating in a male enterprise and employing their beauty as an object of desire. Nyssen upheld alternative conduct in Macrina that stood against the exhibitionist tendencies found in these goddesses. Gregory presented his sister as the antithesis of such indecent sexual appeal. Whereas Hera, Athena, and Aphrodite, for example, showcased their beauty for sordid purposes, in Gregory's story the beauty of Macrina stood for class, piety, and noble manliness (*aretē*). The *agōn* of the former was driven by narcissism; that of Macrina reflected dignity. For Macrina, bodily form was not a commodity to be exploited, but an aspect of being to be considered with caution and to glorify the Creator.

Early in the narrative, Gregory treats Macrina's attractiveness and its effect on men.²⁴⁴ "…though the girl's beauty was concealed, it did not

---

²⁴² For example Aristotle, *N.E.* 1167a 3–4, 1157a 6–10). Konstan, *Beauty*, 67.
²⁴³ D. Fredrick, "Mapping Penetrability in Late Republican and Early Imperial Rome," in *The Roman Gaze: Vision, Power, and the Body*, ed. D. Fredrick (Baltimore: Johns Hopkins University Press, 2002), 237–8, discusses the gaze as a form of penetration that not only represented sexual violation, but also social vulnerability and loss of power.
²⁴⁴ Macrina's physical appeal is foreshadowed in Gregory's portrayal of his mother Emmelia. He describes her body as "in the first flower of beauty," as "the fame of her comeliness (ἐυμορφία) was attracting many suitors." Emmelia recognized the dangers of

escape notice," Gregory writes, nor could "any marvel compare with her beauty (κάλλος) and charm (ἐυμορφία)."[245] As appearance testified to Naucratius' eminence later in the narrative, Macrina's beauty here confirmed her excellence of soul. Men of the region were drawn to her fusion of pedigree, physical desirability, and bearing. Her father, hypersensitive of her beauty, played the admirable role of a patriarch by marrying his daughter to an eligible young man.[246] Thus Macrina is protected, temporarily, from the overtures of other men. But it is only after Macrina's youthful husband met an untimely death that she took charge of her now vulnerable beauty, as several male suitors pursued her because of the "fame of her beauty."[247] Rather than subject herself to further male scrutiny, or allow another man to indulge in her body, Macrina declared herself eternally wed to her deceased husband, whom she declared to be on a journey (spiritually) rather than dead.[248] She never committed herself to temporal marriage again.

Macrina's loyalty to spouse, Georgia Frank has shown, has Homeric antecedents in Penelope's rejection of suitors during her husband Odysseus' wanderings.[249] Macrina's fidelity to her husband, even after his death, also recalls a similar case in the *Ephesian Tale of Anthia and Habrocomes*, a second-century Greek novel by Xenophon of Ephesus.[250] Having believed that her husband Habrocomes had died, and now facing a dreaded upcoming marriage, the wife Anthia determined that her only true spouse would remain Habrocomes. Consequently she planned suicide to avoid a new marriage.[251] This chronicle may have informed

her attraction, "seeing that some, inflamed by her beauty, were preparing to carry her off," and consequently she married Gregory's father Basil (the Elder). She married in order to place herself under the protection and discretion of one man. Thus, Emmelia removed herself from public view and averted male rivalry and sexual violence. See Greg. Ny., *Vit. Macr.* 2.10–20.

[245] Greg. Ny., *Vit. Macr.* 4.1–10 (Silvas, 5.2).   [246] Greg. Ny., *Vit. Macr.* 4.15–20.
[247] Greg. Ny., *Vit. Macr.* 5.5–7 (Silvas, 6.2).   [248] Greg. Ny., *Vit. Macr.* 5.15–20.
[249] In Homer's *Odyssey*, book 16, Penelope staves off advances from multiple suitors as she remains faithful to her absent husband Odysseus: Frank, "Macrina's," 522–5.
[250] Xenophon, *Ephesian Tale*. Discussion on this work and references found in Jones, *Playing*, 112–3, 186–208. For translation, G. Anderson, "Xenophon of Ephesus: An Ephesian Tale," in *Collected Ancient Greek Novels*, ed. B. P. Reardon (Berkeley: University of California Press, 1989), 125–69.
[251] Xenophon, *Ephesian Tale* 3.6.3; Jones, *Playing*, 112, shows that she thus succeeds in maintaining her chastity and fidelity; D. Konstan, "Le courage dans le roman grec: de Chariton à Xénophon d'Ephèse, avec une reference à Philon d'Alexandrie," in *Passions, vertus et vices dans l'ancien roman*, eds. B. Pouderon and C. Bost-Pouderon (Lyon: Maison de l'Orient Méditerranéen, 2009), 123, states that the heroine Anthia's courage is indistinguishable from that of the hero Habrocomes.

Gregory's rendition of Macrina's decision not to re-marry in the sense that in both cases, the woman determined who would enjoy her beauty (and body). In a somewhat parallel manner to Anthia, Macrina exudes courage both through maintaining chastity in the face of sexual pressure, and by managing access to her body. Controlling one's body – and its availability – indicated a manly virtue. Much like Gregory would later claim for Macrina, Anthia proclaims that she has surpassed the expectations of σωφροσύνη (moderation) for a woman.[252] Macrina's fending off admirers likewise represents the unsullied body, which has not been compromised to the eyes of any man.

And in a final demonstration of Macrina's steadfastness, readers learn of a malady, earlier in her life, when she had not allowed doctors to observe her body, She considered that having her nakedness seen by strangers was worse than the harm of the accident.[253] This episode also had antecedents in Nazianzen's portrayal of Gorgonia after her carriage accident, when she would not allow physicians near her because of her modesty.[254] In both cases the women took sacrificial measures to maintain their virtue. The audience learns of Macrina's prior illness – the one from which she recovered – during the aftermath of the sickness that took her life. The reader is taken to the privileged place of her bedside, where Gregory himself is first learning of the previous ailment. As Gregory stands near his sister's post-mortem body, a spiritual dependent of Macrina points out a scar that marks the site where God had healed her of the cancer.[255] Readers familiar with the *Odyssey* were now prompted to recall the story of Odysseus' scar, a blemish identified by the servant Eurycleia.[256] Not only, therefore, does Gregory render Macrina with the sexual probity of Penelope, but also he invests her with the identity of a Greek warrior who has returned home after daring adventures. A major theme in the *Life* is Macrina's spiritual purity. Her impenetrability and boldness now map onto her body piety associated with *aretē*.

In the experiences of Gorgonia and Macrina, the women's bodies were concealed from the view of the general male populace.[257] Thus they remained fortified against the gaze of men. The Gregories may have used themes of circumspection as a metaphor for how they (clergy) protected

---

[252] Xenophon, *Ephesian Tale* 5.8.7.   [253] Greg. Ny., *Vit. Macr.* 31.20–5.
[254] Greg. Naz., *Or.* 8.15.   [255] Greg. Ny., *Vit. Macr.* 31.5–15.
[256] *Odyssey* 19.505–50. Frank, "Macrina's," 526–9.
[257] Or one might say that the authors managed the view of the bodies, through *what* they described. On avoiding passivity of an audience's voyeurism: Cobb, *Dying*, 106.

congregations from corrupting influence (false teaching). While Nyssen composed his account of Macrina while serving as bishop, Nazianzen had delivered the oration on Gorgonia before his episcopacy. But Nazianzen was already an ordained priest and his father was a bishop at the time. He knew the duties of guarding a congregation from malicious teachings. Lay members, meanwhile, were encouraged to follow the examples of Gorgonia and Macrina in guarding their bodies (here a metaphor for the soul) against damaging intrusion. In scripting the stories, that is, the authors created mechanisms of warning audiences of laity about exposing themselves to indiscriminate doctrines. Individuals were being advised to guard true beliefs (represented by "beauty") against violation (heresy).

These portraits of their sisters' physicality accorded closely to New Testament depictions of women as found in the pastoral epistles. Both Gregories developed images of their sisters that approximated instructions to women from I Timothy: "I also want women to dress modestly, with decency and propriety, not with braided hair or gold or pearls or expensive clothes, but with good deeds."[258] The idealized Christian woman coincided with expectations prescribed for men, with reputation coming from actions rather than appearance. The Gregories fashioned Gorgonia and Macrina accordingly. For Macrina, "the only adornment of concern...was a pure life."[259] And for Gorgonia, "Gold, worked up to an excess of beauty by human art, never adorned her," Nazianzen writes, but "the only rouge she valued was the blush of modesty."[260] Nyssen and Nazianzen thus used personal management of beauty to project male qualities onto their sisters. Bodily splendor confirmed the nobility and piety of the women, which the sisters demonstrated through sacred endeavors. Nazianzen, for example, concludes his oration on Gorgonia by affirming his sister as the most beautiful woman.[261] But corporeality was not these women's concern. Beauty was a biproduct of the women's *aretē*; an outcome of the *agōnes* in which they exhibited spiritual discipline. Moreover, it was the episcopal brothers who regulated the physical allure of Gorgonia and Macrina through text and speech. They filtered their sisters' beauty through the lens of their deeds, subsequently drawing consideration to appearance only as a corollary to activity.

The Cappadocians thus ascribed physical beauty to family members, associates, and clergy as a means of illustrating virtue that increasingly

---

[258] I Timothy 2:9–10 (NIV).   [259] Macrina: Greg. Ny., *Vit. Macr.* 29.5–10 (Silvas, 31.2).
[260] Gorgonia: Greg. Naz., *Or.* 8.10 (Daley).   [261] Greg. Naz., *Or.* 8.22 (Daley).

was equated with sanctity. In physiognomy, the essence of a person was discernible through his or her body, with beauty equating moral excellence. But loveliness, that of the noble kind, was susceptible to interpretation. The Gregories inserted themselves into this dialogue by introducing the element of beauty in subjects, and then by serving as translators of this "corporeal code of *aretē*."[262] The bishops were taking on the role of physiognomists, thus showing audiences what an ideal man and woman looked like. With *paideia* a mark of Greekness, nobility, and masculinity, the Cappadocians could expect to accrue significant standing by moderating this discourse. They subsequently framed beauty as a product of two kinds of *paideia*, both masculine, with one for men and one for women. In references to manly beauty, the Cappadocians were confirming the *aretē* of their protagonists, formulated as spiritual excellence. For the males, the Gregories affiliated comeliness with strength and size, assets befitting the athlete and soldier, now transformed into features of pro-Nicene leaders that directed the church and polis. For the women in the hagiographies, beauty also presented both a sign of excellence and an identifier of worthy acts. Such loveliness, however, presented an ambivalence. Although the elegant disposition symbolized virtue, it had to be controlled. In an irony with a long tradition in the classical world, Nazianzen and Nyssen correlated the beauty of the women in their biographies to a determination to keep this praiseworthy attribute off limits to most persons. Thus, as the Gregories preserved physical beauty as a feature of Christian *paideia*, they maintained classical expectations of male and female gender norms.

In the biographies treated in this chapter, the Cappadocians used athletic and martial imagery to depict theology as manly combat, with battle a matter of education, class, and piety. The subjects could be trusted because they had encountered struggles and overcame them. Such representations issued an image of pro-Nicene bishops as well-suited for confrontations within the contentious setting of ecclesiastic, imperial, and civic politics. Nazianzen and Nyssen put *paideia* on display even as they promoted an aesthetic of Christian comportment through their subjects. In staging this ideal, they came to be arbiters of classical philosophy and rhetoric re-situated in the episcopal hierarchy.[263] The authors

---

[262] Phrase used in Hawhee, *Bodily*, 20.
[263] Krueger, *Writing*, 191, states that "Engaging in literary composition, a writer both displayed and produced authorial piety."

accrued spiritual and social capital through their literary constructions of clerical masculinity, as they enfolded elements of *aretē* into sacred figures. Manliness, as imagined through use of the Greek past, conveyed legitimacy in the realm of civic leadership, the church body, and theological dialogue.

The Gregories choreographed feats of strength in their protagonists, taking as a model the Homeric heroes and Greek hoplites; *agathoi* who were invoked as precursors to pro-Nicene clergy.[264] As projections of fortitude and reliability, these personifications conditioned audiences to accredit pro-Nicene clergy in the realm of ecclesial politics. Biblical figures, meanwhile, were re-fashioned to accord with characterizations of classical masculinity, an image that contributed to the coalescence of sanctity and manly virtue in the Cappadocians' subjects. The bishops were attempting to situate theological debate within the episcopacy as tantamount to warfare, with pro-Nicene bishops taking on the role of battle-tried defenders of the truth. For *pepaideumenoi*, who understood *agōnes* as matters of intellectual vigor, the literary portraits showed well-rounded clergy, socialized with the expectations of imperial and provincial elites. Consequently, the Gregories balanced martial-like portrayals with portraits of erudition and refinement.[265] Eloquence and sacred truth, that is, concurred in orthodox leadership.

In accounts of female saints, Nazianzen and Nyssen showed that outward demonstrations of *aretē*, to be sacred, had to be grounded in the internal *paideia* of the domestic sphere. The Cappadocians underscored their own holiness by grafting onto themselves the piety of their female siblings. By guiding audiences into the intimacy of their sisters' trials, the Gregories called to mind the privileged attachment they held with their sisters – a kind of symbiotic bond. They tethered themselves to their sisters, who provided a resource to bodily piety for which the sacred women were known. The familial nexus sanctioned the Cappadocians in the court of public disputation, where theologians sought an identity of manliness that issued from relationship to the Divine; and where doctrinal truth derived from a pure, unsullied source. These accounts also reified the episcopal hierarchy by showing how even the inviolable Gorgonia and Macrina held the priestly office in highest esteem. The hagiographies of

---

[264] Bassi, *Acting*, 215: These figures represented, "the lost and longed-for dominance of an elite masculine ethos defined in terms of martial virtue."

[265] In this approach, they were recalling Athenian orator Pericles' claim, that "we love wisdom without being enervated," Thucydides, *History* 2.40 (Lattimore).

the two women simultaneously made the women into a repository of holiness for saints, while reinforcing the boundary between male/female and clergy/laity in the church. But while intensifying ecclesiastical boundaries, the biographies also made the *aretē* of the sisters accessible to the general church body. Laity, and women, could relate and honor these women because their faith, and acts of manliness, took place in the household. Their acts of sanctity were rendered attainable and they provided a model of faith meant to lay the foundation for every Christian domicile.

Masculinity was also manifested as a concordance of physical beauty and piety, with manly virtue evident in the bodies of both saintly men and women. Nazianzus and Nyssen registered appearance as a denotation of class, gender, and education, elements that in Christianity were enfolded into the ideal of pro-Nicene governance. The link between corporeal features and virtuous life represented a continuity of *paideia* that provided eastern Romans an analogue for thinking about the Divine. As Christians were confronted with thinking about the sacred, this paradigm influenced *how* they imagined saints and *how* they would come to represent them in text and art. As late antique hagiographers associated beauty with nobility and masculinity, audiences increasingly came to envision holiness with aesthetic appeal.

4

Agōn and Theological Authority

Hagiography and Polemics of Identity

While walking the streets of Constantinople in the spring of 381, Gregory of Nyssa observed a scene that he later recounted:

> ... entire households and worthless slaves, even runaways, they solemnly pontificate about incomprehensible subjects. Surely, you are not unaware that the discussion has turned to everybody. For the entire city – alleyways, marketplaces, avenues, roundabouts – has been filled with the likes of these "experts": retailers of garments, officials monitoring the moneychangers, vendors buying and selling food. If you ask someone for a coin, he philosophizes to you about "begotten" and "unbegotten." Ask about the price of bread, and he answers, "The Father is greater, and the Son is inferior." If you ask is the bath prepared, he answers that the being of the Son cannot be divided. I do not know what is fitting to name this evil: debate or madness, or what such evil is among the people, which has caused this folly.[1]

Gregory found nothing redemptive about a spectacle where anybody and everybody was teaching about the nature of the Godhead. Quarrels over the terms "begotten" (*gennētos*/γεννητός) and "unbegotten" (*agennētos*/ἀγέννητος) were leading the urban rabble to minimize the likeness of the Son to the Father, thus exposing them as Heterousians. They were adherents to one-time bishop Eunomius of Cyzicus' teaching that the Son consisted of a separate nature (begotten) from the Father (unbegotten) and thus was fundamentally different from him. Reference to the indivisibility of the Son, meanwhile, implicated another group as Apollinarists.[2]

---

[1] Greg. Ny., *On the Deity of the Son and of the Holy Spirit* (PG 46 557) (my translation).

[2] On Apollinaris, J. Behr, *The Nicene Faith: Formation of Christian Theology*, vol. 2 (Crestwood, NY: St. Vladimir's Seminary, 2004), 377–400 and K. Anatolios, *Retrieving*

The latter were branded as such because of holding to the teachings of bishop Apollinaris of Laodicea (died 382), who believed that the Son had a human body but a divine nature. In his mockery of popular philosophizing about theology, Gregory created an image of chaotic populist speculation.

Similar displeasure was expressed by Gregory of Nazianzus, the resident pro-Nicene bishop at Constantinople from 379 to 381 and the prelate who initially presided over the ecumenical council there in 381.[3] The assembly was called by Emperor Theodosius, roughly a year after Basil's death. Theodosius convened clergy from across the eastern empire to discuss divisions in the church at the imperial capital and to unify eastern Christianity based on a conception of Trinitarianism commensurate with that outlined at the Council of Nicaea in 325.[4] In his first theological oration (before the council, in spring 381), Gregory stated: "Discussion of theology is not for everyone, I tell you, not for everyone – it is no inexpensive or effortless pursuit."[5] Gregory was exhorting his audience to consider the source of dogmas contrary to that of pro-Nicenes, thus placing doubt on the legitimacy of his opponents. Congregants were left to consider exactly who merited teaching about the Godhead. "It [theology] is not for all men," Gregory elaborated, "but only for those who have been tested and have found a sound footing in study, and, more importantly, have undergone, or at the very least are undergoing, purification of body and soul."[6] Nazianzen's theological orations issued reservations over the credentials of philosophers (as theologians) as much as they questioned their actual teachings. While Gregory

---

Nicaea: The Development and Meaning of Trinitarian Doctrine (Grand Rapids, MI: Eerdmans, 2011), 92–7.

[3] On examples of collaboration between Nyssen and Nazianzen, S. Holman, "Healing the Social Leper in Gregory of Nyssa's and Gregory of Nazianzus's 'περιφιλοπτωχίας,'" HTR 92 (1999), 283–4.

[4] R. Staats, *Das Glaubensbekenntnis von Nizäa-Konstantinopel: Historische und theologische Grundlagen* (Darmstadt: Wissenschaftliche Buchgesellschaft, 1996), 1–15; A.-M. Ritter, *Das Konzil von Konstantinopel und sein Symbol* (Göttingen: Vandenhoeck and Ruprecht, 1965) remains a classic treatment of the council; and for a thorough analysis of Nazianzen at Constantinople, see J. McGuckin, *St Gregory of Nazianzus: An Intellectual Biography* (Crestwood, NY: St. Vladimir's Seminary, 2001), 229–370.

[5] Greg. Naz., *Or.* 27.3 (Norris).

[6] Greg. Naz., *Or.* 27.3 (Norris). οὐ πάντων μέν, ὅτι τῶν ἐξητασμένων καὶ διαβεβηκότων ἐν θεωρίᾳ, καὶ πρὸ τούτων καὶ ψυχὴν καὶ σῶμα κεκαθαρμένων, ἢ καθαιρομένων, τὸ μετριώτατον.

does not specify Eunomius or individuals who subscribed to his teachings, he was alluding to them.[7]

We encountered Eunomius in the preceding chapter in an overview of the theological divisions in the eastern empire during the latter half of the fourth century.[8] The teachings of Eunomius and his mentor Aetius contravened the beliefs of the Cappadocians by denying that the Father and Son shared the same essence. On that account alone, they drew antipathy from the Cappadocians. But in addition, Eunomius' and Aetius' paths to theological relevance took a much different route than that of the Cappadocians. The latter had taken part in the *agōn* culture of *paideia*, that is, while Aetius and Eunomius had not engaged with the same extensive curriculum of historical, literary, and philosophic classics that required the highest standard of competition and performance. Aetius' and Eunomius' powers of persuasion, as portrayed by Nazianzen and Nyssen, came by short cut; they lacked the depth that came from experience in legitimate spiritual and intellectual *agōnes*. Their influence derived from having mastered the art of dialectical reasoning, the ability to use a series of questions and answers to win arguments; a useful skill, but shallow without the adequate preparation that came from studying the core texts that informed the mind of a *pepaideumenos*. It was an aptitude, moreover, notorious for its superficiality and misuse.[9]

Although many of the individuals described in Nyssen's account above came from marginalized ranks of society, the problem with such persons involved more than class deficiency. Nyssen and Nazianzen had been raised on traditions that associated accuracy of teaching with an individual's character. The person who had successfully undergone intellectual and spiritual training, a test of *ēthos*, garnered authority to expound on

---

[7] R. Lim, *Public Disputation, Power, and Social Order in Late Antiquity* (Berkeley: University of California Press, 1995), 158–65, does not consider these orations as pointed at any one group, but rather as a general denunciation of populist involvement in theology; thus limiting doctrinal discourse to clergy.

[8] Introduction to Eunomius in R. Vaggione, *Eunomius of Cyzicus and the Nicene Revolution.* (Oxford: Oxford University Press, 2000), 1–11; M. Wiles, "Eunomius: Hair-Splitting Dialectician or Defender of the Accessibility of Salvation?" in *The Making of Orthodoxy: Essays in Honor of Henry Chadwick*, ed. R. Williams (Cambridge: Cambridge University Press, 1989), 157–72.

[9] E. Vandenbussche, "La part de la dialectique dans la théologie d'Eunomius 'le technologue,'" *Revue d'Histoire Ecclésiastique* 40 (1944–5), 47–72, discusses the polemics against Eunomius and the recurring charge, in depictions of his dialectic, that he was a *technologos*; meaning an amateur tinkering with a subject for which he was not equipped. Lim, *Public*, 158–67, offers a particularly insightful discussion of Nazianzen's portrayal of a *theologos* through his theological orations.

matters of the Divine. Like the *agōnes* discussed in our earlier treatment of hagiographic accounts, these struggles revealed an individual's *aretē*; in this case, disclosing an internal disposition that had capacity for contemplation of God (*theōria*/θεωρία) and familiarity with God (*oikeiōsis*/οἰκείωσις).[10] The Cappadocians were familiar with the trope of corporeal restraint as depicted in multiple spokespersons for God in the Old and New Testaments. These figures achieved closeness to the Almighty, a proximity usually accompanied by a period of bodily subjection. The Cappadocians also were influenced by portrayals of philosophic *agōn* by writers of the Second Sophistic; that is, the exposition of divine truth by individuals who had overcome duress, foregoing fame and ease of life in order to wrestle with eternal verities. The Cappadocians thus interwove sacred and classical sources of rhetoric that issued disdain for the untried philosopher/theologian.

While impugning the laxity of opponents in orations and dogmatic works, Nyssen and Nazianzen meanwhile amplified the rigors of pro-Nicene clergy through sacred biographies. These accounts recalled ascetic endeavors and philosophic inquiry that not only showed the spiritual depth of the pro-Nicene subjects, but also reoriented their experiences as agonists by translating them into a component of sacred office. In *Sons of Hellenism*, Susanna Elm explained the cultural rivalry between Emperor Julian and Nazianzen as a matter of correct use of *logoi* (classical philosophy and rhetoric).[11] Elm observed in Gregory's early orations against Julian, and later theological orations against Eunomius, a battle to claim ownership of classical discourse. Gregory, for example, proclaimed that Eunomius had misapplied philosophy and consequently had made spurious arguments about the nature of the Son.[12] By way of comparison, Gregory came from a background of ordered noetic training and thus correct doctrine. Arthur Urbano likewise has shown that intellectuals of the fourth century used biography as an arena of philosophical competition.[13] Christians and Neo-platonists, he asserts, vied with one another to establish a pedigree that linked them to ancient schools of metaphysical interpretation.

---

[10] B. Maslov, "*Oikeiōsis pros Theon*: Gregory of Nazianzus and the Heteronomous Subject of Eastern Christian Penance," ZAC 16 (2012), 317–9.
[11] S. Elm, *Sons of Hellenism, Fathers of the Church: Emperor Julian, Gregory of Nazianzus, and the Vision of Rome* (Berkeley: University of California Press, 2012), 387–413.
[12] Elm, *Sons*, 259–65.
[13] A. Urbano, *The Philosophical Life: Biography and the Crafting of Intellectual Identity in Late Antiquity* (Washington: Catholic University of America Press, 2013), 16–26.

I argue in this chapter that Nazianzen and Nyssen used the genre of sacred biography for a similar indictment of Heterousians by correlating the *aretē* of pro-Nicene bishops to piety and true doctrine that derived from *agōnes*. As a most prominent anti-Trinitarian, Eunomius provided the ideal touchstone against which the Gregories personified masculinized, pro-Nicene clergy. The Gregories contended that Eunomius lacked the development into manhood that came through legitimate *paideia*. He had not engaged in the same kind of *agōnes* as true *pepaideumenoi*. In the invective of the Cappadocians, Eunomius is made to embody the effeminacy of the Heterousians. Against this vilification, the Cappadocians held up noble, manly versions of a true philosopher/theologian by illustrating *aretē* in pro-Nicene saints. In the hagiographic biographies, rightly ordered *paideia* played a key role in the Christological controversies of the day.

The Cappadocians personified their hagiographic persons in a way that distinguished them as approved intellectuals, as holy *agathoi*, thus singling them out against other theologians such as Eunomius. More specifically, Nyssen and Nazianzen correlated the soundness of their subjects' doctrines to their unsullied use of language. Most of their biographies corresponded to the period immediately preceding and following the Council of Constantinople of 381, where dogmatic division and other ecclesiastical polarities prompted the Cappadocians to expound on the profile of a worthy bishop. In the context of contemporary theological invective, these narratives constituted literary contrasts between Heterousian and pro-Nicene exponents of the Divine.[14] Many *pepaideumenoi* among the clergy were familiar with portions of the doctrinal treatises and polemical texts circulating at this time. We will therefore set each of the three biographies in this chapter against contemporary works by Nazianzen and Nyssen that denounced unworthy theologians. Considered through the lens of the doctrinal warfare of the time, the narratives read in part as a critique of non-Trinitarians. The first two hagiographies come from Nazianzen: one chronicling the feats of pro-Nicene bishop Athanasius of Alexandria (c. 298–373); the second is Nazianzen's funeral oration on Basil (from Chapter 3), with our emphasis here on Gregory showing how Basil's *agōnes* sanctioned his use of speech to defend pro-Nicene tenets; and in the third, we return to Nyssen's

---

[14] R. Cribiore, *Libanius the Sophist: Rhetoric, Reality, and Religion in the Fourth Century* (Ithaca: Cornell University Press, 2013), 108, points out that "Invective is the complement of encomium."

biography of Macrina, discussing how her virginity and endurance of hardship reflected the integrity of pro-Nicene theologians.

Choreographing virtual *agōnes*, Nazianzen characterizes Athanasius and Basil as conflations of biblical heroes and classical philosophers who have been substantiated by their actions. In these accounts, Gregory's protagonists set forward piety and culture, while his enemies evoke heresy and duplicity. Set against treatises that feminized heretical opponents and other disputants, Athanasius and Basil come across as exemplars of sacred *aretē*. As individuals disciplined through a manly regimen of spiritual *askēsis*, the pro-Nicene clergy thus emerge as standard bearers of theological discernment. Suzanne Abrams Rebillard's study on Nazianzen's poetry shows why imagery of struggle is especially relevant in such depictions. She argues that Gregory imagined speech – both the use of words and the practice of silence – as a struggle. Rebillard talks about Gregory's period of quietude, for example, as a victor winning a contest over his tongue. Under this conception, physical and spiritual self-control together formed the ascetic basis that purifies and orders speech about the Divine.[15] Athanasius and Basil, as personified in Gregory's hagiographies, underwent a series of such *agōnes* – struggles against rival priests, emperors, as well as somatic hardships redolent of biblical prophets and Christian martyrs. These contests testified to their moral strength and validated their speech as sacred and forceful.

The final biography returns to Nyssen's account of Macrina (also addressed in Chapter 3), in which he imbues his sister with the philosophic acumen of a right-minded Christian leader, with piety guiding her sacred dialogue. In the *Life of Macrina*, Nyssen represents his sister as the embodiment of sanctified speech, which moderates the *paideia* of his episcopal brothers Basil and Peter, as well as himself. In the *Life*, Nyssen personifies his brother Basil as a promising clergyman whose elocution has been tamed by Macrina, and whose bold expositions are subsequently governed by the Divine. These images of well-managed intellect come into focus when set against Nyssen's *Against Eunomius* (*Contra Eunomium*), a lengthy exposition of three books penned to disprove the teachings of Eunomius and his followers.

In these three hagiographies, Nazianzen and Nyssen use ecclesiastical politics, particularly theological polarities, to contribute to their identity as theologians acquitted through philosophic struggle and spiritual

---

[15] S. A. Rebillard, "Speaking for Salvation: Gregory of Nazianzus as Poet and Priest in his Autobiographical Poems," Ph.D. Dissertation, Brown University, 2003, 169.

refinement. The juxtaposition of hagiographic biographies against effete heretics amplified their image of pro-Nicene clergy: sanctified through asceticism that has been masculinized, noble in pedigree, and philosophically and rhetorically conditioned through a course of *agōnes* to contemplate the Godhead while relating attributes of the Divine to laity. As arbiters of these sacred biographies, the Gregories subsumed the social and spiritual status of their subjects, thus enhancing the position of Homoousian Christian leaders and, indeed, their own standing. Each hagiography presents a rhetorical critique of theologians, showing that veritable teaching is an outcome of proximity to the Divine and subsequent sanctification of one's voice. It is a position acquired through *agōnes*, an enterprise characterized in the pro-Nicene subjects as purification through ascetic struggle. As set forth by the Gregories, Athanasius, Basil, and Macrina personify speech that ushers from divinely proven *aretē*, thus bolstering the correctness of Trinitarian doctrine.

THE EUNOMIANS AS FALSE *PEPAIDEUMENOI*

In the preceding chapter, we discussed the theological climate in which Nazianzen and Nyssen constructed paradigms of sacred *aretē*. As we scrutinize the texts more deliberately as theological polemic, it is evident that the ideals represented in the biographies were imagined against non-Trinitarians , and more specifically adherents of Eunomius. As Andrew Radde-Gallwitz notes, moreover, Nyssen may have purposefully linked other opponents to Eunomius, such as moderate Homoians and Apollinarists.[16] Such conflations would have posed an opportunity for Nyssen and Nazianzen, when impugning Eunomians, to elevate pro-Nicene clergy against all Trinitarian adversaries. Before treating the hagiographies, we will consider why Eunomius and his teachings remained on the minds of the Gregories as they penned these portraits.

The backgrounds of Eunomius and his mentor Aetius were similar. Aetius was born around 313 to a family of limited financial means in Syria, and he subsequently took up the uncelebrated craft of goldsmithing to help support his family.[17] By his teens, however, he began a path of

---

[16] A. Radde-Gallwitz, *Gregory of Nyssa's Doctrinal Works: A Literary Study* (Oxford: Oxford University Press, 2018), 13–14.

[17] Philostorgius, *H.E.* 3.1. T. Kopecek, *A History of Neo-Arianism*, vol. 1 (Cambridge, MA: Philadelphia Patristics Foundation, 1979), 62–3, believes that Aetius came from one of the poorer curial families in Antioch. Because eastern *curiales* placed such a high premium

philosophic study while serving under multiple clergy. These prelates supported the Christology of Arius, the theologian targeted by Homoousians at the Nicene Council of 325. While working for pro-Arian clergy, Aetius excelled in studying Aristotelian dialectic, which he used against pro-Nicene theologians.[18] He also studied medicine, a discipline affiliated with logic and refutative argumentation.[19] Aetius never held a bishopric, but he was ordained as deacon around 348 and he presided under pro-Arian bishop George of Cappadocia in Alexandria during the late 350s. Twice, Aetius was exiled because of his teaching that the Son does not share in the essence of the Father. Eunomius likewise came from non-aristocratic origins, born in 335 in an outlying region of Cappadocia. He grew up studying shorthand writing, a respectable career, but not the stuff that would normally produce a civic or church notable.[20] His aptitude and passion for learning took him to Constantinople, where he secured a position as a tutor and honed his literary skills. He eventually pursued an opportunity to study in Antioch and relocated to Alexandria in the mid 350s, where he came under the influence of Aetius.[21] With Aetius as his mentor, Eunomius grew into a masterful debater, which complemented his simultaneous immersion in theology. He later moved to Antioch, where in 358 he was ordained deacon by Eudoxius, a Heterousian prelate who later held the bishopric of Constantinople from 360 to 370.[22] Eunomius was made bishop of Cyzicus in 360, but the extremity of his views in the eyes of some Homoians led to his being deposed only a year into his bishopric.

Both Aetius and Eunomius became major apologists for Heterousians and they also later served as assets to Homoian clergy and emperors who opposed Homoousian and Homoiousian Christological doctrines. Even when theologians did not accept Eunomius' doctrine, his teachings hindered the cause of pro-Nicenes. His view of the Son as subordinate

---

on education, Kopecek's interpretation would explain how Aetius had acquired an education that left him behind that of most *pepaideumenoi* but above the pedagogy available to lower classes.

[18] Lim, *Public*, 122–5, observes that dialectic was associated with the Aristotelian method of inquiry and drew significant reservation because of its widespread misuse. Lim notes, however, that the same concerns did not apply to Aristotle's ontological and scientific research. Lim expands here on the representation of dialectic argumentation as pejorative in Vandenbussche, "La part," 49–53.

[19] Philostorgius, *H.E.* 3.16. Lim, *Public*, 115–6, on overlap between dialectic philosophy and medicine.

[20] Vaggione, *Eunomius*, 6.   [21] Vaggione, *Eunomius*, 209–12.

[22] Eudoxius: ch. 3 n. 25.

to the Father made it easier for imperial and church officials to support Homoian teachings – "likeness" between Father and Son – versus the "sameness of essence" of the extreme Homoousians. A few points about Aetius and Eunomius relate to the Cappadocians' hagiographic biographies. First, the two were exceptionally bright pupils and resourceful in acquiring an education that they parlayed into theological disputation. Second, they epitomized the accomplished social climber of the day, having made their way into influential ecclesiastical circles without having family wealth to expedite their networking. And third, their advancement evoked scorn from the Cappadocians, who expressed contempt for their social mobility as part of invective against Eunomius.[23] Social ascension in the eyes of *pepaideumenoi*, it should be noted, usually generated scorn.[24]

Eunomius elicited opposition for good reason. The premise of his Christology reflected a well-reasoned argument. He asserted that the essence (οὐσία) of God the Father is ἀγέννητος (unbegotten), whereas the Son – created by the Father – is γεννητός (begotten).[25] The corollary to this assertion was that the Son did not share the same substance as the Father. Subsequently the simplicity of the Godhead (the notion of God as one part) was compromised and the Son was relegated to a lower rank of divinity.[26] Pro-Nicene opponents countered that the terms ἀγέννητος and γεννητός conveyed characteristics of the Father and Son – *not* substances – and that Eunomius thus had employed a taxonomy that compromised the

---

[23] R. Van Dam, *Becoming Christian: The Conversion of Roman Cappadocia* (Philadelphia: University of Pennsylvania Press, 2003), 16, states that it would have been infuriating for men of the Cappadocians' social background to have as a theological peer someone of Eunomius' background.

[24] L. Van Hoof. "Performing *Paideia*: Greek Culture as an Instrument for Social Promotion in the Fourth Century A.D.," *CQ* 63 (2013), 402, says that to be truly accepted in higher circles involved more than acquiring facility in Greek philosophy and rhetoric. The individual had to learn the rules of self-representation and interaction with persons of power. A classic case of Aetius not mastering "the game" happened when he humiliated his patron in a public forum and was subsequently fired. See Philostorgius, *H.E.* 3.15.

[25] Greg. Ny., *Contr. Eun.* 2.12–27; much of Eunomius' theology is known from his works *Apology* and *Apol. Apol.*, treatises preserved primarily through citations and direct quotations from, respectively, Basil's *Contr. Eun.* and Nyssen's *Contr. Eun*; for date and occasion of these texts R. Vaggione, *Eunomius: The Extant Works* (Oxford: Clarendon Press, 1987), 82–9.

[26] Vaggione, *Extant*, 124; A. Radde-Gallwitz, *Basil of Caesarea, Gregory of Nyssa, and the Transformation of Divine Simplicity* (Oxford: Oxford University Press, 2009), 7–11; S. Hildebrand, *The Trinitarian Theology of Basil of Caesarea: A Synthesis of Greek Thought and Biblical Truth* (Washington, DC: Catholic University of America Press, 2007), 41–5.

causal relationship between the persons of the Trinity.[27] Eunomius thus directly opposed the pro-Nicene interpretation that the Godhead consists of three distinct entities (*hypostases*/ὑποστάσεις) that share the same essence.[28] There existed a fundamental impasse, then, that could not be breached as long as opposing sides were divided on philosophy of language.[29] According to the philosophical framework he used, Eunomius' doctrinal position was strong.

Over the past fifty years, and especially in the last twenty, scholars have increasingly addressed the significance of Eunomius and Aetius. These studies have changed the trajectory of late-antique studies by showing that Eunomius, in particular, was an influential figure in late-fourth century church politics; that he developed a compelling theology that challenged Homoousians; and that his theology was a legitimate threat to pro-Nicene Christianity at least into the early 380s. Jean Daniélou argued several years ago that Eunomius derived his theory about the origin of language from Neo-platonic philosophers who held to tenets found in Plato's *Cratylus*.[30] More recently, Mark DelCogliano and Andrew Radde-Gallwitz have disputed Daniélou's thesis by finding many disparities between Eunomius' use of name theory and that which he allegedly adapted from *Cratylus*.[31] Still, Daniélou, DelCogliano, and Radde-Gallwitz agree that the philosophy of language was a source of substantial disagreement in the late fourth century and underpinned much of the Christological disagreement between Gregory and Eunomius. The latter taught that the words "begotten" and "unbegotten" corresponded

---

[27] For example Basil, *Contr. Eun.* 2.26 and Greg. Naz., *Or.* 29.13.
[28] C. Beeley, *The Unity of Christ: Continuity and Conflict in Patristic Tradition* (New Haven: Yale University Press, 2012), 199–204, M. Ludlow, *Gregory of Nyssa, Ancient and (Post)modern* (Oxford: Oxford University Press, 2007), 17–22, and J. Zachhuber, *Human Nature in Gregory of Nyssa: Philosophical Background and Theological Significance*, VC 46 (Leiden: Brill, 2000), 73–9.
[29] Eunomius on language: fragments throughout Eunomius, *Apol. Apol.*, in Vaggione, *Extant*, 106–18; especially 1.346.20–347.1; 1.313.16–18; 1.316.6–11; 1.318.10–15; and 1.323.23–6 GNO (Vaggione, 108–9) and 2.96.24–97.5 GNO (Vaggione, 118). Hildebrand, *Trinitarian*, 41–72, discusses at length the logic behind Eunomius' language theory. Also, Frederick Norris, ed., *Faith Gives Fullness to Reasoning: The Five Theological Orations of Gregory of Nazianzus* (Leiden: Brill, 1991), 33–43.
[30] J. Daniélou, "Eunome l'arien et l'exégèse néo-platonicienne du Cratyle," *Revue des Études Grecques* 69 (1956), 412–32.
[31] M. DelCogliano, *Basil of Caesarea's Anti-Eunomian Theory of Names: Christian Theology and Late-Antique Philosophy in the Fourth-Century Trinitarian Controversy* (Leiden: Brill, 2010), 51–6; Radde-Gallwitz, *Gregory*, 139, argues that Gregory himself was more heavily influenced by Plato's *Cratylus* than Eunomius was, and that he was concerned to know how the formation of a name revealed something about its referent.

to the actual essence of the Son and the Father, as designations *ascribed by* God. Gregory, by way of comparison, believed that humans – although divinely guided – were the creators of the words that served theological discourse. As such, theological appellations ultimately reflected *human perception of divine activity* rather than the full nature of God and therefore could not fully account for the complexity and transcendence of the Divine.[32] The etymological disconnect between Nyssen and Eunomius and the persuasiveness of Eunomius' Christology were major concerns for pro-Nicene theologians. Basil, readers will remember, had been attempting to overcome Eunomius' theories since the early 360s. In the early 380s, the Gregories were still fighting the battle. Although the Gregories challenged the intellectual basis for Eunomius' doctrines, they were equally or more assiduous to discount his ability to engage in philosophical thought. For individuals who subscribed to a theory of name origin like that of Eunomius, logic alone was insufficient to defeat his doctrine. Eliminating Eunomius' credentials, however, could mitigate his influence and take attention away from his assertions.

The hagiographic biographies we are investigating in this chapter issued a foil against Eunomius, who is condemned by the Cappadocians in other texts. These narratives contributed to the Cappadocians' self-portrayal as manly, trustworthy, and singular in theological authority. Richard Lim has claimed that the Cappadocians were discouraging doctrinal speculation more generally among the laity.[33] That is, they were not singling out one group, but rather categorically condemning dialectical questioning of God's nature. I remain convinced, however, that many seemingly generalized censures by Nyssen and Nazianzen around 380 in fact were aimed foremost at discrediting the Eunomians, and by association, other heterodox rivals. Although they may have intended the personification of saints as a measure against multiple doctrinal rivals, the Cappadocians composed the biographies foremost with Heterousians in mind.[34] A number of concurrent or near concurrent texts criticized Eunomius (or his mentor Aetius) specifically for deficiencies that disqualified them as worthy philosophers.

---

[32] Radde-Gallwitz, *Gregory*, 136–43.   [33] Lim, *Public*, 150.
[34] Elm, *Sons*, 259–65, gives the example of Nazianzen's *Oration* 2, where Gregory describes deficiencies in priests, thus alluding to Eunomians without designating the group by name.

Nazianzen's hagiographies of Athanasius and Basil, and Nyssen's treatment of Macrina, meanwhile, merged *agōnes* and acts of purification through performances of asceticism. The *aretē* lacking in Eunomius, that is, permeates the narratives, thus amplifying his deficiency. Nyssen's encomium for Basil, we saw in Chapter 3, specifically named Eunomius and Aetius as antitheses to the Caesarean. But even in hagiographic accounts, where he is not specifically designated, the Cappadocians alluded to Eunomius and his lack of qualification. The trope of insufficient training was a common strategy to use against competing philosophers. It was a method, in fact, that the *pepaideumenos* Emperor Julian had used against Christians. Such polemic, however, often did not call its target by name. Nor did it neatly fit into only one genre. Nazianzen and Nyssen did not construct hagiographic narratives with the sole purpose of attacking Eunomius. Yet in the biographies, they created sub-texts that insinuated lack of manliness in Heterousian rivals. By affiliating manly *aretē* with the pro-Nicene camp, the Cappadocians attempted to solidify their doctrine while calling perceptive audiences to consider its absence in their antagonists.

Perhaps the most visible manifestation of the Cappadocians bolstering the authority of pro-Nicene leaders against Eunomians comes in their treatment of monasticism in hagiographic biographies. They attempted both to converge acts of corporeal discipline with conventional ideals of masculinity and they tried to define such discipline as distinctly pro-Nicene. In his extensive study of Eunomius, Richard Vaggione chronicles the battle between Eunomians and pro-Nicenes to coopt and moderate Christian asceticism.[35] In an attempt to define orthodox asceticism, Eunomian supporters branded pro-Nicene monastic communities as over-zealous, excessive, and artificial; even with overtones of barbarism.[36] Such classifications mimicked the same feminizing rhetoric that the Cappadocians used against the Eunomians. For their own part, the Cappadocians labeled Eunomians as anti-monks, a moniker that fit well with their castigation of Heterousians as profligates who coveted fame and wealth.[37] Herein lay the problem, that both sides attempted to claim philosophic authority through regulating ascetic endeavors. With each claiming the ascetic and theological high ground, the Cappadocians referred to the dichotomy between the image of the good and bad orator in Second Sophistic literature to defend their position. A stratagem

---

[35] Vaggione, *Eunomius*, 190–9.   [36] Lim, *Public*, 144–8.
[37] Vaggione, *Eunomius*, 181–2.

adopted by the Gregories (and before them, Basil) to secure their ascetic supremacy was to prompt readers of their works to juxtapose their rival's inferior character against that of their protagonists.

The model was based on a synthesis of two traditions. The first was philosophic portrayals of rightly guided *pepaideumenoi*, as transmitted through Second Sophistic authors. The second was biblical scriptures that framed asceticism as a purifying act that enabled intimacy with God. In these categorizations, the *agōn* motif – the stage for a leading Greek male – was collapsed into the corporeal subjection through which holy persons acquired familiarity with God. Thus, *aretē* exhibited through *agōnes* merges with piety to create the ideal exponent of the Divine. By aligning *paideia* and its attendant decorum with asceticism and portraying Eunomians as anti-monks, the Cappadocians identified pro-Nicenes as guided by true ("manly") philosophy.[38] Through such polemic, the Cappadocians categorized Eunomians not only as the antithesis of ascetics, but also as a blight on their communities, where they were deemed ill-suited for episcopal leadership.

This tactic was pivotal in the conflict between pro-Nicenes and Eunomians because the doctrinal division rested largely on the issue of cultural superiority, verbal proficiency, and language theory.[39] The Cappadocians subsequently attacked Eunomius as much on the misapplication of speech based on his weak character as on the fallibility of his arguments. In the mid 360s, some fifteen years before most of Nyssen's and Nazianzen's hagiographical works and treatises, Basil had penned a rebuttal to Eunomius' *Apology*, which had been completed in 360 or 361, even before Basil's episcopacy.[40] Basil characterized Eunomius as an

---

[38] K. Eshleman, *The Social World of Intellectuals in the Roman Empire: Sophists, Philosophers, and Christians* (Cambridge: Cambridge University Press, 2012), 149–76, treats the construction of heresy during the second and third centuries as a means of self-fashioning by Christian leaders that mimicked patterns of identity formation by contemporary sophists. I argue that Eunomius and the Cappadocians were attempting to coopt elements of Christian monasticism for similar purpose.

[39] Greg. Ny., *Contr. Eun.* 2.125–76; see Vaggione, *Eunomius*, 232–66; DelCogliano, *Basil*, 32–43; K.-H. Uthemann, "Die Sprache der Theologie nach Eunomius von Cyzicus," ZK 104 (1993), 143–75; E. Mühlenberg, *Die Unendlichkeit Gottes bei Gregor von Nyssa: Gregors Kritik am Gottesbegriff der klassischen Metaphysik* (Göttingen: Vandenhoeck & Ruprecht, 1966).

[40] DelCogliano, *St. Basil, Against Eunomius*, 18–35; S. Hildebrand, "A Reconsideration of the Development of Basil's Trinitarian Theology: The Dating of Ep. 9 and "Contra Eunomium," VC 58 (2004), 393–406; Vaggione, *Extant Works*, 5–9; B. Sesboüé, *L'Apologie d'Eunome de Cyzique et le contre Eunome de Basile de Césarée* (Rome: Pontificia Universitas Gregoriana, 1980).

opportunist who "acts neither straightforwardly nor without dishonest intent."⁴¹ The depiction recalls Dio Chrysostom's discourse on speakers "of nimble wit," who offer no substantive instruction, but rather "make gratification (χάρις) the aim of their discourse."⁴² Eunomius was a fraud, Basil says, because he proposed to offer beneficial instruction when in reality he was seeking fame.⁴³ Basil acknowledges him as a clever writer, yet one who abused his talent in hopes of gaining popularity. He was misdirecting Christians through delusory arguments, the kind of deception that Basil warned against in sophists.⁴⁴ Basil paints Eunomius much like the charlatan in Dio Chrysostom's discourse, a person who panders to crowds that welcome novel assessments because they are unfamiliar with sound teaching.⁴⁵ Eunomius thus is made culpable of corrupting the innocent through his fine words, pleasing to the ear but lacking substance.⁴⁶ He thus epitomized what writers such as Lucian had labeled as a false *pepaideumenos*. Lucian described this kind of speaker as convincing by his charming smile, able to entice audiences through the "seductiveness of his tone" (προσηνής τοῦ φθέγματος).⁴⁷ Basil played on the familiarity of this image to undermine his rival. Lucian's caricature of the pseudo-*pepaideumenos* showed elements of effeminacy, shallowness, and demagoguery. His was a persona prone to manipulating for personal advantage.⁴⁸ As he censured his rival, Basil cued readers to recall a similar characterization of a flawed philosopher-theologian.

Twenty years later, when engaging Heterousians in doctrinal confrontation, Nazianzen and Nyssen likewise called on audiences to evaluate the motives and credentials of individuals discoursing on theological truth. The Gregories infused orations and invectives with caution about untried individuals who were veiling erroneous teaching through affectation of style. Nyssen warned against such persons, who persuade by "spicing the lie with verbal pleasure, applying this kind of superfluous polish to the style of the speech like rouge."⁴⁹ Their teachings have plausibility and

---

⁴¹ Basil, *Contr. Eun.* 1.2 (DelCogliano).   ⁴² Dio Chrysostom, *Or.* 33.3 (Cohoon).
⁴³ Basil, *Contr. Eun.* 1.2.   ⁴⁴ Basil, *Contr. Eun.* 1.3.   ⁴⁵ Dio Chrysostom, *Or.* 33.7.
⁴⁶ Basil, *Contr. Eun.* 1.1 (DelCogliano).
⁴⁷ Lucian, *Professor of Public Speaking* 12 (Harmon).
⁴⁸ M. Jones, *Playing the Man: Performing Masculinities in the Ancient Greek Novel* (Oxford: Oxford University Press, 2012), 30, shows that, in portraying the speaker as effeminate, Lucian made an especially powerful critique of gender, because public speeches provided the consummate site for performing masculinity.
⁴⁹ Greg. Ny., *Contr. Eun.* 1.19 (Hall): χρήσιμον ἴσως διὰ τῆς τῶν ῥημάτων ἡδονῆς ὑποφαρμάττειν τὸ ψεῦδος, οἷόν τι φυκίον τὴν τοιαύτην περιεργίαν ἐνδιατρίβοντας τῷ χαρακτῆρι τοῦ λόγου.

gain favor, Gregory asserts, only because hearers are taken in by the artifice of the words. The elegance of presentation masked the falseness that they were disseminating. Contrary to the imposter, Nyssen says, are those who make known "truth pure and unadulterated by any false covering."[50] Nyssen alludes here to the author's assertion in I Corinthians that his preaching derived not from wise and persuasive words, but from the power of the Holy Spirit.[51] Nazianzen offers a similar censure of pseudo-theologians, likewise referring to I Corinthians while inculpating Eunomius. Gregory rebukes the "unctuous fool (ἄφρονα) who in his ignorance takes pride in feats of logic and by his facility with words (διὰ τῆς ἐν λόγοις δυνάμεως) empties the cross of Christ of its power."[52] Nazianzen categorizes logic masquerading as truth as tantamount to blasphemy, as it nullifies the very sacrifice on which the Christian faith is based. He echoes the admonition in I Corinthians that Christians should proclaim the good news of Christ's simultaneous humanity and union with the Father. Above the corrupting tendencies of human arguments, the message of Christ stood on its own merits.[53] The gospel should convict, not in its delivery, but in its veracity. As Paul had cautioned the Christians at Corinth to be wary of wily teachers, Nyssen and Nazianzen personified Eunomius as one such pretender. By allying their positions with the words of the New Testament, and othering their rivals as a threat to sacred writ, the Gregories infused their dogma with the sovereignty of a divine source.

The use of invective against Eunomians appears especially prevalent in Nazianzen's sermons during the months leading up to the Council of Constantinople of 381. Gregory delivered his famous five theological orations in preparation for a gathering that was designed to establish pro-Nicene Trinitarianism as orthodox doctrine for the Roman empire.[54] As both an apologia for the upcoming council and to generate support from a predominantly Homoian citizenry at the capital, Gregory used these speeches to justify the Homoousian position and to exalt pro-Nicene theologians over rivals, notably the Heterousian Eunomians who posed the greatest detractors. The incriminations were unmistakable. He accused the Heterousians of supporting dialecticians (an obvious slight against the Eunomians), thus putting their trust in "the most effeminate

---

[50] Greg. Ny., *Contr. Eun.* 1.19 (Hall): καθαρὰ καὶ ἀμιγὴς παντὸς δολεροῦ προκαλύμματος.
[51] I Corinthians 2:1–5 (NIV). [52] Greg. Naz., *Or.* 32.26 (Vinson).
[53] I Corinthians 1:17 (NIV). [54] Greg. Naz., *Ors.* 27–31.

(πλέον θηλύνας) specimens of the male sex."⁵⁵ The Cappadocians frequently disparaged the Eunomians through such inflections of gender. This form of abuse often occurs implicitly, as for example, in the charge that the unfit theologians are ruled by their tongues: a sign of unmanliness and, according to the book of James, also of unholiness.⁵⁶ Similar insinuations of effeminacy lay behind further condemnations: that the arrivistes lacked *paideia*, and thus were deficient in *aretē*; and that their use of deductive arguments to conceptualize of the divine showed that they were bound by corporeality, a preoccupation with materiality often ascribed to women.⁵⁷

For the Gregories, philosophy and rhetoric were not a threat to the church. Rather persons lacking in *aretē* who misapplied *paideia* to theology posed the problem. In his treatment of Nazianzen's theology, Christopher Beeley states that Gregory's theological orations issued concerns about the relationship between God and the theologian as much as they specified a dogmatic system. Knowledge of God, who is pure, depended on an individual first undergoing purification so that he or she could experience a fuller understanding of the Almighty.⁵⁸ Nazianzen's doctrine of purification was based on a substantial section in Plato's *Phaedrus*, which stipulated the necessity of purification in order to draw near to the Divine.⁵⁹ The influence of Platonic theory helped to shape Gregory's doctrine of *theōsis*, the transformative process leading to union with God.⁶⁰ Gregory was also informed, Beeley shows, by a number of biblical passages, including the maxim by Jesus that "Blessed are the pure in heart. For they shall see God."⁶¹ In this scripture, "to see God" meant to enjoy a higher level of intimacy with the Creator than

---

⁵⁵ Greg. Naz., *Or.* 27.9 (Norris).   ⁵⁶ Greg. Naz., *Or.* 27.9; James 3.
⁵⁷ Greg. Naz., *Or.* 28.7.
⁵⁸ C. Beeley, *Gregory of Nazianzus on the Trinity and Knowledge of God: In Your Light We Shall See Light* (Oxford: Oxford University Press, 2008), 65–72; also J. Plagnieux, *Saint Grégoire de Nazianze Théologien* (Paris: Éditions franciscaines, 1952), 81–113.
⁵⁹ Plato, *Phaedrus* 67b.
⁶⁰ For example C. Moreschini, *Filosofia e letteratura in Gregorio de Nazianzo* (Milan: Vite e Pensiero, 1997), 33–6, argues that Nazianzen's theory of assimilation to God derived largely from Plato. Recently, this interpretation has been criticized as too much of a homogenizing approach. See B. Maslov, "The Limits of Platonism: Gregory of Nazianzus and the Invention of *theōsis*," *Greek, Roman, and Byzantine Studies* 52 (2012), 440–68, who finds other sources for the doctrine. S. Elm, "Gregory of Nazianzus: Mediation between Individual and Community," in *Group Identity and Religious Individuality in Late Antiquity*, eds. É. Rebillard and J. Rüpke (Washington: Catholic University of America Press, 2015), 93, argues that Nyssen's idea of *theōsis* has often been transposed onto Nazianzen.
⁶¹ Beeley, *Gregory*, 75, referring to Matthew 5:8.

most persons. To have this greater familiarity, an individual had to undergo trials that conditioned his or her heart to approach the Divine. The Gregories imagined *agōnes* of the *agathoi* and bodily sacrifices of apostles both as physical struggles that gave credence to an individual's instruction. The apostle Paul provided perhaps the most apparent example of an individual tested by God and thus was given special familiarity with him. Paul's series of ordeals during his missionary journeys, and even the severe nature of his conversion experience, provided an example of how hardships played a major part in qualifying a sacred person to serve as a messenger of the Almighty. His multiple imprisonments, shipwreck, stonings, hunger, sleep deprivation, and repeated beatings prepared him to serve as a voice from God.[62] Nyssen and Nazianzen would show through biography that pro-Nicene saints shared a somewhat similar preparation.

Gregory's conception of purification was therefore closely tied to his advocacy of asceticism and his frequent references to agonistic, classical feats that paralleled ascetic practices. Both kinds of contests demanded bodily and noetic discipline and involved the person in a series of calisthenics that set them apart from the ordinary. Gregory's ideal theologian thus was experienced in spiritual and intellectual ordeals that exhibited *aretē*. Athanasius, Basil, and Macrina, we will see, embodied these attributes. The emphasis on *agōnes* was directed toward audiences who accepted a hierarchy based on superiority in spiritual discernment in certain persons, on the one hand, and civic leadership, on the other. As presented by Nyssen and Nazianzen, these groups often overlapped. Persons falling short of both intellectual refinement and purification of mind subsequently were not fitting sources for civic governance or theology. Such unsuitable individuals, the Gregories suggested, came from the ranks of non-Trinitarians. Unlike some defenders of pro-Nicene orthodoxy, who associated heresy with Greek *paideia*, Nazianzen and Nyssen considered false teaching a matter of misdirected or poor cultivation rather than inherent incompatibilities between classical philosophy and accurate theology.[63] Raised on elite pedagogy, the Cappadocians

---

[62] II Corinthians 11:24–8.

[63] For example Y. Kim, *Epiphanius of Cyprus: Imagining an Orthodox World* (Ann Arbor, MI: University of Michigan Press, 2015), emphasizes that Epiphanius, a contemporary bishop of Cyprus (c. 315–403), produced polemics that correlated heresy directly to classical Greek culture. For Epiphanius, who came from a family of modest means and had minimal training in *paideia*, Paul was to be taken literally as he mocked the "wise man," "scholar," and "philosopher of this age," whom God had "made foolish" (I Corinthians 1:20). Kim writes that "Epiphanius attempted to show that Greek

took a much different approach in condemning Eunomius, one that accorded with their ideal of a classically trained bishop. They reprimanded rival theologians either for having misapplied Greek *paideia*, or for having undergone only a cursory training.[64] Instead of denouncing a culture of *agōn*, Nyssen and Nazianzen believed that demonstrations of intellectual and corporeal contests in pro-Nicene church leaders testified to their fluency in discourses on theology. But the endeavors functioned primarily as a medium of authorization and by nature was limited to select clergy, Homoousians whose asceticism and holiness combined with mental vigor to forge manly leadership. As such, the practice of theology was a limited enterprise, indicative of the hierarchy that governed the church. The *agōn* of purification, that is, enabled discernment.[65]

Nyssen and Nazianzen therefore enlisted disparities often evoked by Second Sophistic authors between the feminine, deceitful speaker and his manly, authentic counterpart.[66] In order to cast a foe as dubious, an antagonist frequently labeled a rival as a "sophist," a verbal showman intent on swaying an audience to his or her opinion, regardless of its validity. Individuals seeking to ingratiate themselves with communities or private courts were notorious for mastering the art of catering to the demands of audiences.[67] Those recognized as engaging in philosophical rhetoric on the other hand, enjoyed the reputation of influencing others, not for the sake of winning the argument per se, or for acquiring favor, but rather to establish a truth.[68] Thus oratory could be used for noble or ignoble purposes depending on intent. In confrontation with Heterousians, Nazianzen called attention to the sycophantic behavior of

---

culture...was the result of human corruption and decline, not progress and evolution" (56).

[64] E. Gunderson, *Staging Masculinity: The Rhetoric of Performance in the Roman World* (Ann Arbor: University of Michigan Press, 2000), 164, suggests that in the Latin West, a similar attitude about rhetoric and philosophy predominated. On the attitude of many literati: "Rhetoric is a fixed term"; he writes. "The only real question is what sort of man will wield its power: a good old Athenian gentleman like Demosthenes or Plato, or a foreign freak."

[65] Plagnieux, *Grégoire*, 88–93, argues that the *pepaideumenoi* at Constantinople would have been receptive to Gregory's emphasis on spiritual discipline as a requisite for teaching moral truth.

[66] Gunderson, *Staging*, 149–53.

[67] F. Norris, "Of Thorns and Roses: The Logic of Belief in Gregory Nazianzen," *CH* 53 (1984), 455–64; Vandenbussche, "La part," 47–72.

[68] G. W. Bowersock, *Greek Sophists in the Roman Empire* (Oxford: Oxford University Press, 1969), 89–100.

his adversaries, while guarding himself against similar retorts: "I am not full of small talk, nor a jester popular with company, nor great hunter of the marketplace, nor given to chatter and gossip with any chance people."[69] Gregory offered up this disclaimer as part of an oration in the months leading up to the Council of Constantinople. He calls out his opposition as crowd pleasers, as individuals bent on gaining favor from the masses. His characterization infers the activities of someone lacking stability, a person unable to shed his base pedigree. Gregory was deliberate to separate himself from theologians that he labeled as morally, theologically, and intellectually inferior. He was also distancing himself from rank and file theologians that sought popular approval.

Such binaries between a virile *pepaideumenos* – often represented as a combatant – and a pretentious syllogizer were rooted in the legacy of Greek anxieties over rhetoricians addressed by writers such as Lucian, Aelius Aristides, Plutarch, and Dio Chrysostom – authors whose personifications were informed by Plato's *Gorgias*. Concerns stemmed from a belief that classical literature could instill bravery or flamboyance in a student depending on the nature of the training and the bearing of the instructor.[70] Aristides, for example, correlated trustworthy orators to athletes, against whom he juxtaposed speakers who cater to their audiences, "twisting and turning like dancing girls."[71] Such persons were an embarrassment to the community and a betrayal of manhood. They cut a pitiful figure because of their absolute loss of control and for drawing untoward attention for their vulgar movements. For Aristides, individuals who were forthright in their message coincided with the vigor of a sportsman, thus distinguishing themselves from those seeking approval in demeaning activities. Dio Chrysostom, meanwhile, described his hypothetical encounters with two men: one "who knows the road," and the other, "some ignorant and charlatan sophist."[72] The former, he says, provides reliable instructions for the journey and enables the traveler to proceed on his journey confidently.[73] The latter, on the other hand, leads

---

[69] Greg. Naz., *Or.* 33.8 (NPNF II): Τὸ δὲ μὴ στωμύλον εἶναι, ποῦ στήσεις, μηδὲ γελοιαστήν τινα, καὶ τοῖς συνοῦσι κεχαρισμένον, μηδὲ ἀγοράζειν τὰ πολλά, μηδὲ λαλεῖν τε καὶ περιλαλεῖν οἷς ἔτυχε.

[70] J. Connolly, "Like the Labor of Heracles: *Andreia* and *Paideia* in Greek Culture Under Rome," in *Andreia: Studies in Manliness and Courage in Classical Antiquity*, eds. R. Rosen and I. Sluiter (Leiden: Brill, 2003), 287–96. On concerns about acceptable education, Plutarch, *Moralia* 14e–37b.

[71] Aristides, *Or.* 34.23 (Behr).

[72] Dio Chrysostom, *Or.* 4.33 (Cohoon): "sophist," ἀγνοοῦντι καὶ ἀλαζόνι σοφιστῇ.

[73] Dio Chrysostom, *Or.* 4.33.

the journeyman all over the place because his own knowledge of the path has come from someone equally ignorant.⁷⁴ Dio was giving a conventional critique of sophists: that many, because they had not undergone sufficient training, concentrated on presentation rather than fact, thereby offering no legitimate guidance. This personification correlated to the road traveled by the majority populace according to the satirist Lucian, a group that included a man with "a mincing gait (διασεσαλευμένον τὸ βάδισμα), a thin neck, a languishing eye, and a honeyed voice (μελιχρὸν τὸ φώνημα), who distils perfume, scratches his head with the tip of his finger, and carefully dresses his hair..."⁷⁵ It is the image of a man whose appearance and habits betray his effeminacy. The man symbolized the life of ease, of pleasure. His was the way that attracted the majority, the weak-willed. Lucian's profile stood in contradiction to the imagery in the Cappadocians' illustrations of athletes and warriors: the foundation of manliness and good order.⁷⁶ Informed by such tropes, Nyssen and Nazianzen repeatedly vilified their opponents as base, effete, and underhanded, utterly unqualified and untrustworthy in their theology. In doing so, the Gregories distinguished themselves from malformed *pepaideumenoi*. They assimilated philosophical rhetoric to the rigors of asceticism, thus redeeming their own use of wordplay as a mechanism of accurate doctrinal instruction.

EXILE AS *AGŌN* IN THE *LIFE OF ATHANASIUS*

Within a year of arriving at Constantinople in 379 to serve as resident bishop of the pro-Nicene community there, Nazianzen delivered a panegyric on Athanasius (296–373), the former Alexandrian bishop who had countered non-Trinitarian teachings throughout an intermittent forty-five year episcopal tenure at the Egyptian city.⁷⁷ The period included five different cases of forced exile. Gregory could relate to the struggles of the now deceased prelate since he had just arrived at Constantinople

---

⁷⁴ Dio Chrysostom, *Or.* 4.33 (Cohoon). ⁷⁵ Lucian, *Professor* 11 (Harmon).
⁷⁶ Gunderson, *Staging*, 149–55, emphasizes that the orator's mannerisms and appearance contributed to or detracted from his manhood.
⁷⁷ T. Barnes, *Athanasius and Constantius: Theology and Politics in the Constantinian Empire* (Cambridge, MA: Harvard University Press, 2001), A. Martin, *Athanase d'Alexandrie et l'Église d'Egypte au IVe siècle (328– 373)* (Paris: École française de Rome, 1996), 394–540, and D. Gwynn, *Athanasius of Alexandria: Bishop, Theologian, Ascetic, Father* (Oxford: Oxford University Press, 2012), 19–54, chronicle and analyze Athanasius' political career.

when the majority of the population there favored Homoian Christianity.[78] Gregory had assumed leadership of the pro-Nicene congregation at the capital with the support of Emperor Theodosius, but he faced recurring opposition from a larger Homoian population during his tenure there. A biography of Athanasius made an especially suitable addendum in a theological rivalry with Heterousians. The Alexandrian bishop had been one of the most consistent proponents of Nicene Trinitarianism since the 320s. Throughout his career, he had repeatedly disputed theologians who denied *homoousios* between Father and Son. Athanasius himself had built a reputation as a champion of Nicene orthodoxy by portraying himself as endlessly persecuted by Arians.[79] He branded such enemies as partisans of Arius, the man largely blamed for propagating the doctrine that the Son lacked the substance of the Father and therefore did not share in his divinity. Many of the individuals labeled as Arians by Athanasius in fact held to different Christological doctrines than Arius.[80] But in grouping together other non-Nicenes with the Heterousian Arius, Athanasius imputed as heretical multiple Christian groups who subordinated the position of the Son to the Father.[81]

Another reason Athanasius made a suitable hagiographic subject is that he had cultivated an alliance with a number of monastic communities in Egypt.[82] His vision of asceticism, in alliance with and under the

---

[78] For Athanasius' influence on Gregory: J. Szymusiak, "Grégoire le théologien, disciple d'Athanase," in *Politique et Théologie chez Athanase d'Alexandrie*, ed. C. Kannengiesser (Paris: Beauchesne, 1974), 356–63. Much like Athanasius, Nazianzen went to much effort to relate his many struggles. On Athanasius' conflicts and identities: M. Tetz, "Zur Biographie des Athanasius von Alexandrien," *ZK* 90 (1979), 158–92. For Nazianzen: N. McLynn, "A Self-Made Holy Man: The Case of Gregory Nazianzen," *JECS* 6.3 (1998), 463–83.

[79] Barnes, *Athanasius*, 121–35, analyzes two such texts that Athanasius used to present himself as suffering part of a systemic persecution by pro-Arians against upholders of true doctrine: *Defense of His Flight*, completed in 357, and *History of the Arians*, finished in 357 and potentially an addendum to *Defense*. Athanasius likened himself to righteous biblical persons that had suffered against villainous figures such as Ahab and Pontius Pilate.

[80] Barnes, *Athanasius*, 128–35, on several misrepresentations in the texts that were used to ridicule adversaries.

[81] C. Shepardson, "Defining the Boundaries of Orthodoxy: Eunomius in the Anti-Jewish Polemic of His Cappadocian Opponents," *CH* 76 (2007), 700–1, shows that the Cappadocians used the heresy of subordinating the Son as part of anti-Jewish rhetoric used against the Eunomians.

[82] D. Brakke, *Athanasius and the Politics of Asceticism* (Baltimore: Johns Hopkins University Press, 1995), 57–9, indicates that aligning Nicene doctrine with the growing ascetic movement was central to Athanasius' vision of establishing a stable orthodoxy.

auspices of Nicene clergy, became one of the legacies of his episcopal career. But the affiliation between asceticism and Nicene Christianity (under Athanasius) had been challenging to cultivate.[83] Later pro-Nicene writers contributed to a narrative that coupled Athanasius and the ascetic movement. Through the pen of Nazianzen, for instance, the nexus came to serve as a mark of manhood and a critique against Eunomians. And finally, Athanasius served as a fitting source of Gregory's biography because the Alexandrian's Arian adversaries were comparable in beliefs and background to Gregory's nemesis Eunomius. Most of the persons criticized in the account, in fact, are best interpreted as a composite representing the shortcomings of Heterousians in 381.[84] Gregory couched vitriol against the Eunomians, through the Arians, in order to show a legacy of pro-Nicene resistance to heretical teachings and to emphasize the magnitude of the conflict in which he was currently battling.

Along with heaping copious praise on Athanasius, Gregory arranged the narrative as a juxtaposition between his protagonist and the Alexandrian's Arian enemies: "illegitimate and intrusive priests...whose preparation for the priesthood cost them nothing, who have endured no inconvenience for the sake of virtue."[85] The triviality of his rivals' spiritual and philosophic formation forms a consistent theme in Gregory's polemic. He fastens on a trope similar to that of second-century Stoic philosopher Epictetus, who taught that goodness (*agathos*) is acquired through confrontation with an opponent; a contest that exercises virtues such as patience and gentleness.[86] Growth in virtue, according to Epictetus, comes through hardship. Lacking the discipline of struggle, Gregory's Arians lack the preparation that makes a valid philosopher. Gregory compares the treatment of theology by the Arians to "dancing before an audience with varied and effeminate contortions (παντοίοις καὶ ἀνδρογύνοις λυγίσμασι)."[87] Gregory minimizes the gravity with which they

---

[83] Gwynn, *Athanasius*, 120–4; S. Elm, "*Virgins of God*": *The Making of Asceticism in Late Antiquity* (Oxford: Clarendon Press, 1994), 348–53, recounts ascetic groups associated with Arius and his followers and the methods by which Athanasius discredited them. The followers of Arius were only one such group against which Athanasius attempted to bring monasticism under Nicene authority.

[84] B. MacDougall. "Arianism, Asianism, and the Encomium of Athanasius by Gregory of Nazianzus," in *Rhetorical Strategies in Late Antique Literature: Images, Metatexts and Interpretation*, ed. A. Puertas (Leiden: Brill, 2017), 104, recognizes that the polemic against the Arians is a barely veiled critique of their successors.

[85] Greg. Naz., *Or.* 21.9 (NPNF II): "endured," μηδὲ τοῦ καλοῦ προταλαιπωρήσαντες.

[86] Epictetus, *Discourse* 2.20.9–19.   [87] Greg. Naz., *Or.* 21.12 (NPNF II).

considered the Divine by painting them as irreverent. He presents a picture of individuals gyrating for the sake of pleasuring their onlookers. Such cavorting also connoted unrestraint: the opposite of the self-control expected of a priest. Seeking to entertain, the Arians were not to be taken seriously. Gregory thus strikes the opponents of Athanasius as driven by love for argument rather than wisdom. It is the exact reproach used repeatedly against Eunomius in other works by Gregory and informing Nyssen's multi-volume theological treatise *Against Eunomius*. Nazianzen mimics a critique by Plutarch, who reprimanded beginners in philosophy for pursuing discussions in order to win fame.[88] It is a complaint that echoes Plato's derision of young men using their skills at disputation to entertain rather than instruct.[89]

Athanasius, by way of contrast, appears as the antithesis of such crowd pleasers. He is the disciplined, purified "champion of the Word" (στάτης τοῦ Λόγου), a hero set apart from his feminized antagonists.[90] He experienced "the unity which is perceived in the Trinity" – that is, the mutual substance of the three persons of the Godhead – a knowledge "which is conferred by true philosophy."[91] Thus Gregory shows Athanasius as discerning the nature of the Trinity in a way that heretics could not. In his evaluation of the Nicene bishop, Gregory foregrounds the noetic and ascetic exertions that distinguished Athanasius from the untried masses. "He was brought up, from the first, in religious habits and practices," Gregory states, "after a brief study of literature and philosophy."[92] Gregory established that from the outset, Athanasius' *paideia* was grounded in a context of devotion to God and used for sacred purpose. This intellectual development contributed to his understanding of the scriptures. "From meditating on every book of the Old and New Testament, with a depth such as none else had applied even to one of them, he grew rich in contemplation (θεωρία)."[93] Athanasius, Gregory is showing, enjoyed an acute comprehension of God because of his cognitive

---

[88] Plutarch, *Moralia* 78f.   [89] Plato, *Republic* 539b.
[90] Greg. Naz., *Or.* 21.14 (NPNF II). U. Oosthout, "La vie contemplative: vie d'ascete ou vie de theologien? Purification et recherche de Dieu chez Athanase d' Alexandrie et Gregoire de Nazianze," in *Fructus Centesimus. Melanges offerts a G. J. M. Bartelinka l'occasion de son soixante-cinquième anniversaire*, eds. A. Bastiaensen, A. Hilhorst, and C. Kneepkens (Dordrecht: Brepols, 1989), 259–67, shows that Basil and Athanasius viewed asceticism as a crucible for theological training. It thus comes as no surprise that Gregory follows these two figures in advancing his own doctrine of purification.
[91] Greg. Naz., *Or.* 21.2 (NPNF II).   [92] Greg. Naz., *Or.* 21.6 (NPNF II).
[93] Greg. Naz., *Or.* 21.6 (NPNF II)..

discipline and his rigorous investigation of sacred writ. First-century Hellenistic philosopher Philo of Alexandria likewise had dictated that only men who had labored through virtuous instruction could hope to transcend their material state and win as a crown the "vision of God" (ὅρασις θεοῦ).[94] According to Philo and Gregory, such fullness in contemplation was necessary to know God.[95] This insight depended on communion with God, an intimacy that Gregory assigns to Athanasius based on his spiritual discipline.

Like Nyssen, Nazianzen lamented the ubiquity of theological discourse among the Constantinopolitan populace. In an oration at the capital nearly concurrent to his panegyric on Athanasius, Gregory warned "But if you are one of the common crowd, the mountain does not admit you. Wait below and seek to hear only the voice and this only after you have been cleansed and purified yourself."[96] Here Gregory alluded to Moses' ascension of Mount Sinai, a recurring trope that he, and later Nyssen, deployed because of the Hebrew prophet's rejection of luxury, his appearance in the presence of God, and his consequent familiarity with the Divine.[97] Few other biblical heroes had undergone such hardship and gained subsequent intimacy with the Almighty. Gregory classifies Athanasius as a philosopher in the manner of Moses, one of the few persons that God deemed worthy of special insight.[98] Gregory includes Athanasius not only alongside Moses, but among a litany of biblical heroes including Noah, Abraham, Isaac, David, and many others.[99] Gregory hereby makes a correlation between Athanasius and select individuals from the Old and New Testaments who enjoyed a special comprehension of God. Gregory casts these paragons of holiness as men of

---

[94] Philo, *On Rewards and Punishments* 27 (Colson); also Greg. Naz., *Or.* 21.2.
[95] Beeley, *Gregory*, 69–71.
[96] Greg. Naz., *Or.* 32.16 (Vinson); reference to Exodus 24. This oration was probably delivered within two months of *Or.* 21.
[97] For example Greg. Naz., *Or.* 2.92; 9.1; 28.2–3; and 31.1. and Greg. Ny., *Life of Moses*; Beeley, *Gregory*, 65–7, C. Rapp, *Holy Bishops: The Nature of Christian Leadership in an Age of Transition* (Berkeley: University of California Press, 2005), 128–33, and A. Sterk, *Renouncing the World Yet Leading the Church: The Monk-Bishop in Late Antiquity* (Cambridge: Harvard University Press, 2004), 62–3, 96–8, 103–5, 116–17, on Moses as a model for fourth-century bishops.
[98] Greg. Naz., *Or.* 21.3 (NPNF II).
[99] Greg. Naz., *Or.* 21.3; R. Flower, *Emperors and Bishops in Late Roman Invective* (Cambridge: Cambridge University Press, 2013), 23–5, discusses the literary commonplace of affiliating an individual with classical or biblical heroes from the past.

intellect, whose renown came from their courageous acts.[100] While standing as friends of God, they also epitomize the ideals of the classical Greek male. Athanasius takes his place among these heroes, even excelling (νικάω) them by emulating their various forms of beauty (κάλλος), here referring to attributes that made them superior men. Gregory fashions Athanasius as part of a limited circle that enjoyed intimacy with the Almighty. Like his forebears, who are cast as *agathoi*, Athanasius applied his intellect as a pious philosopher, subsequently distinguishing himself from doctrinaires motivated by arrogance.[101] Such a figure "could not brook being occupied in vanities, like unskilled athletes (ἀθλητῶν τοῖς ἀπείροις), who beat the air instead of their antagonists and lose the prize."[102] Gregory directs readers to the passage in I Corinthians, of a runner and a wrestler who are unskilled and aimless in their respective sports.[103] He guides readers to associate such futility with unqualified theologians – namely Eunomius (as Arius) – who constituted the foil to his personification of Athanasius.

Gregory furthermore characterizes Athanasius as a "mighty trumpet of truth," an instrument that projected sound broadly.[104] In ancient Greece, the trumpet was used as a call to battle. Athanasius, in other words, spoke truth boldly and he understood that in doing so, he was engaging in warfare. The Alexandrian brought clarity to the pro-Nicene interpretation of the Trinity, doing so in the face of repeated opposition and banishments. "For the illustrious warrior must needs conquer in three struggles," Gregory writes, in reference to three exiles.[105] Athanasius actually had been forced from Alexandria on five occasions, but Gregory prioritizes the number three to symbolize the triad in the Trinitarian doctrine of the pro-Nicenes. As a soldier fighting against impiety, Gregory says, Athanasius was vulnerable because the unrighteous concentrated their assaults against the strongest position of resistance.[106] If the heretics could defeat Athanasius, the strongest, then they would win. Here Gregory personifies Athanasius as a stalwart against a danger to the community, a commonplace in ancient Greek oratory of crafting the image of defender against tyranny.[107] He was the object of attack because he was the most capable of protecting the church.

---

[100] Greg. Naz., *Or.* 21.4.   [101] Greg. Naz., *Or.* 21.4.
[102] Greg. Naz., *Or.* 21.6 (NPNF II).   [103] I Cor. 9:24–6.
[104] Greg. Naz., *Or.* 21.14 and 21.13 (NPNF II): "trumpet," μεγάλη σάλπιγξ τῆς ἀληθείας.
[105] Greg. Naz., *Or.* 21.32 (NPNF II).   [106] Greg. Naz., *Or.* 21.14 (NPNF II).
[107] Flower, *Emperors*, 134.

Athanasius thus undergoes a series of trials that test his faith and comprehension of the nature of the Trinity.

Gregory likewise alludes to occasions when Athanasius was forced out of episcopal office by Arian supporters. In recounting one such episode, the seizure of Athanasius' episcopate at Alexandria by the pro-Arian George of Cappadocia, Gregory differentiates between the two in order to exemplify the steadfastness of the former.[108] Gregory introduces George as a man "who had learned to say and do everything with an eye to his stomach (ἐπὶ τῇ γαστρί)."[109] The pro-Arian appears as a counter-ascetic, preoccupied with the pleasures of food. As a glutton, his body is a slave to the sin of satiety. Gregory invokes the Platonic ideal that pure knowledge requires subjugation of the body.[110] George is cast as a slave to his appetites rather than a man driven by strength of soul. Gregory furthermore casts doubt on his villain's pedigree and class, describing George as "born on our [Cappadocia's] farthest confines, of low birth, and lower mind, whose blood was not perfectly free, but mongrel."[111] Using a common device in invective, Gregory maligns his opponent by recalling his lack of self-control, in this case a product of his base background.[112] This adversary, representing the Heterousian opposition, lacks the lineage and forbearance of the superior pro-Nicene bishop. His theology, therefore, is inferior. The mention of George's hometown was also meant as an oblique slight to Eunomius, who was born at the non-descript town of Oltiseris in northern Cappadocia. Eunomius, he hints, shares the lack of civilization in his Heterousian predecessor.[113]

Meanwhile, Gregory draws an extended likeness between Athanasius and the Hebrew sage Job, a truthful man whose misfortunes defied comparison.[114] Job, it may be recalled, had his family, health, and

---

[108] George was cast as a particularly vile heretic by a number of pro-Nicene authors, in part because he had replaced the revered Athanasius as bishop at Alexandria when the latter was forced into exile. See discussion in Y. Kim, "Reading the *Panarion* as Collective Biography: The Heresiarch as Unholy Man," VC 64 (2010), 399–401, T. Barnes, *Athanasius*, 119–25; and Kopecek, vol. 1, *History*, 138–45.

[109] Greg. Naz., *Or.* 21.16 (NPNF II). I Corinthians 6.12–14; D. Martin, *The Corinthian Body* (New Haven: Yale University Press, 1995), 70.

[110] Plato, *Phaedo* 66e.

[111] Greg. Naz., *Or.* 21.16 (NPNF, 273). See analysis of this invective by R. R. Ruether, *Gregory of Nazianzus: Rhetor and Philosopher* (Oxford: Clarendon Press, 1969), 111–2.

[112] Flower, *Emperors*, 22–3.

[113] Greg. Ny., *Contr. Eun.* 1.34 (Hall), on Eunomius' birth at Oltiseris.

[114] Greg. Naz., *Or.* 21.17 (slight modification of NPNF II).

prosperity taken from him by Satan through a series of disasters. The *Book of Job* ushers a series of dialogues between Job and his friends, with the beleaguered prophet refusing to accept their faulty counsel. Only at the end of the book, after enduring his misery and listening to the wisdom of God, could Job state: "My ears had heard of you but now my eyes have seen you."[115] Alluding to Athanasius through the figure of Job, Gregory considers the Alexandrian's adversities as "the touchstone of virtue" (βάσανον ἀρετῆς).[116] The sufferings, that is, played a part in shaping Athanasius and his understanding of God, much as they had for Job. Travails had given rise to *aretē* in Athanasius, helping to make him privy to the Divine. In addition to likening Athanasius to the biblical personification of acquittal through tribulation, Gregory recalls the Platonic trope that true philosophic nature is acquired through physical toils.[117] A noble disposition, that is, comes to light only after bodily trial. Deposition and exile had created a nature in Athanasius that was able to discern God. Athanasius' teaching was born out of trial. He spoke from experience.

Gregory's depiction of a just, resolute prelate provided audiences at Constantinople with an image of Athanasius as holy man and philosopher. It was the same reputation Gregory wanted for himself as a man under siege from doctrinal enemies at Constantinople. Gregory relates Athanasius' tribulations as those of a martyr and an athlete, roles representative of agonistic feats. "It was a contest between virtue and envy," Gregory writes, "the one straining every nerve to overcome the good, the other enduring everything."[118] The language evokes imagery of taut muscles in a runner or wrestler. The match is set as a battle of righteousness versus wickedness. And mimicking the vocabulary applied to martyr accounts, Gregory declared Athanasius' triumph: "At the end of the contests, He [God] declares the victory of the athlete."[119] True competitors always contended in public. Athanasius had been vindicated

---

[115] Job 42:5. (NIV).
[116] Greg. Naz., *Or.* 21.17 (NPNF II). But as Vaggione shows, non-Nicenes also appealed to the example of Job to advocate for a more restrained form of asceticism. Vaggione, *Eunomius*, 190–2.
[117] Plato, *Republic* 410 b–e.
[118] Greg. Naz., *Or.* 21.18 (NPNF II): "contest," Ἀγὼν γὰρ ἦν ἀρετῆς καὶ φθόνου; see Rapp, *Holy*, 297, on Nazianzen making Athanasius a "martyr for the Orthodox cause."
[119] Greg. Naz., *Or.* 21.18 (NPNF II).

in the most conspicuous of all settings, in the very presence of God. His candid speech had precedents that also appealed to *pepaideumenoi*.[120] Dio Chrysostom, for example, had once fictionalized a meeting between Alexander the Great and the Cynic philosopher Diogenes. After hearing an authentic account of how heartily Diogenes had endured exile, Alexander expressed admiration for the man and his courage.[121] Alexander favored the destitute philosopher, Dio writes, because unlike other sages, Diogenes spoke with absolute sincerity.[122] Gregory invoked these sentiments of consistency and candor in Athanasius, who was steady in "word and deed and thought" (καὶ λόγος, καὶ πρᾶξις, καὶ διανόημα), a strength of disposition also applauded by Demosthenes.[123] Athanasius' contests reflected his entire life of danger, exile, instruction, and leadership.[124] All of his attributes accorded with one another, testifying to an individual of harmony and balance. The contests had confirmed his integrity and validated him as an exemplar of the episcopacy.

Gregory accompanies these performances of perseverance by crediting Athanasius with a record of asceticism, both in practice and in supervision. Thus the Alexandrian engages in "vigils and acts of discipline," an account of spiritual exercises that Gregory uses to portray Athanasius as an ascetic.[125] Such self-renunciation did not mirror the extreme rigors of desert monks, thus requiring Gregory to redress the seeming incongruence between Athanasius and the former. Gregory tempers such extreme cases of ascetic fortitude by situating Athanasius within a civic space. Gregory compensated for any perceived insufficiency, Claudia Rapp points out, by acknowledging other forms of temperance that proved his spiritual excellence.[126] Athanasius serves as a guide, for example, by creating guidelines for monastic living through composition of the hagiographic *Life of*

---

[120] See discussions of *parrēsia*: Flower, *Emperors*, 134–77; Rapp, *Holy*, 266–73, and P. Brown, *Power and Persuasion in Late Antiquity: Towards a Christian Empire* (Madison: University of Wisconsin Press, 1992), 61–70.
[121] Dio Chrysostom, *Or.* 4.6–7.   [122] Dio Chrysostom, *Or.* 4.10.
[123] Greg. Naz., *Or.* 21.17 (NPNF II). Demosthenes, *Or.* 2.12 and 10.3. See discussion on consistency in deeds and words in political leaders in J. Roisman, *The Rhetoric of Manhood: Masculinity in the Attic Orators* (Berkeley: University of California Press, 2005), 139–41. On actions and teaching coinciding in philosophers, P. C. Miller, *Biography in Late Antiquity: A Quest for the Holy Man* (Berkeley: University of California Press, 1983), 49–51.
[124] Greg. Naz., *Or.* 21.30.   [125] Greg. Naz., *Or.* 21.36 (NPNF II).
[126] Rapp, *Holy*, 297.

Antony. He also instructs Egyptian eremitic monks on reconciliation of solitary and communal living.[127] Gregory's Athanasius, then, is an ascetic of a different sort.[128] His exiles in the name of theological orthodoxy – a form of martyrdom – constitute his *agōn* and set him apart as a holy man, equipped with the ability to speak with forcefulness and inspiration. His authorial piety and monastic governance are validated by his endurance for the sake of truth. The opposition he faced, moreover, harmonized with the clerical hardships faced by current pro-Nicene bishops such as Gregory, who were contending not with demons in the wilderness, but with exponents of false doctrine.[129]

Athanasius' exilic asceticism, fashioned as *agōn*, offered readers a lens through which to consider Gregory's own contests that he was waging as a theologian.[130] Through the person of Athanasius, Gregory continues his quest to associate asceticism with pro-Nicene Christianity. His interpretation of Athanasius' asceticism countered criticisms by Eunomians, who chastised eremitic monasticism as extreme and threatening to the social order of the church and city.[131] By gathering desert monks under the polity of the city and church, and by moderating asceticism for lay Christians, Athanasius assuages concerns that monks were undermining the church hierarchy and community.[132] In reconciling monasticism and civic membership through Athanasius, Gregory continues to render asceticism as an enterprise consonant with classical expectations of masculinity. Gregory sets forth exile as Athanasius' version of *agōn* because as a bishop facing broad opposition at Constantinople, he could identify with the adversity. Gregory's representation of Athanasius not only helped to fashion himself as an ascetic, but also to set forth pro-Nicene bishops in general as the beleaguered party in an empire-wide theological conflict. Their teachings would carry more gravitas when coming as fighters of tyranny, ascetics contending for the well-being of the church and city.

Through displays of steadfastness in Athanasius, Gregory builds an overriding code of comportment rooted in noetic and bodily self-control,

---

[127] Greg. Naz., *Or.* 21.5 and 21.19.
[128] This form of asceticism seems to vary significantly from that espoused by Athanasius himself. See Brakke, *Athanasius*, 182–200.
[129] On the eremitic "holy man," Peter Brown, "The Rise and Function of the Holy Man in Late Antiquity," in P. Brown, *Society and the Holy in Late Antiquity* (London: Faber & Faber, 1982), 103–52.
[130] McLynn, "Self-Made," 475.   [131] Vaggione, *Eunomius*, 189–91.
[132] Brakke, *Athanasius*, 261–2.

thereby authorizing his own voice (and the veracity of his teaching) against the error of current Heterousians. Through his characterization of Athanasius, Gregory ascribed his own eloquence and philosophy to sacred origin. Surrounded by spurious teachers, Athanasius offered true philosophy because he ushered words from a purified mouth.[133] The soundness of the Alexandrian's theology correlated to his corporeal (the tongue) and cognitive (*paideia*) discipline. With the matter of language playing a major role in the polarization between Heterousians and pro-Nicenes, the issue of speech played a central role in Gregory's rendition of Athanasius. In another oration delivered recently, in 379, Gregory had exhorted church leaders to be "keepers over both our speech and our silence."[134] Both forms of communication and authority required composure. All speech is imperfect for communicating, Gregory warned, but discussion about God's nature is especially insufficient because it is so much more complex than any other subject.[135] Language was by nature elusive, and particularly susceptible to deficiency in discourse about the Divine. The issue was compounded, moreover, by theologians whose emotions guided their words.[136] Gregory pointed to the danger of unrestrained talk to highlight the integrity of speech in Athanasius.

Before focusing on the supremacy of language in Athanasius, Gregory first inveighs against the misapplication of language in the Alexandrian's Heterousian opponents. He chastises the Arians as heretics who infected the churches with their "babbling" (φλυαρία) and who undermined the glory of the church through "utterances and deeds of impiety."[137] The latter charge was based on a passage from Romans, when the author condemns "deceitful tongues" in those persons who have stopped seeking God.[138] Gregory likewise derides Arius for "his unbridled tongue (ἀκολάστου γλώσσης)," a reference to the censure in James of the person who cannot keep a rein on his tongue.[139] In each of these cases, by impugning Arius, Gregory is actually rebuking Eunomius. And in every charge, Gregory equates Arius' misdirected teachings to his inability to manage his speech. According to the case made by Gregory, Arius'

---

[133] Beeley, *Gregory*, 65–90: A predominant theme in Nazianzen's theology was that the theologian must be purified to contemplate God.
[134] Greg. Naz., *Or.* 32.14 (Vinson): ταμιεύειν ἑαυτῷ καὶ λόγον καὶ σιωπήν.
[135] Greg. Naz., *Or.* 32.14 (Vinson).
[136] Norris, *Fullness*, 33–9, on Gregory's theory of language.
[137] Greg. Naz., *Or.* 21.12 (NPNF II): "babbling"; *Or.* 21.26 (NPNF II): utterances," τοῖς τῆς ἀσεβείας ἐνετρύφων δόγμασί τε καὶ πράγμασι.
[138] Romans 3:13 (NIV). [139] Greg. Naz., *Or.* 21.13 (NPNF II). James 1:26 (NIV).

teachings came from a place of recalcitrance. His doctrine was an extension of his mouth, an organ of disorder. Arius' insufficient control over his speech conveyed his effeminacy. Gregory is directing audiences to consider that a core problem with Arius' doctrines was his lack of sufficient *paideia*, the cultivation that moderated intercourse and checked garrulity. When characterizing the pro-Arian George the Cappadocian as "without culture, without fluency in conversation," Gregory is assigning him the same fallibility as his predecessor Arius and his successor, Eunomius.[140] Flawed education and blasphemy combined in these figures to produce disordered language that resulted in heresy. Because such false teachers lacked *paideia*, Gregory analogizes their words to barbarisms. These individuals are flamboyant in their speech, Gregory says. Lacking spiritual and intellectual conditioning, they have no credibility. Their excessiveness of speech correlated to baseness and impiety.

Athanasius, on the other hand, speaks in moderation. Unlike the frenzied heretics, Gregory points out, Athanasius was "brought up and trained, as even now those should be who are to preside over the people."[141] The juxtaposition brings to light the difference between untrained and managed speech. Athanasius had undergone a regimen that made him a reputable prelate. His words had substance. And it was a pedigree that Gregory could claim for himself. The forbearance of Athanasius reaches a crescendo at the end of the panegyric when Gregory praises him for illustrating "the due proportions of speech and of silence."[142] Gregory says that contrary to the intemperance of his opponents, Athanasius' "verbal stillness" made him a forceful Nicene proponent.[143] Such restraint found parallels in Plutarch's adage about the superiority of timely silence over speech.[144] The apostle Paul similarly had admonished Christians at Thessaly to practice quietude as a behavior that would earn respect from non-Christians.[145] Brad Storin has shown

---

[140] Greg. Naz., *Or.* 21.16 (NPNF II). [141] Greg. Naz., *Or.* 21.7 (NPNF II).
[142] Greg. Naz., *Or.* 21.37 (NPNF II). Gregory's portrayal of Athanasius reflects the temperance of the rhetorician outlined by Lucian: "a vigorous man with hard muscles and a manly stride, who shows heavy tan on his body, and is bold-eyed and alert." Lucian, *Professor* 9 (Harmon).
[143] On "verbal stillness" as a literary strategy, B. Storin, "In a Silent Way: Asceticism and Literature in the Rehabilitation of Gregory of Nazianzus," *JECS* 19:2 (2011), 225–57 and F. Gautier, "Le Carême de silence de Grégoire de Nazianze: une conversion à la littérature?" *Revue des Études Augustiniennes* 47 (2001), 97–143.
[144] Plutarch, *Moralia* 10f. (Babbitt): "For timely silence is a wise thing, and better than any speech."
[145] I Thessalonians 4:11 (my translation).

how Gregory himself later reclaimed his honor after his unceremonious departure from Constantinople by engaging in an extended period of silence.[146] Gregory elevates such management of the tongue, already here in 381, in his portrayal of Athanasius. By subjecting the physical self (the tongue) to the transcendent self (the mind under direction of God), Athanasius exerted command of faculties that validated his doctrine of the Trinity.[147] Listening to God in quietness and humility was an undertaking that consecrated his voice, thus making it all the more revered.[148]

With such careful supervision of his words, Athanasius had developed a voice that commanded renown. When he returned from one of his exiles, Gregory observes, the Alexandrians and Egyptians in nearby regions flocked to the city just to hear his voice.[149] Athanasius' mouth had come to represent his cumulative excellence – his *aretē* – and his connection to God. His temperance in speaking also amplified the fierceness of his refuting heresy. Gregory places the Alexandrian among those sacred heroes who remain calm until they hear of a threat to the church.[150] At that point, Gregory says, they suspend their silence to take up the fight.[151] Using an economy of words, Athanasius presented an imposing figure when provoked to defend the church against false teaching. He remains in control of his tongue, but when danger arises, he unleashes the full force of his voice as a weapon. Here, the warrior ideal comes to the forefront, with Gregory attributing Athanasius' martial-like valor to his role as overseer of the church and the city. His spoken words are thus channeled into a display of physical exertion, an image of heroic combat for Gregory's audiences to visualize.

Gregory's narrative of Athanasius enabled the Cappadocian to reflect on the gulf between the true philosopher – the rightly guided theologian – and the upstart. The former spoke from a position of experience, from training, from trials, and from closeness to God. The other expounded from a position of deficiency, unproven, unsure of himself and inclined

---

[146] Storin, "Silent," 242–52.
[147] Rebillard, *Speaking*, 149–50, presents a similar strategy of self-representation in Nazianzen's poetry.
[148] Here Nazianzen echoes Old Testament passages to "Be still and know that I am God" (Psalm 46:10) and "Let him sit alone in silence, for the Lord has laid it on him," (Lamentations 3:28) (NIV).
[149] Greg. Naz., *Or.* 21.27 (NPNF II). The apparent aesthetic appeal of Athanasius' voice recalls the story of the philosopher Pythagoras' teaching method as chronicled by Diogenes Laertius. See Chap. 2 n. 134.
[150] Greg. Naz., *Or.* 21.25 (NPNF II).   [151] Greg. Naz., *Or.* 21.25 (NPNF II).

towards popular approval. In the characterizations of Athanasius and his rivals, Gregory sets the former in a series of contests that hone his *aretē*, preparing him to serve as God's spokesperson for theological truth. For Gregory, purity of the tongue corresponded to purity of the mind. The refinement of speech activated the divine part of his humanity (*nous*), thus enabling him to comprehend realities that transcended his intellectual capacity.[152] Many philosophers believed that nearness to the divine enabled discernment of the otherwise incomprehensible.[153] Athanasius's *Life of Antony*, in Gregory's view, set forth an extreme form of discipline. Gregory was promoting the stringency of Antony's asceticism, not to advocate such severe measures on clergy (or laity), but rather to join his special intimacy with God to the pro-Nicene community of Athanasius, and by association, himself. The biography of Athanasius helped further to establish the pedigree of the virile, authentic theologian against his effeminate, deceitful counterpart. As audiences imagined Athanasius, they realized that Gregory had inscribed himself into the persona of the noble prelate. Gregory was the source of knowledge and surety mirrored in his Alexandrian counterpart. As a mutual affiliate of the Divine, because of his own *agōnes*, Gregory further postured pro-Nicene clergy as a source of sacred *aretē*.

BASIL'S VOICE AS THEOLOGICAL CONDITIONING

During his tenure at Constantinople, we have seen, Nazianzen disparaged Eunomius and his adherents through an array of literary strategies. Foremost was his reproach of their unworthiness, particularly in use of language about the Divine. Such invective augmented Gregory's vision of a pro-Nicene episcopacy, a model he set forth in the oration on Athanasius. He did not stop promoting his ideal after his retirement to Cappadocia. In fact, he used the circumstances of his resignation from the council in 381 to compose several literary treatises that reinforced the juxtaposition between false clergy and authentic philosopher/theologians. Less than two years after delivering his oration on Athanasius, in July 381 Gregory returned to Cappadocia following a harrowing tenure at the capital. In addition to opposition from Homoians at Constantinople,

---

[152] Rebillard, *Speaking*, 152, 178.
[153] E. Watts, *City and School in Late Antique Athens and Alexandria* (Berkeley: University of California Press, 2008), 87–9, 177–81.

fellow pro-Nicene and one-time friend Maximus the Cynic had attempted unsuccessfully to replace him as patriarch at Constantinople in 380, thus undermining his support. Although he held on to the see, he later faced another blow to his episcopal career. Meletius, the prelate presiding over the Council of Constantinople, died in 381. Gregory was appointed by Emperor Theodosius to replace Meletius in the supervisory role, but after opponents called for his removal shortly after his selection, he resigned a few months later. Detractors had arrived during the council and questioned the legality of his holding a priesthood at Constantinople concurrent to his installation back at Sasima in Cappadocia. Gregory had subsequently given up the post at the capital, and with it, leadership of the council. The chaotic period culminated in his withdrawal to Nazianzus in summer 381.[154]

As disheartening as it was to leave under a cloud of opposition, more unpalatable yet was the fact that Emperor Theodosius replaced Gregory as bishop of Constantinople and head of the council with Nectarius, an unbaptized, imperial official (the praetor of Constantinople), who had no theological training and no experience as an ascetic.[155] Distressed by the elevation of Nectarius and clergy serving under him, Gregory composed reflections on his experiences in Constantinople. These included a poetic treatise *Concerning Himself and the Bishops*, which addressed the unsuitability of individuals recently elevated to the clergy: "people whose worth has not been demonstrated by the test of time, or fire."[156] This text represents only one of Gregory's ninety-nine autobiographical poems, most of which he penned after Constantinople. Unlike his orations, spoken to crowds and only thereafter passed around in writing, Gregory sent the poems to *pepaideumenoi* in Constantinople in order to be circulated among the imperial officials there.[157] Although scholars have rightfully focused on Nectarius as the subject of Gregory's acrimony, I propose that in *Concerning Himself* Gregory also was still waging a campaign against the Eunomians at Constantinople. Gregory reproached Nectarius by using much of the same polemic he used elsewhere against Eunomius. In other words, he simultaneously castigated Nectarius and his

---

[154] McGuckin, *Gregory*, 311–69; B. Daley, *Gregory of Nazianzus* (London: Routledge, 2006), 14–25; Norris, *Faith*, 8–12.
[155] Chap. 1 n. 115.
[156] Greg. Naz., *Concerning Himself and the Bishops* 380–2 (Meehan). See McGuckin, *Gregory*, 381–4, for recognition of passages that allude specifically to Nectarius.
[157] Rebillard, *Speaking*, 79–80, argues that Gregory used the poetry to continue his influence in the capital, particularly to advocate to the laity on proper devotion to God.

supporters and Eunomius and his sympathizers with the same barely veiled invective. By using similar denouncements against Nectarius, Gregory continued to coerce Constantinopolitan elites both to eschew Eunomius and to associate Nectarius with the long-time enemy of pro-Nicenes. Part of the brilliance of Gregory was to disparage both Heterousians and his successor at Constantinople, but without directly specifying either. His readers were left to determine for themselves when he was referring to one, both, or neither. The imprecision forced the reader, then, to weigh his comments carefully and consider his points.

Meanwhile, frustrated with the influence of such prelates, Gregory drafted the eulogy of his friend Basil, which he delivered in January 382 in Caesarea. He penned the oration at, or near, the same time that he composed *Concerning Himself* in late summer/early fall 381. After presenting portions of the eulogy by speech at Caesarea, he most likely sent the full text to Constantinople in early 382 to be shared with the same circle of imperial elites that read *Concerning Himself*.[158] We have already set Nazianzen's funeral oration for Basil into the context of theological struggle. But treating it as part of the Eunomian/Nectarian polemic shows how Gregory further elevated his deceased friend as a testimony of *aretē* and sound teaching, a portrait that would stand against heterodox foils in Gregory's other texts. After characterizing the Constantinopolitan clergy as unprepared for episcopal office, Gregory renders Basil as the exemplar of a proven leader.[159] Recent events at the capital had afforded a platform to question even more the competency of the episcopacy there, where Gregory says "the empty masks of yesterday are the actors of today."[160] Gregory was bemoaning that the offices at Constantinople had been filled indiscriminately, thus offering the church a poor source of guidance. Nectarius' ordination at Constantinople and the continued presence of Eunomians there served as a catalyst for him to expand the details of his conceptualized church leader.

The panegyric on Basil provided an immediate forum for a narrative that honored a like-minded friend and mutual adversary of Eunomius.

---

[158] S. Elm, "A Programmatic Life: Gregory of Nazianzus' Orations 42 and 43 and the Constantinopolitan Elites," *Arethusa* 33:3 (2000), 426.

[159] Greg. Naz., *Or.* 43.70 (McCauley): "completely tested in a complete life."

[160] Greg. Naz., *Concerning Himself* 360-3 (Meehan); F. Norris, "Your Honor, My Reputation," in *Greek Biography and Panegyric in Late Antiquity*, eds. T. Hägg and P. Rousseau (Berkeley: University of California Press, 2000), 140-59 and J. Bernardi, *La Prédication des pères cappadociens: le prédicateur et son auditoire* (Marseille: Presses universitaires de France, 1968), 238-46.

Gregory conceived of this biography as an extension of the theme of theological qualification in Athanasius. But whereas he accredits Athanasius by focusing on his feats of exilic asceticism, Gregory sanctions Basil based on his rigorous rhetorical and philosophic training as a *pepaideumenos*. Basil speaks theological truth because he has mastered the use of language under the authority of God. His voice serves as a physical and spiritual manifestation of the *agōn* that distinguishes him as God's select. Gregory imbues Basil with the very attributes lacking in the unproven priests whom he casts as effete.[161] The narrative of Basil's life, that is, serves as an antithesis of the bishops that Gregory decried only weeks earlier in *Concerning Himself*. These texts, among others, focused on the characteristics distinguishing Gregory's ideal bishop from the many charlatans who were springing forth.[162] Like the idealized, manly orator of Second Sophistic typology, Gregory's Basil conveys truth borne out of a life of exertion. Thus, Gregory develops more fully his idea of legitimate theology that derives from *paideia*, philosophy and rhetoric that have been consecrated to God. As in the oration on Athanasius, ascetic severity merges with piety to authorize a pro-Nicene bishop as spokesperson for God.

Continuing the theme of discipline and purification introduced in the oration on Athanasius, Gregory advances Basil through a progression of pedagogical, philosophical, and spiritual experiences that enable him "to unite with God, to gain the things above (comprehension of divine nature) by means of the things below (mind)."[163] Gregory returns to the Platonic theme that the human mind must be conditioned in order to relate to the Divine.[164] Communion with God (θέωσις) requires exercises that direct the body and the mind to the presence of God. More than in the account of Athanasius, Gregory extols Basil for his immersion in *paideia*.[165] Indeed, proper training in rhetoric and philosophy rewarded Basil's passion for learning by equipping him with the "power necessary for the

---

[161] Greg. Naz., *Concerning Himself* 392 (Meehan): "totally untrained, but all ready-made in dignity."

[162] Elm, "Programmatic," 420, discusses these works in the context of *Or.* 42 and *Concerning His Own Life*, works Nazianzen finished within a few months of *Concerning Himself* and *Or.* 43. Elm remarks that the four texts "are united by one central theme: the characteristics of a true Christian leader, his internal and external attributes, and what distinguishes the model bishop from his opposite."

[163] Greg. Naz., *Or.* 43.13 (McCauley).   [164] Plato, *Republic* 410b.

[165] Greg. Naz., *Or.* 43.11 (McCauley): "the external culture which many Christians by an error of judgment scorn as treacherous and dangerous and as turning away from God."

exposition of thought."[166] He secured the capacity to postulate, that is, on complex issues such as Trinitarianism. Gregory also foreshadows Basil's virtuous speech early in the narrative when he recounts his and Basil's coming home to Cappadocia after years of study at Athens. Others departed this center of philosophy, Gregory says, with ambitions of winning the admiration of the masses.[167] Basil and he, however, acquired no such "love for theatrical display."[168] Once again, Gregory distinguishes pro-Nicenes from their rivals, whose speech was oriented toward entertaining spectators. While other young men succumbed to the allures of popularity engendered by rhetoric, Basil and Gregory came away from their studies "independent, and accounted men instead of beardless youths, advancing in more manlike fashion in philosophy (ἀνδρικώτερος τῇ φιλοσοσοφίᾳ)."[169] In intellect they had graduated past the need for popular validation, and now pursued philosophy with depth of mind free of pretense.[170] Having devoted their noetic exercises to the service of God, the two friends gained a resolve for truth that distinguished them from intellectuals who had compromised the calling of a true philosopher.

The image of Basil as *pepaideumenos* stands at variance with the unlettered bishop of *Concerning Himself*, who lacks the regimen that taught command of the mind and ability to discern the Divine. The inferior bishop "sported, he sang, he pandered to the appetites of the belly, he surrendered all pleasures, unlocked the door to all sensations, was a colt without restraint."[171] Gregory maligns this bishop as indulgent, as slave to a variety of bodily gratifications. The reference to immoderate eating, which we encountered in Gregory's denunciation of George of Cappadocia (*Or.* 21.16), was standard invective that signaled total lack of self-control.[172] Such a person thus has no stability; no reliability. He cannot be taken seriously. The intemperate man is not only obsessed with personal appetite, moreover, but also craves popularity with the masses. Thus he may acquire affirmation from the masses, but his wisdom has no credibility.[173] Such lack of sophistication leads him to

---

[166] Gregory calls his passion for learning "noble training," Greg. Naz., *Or.* 43.14 (McCauley); on "power," *Or.* 43.13 (McCauley).
[167] Greg. Naz., *Or.* 43.25 (McCauley).   [168] Greg. Naz., *Or.* 43.25 (McCauley).
[169] Greg. Naz., *Or.* 43.25 (McCauley).   [170] Plutarch, *Moralia* 79b.
[171] Greg. Naz., *Concerning Himself* 60–4 (Meehan).
[172] C. Brown, "Pindar on Archilochus and the Gluttony of Blame (Pyth. 2.52–6)," *Journal of Hellenic Studies* 126 (2006), 36–46, states that one of the worst implications of gluttony was that a person put all other needs aside for his quest for food and drink.
[173] Greg. Naz., *Concerning Himself* 69–70 (Meehan).

fixate on pushing forward his own agenda without concern for its merits.[174] This caricature corresponds to Dio Chrysostom's illustration of a hedonistic figure who captivated listeners through the inflections of his voice. He gained status and high rank because of his ability to mesmerize.[175] But playing a spurious role, he ultimately is unmasked by his "breathing of myrrh and wine, in a saffron robe...reeling in his gait, dancing and singing an effeminate tuneless song."[176] Dio's charlatan eventually is exposed for his unmanliness. Gregory treats the inept bishops in his account with similar dismissiveness, vilifying them as inept, caught up in love for petty arguments rather than substantive dialogue. The vilification harks back to Gregory's reference in a theological oration to prelates who try to show off their fluency by attempting to disprove noble doctrines.[177] Here, in *Concerning Himself*, Gregory brings the same allegation to bear on Nectarius, and by analogy, the Eunomians. Gregory thus engages audience distaste for pretenders, particularly an aversion for individuals who engage in discourse that is out of their depth.

Basil, meanwhile, comes across in Gregory's funeral oration as the personification of a teacher whose words usher service to God. In this capacity, he was accounted as outstanding among all ranks of *pepaideumenoi*, regardless of affiliation. Gregory calls him "an orator among orators, even before the lecturer's chair, a philosopher among philosophers even before advancing doctrines."[178] In Basil's life, education plays a crucial role in his development as a theologian. He had graduated from a program of studies that fashioned men according to classical ideals. For Basil, the austerity of *paideia* had been subsumed into his identity as a Christian. The *agōnes* of education had shaped his mind and his tongue for confronting false instruction. The pedagogy thus contributed to a "constancy of character," which enabled him to hold fast to true doctrine.[179] Well-rounded instruction was pivotal in his theology since it enabled him both to defend his position and to expound on the

---

[174] Greg. Naz., *Concerning Himself* 254–6 and 275–80 (Meehan): "to simply get hopelessly involved in [his] own arguments."

[175] Dio Chrysostom, *Or.* 4.108 (Cohoon): "emerged as a general or as a popular figure with shrill and piercing voice."

[176] Dio Chrysostom, *Or.* 4.110 (Cohoon): "reeling," πλάγιος φερόμενος, ὀρχούμενός τε καὶ ᾄδων θῆλυ καὶ ἄμουσον μέλος.

[177] Greg. Naz., *Or.* 27.1 (Norris): "versatile tongues...resourceful in attacking doctrines nobler and worthier than their own."

[178] Greg. Naz., *Or.* 43. 13 (McCauley).

[179] Greg. Naz., *Or.* 43.13 (McCauley): τοῦ ἤθους πῆξιν.

complexity of the Godhead.[180] In order not only to contemplate God, but also to teach about the Trinity, Basil had to be able to make explanations of the Divine comprehensible. The curriculum of grammar, scriptural study, philosophy, and rhetoric coincided with a life of corporeal discipline, whereby Basil was free "from the tyranny of pleasures and from the servitude of that cruel and degrading master, the belly."[181] Here Gregory establishes the ascetic credentials in *paideia* that confirm Basil's holiness and the *parrēsia* (frankness) of his philosophy. The tongue, Basil's instrument of proclaiming wisdom, excelled because he has subdued hedonism and need for popular approval; vices he has overcome even as he has subjected the stomach. Basil emerges as the analogue to Gregory's manly priest in *Concerning Himself*: "a man who has eked out a life of toil."[182] The nature of these bishops, Gregory says, was formed by "groans, vigils, limbs wasted by tears...anxieties of the spirit, study of sacred writ."[183] Basil is one such pontiff, the counterpart of the lax church leader that had not endured a series of noetic and corporeal challenges.[184] Gregory's implication was that "soft" bishops either were susceptible to shallow theology or too intellectually and spiritually weak to stand up to it. Basil is the *pepaideumenos*, the philosopher whose pedagogical regimen mirrors other forms of ascetic discipline, thus making him credible as a prelate and sanctioning his speech.

In effect, Gregory sets Basil as the converse of the priests he denounces in *Concerning Himself*. "Who was like him [Basil] in rhetoric," Gregory asks, "...though his character differed from that of the rhetoricians?"[185] Basil strikes an appealing figure for Gregory's educated Christian audiences because he subjected his elocution to true philosophy.[186] *Pepaideumenoi* were familiar with Gorgias' enduring admonition, in Plato's work, to use rhetoric justly, as an accessory to communicate philosophy.[187] This recurring feature of Platonic teaching informs Gregory's version of the noble bishop. For Basil, purity of thought and fluency of speech combine to advance the mission of the church. Gregory accordingly celebrates Basil as a master of Greek grammar; the medium,

---

[180] Greg. Naz., *Or.* 43.13 (McCauley).   [181] Greg. Naz., *Or.* 43.61 (McCauley).
[182] Greg. Naz., *Concerning Himself* 54 (Meehan).
[183] Greg. Naz., *Concerning Himself* 55–9 (Meehan).
[184] Greg. Naz., *Concerning Himself* 68–9 (Meehan): "who had the smooth course all the way."
[185] Greg. Naz., *Or.* 43.23 (McCauley).
[186] Greg. Naz., *Or.* 43. 13 (McCauley): "eloquence was only an accessory."
[187] Plato, *Gorgias* 457a.

he says, of literati, historians, poets, and philosophers.[188] This praise for Basil's command of language – perhaps the most treasured heritage of the Greek past – prompts the audience to consider his theological instruction within the lineage of the great historians, philosophers, and poets. By attributing to Basil a record of excellence across the foundational disciplines of Greek intellectual culture, Gregory paints him as the principal figure of a stable city, an *agathos*. In this characterization, elite audiences found one of their own, a Hellene who had confirmed his position through mastery of an unfailing pedagogy. Basil fares well indeed, especially when set against Gregory's effeminate bishops, who had just recently "performed at weddings with a chorus of Lydian girls, crooning ditties and getting high in your cups."[189] Gregory's caricature of such newly ordained prelates questioned the reliability, the manliness, of church leaders that were masquerading as experts on the nature of God.[190] Basil's long record of service in the church and his success in the cutthroat world of *paideia* must have seemed all the more appealing in light of such invective. In *Concerning Himself*, Gregory simultaneously incriminated Nectarius and Eunomius, painting Nectarius as the same hedonistic, unlearned misfit as the Heterousian. Having called out ongoing unsuitability in the episcopacy, Gregory exhibited Basil as a model that activated the sensibilities of the east Roman intelligentsia. He made Basil the link to the civic ethos of erudition, frankness, and self-control with which the aristocracy of eastern Rome identified.

In the exemplar of Basil and in *Concerning Himself*, Gregory affiliates noetic facility in clergy with the ability to contemplate and speak about the Godhead. This aptitude reflects Gregory's high appraisal of *paideia*, as well as his concerns about social mobility, a theme that he continues to use as invective against the Eunomians. Low birth, Gregory suggests, makes one more susceptible to vacillation when interacting with individuals of wealth and power. Thus, Gregory frees Basil from such penchant

---

[188] Greg. Naz., *Or.* 43.23 (McCauley): "Who was like him in grammar, which makes us Greeks in language, which composes history, which presides over meters and makes laws for poems? Who was like him in philosophy?"

[189] Greg. Naz., *Concerning Himself* 425–30 (Meehan).

[190] Greg. Naz., *Or.* 27.9 (Norris): Gregory's reflection on the elevation of untrained men into the episcopacy recalled a grievance he had made in the months leading up to the Council of Constantinople in 381. In *Or.* 27.9, directed against Eunomians, he had similarly lamented how Heterousian bishops had neither the credentials nor the longevity of service that were requisite for theology: "Why do you then try to mold men into holiness overnight, appoint them theologians, and as it were, breathe learning into them, and thus produce ready-made any number of Councils of ignorant intellectuals?"

for flattery, particularly in his role as theologian. By acting "courageously and nobly" (νεανικῶς καὶ μεγαλοπρεπῶς), Basil was elevated above the servility of the others.[191] *Parrēsia* and high birth merge in the man who Gregory notes came from aristocratic origins, yet did not act prideful of that pedigree.[192] Basil's superior social rank comes into focus when considered in the context of *Concerning Himself*, where Gregory alludes to the inferior backgrounds of the clergy. Gregory issues a description of the rank and file whose origins cast doubt on suitability for office:

> Some of them are the offspring of tribute-mongers, whose only concern is falsification of accounts. Some come straight from the tax booth...some from the plough, with their sunburn still fresh...some again from day-long exertions with the mattock and the hoe: some have just left the galleys or the army.[193]

The generalization, aimed at Nectarius and the current clergy, prompted readers to remember Nyssen's earlier portrayal of Eunomius' background as the son of an overburdened farmer, bent low over his plough.[194] The problem with such individuals, Gregory states, is that they have been assigned a task for which they are incapable, and yet they remain stubbornly dogmatic about their teachings.[195] For Gregory the ignoble bishop constitutes a danger to the church and the polis because he has been raised to office without the requisite socialization and education that comes with pedigree. The insinuation was that persons from these occupations were notoriously greedy, low-born, or both. Such unqualified priests offer "facile assertions about things that were better kept private and unspoken" and they refuse to modify their arguments.[196] Gregory likens their inabilities as theologians to "boxers who haven't had previous training and made a study in good time of contests" and "a track-runner who hasn't exercised his legs."[197] Sending an unconditioned individual into competition was foolish and promised failure. In treatment of the Godhead, it was inexcusable to allow such absurdity. The athletic metaphors contributed to the imagery of insufficiency because the nexus between *paideia*, masculine identity, and sports remained a commonplace

---

[191] Greg. Naz., *Or.* 43.40 (McCauley).   [192] Greg. Naz., *Or.* 43.3 (McCauley).
[193] Greg. Naz., *Concerning Himself* 155–60 (Meehan).
[194] Greg. Ny., *Contr. Eun.* 1.49 (Hall): "[a] farmer bending at the plough and burdened with countless tasks."
[195] Greg. Naz., *Concerning Himself* 162–4 (Meehan): "they have blossomed into captains of the people, and generals resolved not to yield an inch."
[196] Greg. Naz., *Concerning Himself* 252–6 (Meehan).
[197] Greg. Naz., *Concerning Himself* 555–7 (Meehan).

among late-antique audiences.[198] The lack of physical fitness indicated a body, mind, and soul that had not been purified. The individual remained occluded from any legitimate conception of the Divine.

Gregory thus underscored the insufficiency of a group of priests partly by playing on audience anxieties about raising "new men" to powerful positions.[199] "We manufacture holy men in a day," Gregory laments, "and we bid them to be wise, when they have had no training in wisdom."[200] Gregory's expectations for bishops included combining a life of piety with a course of study generally available only to the provincial aristocracy. Such literati came from established families, unlikely to be deterred from duties to church and city because of a need for acclamation or money. Gregory admonishes listeners/readers to understand clergy who "dishonor education" as being "ignorant and uncultured," and thus falling into the deficiencies of the uncultured masses.[201] Once again, he correlates a dearth of sophistication with refinement and class. With little wisdom and financial security, clergy from this background appear more susceptible to the whims of the wealthy and influential. Gregory, as one might expect, showed that Basil faced no such hindrances. "There was his independence toward magistrates and the most powerful men in the city."[202] Basil was his own man, or rather God's man, because of his spiritual and philosophical transformations, undertakings afforded to him largely because of his family's wealth and standing. He was not, therefore, preoccupied with image: "For he strove not to seem but to be excellent."[203] This phrase, borrowed from the Greek tragedian Aeschylus, conveyed the idea of appearing consonant to one's nature, thus avoiding pretentiousness.[204] Contrary to ostentation, Basil enjoyed assurance in his heritage and his upbringing, thereby releasing him from distractions of class inferiority. Basil's *paideia* reflected the collective sense of *aretē* that civic aristocrats claimed as a badge of honor; the reputation came from *agōnes* made possible partly by his family

---

[198] O. Van Nijf, "Athletics and Paideia: Festivals and Physical Education in the World of the Second Sophistic," in *Paideia: The World of the Second Sophistic*, ed. B. Borg (Berlin: de Gruyter, 2004), 210–2.

[199] Elm, "Programmatic," 423, writes that Gregory reproached them for being "low-born, lacking in education, wholly unprepared, badly mannered, and motivated solely by greed and blind ambition."

[200] Greg. Naz., *Or.* 43.26 (McCauley).   [201] Greg. Naz., *Or.* 43.11 (McCauley).

[202] Greg. Naz., *Or.* 43.34 (McCauley).

[203] Greg. Naz., *Or.* 43.60 (McCauley): Εἶναι γάρ, οὐ δοκεῖν, ἐσπούδαζεν ἄριστος.

[204] Aeschylus, *Seven Against Thebes* 599.

background. Invoked for sacred cause, family honor, education, and wealth contributed to a manly image and made for substantial assets in an episcopal career.

In Basil, an exacting program of training thus marked his manhood and his class distinction. Gregory places emphasis on his background and education ultimately to authorize his speech, the issue around which so much theological controversy revolved. A noble background added gravitas to Basil's words, as when Gregory described him as a rhetorician "breathing forth the might of fire."[205] According to ancient medical theories, the breath formed the avenue for *pneuma* (vital substance) to enter and exit the body. The breath was also closely tied to the voice, which when speaking, externalized the essence of the person through speech.[206] The porous boundaries between the internal body and the outside meant that the voice constituted the embodiment of the individual's essence. Basil's "breathing forth the might of fire," then, symbolized the power of his words, which confirmed his manliness and the truth of his message. The metaphor stands for the forcefulness in Basil and it also serves as an extension of the purifying agent of fire within him, a man ennobled through self-restraint. Fourth-century *pepaideumenoi*, Stefan Hodges-Kluck points out, "conceived of education as a series of practices that created the physical, mental, and spiritual conditions necessary to lead the soul toward the Divine through the power of words."[207] Purification of speech carried not only a figurative connotation, but also connoted a series of vocal exercises that rendered the faculty of speaking valid. The exertions of *paideia* and spiritual *askēsis* in Basil thus validated his use of language.

At the outset of the narrative, Gregory stresses the sanctification of his own tongue before divulging the life of Basil. "I shrank from speaking," he says, "before I, like those who approach the holy places, had cleansed my voice and my mind."[208] Gregory thus merges the idea of vocal conditioning, a form of corporeal control in *paideia*, with the piety he accrued through acts of spiritual modification.[209] Gregory had prepared to speak

---

[205] Greg. Naz., *Or.* 43.23 (McCauley): τὴν πυρὸς μένος πνέουσαν; see "breathing fire" in *Iliad* 6.186.
[206] Martin, *Corinthian*, 32–3.
[207] S. Hodges-Kluck, "Religious Education and the Health of the Soul according to Basil of Caesarea and the Emperor Julian," *SP* 81 (2017), 101.
[208] Greg. Naz., *Or.* 43.2 (McCauley).
[209] M. Gleason, *Making Men: Sophists and Self-Presentation in Ancient Rome* (Princeton: Princeton University Press, 1995), 88–94, on the breath as *pneuma*, and the relevance of vocal conditioning to status.

on the sanctity of his friend, but he goes a step further to bolster his claims, by "choosing his [Basil's] God as the guide of my discourse."[210] Patterning himself after a figure of sacred authority such as Moses or Elijah, Gregory makes the Almighty the source of his words. After establishing his own credentials, Gregory introduces Basil as "that noble champion of the truth, whose very breath was pious doctrine."[211] Speech, essence, and theological truth merge in this characterization of Basil's voice. As he proceeds to narrate Basil's holiness and erudition throughout the oration, Gregory leads the audience to consider his friend's proximity to God. The plentiful examples of Basil's superior education and affiliation with the Divine show that his mind (νοῦς) has been nobly transformed. The *pneuma* (breath) ushering from within, therefore, conveys the truth that comes only from a divine source. Basil's wisdom stands apart from the "babbling tongues and complicated errors" of the heretics deplored by Gregory in *Concerning Himself*.[212] The vulgarity ushering from their mouths divulged their status. They had been immersed in fleeting pleasures, in unrestrained luxury, so that their speech derived from a tainted soul incapable of expressing the complex miracle of a God who "is one but yet divided, one majesty, one nature, a unity and a trinity."[213] With few able to articulate such a profound marvel, Gregory elevates Basil above the indiscriminate masses, where "unbridled tongues" constituted a source of confusion and misguidance.[214]

Control of the voice – the tongue – testifies to the accuracy of Basil's (and Gregory's) theology. Using this imagery, associated with illustrations of revelatory light, Gregory presents his tongue, his speech that is, as an instrument that brings truth.[215] Gregory's portrayal of Basil's asceticism

---

[210] Greg. Naz., *Or.* 43.2 (McCauley).
[211] Greg. Naz., *Or.* 43.2 (McCauley): ἐκείνῳ τῷ γενναίῳ τῆς ἀληθείας ἀγωνιστῇ καὶ μηδὲν ἕτερον ἀναπνεύσαντι ὅτι μὴ λόγον εὐσεβῆ.
[212] Greg. Naz., *Concerning Himself* 85–7 (Meehan).
[213] Greg. Naz., *Concerning Himself* 310–11 (Meehan).
[214] Greg. Naz., *Concerning Himself* 184–6 (Meehan).
[215] Rebillard, *Speaking*, 81–5, on Nazianzen's use of the theme of "light and flow" in his poetry. J. Mossay, *La Mort et l'au-delà dans Saint Grégoire de Nazianze* (Louvain: Publications Universitaires, 1966), 110–68, traces the widespread use of light imagery from a series of classical and patristic sources. C. Moreschini, "Luce e purificazione nella dottrina di Gregorio Nazianzeno," *Augustinianum* 13 (1973), 535–49, finds precedents for Gregory's specific use of light imagery in scripture and in Platonic explanations of human perception.

and intellectual training serves the important purpose of translating his friend's tongue into a mouthpiece of illumination.[216] Gregory idealizes Basil as a doctrinal exponent because the Caesarean had communed with God. While the multitude had pursued the "short easy road" of Lucian's effete sophist, Basil had been subjected to trials that affiliated him with the Divine.[217] "Who purified himself more for the Spirit and was better prepared to explain divine things?" Gregory asks.[218] Basil triumphs as arbiter of truth partially because of his eloquence, a hard-won faculty given over to Christ to instruct his body the church. This fluidity of speech construed the vehicle through which he imparted his knowledge of the Divine. Thus, Gregory encounters God whenever he reads Basil's words. Gregory rejoices that "Whenever I peruse his moral and practical treatises, I am purified, soul and body."[219] An accomplished *pepaideumenos*, Basil was a transmitter of the Divine, "his pen guided as though it belonged to the Spirit."[220] As we have seen earlier, the pen often correlated to the mouth, an organ that often was imagined as a weapon and certainly a vehicle of *aretē*. Basil's armament, a metaphor for his manhood, fought under the direction of the Holy Spirit. Through Gregory's portrayal, Basil preserved the mystery of the Godhead while introducing a notion of its miraculous unity to laity. The certitude of his voice, the strength of his intellect, and intimacy with the Divine converged to authorize Basil as Gregory's version of the manly theologian.

MACRINA AND AETIUS AS CONTRASTING MODERATORS OF THEOLOGY

The issue of speech also plays a major theme in Nyssen's *Life of Macrina*. After his brother Basil's death in 379, Nyssen took an increasingly active role in theological politics, and he served as one of the principal advocates of pro-Nicene orthodoxy at the Council of Constantinople. Over the course of two to three years, he composed his lengthy rebuttal of the Heterousian Eunomius in *Against Eunomius*. He completed Books I and II in 380, with the third tome finalized between 381 and 383, after the council. Sometime during the latter period, he also completed the

---

[216] Beeley, *Gregory*, 109–11, on illumination that comes as a result of purification.
[217] Lucian, *Professor* 10 (Harmon).   [218] Greg. Naz., *Or.* 43.65 (McCauley).
[219] Greg. Naz., *Or.* 43.67 (McCauley).   [220] Greg. Naz., *Or.* 43.68 (McCauley).

Life.²²¹ As we discussed in the previous chapter, Gregory presented the *Life* as a model of sacred *aretē*. Through a series of *agōnes*, Macrina personified a manly woman in terms of her moral excellence, thus bringing to light Gregory's ideal of a pro-Nicene *agathos*. Gregory also used the ascetic struggles of Macrina to model the philosophical conditioning required of bishops. The voice of Macrina represents the foundations of untainted theology in her priestly brothers Basil, Nyssen, and Peter. The image of Macrina as spiritual pedagogue ushers a reminder to Christian *pepaideumenoi* that the theologian requires purification, first to discern mysteries of the divine, and second, to teach about them.

Gregory accordingly crafts a portrait of Macrina as an ascetic and a philosophic guide to moderate the *paideia* of her brothers. He prompts readers to consider his sister as a model of theology that reveals the fallacy of Heterousians such as Eunomius and his mentor Aetius. Macrina appears particularly noble when read against portrayals of Eunomius and Aetius in *Against Eunomius*, in which Gregory includes invective against the two to undermine their doctrines. Considered within the theological disputes of the early 380s, the *Life* enlists Macrina as a source of spiritual refinement in opposition to heretical opponents. Writing during the immediate aftermath of Constantinople, at about the same time he was composing the final volume of *Against Eunomius*, Gregory consciously scripted his family in the *Life* as a counterpoint to the heretics chronicled in *Against*. He used the latter text partly as an antipode, from which he crafted his ideal theologian in the *Life*. For audiences familiar with his invective against the Eunomians, Gregory was likening his sister's ascetic feats to a series of *agōnes*, contests authorizing pro-Nicene theology against the teachings of the Heterousians. With Macrina playing the guiding role as Lady Wisdom, Gregory lays stress upon the self-discipline and social rank through which his sister conditioned purified speech in him and his episcopal brothers.²²² He thus uses rhetorical devices to attest that his siblings, arbiters of pro-Nicene theology, represented *logos* (doctrine) that was subjugated to and directed by the Divine.

The figure of Macrina stands in part as castigation of wisdom and rhetoric in persons driven by ambition rather than divine purpose.²²³ In

---

²²¹ Chronology of these works: *The Brill Dictionary of Gregory of Nyssa*, eds. G. Maspero and L. Mateo-Seco (Leiden: Brill, 2009), 153–60 and A. Silvas, *Macrina the Younger: Philosopher of God* (Turnhout: Brepols, 2008), 102.
²²² W. Helleman, "Cappadocian Macrina on Lady Wisdom," *SP* 37 (2001), 86–102.
²²³ Urbano, *Philosophical*, 254–6, states that the absence of *paideia* in biographies of women does not necessarily cast intellectual training in a negative light. The point, in

the *Life*, Macrina moderates the speech of her pro-Nicene brothers, with her voice serving as a metonym for doctrine that is tested, pure, and masculine. It is one of multiple ways that Gregory cast Macrina as a spiritual guide in his writings.[224] But for her to play the part, she first had to meet the qualifications. Gregory thus turns to her education early in the narrative, suggesting that misdirected instruction of children formed the start of flawed theology. He then commends Macrina for excelling in her early childhood studies, emphasizing that her mother Emmelia safe-guarded her against the moral dangers of classical poetry, the unscrupulous rivalries in the comedies, and the duplicitous behavior in Homer's epics.[225] Emmelia insulated Macrina from stories that might corrupt her daughter's mind. A key component of Nyssen's theology relied on preserving the character of the theologian, much as earlier philosophers had advocated censorship to keep intact a youth's dignity. Emmelia's guarding of Macrina's pedagogy echoes similar admonitions about children's instruction by Plutarch and Plato.[226] The former devoted an entire treatise to the subject.[227] "Let us keep a very close watch over them [young men]," Plutarch advises, "in the firm belief that they require oversight in their reading even more than in the streets."[228] Plutarch's concern was that the rectitude of youth would be compromised by indiscriminate stories and inadequate oversight over morally pliable tales. In one passage, Plutarch specified the dissolute ploys of the Euripidean women Phaedra (from *Hippolytus*) and Helen (from *Trojan Women*).[229] He wanted young men to recognize treachery for what it was, as malfeasance rather than cleverness.[230] Gregory imbues the *Life* with a similar trope by disavowing any favorable depiction of such perfidy. For him, the best way to preserve the unsullied Macrina was to withhold such tales from her.

Gregory also reflects Plato's discourse on education in the *Republic*: "We must make it of prime importance that the first stories they hear are

---

Macrina for example, is that her character was such that she acquired philosophical insight that men normally acquired through *paideia*. The purity of her soul outweighs educational credentials; and that philosophical and rhetorical training was adverse when misapplied.

[224] Burrus, "Begotten," 112–22, J. W. Smith, "Macrina, Tamer of Horses and Healer of Souls: Grief and Therapy of Hope in Gregory of Nyssa's *De Anime et Resurrectione*," *JTS* 52 (2001), 37–60, and Helleman, "Cappadocian," 86–102.
[225] Greg. Ny., *Vit. Macr.* 3.5–15 (Silvas, 4.2).
[226] Plutarch *Moralia* 14e–37b and Plato, *Republic* 2–3. See Silvas, *Macrina*, 113 n 21.
[227] Plutarch, *Moralia* 14e–37b.   [228] Plutarch, *Moralia* 15a (Babbitt).
[229] Plutarch, *Moralia* 28a.   [230] Plutarch, *Moralia* 28b (Babbitt).

the finest tales possible to encourage their sense of virtue."[231] The best way to inculcate virtuous conduct, according to Plato, was to offer examples to emulate. Gregory suggests hazards implicit in poetry that dramatized reprobates, his concern being that authors were susceptible to taking on the personas of their cast.[232] Showing awareness of potential moral pitfalls in such literature, Gregory credits Macrina with a salutary course of study. Her focus was on texts that created closeness to God, such as Old Testament wisdom poetry: "She had the Psalter with her at all times," Gregory says, "like a good and faithful traveling companion."[233] Gregory thus shows Macrina's exposure limited to sources that promoted sacred intimacy.[234] The poetry of the *Psalms*, for example, issued a commendable example of mimetic speech. Unlike the bawdy works proscribed by Plato, songs of adoration for God afforded Macrina a language for expressing affiliation with the Divine. Because of careful regulation, Macrina's wisdom developed from a divine source, inspired scripture.[235] As a parallel, Eunomius lacked a governing figure to filter such unseemly readings. An underlying motif in the *Life* involves guardianship, with authority coming from well-ordered speech. The text insinuated that individuals without such tutelage were not equipped for theology.

In other ways, Gregory portrays Macrina's sagacity as overshadowing the conventional training of young men. When she came of age, for example, her father (Basil the Elder) betrothed her to a young lawyer, a rising forensic star who used his renowned eloquence to defend those who had been wronged.[236] By all accounts, the barrister was the ideal mate for Macrina. The young man died before the marriage, however, an apparent tragedy that robbed Macrina of union with a *pepaideumenos* who would have provided her a partner in piety, as well as a source of security and prestige.[237] But as the narrative progresses, the reader considers that her

---

[231] Plato, *Republic* 2.378e (Emlyn-Jones and Preddy).
[232] See Plato, *Republic* 3.393c (Shorey): "effecting their narration through imitation."
[233] Greg. Ny., *Vit. Macr.* 3.20–25 (Callahan).
[234] D. Krueger, *Writing and Holiness: The Practice of Authorship in the Early Christian East* (Philadelphia: University of Pennsylvania Press, 2004), 124–7, argues that in narrating Macrina's life, Gregory was performing an act of worship, which produced in himself a holy identity akin to that of his sister.
[235] Yet ironically, Gregory's performance in illustrating his sister's sacred philosophy is meant to validate the use of non-Christian texts for Christian *pepaideumenoi*. For a similar argument, E. Muehlberger, "Salvage: Macrina and the Christian Project of Cultural Reclamation," *CH* 81:2 (2012), 273–7.
[236] Greg. Ny., *Vit. Macr.* 4.15–25 (Silvas, 5.4).   [237] Greg. Ny., *Vit. Macr.* 4.22–5.

betrothed's early demise preserved Macrina's uncompromised virginity, a status that later contributed to her mentoring of family, as well as her patronage over a community of ascetics. Her maidenhood also reads as a symbol of untainted theology, which is not dependent on popular appeal. Rather than remarry, Macrina practiced sexual renunciation, whereby she guided her mother, and later her brothers, "towards the philosophical and unworldly way of life."[238] The decision to remain outside her father's household, and not to join that of another husband, signaled Macrina's complete dependence on God as her sustainer.[239] It was an act of spiritual bravery, a statement that in Gregory's narrative indicates assurance in an unconventional way of life. It was a struggle that formed her philosophy in Christ, a counterpoint to worldly wisdom.[240] Gregory used the passing of Macrina's betrothed as a metaphor for the secondary merits of worldly erudition. Macrina's earthly spouse, who signified elocution, was replaced by the heavenly bridegroom Christ, a provider of transcendent shelter, glory, and knowledge.

Much later in the narrative, after Macrina's death, one of her attendants related an experience to Gregory that also suggested his sister's immersion in sacred wisdom. A painful sore had developed on Macrina that threatened to cause serious illness if not removed by a physician. Emmelia urged her daughter to seek the services of a doctor, imploring her to accept the discipline of medicine as a gift from God.[241] Yet Macrina still declines the assistance, in part, for the sake of her modesty.

---

[238] Greg. Ny., *Vit. Macr.* 11.6–8 (Callahan).

[239] P. Rousseau, "The Pious Household and the Virgin Chorus: Reflections on Gregory of Nyssa's Life of Macrina," *JECS* 13 (2005), 174–5, makes the point that by not returning to her father's household after the death of her betrothed, Macrina assumed a kind of independent status akin to that of a man no longer under his father's legal authority. On the social ramifications of virginity, K. Cooper, *The Virgin and the Bride: Idealized Womanhood in Late Antiquity* (Cambridge, MA: Harvard University Press, 1999), 74–91. See analysis of Macrina's virginity and ascetic community in Elm, "*Virgins*," 78–105.

[240] Calling readers to consider the passages II Corinthians 4:7: "jars of clay," and I Corinthians 3:19: "wisdom of the world is foolishness," (NIV).

[241] Greg. Ny., *Vit. Macr.* 31.15–20 (Silvas, 33.3). Medicine formed a core part of *paideia*, and medical theory, philosophy, and theology were interrelated: P. Van der Eijk, *Medicine and Philosophy in Classical Antiquity: Doctors and Philosophers on Nature, Soul, Health and Disease* (Cambridge: Cambridge University Press, 2010), 10–23, and G. E. R. Lloyd, *In the Grip of Disease: Studies in the Greek Imagination* (Oxford: Oxford University Press, 2004), 191–220. Basil also addresses the functional role of medicine for Christians in his monastic guidelines: *The Longer Rules* 55.

She considered the affliction less unbearable than allowing a stranger to view her nakedness.[242] As part of an overall image of *aretē*, Gregory shows that Macrina remains unwilling to accept the invasion of another's eyes, a form of visual penetration; and here, perhaps signifying corruption of pure philosophy in Christ. Rather than accepting a standard cure, Macrina chooses an alternative. She has her mother put her hand inside her cloak and apply the sign of the cross. The sore subsequently disappeared.[243] The tumor is vanquished, therefore, through a divine remedy over a more standard course of healing. In the aftermath of the ordeal, a mark remained on the location of the tumor, "as a memorial," Gregory writes, "of the divine visitation, a cause and a subject of continual thanks to God."[244] The spot signified her proximity to God and showed her utter reliance on him alone. This anecdote, as well as the story of her engagement, shows that Macrina's dependence on God informs her philosophy. She derived wisdom not through a traditional regimen of study, but through participation (μετουσία) in activities (ἐναργείαι) that enabled intimacy with the divine.[245] Through Macrina, Gregory's readers were left to think of theology as an issue of relation more than argument.

Gregory thus characterizes Macrina as a source of philosophy that will come to moderate the *paideia* of her episcopal brothers Basil, Gregory, and Peter. Because of proximity to the Divine, Macrina is well-positioned to carry out a generative role in their theology and speech, a place that also prompts readers to call to mind Eunomius' malpractice of philosophy and that of his teacher Aetius. For individuals who had read book One of *Against Eunomius*, the *Life* brings into focus the issue of failed theological influence in Gregory's adversaries. Virginia Burrus

---

[242] Greg. Ny., *Vit. Macr.* 31.20–5 (Silvas, 33.3).
[243] Greg. Ny., *Vit. Macr.* 31.30–5 (Silvas, 33.6).
[244] Greg. Ny., *Vit. Macr.* 31.12–16 (Silvas, 33.7). V. Burrus, "Macrina's Tatoo," in *The Cultural Turn in Late Antique Studies*, eds. D. Martin and P. C. Miller (Durham, NC: Duke University Press, 2005), 103–16, calls attention to the mark in this text as an inversion of tattooing normally applied to Roman slaves or gladiators. Macrina's mark thus reorients a signal of (former) passivity into a sign of agency and a testimony of bravery; G. Frank, "Macrina's Scar: Homeric Allusion and Heroic Identity in Gregory of Nyssa's *Life of Macrina*," *JECS* 8.4 (2000), 511–20, argues that the mark invests his sister with a heroic identity that has precedents in martyr accounts and Greek mythology.
[245] On early Christian views of participation (μετουσία) in the divine: T. Tollefsen, *Activity and Participation in Late Antique and Early Christian Thought* (Oxford: Oxford University Press, 2012), 97–101, discusses, among others, Nyssen's theology on the issue; also D. Balás, Μετουσια Θεου: *Man's Participation in God's Perfections according to Saint Gregory of Nyssa* (Rome: Herder, 1966).

shows that in *Against*, Gregory framed Eunomius' doctrine as an example of failed sonship: "a bastard text, begotten not through intense intellectual intercourse with a worthy spiritual master but in an unseemly act of rebellion against that noble lover."[246] The heretic Eunomius, in other words, had no solid foundation for his doctrine, his "bastard text." His spiritual guide Aetius had not modeled the rigor that was necessary for philosophical discourse. Eunomius' theology had no worthy parentage. Through the text of Book 1, Burrus asserts, "Eunomius' *specular* function, as a distorted mirror of Gregory's own role, becomes more evident."[247] As we will see below, Gregory continues to draw on this counter-image of spiritual parentage as he scripts Macrina in the *Life* as the inverse of his depiction of Aetius.[248] Aetius, that is, constitutes a negative example. Macrina was everything that he was not.

In the brief overview of Aetius' life from *Against*, Gregory begins by saying that he had fallen into heresy because he was seeking financial stability.[249] In the succeeding passages, Gregory explains Aetius' deceptive instruction as an innovation that would provide a comfortable livelihood.[250] His teachings, that is, were driven by material interests. In this context, the term "innovation" or "craft" (τέχνη) denotes the work of somebody lacking the refinement of a nuanced education. As Ludlow has documented, literati prided themselves on their craft and built communities and workshops to sharpen each other's eloquence.[251] When applied to an unlettered individual, however, τέχνη often implied a person adept at one particular skill, and thus lacking well-roundedness. It was a designation attributed to dialecticians by their opponents because the term carried a sense of moral and intellectual baseness.[252] Gregory then chronicles Aetius' career advancement, imputing his rise to monetary aspirations. Social mobility here carried a pejorative sense, since individuals seeking higher rank were motivated by wealth and status, instead of sincere instruction. Gregory points out that Aetius had served as a slave, a rhetorical strike by Gregory designed to discredit him completely.[253]

---

[246] Burrus, "Begotten," 101.   [247] Burrus, "Begotten," 102.
[248] On Aetius: Vaggione, *Eunomius*, 14–29; Lim, *Public*, 112–22; Kopecek, *History*, vol. 2, 396–440.
[249] Greg. Ny., *Contr. Eun* 1.36 (Hall).   [250] Greg. Ny., *Contr. Eun* 1.38 (Hall).
[251] Ludlow, *Art*, 222–32.
[252] Lim, *Public*, 125–48, for analysis of how pro-Nicene opponents vilified Aetius and Eunomius in this sense.
[253] Greg. Ny., *Contr. Eun.* 1.38 (Hall). Claims of Aetius' lowly origins, Vaggione emphasizes, must not be accepted at face value. See his assessment of Aetius' background. Vaggione, *Eunomius*, 14–16.

Having acquired his freedom, in some unspecified manner, Aetius began a series of menial jobs, becoming "at first a smith, engaged in this hot and dirty manual work, with short hammer and little anvil sitting under a hair tent as he eked out a mean and laborious living at this trade."[254] The reference to diminutive tools conjured an image of a minuscule man, and may have alluded to his limited mental faculties. Aetius' "dirty (βάναυσος) work," moreover, suggested that his earliest jobs were vulgar and exhausting, leaving him covetous of an easier way of life. Gregory's initial picture of Aetius seems to offer some empathy, maybe even pity for the destitute man. But the struggling man loses all favor when Gregory shows that he responded to his poverty through dishonorable means. Here, early in his career, Aetius already appears as a cheat. Gregory recounts Aetius swindling a woman who had brought in a gold necklace for repair by keeping it and giving her a cheaper facsimile.[255] After his crime was detected, he faced prosecution and punishment. Instead of accepting the consequences of his own indiscretion, however, Aetius deflects the blame by saying it was the fault of his trade. He subsequently quits his job.[256] Throughout the rest of his account of Aetius, Gregory brands him a perpetual deceiver, a money-monger polluted by the temptations that appeal to an individual who lacks the cultivation of a gentleman.

At one point along his sundry employments, Gregory writes, Aetius found the opportunity to dabble in the art of medicine, a discipline that was associated with dialectic philosophy. Many physicians were highly respected. But the ranks of doctors had been notoriously breached by individuals who dazzled with logical arguments, while remaining grossly inadequate in practice. The stereotype of such frauds was not unlike the binary between that of the genuine philosopher versus the sycophantic sophist.[257] In a similar capacity, without sufficient training, Aetius inveigled an unsuspecting foreigner into hiring him as a physician. As a novice within the medical community, Gregory writes, Aetius gained a following, winning debates as "one of the noisy ones" (τῶν βοώντων εἷς).[258] Gregory insults his demeanor and challenges his actual medical knowledge. Gregory calls readers to consider his loudness (βόαμα), a flaw that reflected the incontinence of Aetius' voice, and by association, his theology. Gregory uses Aetius' shouting as a metaphor for his doctrines, which enjoy favor among those "who hire loud mouths to promote their

---

[254] Greg. Ny., *Contr. Eun.* 1.38 (Hall). [255] Greg. Ny., *Contr. Eun.* 1.40.
[256] Greg. Ny., *Contr. Eun.* 1.41. [257] Lim, *Public*, 115–21; Vaggione, *Eunomius*, 25.
[258] Greg. Ny., *Contr. Eun.* 1.44 (Hall).

own quarrels."²⁵⁹ The overriding criticism again surfaces, that his theology was driven by desire for fame and profit. The discord of his voice, his teachings, appealed to people attracted to boisterousness. The teachings gained support based on his yelling them. Therefore, Gregory also maligns those who gave credence to the pretender. A believer, that is, remains culpable for doctrinal error when he or she confides in persons such as Aetius. Gregory compares supporters of Heterousian doctrines to the falsifiers in I Timothy who accept as sound teaching "what their itching ears want to hear."²⁶⁰ Returning to Macrina's miraculous healing in the *Life*, readers were prompted to interpret her rejection of medical help as a dismissal of theological syllogisms by duplicitous individuals such as Aetius. The image of Aetius also recalls Plato's damning account of disingenuous sophistry, a prominent theme in his writings. In *Against*, Aetius epitomizes Plato's charlatan, who has discovered the "persuasive device" that enables an ignorant man to appear as an expert.²⁶¹ Aetius had honed the "device" and now he pandered his craft, according to Gregory, to patrons who valued his cleverness.

Not only did Aetius typify a sycophant, according to such rendering, but also he represented the shortcomings of a man masquerading as a *pepaideumenos*, lacking the discernment that came from experience in *agōnes*. Aetius' lack of *paideia* contributed to his flawed use of rhetoric and philosophy. His shortcoming of character formed the source of his unorthodoxy. "Heresy," as Richard Vaggione states, "could only be a defective orientation or habitus working itself out in doctrinal terms."²⁶² Vaggione is right, that opponents of Aetius and Eunomius pointed to their philosophical regimen as misshapen; their doctrine derived from defective pedagogy.²⁶³ From servile origins, Aetius had never received counsel on

---

²⁵⁹ Greg. Ny., *Contr. Eun.* 1.44 (Hall). τὸ ἀναιδὲς τῆς φωνῆς πρὸς τὰς ἑαυτῶν φιλονεικίας ἐκμισθουμένων.
²⁶⁰ I Timothy 4:3 (NIV): "The time will come when men will not put up with sound doctrine. Instead, to suit their own desires, they will gather around them a great number of teachers to say what their itching ears want to hear."
²⁶¹ Plato, *Gorgias* 459b (Irwin): "There is no need for it [sophistry] to know how things actually are," the figure of Socrates states in *Gorgias*, "but only to have found some persuasive device so that those who don't know it will seem to know more than those who know."
²⁶² Vaggione, *Eunomius*, 97.
²⁶³ Such incomplete and misdirected pedagogy represented a deficiency critiqued by Plato, *Gorgias* 506d (Irwin). Through the mouthpiece of Socrates, Plato states "But now, the virtue of each thing...doesn't come to be present in the best way just at random, but by some structure and correctness and craft."

how rightly to use philosophy and rhetoric. He was too preoccupied with finding a means to a more comfortable living. Ultimately, it was Aetius' fixation on comfort that disqualified him as a theologian, and subsequently invalidated the dogmas of his protégé Eunomius. His education and eloquence were based on deceit and self-indulgence, vices meant to be erased through a program of *paideia* derived from nobility. Lacking such pedigree, however, Aetius epitomized untruth.

Gregory meanwhile portrays Eunomius as likewise coming from a family of modest means. Eunomius' father is a hard-working farmer, an outstanding man, but overburdened trying to make a living. Perhaps the most scathing indictment in *Against* comes in the next lines. Gregory states that with his father laboring as a farmer, "bending at the plough and working very hard," Eunomius gravitated toward the guidance of Aetius.[264] Eunomius recognized the social and financial elevation that Aetius had acquired by currying favor with powerful individuals. He wanted the same for himself, even if it meant abandoning his own father, a man of honest work ethic. Gregory meant for the rejection to signal Eunomius' ultimate betrayal of masculinity. Gregory furthermore explains Eunomius' acceptance of Aetius' theology as a natural outcome for a man seeking the quickest path to status and affluence. Gregory claims that Eunomius mimicked Aetius' art of attracting followers by "setting aside the uphill and burdensome aspects of virtue as dissuading acceptance of the mystery."[265] Eunomius followed his predecessor's lead, foregoing the demanding intellectual and spiritual work required of a theologian. An unwillingness to participate in the struggles of philosophical inquiry matched his teachings, which were designed to win supporters through simplistic arguments.

The provenance of Eunomius' theology, therefore, was a paternal figure who lacked the *aretē* of a *pepaideumenos*. Eunomius followed Aetius' example of evading *agōnes* that forged moral vigor. It is a damning account of his spurious *paideia*. He wins arguments, Gregory acknowledges, but only because he is a "wordy hack" (τρίβωνα λόγων).[266] Eunomius sacrifices investigation of God's truth in favor of the "juvenile competition" (μειρακιώδης ἡ φιλοτιμία) of winning a battle of words.[267] He abuses language, moreover, by descending to the level of a brute when slandering respectable bishops, even "uttering wagon-talk" against

---

[264] Greg. Ny., *Contr. Eun.* 1.49 (Hall).   [265] Greg. Ny., *Contr. Eun.* 1.53 (Hall).
[266] Greg. Ny., *Contr. Eun.* 1.12 (Hall); on this term from Euripides, see Hall, 75, n. 5.
[267] Greg. Ny., *Contr. Eun.* 1.11 (Hall).

them.²⁶⁸ The cumulative description shows a theologian acting like an unstable adolescent; completely out of his depth, but quick-witted enough to attract the weak-minded. Gregory's allegations are directed as much against the followers of Eunomius as they are the person. *Paideia* involved competitions that instilled superior *ēthos* in young men. Eunomius, however, had never reached manhood because intellectually and socially he had never engaged in virtuous contests. His disputation was typecast as mere wordplay, a manipulation of discourse that lacked substance, and indeed, promoted error. He was the product of a nefarious role model in Aetius.

Gregory depicts Macrina, in counterpoint to Aetius, as a proper theological authority and guide for her fraternal *pepaideumenoi* because she is not confined by physicality, desire, and fame. As a woman, Macrina might have been expected to yield to her natural yearnings, such as pursuing another lover after the death of her spouse. Her decision not to remarry testified to her preoccupation with the eternal. She was neither obsessed with status, as seen in her renunciation of earthly marriage, nor overly concerned with the body, as her response to a cancerous tumor has shown. The undercurrent of class also colors Nyssen's narrative in the *Life*. Macrina came from a family that owned property in three provinces.²⁶⁹ Coming from a family that had paid taxes to three governors, and now serving over an ascetic community of her family's former servants, Macrina enjoyed a certain gravitas, a moral formation associated with status, education, and the responsible management of resources.²⁷⁰ A person from such a background exuded stability in the eyes of late-Roman audiences. Unlike the arrivistes that Gregory depicted in Aetius and Eunomius, Macrina did not acquiesce to patrons. She felt no need to cater to multiple beneficiaries. The words ushering from such a woman would not be dependent on acquiring financial profit or social advancement. In this sense, Macrina symbolized pro-Nicene theology that was unaffected by appeals to populist demands.

---

²⁶⁸ Greg. Ny., *Contr. Eun.* 1.32. (slight alteration of Hall): φωνῇ τὰ ἐκ τῆς ἁμάξης προφέρει; "wagon-talk" here refers to abusive language expected of rowdy young men.

²⁶⁹ Greg. Ny., *Vit Macr.* 5.35–45. On the financial status of the family, Elm, "*Virgins*," 89–93.

²⁷⁰ Lim, *Public*, 183 on the nexus between authentic *paideia* and class ideology: "The notion of *paideia*, allied with the strict moral code that traditionally accompanied inherited wealth and leisure, distinguished the well-born few from the common man." Moral formation is also linked to *paideia* in J. M. André, *L'Otium dans la vie morale et intellectuelle romaine des origines à l'époque augustéenne* (Paris: Presses Universitaires de France, 1966), 125–40.

Her brothers, meanwhile, make ideal apprentices because each had undergone rigorous training that had potential to be reoriented towards sacred teaching. Macrina's own *agōnes* act as a medium for sanctifying her brothers' philosophical development. She embodies sacred *paideia*, with her "complete ease of speech" (εὐκολίᾳ πάσῃ τοῦ λόγου) opposing the loud ramblings of the Heterousians in *Against*.[271] Virginia Burrus argues that in *Against Eunomius*, Gregory cast himself in a filial role to Basil as part of a contest of masculinities to show a "superior theological progeny."[272] In *On the Soul and the Resurrection*, Burrus contends, Gregory appears as the offspring of Macrina's paternity and maternity, thus issuing a masculine identity made complete through elements of femininity.[273] In the *Life*, I believe that in a similar way Gregory sets Basil, Peter, and himself as sons to Macrina, whose paternal role is made evident through ascetic feats re-fashioned as manly contests.[274] She thus appears as a begetter of her brothers' piety, stabilizing her family and shaping the faculties of her siblings toward divine purposes. When Basil came to the family home at Annesi in Pontus, proud of his hard-earned education, Macrina guided him toward philosophy that "despised the applause to be gained through eloquence."[275] She tempered his erudition, that is, with another form of contested *aretē*, her spiritual trials. Her direction thus reflected the adage from Proverbs that fearing God promotes wisdom, and humility precedes honor.[276] Her rectification also recalled a dictum by Plutarch that it was a "point of good sense not to be puffed up with fame, nor to be excited and elated by popular praise."[277] Again, Gregory projects the theme of speech (theology) directed toward truth as superior to words that win renown.

In curbing her brother's pride, moreover, Macrina led Basil to work with his own hands and to embrace poverty as a path to virtue.[278] Such

---

[271] Greg. Ny., *Vit. Macr.* 18.20-2 (Silvas, 20.6).   [272] Burrus, "Begotten," 110.
[273] Burrus, "Begotten," 112–22.
[274] Urbano, *Philosophical*, 267, on the transformation of Macrina's "reproductive role from bearing biological offspring to producing philosophical offspring joined to male philosophical lineage."
[275] Greg. Ny., *Vit. Macr.* 6.1–15 (Silvas, 8.3); L. Coon, *Sacred Fictions: Holy Women and Hagiography in Late Antiquity* (Philadelphia: University of Pennsylvania Press, 1997), 146, on the "leitmotif of inversion to castigate masculine pride"; also V. Harrison, "Male and Female in Cappadocian Theology," *JTS* 41 (1990), 442–5.
[276] Proverbs 15:33 (NIV): "The fear of the Lord teaches a man wisdom, and humility comes before honor." The phrase "humility before honor" also appears in Proverbs 18.12.
[277] Plutarch, *Moralia* 32d. With Plutarch making a reference to Aeschylus, *Seven Against Thebes*, 599.
[278] The choice of poverty and doing manual labor were forms of asceticism. Harrison, "Male," 444–5, argues that such acts of asceticism were re-ordered as masculine enterprises thus opening new avenues for women to exhibit virtue.

striving for *aretē* contrasted with Aetius and Eunomius' fixation on a life made easy by worldly wealth, and in fact, a renunciation of hard work. Macrina likewise molded the education of her younger brother Peter, channeling his education towards "sacred studies" in order to prevent him from succumbing to vanity.[279] As she had done with Basil, Macrina guided Peter to the "lofty goal of philosophy" so that the future bishop of Sebaste participated in ascetic pursuits alongside his sister and mother.[280] In a famous passage recording her all-encompassing roles, Macrina became "all things to the lad [Peter] – father, teacher, guardian, mother, counsellor of every good."[281] She inverted the childless quality of chastity into a means of engendering a future cleric. As a conqueror of nature itself – having overcome the urges of procreation – a virgin had to exhibit extraordinary self-control, particularly over her body and the senses. Macrina transcended her sex by attaining sacred *aretē* through her intimacy with the Divine. Thus she made for an effective moderator of her brothers' intellectual skills.[282] Unlike Eunomius, whose career was rooted in counsel from a man seeking the easy life, Gregory, Basil, and Peter learned sacred manhood through a sister who was experienced in facing ordeals.[283]

Macrina thus embodied spiritualized *paideia*: the wisdom and deportment of a Christian *pepaideumenos*, through the weaker vehicle of the female body. Consequently, she served as a textual reminder that proper philosophy ultimately derived from and belonged to God rather than human aptitude.[284] Gregory depicted his virginal sibling as a counterpoint to figures of highest eloquence, yet the cumulative effect of her guidance was in fact to redeem the rhetorical practice of her brothers, who became episcopal authorities. In doing so, he places priority on sacred capital as the criterion for effective theology. Macrina is removed from the public arena in which bishops operated, yet she exhibits *aretē* more than any male ecclesiastic. She makes the perfect candidate, therefore, to instruct on theology understood as an adjunct to relation with the Divine. Having been chastened by Macrina's instruction, Gregory, Basil, and Peter can now deliver theology that is reasoned through *paideia* and

---

[279] Greg. Ny., *Vit. Macr.* 12.5–15 (Silvas, 14.2).
[280] Greg. Ny., *Vit. Macr.* 12.15–30 (Silvas, 14.3–5).
[281] Greg. Ny., *Vit. Macr.* 12.10–13 (Silvas, 14.2).
[282] R. Williams, *The Wound of Knowledge: Christian Spirituality from the New Testament to St. John of the Cross* (London: Darton, Longman and Todd, 1979), 58–9.
[283] Burrus, "Begotten," 100–3, referring to Eunomius' rejection of Basil's teachings.
[284] Recalling I Corinthians 2:1–5.

formed through divine intimacy. Unlike orations, as a letter, the *Life* was circulated among a more limited group that consisted primarily of fellow *pepaideumenoi* and pro-Nicene clergy. In effect, Gregory composed the work as a dictate to episcopal colleagues and potential aristocratic converts that true philosophy (here meaning pro-Nicene theology) and rhetoric were rooted in a sacred source. With his brothers and himself serving as exemplars, Gregory was identifying pro-Nicene bishops with *paideia* derived from divine affiliation.

Plutarch once instructed young men on evaluating a philosopher's words by observing the bearing of the instructor. "No, rather it is both [his] character and speech, or character by means of speech," Plutarch claimed, "just as a horseman uses a bridle, or a helmsman uses a rudder, since virtue has no instrument so humane or so akin to itself as speech."[285] The Cappadocians invoked a similar trope as they constructed hagiographic lives during the era of the Council of Constantinople. Nazianzen and Nyssen framed late fourth-century theological conflict as a battle between true and false philosophy, illustrated through metaphors of the voice and speech. The truth of the theology was confirmed in the *aretē* of their attendant subjects. The arduous tests endured by saints in these narratives validated the discourse of their pro-Nicene authors. Against the backdrop of a dissolute theologian such as Eunomius, the Gregories and their hagiographic subjects fared well in the forum of public disputation. The overriding issue in this apposition concerned the use of language, a matter in which pro-Nicene saints proved superior at every turn in these hagiographies. The Gregories used the medium of rhetorical biography, itself a performative act, to promote the version of a prelate whose theology is sanctioned by his rectitude and holiness. Such imagery coincided with conceptions of *aretē* associated with the rigors of bodily *askēsis*, a theme that shadowed much of pro-Nicene hagiography.

In the final pages of the *Life*, Nyssen celebrated the effects of speech that has been properly oriented. He narrates how, following his participation in the Council of Antioch of 379, he returned to Annesi. When he arrived, he discovered Macrina seriously ill and dying. Gregory had been prevented from seeing his sister for almost eight years, an absence he blames on opposition from "the leaders of heresy."[286] He situated the meeting against the backdrop of persecution by rival prelates. In this final

---

[285] Plutarch, *Moralia* 33f. (Babbitt).   [286] Greg. Ny., *Vit. Macr.* 15.5–9 (Silvas, 17.2).

encounter with his sister, Gregory was enlightened by his sister's piety and wisdom, as Macrina discoursed on many issues, including "the divine economy hidden in disasters."[287] As Macrina approaches death, she emboldens her brother, so that his soul "was elevated by her words above human nature and set down through the guidance of her discourse within the heavenly sanctuary."[288] Devoid of the worldly sophistication of her brother, Macrina nevertheless apprises Gregory on the soul, life, the flesh, and death. She explains it all to him, and Gregory defers completely to the power of his sister's teaching, her "beautiful" words.[289] Through conquest over suffering, Macrina had acquired a spiritual authority with verbal fluency that transcended that of rhetoricians. The figure of Macrina offered a parallel to the composure of a *pepaideumenos*, with her bodily exertions surpassing the *aretē* of the manly orator.[290] Her teaching derived from the crucible of agonistic, selfless devotion to the Divine and was punctuated by her theological discourse in the painful last hours of life. Gregory thus became the beneficiary of a theology that had been purified through the severest of agonies in the form of disease and death. He would submit his elocution to God.

Nazianzen's Athanasius and Basil, as we have seen, represented a convergence of martyr-like courage and classical expectation of moderation and self-control. These acts of spiritual discipline confirmed the piety of these bishops. The feats also appealed to the sensibilities of aristocratic elites, who found in this conception of monastic activity a parallel to the *aretē* associated with the pedagogy that developed civic leaders. The intellectual regimen undergone by *pepaideumenoi* constituted an analogue to the arduous asceticism that cleansed individuals, thus enabling them to contemplate the Divine. For the Cappadocians, mastery of speech (*logos*) comprised an essential distinction of pro-Nicene theologians. In the wake of Constantinople and debates over the function of speech in the Eunomian controversy, it was particularly advantageous for Nazianzen and Nyssen to differentiate noble, sacred *paideia* from the vagaries of the Heterousians. The Cappadocians thereby accentuated

---

[287] Greg. Ny., *Vit. Macr.* 17.20–7 (Silvas, 20.2). Significant elements of the dialogue are based on Plato's *Symposium*, *Phaedo*, and *Phaedrus*. See Ludlow, *Gregory*, 206–19; R. Williams, "Macrina's Deathbed Revisited: Gregory of Nyssa on Mind and Passion," in *Christian Faith and Greek Philosophy in Late Antiquity: Essays in Tribute to George Christopher Stead*, eds. L. R. Wickham and C. Bammel (Leiden: Brill, 1993), 227–46.

[288] Greg. Ny., *Vit. Macr.* 17.28–30 (Silvas, 20.2).

[289] Greg. Ny., *Vit. Macr.* 22.12–14 (Silvas, 24.1).

[290] Muehlberger, "Salvage," 282–5, on the trope of bravery in Macrina's deathbed scene.

the superiority of voice in protagonists as a condemnation of heretics. Nyssen and Nazianzen scripted Athanasius, Basil, and Macrina as embodiments of sacred *aretē* to be associated with pro-Nicene theology. By simultaneously undermining the gender, class, and sanctity of rivals, the Cappadocians were prodding elite eastern Romans to identify the pro-Nicene episcopacy as *agathoi* : the brave; the upright, the heirs of rightly ordered classical philosophy and theology.

Epilogue

Classical Masculinity in Early Medieval and Byzantine Christianity

In late antique Christianity, performances of manliness ushered moral authority, hierarchy, and philosophic legitimacy. Status in the culture of *paideia* thus was connected to one's place on the rhetorical spectrum between the masculine and the feminine. Occasions for posturing as a classical male during the Second Sophistic took additional forms during the late fourth century, particularly for Christian clergy. Against a backdrop of the battle to determine theological orthodoxy, the Cappadocians composed epistles and hagiographic biographies that tethered pro-Nicene theology to classical masculinity. These demonstrations of contest made for a powerful episcopal tool of self-presentation, particularly during the Christological debates of the fourth century.

The rhetoric of *agōn* applied to multiple methods of identity formation. In epistolary exchange, authors engaged in a dialogue that reenacted questing after *aretē* through contests of writing. Correspondents prompted each other to exhibit literary excellence as an indication of friendship, a bond underpinned sometimes by shared faith, and at other times by a mutual conception of manhood based on *paideia*. In a dialogue on *philia*, where letters were meant to bridge the distance between absent parties, participants showcased their ability to orchestrate sensory experiences in order to create virtual encounters and congruence of soul. In epistolary *agōnes*, the Cappadocians reinforced their membership among a new era of *agathoi*, pro-Nicene leaders established in part by repeated displays of merit and consensus about the attributes that defined a classical Christian male.

The Cappadocians also used the *agōn* trope in personifications of sacred *aretē* as they situated pro-Nicene friends, family members, and bishops in narratives of struggle. Nazianzen and Nyssen situated most of these hagiographies within the context of theological rivalry between pro-Nicenes and their detractors. They subsequently prompted readers to contrast protagonists against Heterousian rivals such as Eunomius of Cyzicus and, by association, other opponents. Gregory of Nyssa, for example, recast third-century bishop Gregory Thaumaturgus by writing him into the fourth-century theological debates as a defender of Nicene orthodoxy. Nyssen's version of Thaumaturgus exuded the qualities of a Greek warrior as Thaumaturgus both defended and articulated the creedal elements of Nicaea that propagated Homoousian dogma against other doctrines. The hagiography thus merged in Thaumaturgus the heroism of an Archaic Greek combatant and the piety of an Old Testament patriarch. In similar manner, Nazianzen held up his brother Caesarius as a member of his family's pro-Nicene dynasty. Caesarius outshined rivals at the imperial capital, using his intellectual prowess to ward off Emperor Julian's attempts to turn him away from his faith. Nazianzen repeatedly likened him to an athlete straining to gain victory, a reflection of Pauline spiritual imagery, as well as a reenactment of Second Sophistic verbal dueling.

In his oration for his sister, Nazianzen likewise invested Gorgonia with an aura of manliness as she overcame the pain of a tragic accident and illness while exhibiting the composure of a *pepaideumenos*. The portrait enhances Gregory's own capital as an emerging clergyman and advocate of pro-Nicene doctrine. And in a biography of his sister, Nyssen shows Macrina as exuding courage, with her response to illness and imminent death authorizing her as a master of true philosophy. Readers of the *Life of Macrina* were left to consider Macrina's purification, with Macrina embodying pro-Nicene sanctity acquired through a conflation of asceticism and athletic vigor. Thus, her *aretē* is confirmed through a series of *agōnes*, while posing a contrast to the degeneracy of the Heterousian Eunomius as impugned in Nyssen's and Nazianzen's polemics. Meanwhile both Nyssen and Nazianzen created hagiographic accounts of Basil that pitted him in contests against non-Nicene antagonists, most notably in direct confrontation against Emperor Valens. The emphasis on Basil's refutation of Valens amplified Basil's defiance against impiety as he defends true belief.

In both epistles and in hagiographic accounts, the Cappadocians used illustrations of *agōnes* to identify with the idealized male, and thus to accrue social and theological authority. For a limited readership of *pepaideumenoi*, the Cappadocians staged letter exchanges as contests to show that they valued the culture of verbal sparring and recognized the role of such ventures in producing *aretē*. For broader audiences of hagiographic narratives, Nyssen and Nazianzen represented pro-Nicene subjects through a series of *agōnes* that aligned the bishops with leadership based on piety in congruence with performances of manhood. Depending on the use of the *agōn* theme, the Cappadocians were claiming membership in a social group of imperial and provincial elites or identifying with expectations of leadership that informed the broader population in the eastern empire.

The subject of *agōn* rhetoric also applies to studies of other epochs and settings within the late antique and medieval Christian church. Recent scholarship has shown, for example, how classical models of manhood influenced choice of apparel by fifth-century clergy, as well as the gendering of liturgy in early medieval Benedictine communities. In "Sizing-Up the Philosopher's Cloak," Arthur Urbano has shown how late antique Christian intellectuals invoked the *tribōn* (the traditional philosopher's cloak) as a method of identity construction. Gregory of Nazianzus referred to the garment as a mark of learning, of status, of manhood, thus reifying his own position among philosophical circles. Nazianzen made such claims not only as part of a contest with non-Christians for intellectual status, but also to advocate for pro-Nicene theology at the time of the Council of Constantinople.[1] Lynda Coon, meanwhile, has argued in *Dark Age Bodies* that in the medieval Carolingian monastery of Fulda, architectural design and *lectio* (public reading of scripture) combined to order space and liturgy according to classical norms of masculinity; here perfected through the sacrifice of Christ as translated through the Benedictine Rule. In a community of male ascetics, the monastery's loggias were designed to exhibit the abbot's worldly power, even while other features of the Plan emphasized expressions of humility.[2] Lectors chosen to conduct sacred public readings likewise mimicked ancient orators in acquiring status through control of their voices and by delivering eloquent performances.[3] The discharge of liturgical duties was carried out by individuals that had proven their *virtus* (manly virtue) after having undergone the hardships of physical, intellectual, and spiritual exercise.

The legacy of classical manhood furthermore came to inform middle Byzantine representations of certain bishops, particularly in liturgical

---

[1] A. Urbano, "Sizing Up the Philosopher's Cloak: Christian Verbal and Visual Representations of the Tribon," in *Dressing Judeans and Christians in Late Antiquity*, eds. K. Upson-Saia, C. Daniel-Hughes, and A. J. Batten (Farnham: Ashgate, 2014), 185–6.
[2] L. Coon, *Dark Age Bodies: Gender and Monastic Practice in the Early Medieval West* (Philadelphia: University of Pennsylvania Press, 2011), 184–9.
[3] Coon, *Dark*, 65–71.

Epilogue

Gregory of Nyssa (Left) and Gregory of Nazianzus (Right) (Codex 61, fol. 113r., Dionysiou Monastery, Mount Athos, 11th century)

volumes that were commissioned for a restricted viewership of clergy, monks, or imperial officials.[4] The manuscript illustration featured on the cover of this book is a case in point (see image on p. 275). Part of an eleventh-century codex, the image accompanies Nazianzen's eleventh oration. The text was a sermon by Nazianzen in 372, responding to Gregory of Nyssa's exhortation to Nazianzen to take on the burden of episcopal duties at Sasima even though Nazianzen believed he had been unjustly appointed.[5] The picture evokes many of the same ideals we have encountered about the circulation of status among fourth-century *pepaideumenoi* and Christian clergy. In the illustration, the two bishops face each other, sitting down, holding large books while engaging in discourse. The seated position suggests spiritual authority, as well as social and spiritual equivalence. The volumes in their hands testify to their wisdom and erudition. Nazianzen gestures with his right hand and Nyssen holds his right hand to his chest as a sign of respect.[6]

The image resonates with the theme of friendship, here rooted in love of God and congregation. While Nyssen has challenged Nazianzen to persevere through the hardships of his office, Nazianzen takes to heart his colleague's exhortation. "A faithful friend is a sturdy shelter, a fortified palace," the homily reads. "A faithful friend is worth more than gold and much precious stone."[7] Further into the speech, Nazianzen asserts his willingness to "struggle against the principalities, against the powers, against lurking tyrants and persecutors."[8] As Leslie Brubaker has argued, miniatures in liturgical texts often did not correlate exactly to the text that they illustrated. More often illustrations conveyed a specific meaning to the viewer for which the codex was commissioned.[9] In this particular portrayal, the artist has emphasized the reciprocal nature of the friendship bond, even though the illuminator might just as well have given precedence to Nazianzen, as the voice of the text, justifying his outrage at his

---

[4] L. Brubaker, *Vision and Meaning in Ninth-Century Byzantium: Image as Exegesis in the Homilies of Gregory of Nazianzus* (Cambridge: Cambridge University, 1999), 23–4, on the limited viewership of miniatures, images that adorned liturgical texts.

[5] Codex 61, fol. 113r., Dionysiou Monastery, Mount Athos; GNz, *Or.* 11. (*Homily* 12, PG 35, 832).

[6] G. Galavaris, *The Illustrations of the Liturgical Homilies of Gregory Nazianzenus* (Princeton: Princeton University Press, 1969), 53–4.

[7] GNz, *Or.* 11.1 (Vinson); reference to Psalm 19:10.   [8] GNz, *Or.* 11.4 (Vinson).

[9] Brubaker, *Vision*, 19–26.

forced ordination. As part of a larger gift that bestowed honor and provided instruction, this miniature reminds the viewer that the pursuit of spiritual *aretē* constitutes a joint venture between virtuous individuals. The bishops wear distinctive priestly robes, rich in color. Coupled with the surrounding architecture and ornate curtain, the picture of the two bishops projects beauty coordinate with sacred *aretē*. The portrayal of these idealized bishops authorizes them as overseers of the mysteries of God. Thus, they are equipped to enter the sacred space, guarded here by the veil of the resplendent curtain.

In depictions of late antique clothing, in early Latin monasteries, and in middle Byzantine art, such symbols of classical masculinity were situated into a Christian context in order to evoke an identity of power and authority within the hierarchy of the church. Like fourth-century *agōn* rhetoric that resonated with authority, these trappings of masculinity provided a language of hierarchy for church leaders to integrate into a faith that lacked comparable platforms for displays of social distinction. The Cappadocians represented a late antique tradition of Christianity that re-oriented and subsumed male identity into their position as clergy. Studies of medieval Latin Christianity and Byzantium are finding increasing evidence that this model of gender continued to shape the postclassical church.

References

ANCIENT SOURCES

Aelius Aristides. *Orations*. In *The Complete Works: Orations xvii–liii (English and Ancient Greek Edition)*. Translated by C. Behr. Leiden: Brill, 1997.
Aelius Theon. *Progymnasmata*. Translated by M. Patillon. Série grecque 374. Paris: Les Belles Lettres, 2002.
Aeschylus. *Persians. Seven against Thebes. Suppliants. Prometheus Bound*. Edited and Translated by A. H. Sommerstein. LCL 145 (2009).
Aeschylus. *Prometheus Bound*. Translated by D. Roberts. Indianapolis: Hackett, 2012.
Ammianus Marcellinus. *History, Volume III: Books 27–31. Excerpta Valesiana*. Translated by J. C. Rolfe. LCL 331 (1939).
Aphthonius. *Progymnasmata*. Text and Translation in G. Kennedy. *Progymnasmata: Greek Textbooks of Prose Composition and Rhetoric*. Atlanta: SBL, 2003.
Aristophanes. *Knights*. In *Aristophanes: The Birds and Other Plays*. Translated by D. Barrett. London: Penguin, 2003.
Aristotle. *Nicomachean Ethics*. Translated by J. A. K. Thomson. London: Penguin, 2004.
Aristotle. *On the Soul. Parva Naturalia. On Breath*. Translated by W. S. Hett. LCL 288 (1957).
Aristotle. *Poetics*. Translated by Stephen Halliwell. London: Duckworth, 1987.
Aristotle. *Rhetoric*. Translated by David Ross. Oxford: Clarendon, 1959.
Athanasius. *Defense of His Flight*. In *Select Writings and Letters of Athanasius, Bishop of Alexandria*. Edited by A. Robertson. NPNF II: 4 (1892; reprint 2004).
Athanasius. *History of the Arians*. In *Select Writings and Letters of Athanasius, Bishop of Alexandria*. Edited by A. Robertson. NPNF II: 4 (1892; reprint 2004).
Augustine. *Confessions*. Translated by H. Chadwick. Oxford: Oxford University Press, 2009.

Basil. *Address to Young Men*. In *Letters, Volume IV: Letters 249–368. On Greek Literature*. Translated by Roy J. Deferrari and M. R. P. McGuire. LCL 270 (1934).
Basil. *Against Eunomius*. In *Basile de Césarée: Contre Eunome*. 2 Vols. Translated and Edited by B. Sesboüé, G.-M. de Durand, and L. Doutreleau. SC 299 and 305 (1982–1983). And *St. Basil of Caesarea: Against Eunomius*. Translated by M. DelCogliano and A. Radde-Gallwitz. FC 122 (2011).
Basil. *The Asketikon, The Longer Rules, and The Shorter Rules*. In *The Asketikon of St. Basil the Great*. Translated by Anna Silvas. OECS. Oxford: Oxford University Press, 2005.
Basil. *Epistles*. In *Basil: Letters*. 4 Volumes. Translated by Roy J. Deferrari and M. R. P. McGuire. LCL 190, 215, 243, 270. (1926–1934). And *Saint Basile. Lettres*. 3 Volumes. Translated by Y. Courtonne. Paris: Les Belles Lettres, 1957–1966.
Basil. *Homily on Gordius* and *Homily on the Forty Martyrs of Sebaste*. In *"Let Us Die That We May Live": Greek Homilies on Christian Martyrs from Asia Minor, Palestine and Syria (c. 350–c. 450 AD)*. Edited and Translated by P. Allen, W. Mayer, J. Leemans, and B. Dehandschutter. London: Routledge, 2003.
Cicero. *Letters to Friends*. In *Greek and Latin Letters: An Anthology, with Translation*. Translated by M. Trapp. Cambridge: Cambridge University Press, 2003. And Malherbe, *AET* (1988).
Demetrius. *On Style*. In Malherbe, *AET* (1988).
Demosthenes. *Orations, Volume I: Orations 1–17 and 20*. Translated by J. H. Vince. LCL 238 (1930).
Demosthenes. *Orations, Volume II: Orations 18–19*. Translated by C. A. Vince and J. H. Vince. LCL 155 (1926).
Demosthenes. *Orations, Volume III: Orations 21–26*. Translated by J. H. Vince. LCL 299 (1935).
Demosthenes. *Orations, Volume VII: Orations 60–61*. Translated by N. W. De Witt and N. J. De Witt. LCL 374 (1949).
Diogenes Laertius. *Lives of Eminent Philosophers, Volume II: Books 6–10*. Translated by R. D. Hicks. LCL 185 (1925).
Dio Chrysostom. *Discourses 1–11*. Translated by J. W. Cohoon. LCL 257 (1932).
Dio Chrysostom. *Discourses 12–30*. Translated by J. W. Cohoon. LCL 339 (1939).
Dio Chrysostom. *Discourses 31–36*. Translated by J. W. Cohoon and H. Lamar Crosby. LCL 358 (1940).
Epictetus. *Discourses, Books 1–2*. Translated by W. A. Oldfather. LCL 131 (1925).
Epiphanius. *Panarion*. In *The Panarion of Epiphanius of Salamis. Book I (Sects 1–46)*. Translated by F. Williams. Leiden: Brill, 2009.
Eunapius. *Lives of the Philosophers and Sophists*. Translated by Wilmer C. Wright. LCL 134 (1921).
Eunomius of Cyzicus. *Apology for the Apology*. In *L'Apologie d'Eunome de Cyzique et le Contre Eunome de Basile de Césarée*. Edited by B. Sesboüe.

SC 299 (1980). And *Eunomius: The Extant Works*. Translated by R. Vaggione. Oxford: Clarendon Press, 1987.
Euripides. *Bacchae. Iphigenia at Aulis. Rhesus*. Edited and Translated by D. Kovacs. LCL 495 (2003).
Euripides. *Medea*. In *Medea and Other Plays*. Translated by J. Morwood. Oxford: Oxford University Press, 2009.
Galen. *Hygiene, Volume I: Books 1–4*. Edited and Translated by I. Johnston. LCL 535 (2018).
Gregory of Nazianzus. *Gregory of Nazianzus: Autobiographical Poems*. Edited and Translated by C. White. Cambridge: Cambridge University Press, 2005.
Gregory of Nazianzus. *Epigrams*. In *The Greek Anthology, Volume II: Book 7: Sepulchral Epigrams. Book 8: The Epigrams of St. Gregory the Theologian*. Translated by W. R. Paton. LCL 68 (1917).
Gregory of Nazianzus. *Epistles*. In *Grégoire de Nazianze: Lettres*. Translated by P. Gallay. Paris: Les Belles Lettres, 1964. And *Gregory of Nazianzus's Letter Collection: The Complete Translation*. Translated by B. Storin. Berkeley: University of California Press, 2019.
Gregory of Nazianzus. *Gregory Nazianzus. Three Poems: Concerning His Own Affairs, Concerning Himself and the Bishops, Concerning His Own Life*. Translated by D. Meehan. FC 75 (1987).
Gregory of Nazianzus. *Gregor von Nazianz. De vita sua*. Translated by C. Jungck. Heidelberg: Winter, 1974.
Gregory of Nazianzus. *Orations 1–3*. In *Grégoire de Nazianze. Discours 1–3*. Edited and Translated by J. Bernardi. SC 247 (1978).
Gregory of Nazianzus. *Orations 4–5*. In *Grégoire de Nazianze. Discours 4–5*. Edited and Translated by J. Bernardi. SC 309 (1983).
Gregory of Nazianzus. *Orations 6–12*. In *Grégoire de Nazianze. Discours 6–12*. Edited and Translated by M.-A. Calvet-Sébasti. SC 405 (1995).
Gregory of Nazianzus. *Orations 7, 8, 18, and 43*. In *Funeral Orations by Saint Gregory Nazianzen and Saint Ambrose*. Translated by L. McCauley. FC 22 (1953).
Gregory of Nazianzus. *Oration 8*. In *Gregory of Nazianzus*. Translated by B. Daley. London: Routledge, 2006.
Gregory of Nazianzus. *Orations 12, 15, 32*. In *Gregory of Nazianzus: Select Orations*. Translated by M. Vinson. FOC 107 (2003).
Gregory of Nazianzus. *Orations 20–23*. In *Grégoire de Nazianze. Discours 20–23*. Edited and Translated by J. Mossay. SC 270 (1980).
Gregory of Nazianzus. *Oration 21*. In *S. Cyril of Jerusalem. S. Gregory Nazianzen*. Translated by C. G. Browne and J. E. Swallow. NPNF II: 7 (1893; reprint 2004).
Gregory of Nazianzus. *Orations 24–26*. In *Grégoire de Nazianze. Discours 24–26*. Edited and Translated by J. Mossay. SC 284 (1981).
Gregory of Nazianzus. *Orations 27–31*. In *Grégoire de Nazianze. Discours 27–31*. Edited and Translated by P. Gallay. SC 250 (1978).
Gregory of Nazianzus. *Orations 27–31*. In *Faith Gives Fullness to Reasoning: The Five Theological Orations of Gregory of Nazianzus*. Edited by F. Norris. Translated by L. Wickham and F. Williams. VCS 13. Leiden: Brill, 1991.

Gregory of Nazianzus. *Orations 32–37*. In *Grégoire de Nazianze. Discours 32–37*. Edited and Translated by P. Gallay and C. Moreschini. SC 318 (1985).
Gregory of Nazianzus. *Oration 33*. In *S. Cyril of Jerusalem. S. Gregory Nazianzen*. Translated by C. G. Browne and J. E. Swallow. NPNF II: 7 (1893; reprint 2004).
Gregory of Nazianzus. *Orations 38–41*. In *Grégoire de Nazianze. Discours 38–41*. Edited and Translated by C. Moreschini and P. Gallay. SC 358 (1990).
Gregory of Nazianzus. *Orations 42–43*. In *Grégoire de Nazianze. Discours 42–43*. Edited and Translated by J. Bernardi. SC 384 (1992).
Gregory of Nazianzus. *Poems*. In *St Gregory of Nazianzus. Poemata Arcana*. Translated by C. Moreschini and D. A. Sykes. Oxford: Clarendon, 1997.
Gregory of Nyssa *Against Eunomius Book 1*. GNO 1.1 (1960); *Contra Eunomium I*. Translated by S. G. Hall. Edited by M. Brugarolas. VCS 148. Leiden: Brill, 2018; and *Select Writings and Letters of Gregory, Bishop of Nyssa*. Translated by W. Moore, H. C. Ogle, and H. A. Wilson. NPNF II: 5 (1893; reprint 1994).
Gregory of Nyssa. *Against Eunomius Book 2*. GNO 2.2 *(1960); Gregory of Nyssa: Contra Eunomium II: An English Version with Supporting Studies. Proceedings of the 10th International Colloquium on Gregory of Nyssa (Olomouc, September 15–18, 2004)*. Translated by S. G. Hall. Edited by L. Karfiková, S. Douglass, and J. Zachhuber. VCS 82 Leiden: Brill, 2007.
Gregory of Nyssa. *The Deity of the Son and the Holy Spirit*. PG 46 557.
Gregory of Nyssa. *Encomium on Basil*. In *Encomium of Saint Gregory, Bishop of Nyssa, on his Brother Saint Basil, Archbishop of Cappadocian Caesarea: A Commentary, with a Revised Text, Introduction, and Translation*. Translated by James Stein. Washington: Catholic University of America Press, 1928.
Gregory of Nyssa. *Epistles*. In *Grégoire de Nysse: Lettres*. Edited and Translated by P. Maraval. SC 363 (1990). And *Gregory of Nyssa: The Letters*. Translated by Anna Silvas. VCS 83. Leiden: Brill, 2006.
Gregory of Nyssa. *Homilies on the Song of Songs*. Translated by R. Norris. Atlanta: SBL, 2012.
Gregory of Nyssa. *Homily on the 40 Martyrs*. In *"Let Us Die That We May Live": Greek Homilies on Christian Martyrs from Asia Minor, Palestine and Syria (c. 350–c. 450 AD)*. Edited and Translated by P. Allen, W. Mayer, J. Leemans, and B. Dehandschutter. London: Routledge, 2003.
Gregory of Nyssa. *Life of Gregory Thaumaturgus*. In *Grégoire de Nysse, éloge de Grégoire le thaumaturge, Éloge de Basile*. Edited and Translated by P. Maraval. SC 573 (2014). And *St. Gregory Thaumaturgus: Life and Works*. Translated by M. Slusser. FC (1998).
Gregory of Nyssa. *Life of Macrina*. In *Grégoire de Nysse: vie de sainte Macrine*. SC 178 (1971); *Macrina the Younger: Philosopher of God*. Translated by Anna Silvas. Turnhout: Brepols, 2008; and *Gregory of Nyssa: Ascetical Works*. Translated by V. W. Callahan. FC 58 (1967).
Gregory of Nyssa. *Life of Moses*. In *Grégoire de Nysse: la vie de Moïse*. Edited and Translated by J. Daniélou. SC 1 (1942); and *Gregory of Nyssa: The Life*

of Moses. Translated by A. Malherbe and E. Ferguson. New York: Paulist Press, 1978.

Hermogenes. *On Types of Style*. Translated by C. Wooten. Chapel Hill: University of North Carolina Press, 1987.

Hermogenes. *Progymnasmata*. Text and Translation in G. Kennedy. *Progymnasmata: Greek Textbooks of Prose Composition and Rhetoric*. Atlanta: SBL, 2003.

Herodotus. *Histories*. Translated by A. de Sélincourt. London: Penguin, 2003.

Hesiod. *Theogony. Works and Days. Testimonia*. Edited and Translated by Glenn W. Most. LCL 57 (2018).

Himerius. *Orations*. In *Man and the Word: The Orations of Himerius*. Translated by R. Penella. Berkeley: University of California Press, 2007.

Hippocrates. *Ancient Medicine. Airs, Waters, Places. Epidemics 1 and 3. The Oath. Precepts. Nutriment*. Translated by W. H. S. Jones. LCL 147 (1923).

Homer. *Iliad*. Translated by S. Lombardo. Indianapolis: Hackett, 1997.

Homer. *Odyssey*. Translated by S. Lombardo. Indianapolis: Hackett, 2000.

John Chrysostom. *Homily on the 40 Martyrs*. In *"Let Us Die That We May Live": Greek Homilies on Christian Martyrs from Asia Minor, Palestine and Syria (c. 350–c. 450 AD)*. Edited and Translated by P. Allen, W. Mayer, J. Leemans, and B. Dehandschutter. London: Routledge, 2003.

Julian. *Epistles*. In *Julian: Letters. Epigrams. Against the Galilaeans. Fragments*. Translated by W. C. Wright. LCL 157 (1923) and in S. Stowers. *Letter-Writing in Greco-Roman Antiquity*. Philadelphia: Westminster, 1986.

Julius Victor. *Art of Rhetoric*. In Malherbe. AET (1988).

Libanius. *Autobiography*. In *Libanius: Autobiography and Selected Letters, Volume I*. Translated by A. F. Norman. LCL 478 (1992).

Libanius. *Epistles*. In *Libanii Opera*, Vols. 10–11. Edited by R. Foerster. Leipzig: Teubner, 1921–1922; *Libanius. Autobiography and Selected Letters, Volume I: Autobiography. Letters 1–50 and Volume II: Letters 51–193*. Edited and Translated by A. F. Norman. LCL 478 and 479 (1992); and *Selected Letters of Libanius from the Age of Constantius and Julian*. Translated by S. Bradbury. Liverpool: Liverpool University Press, 2004.

Libanius. *Libanii Opera*. 4 Volumes. Edited by R. Foerster. Leipzig: Teubner, 1903–1908.

Libanius. *Libanius's Progymnasmata: Model Exercises in Greek Prose Composition and Rhetoric*. Translated by Craig Gibson. Atlanta: SBL, 2008.

Life and Miracles of Thecla. In *Vie et miracles de Sainte Thècle*. Translated by G. Dagron. Paris: Société des Bollandistes, 1978; and *Acts of Paul and Thecla* in *The Apocryphal New Testament*. Translated by M. R. James. Oxford: Clarendon Press, 1924.

Lucian. *Anacharsis or Athletics*. Translated by A. M. Harmon. LCL 162 (1925).

Lucian. *The Eunuch*. Translated by A. M. Harmon. LCL 302 (1936).

Lucian. *Hermotimus or Concerning the Sects*. Translated by K. Kilburn. LCL 430 (1959).

Lucian. *Lexiphanes*. Translated by A. M. Harmon. LCL 302 (1936).

Lucian. *A Professor of Public Speaking*. Translated by A. M. Harmon. LCL 162 (1925).

Martyrdom of Polycarp. In *Polycarp's Epistle to the Philippians and the Martyrdom of Polycarp: Introduction, Text, and Commentary*. Edited by P. Hartog. Oxford: Oxford University Press, 2013.
Menander Rhetor. *Menander Rhetor: A Commentary*. Translation and Commentary by D. A. Russell and N. G. Wilson. Oxford: Oxford University Press, 1981.
Origen. *The Song of Songs: Commentary and Homilies*. Translated by R. P. Lawson. ACW 26. New York: Newman, 1957.
Palladas. *Poem*. Translated in P. Rosenmeyer, *Ancient Epistolary Fictions: The Letter in Greek Literature*. Cambridge: Cambridge University Press, 2001.
Philo. *On Abraham. On Joseph. On Moses*. Translated by F. H. Colson. LCL 289 (1935).
Philo. *On the Special Laws, Book 4. On the Virtues. On Rewards and Punishments*. Translated by F. H. Colson. LCL 341 (1939).
Philostorgius. *Ecclesiastical History*. In *Philostorgius: Church History*. Translated by P. Amidon. Atlanta: SBL, 2007.
Philostratus. *Lives of the Sophists*. Translated by W. C. Wright. LCL 134 (1921).
Philostratus. *On Letters*. In Malherbe, *AET* (1988).
Pindar. *Olympian Odes*. In *Odes for Victorious Athletes*. Translated by A. P. Burnett. Baltimore: Johns Hopkins University Press, 2010.
Plato. *Euthyphro. Apology. Crito. Phaedo. Phaedrus*. Translated by H. N. Fowler. LCL 36. (1914).
Plato. *Gorgias*. Translated by T. H. Irwin. Oxford: Oxford University Press, 1989.
Plato. *Laches. Protagoras. Meno. Euthydemus*. Translated by W. R. M. Lamb. LCL 165 (1924).
Plato. *Laws, Volume II: Books 7–12*. Translated by R. G. Bury. LCL 192 (1926).
Plato. *Lysis. Symposium. Gorgias*. Translated by W. R. M. Lamb. LCL 166 (1925).
Plato. *Republic, Volume I: Books 1–5*. Edited and Translated by C. Emlyn-Jones and W. Preddy. LCL 237 (2013).
Plato. *Republic, Volume II: Books 6–10*. Edited and Translated by C. Emlyn-Jones, W. Preddy. LCL 276 (2013).
Plato. *Theaetetus. Sophist*. Translated by H. N. Fowler. LCL 123 (1921).
Plato. *Timaeus*. Translated by D. Zeyl. Indianapolis: Hackett, 2000.
Plotinus. *Enneads*. Translated by S. MacKenna. New York: Larson, 1992. And *Ennead, Volume I: Porphyry on the Life of Plotinus. Ennead I*. Translated by A. H. Armstrong. LCL 440 (1969).
Plutarch. *Lives, Volume III: Pericles and Fabius Maximus*. Translated by B. Perrin. LCL 65 (1916).
Plutarch. *Lives, Volume VII: Demosthenes and Cicero. Alexander and Caesar*. Translated by B. Perrin. LCL 99 (1919).
Plutarch. *Moralia*, 16 Volumes. Translated by F. Babbitt. LCL 197, 222, 245, 305, 306, 321, 337, 405, 406, 424–429, 470, 499 (1927–1976).
Polemon. *Physiognomy*. In *Seeing the Face, Seeing the Soul: Polemon's Physiognomy from Classical Antiquity to Medieval Islam*. Edited by S. Swain. Translated by R. Hoyland. Oxford: Oxford University Press, 2007.

Porphyry. *Life of Pythagoras.* In *Porphyrii philosophi Platonici opuscula selecta.* Edited by A. Nauck. Leipzig: Teubner, 1886.
Porphyry. *On Abstinence from Killing Animals.* Translated by G. Clark. New York: Bloomsbury, 2014.
Pseudo-Aristotle. *Physiognomics.* In *Aristotle: Minor Works.* Translated by W. S. Hett. LCL 307 (1936).
Pseudo-Athanasius. *Life of Syncletica.* In *The Life and Regimen of the Blessed and Holy Syncletica, Part One: The Translation.* Translated by E. B. Bongie. Eugene: Wipf and Stock, 2005.
Pseudo-Demetrius. *Epistolary Types.* In Malherbe, *AET* (1988).
Pseudo-Libanius. *Epistolary Styles.* In Malherbe, *AET* (1988).
Seneca. *Moral Epistles.* In Malherbe, *AET* (1988).
Themistius. *Politics, Philosophy, and Empire in the Fourth Century: Select Orations of Themistius.* Translated by P. Heather and D. Moncur. Liverpool: Liverpool University Press, 2001.
Themistius. *Themistii orationes quae supersunt.* Edited by G. Downey and H. Schenkl. Leipzig: Teubner, 1965.
Theodoret. *Ecclesiastical History.* In *Theodoret, Jerome, Gennadius, Rufinus: Historical Writings, Etc.* Translated by B. Jackson. NPNF 3 (1892; reprinted 1989).
Thucydides. *History of the Peloponnesian War.* Translated by S. Lattimore. Indianapolis: Hackett, 1998.
Xenophon. *Hiero. Agesilaus. Constitution of the Lacedaemonians. Ways and Means. Cavalry Commander. Art of Horsemanship. On Hunting. Constitution of the Athenians.* Translated by E. C. Marchant and G. W. Bowersock. LCL 183 (1925).
Xenophon. *Memorabilia. Oeconomicus. Symposium. Apology.* Translated by E. C. Marchant, O. J. Todd. Revised by J. Henderson. LCL 168 (2013).
Xenophon of Ephesus. *Ephesian Tale.* In "Xenophon of Ephesus: An Ephesian Tale." Translated by G. Anderson. In *Collected Ancient Greek Novels.* Edited by B. P. Reardon. Berkeley: University of California Press, 1989.

SECONDARY SOURCES

Abramowski, Luise. "Das Bekenntnis des Gregor Thaumaturgos bei Gregor von Nyssa und das Problem seiner Echtheit." ZK 87 (1976): 145–66.
Agapitos, Panagiotis. "Ancient Models and Novel Mixtures: The Concept of Genre in Byzantine Funerary Literature from Photios to Eustathios of Thessalonike." In *Modern Greek Literature: Critical Essays.* Edited by Gregory Nagy and Anna Stavrakopoulou. New York: Routledge, 2003: 5–23.
Alcock, Susan. *Archaeologies of the Greek Past: Landscape, Monuments, and Memories.* Cambridge: Cambridge University Press, 2002.
Alexandre, Monique. "Les Nouveaux Martyrs: motifs martyrologiques dans la vie des saints et thèmes hagiographiques dans l'éloge des martyrs chez Grégoire de Nysse." In *The Biographical Works of Gregory of Nyssa.*

Edited by Andreas Spira. Philadelphia: Philadelphia Patristic Foundation, 1984: 33–70.
Allen, Pauline and Bronwen Neil. *Greek and Latin Letters in Late Antiquity: The Christianisation of a Literary Form*. Cambridge: Cambridge University Press, 2020.
Amato, Eugenio, ed. *Approches de la troisième sophistique: hommages à Jacques Schamp*. Brussels: Peeters, 2006.
Anatolios, Khaled. *Athanasius: The Coherence of his Thought*. New York: Routledge, 1998.
Anatolios, Khaled. *Retrieving Nicaea: The Development and Meaning of Trinitarian Doctrine*. Grand Rapids: Eerdmans, 2011.
Anderson, Graham. "Lucian's Classics: Some Short Cuts to Culture." *Bulletin of the Institute of Classical Studies* 23 (1976): 59–68.
Anderson, Graham. *The Second Sophistic: A Cultural Phenomenon in the Roman Empire*. New York: Routledge, 1993.
Anderson, Graham. "Xenophon of Ephesus: An Ephesian Tale." In *Collected Ancient Greek Novels*. Edited by B. P. Reardon. Berkeley: University of California Press, 1989: 125–69.
Anderson, John K. *Ancient Greek Horsemanship*. Berkeley: University of California Press, 1961.
André, Jean Marie. *L'Otium dans la vie morale et intellectuelle romaine des origines à l'époque augustéenne*. Paris: Presses Universitaires de France, 1966.
Angenendt, Arnold. "Mit reinen Händen: Das Motiv der kultischen Reinheit in abendländische Askese." In *Herrschaft, Kirche, Kultur: Beoträge zur Geschichte des Mittelalters – Festschrift für Friedrich Prinz zu seinem 65 Geburtstag*. Edited by Georg Jenal. Stuttgart: Hiersemann, 1993: 296–316.
Apostolopoulos, Charalambos. *Phaedo Christianus: Studien zur Verbindung und Abwägung des Verhältnisses zwischen dem platonischen "Phaidon" und dem Dialog Gregors von Nyssa "Über die Seele und die Auferstehung."* Frankfurt: Peter Lang, 1986.
Appadurai, Arjun, ed. *The Social Life of Things: Commodities in Cultural Perspective*. Cambridge: Cambridge University Press, 1986.
Ashanin, Charles. "Christian Humanism of the Cappadocian Fathers." *Patristic and Byzantine Review* 6:1 (1987): 44–52.
Athanassiadi-Fowden, Polymnia. *Julian and Hellenism: An Intellectual Biography*. Oxford: Clarendon Press, 1981.
Austin, Norman. "Hellenismos." *Arion: A Journal of Humanities and the Classics* 20:1 (2012): 5–36.
Ayres, Lewis. *Nicaea and its Legacy: An Approach to Fourth-Century Trinitarian Theology*. Oxford: Oxford University Press, 2004.
Ayres, Lewis, ed. *The Passionate Intellect: Essays on the Transformation of Classical Traditions*. Princeton, NJ: Transaction Publishers, 1995.
Bagnall, Roger, ed. *The Oxford Handbook of Papyrology*. Oxford: Oxford University Press, 2009.
Bagnall, Roger. *Reading Papyri, Writing Ancient History*. London: Routledge, 1995.

Balás, David. Μετουσια Θεου: *Man's Participation in God's Perfections according to Saint Gregory of Nyssa*. Rome: Herder, 1966.
Balot, Ryan. *Courage in the Democratic Polis: Ideology and Critique in Classical Athens*. Oxford: Oxford University Press, 2014.
Banchich, Thomas. "Julian's School Laws: *Cod. Theod.* 13.3.5 and *Ep.* 42." *Ancient World* 24 (1993): 5–14.
Bardy, Gustave. "'Philosophie' et 'philosophe' dans le vocabulaire chrétien des premiers siècles." *Revue d'ascétique et de mystique* 25 (1949): 97–108.
Barnes, Michel. "Eunomius of Cyzicus and Gregory of Nyssa: Two Traditions of Transcendent Causality." *VC* 52 (1998): 59–87.
Barnes, Michel and Daniel Williams, eds. *Arianism after Arius: Essays on the Development of the Fourth Century Trinitarian Conflicts*. Edinburgh: T&T Clark, 1993.
Barnes, Timothy. *Athanasius and Constantius: Theology and Politics in the Constantinian Empire*. Cambridge, MA: Harvard University Press, 2001.
Barnes, Timothy. "The Date of the Council of Gangra." *JTS* 40:1 (1989): 121–4.
Barnes, Timothy. "Himerius and the Fourth Century." *CP* 82 (1987): 206–25.
Barrett, Richard. "Sensory Experience and the Women Martyrs of Najran," *JECS* 21:1 (2013): 93–109.
Bartin, Carlin. "Being in the Eyes: Shame and Sight in Ancient Rome." In *The Roman Gaze: Vision, Power, and the Body*. Edited by David Fredrick. Baltimore: Johns Hopkins University Press, 2002: 216–35.
Barton, Tamsyn. *Power and Knowledge: Astrology, Physiognomics and Medicine under the Roman Empire*. Ann Arbor: University of Michigan Press, 1995.
Bassi, Karen. *Acting Like Men: Gender, Drama and Nostalgia in Ancient Greece*. Ann Arbor: University of Michigan Press, 1998.
Bassi, Karen. "The Semantics of Manliness in Ancient Greece." In *Andreia: Studies in Manliness and Courage in Classical Antiquity*. Edited by Ralph Rosen and Ineke Sluiter. Leiden: Brill, 2003: 25–58.
Bastiaensen, A., A. Hilhorst, and C. Kneepkens, eds. *Fructus Centesimus. Melanges offerts a G.J.M. Bartelink à l'occasion de son soixante-cinquieme anniversaire*. Dordrecht: Brepols, 1989.
Beagon, Philip. "The Cappadocian Fathers, Women and Ecclesiastical Politics." *VC* 49 (1995): 165–79.
Beagon, Philip. "Some Cultural Contacts of St. Basil at Antioch." *SP* 32 (1996): 67–71.
Beeley, Christopher. *Gregory of Nazianzus on the Trinity and Knowledge of God: In Your Light We Shall See Light*. Oxford: Oxford University Press, 2008.
Beeley, Christopher, ed. *Re-Reading Gregory of Nazianzus: Essays on History, Theology, and Culture*. Washington, DC: Catholic University of America Press, 2012.
Beeley, Christopher. *The Unity of Christ: Continuity and Conflict in Patristic Tradition*. New Haven: Yale University Press, 2012.
Behr, John. *The Nicene Faith, Part Two, Formation of Christian Theology*. 2 Vols. Crestwood, NY: St. Vladimir's Seminary, 2004.
Belfiore, Elizabeth. *Tragic Pleasures: Aristotle on Plot and Emotion*. Princeton: Princeton University Press, 1992.

Benestad, Brian, ed. *Ernest L. Fortin: Collected Essays*. Lanham, MD: Rowman and Littlefield, 1996.

Bérenger Agnès. "L'Adventus des gouverneurs de province." In *Les Entrées royales et impériales: histoire, représentation et diffusion d'une cérémonie publique, de l'Orient ancien à Byzance*. Edited by Agnès Bérenger and Éric Perrin-Saminadayar. Paris: de Boccard, 2009.

Bérenger Agnès and Éric Perrin-Saminadayar, eds. *Les Entrées royales et impériales: histoire, représentation et diffusion d'une cérémonie publique, de l'Orient ancien à Byzance*. Paris: de Boccard, 2009.

Bernardi, Jean. "Nouvelles perspectives sur la famille de Grégoire de Nazianze." *VC* 38 (1984): 352–9.

Bernardi, Jean. *La Prédication des pères cappadociens: le prédicateur et son auditoire*. Marseille: Presses universitaires de France, 1968.

Bernardi, Jean. *Saint Grégoire de Nazianze: le théologien et son temps*. Paris: Cerf, 1995.

Bloomer, W. Martin. "Schooling in Persona: Imagination and Subordination in Roman Education." *Classical Antiquity* 16 (1997): 57–78.

Blowers, Paul. "Maximus the Confessor, Gregory of Nyssa, and the Concept of 'Perpetual Progress.'" *VC* 46 (1992): 151–71.

Boeft, J. Den and A. Hiljhorst, eds. *Early Christian Poetry: A Collection of Essays*. Leiden: Brill, 1993.

Boegehold, Alan. *When a Gesture Was Expected: A Selection of Examples from Archaic and Classical Greek Literature*. Princeton: Princeton University Press, 1999.

Boersma, Hans. *Embodiment and Virtue in Gregory of Nyssa: An Anagogical Approach*. Oxford: Oxford University Press, 2013.

Borg, Barbara, ed. *Paideia: The World of the Second Sophistic*. Berlin: de Gruyter, 2004.

Børtnes, Jostein and Tomas Hägg, eds. *Gregory of Nazianzus: Images and Reflections*. Copenhagen: Museum Tusculanum, 2006.

Børtnes, Jostein. "Eros Transformed: Same-Sex Love and Divine Desire: Reflections on the Erotic Vocabulary in St. Gregory of Nazianzus's Speech on St. Basil the Great." In *Greek Biography and Panegyric in Late Antiquity*. Edited by Thomas Hägg and Philip Rousseau. Berkeley: University of California Press, 2000: 180–93.

Børtnes, Jostein. "Rhetoric and Mental Images in Gregory." In *Gregory of Nazianzus: Images and Reflections*. Edited by Jostein Børtnes and Tomas Hägg. Copenhagen: Museum Tusculanum, 2006: 37–57.

Bouffartigue, Jean. *L'Empereur Julien et la culture de son temps*. Paris: Institut d'Études Augustiniennes, 1992.

Bourdieu, Pierre. *Ce que parler veut dire: l'économie des échanges linguistiques*. Paris: Librairie Arthème Fayard, 1982.

Bourdieu, Pierre. *The Field of Cultural Production: Essays on Art and Literature*. Edited and Introduced by Randal Johnson. New York: Columbia University Press, 1993.

Bourdieu, Pierre. *Language and Symbolic Power*. Edited and Introduction by John B. Thompson. Translated by Gino Raymond and Matthew Adamson. Cambridge, MA: Harvard University Press, 1991.

Bowersock, Glen W. *Greek Sophists in the Roman Empire*. Oxford: Oxford University Press, 1969.
Bowersock, Glen W. *Julian the Apostate*. Cambridge: Harvard University Press, 1978.
Bowersock, Glen W. *Hellenism in Late Antiquity*. Cambridge: Cambridge University Press, 1990.
Bowersock, Glen W. *Martyrdom and Rome*. Cambridge: Cambridge University Press, 1995.
Boyarin, Daniel. *Dying for God: Martyrdom and the Making of Christianity and Judaism*. Stanford: Stanford University Press, 1999.
Brakke, David. *Athanasius and the Politics of Asceticism*. Baltimore: Johns Hopkins University Press, 1995.
Brakke, David. *Demons and the Making of the Monk: Spiritual Combat in Early Christianity*. Cambridge, MA: Harvard University Press, 2006.
Brakke, David. "Lady Appears: Materializations of 'Woman' in Early Monastic Literature." In *The Cultural Turn in Late Antique Studies*. Edited by Dale Martin and Patricia Cox Miller. Durham, NC: Duke University Press, 2005: 25–39.
Brennecke, Hanns Christof. *Studien zur Geschichte der Homöer: Der Osten bis zum Ende der Homöischen Reichskirche*. Tübingen: 1988.
Brown, Adam. "Homeric Talents and the Ethics of Exchange." *Journal of Hellenic Studies* 118 (1998): 165–72.
Brown, Christopher. "Pindar on Archilochus and the Gluttony of Blame (Pyth. 2.52–6)." *Journal of Hellenic Studies* 126 (2006): 36–46.
Brown, Frank B. *Religious Aesthetics: A Theological Study of Making and Meaning*. Princeton: Princeton University Press, 1989.
Brown, Peter. *The Body and Society: Men, Women, and Sexual Renunciation in Early Christianity*. New York: Columbia University Press, 1988.
Brown, Peter. "Enjoying the Saints in Late Antiquity." *Early Medieval Europe* 9:1 (2000): 1–24.
Brown, Peter. *Poverty and Leadership in the Later Roman Empire (The Menahem Stern Jerusalem Lectures)*. Waltham, MA: Brandeis University Press, 2001.
Brown, Peter. *Power and Persuasion in Late Antiquity: Towards a Christian Empire*. Madison: University of Wisconsin Press, 1992.
Brown, Peter. "The Rise and Function of the Holy Man in Late Antiquity." In Peter Brown, *Society and the Holy in Late Antiquity*. London: Faber & Faber, 1982: 103–52.
Brown, Peter. *Through the Eye of a Needle: Wealth, the Fall of Rome, and the Making of Christianity in the West, 350–550 AD*. Princeton: Princeton University Press, 2012.
Browning, Robert. *The Emperor Julian*. Berkeley: University of California Press, 1976.
Brubaker, Leslie and Shaun Tougher, eds. *Approaches to the Byzantine Family*. Farnham: Ashgate, 2013.
Brubaker, Leslie. *Vision and Meaning in Ninth-Century Byzantium: Image as Exegesis in the Homilies of Gregory of Nazianzus*. Cambridge: Cambridge University Press, 1999.

Burrus, Virginia. *"Begotten, Not Made": Conceiving Manhood in Late Antiquity.* Stanford, CA: Stanford University Press, 2000.
Burrus, Virginia. "Life after Death: The Martyrdom of Gorgonia and the Birth of Female Hagiography." In *Gregory of Nazianzus: Images and Reflections.* Edited by Jostein Børtnes and Tomas Hägg. Copenhagen: Museum Tusculanum, 2006: 153–70.
Burrus, Virginia. "Macrina's Tatoo." In *The Cultural Turn in Late Antique Studies.* Edited by Dale Martin and Patricia Cox Miller. Durham, NC: Duke University Press, 2005: 103–16.
Burrus, Virginia. "Rhetorical Stereotypes in the Portrait of Paul of Samosata." VC 43 (1989): 215–25.
Burrus, Virginia. *The Sex Lives of Saints: An Erotics of Ancient Hagiography.* Philadelphia: University of Pennsylvania Press, 2008.
Butler, Judith. *Gender Trouble: Feminism and the Subversion of Identity.* New York: Routledge, 1990.
Bynum, Caroline Walker. *Jesus as Mother: Studies in the Spirituality of the High Middle Ages.* Berkeley: University of California Press, 1982.
Cadenhead, Raphael. *The Body and Desire: Gregory of Nyssa's Ascetical Theology.* Oakland: University of California Press, 2018.
Calvet-Sebasti, Marie-Ange. "Comment écrire à païen: l'exemple de Gregoire de Nazianze et de Théodoret de Cyr." In *Les Apologists chrétiens et la culture grecque.* Edited by Bernard Pouderon and Joseph Doré. Paris: Beauchesne, 1998: 369–81.
Calvet-Sebasti, Marie-Ange. *Grégoire de Nazianze, théoricien de la lettre. Actes du Colloque sur les lettres dans la Bible et la littérature (3–5 juillet 1996).* Edited by Louis Panier. Lyon: Les Éditions du Cerf, 1999.
Cameron, Averil. "Christianity and Communication in the Fourth Century: The Problem of Diffusion." *Aspects of the Fourth Century A.D.: proceedings of the symposium "power and possession: state, society, and church in the fourth century A.D."* Edited by Henri Pleket and Arthur Verhoogt. Leiden: Brill, 1997.
Cameron, Averil. *Christianity and the Rhetoric of Empire: The Development of Christian Discourse.* Berkeley: University of California Press, 1991.
Cardman, Francine. "Whose Life is It? The *Vita Macrinae* of Gregory of Nyssa." SP 37 (2001): 33–50.
Carey, Chris. "Pindar and the Victory Ode." In *The Passionate Intellect: Essays on the Transformation of Classical Traditions.* Edited by Lewis Ayres. Princeton: Transaction Publishers, 1995: 85–101.
Carruthers, Mary. *The Craft of Thought: Meditation, Rhetoric, and the Making of Images, 400–1200.* Cambridge: Cambridge University Press, 1998.
Cassia, Margherita. *Cappadocia romana: strutture urbane e strutture agrarie alla periferia dell'impero.* Catania: Edizioni del Prisma, 2004.
Castelli, Elizabeth. *Martyrdom and Memory: Early Christian Culture Making.* New York: Columbia University Press, 2004.
Cavallo, Guglielmo. "Greek and Latin Writing in the Papryi." In *The Oxford Handbook of Papyrology.* Edited by Roger Bagnall. Oxford: Oxford University Press, 2009: 101–48.

Cavallo, Guglielmo, Giuseppe de Gregorio, and Marilena Maniaci, eds. *Scritture, libri e testi nelle aree provinciali di Bisanzio: atti del seminario di Erice (18-25 settembre 1988)*. Spoleto: Centro italiano di studi sull'alto Medioveco, 1991.

Cavallo, Guglielmo and Herwig Maehler. *Greek Bookhands of the Early Byzantine Period A.D. 300-800*. London: University of London Institute of Classical Studies, 1987.

Chin, Catherine. *Grammar and Christianity in the Late Roman World*. Philadelphia: University of Pennsylvania Press, 2007.

Christol, Michel, Ségolène Demougin, Yvette Duval, Claude Lepelley and Luce Pietri, eds. *Institutions, société et vie politique dans l'empire romain au IVe siècle ap. J.-C. Actes de la table ronde autour de l'œuvre d'André Chastagnol (Paris, 20-21 janvier 1989)*. Rome: École française de Rome, 1992.

Cixous, Hélène. "Sorties: Out and Out: Attacks/Ways Out/Forays." In *The Newly Born Woman*. Edited by Hélène Cixous and Catherine Clement. Translated by Betsy King. Minneapolis: University of Minnesota Press, 1986: 63-134.

Cixous, Hélène and Catherine Clement, eds. *The Newly Born Woman*. Translated by Betsy King. Minneapolis: University of Minnesota Press, 1986.

Clark, Elizabeth. "Holy Women, Holy Words: Early Christian Women, Social History and the 'Linguistic Turn.'" *JECS* 6:3 (1998): 413-30.

Clark, Elizabeth. "A Lady Vanishes: Dilemmas of a Feminist Historian after the 'Linguistic Turn.'" *CH* 67 (1998): 1-31.

Clark, Elizabeth. *Reading Renunciation: Asceticism and Scripture in Early Christianity*. Princeton: Princeton University Press, 1999.

Clark, Elizabeth. "Women, Gender, and the Study of Christian History." *CH* 70 (2001): 395-426.

Clark, Gillian. "The Old Adam: The Fathers and the Unmaking of Masculinity." In *Thinking Men: Masculinity and its Self-Representation in the Classical Tradition*. Edited by Lin Foxhall and John Salmon. London: Routledge, 2011: 170-82.

Clark, Gillian. *Women in Late Antiquity: Pagan and Christian Life-styles*. Oxford: Clarendon Press, 1993.

Coakley, Sarah. "Gregory of Nyssa." In *The Spiritual Senses: Perceiving God in Western Christianity*. Edited by Paul Gavrilyuk and Sarah Coakley. Cambridge: Cambridge University Press, 2012: 36-55.

Coakley, Sarah, ed. *Re-thinking Gregory of Nyssa*. Boston: Blackwell, 2003.

Cobb, L. Stephanie. *Dying to Be Men: Gender and Language in Early Christian Martyr Texts*. New York: Columbia University Press, 2008.

Connell, Raewyn. *Masculinities*. Cambridge: Polity, 1995.

Connolly, Joy. "Like the Labor of Heracles: *Andreia* and *Paideia* in Greek Culture Under Rome." In *Andreia: Studies in Manliness and Courage in Classical Antiquity*. Edited by Ralph Rosen and Ineke Sluiter. Leiden: Brill, 2003: 287-317.

Conring, Barbara. *Hieronymus als Briefschreiber: Ein Beitrag zur spätantiken Epistolgraphie*. Tübingen: Mohr Siebeck, 2001.

Constable, Giles. *Letters and Letter-Collections*. Turnhout: Brepols, 1976.

Conway, Colleen. *Behold the Man: Jesus and Greco-Roman Masculinity*. Oxford Oxford University Press, 2008.
Coon, Lynda. *Dark Age Bodies: Gender and Monastic Practice in the Early Medieval West*. Philadelphia: University of Pennsylvania Press, 2011.
Coon, Lynda. *Sacred Fictions: Holy Women and Hagiography in Late Antiquity*. Philadelphia: University of Pennsylvania Press, 1997.
Cooper, J. Eric, and Michael Decker. *Life and Society in Byzantine Cappadocia*. New York: Palgrave Macmillan, 2012.
Cooper, Kate. "Insinuations of Womanly Influence: An Aspect of the Christianization of the Roman Aristocracy." *Journal of Roman Studies* 82 (1991): 150–64.
Cooper, Kate. *The Virgin and the Bride: Idealized Womanhood in Late Antiquity*. Cambridge, MA: Harvard University Press, 1999.
Corbeill, Anthony. *Nature Embodied: Gesture in Ancient Rome*. Princeton: Princeton University Press, 2003.
Corrigan, Kevin. *Evagrius and Gregory: Mind, Soul and Body in the 4th Century*. Farnham: Ashgate, 2009.
Cribiore, Raffaella. *Gymnastics of the Mind: Greek Education in Hellenistic and Roman Egypt*. Princeton: Princeton University Press, 2005.
Cribiore, Raffaella. *Libanius the Sophist: Rhetoric, Reality, and Religion in the Fourth Century*. Ithaca: Cornell University Press, 2013.
Cribiore, Raffaella. *The School of Libanius in Late Antique Antioch*. Princeton: Princeton University Press, 2007.
Cribiore, Raffaella. "Vying with Aristides in the Fourth Century." In *Aelius Aristides between Greece, Rome, and the Gods*. Edited by William Harris and Brooke Holmes. Leiden: Brill, 2009: 263–78.
Crislip, Andrew. *Thorns in the Flesh: Illness and Sanctity in Late Ancient Christianity*. Philadelphia: University of Pennsylvania Press, 2013.
Cross, Frank, ed. *The Oxford Dictionary of the Christian Church*. Third edition edited by Elizabeth Livingston. Oxford: Oxford University Press, 2005.
Currie, Bruno. *Pindar and the Cult of Heroes*. Oxford: Oxford University Press, 2005.
Daley, Brian. "Building a New City: The Cappadocian Fathers and the Rhetoric of Philanthropy." *JECS* 7 (1999): 431–61.
Daley, Brian. "Divine Transcendence and Human Transformation: Gregory of Nyssa's Anti- Apollinarian Christology." *SP* 32 (1997), 87–95.
Daley, Brian. *Gregory of Nazianzus*. London: Routledge, 2006.
Daniélou, Jean. "Eunome l'arien et l'exégèse néo-platonicienne du Cratyle." *Revue des Études Grecques* 69 (1956): 412–32.
Daniélou, Jean. "Grégoire de Nysse à travers les lettres de Saint Basile et de Saint Grégoire de Nazianze." *VC* 19 (1965): 31–41.
Daniélou, Jean. *Platonisme et théologie mystique: doctrine spirituelle de Saint Grégoire de Nysse*. Paris: Aubier, 1944.
Davis, Stephen. *The Cult of St. Thecla: A Tradition of Women's Piety in Late Antiquity*. Oxford: Oxford University Press, 2001.
Deissmann, Adolf. *Licht vom Osten: Das Neue Testament und die neuentdeckten texte der hellenistisch-römischen welt*. Tübingen: Mohr Siebeck, 1909.

Dekkers, Eligius. "Les Autographes des pères latins." In *Colligere fragmenta: Festschrift Alban Dodd*. Edited by Bonifatius Fischer and Virgil Fiala. Beuron: Beuroner Kunstverlag, 1952: 127–39.

DelCogliano, Mark. *Basil of Caesarea's Anti-Eunomian Theory of Names: Christian Theology and Late-Antique Philosophy in the Fourth-Century Trinitarian Controversy*. VCS 103. Leiden: Brill, 2010.

DelCogliano, Mark. "The Influence of Athanasius and the Homoiousians on Basil of Caesarea's Decentralization of 'Unbegotten'." *JECS* 19:2 (2011): 197–223.

DelCogliano, Mark and Andrew Radde-Gallwitz. *St. Basil of Caesarea: Against Eunomius*. Washington, DC.: Catholic University of America Press, 2011.

Delehaye, Hippolyte. *The Legends of the Saints*. Translated by Donald Attwater. New York: Fordham University Press, 1962.

Demoen, Kristoffel. *Pagan and Biblical Exempla in Gregory Nazianzen: A Study in Rhetoric and Hermeneutics*. Brepols: Turnhout, 1996.

Dennis, George. "Gregory of Nazianzus and the Byzantine Letter." In *Diakonia: Studies in Honour of Robert T. Meyer*. Edited by Thomas Halton and Joseph Williman. Washington, DC: Catholic University of America Press, 1986: 3–13.

Deslauriers, Marguerite. "Aristotle on *Andreia*, Divine and Sub-Human Virtues." In *Andreia: Studies in Manliness and Courage in Classical Antiquity*. Edited by Ralph Rosen and Ineke Sluiter. Leiden: Brill, 2003: 187–211.

Donlan, Walter. "Political Reciprocity in Dark Age Greece: Odysseus and his Hetairoi." In *Reciprocity in Ancient Greece*. Edited by Christopher Gill, Norman Postlethwaite, and Richard Seaford. Oxford: Oxford University Press, 1998: 51–71.

Donlan, Walter. "Reciprocities in Homer." *Classical World* 75 (1981): 137–75.

Dostálová Ruzena., "Christentum und Hellenismus: Zur Herausbildung einer neuen kulturellen Identität im 4. Jahrhundert." *Byzantinoslavica* 44 (1983): 1–12.

Drake, Harold. *Constantine and the Bishops: The Politics of Intolerance*. Baltimore: Johns Hopkins University Press, 2000.

Drecoll, Volker. *Die Entwicklung der Trinitätslehre des Basilius von Cäsarea: sein Weg vom Homöusianer zum Neonizäner*. Göttingen: Vandenhoeck & Ruprecht, 1996.

Drijvers, Jan and John Watt, eds. *Portraits of Spiritual Authority: Religious Power in Early Christianity, Byzantium and the Christian Orient*. Leiden: Brill, 1999.

Eadie, John and Josiah Ober, eds. *The Craft of the Ancient Historian*. Lanham, MD: University Press of America, 1985.

Ebbeler, Jennifer. *Disciplining Christians: Correction and Community in Augustine's Letters*. Oxford: Oxford University Press, 2012.

Edwards, Mark and Simon Swain, eds. *Portraits: Biographical Representation in the Greek and Latin Literature of the Roman Empire*. Oxford: Clarendon Press, 1997.

Elm, Susanna. "Church-Festival-Temple: Reimagining Civic Topography in Late Antiquity." In *The City in the Classical and Post-Classical World: Changing*

Contexts of Power and Identity. Edited by Claudia Rapp and Harold Drake. Cambridge: Cambridge University Press, 2014: 167–82.

Elm, Susanna. "Family Men: Masculinity and Philosophy in Late Antiquity." In *Transformations of Late Antiquity: Essays for Peter Brown*. Edited by Philip Rousseau and Manolis Papoutsakis. Farnham: Ashgate, 2009: 279–302.

Elm, Susanna. "Gregory of Nazianzus: Mediation between Individual and Community." In *Group Identity and Religious Individuality in Late Antiquity*. Edited by Éric Rebillard and Jörg Rüpke. Washington, DC: Catholic University of America Press, 2015: 89–107.

Elm, Susanna. "Gregory's Women: Creating a Philosopher's Family." In *Gregory of Nazianzus: Images and Reflections*. Edited by Jostein Børtnes and Thomas Hägg. Copenhagen: Museum Tusculanum Press, 2006: 171–91.

Elm, Susanna. "Hellenism and Historiography: Gregory of Nazianzus and Julian in Dialogue." *Journal of Medieval and Early Modern Studies* 33:3 (2003): 493–515.

Elm, Susanna. "A Programmatic Life: Gregory of Nazianzus' Orations 42 and 43 and the Constantinopolitan Elites." *Arethusa* 33:3 (2000): 411–27.

Elm, Susanna. *Sons of Hellenism, Fathers of the Church: Emperor Julian, Gregory of Nazianzus, and the Vision of Rome*. Berkeley: University of California Press, 2012.

Elm, Susanna. *"Virgins of God": The Making of Asceticism in Late Antiquity*. Oxford: Clarendon Press, 1994.

Elsner, Jás. "The Genres of Ekphrasis." *Ramus* 31 (2002): 1–18.

Elsner, Jás. *Imperial Rome and Christian Triumph: The Art of the Roman Empire AD 100–450*. Oxford: Oxford University Press, 1998.

Eshleman, Kendra. *The Social World of Intellectuals in the Roman Empire: Sophists, Philosophers, and Christians*. Cambridge: Cambridge University Press, 2012.

Fedwick, Paul Jonathan, ed. *Basil of Caesarea: Christian, Humanist, Ascetic: A Sixteen-Hundredth Anniversary Symposium*. 2 Vols. Toronto: Pontifical Institute of Mediaeval Studies, 1981.

Fedwick, Paul Jonathan. *Bibliotheca Basiliana Universalis: A Study of the Manuscript Tradition, Translations and Editions of the Works of Basil of Caesarea*. 2 Vols. Brepols: Turnhout, 1993.

Fedwick, Paul Jonathan. "A Chronology of the Life and Works of Basil of Caesarea." In *Basil of Caesarea: Christian, Humanist, Ascetic: A Sixteen-Hundredth Anniversary Symposium* Edited by P. J. Fedwick. 2 Vols. Toronto: Pontifical Institute of Mediaeval Studies, 1981: 13–19.

Festugière, André-Jean. *Antioche païenne et chrétienne*. Paris: de Boccard, 1959.

Finkelberg, Margalit. "Timē and Aretē in Homer." *CQ* 48:1 (1998): 14–28.

Finley, Moses. *The World of Odysseus*. New York: Viking Press, 1954.

Fischer, Bonifatius and Virgil Fiala, eds. *Colligere fragmenta: Festschrift Alban Dodd*. Beuron: Beuroner Kunstverlag, 1952.

Fitzgerald, John, Thomas Olbricht, and L. Michael White, eds. *Early Christianity and Classical Culture: Comparative Studies in Honor of Abraham Malherbe*. Leiden: Brill, 2003.

Fleury, Eugène. *Hellénisme et Christianisme. Saint Grégoire de Nazianze et son temps*. Paris: Beauchesne, 1930.
Flower, Harriet, ed. *The Cambridge Companion to the Roman Republic*. Cambridge: Cambridge University Press, 2004.
Flower, Harriet. "Spectacle and Political Culture in the Republic." In *The Cambridge Companion to the Roman Republic*. Edited by Harriet Flower. Cambridge: Cambridge University Press, 2004: 322–43.
Flower, Richard. *Emperors and Bishops in Late Roman Invective*. Cambridge: Cambridge University Press, 2013.
Fortin, Ernest. "Christianity and Hellenism in Basil the Great's Address ad Adulescentes." In *Ernest L. Fortin: Collected Essays. Vol. 1: The Birth of Philosophic Christianity: Studies in Early Christian and Medieval Thought*. Edited by J. Brian Benestad. Lanham, MD: Rowman and Littlefield, 1996: 137–51.
Fowler, Ryan, ed. *Plato and the Third Sophistic*. Boston: de Gruyter, 2014.
Fox, Robin Lane. *Pagans and Christians*. New York: Alfred A. Knopf, 1987.
Foxhall, Lin and John Salmon, eds. *Thinking Men: Masculinity and its Self-Representation in the Classical Tradition*. London: Routledge, 2011.
Frank, Georgia. "Macrina's Scar: Homeric Allusion and Heroic Identity in Gregory of Nyssa's *Life of Macrina*." *JECS* 8.4 (2000): 511–30.
Frank, Georgia. *The Memory of the Eyes: Pilgrims to Living Saints in Late Antiquity*. Berkeley: University of California Press, 2000.
Frankfurter, David. "Martyrology and the Prurient Gaze." *JECS* 17:2 (2009): 215–46.
Fredal, James. *Rhetorical Actions in Ancient Athens: Persuasive Artistry from Solon to Demosthenes*. Carbondale: Southern Illinois University Press, 2006.
Fredrick, David. "Mapping Penetrability in Late Republican and Early Imperial Rome." In *The Roman Gaze: Vision, Power, and the Body*. Edited by David Fredrick. Baltimore: Johns Hopkins University Press, 2002: 236–64.
Fredrick, David, ed. *The Roman Gaze: Vision, Power, and the Body*. Baltimore: Johns Hopkins University Press, 2002.
Freyburger, Géra amd Laurent Pernot, eds. *Du héros païen au saint chrétien (Strasbourg 1–2 déc. 95)*. Paris: Institut d'études augustiniennes, 1997.
Fruchtman, Diane. "Modeling a Martyrial Worldview: Prudentius' Pedagogical Ekphrasis and Christianization." *JLA* 7:1 (2014): 131–58.
Gaca, Kathy. *The Making of Fornication: Eros, Ethics, and Political Reform in Greek Philosophy and Early Christianity*. Berkeley: University of California Press, 2003.
Gain, Benoît. *L'Église de Cappadoce au IVe siècle d'après la correspondance de Basile de Césarée*. Rome: Pontificium Institutum Orientale, 1985.
Galavaris, George. *The Illustrations of the Liturgical Homilies of Gregory Nazianzenus*. Princeton: Princeton University Press, 1969.
Gamble, Harry. *Books and Readers in the Early Church: A History of Early Christian Texts*. New Haven: Yale University Press, 1995.
Gautier, Francis. "Le Carême de silence de Grégoire de Nazianze: une conversion à la littérature?" *Revue des Études Augustiniennes* 47 (2001): 97–143.

Gautier, Francis. *La Retraite et le sacerdoce chez Grégoire de Nazianze.* Turnhout: Brepols, 2002.

Gavrilyuk, Paul and Sarah Coakley, eds. *The Spiritual Senses: Perceiving God in Western Christianity.* Cambridge: Cambridge University Press, 2012.

Gemeinhardt, Peter, Lieve van Hoof, and Peter van Nuffelen, eds. *Education and Religion in Late Antique Christianity: Reflections, Social Contexts and Genres.* London: Routledge, 2016.

Giannarelli, Elena. "La biografia femminile: temi e problemi." In *La donna nel pensiero cristiana antico.* Edited by Umberto Mattioli. Genoa: Marietti, 1992: 223–45.

Giet, Stanislas. *Les Idées et l'action sociales de Saint Basile.* Paris: Gabalda, 1941.

Giet, Stanislas. "Saint Basile et le concile de Constantinople de 360." *JTS* 6 (1955): 94–99.

Gill, Christopher, Norman Postlethwaite, and Richard Seaford, eds. *Reciprocity in Ancient Greece.* Oxford: Oxford University Press, 1998.

Gleason, Maud. "By Whose Gender Standards (If Anybody's) Was Jesus a Real Man?" In *New Testament Masculinities.* Edited by Stephen Moore and Janice Anderson. Atlanta: SBL, 2003: 325–27.

Gleason, Maud. "Elite Male Identity in the Roman Empire." In *Life, Death, and Entertainment in The Roman Empire.* Edited by David Potter and David Mattingly. Ann Arbor: University of Michigan Press, 1999: 67–84.

Gleason, Maud. *Making Men: Sophists and Self-Presentation in Ancient Rome.* Princeton: Princeton University Press, 1995.

Goehring, James. *Ascetics, Society, and the Desert: Studies in Early Egyptian Monasticism.* Harrisburg: T&T Clark, 1999.

Goldhill, Simon, ed. *Being Greek Under Rome: Cultural Identity, the Second Sophistic and the Development of Empire.* New York: Cambridge University Press, 2001.

Goldhill, Simon. "The Erotic Eye: Visual Stimulation and Cultural Conflict." In *Being Greek Under Rome: Cultural Identity, the Second Sophistic and the Development of Empire.* Edited by Simon Goldhill. New York: Cambridge University Press, 2001: 154–94.

Goldhill, Simon. "Introduction: Setting an Agenda: 'Everything is Greek to the Wise.'" In *Being Greek Under Rome: Cultural Identity, the Second Sophistic and the Development of Empire.* Edited by Simon Goldhill. New York: Cambridge University Press, 2001: 1–25.

Goldhill, Simon. "Rhetoric and the Second Sophistic." In *Cambridge Companion to Ancient Rhetoric.* Edited by Erik Gunderson. Cambridge: Cambridge University Press, 2009: 228–41.

Goody, Jack. *Representations and Contradictions: Ambivalence toward Images, Theatre, Fiction, Relics and Sexuality.* Oxford: Wiley-Blackwell, 1997.

Gray, Allison. *Gregory of Nyssa as Biographer.* Tübingen: Mohr Siebeck, 2001

Graziosi, Barbara and Johannes Haubold. "Homeric Masculinity: HNOREH and ΑΓΗΝΟΡΙΗ." *The Journal of Hellenic Studies* 123 (2003): 60–76.

Gregg, Robert. *Consolation Philosophy: Greek and Christian Paideia in Basil and the Two Gregories.* Washington: Catholic University of America Press, 1975.

Gribomont, Jean. *Saint Basile: évangile et église. Mélanges.* 2 Vols. Bégrolles-en-Mauges: Abbaye de Bellefontaine, 1984.

Guignet, Marcel. *Saint Grégoire de Nazianze et la rhétorique.* Paris: Picard, 1911.

Gunderson, Erik, ed. *Cambridge Companion to Ancient Rhetoric.* Cambridge: Cambridge University Press, 2009.

Gunderson, Erik. *Staging Masculinity: The Rhetoric of Performance in the Roman World.* Ann Arbor: University of Michigan Press, 2000.

Gutzwiller, Kathryn. *A Guide to Hellenistic Literature.* Malden, MA: Blackwell, 2007.

Gwynn, David. *Athanasius of Alexandria: Bishop, Theologian, Ascetic, Father.* Oxford: Oxford University Press, 2012.

Gygax, Marc Domingo and Arjan Zuiderhoek, eds. *Benefactors and the Polis: The Public Gift in the Greek Cities from the Homeric World to Late Antiquity.* Cambridge: Cambridge University Press, 2020.

Hagendahl, Harald. "Die Bedeutung der Stenographie für die spätlateinischen christliche Literatur." In *Jahrbuch für Antike und Christentum* 14 (1971): 24–38.

Hägg, Tomas. *The Art of Biography in Antiquity.* Cambridge: Cambridge University Press, 2012.

Hägg, Tomas. "Playing with Expectations: Gregory's Funeral Orations on his Brother, Sister, and Father." In *Gregory of Nazianzus: Images and Reflections.* Edited by Jostein Børtnes and Tomas Hägg. Copenhagen: Museum Tusculanum Press, 2006: 133–51.

Hägg, Tomas and Philip Rousseau, eds. *Greek Biography and Panegyric in Late Antiquity.* Berkeley: University of California Press, 2000.

Haines-Eitzen, Kim. "Girls Trained in Beautiful Writing: Female Scribes in Roman Antiquity and Early Christianity." *JECS* 6 (1998): 629–46.

Haines-Eitzen, Kim. *Guardians of Letters: Literacy, Power, and Transmitters of Early Christian Literature.* Oxford: Oxford University Press, 2000.

Halton, Thomas and Joseph Williman, eds. *Diakonia: Studies in Honour of Robert T. Meyer.* Washington: Catholic University of America Press, 1986:

Harper, Kyle. *From Shame to Sin: The Christian Transformation of Sexual Morality in Late Antiquity.* Cambridge, MA: Harvard University Press, 2013.

Harris, William. *Ancient Literacy.* Cambridge, MA: Harvard University Press, 1989.

Harris, William and Brooke Holmes, eds. *Aelius Aristides between Greece, Rome, and the Gods.* Leiden: Brill, 2009.

Harrison, Verna. "Male and Female in Cappadocian Theology." *JTS* 41 (1990): 441–71.

Harvey, Susan Ashbrook. *Sensing Salvation: Ancient Christianity and the Olfactory Imagination.* Berkeley: University of California Press, 2006.

Hatlie, Peter. "Redeeming Byzantine Epistolography." *Byzantine and Modern Greek Studies* 20 (1996): 213–48.

Hawhee, Debra. "Agonism and Arete." *Philosophy and Rhetoric* 35.3 (2002): 185–207.

Hawhee, Debra. *Bodily Arts: Rhetoric and Athletics in Ancient Greece.* Austin: University of Texas Press, 2005.

Helleman, Wendy. "Cappadocian Macrina on Lady Wisdom." *SP* 37 (2001): 86–102.

Helleman, Wendy. "Penelope as Lady Philosophy." *Phoenix* 49 (1995): 283–302.
Helmbold, William and Edward O'Neil. *Plutarch's Quotations*. Oxford: American Philological Association, 1959.
Hildebrand, Stephen. "A Reconsideration of the Development of Basil's Trinitarian Theology: The Dating of Ep. 9 and "Contra Eunomium." *VC* 58 (2004): 393–406.
Hildebrand, Stephen. *The Trinitarian Theology of Basil of Caesarea: A Synthesis of Greek Thought and Biblical Truth*. Washington: Catholic University of America Press, 2007.
Hobbs, Angela. *Plato and the Hero: Courage, Manliness and the Impersonal Good*. Cambridge: Cambridge University Press, 2000.
Hodges-Kluck, Stefan. "Religious Education and the Health of the Soul according to Basil of Caesarea and the Emperor Julian." *SP* 81 (2017): 91–107.
Hodkinson, Owen. "Better than Speech: Some Advantages of the Letter in the Second Sophistic." In *Ancient Letters: Classical and Late Antique Epistolography*. Edited by Ruth Morello and A. D. Morrison. Oxford: Oxford University Press, 2007: 283–300.
Holl, Karl. *Amphilochius von Ikonium in seinem Verhältnis zu den großen*. Tübingen: Mohr Siebeck, 1904.
Holman, Susan. "Healing the Social Leper in Gregory of Nyssa's and Gregory of Nazianzus's "περιφιλοπτωχίας." *HTR* 92 (1999): 283–309.
Holman, Susan. *The Hungry are Dying: Beggars and Bishops in Roman Cappadocia*. Oxford: Oxford University Press, 2001.
Holman, Susan. "Taxing Nazianzus: Gregory and the Other Julian." *SP* 37 (2001): 103–9.
Hopkins, Julie, and Elizabeth Dieckmann. *Feministische Christologie: Wie Frauen Heute Von Jesus Reden Können*. Mainz: Matthais-Grünewald Verlag, 1996.
Howard, Nathan. "Epistolary *Agōn* in the Cappadocian Fathers." *SP* 115 (2021): 11–17.
Howard, Nathan. "Gifts Bearing Greekness: Epistles as Cultural Capital in Fourth-Century Cappadocia." *JLA* 6 (2013): 37–59.
Howard, Nathan. "Preserving Family Honour: Gregory of Nyssa's *Life of Macrina* as Theological Polemic." In *Approaches to the Byzantine Family*. Edited by Leslie Brubaker and Shaun Tougher. Farnham: Ashgate, 2013: 91–108.
Howard, Nathan. "Sacred Spectacle in the Biographies of Gorgonia and Macrina." *SP* 91 (2017): 267–74.
Jaeger, Werner. *Paideia: The Ideals of Greek Culture*. Translated by Gilbert Highet. 3 Vols. New York: Oxford University Press, 1945.
Janes, Dominic. *God and Gold in Late Antiquity*. Cambridge: Cambridge University Press, 2011.
Jensen, Robin. *Face to Face: Portraits of the Divine in Early Christianity*. Minneapolis: Fortress, 2004.
Johnson, Aaron. *Religion and Identity in Porphyry of Tyre: The Limits of Hellenism in Late Antiquity*. Cambridge: Cambridge University Press, 2013.
Johnson, Elizabeth. *She Who Is: The Mystery of God in Feminist Theological Discourse*. New York: Crossroad, 1992.

Johnston, Scott, ed. *Greek Literature in Late Antiquity: Dynamism, Didacticism, Classicism*. Aldershot: Ashgate, 2006.

Johnson, Scott. *The Life and Miracles of Thekla: A Literary Study*. Cambridge, MA: Harvard University Press, 2006.

Johnstone, Christopher. *Listening to the Logos: Speech and the Coming of Wisdom in Ancient Greece*. Columbia: University of South Carolina Press, 2009.

Jones, A. H. M. *The Later Roman Empire, 284–602: A Social, Economic, and Administrative Survey*. 3 vols. Oxford: Basil Blackwell, 1964.

Jones, Meriel. *Playing the Man: Performing Masculinities in the Ancient Greek Novel*. Oxford: Oxford University Press, 2012.

Kaldellis, Anthony. *Hellenism in Byzantium: The Transformation of Greek Identity and the Reception of the Classical Tradition*. Cambridge: Cambridge University Press, 2007.

Kannengiesser, Charles, ed. *Politique et Théologie chez Athanase d'Alexandrie*. Paris: Beauchesne, 1974.

Kaster, Robert. *Guardians of Language: The Grammarian and Society in Late Antiquity*. Berkeley: University of California Press, 1988.

Kelly, Christopher. *Ruling the Later Roman Empire*. Cambridge: Cambridge University Press, 2004.

Kennedy, George. *Greek Rhetoric Under Christian Emperors*. Princeton: Princeton University Press, 1983.

Kennedy, George. *A New History of Classical Rhetoric*. Princeton: Princeton University Press, 1994.

Kennedy, George. *Progymnasmata: Greek Textbooks of Prose Composition and Rhetoric*. Atlanta: SBL, 2003.

Kerferd, George. *The Sophistic Movement*. Cambridge: Cambridge University Press, 1981.

Kim, Young. *Epiphanius of Cyprus: Imagining an Orthodox World*. Ann Arbor: University of Michigan Press, 2015.

Kim, Young. "Reading the *Panarion* as Collective Biography: The Heresiarch as Unholy Man." *VC* 64 (2010): 382–413.

Kimball, Paul. "The Third Sophistic: New Approaches and Rhetoric in Late Antiquity." *JLA* 3.2 (2010): 262–3.

Kindstrand, Jan Fredrik. *Homer in der Zweiten Sophistik. Studien zu der Homerlektüre und dem Homerbild bei Dion von Prusa, Maximos von Tyros und Ailios Aristeides*. Stockholm: University of Uppsala Press, 1973.

Klauck, Hans-Josef and Daniel Bailey. *Ancient Letters and the New Testament: A Guide to Content and Exegesis*. Waco, TX: Baylor University Press, 2006.

Klingshirn, William and Linda Safran, eds. *The Early Christian Book*. Washington: Catholic University of America Press, 2008.

Klock, Christoph. *Untersuchungen zu Stil und Rhythmus bei Gregor von Nyssa: Ein Beitrag zum Rhetorikverstandnis der griechischen Väter*. Frankfurt a. Main: Athenaeum Verlag, 1987.

König, Jason. *Athletics and Literature in the Roman Empire*. Cambridge: Cambridge University Press, 2005.

Konstan, David. *Beauty: The Fortunes of an Ancient Greek Idea*. Oxford: Oxford University Press, 2014.

Konstan, David. "Le Courage dans le roman grec: de Chariton à Xénophon d'Ephèse, avec une reference à Philon d'Alexandrie." In *Passions, vertus et vices dans l'ancien roman*. Edited by Bernard Pouderon and Cécile Bost-Pouderon. Lyon: Maison de l'Orient Méditerranéen, 2009: 117–26.

Konstan David. *Friendship in the Classical World*. Cambridge: Cambridge University Press, 1997.

Konstan, David. "How to Praise a Friend: St. Gregory of Nazianzus's Funeral Oration for St. Basil the Great." In *Greek Biography and Panegyric in Late Antiquity*. Edited by Thomas Hägg and Philip Rousseau. Berkeley: University of California Press, 2000: 160–79.

Konstan, David. "Patrons and Friends." *CP* 4 (1995): 328–42.

Konstan, David. "Problems in the History of Christian Friendship." *JECS* 4:1 (1996): 82–113.

Konstan, David. "Reciprocity and Friendship." In *Reciprocity in Ancient Greece*. Edited by Christopher Gill, Norman Postlethwaite, and Richard Seaford. Oxford: Oxford University Press, 1998: 279–301.

Kopecek, Thomas. "The Cappadocian Fathers and Civic Patriotism." *CH* 43 (1974): 293–303.

Kopecek, Thomas. *A History of Neo-Arianism*. 2 Vols. Cambridge, MA: Philadelphia Patristic Foundation, 1979.

Kopytoff, Igor. "The Cultural Biography of Things: Commoditization as Process." In *The Social Life of Things: Commodities in Cultural Perspective*. Edited by Arjun Appadurai. Cambridge: Cambridge University Press, 1986: 64–92.

Korom, Frank, ed. *The Anthropology of Performance: A Reader*. Boston: Wiley-Blackwell, 2013.

Koskenniemi, Heikki. *Studien zur Idee und Phraseologie des greichischen Briefes bis 400 n. Chr*. Helsinki: Suomalainen Tiedeakatemia, 1956.

Krueger, Derek. *Writing and Holiness: The Practice of Authorship in the Early Christian East*. Philadelphia: University of Pennsylvania Press, 2004.

Krueger, Derek. "Writing and the Liturgy of Memory in Gregory of Nyssa's *Life of Macrina*." *JECS* 8:4 (2000): 483–510.

Kube, Jörg. *TEXNH und APETH: Sophistisches und platonisches Tugendwissen*. Berlin: de Gruyter, 1969.

Kuefler, Mathew. *The Manly Eunuch: Masculinity, Gender Ambiguity, and Christian Ideology in Late Antiquity*. Chicago: University of Chicago Press, 2001.

Kurke, Leslie. *The Traffic in Praise: Pindar and the Poetics of Social Economy*. Ithaca: Cornell University Press, 1991.

Laird, Martin. "Gregory of Nyssa and Divinization: A Reconsideration." *SP* 47 (2010): 33–38.

Laird, Martin. *Gregory of Nyssa and the Grasp of Faith: Union, Knowledge, and Divine Presence*. Oxford: Oxford University Press, 2004.

LaMarre, Thomas. *Uncovering Heian Japan: An Archaeology of Sensation and Inscription*. Durham, NC: Duke University Press, 2000.

Larmour, David. *Stage and Stadium: Drama and Athletics in Ancient Greece*. Hildesheim: Weidmann, 1999.

Laniado, Avshalom. *Recherches sur les notables municipaux dans l'empire protobyzantin*. Paris: Association des Amis du Centre d'Histoire et Civilisation de Byzance, 2002.

Lateiner, Donald. *Sardonic Smile: Nonverbal Behavior in Homeric Epic.* Ann Arbor: University of Michigan Press, 1998.

Latham, Jacob. *Performance, Memory, and Processions in Ancient Rome: The pompa circensis from the Late Republic to Late Antiquity.* Cambridge: Cambridge University Press, 2016.

Lendon, Jon. *Empire of Honour: The Art of Government in the Roman World.* Oxford: Clarendon Press, 2002.

Lenski, Noel. "Basil and the Isaurian Uprising of A.D. 375." *Phoenix* 53 (1999): 308–29.

Lenski, Noel. *Failure of Empire: Valens and the Roman State in Fourth Century A.D.* Berkeley: University of California Press, 2003.

Leyerle, Blake. *Theatrical Shows and Ascetic Lives: John Chrysostom's Attack on Spiritual Marriage.* Berkeley: University of California Press, 2001.

Leyser, Conrad. *Authority and Asceticism from Augustine to Gregory the Great.* Oxford: Oxford University Press, 2000.

Liebeschuetz, John H. W. G. *Ambrose and John Chrysostom: Clerics between Desert and Empire.* Oxford: Oxford University Press, 2011.

Liebeschuetz, John H. W. G. *Antioch: City and Imperial Administration in the Later Roman Empire.* Oxford: Oxford University Press, 1972.

Liebeschuetz, John H. W. G *Decline and Fall of the Roman City.* Oxford: Oxford University Press, 2001.

Liebeschuetz, John H. W. G "Letters of Ambrose of Milan (374–397), Books I–IX." In *Collecting Early Christian Letters: From the Apostle Paul to Late Antiquity.* Edited by Bronwen Neil and Pauline Allen. Cambridge: Cambridge University Press, 2015: 97–112.

Lim, Richard. *Public Disputation, Power, and Social Order in Late Antiquity.* Berkeley: University of California Press, 1995.

Limberis, Vasiliki. *Architects of Piety: The Cappadocian Fathers and the Cult of the Martyrs.* Oxford: Oxford University Press, 2011.

Lizzi Testa, Rita. *Il potere episcopale nell'Oriente romano: Rappresentazione ideologica e realtà politica (IV–V sec. d. C.).* Rome: Edizioni dell'Ateneo, 1987.

Lizzi Testa, Rita., ed. *Trasformazioni delle élites en età tardoantica.* Rome: L'Erma di Bretschneider, 2006.

Lloyd, Geoffrey. *In the Grip of Disease: Studies in the Greek Imagination.* Oxford: Oxford University Press, 2004.

Louth, Andrew. "The Cappadocians." In *The Cambridge History of Early Christian Literature.* Edited by Francis Young, Lewis Ayres, and Andrew Louth. Cambridge: Cambridge University Press, 2004: 289–301.

Louth, Andrew. "Eros and Mysticism: Early Christian Interpretation of the Song of Songs." In *Jung and the Monotheists: Judaism, Christianity, and Islam.* Edited by Joel Ryce-Menuhim. London: Routledge, 1994: 241–254.

Ludlow, Morwenna. *Art, Craft, and Theology in Fourth-Century Christian Authors.* Oxford: Oxford University Press, 2020.

Ludlow, Morwenna. *Gregory of Nyssa, Ancient and (Post)modern.* Oxford: Oxford University Press, 2007.

Ludlow, Morwenna. "Texts, Teachers and Pupils in the Writings of Gregory of Nyssa." In *Literature and Society in the Fourth Century AD: performing paideia, constructing the present, presenting the self*. Edited by Lieve Van Hoof and Peter Nuffelen. Leiden: Brill, 2014: 83–102.

Lugaresi, Leonardo. "Ambivalenze della rappresentazione: riflessioni patristiche su riti e spettacoli." *ZAC* 7:2 (2003): 281–309.

Lyman, Rebecca. "2002 NAPS Presidential Address: Hellenism and Heresy." *JECS* 11:2 (2003): 209–22.

MacCormack, Sabine. *Art and Ceremony in Late Antiquity*. Berkeley: University of California Press, 1981.

MacDougall, Byron. "Arianism, Asianism, and the Encomium of Athanasius by Gregory of Nazianzus." In *Rhetorical Strategies in Late Antique Literature: Images, Metatexts and Interpretation*. Edited by Alberto Quiroga Puertas. Leiden: Brill, 2017: 104–16.

MacDougall, Byron. *Gregory of Nazianzus and Christian Festival Rhetoric*. Ph.D. Dissertation. Brown University, 2015.

MacMullen, Ramsay. "Personal Power in the Roman Empire." *American Journal of Philology* 107 (1986): 513–24.

Malherbe, Abraham. *Ancient Epistolary Theorists*. Atlanta: SBL, 1988.

Malingrey, Anne Marie. *'Philosophia': étude d'un groupe de mots dans la littérature grecque des présocratiques au IVe siècle après J.C*. Paris: Klincksiek, 1961.

Malosse, Pierre-Louis and Bernard Schouler. "Qu'est-ce la troisieme sophistique?" *Lalies* 29 (2009): 161–224.

Mansfield, Jaap. "Diogenes Laertius on Stoic Philosophy." *Elenchos* 7 (1986): 297–382.

Maraval, Pierre. "La 'Vie de Saint Macrine' de Grégoire de Nysse: continuité et nouveauté d'un genre littéraire." In *Du héros païen au saint chrétien (Strasbourg 1–2 déc. 95)*. Edited by Géra Freyburger and Laurent Pernot. Paris: Institut d'Études Augustiniennes, 1997: 133–8.

Marrou, Henri-Irénée *A History of Education in Antiquity*. Translated by George Lamb. New York: Mentor, 1956.

Martin, Annick. *Athanase d'Alexandrie et l'église d'Egypte au IVe siècle (328–373)*. Paris: École française de Rome, 1996.

Martin, Dale. *The Corinthian Body*. New Haven: Yale University Press, 1995.

Martin, Dale and Patricia Cox Miller, eds. *The Cultural Turn in Late Antique Studies*. Durham, NC: Duke University Press, 2005.

Maslov, Boris. "The Limits of Platonism: Gregory of Nazianzus and the Invention of *theōsis*." *Greek, Roman, and Byzantine Studies* 52 (2012): 440–68.

Maslov, Boris. "*Oikeiōsis pros Theon*: Gregory of Nazianzus and the Heteronomous Subject of Eastern Christian Penance." *ZAC* 16 (2012): 311–43.

Maspero, Giulio. *Trinity and Man: Gregory of Nyssa's Ad Ablabium*. Leiden: Brill, 2007.

Mateo-Seco, Lucas. "El cristiano ante la vida y ante la morte: Estudio del Panegírico de Gregorio de Nisa sobre Gregorio Taumaturgo." In *The Biographical works of Gregory of Nyssa: Proceedings of the Fifth*

International Colloquium on Gregory of Nyssa, Mainz, 6–10 September 1982. Edited by Andreas Spira. Cambridge, MA: Philadelphia Patristic Foundation, 1984: 197–219.

Mateo-Seco, Lucas and Giulio Maspero, eds. *The Brill Dictionary of Gregory of Nyssa.* Leiden: Brill, 2009.

Mathisen, Ralph. *Roman Aristocrats in Barbarian Gaul: Strategies for Survival in an Age of Transition.* Austin: University of Texas Press, 1993.

Mattioli, Umberto, ed. *La donna nel pensiero cristiana antico.* Genoa: Marietti, 1992.

Mauss, Marcel. *The Gift: Forms and Functions of Exchange in Archaic Societies.* Translated by Ian Cunnison. New York: W. W. Norton and Company, 1967.

Maxwell, Jaclyn. *Christianization and Communication in Late Antiquity: John Chrysostom and his Congregation in Antioch.* Cambridge: Cambridge University Press, 2009.

Mayer, Wendy. "The Ins and Outs of the Chrysostom Letter-Collection: New Ways of Looking at a Limited Corpus." In *Collecting Early Christian Letters: From the Apostle Paul to Late Antiquity.* Edited by Bronwen Neil and Pauline Allen. Cambridge: Cambridge University Press, 2015: 129–53

McCall, Richard. *Do This: Liturgy as Performance.* Notre Dame, IN: Notre Dame University Press, 2007.

McDonnell, Myles. "Roman Mean and Greek Virtue." In *Andreia: Studies in Manliness and Courage in Classical Antiquity.* Edited by Ralph Rosen and Ineke Sluiter. Leiden: Brill, 2003: 235–61.

McDonnell, Myles. "Writing, Copying, and Autograph Manuscripts in Ancient Rome." *CQ* 46 (1996): 469–91.

McGuckin, John. *St Gregory of Nazianzus: An Intellectual Biography.* Crestwood, NY: St. Vladimir's Seminary, 2001.

McInerney, Jeremy. "Plutarch's Manly Women." In *Andreia: Studies in Manliness and Courage in Classical Antiquity.* Edited by Ralph Rosen and Ineke Sluiter. Leiden: Brill, 2003: 319–44.

McKitterick, Rosamond, ed. *The Uses of Literacy in Early Medieval Europe.* Cambridge: Cambridge University Press, 1990.

McLynn, Neil. "Among the Hellenists: Gregory and the Sophists." In *Gregory of Nazianzus: Images and Reflections.* Edited by Jostein Børtnes and Thomas Hägg. Copenhagen: Museum Tusculanum Press, 2006: 213–38.

McLynn, Neil. "Curiales into Churchmen: The Case of Gregory Nazianzen." In *Le trasformazioni delle élites en età tardoantica.* Edited by Rita Lizzi Testa. Rome: L'Erma di Bretschneider, 2006: 277–95.

McLynn, Neil. "Gregory Nazianzen's Basil: The Literary Construction of a Christian Friendship," *SP* 34 (2001): 178–93.

McLynn, Neil. "A Self-Made Holy Man: The Case of Gregory Nazianzen." *JECS* 6.3 (1998): 463–83.

Meredith, Anthony. *The Cappadocians.* Crestwood, NY: St. Vladimir's Seminary Press, 1997.

Meredith, Anthony. "A Comparison between the Vita Sanctae Macrinae of Gregory of Nyssa and the Vita Plotini of Porphyry and the De Vita Pythagorica of Iamblichus." In *The Biographical works of Gregory of*

Nyssa: *Proceedings of the Fifth International Colloquium on Gregory of Nyssa, Mainz, 6–10 September 1982*. Edited by Andreas Spira. Cambridge, MA: Philadelphia Patristic Foundation, 1984: 181–95.
Meredith, Anthony. "Divine Incomprehensibility in Gregory of Nyssa and Augustine." *SP* 47 (2010): 3–7.
Meredith, Anthony. *Gregory of Nyssa*. London: Routledge, 1999.
Méridier, Louis. *L'Influence de la seconde sophistique sur l'oeuvre de Grégoire de Nysse*. Paris: Libraire Hachette, 1906.
Métivier, Sophie. *La Cappadoce (IVe–VIe siècle): Une histoire provinciale de l'Empire romain d'Orient*. Paris: Publications de la Sorbonne, 2005.
Mifsud, Marilee. "On Rhetoric as Gift/Giving." *Philosophy and Rhetoric* 40:1 (2007): 89–107.
Millar, Fergus. *A Greek Roman Empire: Power and Belief Under Theodosius II 408-450*. Berkeley: University of California Press, 2006.
Miller, Patricia Cox. *Biography in Late Antiquity: A Quest for the Holy Man*. Berkeley: University of California Press, 1983.
Miller, Patricia Cox. *The Corporeal Imagination: Signifying the Holy in Late Ancient Christianity*. Philadelphia: University of Pennsylvania Press, 2009.
Miller, Stephen. *Arete: Greek Sports from Ancient Sources*. Berkeley: University of California Press, 2012.
Mitchell, Margaret. *Paul and the Rhetoric of Reconciliation: An Exegetical Investigation of the Language and Composition of I Corinthians*. Louisville, KY: John Knox, 1991.
Mitchell, Stephen. *Anatolia: Land, Men, and Gods in Asia Minor*. 2 Vols. Oxford: Clarendon Press, 1993.
Mitchell, Stephen. "The Life and *Lives* of Gregory Thaumaturgus." In *Portraits of Spiritual Authority: Religious Power in Early Christianity, Byzantium and the Christian Orient*. Edited by Jan Drijvers and John Watt. Leiden: Brill, 1999: 99–138.
Momigliano, Arnaldo. *The Development of Greek Biography*. Cambridge, MA: Harvard University Press, 1971.
Momigliano, Arnaldo. "The Life of St. Macrina by Gregory of Nyssa." In *The Craft of the Ancient Historian: Essays in Honor of Chester G. Starr*. Edited by John Eadie and Josiah Ober. Lanham, MD: University Press of America, 1985: 443–58.
Moore, Stephen and Janice Anderson, eds. *New Testament Masculinities*. Atlanta: SBL, 2003.
Morello, Ruth and A. D. Morrison, eds. *Ancient Letters: Classical and Late Antique Epistolography*. Oxford: Oxford University Press, 2007.
Moreschini, Claudio. *Filosofia e letteratura in Gregorio de Nazianzo*. Milan: Vite e Pensiero, 1997.
Moreschini, Claudio. "Is it Possible to Speak of 'Cappadocian Theology' as a System?" *SP* 95 (2017): 139–63.
Moreschini, Claudio. "Luce e purificazione nella dottrina di Gregorio Nazianzeno." *Augustinianum* 13 (1973): 535–49.
Morris, Ian. "Gift and Commodity in Archaic Greece." *Man* 21:1 (1986): 1–17.
Moss, Candida. *Ancient Christian Martyrdom: Diverse Practices, Theologies, and Traditions*. New Haven: Yale University Press, 2012.

Mossay, Justin. *La Mort et l'au-delà dans Saint Grégoire de Nazianze*. Louvain: Publications Universitaires, 1966.
Muehlberger, Ellen. "Salvage: Macrina and the Christian Project of Cultural Reclamation." *CH* 81:2 (2012): 273–97.
Muehlberger, Ellen. "Simeon and Other Women in Theodoret's *Religious History*: Gender in the Representation of Late Ancient Christian Asceticism." *JECS* 23:4 (2015): 583–606.
Mühlenberg, Ekkehard. *Die Unendlichkeit Gottes bei Gregor von Nyssa: Gregors Kritik am Gottesbegriff der klassischen Metaphysik*. Göttingen: Vandenhoeck & Ruprecht, 1966.
Muir, John. *Life and Letters in the Ancient Greek World*. London; Routledge, 2009.
Mullett, Margaret. "The Classical Tradition in the Byzantine Letter." In *Byzantium and the Classical Tradition*. Edited by Margaret Mullett and Roger Scott. Birmingham: Centre for Byzantine Studies, 1981.
Mullett, Margaret. *Theophylact of Ochrid: Reading the Letters of a Byzantine Archbishop*. Aldershot: Ashgate, 1997.
Mullett, Margaret. "Writing in Early Medieval Byzantium." In *The Uses of Literacy in Early Medieval Europe*. Edited by Rosamond McKitterick, Cambridge: Cambridge University Press, 1990: 183–4.
Mullett, Margaret and Roger Scott, eds. *Byzantium and the Classical Tradition*. Birmingham: Centre for Byzantine Studies, 1981.
Nagy, Gregory and Anna Stavrakopoulou, eds. *Modern Greek Literature: Critical Essays*. New York: Routledge, 2003.
Naldini, Mario, ed. *Basilio di Cesarea, Discorso ai Giovani (Oratio ad adulescentes), con la versione latina di Leonardo Bruni*. Florence: Nardini, 1984.
Naldini, Mario. "Paideia origeniana nella 'Oratio ad adolescentes' di Basilio Magno." *Vetera Christianorum* 13 (1976): 297–318.
Naldini, Mario. "Sulla 'Oratio ad adolescentes' di Basilio Magno." *Prometheus* 4 (1978): 36–44.
Nautin, Pierre. "L'Éloge funèbre de Basile par Grégoire de Nazianze: remarques sur le texte et l'interprétation." *VC* 48 (1994): 332–40.
Neil, Bronwen and Pauline Allen, eds. *Collecting Early Christian Letters: From the Apostle Paul to Late Antiquity*. Cambridge: Cambridge University Press, 2015.
Nicholson, Nigel. *Aristocracy and Athletics in Archaic and Classical Greece*. Cambridge: Cambridge University Press, 2005.
Norman, A. F. "Gradations in Later Municipal Society." *Journal of Roman Studies* 1:2 (1958): 79–85.
Norris, Frederick. "Gregory Contemplating the Beautiful: Knowing Human Misery and Divine Mystery through and Being Persuaded by Images." In *Gregory of Nazianzus: Images and Reflections*. Edited by Jostein Børtnes and Tomas Hägg. Copenhagen: Museum Tusculanum, 2006: 19–35.
Norris, Frederick. "Of Thorns and Roses: The Logic of Belief in Gregory Nazianzen." *CH* 53 (1984): 455–464.
Norris, Frederick. "Your Honor, My Reputation." In *Greek Biography and Panegyric in Late Antiquity*. Edited by Thomas Hägg and Philip Rousseau. Berkeley: University of California Press, 2000: 140–59.

Oosthout, Henri. "La Vie contemplative: vie d'ascète ou vie de théologien? Purification et recherche de Dieu chez Athanase d' Alexandrie et Grégoire de Nazianze." In *Fructus Centesimus. Mélanges offerts a G. J. M. Bartelink à l'occasion de son soixante-cinquième anniversaire.* Edited by A. Bastiaensen, A. Hilhorst, and C. Kneepkens. Dordrecht: Brepols, 1989: 259–67.
Pack, Edgar. *Städte und Steuern in der Politik Julians. Untersuchungen zu den Quellen eines Kaiserbildes.* Brussels: Revue d'Études Latines, 1986.
Panier, Louis, ed. *Grégoire de Nazianze, théoricien de la lettre. Actes du Colloque sur les lettres dans la Bible et la littérature (3–5 juillet 1996).* Lyon: Les Éditions du Cerf, 1999.
Parani, Maria. "Mediating Presence: Curtains in Middle and Late Byzantine Imperial Ceremonial and Portraiture." *Byzantine and Modern Greek Studies* 42:1 (2018): 1–25.
Pelikan, Jaroslav. *Christianity and Classical Culture: The Metamorphosis of Natural Theology in the Christian Encounter with Hellenism.* New Haven: Yale University Press, 1993.
Penella, Robert. *Greek Philosophers and Sophists in the Fourth Century A.D.: Studies in Eunapius of Sardis.* Leeds: Francis Cairns, 1990.
Penella, Robert. "Julian the Persecutor in Fifth-Century Church Histories." *Ancient World* 24 (1993): 31–43.
Penella, Robert. *Man and the Word: The Orations of Himerius.* Berkeley: University of California Press, 2007.
Penella, Robert. *The Private Orations of Themistius.* Berkeley: University of California Press, 2000.
Pernot, Laurent. *La Rhétorique de l'éloge dans le monde gréco-romain.* 2 Vols. Paris: Institut d'Études Augustiniennes, 1993.
Petit, Paul. *Les Étudiants de Libanius.* Paris: Nouvelles Editions latines, 1957.
Petit, Paul. *Libanius et la vie municipale à Antioche au IVe siècle après J.-C.* Paris: Librairie Orientaliste Paul Geuthner, 1955.
Pfitzner, Victor. *Paul and the Agon Motif: Traditional Athletic Imagery in Pauline Literature.* Leiden: Brill, 1967.
Plagnieux, Jean. *Saint Grégoire de Nazianze théologien.* Paris: Éditions franciscaines, 1952.
Pleket, Henri and Arthur Verhoogt, eds. *Aspects of the Fourth Century A.D.: Proceedings of the Symposium "Power and Possession: State, Society, and Church in the Fourth Century A.D."* Leiden: Brill, 1997.
Polanyi, Karl. *The Great Transformation.* Boston: Beacon Press, 1968.
Polanyi, Karl, Conrad Arensberg, and Harry Pearson, eds. *Trade and Market in the Early Empires: Economies in History and Theory.* New York: Free Press, 1957.
Porter, James. "Rhetoric, Aesthetics, and the Voice." In *Cambridge Companion to Ancient Rhetoric.* Edited by Erik Gunderson. Cambridge: Cambridge University Press, 2009: 92–108.
Porter, James. *The Origins of Aesthetic Thought in Ancient Greece.* Cambridge: Cambridge University Press, 2010.
Porter, Stanley, ed. *Handbook of Classical Rhetoric in the Hellenistic Period 330 B.C.–A.D. 400.* Leiden: Brill, 1997.

Potter, David. "Martyrdom and Spectacle." In *Theatre and Society in the Classical World*. Edited by Ruth Scodel. Ann Arbor: University of Michigan Press, 1993: 53–88.

Potter, David and David Mattingly, eds. *Life, Death, and Entertainment in the Roman Empire*. Ann Arbor: University of Michigan Press, 1999.

Pouchet Robert. *Basile le Grand et son univers d'amis d'après sa correspondance: une stratégie de communion*. Roma: Institutum Patristicum Augustinianum, 1992.

Pouderon, Bernard and Joseph Doré, eds. *Les Apologists chrétiens et la culture grecque*. Paris: Beauchesne, 1998.

Pouderon, Bernard and Cécile Bost-Pouderon, eds. *Passions, vertus et vices dans l'ancien roman*. Lyon: Maison de l'Orient Méditerranéen, 2009.

Poulakos, John. *Sophistical Rhetoric in Classical Greece*. Columbia: University of South Carolina Press, 1995.

Preston, Rebecca. "Roman Questions, Greek Answers; Plutarch and the Construction of Identity." In *Being Greek Under Rome: Cultural Identity, the Second Sophistic and the Development of Empire*. Edited by Simon Goldhill. New York: Cambridge University Press, 2001: 86–118.

Price, A. W. *Love and Friendship in Plato and Aristotle*. Oxford: Clarendon Press, 1989.

Puertas, Alberto. *The Dynamics of Rhetorical Performances in Late Antiquity*. London: Routledge, 2018.

Puertas, Alberto. "From Sophistopolis to Episcopolis: The Case for a Third Sophistic." *Journal for Late Antique Religion and Culture* 1 (2007): 31–42.

Puertas, Alberto, ed. *Rhetorical Strategies in Late Antique Literature: Images, Metatexts and Interpretation*. Leiden: Brill, 2017.

Radde-Gallwitz, Andrew. *Basil of Caesarea, Gregory of Nyssa, and the Transformation of Divine Simplicity*. Oxford: Oxford University Press, 2009.

Radde-Gallwitz, Andrew. "*Epinoia* and Initial Concepts: Re-assessing Gregory of Nyssa's Defense of Basil." *SP* 47 (2010): 21–26.

Radde-Gallwitz, Andrew. *Gregory of Nyssa's Doctrinal Works: A Literary Study*. Oxford Oxford University Press, 2018.

Radde-Gallwitz. Andrew. "The Letter Collection of Basil of Caesarea." In *Late Antique Letter Collections*. Edited by Cristiana Sogno, Bradley Storin, and Edward Watts. Berkeley: University of California Press, 2017: 69–80.

Radde-Gallwitz. Andrew. "The Letter Collection of Gregory of Nyssa." In *Late Antique Letter Collections*. Edited by Cristiana Sogno, Bradley Storin, and Edward Watts. Berkeley: University of California Press, 2017: 102–13.

Rapp, Claudia. "Christians and their Manuscripts in the Greek East in the Fourth Century." In *Scritture, libri e testi nelle aree provinciali di Bisanzio: atti del seminario di Erice (18–25 settembre 1988)*. Edited by Guglielmo Cavallo, Giuseppe de Gregorio, and Marilena Maniaci. Spoleto: Centro italiano di studi sull'alto Medioveco, 1991: 131–43.

Rapp, Claudia. "The Elite Status of Bishops in Late Antiquity in Ecclesiastical, Spiritual, and Socal Contexts." *Arethusa* 33 (2000): 379–99.

Rapp, Claudia. "Hellenic Identity, Romanitas, and Christianity in Byzantium." In *Hellenisms: Culture, Identity, and Ethnicity from Antiquity to Modernity*. Edited by Katarina Zacharia. Aldershot: Ashgate, 2008: 127–47.

Rapp, Claudia. *Holy Bishops: The Nature of Christian Leadership in an Age of Transition*. Berkeley: University of California Press, 2005.

Rapp, Claudia and Harold Drake, eds. *The City in the Classical and Post-Classical World: Changing Contexts of Power and Identity*. Cambridge: Cambridge University Press, 2014.

Reardon, B. P., ed. *Collected Ancient Greek Novels*. Berkeley: University of California Press, 1989.

Rebillard, Éric. *Christians and Their Many Identities in Late Antiquity, North Africa, 200–450 CE*. Ithaca: Cornell University Press, 2012.

Rebillard, Éric and Jörg Rüpke, eds. *Group Identity and Religious Individuality in Late Antiquity*. Washington, DC: Catholic University of America Press, 2015.

Rebillard, Suzanne Abrams. "Let Me Cry Out in Tragic Voice: Gregory of Nazianzus' Use of Tragic Pathos." Paper Presentation at the International Conference on Patristic Studies. Oxford, 2015.

Rebillard, Suzanne Abrams. "Speaking for Salvation: Gregory of Nazianzus as Poet and Priest in his Autobiographical Poems." Ph.D. Dissertation. Brown University, 2003.

Rebillard, Suzanne Abrams. "The Speech Act of Swearing: Gregory of Nazianzus's Oath in *Poema* 2.1.2 in Context." *JECS* 21 (2013): 177–207.

Reeser, Todd. *Moderating Masculinity in Early Modern Culture*. Chapel Hill: University of North Carolina Press, 2006.

Remijsen, Sofie. *The End of Greek Athletics in Late Antiquity*. Cambridge: Cambridge University Press, 2015.

Reynolds, L. D., and N. G. Wilson. *Scribes and Scholars: A Guide to the Transmission of Greek and Latin Literature*. Second Edition. Oxford: Clarendon Press, 1974.

Rist, John. "Basil's 'Neoplatonism': Its Background and Nature." In *Basil of Caesarea: Christian, Humanist, Ascetic: A Sixteen-Hundredth Anniversary Symposium*. Edited by P. J. Fedwick. 2 Vols. Toronto: Pontifical Institute of Mediaeval Studies, 1981: 137–220.

Ritter, Adolf-Martin. *Das Konzil von Konstantinopel und sein Symbol*. Göttingen: Vandenhoeck and Ruprecht, 1965.

Roberts, Colin. *Greek Literary Hands 350 B.C.–A.D. 400*. Oxford: Clarendon Press, 1955.

Roberts, Michael. *The Jeweled Style: Poetry and Poetics in Late Antiquity*. Ithaca: Cornell University Press, 1989.

Robertson, George. "The *Andreia* of Xenocles: *Kouros, Kallos* and *Kleos*." In *Andreia: Studies in Manliness and Courage in Classical Antiquity*. Edited by Ralph Rosen and Ineke Sluiter. Leiden: Brill, 2003: 59–76.

Roisman, Joseph. "The Rhetoric of Courage in the Athenian Orators." In *Andreia: Studies in Manliness and Courage in Classical Antiquity*. Edited by Ralph Rosen and Ineke Sluiter. Leiden: Brill, 2003: 127–43.

Roisman, Joseph. *The Rhetoric of Manhood: Masculinity in the Attic Orators*. Berkeley: University of California Press, 2005.

Roisman, Joseph. "Rhetoric, Manliness and Contest." In *A Companion to Greek Rhetoric*. Edited by Ian Worthington. Malden, MA: Blackwell, 2007: 393–410.

Rosen, Ralph and Ineke Sluiter, eds. *Andreia: Studies in Manliness and Courage in Classical Antiquity.* Leiden: Brill, 2003.

Rosenmeyer, Patricia. *Ancient Epistolary Fictions: The Letter in Greek Literature.* Cambridge: Cambridge University Press, 2001.

Rosenwein, Barbara. *Emotional Communities in the Early Middle Ages.* Ithaca: Cornell University Press, 2006.

Rossiter, Jeremy. "Roman Villas of the Greek East and the Villa in Gregory of Nyssa Ep. 20." *Journal of Roman Archaeology* 2 (1989): 101–10.

Rousseau, Philip. "Antony as Teacher in the Greek Life." In *Greek Biography and Panegyric in Late Antiquity.* Edited by Thomas Hägg and Philip Rousseau. Berkeley: University of California Press, 2000: 89–109.

Rousseau, Philip. *Ascetics, Authority, and the Church in the Age of Jerome and Cassian.* Oxford: Oxford University Press, 1978.

Rousseau, Philip. *Basil of Caesarea.* Berkeley: University of California Press, 1994.

Rousseau, Philip. "The Pious Household and the Virgin Chorus: Reflections on Gregory of Nyssa's Life of Macrina." *JECS* 13 (2005): 165–86.

Rousseau, Philip and Manolis Papoutsakis, eds. *Transformations of Late Antiquity: Essays for Peter Brown.* Farnham: Ashgate, 2009.

Rubarth, Scott. "Competing Constructions of Masculinity in Ancient Greece." *Athens Journal of Humanities and Fine Arts* 1 (2014): 21–32.

Rubenson, Samuel. "Philosophy and Simplicity: The Problem of Classical Education in Early Christian Biography." In *Greek Biography and Panegyric in Late Antiquity.* Edited by Thomas Hägg and Philip Rousseau. Berkeley: University of California Press, 2000: 110–39.

Ruether, Rosemary Radford. *Gregory of Nazianzus: Rhetor and Philosopher.* Oxford: Clarendon Press, 1969.

Russell, Donald. *Greek Declamation.* Cambridge: Cambridge University Press, 2009.

Ryce-Menuhim, Joel, ed. *Jung and the Monotheists: Judaism, Christianity, and Islam.* London: Routledge, 1994.

Salzman, Michele. *The Making of a Christian Aristocracy: Society and Religious Change in the Western Empire.* Cambridge, MA: Harvard University Press, 2002.

Saïd, Suzanne. *Hellenismos: quelques jalons pour une histoire de l'identité grecque: Actes du Colloque de Strasbourg, 25–27 octobre 1989.* Leiden: Brill, 1991.

Sandwell, Isabella. *Religious Identity in Late Antiquity: Greeks, Jews and Christians in Antioch.* Cambridge: Cambridge University Press, 2011.

Schmitz, Thomas. *Bildung und Macht: Zur sozialen und politischen Funktion der zweiten Sophistik in der griechischen Welt der Kaiserzeit.* Munich: Beck, 1997.

Schoedel, William and Robert Wilken, eds. *Early Christian Literature and the Classical Tradition: In Honorem Robert M. Grant.* Paris: Beauchesne, 1979.

Schönborn, Christoph von. *L'icône du Christ: fondements théologiques élaborés entre le 1er et le 2e Concile de Nicée (325–787).* Fribourg: Éditions universitaires, 1976.

Schor, Adam. "Becoming Bishop in the Letters of Basil and Synesius: Tracing Patterns of Social Signaling across Two Full Epistolary Collections." *JLA* 7:2 (2014): 298–328.
Schor, Adam. "The Letters of Theodoret of Cyrrhus: Personal Collections, Multi-Author Archives and Historical Interpretation." In *Collecting Early Christian Letters: From the Apostle Paul to Late Antiquity*. Edited by Bronwen Neil and Pauline Allen. Cambridge: Cambridge University Press, 2015: 154–71.
Schor, Adam. "Patronage Performance and Social Strategy in the Letters of Theodoret, Bishop of Cyrrhus." *JLA* 2:2 (2009), 274–99.
Schor, Adam. *Theodoret's People: Social Networking and Religious Conflict in Late Roman Syria*. Berkeley: University of California Press, 2011.
Schouler, Bernard. "Hellénismos et humanisme chez Libanios." In *Hellenismos: quelques jalons pour une histoire de l'identité grecque: Actes du Colloque de Strasbourg, 25–27 octobre 1989*. Edited by Suzanne Saïd. Leiden: Brill, 1991: 267–85.
Schwartz, Daniel. *Paideia and Cult: Christian Initiation in Theodore of Mopsuestia*. Washington, DC: Center for Hellenic Studies, 2013.
Scodel, Ruth, ed. *Theatre and Society in the Classical World*. Ann Arbor: University of Michigan Press, 1993.
Seaford, Richard. *Reciprocity and Ritual: Homer and Tragedy in the Developing City-State*. Oxford: Oxford University Press, 1994.
Sesboüé, Bernard. *L'Apologie d'Eunome de Cyzique et le contre Eunome de Basile de Césarée*. Rome: Pontificia Universitas Gregoriana, 1980.
Sesboüé, Bernard. *Saint Basile et la Trinité, un acte théologique au IVe siècle: le rôle de Basile de Césarée dans l'élaboration de la doctrine et du langage trinitaires*. Paris: Desclée, 1998.
Sestili, Antonio. *L'equitazione nella Grecia antica: i trattati equestri di Senofonte e i frammenti di Simone*. Scandicci: Firenze Atheneum, 2006.
Shaw, Brent. "Body/Power/Identity: Passions of the Martyrs." *JECS* 4:3 (1996): 269–312.
Shepardson, Christine. *Controlling Contested Places: Late Antique Antioch and the Spatial Politics of Religious Controversy*. Berkeley: University of California Press, 2014.
Shepardson, Christine. "Defining the Boundaries of Orthodoxy: Eunomius in the Anti-Jewish Polemic of His Cappadocian Opponents." *CH* 76 (2007): 699–723.
Sheppard, Anne. *The Poetics of Phantasia: Imagination in Ancient Aesthetics*. London: Bloomsbury, 2015.
Silvas, Anna. "The Letters of Basil of Caesarea and the Role of Letter-Collection in their Transmission." In *Collecting Early Christian Letters: From the Apostle Paul to Late Antiquity*. Edited by Bronwen Neil and Pauline Allen. Cambridge: Cambridge University Press, 2015: 113–28.
Silvas, Anna. *Macrina the Younger: Philosopher of God*. Turnhout: Brepols, 2008.
Skeat, T. C. "Was Papyrus Regarded as 'Cheap' or 'Expensive' in the Ancient World?" *Aegyptus* 75 (1995): 88–105.
Slootjes, Daniëlle. "Bishops and Their Position of Power in the Late Third Century CE: The Cases of Gregory of Thaumaturgus and Paul of Samosata." *JLA* 4.1 (2011), 100–15.

Slootjes, Daniëlle. *The Governor and His Subjects in the Later Roman Empire*. Leiden: Brill, 2006.
Smith, J. Warren. "A Just and Reasonable Grief: The Death and Function of a Holy Woman in Gregory of Nyssa's *Life of Macrina*." *JECS* 12 (2004): 57–84.
Smith, J. Warren. "Macrina, Tamer of Horses and Healer of Souls: Grief and Therapy of Hope in Gregory of Nyssa's *De Anime et Resurrectione*." *JTS* 52 (2001): 37–60.
Smith, Rowland. *Julian's Gods: Religion and Philosophy in the Thought and Action of Julian the Apostate*. London: Routledge, 1995.
Smoes, Étienne. *Le Courage chez les Grecs d'Homère à Aristotle*. Brussels: Ousia, 1995.
Smith, R. R. R. "Cultural Choice and Political Identity in Honorific Portrait Statues in the Greek East in the Second Century A.D." *Journal of Roman Studies* 88 (1998): 56–93.
Sogno, Cristiana, Bradley Storin, and Edward Watts, eds. *Late Antique Letter Collections*. Berkeley: University of California Press, 2017.
Soler, Emmanuel. *Le Sacré et le salut à Antioche au IVe siècle apr. J.-C.: pratiques festives et comportements religieux dans le processus de christianisation de la cité*. Beirut: Institut français du Proche-Orient, 2006.
Spadavecchia, Carla. "Some Aspects of Saint Basil of Caesarea's Views on Friendship, Compared with Those of his Pagan Contemporaries." *Kleronomia* 15 (1983): 303–17.
Spira, Andreas, ed. *The Biographical works of Gregory of Nyssa: Proceedings of the Fifth International Colloquium on Gregory of Nyssa, Mainz, 6–10 September 1982*. Cambridge, MA: Philadelphia Patristic Foundation, 1984.
Spira, Andreas. "Volkstümlichkeit und Kunst in der griechischen Väterpredigt des 4. Jahrhunderts." *Jahrbuch der österreichischen Byzantinistik* 35 (1985): 55–73.
Staats, Reinhart. *Das Glaubensbekenntnis von Nizäa-Konstantinopel: Historische und theologische Grundlagen*. Darmstadt: Wissenschaftliche Buchgesellschaft, 1996.
Starr, Raymond. "The Circulation of Literary Texts in the Roman World." *CQ* 37:1 (1987): 213–23.
Stenger, Jan. *Hellenische Identität in der Spätantike: pagane Autoren und ihr Unbehagen an der eigenen Zeit*. Berlin: de Gruyter, 2009.
Sterk, Andrea. "On Basil, Moses, and the Model Bishop: The Cappadocian Legacy of Leadership." *CH* 67 (1998): 227–53.
Sterk, Andrea. *Renouncing the World Yet Leading the Church: The Monk-Bishop in Late Antiquity*. Cambridge, MA: Harvard University Press, 2004.
Stewart, Michael Edward. *The Soldier's Life: Martial Virtues and Manly Romanitas in the Early Byzantine Empire*. Leeds: Kismet, 2016.
Stinger, Charles. *Humanism and the Church Fathers: Ambrogio Traversari (1386–1439) and Christian Antiquity in the Italian Renaissance*. Albany: State University of New York Press, 1977.
Stirewalt, M. Luther. *Studies in Ancient Greek Epistolography*. Atlanta: Scholars, 1993.

Storin, Bradley. *The Letters of Gregory of Nazianzus: Discourse and Community in Late Antique Epistolary Culture*. Ph.D. Dissertation. Indiana University, 2012.
Storin, Bradley. "In a Silent Way: Asceticism and Literature in the Rehabilitation of Gregory of Nazianzus." *JECS* 19:2 (2011): 225–57.
Storin, Bradley. "The Letter Collection of Gregory of Nazianzus." In *Late Antique Letter Collections*. Edited by Cristiana Sogno, Bradley Storin, and Edward Watts. Berkeley: University of California Press, 2017: 81–101.
Storin, Bradley. *Self-Portrait in Three Colors: Gregory of Nazianzus's Epistolary Autobiography*. Oakland: University of California Press, 2019.
Stowers, Stanley. *Letter Writing in Greco-Roman Antiquity*. Philadelphia: Westminster Press, 1986.
Struck, Peter. "The Ordeal of the Divine Sign: Divination and Manliness in Archaic and Classical Greece." In *Andreia: Studies in Manliness and Courage in Classical Antiquity*. Edited by Ralph Rosen and Ineke Sluiter. Leiden: Brill, 2003: 167–86.
Swain, Simon. "Biography and Biographic in the Literature of the Roman Empire." In *Portraits: Biographical Representation in the Greek and Latin Literature of the Roman Empire*. Edited by Mark Edwards and Simon Swain. Oxford: Clarendon Press, 1997: 1–17.
Swain, Simon. *Hellenism and Empire: Language, Classicism, and Power in the Greek World AD 50–250*. Oxford: Clarendon Press, 1996.
Swain, Simon. "Polemon's Physiognomy." In *Seeing the Face, Seeing the Soul: Polemon's Physiognomy from Classical Antiquity to Medieval Islam*. Edited by Simon Swain. Oxford: Oxford University Press, 2007: 125–201.
Swain, Simon, ed. *Seeing the Face, Seeing the Soul: Polemon's Physiognomy from Classical Antiquity to Medieval Islam*. Oxford: Oxford University Press, 2007.
Swain, Simon. "Sophists and Emperors: The Case of Libanius." In *Approaching Late Antiquity: The Transformation from Early to Late Empire*. Edited by Simon Swain and Mark Edwards. Oxford: Oxford University Press, 2006: 355–400.
Swain, Simon and Mark Edwards, eds. *Approaching Late Antiquity: The Transformation from Early to Late Empire*. Oxford: Oxford University Press, 2006.
Szymusiak, Jan. "Grégoire le théologien, disciple d'Athanase." In *Politique et Théologie chez Athanase d'Alexandrie*. Edited by Charles Kannengiesser. Paris: Beauchesne, 1974: 356–63.
Temmerman, Koen De and Kristoffel Demoen. *Writing Biography in Greece and Rome: Narrative Technique and Fictionalization*. Cambridge: Cambridge University Press, 2016.
Tetz, Martin. "Zur Biographie des Athanasius von Alexandrien." *ZK* 90 (1979): 158–92.
Thomas, Rosalind. "Performance and Written Literature in Classical Greece: Envisaging Performance from Written Literature and Comparative Contexts." In *The Anthropology of Performance: A Reader*. Edited by Frank Korom. Malden, MA: Wiley Blackwell, 2013: 26–35.

Thraede, Klaus. *Grundzüge griechisch-römische Brieftopik*. Munich: Beck, 1970.
Tollefsen, Torstein. *Activity and Participation in Late Antique and Early Christian Thought*. Oxford: Oxford University Press, 2012.
Torrance, Alexis. "Precedents for Palamas' Essence-Energies Theology in the Cappadocian Fathers." *VC* 63 (2009): 47–70.
Trapp, Michael, ed. *Greek and Latin Letters: An Anthology with Translation*. Cambridge: Cambridge University Press, 2003.
Treu, Kurt. "Φιλία und Ἀγάπη: zur Terminologie der Freundschaft bei Basilius und Gregor von Nazianz." *Studii Clasice* 3 (1961): 421–7.
Trout, Dennis. *Paulinus of Nola: Life, Letters and Poems*. Berkeley: University of California Press, 1999.
Turner, Eric. *Greek Manuscripts of the Ancient World*. Princeton: Princeton University Press, 1971.
Upson-Saia, Kristi, Carly Daniel-Hughes, and Alicia J. Batten, eds. *Dressing Judeans and Christians in Late Antiquity*. Farnham: Ashgate, 2014.
Urbano, Arthur. *The Philosophical Life: Biography and the Crafting of Intellectual Identity in Late Antiquity*. Washington, DC: Catholic University of America Press, 2013.
Urbano, Arthur. "Sizing-Up the Philosopher's Cloak: Christian Verbal and Visual Representations of the Tribon." In *Dressing Judeans and Christians in Late Antiquity*. Edited by Kristi Upson-Saia, Carly Daniel-Hughes, and Alicia J. Batten. Farnham: Ashgate, 2014: 174–94.
Uthemann, Karl-Heinz. "Die Sprache der Theologie nach Eunomius von Cyzicus," *ZK* 104 (1993): 143–75.
Vaggione, Richard. *Eunomius of Cyzicus and the Nicene Revolution*. Oxford: Oxford University Press, 2000.
Vaggione, Richard. "Of Monks and Lounge Lizards: 'Arians,' Polemics and Asceticism in the Roman East." In *Arianism after Arius: Essays on the Development of the Fourth Century Trinitarian Conflicts*. Edited by Michel Barnes and Daniel Williams. Edinburgh: T&T Clark, 1993: 197–214.
Van Dam, Raymond. *Becoming Christian: The Conversion of Roman Cappadocia*. Philadelphia: University of Pennsylvania Press, 2003.
Van Dam, Raymond. "Emperor, Bishops, and Friends in Late Antique Cappadocia." *JTS* 37 (1986): 53–77.
Van Dam, Raymond. *Families and Friends in Late Roman Cappadocia*. Philadelphia: University of Pennsylvania Press, 2003.
Van Dam, Raymond. "Governors of Cappadocia during the Fourth Century." *Medieval Prosopography* 17 (1996): 7–93.
Van Dam, Raymond. "Hagiography and History: The Life of Gregory Thaumaturgus." *Classical Antiquity* 1:2 (1982): 272–308.
Van Dam, Raymond. *Kingdom of Snow: Roman Rule and Greek Culture in Cappadocia*. Philadelphia: University of Pennsylvania Press, 2002.
Van Dam, Raymond. *The Roman Revolution of Constantine*. Cambridge: Cambridge University Press, 2007.
Van Dam, Raymond. "Self-Representation in the Will of Gregory of Nazianzus." *JTS* 46 (1995): 118–48.

Van der Eijk, Philip. *Medicine and Philosophy in Classical Antiquity: Doctors and Philosophers on Nature, Soul, Health and Disease*. Cambridge: Cambridge University Press, 2010.
Van Hoof, Lieve. "Falsification as a Protreptic to Truth: The Force of the Forged Epistolary Exchange between Basil and Libanius." In *Education and Religion in Late Antique Christianity: Reflections, Social Contexts and Genres*, Edited by Peter Gemeinhardt, Lieve van Hoof, and Peter van Nuffelen. London: Routledge, 2016: 116–30.
Van Hoof, Lieve, ed. *Libanius: A Critical Introduction*. Cambridge: Cambridge University Press, 2014.
Van Hoof, Lieve. "Performing Paideia: Greek Culture as an Instrument for Social Promotion in the Fourth Century A.D." *CQ* 63 (2013): 387–406.
Van Hoof, Lieve, and Peter Nuffelen, eds. *Literature and Society in the Fourth Century AD: Performing Paideia, Constructing the Present, Presenting the Self*. Leiden: Brill, 2014.
Van Hoof, Lieve and Peter Nuffelen. "The Social Role and Place of Literature in the Fourth Century AD." In *Literature and Society in the Fourth Century AD: Performing Paideia, Constructing the Present, Presenting the Self*. Edited by Lieve Van Hoof and Peter Nuffelen. Leiden: Brill, 2014: 1–15.
Van Nijf, Onno. "Athletics and Paideia: Festivals and Physical Education in the World of the Second Sophistic." In *Paideia: The World of the Second Sophistic*. Edited by Barbara Borg. Berlin: de Gruyter, 2004: 203–27.
Van Nijf, Onno. "Athletics, *Andreia* and the Askêsis-Culture in the Roman East." In *Andreia: Studies in Manliness and Courage in Classical Antiquity*. Edited by Ralph Rosen and Ineke Sluiter. Leiden: Brill, 2003: 263–86.
Van Nijf, Onno. "Festivals and Benefactors." In *Benefactors and the Polis: The Public Gift in the Greek Cities from the Homeric World to Late Antiquity*. Edited by Marc Domingo Gygax and Arjan Zuiderhoek. Cambridge: Cambridge University Press, 2020: 243–64.
Vandenbussche, E. "La Part de la dialectique dans la théologie d'Eunomius 'le technologue.'" *Revue d'Histoire Ecclésiastique* 40 (1944–45): 47–72.
Vasileiou, Fotis. "At a Still Point of a Turning World: Privacy and Asceticism in Gregory of Nyssa's *Life of St. Macrina*." *Byzantion* 82 (2012): 451–63.
Vogler, Chantal. "L'Administration impériale dans la correspondance de Saint Basile et Saint Grégoire de Naziance." In *Institutions, Société et vie politique dans l'Empire romain au IV siècle ap. J.-C. Actes de la table ronde autour de l'oeuvre d'André Chastagnol (Paris, 20–21 janvier 1989)*. Edited by Michel Christol, Ségolène Demougin, Yvette Duval, Claude Lepelley and Luce Pietri Vogler. Rome: École Française de Rome, 1992: 447–64.
Vössing, Konrad. "Schreiben lernen, ohne lesen zu können? Zur Methode des antiken Elementarunterrichts." *Zeitschrift für Papyrologie und Epigraphik* 123 (1998): 121–5.
Wallace-Hadrill, Andrew. *Patronage in Ancient Society*. London: Routledge, 1989.
Watts, Edward. *City and School in Late Antique Athens and Alexandria*. Berkeley: University of California Press, 2008.

Watts, Edward. *The Last Final Pagan Generation*. Berkeley: University of California Press, 2015.
Webb, Ruth. *Ekphrasis, Imagination and Persuasion in Ancient Rhetorical Theory and Practice*. Farnham: Ashgate, 2009.
Wenzel, Aaron. "Libanius, Gregory of Nazianzus, and the Ideal of Athens in Late Antiquity." *JLA* 3:2 (2010): 264–85.
White, Carolinne. *Christian Friendship in the Fourth Century*. Cambridge: Cambridge University Press, 1992.
White, L. Michael. "Rhetoric and Reality in Galatians: Framing the Social Demands of Friendship." In *Early Christianity and Classical Culture: Comparative Studies in Honor of Abraham Malherbe*. Edited by John Fitzgerald, Thomas Olbricht, and L. Michael White. Leiden: Brill, 2003: 307–50.
Whitmarsh, Tim. *Greek Literature and the Roman Empire: The Politics of Imitation*. Oxford: Oxford University Press, 2001.
Whitmarsh, Tim. *The Second Sophistic*. Oxford: Oxford University Press, 2005.
Wickham, Lionel. "The Date of Eunomius' Apology: A Reconsideration." *JTS* 20 (1969): 231–40.
Wickham, Lionel. "The *Syntagmation* of Aetius the Anomean." *JTS* 19 (1968): 532–69.
Wickham, Lionel and Caroline Bammel, eds. *Christian Faith and Greek Philosophy in Late Antiquity: Essays in Tribute to George Christopher Stead: In Celebration of His Eightieth Birthday*. Leiden: Brill 1993.
Wilcox, Amanda. *The Gift of Correspondence in Classical Rome: Friendship in Cicero's Ad Familiares And Seneca's Moral Epistles*. Madison: University of Wisconsin Press, 2012.
Wiles, Maurice. "Eunomius: Hair-Splitting Dialectician or Defender of the Accessibility of Salvation?" In *The Making of Orthodoxy: Essays in Honor of Henry Chadwick*. Edited by Rowan Williams. Cambridge: Cambridge University Press, 1989: 157–72.
Williams, Joe. "Letter Writing, Materiality, and Gifts in Late Antiquity: Some Perspectives on Material Culture." *JLA* 7:2 (2014): 351–59.
Williams, Rowan. *Arius: Heresy and Tradition*. Grand Rapids, MI: Eerdmans, 2002.
Williams, Rowan. "Macrina's Deathbed Revisited: Gregory of Nyssa on Mind and Passion." In *Christian Faith and Greek Philosophy in Late Antiquity: Essays in Tribute to George Christopher Stead*. Edited by Lionel Wickham and Caroline Bammel. Leiden: Brill, 1993: 227–46.
Williams, Rowan, ed. *The Making of Orthodoxy: Essays in Honor of Henry Chadwick*. Cambridge: Cambridge University Press, 1989.
Williams, Rowan. *The Wound of Knowledge: Christian Spirituality from the New Testament to St. John of the Cross*. London: Darton, Longman and Todd, 1979.
Wilson, Brittany. *Unmanly Men: Refigurations of Masculinity in Luke-Acts*. Oxford: Oxford University Press, 2015.

Worthington, Ian, ed. *A Companion to Greek Rhetoric*. Malden, MA: Blackwell, 2007.
Young, Francis, Lewis Ayres, and Andrew Louth, eds. *The Cambridge History of Early Christian Literature*. Cambridge: Cambridge University Press, 2004.
Zacharia, Katarina, ed. *Hellenisms: Culture, Identity, and Ethnicity from Antiquity to Modernity*. Aldershot: Ashgate, 2008.
Zachhuber, Johannes. *Human Nature in Gregory of Nyssa: Philosophical Background and Theological Significance*. Leiden: Brill, 2000.

Index

abbot (Benedictine), 274
Ablabius (rhetorician), 98–9
Abraham (O.T. patriarch), 58–9, 235
absence, 49
  as literary trope for friendship, 53, 61, 104, 110–11
Aburgius (imperial magistrate from Cappadocia), 7
Achilles (Greek warrior), 2, 10, 72–4, 86, 93–4, 175, 203
Acts (N.T.), 129, 139–40
Adamantius (priest), 98
Adelphius (friend of Nyssen), 123–4
adolescence, 25, 43, 70–2, 101
  and training for manhood, 70–2
  as undeveloped, 266
adventus, 3
Aelius Aristides (orator), 68, 72, 127, 176, 230–1
Aelius Theon (rhetorician), 54, 123
Aeschylus (Greek tragedian), 78, 138, 253, 267
aesthetic. *See* beauty
  of friendship, 104, 111, 143, 152
  of manhood, 61, 106, 118, 158, 209
Aetius (theologian), 162, 173, 214, 220
  abuse of language, 262–5
  as foil to Macrina, 257, 266–8
  background and contrast to Cappadocians, 218–23
  lacking *aretē* as mentor to Eunomius, 261–6
Agamemnon (king of Mycenae), 92, 174
agapē, 107

agathos/agathoi, 10–12, 39, 58, 61–2, 65–6, 82–4, 92, 99, 101, 103–4, 144, 154, 174, 214, 233, 251, 257
agōn. *See* virtual; *agōn*, *See* exhibition; as *agōn*, *See* asceticism, *See* purification; *agōn* as, *See* *aretē*; product of *agōn*
  and identity, 10–14, 86–96
  and theological authority, 214–18, 223–44, 247
  classical, 9–14, 44–5
  epistolary exchange as, 3–4, 17–18, 40–1, 48–56, 77–86
  euergetism as, 35
  gift exchange as, 145
  in friendship, 103–8
  in hagiography, 5, 20–1, 44, 56–61, 158–60, 186–200
  Second Sophistic antecedents, 67–70
agora, 128
Ahab (Israelite king), 173, 232
Ajax (Greek hero), 96, 103, 145
Alexander the Great, 54–6, 239
Alexandria (city), 23, 26, 165, 216, 219, 236–7, 243
Amalekites (enemy of Israel), 175–6
Ambrose of Milan, 112
Ammianus Marcellinus (historian), 182
Amphilochius the Elder, 25
Amphilochius the Younger, 24–5, 28, 84, 91, 96–7, 100, 132, 134, 138–9, 141
Andronicus (Governor of Armenia), 49
Annesi (town in Pontus), 267, 269
Antioch, 47, 218–19, 269

Index

Antiochanus (addressee of Nyssen), 54–5
antithesis, 42, 59, 64, 89, 99, 183, 205, 224, 234, 247
Aphrodite (goddess), 90, 205
Apollinaris (bishop), 213
Apollinarists, 212
Apollo (god), 84
apologist, 153, 172, 219
appetite, 237, 248
arbiter, 4, 117, 144, 256
   Cappadocians as judges of literary style, 95
aretē. *See* exhibition; of *aretē*, *See* family; and shared *aretē*, *See* beauty; and *aretē*, *See* character; as moral virtue
   and masculinity, 12, 91–101
   and theological rivalry, 223–4, 238, 243–4, 256–7
   as source of friendship, 103–18, 124, 145, 148–9
   classical, 3–5, 9–14, 32, 44, 54–6
   handwriting and, 141–5
   in female saints, 186–200
   manifest in the body, 200–1
   product of *agōn*, 11–21, 77–86
   sacred, 48, 56–61, 155–60, 172–200, 216–18, 253, 272–4
Arian/Arians, 165, 219
   as inferior to Nicene bishop Athanasius, 232–4
   and flawed language, 241–2
   as counter ascetics, 237
Arianzus (Cappadocian town), 23
Ariminum (Coucil of), 161–2
aristocracy/aristocrat
   and athletics, 166, 187
   and masculine deportment, 11–12, 37, 84, 158
   association with *paideia*, 21–2, 67, 270
   expectations of provincial, 25, 32–5, 41, 167, 253–4
   horses associated with, 2
   hunting as an activity of, 86
   image of, 106, 108, 118, 191, 198–200, 251–2
   provincial, bishops coming from ranks of, 6–7
Aristophanes (playwright), 3, 95, 109
Aristotle, 16, 112, 200
   and *aretē*, 11–12, 19, 85
   and friendship, 103

   andreia and endurance, 191
   as a source of erudition, 171
   beauty and vision, 119, 205
   dialectic, 219
   epistles as a gift, 150
   friendship, 109
   hands and gestures, 137
   hierarchy of the senses, 154
   intimacy, 98
   on verbal description, 203
   physiognomy, 113
   sound and voice, 133
   synkrisis, 184
   teacher of Alexander the Great, 55
Arius (theologian), *See* Arian/Arians
Armenia/Armenians, 24, 42, 49, 178, 182–3
   characterized as theological rivals, 178
asceticism, 4, 20, 25, 29
   and masculinity, 36–45
   and purification, 217–18
   as *agōn*, 45, 228–9
   in female saints, 160, 186–90, 193–9
   in *Life of Macrina*, 257–60
   as authorization, 215–18, 223–4
   Athanasius and, 232–40
   Basil and, 41–4
   Eunomians as antithesis of, 223–4
   Macrina as contrast to Eunomius, 266–8
   paideia in Basil as asceticism, 247–50, 255
   silence as, 131–2
Ascholius (Bishop of Thessalonica), 119
Asianism, 89
   as effeminate style, 64, 89
Asterius (Cappadocian magistrate), 136
Athanasius (bishop). *See* biography; oration on Athanasius, *See* asceticism; Athanasius and, *See* Egypt; and Athanasius
   and pure speech, 242–4
   as pro-Nicene hero, 217–18, 232–5
   asceticism and, 43, 232, 234
   in fourth-century theology, 163, 235–9
   Life of Antony, 43, 239, 244
Athena (goddess), 136, 205
Athens
   and *paideia*, 7
   Athena myth, 136
   Basil and Nazianzen at, 22, 27–8, 70–4, 78, 88, 100, 177–8, 248
   classical, 82, 97, 173

Athens (cont.)
  generals from, 96, 98
  Libanius at, 47
athlete
  and *paideia*, 159–60, 230
  ascetic as, 20, 159
  Athanasius as, 236, 238
  beauty in, 209
  Caesarius as, 168, 170–1, 273
  Gregory Thaumaturgus as, 156–7, 166–8
  female saints as, 38, 188
  idealized masculinity, 11–14, 44, 66, 71–2, 170
  Macrina as, 194–6
  martyr as, 159, 187
  Olympic, 137
athletics
  and *aretē*, 16–18, 159–60, 167
  and aristocracy, 166, 187
  as *agōn*, 11–12, 16, 78–82, 108, 145
Atticism (literary style), 53, 64, 148
Ayres, Lewis, 3, 162, 165

Baal (Canaanite god), 185
Balios and Xanthos (Achilles' horses), 2, 93
barbarian, 31, 100, 179
  antithesis of Greek, 31, 99–100, 128, 223, 242
  as effeminate, 19, 55, 183
  as heresy, 177, 179
Barnes, Timothy, 27, 42, 232
Basil. *See* Athens; Basil and Nazianzen at
  Address to Young Men, 79–80
  advises friend Leontius on handwriting, 144
  Against Eunomius, 164, 220, 225
  agōn produces superior speech in, 254–6
  antithesis of unmanly bishops, 246–56
  as authentic theologian, 244–56
  as bishop, 5–6
  as combatant, 58–9, 172–84
  as Moses, 184–5
  asceticism of, 41–4
  Asketikon, 42
  beauty in friends as virtue and piety, 106, 109–13, 118–23
  beauty of, 201–2
  body and soul in letter to Maximus the Philosopher, 111–12
  ceremony of letter delivery to Magninianus, 149
  combat against Heterousians, 172–5
  compared to Old Testament heroes, 184–6
  correspondence with Libanius, 27, 63
  counters Homoians, 184–5
  depicted in lineage of biblical protagonists, 58
  education at Constantinople, 26
  epistolary collection, 52, 90–1
  exhorts like Nestor and Themistocles, 96–7
  family of, 24–5, 261, 266–70
  friendship with Nazianzen, 25–7, 73–5, 105–6
  influenced by Eustathius of Sebaste, 42, 162–3
  laments Valens' administrative division of Cappadocia, 124–8
  likened to Israelite kings, 176
  likened to O.T. prophet Job, 185
  Macrina as guide for, 266–9
  Magninianus' daughter Icelium as letter carrier, 149
  medical theory in letter to Eustathius the physician, 83
  on *agōn* and *aretē*, 79–80
  opposes Eunomius, 224–5
  opposes Valens' religious policies in Cappadocia, 164, 175–6, 178–86, 273
  paideia as asceticism in, 246–50, 255–6
  petition for friend Domitian, 49–50
  petitions Governor Andronicus through letter, 49–50
  pleads to Martinianus on behalf of Cappadocia, 124–9
  sensual appeal of correspondence, 115–16
  shepherds congregation at Satala through letter, 49–50
  studied through network theory, 51–2
  study under Libanius, 26
  subject in *Encomium* by Nyssen, 58–60, 172–7, 184–5, 194, 201–2, 223
  subject of *Oration* 43 by Nazianzen, 177–86, 202, 246–56
  the *Basiliad* (hospital), 33, 183
  theology of, 163–4, 180–1, 246–50
  training in *paideia*, 25–8, 44–5, 71, 73–5, 177–8, 246–56
  transcendent masculinity, 40–4
  use of *ekphrasis*, 124–6

use of hands and voice in letter to
    Amphilochius, 139–40
uses metaphor of light, 121–2
voice depicted as fire, 254
Basil of Ancyra (bishop), 162
Basil the Elder, 24, 259
Basiliad (Basil's hospital), 33
Bassi, Karen, 14, 66, 96–7, 158
beauty (*kalos; kallos*)
    and *aretē*, 113–18, 200–11
    and materiality, 106, 121
    and vision, 118–27
    as sign of moral virtue, 20, 124, 236
    of voice, 132
Beeley, Christopher, 227
begotten/unbegotten (*gennētos/agennētos*), 212–13, 220–2
Benedictine monastic order, 274
Bernardi, Jean, 41, 157–8
best (*aristos*), 16, 66, 74, 118, 137, 167, 191
    to outdo (as a verb), 11, 15
biography
    and audience, 157
    and masculinity, 159
    arbiters of, 218
    as polemic, 160, 173, 218–25, 244–69
    encomium, 56, 157
    Encomium on Basil by Nyssen, 172–7, 194, 223
    hagiographic (saints' lives), 56–61
    letters as, 91
    letters as autobiography, 51–2, 151
    Life of Gregory Thaumaturgus, 166–8
    Life of Macrina, 194–200, 256–69
    Nazianzen's *Oration on Basil* (Or. 43), 172–84, 244–56
    Nazianzen's *Oration on Athanasius* (Or. 21), 231–44
    Nazianzen's *Oration on Caesarius* (Or. 7), 168–72
    Nazianzen's *Oration on Gorgonia* (Or. 8), 190–4
    of female saints, 186–90, 203, 209, 211
    pro-Nicene, 161, 166, 215–17, 272
bishops
    and *paideia*, 6, 8, 49, 54, 76–7, 209, 253
    as provincial administrators, 6
    as shifty, 63
    asceticism and, 257, 269–70
    Moses as a model for, 235
    New Testament descriptions of, 100

non-Trinitarian, 161–2
pro-Nicene, 59, 62, 157–8, 209–10, 240, 273
theological rivalries, 166, 180–1
unqualified, 253
body/corporeality, 116
    and fellowship, 153–4
    and *paideia*, 140, 211, 241
    and soul, 104, 109–15, 130–1, 133, 213
    and training, 79, 83
    as measure of manhood, 17, 19–20, 106, 112, 118, 203–9
    as society, 125, 128
    as text, 108, 115
    as the church, 125, 173, 210, 256
    association with femininity, 188, 202, 227, 268
    beauty of, 202–3
    control of, 159, 193, 195–7, 199, 215, 223–4, 250, 254, 268
    elevated status of, 117–18, 141, 153
    hierarchy within, 113
    imagery in friendship, 108–24, 134–7, 145
    in *ekphrasis*, 120–5
    body language, 43, 61, 110, 115, 136, 149, 153, 238
    management of in female saints, 203–7
    of Christ, 116
    punishment, 70
    rhetoric as struggle of, 78
    soul and, 72
    struggle within, 160, 188, 191–2, 196
    training of, 74, 81, 247
    unmanliness in, 200, 237
    voice as part of, 129, 241, 243, 254
boldness
    in speech (*parrēsia*), 87, 128, 176
    sign of masculinity, 99, 143, 158, 166–7, 169, 183, 199
Bourdieu, Pierre, 4, 6, 66–7
Brakke, David, 20–1, 45, 232
breath
    and *pneuma*, 254–5
    and voice, 134, 254
    of Zeus, 93–4
Brown, Peter, 6, 8
Burrus, Virginia, 36–40, 189, 192, 261–2, 267
Byzantine
    illustrations of bishops, 274, 277

Cadenhead, Raphael, 38–40
Caesarea (capital of Cappadocia), 23, 26, 29, 33
  and administrative divison of Cappadocia, 125
  as patron, 26
  Basil and Nazianzen defend against Valens' policies, 164, 173, 180–1, 183
  Basil laments harm from administrative division, 125–8
  Basiliad at, 33
Caesarius, 23, 59, 88, 114–15, 273
  beauty of, 200–1
  Nazianzen's *Oration* 7, 168–72
Callimachus (Athenian general at Marathon), 98
Calvet-Sebasti, Marie-Ange, 65
Cameron, Averil, 153
Candidianus (Governor of Cappadocia), 1–3, 146
Carolingian
  monastery, 274
ceremony
  letter as choreographing, 3, 126
  letter delivery as, 148–9
Chaeronea (Battle of), 176
champion
  as defender, 232, 234, 255
  as masculine figure, 27, 108, 156, 166
character/disposition (*ēthos*)
  as essence of an individual, 73, 90, 104–13, 119–20, 123–9, 198, 201, 209, 239
  as moral virtue, 9, 17, 60, 82–4, 137, 141, 153, 165, 175, 188, 214–17, 229, 243, 249–50, 258, 269
  lack of moral formation in rivals, 224, 264–6
charlatan
  as unmanly, 249
  Heterousians depicted as, 217, 225, 264
  sophist as, 230
  unqualified bishops as, 247
cheat
  Aetius portrayed as a, 263
Christ, 13, 116, 121, 226, 274, *See* Jesus Christ
  as bridegroom to Macrina, 260
  as counterpoint to philosophy, 260
  as cure for Gorgonia, 193
  as the true male, 43

Cappadocians as followers of, 34, 58, 111, 170–1, 179, 196
  clergy submitting to, 37
  divinity of, 185
  eloquence submitted to, 256
  message of, 226
  prize of salvation in, 159
  pure philosophy in, 261
  reliance on, 196
  tempted by Satan, 167
Christology
  and Valens, 179
  of Arius, 219
  of Eunomius, 220–2
  theological rivalry over, 161–6
Cicero (Latin rhetorician), 96, 130
Clark, Elizabeth, 37, 43, 54, 198
Clement of Alexandria (theologian), 107
clothing
  and masculinity, 277
  of letter deliverer, 149
Cobb, L. Stephanie, 20–1, 45, 60, 160, 187–8
collective, 181
  aretē, 11
  identity, 6
  memory, 181
  munificence, 34
  sense of manhood, 25, 97, 108, 114, 128, 184, 253
  suffering of Cappadocia, 126
  values, 15, 76, 97, 128, 167
Colossians (N.T. book), 13, 111, 143
combat, 2, 10–12, 14, 20, 37, 64, 70, 72–3, 96, 145, 174, 181, 199, 209, 243
  against demons, 20
  against heresy, 167, 209, 273
  and honor, 10–15, 59, 151, 243
  and horses, 2
  and piety, 273
  and trustworthiness, 94, 160, 174, 199
  close rank, 174–5
  gymnasium as training for, 81
  in *Iliad*, 64, 103, 145
  paideia as, 70, 230
  verbal, 15, 29, 53, 71–3, 86, 132, 178
Commodus (Emperor), 127
composure
  as masculinity, 132, 144, 187, 191–2
  in female saints, 187–97, 270
Constantine (Emperor), 32

Index

Constantinople
  Basil's training at, 26
  Council of 381, 22, 24, 45, 51, 165–6, 216, 226, 274
  Libanius teaches at, 47
  Nazianzen bishop at, 213, 226, 230–44
  Nazianzen's dismissal and response, 131, 244–6, 270
  Nyssen writing during Council of, 257
  populist theologians in 381, 212
  Synod of 360, 41, 162, 164, 180
Constantius II (Emperor), 23, 161
  as supporter of Homoianism, 161–2
contemplation of God (*theōria*), 215, 234
contest. *See agōn*
conversation
  letter as, 130, 134
Coon, Lynda, 58, 133, 190, 274
courage/bravery (*andreia*)
  against sexual temptation, 207
  and *paideia*, 230
  and piety, 61, 187, 270
  as basis for manhood, 10–12, 17, *118*, *171*
  as emulated from the past, 55, 66, 78, *103*, *236*
  in warriors, 64, 78, *145*, 174–8, 181
  associated with pro-Nicenes, 158
  based in the soul, 113
  dependence on God, 260
  during suffering, *190*–9, *199*, 270, 273
  in exile, 239
  in N.T., 10
  in predecessors, 98
  inner, *189*
craftsmanship (*technē*)
  dishonorable, 262–4
  epistolary composition as, 18, 89, 101, 127, 147–8
  rhetoric as, 64, 69–71, 81, 110, 262
Cribiore, Raffaella, 1, 47, 66, 76, 80
Croesus (King of Lydia), 50
crucifixion, 139
cultural capital
  among provincial elites, 6
  and bestowal of honor, 8
  epistles as, *61, 148, 160*
  in early Greece, 9
  in Pierre Bourdieu, 6
curiales (local magistrates)
  Cappadocians as, 23

  emphasis on *paideia*, 218
  expectations of patronage, 25
  local aristocracy, 6
  performance of civic duty, 32–5
Cynegirus (Athenian general at Marathon), 98
Cynic/Cynicism (philosophy)
  Diogenes, 239
  Maximus, 245
  on acquiring virtue, 12–13
Cyrus (King of Persia), 50

Daley, Brian, 204
dance,
  expression of excitement, 117
  as image of effeminacy, 125, 230, 233, 249
Daniélou, Jean, 221
Darius (King of Persia), 181
David (King of Israel)
  Athanasius likened to, 235
  Basil likened to, 176
  friendship with Jonathan, 109
  at right hand of Yahweh, 140
declamation, 18, 53, 64, 128
  as advertising manhood, 71
  as athletic event, 73, 75
decorum
  as noble woman, 191
  as superior behavior, 6, 192, 194, 200, 204, 211
  of classical male, 45, 224
decurion. *See curiales*
DelCogliano, Mark, 163, 221
Demetrius of Phalerum (rhetorician), 89
demons, 240
  conquest of, 20–1, 157
Demosthenes (Emperor Valens' official), 164, 182
  portrayed as effeminate, 182
Demosthenes (orator), 69
  favors weapons of footsoldier, 175
  on dying nobly, 176
  on word and deed, 155, 239
  portrayed as warrior, 72–3
  training his voice, 133
dialectic, 214, 219, 263
  and Heterousians, 226
  as insufficient means of knowledge, 169, 214, 222, 226, 262

dialectic (cont.)
  associated with practice of medicine, 219, 263
  use by Aetius, 219
Dianius (Cappadocian bishop), 180
Dio Chrysostom (orator), 33
  athletics and manhood, *170*
  body signifying manhood, *118*
  on false teachers, 225, 230–1, 249
  meeting between Alexander the Great and Diogenes the Cynic, 239
Diogenes the Cynic (philosopher), 239
Diogenes Laertius (biographer), 129
Diomedes (Greek warrior), 135
Dionysus (god of wine), 125
disputation, public
  and influence of holy women, 189, 210
  as entertainment, 234, 266
  as site of *agōn*, 159
  in Second Sophistic, 169
  theological, 180, 220, 269
domestic sphere
  emphasized in female saints, 40, 187, 194, 210
Domitian (friend of Basil), 49–50

effeminacy
  and lack of civic responsibility, 41, 175
  asceticism as, 42–3
  Athanasius in contrast to, 244
  characteristics of described by Lucian, 63, 231
  Christianity interpreted as, 35
  dancing as. *See* dancing
  Eunomians associated with, 225–7
  heresy as, 21, 60
  in Heterousians, 216, 233, 242
  in Nazianzen's description of bishops, 251
  in opponents of pro-Nicenes, 5, 99, 160, 177, 182
  luxury as, 179
  Persia as metaphor for, 98
Egypt/Egyptians
  and Athanasius, 164, 231–43
  Homoians represented as, 185
  Joseph provides grain for, 186
  monks in, 20
ekphrasis, 104, 120, 123
  in letters of friendship, 123–7
  in recounting suffering, 124–7, 188, 191, 196

Elijah (Israelite prophet), 58–9, 173, 185, 255
Elm, Susanna, 5, 36
  and "new masculinity", 189
  and Nazianzen's philosophical family, 169
  Nazianzen's vision of empire, 59, 247
  significance of *paideia* to theology, 9, 215
eloquence. *See* warfare; eloquence and, *See* exertion; sweat of eloquence, *See* self-representation; in *paideia*
  and *agōn*, 71–5, 78–80, 86, 101, 256, 262
  as source of identity, 7, 9, 11, 25, 30–1, 51–4, 65, 95, 198–9
  shallow, 89, 265
emasculation
  of church leaders by Emperor Julian, 4, 172
  of Jesus, 35
Emmelia (mother of Basil and Nyssen), 24
  manages her beauty, 205
  oversees Macrina's education, 258
  urges Macrina to accept medical help, 260
emotion
  associated with Asianic literary style, 89
  control over, 188
  directing, 111, 123, 127, 146
  Gorgonia's restraint of, 191–3
  letters as evoking, 145, 191–3
  theology compromised by, 241
encomium. *See* oration, *See* panegyric, *See* biography
Ephesians (N.T. book), 121, 135
Ephraim (son of Jacob the Israelite), 139
Epictetus (philosopher), 233
Epicurus (philosopher), 171
epinician (victory ode), 167–8
Epiphanius (Bishop of Salamis, Cyprus), 228
Epiphanius (friend of Nazianzen), 135
epistle/epistolary exchange. *See agōn*; epistolary exchange as, *See* craftsmanship; epistolary composition as, *See* gamesmanship; epistolary exchange as
  and erotic imagery, 114–18
  and friendship, 104–14
  and identity formation, 48–56, 86–8, 132–4, 141–4

Index 323

and sensory rhetoric, 118–41
as gift exchange, 145
collections, 89–91
exhibition of, 4–16, 63–7, 82–6
genre of, 50–4
network of, 50–2
eroticism/sensuality (*erōs*)
and perfected manhood, 37
in epistolary exchange, 114–21
of body and soul, 153
Esau (O.T. son of Isaac), 176
Eshleman, Kendra, 46, 224
Euclid (mathematician), 171
Eudoxius (rhetorician from Cappadocia), 17
correspondent of Nazianzen, 84–6, 95–6
Eudoxius of Antioch (Bishop of Constantinople), 162, 173, 219
euergetism/benefactor. *See* honor; through euergetism
and humility, 34
and pride, 31–4
as *agōn*, 31–2
Eugenius (deacon in Cappadocia), 140
Eunapius of Sardis (historian), 7, 27, 63, 71, 74–5
Eunomius, 5, 22, *See* Aetius; as mentor to Eunomius, *See* polemic; against Eunomius
and distorted *paideia*, 59, 224–7, 264–6
as contrast to pro-Nicenes, 216, 243–56, 261–2
as flawed theologian, 214–15, 222–4, 227–31, 261–2
as opponent of pro-Nicenes, 218–22
family and background, 219–20, 265
theology of, 162–6, 173, 212, 220–2
Eupatrius (lawyer from Pontus), 94–5
Euripides (playwright), 68, 125, 138, 148
Eurybiades (Spartan naval commander), 96
Eurycleia (servant of Odysseus), 207
Eusebius (Bishop of Caesarea in Cappadoca), 24, 179–80
Eustathius (physician and friend of Basil), 83
Eustathius of Sebaste (bishop from Armenia), 42, 162–3
Eustochius (Cappadocian rhetorician), 92–3, 132
Eutropius (Proconsul of Asia), 151–2

exertion/labor
as manhood, 80–2
asceticism as, 158, 187, 234, 270
classical precedents, 79
indicative of *paideia*, 149, 235, 243, 247, 254
letter writing as, 17, 48, 61, 67, 78, 100, 147
"sweat of eloquence", 63, 71, 78–9, 88
exhibition/display
and *aretē*, 59
as *agōn*, 86, 92, 243
as moral superiority, 30
epistolary composition as, 4, 15, 21, 47, 67
hagiographic biography as, 172, 175, 188, 199
in female saints, 187, 188, 191, 194, 199, 205
in friendship, 103, 127, 145, 152
in Second Sophistic, 75–7, 77
of *aretē*, 14, 32, 44, 62, 76, 82, 135, 158
of cultural capital, 8
of masculinity, 21, 99, 191, 195
oratorical, 14, 18–19, 30, 53, 66, 71, 134
the body as, 113, 117, 124, 144, 158, 201
exile
as asceticism, 240
of Aetius, 219
of Athanasius, 163, 231–44
of Diogenes the Cynic, 239
of Gregory of Nyssa, 164
of pro-Nicene bishops by Valens, 165, 180
Exodus (O.T. book), 129, 140, 168, 176, 186
eyes/seeing/vision, 167
and discernment, 16, 110, 119–20, 168, 235, 238
and *ekphrasis*, 123–8
and penetration, 207, 261
as portal for *erōs*, 204
as virtuous, 154
direct contact and reciprocity among friends, 122–3
highest sense of corporeal hierarchy, 113, 118–19
relationship to hands, 201
face
expression of, 136, 200

face (cont.)
  face-to-face nature of *agōn*, 82, 106, 122, 130, 174
  in conversations, 130
  in hierarchy of the body, 119
  measure of the body, 113
family/families
  and *agōn*, 31–2
  and guest friendship (*xenia*), 103, 135
  and shared *aretē*, 45, 48, 97, 158, 187, 190–1, 253–4, 272
  beauty depicted in, 203, 208
  in hagiography, 57, 200, 210, 267
  Macrina's consolation of, 194
  of Aetius and Eunomius, 218–20, 265
  of Basil and Gregory of Nyssa, 24–5, 266
  of Gregory of Nazianzus, 23–4, 257
  of Libanius, 47
  philosophical. *See* Elm, Susanna
  provincial elite, 6, 23, 33–5
  sacred pedigree in, 156–7, 164, 177
  theological and rhetorical education from, 25
fellowship (*koinōnia*)
  based on Christian identity, 61, 102, 111, 135, 143
  of *pepaideumenoi*, 15, 102, 147
female/femininity. *See* domestic sphere; emphasized in female saints, *See* exhibition; in female saints, *See* modesty; in female saints
  and male, dichotomy of, 18, 40–1
  and male, fluidity between, 38–9, 60
  as instructive device, 37, 54
  as masculine, 187–90, 199
  asceticism as *agōn*, 186–90, 192–9
  body, in martyr accounts, 187–8, 191–4
  body, management of, 202–8
  conventional characteristics of, 10, 188, 193, 205
  in gender hierarchy, 43–4, 191
  saint as athlete, 38, 188
  saints and *aretē*, 186–99
  saints, biography and, 186–90, 203–4, 208–11
  saints, honor in, 188, 198–205, 211
  saints, piety associated with, 211
  soul as, 38
  vanity, 205

festival
  athletic, 85
  Gorgonia's deathbed as, 194
  letter reception as, 146
Finley, Moses, 145
fire
  as a medium for testing, 245
  Basil's breath as, 254
  light of as a beacon, 121
  tongue compared to, 132
I Corinthians (N.T. book), 111–12, 159, 226, 228, 237, 260, 268
I Kings (O.T. book), 173
I Peter (N.T. book), 77
I Samuel (O.T. book), 109, 129, 176
I Thessalonians (N.T. book), 242
I Timothy (N.T. book), 100, 190, 196, 264
Fortunatus (friend of Nazianzen), 137
Fourth Maccabees (book of), 13, 159
Frank, Georgia, 122, 206
friendship/friend (*philia/philos*). *See* literature; friendship in, *See* nobility; in friendship, *See* Homer; friendship in, *See* reciprocity; in friendship
  among *pepaideumenoi*, 103–14
  and *agōn*, 103–8
  and honor, 103–8
  and reordering of materiality, 61, 108–10, 152–3
  and rhetoric of gift-giving, 145–52
  and sensory pleasure, 115–18
  and the senses, 113–34, 152–3
  and the soul, 108–27
  and the voice, 131–4
  ekphrasis in, 123–7
  family/guest (*xenia*), 103, 135
  imagery of body in, 109–24, 134–7
  in Aristotle, 85, 103, 119
  in Second Sophistic, 105–6, 109, 118
  networking in, 106–8
  philosophy of, 103–4
  rhetoric of, 103–8
  symbolism of the hand in, 134–8
  through epistolary exchange, 104–14
  with basis in *aretē*, 103–8, 124, 145, 148–9
Fruchtman, Diane, 188
Fulda (Benedictine monastery), 274

Galatians (N.T. book), 35, 135, 143, 195
Galen (physician), 83, 171

gamesmanship
  epistolary exchange as, 63–5, 84–6, 91–3
Gangra (Council of), 42
Gautier, Francis, 2, 17, 77
gaze
  as act of masculinity, 98–9, 122, 207
  as penetration, 122, 205
gender
  and *aretē*, 14, 133
  and asceticism, 38, 41–3
  and voice, 95, 98, 128
  classical conventions of, 4, 18–21, 57, 80, 171, 186–7, 209
  fluidity/reversal, 80–1, 97, 182, 227, 272
  hierarchy in, 39–44, 177, 198
  in Benedictine liturgy, 274
  moral element of, 10, 13, 195, 211
  reconfigured, 35–9, 60, 189
Genesis (O.T. book), 139, 185
geometry, 169
George of Cappadocia (Arian Bishop of Alexandria), 219, 237
gesture
  and mutual respect, 276
  as complement to text, 136–7
  as index of gender, 43, 140
  vision as, 122
gift
  as patronage, 31
  epistle as, 61, 145–53
  epistolary collection as, 24, 68, 90
  exchange of between Homeric warriors, 103, 145
  hagiographic narrative as, 201
  rhetoric of in friendship, 106, 145, 277
Glaukos (Trojan warrior), 135
Gleason, Maud, 14, 80, 254
gluttony
  as disqualification for theologians, 237, 248, 250
Goldhill, Simon, 14, 29, 124
Gorgonia, 24, 39–40, 190, See also biography; oration on Gorgonia
  aretē of body, 186–90, 194
  beauty of, 175–208
  biblical women as model for, 187
  control of body, 207–8
  reconfigured masculinity in, 199–200
Greekness/Hellenism, 55, 183–4, 209

Gregory of Nazianzus. *See* Nazianzen
Gregory of Nyssa. *See* Nyssen
Gregory Thaumaturgus. *See* also athlete; Gregory Thaumaturgus as
  agōnes, 167–8
  aretē in, 59, 61, 166–7
  as man of deeds, 155
  as pro-Nicene, 168, 273
  Life of Gregory Thaumaturgus. *See* also biography; *Life of Gregory Thaumaturgus*
Gunderson, Erik, 63, 80, 129, 229, 231
gymnasium, 127
  as crucible of masculinity, 81, 170, 186, 202

habit, 7, 187, 231, 234
habitus in Pierre Bourdieu, 4
heresy as, 264
moral goodness as, 12, 17, 82
paideia as, 36, 66, 143, 153
hand/touch
  and participation, 147
  as active, 134
  as medium of sanctity, 138–40, 154, 201
  as most terrene of senses, 141, 153
  commanded by higher senses, 119
  exceeding materiality, 140–1
  honor of right hand, 135, 138–41, 276
  in friendship, 134–8
  in mediation, 136
  inferiority of left hand, 138
  significance in writing, 141–5, 150
handwriting/penmanship, 141–5
  autograph, 143–4
  calligrapher, 142
  sign of *aretē*, 143–4
  stenographer, 142–3
Harrison, Verna, 38–41, 187, 267
Harvey, Susan Ashbrook, 109
Hawhee, Debra, 17, 85
Hector (Trojan warrior), 10, 103, 145, 174
heir
  of classical intellectuals, 47, 61–2, 67, 69, 169, 186, 271
Helen (of Sparta), 258
Helladius (Bishop of Caesarea in Cappadocia), 146
Hephaestion (rhetorician/rival of Prohaeresius), 74
Hera (goddess), 205

Heracles (Greek hero), 80
heresy, 177, 184, 224, 232, 243, 269, *See*
  habit; heresy as, *See* barbarian; as
  heresy, *See* combat; heresy as, *See*
  effeminacy; in opponents of pro-
  Nicenes, *See* effeminacy; heresy as
  as disordered *paideia*, 242
  associated with *paideia*, 228
Hermogenes (rhetorician), 123
hero/heroes, 158, 173, 234
  as pro-Nicene, 161, 166
  athlete as, 158, 195
  best man, 97, 167
  biblical, 58–9, 184, 217, 235–6, 243, 273
  Homeric, 73–4, 94, 96, 145, 203, 210
Hero (mathematician), 171
Herod (King of Judea), 185
Herodes Atticus (rhetorician), 72
Herodotus (historian), 50, 64, 68, 98
heroic, 2, *See* combat; and honor
  combat, 2, 86, 97, 99, 167, *See also*
    combat; and honor
  past, 45, 65, 81, 99, 186, 189
heroine
  as athlete, 158
  as pro-Nicene, 158, 161, 166
  biblical, 58–9
  spiritual, 190
Hesiod (poet), 68, 79, 85
hetaireia (companion), 7
Heterousian/s, 212, 246, 251, 270
  as Basil's enemies, 172–6
  as counterpoint to Macrina, 256–67, 273
  as foil to pro-Nicene bishops, 216–44, 273
  as unmanly, 204
  in fourth-century theology, 162–6
hierarchy, 13, 46, 118, 133, 197, *See*
  gender; and asceticism, *See* gender;
  hierarchy in
  episcopal, 43, 100, 210, 214, 228–9, 240, 277
  of body, 118–19, 127, 133, 153
  of *pepaideumenoi*, 21–2, 34, 78, 88, 134, 148, 153, 160
Hildebrand, Stephen, 162–3, 221
Himerius (rhetorician), 27
Hippocrates (physician), 171
history
  as subject of *paideia*, 6, 14, 47, 65, 101

Hodges-Kluck, Stefan, 133, 254
Homer, 64, 151, 206, 258, *See* hero;
  Homeric, *See* combat; close rank, *See*
  combat; in *Iliad*
  aretē in, 10–11, 65, 81, 95
  friendship in, 135–6, 138, 152
  in Second Sophistic, 68
Homoian/s
  Basil battles against, 184–5
  Eunomius as, 219–20
  in fourth-century theology, 161–6
  Nazianzen faces at Constantinople, 226, 232
  Valens as supporter of, 175–84
Homoiousian/s
  against Eunomius, 219
  and Valens, 175–84
  in fourth-century theology, 163–4
Homoousian/s, 165
  and Cappadocian biography, 218, 226, 229, 273
  and Valens, 182
  Eunomius against, 218–21
  in fourth-century theology, 161–6
honor. *See* courage; as warriors, *See* hand;
  honor of right hand, *See* cultural
  capital; and bestowal of honor, *See*
  combat; and honor, *See* gift; exchange
  of between Homeric warriors
  agōn as, 85
  among *pepaideumenoi*, 6–8, 15, 54, 81, 253
  as *agōn*, 159
  based on classical precedents, 9–15, 95, 112
  epistolary exchange and, 3–5, 66, 77, 84, 146–53
  eyes and, 119
  family, 190
  in female saints, 188, 198–205, 211
  in friendship, 85, 103–8
  of orators, 30, 66, 72
  of parents, 135
  through euergetism, 32
hoplite, 11, 176–7, *See* combat; and honor,
  See combat; close rank, *See* courage;
  as warriors, *See* hero; Homeric
  as symbol of masculinity, 20, 174–5, 194, 210
horse. 2, 26, 72, 85, 93, *See* combat; and
  horses, *See* Balios and Xanthos
  (Achilles' horses)

Cappadocian pride in, 2
control of, 269
racing of, 73, 116
hunting, 25
    activity of *pepaideumenos*, 86
    for *aretē*, 86
hypostaseis (persons of the Trinity)
    in fourth-century theology, 221
Hypsistarii, 23

Iamblichus (philosopher), 116
Icelium (letter carrier for Basil), 149
Iconium (city in Lycaonia), 24, 96–7, 100, 138–9
identity. *See* fellowship; based on Christian identity, *See* literature; and identity, *See* self-representation; and identity formation, *See* voice; as identity
    agōn forms, 9–14, 86–96, 272–7
    and asceticism, 41–4
    as pro-Nicene, 5, 21, 47, 98–100
    based on eloquence, 7–11, 25, 30–1, 51–4, 65, 95, 197–9
    epistles in formation of, 48–56, 86–8, 132–4, 141–5
    formation among *pepaideumenoi*, 41–55, 62, 145
    formation and genre, 48–61
    formation through martyr texts, 20–1, 46, 270
Iliad, 2, 64, 74, 86, 90, 92–3, 174, *See* Homer; friendship in, *See* gift; exchange of between Homeric warriors, *See* hero; Homeric, *See* combat; in Iliad, *See* combat; close rank
illness
    and *ekphrasis*, 196
    in Gorgonia, 273
    in Macrina, 195–6, 207, 260
image. *See* body; imagery in friendship, *See* aristocracy/aristocrat; image of
    martial, 17, 86, 97, 103, 175, 236, 243
    of classical masculinity, 12, 45, 172, 231, 261, 273
    of contest, 81–2, 158, 161, 166, 194, 196, 209–10, 217, 238
    of false theologian, 225, 231, 252, 263–4
    of humility, 77
    of philosopher, 238, 255, 257
    of pro-Nicene clergy as ideal leaders, 218
    of transcendent masculinity, 43–4, 189, 262
    paideia and, 62, 77, 93, 99, 144, 148, 248
    scriptural, 208, 273
    through letter collection, 51
imitation
    of classical Greece, 14, 69
intimacy
    among friends, 104, 131, 134, 143, 153
    in hagiographic biography, 210, 268–9
    letters promoting, 145
    with ancient Greeks, 3, 9, 98, 153
    with God (*theosis*), 224, 227, 235–6, 244, 256, 259, 261
invective. *See* polemic
Isaac (O.T. patriarch), 235
Isaiah (O.T. book), 140

Jacob (O.T. patriarch), 139, 185
James (N.T. book), 131, 227, 241
Jeremiah (Israelite prophet), 179
Jeremiah (O.T. book), 179, 182
Jesus Christ, 116, 129–30, 227, *See* Christ, *See* emasculation; of Jesus
    hands of, 139
    healing through touch, 139
    Satan tests, 167
Jewish
    anti-Jewish polemic by Cappadocians, 232
    exiles under King Nebuchadnezzar, 182
    martyrs, 13
Job (O.T. book), 129, 186, 197
Job (O.T. prophet)
    Athanasius likened to, 237–8
    Basil likened to, 185–6
    Macrina likened to, 197, 199
John (N.T. book), 121, 139, 171
John the Baptist, 58, 185
Joseph (O.T. son of Jacob), 186
Joshua (Israelite leader), 139, 176, 186
Joshua (O.T. book), 186
Jovinus (Count of the East), 119
Judaism
    influence on Hypsistarii, 23
    significance of hands in, 138
Julian (Emperor), 23, 59, 180, *See* emasculation; of church leaders by Emperor Julian
    and Nazianzen in rivalry, 5, 215
    and *paideia*, 47, 62, 116, 189, 223

Julian (Emperor) (cont.)
  as letter writer, 120
  Caesarius outperforms in *paideia*, 170–2, 273
  prohibits Christians from teaching classical *paideia*, 1–5
Julianus (Cappadocian rhetorician), 27
Julius Victor (rhetorician), 65, 130
Justinian (Emperor), 32

Konstan, David
  beauty in actions, 200
  courage of heroines, 206
  friendship between Basil and Nazianzen, 178
  on *philia*, 8
  vision and beauty, 119
  vocabulary for friendship, 105
Koskenniemi, Heikki, 51, 104
Krueger, Derek, 108, 115, 155, 259
Kurke, Leslie, 153

labor. *See* exertion
Laertes (King of Ithaca), 94–5
Lamachus (Greek general), 98
Lamentations (O.T. book), 243
language. *See* Arians; and flawed language, *See* body; language, *See* combat; verbal, *See* Latin; language as threat to Greek culture
  abuse of in Eunomius, 265–6
  and theology, 216–24, 241–2, 244, 259, 269
  as core of *paideia*, 101, 251, 254
  biblical, 105
  command of, 73, 95, 148, 247, 251
  figural, 153
  of giftedness, 106, 145
Latin
  language as threat to Greek culture, 30–1
  medieval Christianity, 277
  monasteries, 277
  physical performance, 19
lectio (liturgical reading), 274
lector (public reader), 133, 274
leitourgia. *See* euergetism (benefactors)
Leonidas (King of Sparta), 179
Leontius (rhetorician and friend of Basil), 144
letter. *See* epistle
Libanius. *See* Athens; Libanius, *See* Constantinople; Libanius teaches at, *See* family; of Libanius

and epistolary exchange, 83–4, 120
Basil's training under, 26
emphasis on Greek *paideia*, 3, 30–1
identity similar to that of Cappadocians, 46–8
influence on Gregory of Nyssa, 28
library of, 69
pursuit of friendship, 86, 116
reputation of, 18, 53, 147–8
Life and Miracles of Saint Thecla, 187
Life of Syncletica, 192
light
  as good (versus evil), 20, 121
  as revelation, 121
  classical and patristic sources for, 255
Lim, Richard, 214, 219, 222
Limberis, Vasiliki, 123–4
literature
  and identity, 4, 11, 19, 61, 67, 103
  friendship in, 103, 106, 109, 115, 140
  in *paideia*, 1, 6, 14, 47, 65, 88, 101
literatus/literati. *See pepaideumenos/ pepaideumenoi*
liturgy, 274
loggia, 274
Louth, Andrew, 115
loyalty, 33, 126, 152, 173–4, 206
Lucian of Samosata (rhetorician), 68, 111, *See* effeminacy; characteristics of described by Lucian
  athletics and manliness, 16, 82
  false orator, 225, 230–1, 256
  masculine orator, 80, 225, 242
Ludlow, Morwenna, 28, 70, 200–1, 262
luxury. *See* effeminacy; luxury as
Lycaonia (eastern Roman province), 24, 139
lyre/plectrum, 134
  instrument of manhood, 84

MacDougall, Byron, 64, 89, 146
Macrina, 5, 24, *See* virgin, *See* biography; *Life of Macrina*
  and Emmelia, 258, 260
  and illness, 195–7, 207–8, 260–1
  as athlete, 194–6
  as contrast to Heterousians, 256–67
  as foil to Aetius, 265–8
  as philosopher, 198, 256–61, 266–70
  asceticism of, 256–60
  compared to Job, 197–9
  guide for brothers, 266–8

Maenads (devotees of god Dionysus), 125
Magninianus (imperial magistrate and correspondent of Basil), 149
male/masculinity. *See* nobility; synonomous with classical masculinity, *See* boldness; sign of masculinity, *See pepaideumenos/pepaideumenoi*; masculinity of, *See* female; and male, *See* female; as masculine
  aretē as, 11–14, 90–9
  as pedigree, 4, 94–5
  asceticism and, 36–44
  associated with *paideia*, 6–9, 65–7, 69–75, 168–72, 177–84, 247–52
  athlete as idealized, 11–14, 170–1
  athletics and, 16–17, 82
  classical, characteristics of, 4–9, 13–15, 18–21, 30, 43–5, 99–101, 106, 254, 277
  clothing of, 277
  composure as trait of, 132, 144, 187, 191–2
  decorum as trait of, 45, 224
  exhibition of, 21, 98–9, 191, 195
  gaze as an act of, 98–9, 122–3, 207
  gymnasium as crucible of, 80–1, 170, 186, 202
  hoplite as emblematic of ideal, 20, 172–5, 209–10
  illustrated by *agōn*, 14–18, 44–5, 53–4, 66–70, 86–8
  images of classical, 12, 44–5, 172, 231, 261, 273
  in biography, 159
  of monks, 20–1, 46
  orator, 80
  personified as champion, 28, 108, 156, 166
  "play the man", 10, 39, 96–7
  self-control as trait of, 11, 19, 185, 240, 248, 251, 270
  self-control in transcendent, 189, 217, 268
  transcendent, 36–45, 188–90
  virtus (Latin), 274
  warfare as performance of, 3, 173–4
manuscript
  Codex 61 fol. 113r. Dionysiou Monastery, Mount Athos, 276
  of texts by classical authors, 68
Marathon (Battle of), 98

Maraval, Pierre, 54, 187, 199
Marcus Aurelius (Roman emperor), 127
Martin, Dale, 110, 113
Martinianus (Cappadocian nobleman and retired imperial official), 124–8
martyr/martyrdom, 194
  accounts of as identity forming texts, 20–1, 46, 270
  and struggle, 158, 192, 194, 217, 238–40
  as soldier, 38
  Christian martyrs as more masculine than pagan, 160
  exerting control, 60, 193, 199
  Jewish, 13
  role of body in female martyrologies, 187–8, 192
Martyrdom of Polycarp, 193
materiality. *See* beauty; and materiality, *See* hand; exceeding materiality, *See* memory; letter as material
  critique of teaching rooted in, 262, 268
  in letters, 106, 112, 121, 137
  Macrina exceeding, 196
  of texts, 115
  reordered in friendship, 61, 109, 134, 153
  the material turn, 108–9
  transcending, 235
mathematics, 169, 171
Matthew (N.T. book), 10, 112, 121, 129–30, 139, 167, 227
Mauss, Marcel, 145
Maximus the Cynic (rival to Nazianzen for bishopric at Constantinople), 245
Maximus the Philosopher (friend of Basil), 111–12
McGuckin, John, 34, 165, 170, 178, 245
McLynn, Neil, 52, 91
medicine. *See* dialectic; associated with practice of medicine
  as part of *paideia*, 6, 169, 193
  Macrina's rejection of, 260
Meidias (Demosthenean character) as antithesis of hoplite, 175
Meletius (Bishop of Antioch), 245
memory. *See* collective; memory
  letter as material, 52, 150–1
  of bravery, 103
  of shared *paideia*, 88
  pen and papyrus as medium for, 142
Menander Rhetor (rhetorician), 57, 123
Menelaus (King of Sparta), 64

metousia (participation in the Divine), 261
Miller, Patricia Cox, 108, 120, 239, 261
Miltiades (Greek general at Marathon), 98
miniature (image adorning manuscript), 276–7
moderation (*sōphrosunē*), 207
  in Athanasius, 239, 242–3, 270
  in Gorgonia, 192, 204
Modestus (Prefect of the East), 16, 136, 181–3
modesty
  in female saints, 192, 203, 207–8, 260
  in hagiographic subjects of Cappadocians, 191
monks, 32, 276, See Egypt; monks in
  and civic leadership, 42
  Eunomians as antithesis of, 223–34
  masculinity of, 20–1, 46
  under pro-Nicene church management, 43, 239–40
Moreschini, Claudio, 22, 227, 255
Moses (O.T. prophet), 36, 58–9, 129, 139, 168, 176, 185, 235, 255, See bishops; Moses as a model for
Mossay, Justin, 192, 255
Mount Sinai, 129, 168, 235
mouth. *See* voice
movement
  depictions of bodily, 106, 114, 134, 136, 138, 141, 230
  eyes as ushering, 122
  writing as kinetic, 53
Muehlberger, Ellen, 38, 194
mystagogy (a divine vision), 168

Nabuzardan (Babylonian general), 182
nakedness
  as source of shame in O.T., 159
  Macrina safeguards, 207, 261
Naucratius (Basil and Nyssen's brother), 25, 203, 206, See body; beauty of
Nazianzen. *See* Athens; Basil and Nazianzen at
  acknowledges virtue in Eudoxius the rhetorician, 95–6
  as bishop, 5–6, 33
  asceticism of, 43
  assumes the role of Nestor, 135–6
  beauty in family and friends as virtue and piety, 106, 200–5
  Bishop at Constantinople, 213–14, 226, 230–45

Concerning Himself and the Bishops, 245–53, 255
Concerning His Own Affairs, 41
Concerning His Own Life, 41
  dispute between teachers over Nicobulus, 92–3
  episcopacy at Constantinople challenged by Maximus the Cynic, 245
  epistle as handshake with Epiphanius, 135–6
  epistles as *agōn*, 91
  epistles as self-portrait, 51–2, 90–1
  epistolary banter with Eudoxius the rhetorician, 135–6
  family of, 23–4, 200–1, 203–5, 208–9, 273
  friendship with Basil, 22, 25–7, 73–5, 105–6
  friendship with Eutropius represented as between Greek warriors, 151–2
  friendship with Nyssen, 276
  honors Caesarius through correspondence with Philagrius, 87–8, 114–15
  includes Aristotle's epistles as a gift, 150
  instructs Nicobulus on epistolary *agōn*, 89–90
  on effeminate bishops, 251
  on flawed bishops and theologians, 226–56
  opposes Valens' religious policies in Cappadocia, 178–83
Oration 2, 276
Oration 11, 189
Oration 15, 124
Oration 18, 41, 222
Oration 26, 41
Oration 27, 213–14, 226–7, 249, 251
Oration 28, 227
Oration 29, 221
Oration 32, 226, 235, 241
Oration 33, 230
Oration 35, 125
Oration on Athanasius (Or. 21), 231–44
Oration on Basil (Or. 43), 177–86, 202, 246–56
Oration on Caesarius (Or. 7), 168–72, 200–1
Oration on Gorgonia (Or. 8), 190–4, 203–5, 207–9
  plays the role of Zeus, 93–4

polemic against theological rivals at
  Constantinople, 208–9, 233–56
references to Greek generals, 98–9
responds to Julian's measures against
  Christian *pepaideumenoi*, 1–5, 62, 215
response after departure from
  Constantinople, 131, 244–7, 270
response to unjust ordination at Sasima,
  276
self-imposed silence, 45, 131–2
sends letter collection to Nicobulus, 90–1
sensual appeal of correspondence,
  114–15
simulates handshake with Procopius
  through letter, 140
theology of, 22, 164–6, 177–84, 203–5,
  213–14, 226–9, 234–44, 247–50
training in *paideia*, 25–8, 44–5, 70–1,
  73–5, 177–8, 248
transcendent masculinity, 40–5
use of *synkrisis*, 93
vision of pro-Nicene empire, 59
voice as measure of virtue, 129–32
Nazianzus (Cappadocian town), 23–4, 245
Nebuchadnezzar (King of Babylon), 182
Nectarius (Bishop of Constantinople),
  245–6, 249, 251–2
Nectarius (friend of Basil), 87
Neo-Caesarea (city in Pontus), 156, 168
Neo-platonism, 47, 54, 199, 215, 221
Nestor (King of Pylos), 96, 135, 176
network, 220
  and friendship, 107–8
  based on *paideia*, 6–8, 22, 40–1, 83, 153
  epistolary, 4, 50–1
  theory, 8, 51
Nicaea (Council of), 161, 213
  Nicene Creed, 3–4, 273
Nicias (Greek general), 12
Nicobulus (grandnephew of Nazianzen), 24
  Nazianzen intervenes in teachers' dispute
    over, 92
  Nazianzen petitions for, 136
  Nazianzen's correspondence with, 89–90
  receives letter collection from Nazianzen,
    90–1, 151
Noah (O.T. patriarch), 185, 235
nobility
  and *aretē*, 7, 11, 59, 98, 155, 158, 192,
    209
  as related to *paideia*, 22, 190, 265

in death, 193
in friendship, 122, 127, 145
synonymous with classical masculinity,
  21, 40, 54, 62, 73, 86, 95, 97, 100,
  153, 168, 190, 205, 216, 250
visible in body, 110, 202, 208, 211
voice associated with, 19
Nonna (mother of Nazianzen), 23, 39–40
Norris, Frederick, 41, 57, 157, 184
  friendship between Basil and Nazianzen,
    178
Numbers (O.T. book), 139
Nyssa (Cappadocian town), 6, 24, 164
Nyssen
  Against Eunomius, 41, 162, 182, 220,
    224, 226, 237, 252, 262–6
  and Naucratius, 202–3, 206
  as bishop, 6
  as *pepaideumenos*, 28–9
  assumes role as King Laertes, 94–5
  beauty in family and friends as virtue and
    piety, 108–24, 201–3, 205–7
  considers epistle from Libanius a treasure,
    147–8
  correspondence with Libanius, 18, 84
  deploys Macrina to chastise Eunomius,
    257–8
  Encomium on Basil, 58–60, 172–7,
    184–5, 194, 201–2, 223
  exhorts Nazianzen after ordination at
    Sasima, 276–7
  exile of, 164
  family of, 6, 24–5, 201–3, 208–9, 266–70
  friendship with Nazianzen, 276
  gamesmanship with Stagirius, 63–7
  Homilies on the Song of Songs, 115, 130
  Libanius influence on, 28–9
  Life of Gregory Thaumaturgus, 155–7,
    166–8, 273
  Life of Macrina, 60–1, 194–200, 202–3,
    205–8, 256–70, 273
  Life of Moses, 38, 235
  on flawed bishops and theologians,
    212–26, 256–69
  On the Soul and the Resurrection, 37
  On Virginity, 37
  sensual appeal of correspondence, 120–2
  The Deity of the Son and the Holy Spirit,
    212
  theology of, 21–3, 164–6, 168, 172–7,
    212–13

Nyssen (cont.)
  transcendent masculinity, 37–40, 43–4
  use of Alexander the Great, 54–6
  use of *ekphrasis*, 123–4
  use of *synkrisis*, 184
  writings in relationship to Constantinople, 165, 168, 257

Odysseus (Greek warrior), 92, 94–5, 132, 206–7
Odyssey, 68, 94–5, 135, 138, 145, 193, 206–7
oikeiōsis (intimacy with God), 215
olive branch
  as gift included with letter, 136
Oltiseris (Cappadocian town), 237
Olympian
  as symbol of a competitor, 81, 157
Olympianus (Governor of Cappadocia), 150
Olympius (Governor of Cappadocia, 95, 114
Oosthout, Henri, 234
oration
  advocacy of pro-Nicene theology, 5, 56–61, 214–18, 240–1, 246–51
  as condemnation of non-Trinitarians, 226–31, 233–4, 237, 241–2
  Encomium on Basil (by Nyssen), 172–7
  genre of, 157–9
  on Athanasius by Nazianzen(*Or.* 21), 231–44
  on Basil by Nazianzen(*Or.* 43), 177–84, 244–56
  on Caesarius by Nazianzen(*Or.* 7), 168–72
  on Gorgonia by Nazianzen(*Or.* 8), 190–4
orator, 75, 77, *See* Lucian; false orator, *See* Lucian; masculine orator, *See* exhibition; oratorical, *See* honor; of orators
  and *agōn*, 3, 11, 18, 181
  and artifice, 17
  and *paideia*, 6
  as performance of manhood, 13–15, 30, 53, 67, 75, 98, 144, 171, 270, 274
  in Second Sophistic, 13–15, 89, 123, 169, 192, 217, 223, 247
  writer as, 90, 106
Origen (theologian), 115
othering
  as a means of undermining, 226

Otreius (bishop and friend of Nyssen), 122, 139
ousia (essence), 162–3

paideia. *See pepaideumenos/pepaideumenoi*
  and image, 62, 77, 93, 99, 144, 148
  and self-representation, 14, 29, 44, 73
  as habit, 36, 66, 143, 153
  Basil excelling in, 246–52
  bishops and, 5–8, 49, 75–7
  Caesarius greater than Julian, 168–72
  definition of, 6–9
  history in, 6, 14, 47, 65, 101
  Julian proscribes Christians from teaching, 1–5
  literature in, 1, 4, 6, 14, 47, 65, 88, 101
  pedigree of, 28, 68, 133
  philosophy in, 1, 6, 9, 14, 47, 65, 101, 200
  priests trained in, 7, 22, 25, 91
pain. *See* suffering
Palladas (Greek poet), 141
panegyric, 201, *See* biography; oration on Athanasius, *See* biography; Nazianzen oration on Basil
  epistle as, 2, 114, 149
  genre, 157
  oration as, 190
paper, 142
  record of the hand writing, 141
  recording of visual experience, 53, 110
  representation of voice, 130, 141
Paris (Trojan warrior), 64, 205
parrēsia, *See* boldness; in speech
passion. *See* emotion
Patroclus (Greek warrior and Achilles' companion), 93
patronage. *See* euergetism
Paul (apostle and N.T. author), 58–9, 111, 116, 143, 196, 226, 228, 242, 273
pedigree. *See* family; sacred pedigree in
  and contempt for social mobility, 220, 251, 262
  and masculine identity, 4, 95–6
  aristocratic, 252
  inferior in false theologian, 230, 237, 244, 265
  in Macrina, 206
  of *paideia*, 28, 68, 133
  philosophical, 15, 215
  sacred, 186, 218, 242

Index

Peloponnesian War, 98
Pelops (King from Peloponessus), 129
pen/stylus. *See* memory; pen and papyrus as medium for, *See* handwriting/penmanship
   as extension of a person, 141
   as instrument of virtual *agōn*, 53–4, 61, 86
   as the tongue, 142, 256
Penella, Robert, 27, 74
Penelope (wife of Odysseus), 94, 206–7
Pentheus (King of Thebes), 125
pepaideumenos/pepaideumenoi. *See* honor; among *pepaideumenoi*, *See* hierarchy; of *pepaideumenoi*
   and *agōn*, 6–21, 30–5, 77–82, 210–11
   and identity, 40–55, 62–7, 146–8
   and Second Sophistic, 67–77
   Basil as authentic, 246–54
   false, 218–31, 264–6
   friendship among, 103–14
   masculinity of, 96–7, 127–34, 145–6, 159–61
   the Cappadocians as, 25–9
performance, 77, *See* orator; as performance of manhood
   as measure of *aretē*, 14, 23, 43, 105, 158, 214, 274
   asceticism as, 223, 239
   epistolary, 5, 15, 18–19, 44, 53, 66–7, 83, 103, 121, 136, 148
   hagiographic, 195, 199, 259
   intensity of, 70, 90
   of letter carrier, 149
   of *paideia*, 66, 73–4, 133
   recurrent, 82
Pernot, Laurent, 14, 57, 75, 157
Perpetua (martyr from Carthage), 158, 188
Persia. *See* Cyrus (King of Persia), *See* Darius (King of Persia), *See* Xerxes (King of Persia); *See* effeminacy; Persia as metaphor for
   antithesis of Greekness, 55, 64, 96, 98–9, 181–2
   as metaphor for heresy, 99, 179, 273
Peter (N.T. apostle), 129, 140
Peter of Sebaste (Basil and Nyssen's brother), 25
   under Macrina's guidance, 43, 217, 257, 261, 267–9
Pfitzner, Victor, 12, 159

Phaedra (wife of King Theseus in *Hippolytus*), 258
Pheidias (sculptor), 111
Philagrius (childhood friend of Nazianzen), 78, 87–8, 114, 141
Philemon (N.T. book), 143
Philippi (city in Macedonia), 116
Philippians (N.T. book), 77, 111, 116, 143
Philo of Alexandria (philosopher), 12–13, 36, 122, 235
philosopher
   as distinct from sophist, 29, 77, 87, *101*, 156, 184, 213, 215
   as guide, 50
   as honorable role, 176, 178, 216–17, 235–6, 238, 251
   Macrina as, 198, 257–8
   pro-Nicene as true, 243–4, 248–50, 263, 269
   Trinitarian rivals as flawed, 222–3, 225, 233
philosophy
   and *aretē*, 9–14, 93
   as theology, 59, *196*, 269
   asceticism as guide for, 227–31, 234, 241, 260, 267–9
   in *paideia*, 1, 6, 9, 14, 47, 65, *101*, 200
   misapplication by heretics, 215, 234, 261–6
   of friendship, 103–4
   of language in theology, 219–22
   paideia in, 220
   true in pro-Nicenes, 247–51, 260–1, 271, 273
Philostorgius (church historian), 162, 218–20
Philostratus of Athens (rhetorician), 14–15, 53, 71–3
physician, 33, 125, *See* Galen (physician), *See* Hippocrates (physician), *See* Eustathius (physician and friend of Basil)
   Aetius as, 263
   Caesarius as, 23, 170
   Gorgonia's refusal of treatment from, 192, 207
   Macrina's refusal of treatment from, 260
physiognomy, 113, 200–1, 203, 209, *See* Aristotle; physiognomy, *See* Pseudo-Aristotle; *Physiognomonics*
piety. *See* combat; and piety, *See* courage; and piety
   and *agōn*, 13, 43–4, 274

piety. (cont.)
    Arians as impious, 236, 241–2, 273
    associated with *aretē*, 5, 62, 156–60, 224, 253
    authorial, 209, 240
    in family, 58–60, 169–71, 189, 191–200, 217, 267, 270
    in laity, 198
    through bodies of female saints, 207–8, 210–11
Pindar (poet), 3, 68, 167
Plato, 2, 16, 37, 109, 113, 115, 122, 133, 136, 171, 255, 264, 270
    agōn in, 16, 79
    and eloquence, 69, 250
    and love of the Beautiful, 104, 117–18
    elevated status of eyes, 118–19
    on bravery, 11–12
    on character of an instructor, 230, 234
    on disingenuous sophistry, 264
    on education, 258–9
    on *sōphrosunē*, 191
    purification in experiencing the divine, 227, 247
    subjugation of the body, 237–8
    theory of language, 221
    words as gateway to the Soul, 129
pleasure
    as indulgence and weakness, 231, 237, 248–50, 255
    from correspondence, 114, 139, 142, 146
    of the senses in friendship, 115–21
Plotinus (philosopher), 118
Plutarch, 54, 72, 85, 90, 112, 133, 188, 200, 248, 267, 269
    aretē as habit, 17, 82, 131
    importance of childhood instruction, 258
    on care of body, 26
    on self-restraint, 55
    on silence, 132, 242
    suspicion of sophists, 176, 230, 234, 267, 269
    voice and self-presentation, 133
Pneumatomachi, 165
Polanyi, Karl, 145
polemic, 228, 237, *See* biography; and polemic, *See* biography; as polemic against Eunomius, 163, 165, 214, 216, 220, 223, 225–7, 251, 257
    in Second Sophistic, 72
    theological, 59, 61, 216, 218

Polemon of Laodicea (rhetorician), 71–2, 113–14, 201
polis (Greek city-state), 11, 31, 34, 42
    as thriving, 128
    biblical figures situated in, 185
    church and, 194, 209, 252
    as crucible of *aretē*, 66, 81–2, 133, 167, 192
    Macrina secluded from, 197
    sacrificing on behalf of, 174
polytheists
    non-Trinitarians branded as, 185
Pontus (eastern Roman province), 94, 168
    family home of Basil and Nyssen, 24–6, 43, 156, 267
Porphyry (philosopher), 54, 134, 199
Porter, James, 130, 197, 243
posture, 136
    as indicative of manhood, 99, 143
priest/s
    asceticism in, 132
    Heterousian as illegitimate, 222, 233–4, 247, 252–3
    non-Trinitarians as pagan, 173, 184
    provincial aristocracy as, 32–4
    reverence for office of, 190, 198, 210
    safeguarding Trinitarian Christianity, 178, 217
    sanctity of hands, 139
    training in *paideia*, 7, 22, 25, 91
Priscus (rhetorician), 116
prize
    aretē as, 86
    classical literature as, 150
    epistles as, 94, 147
    salvation in Christ, 159
Procopius (Cappadocian magistrate and friend of Nazianzen), 140
Procopius (general of Emperor Julian), 180
Prohaeresius (rhetorician), 27, 75, 100
prompt
    to participate in epistolary exchange, 67, 100–1, 123–4, 272
pro-Nicene, 3, *See* biography; pro-Nicene, *See* bishops; pro-Nicene, *See* courage; associated with pro-Nicenes, *See* effeminacy; in opponents of pro-Nicenes, *See* exile; of pro-Nicene bishops by Valens, *See* monks; under pro-Nicene church management, *See* hero; as pro-Nicene, *See* heroine; as

pro-Nicene, *See* Heterousian/s; as foil to pro-Nicene bishops, *See* image; of pro-Nicene clergy as ideal leaders, *See* vision (as an ideal); conception of pro-Nicene leadership
   affiliation with asceticism, 223–34
   as antithesis of non-Trinitarians, 59–60, 218
   as category of identity formation, 4–5, 21, 47, 99–100
   as true Christianity, 58, 100, 176, 216–17, 228, 256–7
   community at Constantinople, 231
   in opposition to Valens, 178–81
   theology of, 168, 173, 220, 222, 269
prophet, 160, 173, 179, 185
   and *aretē*, 184, 217
   godly versus pagan, 185
   rejection of luxury, 235
prostitution
   verbal trickery as, 171
Proverbs (O.T. book), 77, 204, 267
provincial nobility. *See* aristocracy/aristocrat
Psalms (O.T. book), 140, 142, 243, 276
Pseudo-Aristotle, *Physiognomonics*, 113, 128
Pseudo-Libanius, *Epistolary Styles*, 63, 65, 116
Ptolemy (mathematician), 171
Puertas, Alberto, 87, 101
purification, 234, *See* Plato; purification in experiencing the divine
   agōn as, 223, 228–9, 247, 254
   and asceticism, 213, 218, 227–8, 273
   of theologian, 257
   through silence, 132
Pythagoras (philosopher), 129, 243

quest
   for *aretē*, 4, 17, 60, 85, 108, 272
   for family honor, 190
Quintilian (rhetorician), 130

Radde-Gallwitz, Andrew, 48, 90, 163, 218, 221
Rapp, Claudia, 9, 235, 238–9
Rebillard, Éric, 46, 227
Rebillard, Suzanne Abrams, 127, 131–2, 140, 217, 243, 245
reciprocity
   in epistolary *agōn*, 82, 91, 145

   in friendship, 104, 124, 133, 147, 152
Remijsen, Sofie, 20, 159
repetition (as habit). *See* habit; *paideia* as in epistolary exchange, 82
rhetoric
   and likeness of soul, 108–14
   and philosophy, 227–31, 247–54, 264
   as a weapon, 70–7, 132
   as craftsmanship, 63–72
   of contest (*agōn*), 3, 21, 62, 86, 88, 134, 160, 178, 272
   of erotic attraction, 114–18
   of friendship, 103–8
   of gift exchange, 145–52
   of gift-giving, 106
   of hands, 134–41
   of the voice, 127–34
   visual, 118–27
Ritter, Adolf-Martin, 163, 165, 213
rivalry. *See agōn*
Roisman, Joseph, 81, 155, 174
Romans (N.T. book), 195, 241
rose
   symbolic of beauty, 120–1
Rousseau, Philip, 26, 33, 42, 138, 161, 178, 260
Ruether, Rosemary Radford, 120, 127, 159, 192, 237
runner, 16, 72, 133, 157, 159, 196, 236, 252, *See* athlete, *See* Olympian

saints. *See* asceticism; and masculinity, *See* asceticism; as authorization, *See* biography; hagiographic (saints' lives)
Salamis (Battle of), 96, 182
Sasima (Cappadocian town), 6, 24, 164, 245, 276
Satala (town in Roman province Armenia minor), 49–50
Saul (King of Israel), 176
Schmitz, Thomas, 66, 71
Schor, Adam, 8, 49, 51, 90, 136–7
Scipio Africanus (Roman general), 200
Sebaste (city in Roman province Armenia minor), 25, 268
II Chronicles (O.T. book), 77
II Corinthians (N.T. book), 111, 137, 228, 260

Second Sophistic, 14–18, *See* disputation, public; in Second Sophistic, *See* exhibition; in Second Sophistic, *See* orator; in Second Sophistic
  and *agōn*, 29, 44, 229
  and classical authors, 66–9, 97, 224
  and friendship, 105–6, 109, 113, 118
  and rhetoric of combat, 70–3
  and the Cappadocians, 73–5
  and Third Sophistic, 75–7
  cultural influence on Nyssen philosophy, 28
  epistolary in, 53, 61, 75–7
  intellectual pedigree, 69–70, 272
II Thessalonians (N.T. book), 171
Seleucia (Council of), 161–2
self-control, 234, 237
  feature of masculinity, 11, 19, 170, 185, 240, 248, 251, 270
  in I Timothy and Titus, 100
  in transcendent masculinity, 189, 217, 268
  of martyrs, 21, 193, 200
  of O.T. patriarchs, 13
  silence as, 82
self-representation, 76, 105, 133–4, 153
  and identity formation, 9, 21–2, 44, 52, 62, 84, 130, 220, 272
  in *paideia*, 14, 29, 44, 73
Seneca (philosopher), 89, 112, 120
sense/sensory, 52–3, *See* hand, *See* eyes, *See* voice
  and rhetoric, 61, 106, 176, 192, 200, 272
  in encounters, 134–45
  in friendship, 114–34, 152–3
  revalorization of, 104–53
Shepardson, Christine, 47, 232
silence, 82, 243
  as self-control, 217, 241
  as superior to speech, 131–2, 242–3
  Nazianzen's self-imposed, 45, 131
Silvas, Anna, 24, 31, 48, 90, 124, 164
Smoes, Étienne, 11, 176
Song of Songs (O.T. book), 115, 117, 121, 130
sophist/sophistry. *See* orator, *See* Plato; on disingenuous sophistry, *See* Lucian; false orator, *See* Second Sophistic; rhetoric of combat, *See* Plutarch; suspicion of sophists
  definition of during Second Sophistic, 14–16

  denunciation of, 29–30, 77, 87, 101, 177, 229–31
Sophronius (imperial magistrate from Cappadocia), 32–3, 130
soul. *See* body; and soul
  and friendship, 108–27
  as guiding element of Macrina, 196–9, 208, 258, 267, 270
  paideia as training, 254
Sparta (Greece), 64, 96, 129, 179, 273
spectator, 248
  at athletic games, 20, 73
  hagiographic trope of, 170–1, 175, 196
speech. *See* boldness; in speech, *See* language
  as index of character, 2, 4, 61, 73, 79–80, 87, 90, 128–34, 197–8, 216–18, 241–57
  excellence of, 10, 46
  misapplication of, 156, 204, 224–6, 241–2
speech (public presentation). *See* oration, *See* declamation
stadium
  site of performance, 81, 171, 196
Stagirius (Cappadocian rhetorician), 63–6, 114, 117, 132
Sterk, Andrea, 42–3, 235
Stewart, Michael Edward, 20, 42
Stoic/Stoicism, 12–13, 117, 120, 233
stomach. *See* gluttony
Storin, Bradley, 29, 51–2, 111, 135
  epistles as self-portrait, 51–2, 90, 111
  verbal stillness in Nazianzen, 45
strength, 45
  from God, 156
  letter writing as exhibition of, 101
  of body as symbol of *aretē*, 17, 110, 118, 133, 170, 174, 209–10
  of soul, 39, 186, 188, 193, 195, 204, 237
  of speech, 133, 172
  of voice, 128
struggle, 78, 82, 158, 167, 190, 194, 209, 228, *See* martyr; and struggle, *See* body; struggle within, *See agōn*
  agonistic vs. antagonistic, 85
Swain, Simon, 56, 59, 63, 89
sweat. *See* exertion
synkrisis (rhetorical device), 54, 93, 184

Telchine (from Greek mythology), 92
Telemachus (son of Odysseus), 94–5

telos, 31, 79, 82
temperance
  in I Timothy and Titus, 100
theatre
  and classical Greek ideal, 97
  site of gender instability, 81
Thecla (saint), 187, 194
Themistius (rhetorician), 101, 129–30
Themistocles (Athenian general), 96
Theodore (Bishop of Tyana in Cappadocia), 146
Theodoret (Bishop of Cyrrhus), 38, 136
Theodosius (Emperor), 165–6, 213, 232, 245
theology. *See* warfare; theology depicted as, *See* language; and theology, *See* oration; advocacy of pro-Nicene theology
  and asceticism, 36–9, 62, 257–61, 268–70
  Basil and, 163–4, 172–83
  conflicts in fourth century, 160–6
  Nazianzen and, 164–6, 177–83
  Nyssen and, 164–6, 168, 172–7
  of Athanasius, 163–4, 231–9
  of Eunomius, 162–6, 220–2
  paideia and, 227–31, 247–56
  pro-Nicene, 168, 172–83, 219–22
  similarities among Cappadocians, 22–3
theōria (contemplation of God), 197, 215, 234
theōsis (communion with God), 227
Thermopylae (Battle), 64, 179
Third Sophistic, 14–15, 75–7
Thomas (N.T. apostle), 139
Timothy (correspondent of Nazianzen), 86
Titus (N.T. book), 100
tongue. *See* pen; as the tongue
  and hierarchy, 133
  as a weapon, 72, 132
  as instrument of truth, 255–6
  control of, 131–2, 217, 241–3, 249–50
  lack of control over, 227, 241, 255
  purity of, 244, 254
  representative of the individual, 131
touch. *See* hand
toughness
  outcome of *paideia*, 71, 193
tribōn (cloak), 274
Trinitarian. *See* pro-Nicene, *See* biography; pro-Nicene, *See* biography; and polemic, *See* bishops; pro-Nicene

  Cappadocian Fathers as, 22–3
  doctrinal development in fourth century, 161–6
Trinity (pro-Nicene doctrine), 38–9, 163, 168, 221, 234, 236–7, 250, 255
Trojan/Trojan War, 103, 135, 145, 205
trumpet
  Athanasius as a trumpet of truth, 236
  used as call to battle, 236
Tyana (Cappadocian city), 146
tyranny
  as antithesis of Greekness, 99, 174, 236, 240

unbegotten. *See* begotten/unbegotten
Urbano, Arthur, 9, 257
  biography as arena of competition, 62, 215
  on the philosopher's cloak and identity formation, 274

Vaggione, Richard, 162, 223, 238, 262, 264–5
Valens (Emperor), 23, *See* exile; of pro-Nicene bishops by Valens, *See* pro-Nicene; in opposition to Valens, *See* Homoian; Valens as supporter of administrative division of Cappadocia, 124
Van Dam, Raymond, 28, 136, 138, 156, 158, 166, 182
  division of Cappadocia, 125
  on Amphilochius as the Fourth Cappadocia Father, 24
  on challenges of letter exchange, 137
  on Emperor Valens' religious policies in Cappadocia, 175
Van Hoof, Lieve, 27, 76, 220
Van Nijf, Onno, 167
Vandenbussche, E., 214, 219
Venota (Cappadocian town), 124
victory
  as management of internal self, 20, 159, 199
  in hagiography, 158, 167–72, 192, 195, 238
  Olympic, 137
  over heresy, 60, 177–84, 256
  rhetorical, 73–5, 81, 85, 94, 108, 273
virgin/virginity, 189, 260
  as potential loss of manhood, 42

virgin/virginity (cont.)
  community of virgins under Macrina, 43,
    196, 198–200
  Macrina as, 25, 60–1, 198, 200, 260,
    267–9
virtual
  agōn, 3, 53, 67, 106, 158, 160, 170, 217
  text as person, 108, 110, 112, 168, 272
vision (as an ideal)
  Basil's conception of a perfect society, 38
  conception of pro-Nicene leadership,
    59–60, 62, 77, 100, 158, 232, 244
vision (sight). *See* eyes
voice. *See* body; voice as part of, *See* breath;
    and voice, *See* gender; and voice
  and friendship, 131–4, 139
  as a weapon, 132, 243
  as effeminate, 231, 249, 263
  as identity, 128–31, 133, 141, 197–8,
    247, 254–5
  as measure of truth, 255–6, 269, 271
  highest sense, 153
  performance of, 19
  purification of, 218, 235, 243, 254,
    257–8
  sound of as sign of strong society, 127–8
voyeurism, 207

warfare. *See* Second Sophistic; and rhetoric
    of combat, *See* combat, *agōn* as, 73, 78,
    82
  as antagonistic, 85
  eloquence and, 75, 183
  performance of masculinity as, 3, 173
  theology depicted as in hagiography,
    177–84, 210, 216–17, 236–7
warrior. *See* courage; as warriors, *See*
    hoplite, *See* combat, *See* warfare
Watts, Edward, 7, 27, 74
weapon. *See* tongue; as a weapon
  as a gift, 145
  patronage as, 64
  rhetoric as, 72–4, 86, 93, 132
  voice as, 243, 256
Webb, Ruth, 55, 104, 123
White, Carolinne, 104, 106–7, 111
Whitmarsh, Tim, 69, 89
wickedness
  of heresy, 168, 173, 238
wilderness
  as place of hardship, 185, 240
wrestler, 72, 236, *See* athlete
  and *agōn*, 16, 72, 82, 133, 238

xenia. *See* family; and guest friendship
    (*xenia*)
Xenophon (historian), 2, 85–6
Xenophon of Ephesus (novelist), 206
Xerxes (King of Persia), 181–3

Yahweh (Hebrew name for God), 129, 140,
    168, 179

Zeus (god), 23, 109

For EU product safety concerns, contact us at Calle de José Abascal, 56–1°, 28003 Madrid, Spain or eugpsr@cambridge.org.

www.ingramcontent.com/pod-product-compliance
Lightning Source LLC
LaVergne TN
LVHW041619060526
838200LV00040B/1348